BAKER'S
Student
Encyclopedia
of
Music

BAKER'S
Student Encyclopedia of Music

of

Music

Compiled by Laura Kuhn

H-Q

VOLUME TWO

SCHIRMER BOOKS

An Imprint of Macmillan Library Reference USA

New York

SCHIRMER BOOKS
An Imprint of Macmillan Library Reference USA
1633 Broadway
New York, NY 10019

Library of Congress Catalog Card Number: 99-31758

Printed in the United States of America

Printing number
1   2   3   4   5   6   7   8   9   10

Library of Congress Cataloging-in-Publication Data
Baker's student encyclopedia of music / edited by Laura Kuhn
    p. cm.
    Includes index.
    ISBN 0-02-865315-7 (all). — ISBN 0-02-865415-3 (vol. 1). — ISBN 0-02-865416-1 (vol. 2). — ISBN 0-02-865421-8 (vol. 3)
1. Music Dictionaries. I. Kuhn, Laura Diane. II. Title: Student encyclopedia of music.
ML100.B26 1999
780′.3—dc21
                                                      99-31758
                                                      CIP

This paper meets the requirements of ANSI/NISO Z39.48-1992 (Permanence of Paper).

H

H. 1. In scores, FRENCH HORN. 2. In organ music, heel. 3. In keyboard music, hand (r.h., l.h.). 4. (Ger.). The note B. *H dur,* B major; *H moll,* B minor.

habanera (often misspelled *habañera*). The dance of Havana, in DUPLE meter, at a moderately slow tempo. The meter of the habanera is $\frac{2}{4}$ and its most characteristic rhythmic figure is a dotted eighth note followed by a sixteenth note and two eighth notes.

häh-bäh-nâ′răh

The origin of the habanera as a folk dance is unknown. The most popular theory is that the habanera was an offspring of the English country dance. According to this theory, country dance became *contredanse* in France and *contradanza* in Spain, the name that was abbreviated to *danza* in 1800. In 1825, it appeared in Cuba as *danza habanera,* and later simply as *habanera.*

Perhaps the most famous habanera is the one that Carmen sings in GEORGES BIZET's opera, but it was not Bizet's tune. He picked it up from a collection of songs by the Spanish composer SEBASTIÁN YRADIER, published in 1864, in which it appeared under the title *El Arreglito,* with a French subtitle, *Chanson havanaise.* (Yradier also composed the famous habanera, *La Paloma.*) But since the action of *Carmen* takes place in southern Spain, what is a ditty from Havana, Cuba, doing in it anyway?

Among other composers who wrote dances in the rhythm of the habanera are ISAAC ALBÉNIZ, CLAUDE DEBUSSY, MAURICE RAVEL, EMMANUEL CHABRIER, and MANUEL DE FALLA.

The famous habanera in CARMEN was inserted in the opera at the last minute by Bizet. The opera's producers were unhappy with the score, and begged the composer to add a song that would appeal to the crowds. The result was the most memorable song in the opera, and one of the most recognizable melodies in all classical music.

Haffner Serenade. A work by WOLFGANG AMADEUS MOZART, 1776 (K.250). This is a light and charming piece in D major written for the wedding of the daughter of the Bürgomaster of Salzburg named Haffner. (Mozart himself was her secret admirer.) Thus was immortality acquired by the modest Haffner family.

The Serenade has eight movements, and lasts longer than some of Mozart's full-fledged symphonies.

Haffner Symphony. Symphony No. 35 by WOLFGANG AMADEUS MOZART, 1782 (K.385). Haffner strikes twice. The key is D major, the same as is used for the *Haffner Serenade.* This work was jotted down by Mozart in a couple of weeks, eight years after the composition of the *Serenade.* Haffner, the Bürgomaster of Salzburg, endeared himself to Mozart by his many kindnesses to him.

Haggard, Merle (Ronald), American country singer, songwriter, fiddler, and guitarist; b. Bakersfield, Cal., Apr. 6, 1937. Haggard's impoverished family moved to California, where they lived in an abandoned boxcar near Bakersfield.

Haggard started early on a criminal career. He escaped seven times from reform schools, stole cars, and held up a bar. He finally ended up at San Quentin as prisoner No. 845,200. There he met the notorious "red-light bandit" Caryl Chessman, eventually executed for a series of brutal rapes. Chessman exercised a profound influence on Haggard, who began improvising songs of destitution, despair, and crime, exemplified by the autobiographical line, "Did you ever steal a quarter when you was ten years old?"

Haggard reformed himself on his release in 1960, and began performing in the Bakersfield area. He made his first recordings for the tiny Tally label, scoring a minor hit in 1963 with *Sing a Sad Song.* Capitol bought out his contract, and he made it to the top of the country charts with 1965's *(All My Friends Are Going to Be) Strangers;* he immediately named his backup band the Strangers in honor of the song. *I'm a Lonesome Fugitive,* based on his prison experiences, followed in 1966.

Haggard reached the height of his fame—and notoriety—with the release in 1968 of the anti-antiwar song, *Okie from Muskogee.* In it, Haggard criticized the hippie movement, and those who opposed the draft and preached free love. He also released *The Fightin' Side of Me* as another expression of his support for the Vietnam War.

PEOPLE IN MUSIC

In the late '60s and early '70s, Haggard made several theme albums to celebrate influential figures in country music history, including "the singing brakeman," JIMMIE RODGERS and Western Swing pioneer BOB WILLS. In terms of commercial success, his greatest period was the early '70s, when he scored nine No. 1 country hits in a row.

Haggard's chart-topping days ended, though, by the mid-'70s. Despite his lack of status as a record seller, Haggard continues to tour tirelessly, and is a popular performer on the country circuit. Occasional divorces, bankruptcies, and other crises only sharpen his image as the weathered country star he has become.

Hahn, Reynaldo, Venezuelan-born French conductor, music critic, and composer; b. Caracas, Aug. 9, 1874; d. Paris, Jan. 28, 1947. Hahn's father, a merchant from Hamburg, settled in Venezuela around 1850. The family moved to Paris when Reynaldo was five years old. He studied singing, and a recording he made in 1910 testifies to his beautiful voice.

Hahn studied theory and composition at the Paris Conservatory, numbering among his teachers the opera composer JULES MASSENET, who had a strong influence on the young musician. Hahn also studied conducting, achieving a high professional standard as an opera conductor. In 1934 he became music critic of *Le Figaro.*

Hahn remained in France during the Nazi occupation at a considerable risk to his life, because he was Jewish on his father's side. In 1945 he was named a member of the Institut de France and in 1945–46 was music director of the Paris Opéra.

Hahn's music is distinguished by flowing melodies and fine ROMANTIC flair. Socially, he was known in Paris for his brilliant wit. He maintained a passionate youthful friendship with the author Marcel Proust, who portrayed him as a poetic genius in his novel *Jean Santeuil.* Their intimate correspondence was published in 1946. Hahn was a brilliant journalist, and his articles were published in several collections.

Hahn wrote primarily for the stage, including operas, operettas, incidental music, and ballets. He also composed

PEOPLE IN MUSIC

concertos for violin, piano, and cello, a Piano Quintet and String Quartet, and piano pieces, among them a suite, composed in 1894 called *Portraits des peintres* (Portraits of painters), inspired by poems of Proust.

Hail, Columbia. A patriotic song with words by Joseph Hopkinson (1770–1842), set to the melody of the *President's March,* attributed to Philip Phile. It was first sung as a finale to a play, *The Italian Monk,* produced in Philadelphia in 1798. It gradually acquired popularity as a patriotic American ANTHEM.

Hail, Hail, the Gang's All Here. American version, published in 1908, of a chorus from Gilbert and Sullivan's THE PIRATES OF PENZANCE (1879). It has become a popular song to sing at social gatherings.

Hail to the Chief. American marching song of unknown authorship that traditionally accompanies the entrance of the President of the U.S. on state occasions.

The 1993 London revival production of Hair. *(Robbie Jack/Corbis)*
▶

Hair. Rock musical by GALT MAC-DERMOT, 1967, with book and lyrics by Gerome Ragni and James Rado. Billed as "the American tribal love-rock musical," it was first performed off Broadway, then radically rewritten and presented on Broadway in 1968.
   The play was shocking and

scandalous for its time, because of the use of profanities, a brief scene (before the curtain falls on the first act) when the cast appeared nude, and its preaching of peace, love, and happiness.

Plotwise, *Hair* is a "nonbook musical," that is, it has no coherent storyline. But, lurking beneath the messages of peace and love is a strong commentary on the evils of the Vietnam War, capitalist society, and racism.

There are two categories of songs: those defiantly challenging of stereotypes (*Sodomy, Colored Spade, White Boys/Black Boys, I'm Black/Ain't Got No*), and those fusing rock with popular song (the title song, *Aquarius, Frank Mills, Where Do I Go?, Easy to Be Hard, Good Morning Starshine, Let the Sunshine In*).

Haitink, Bernard (Johann Herman), eminent Dutch conductor; b. Amsterdam, March 4, 1929. Haitink studied violin at the Amsterdam Conservatory, then played in the Radio Philharmonic Orchestra. In 1954–55 he attended the conducting course of FERDINAND LEITNER, sponsored by the Netherlands Radio. In 1955, he was appointed to the post of second conductor of the Radio Philharmonic Orchestra, becoming its principal conductor in 1957. In 1956 he made his first appearance as a guest conductor with the Concertgebouw Orchestra of Amsterdam.

Haitink made his U.S. debut with the Los Angeles Philharmonic Orchestra in 1958. In 1959 he conducted the Concertgebouw Orchestra in England, of which, in 1961, he became co-principal conductor. That same year he led it on a tour of the U.S., followed by one to Japan in 1962. In 1964 he became chief conductor of the Concertgebouw Orchestra, a position he held with great distinction until 1988. In 1967, Haitink also assumed the post of principal conductor and artistic adviser of the London Philharmonic Orchestra, serving as its artistic director from 1969 to 1978.

Haitink made his first appearance at the Glyndebourne Festival in 1972, and from 1978 to 1988 was its music director. In 1987 he became music director of the Royal Opera House at London's Covent Garden. He also appeared as a guest conductor with the Berlin Philharmonic, Vienna Philharmonic, N.Y. Philharmonic, Chicago Symphony,

So contagious was the stage show that one N.Y. critic actually undressed himself during *I Got Life* (where most of the cast went naked under dimmed stage lights) to demonstrate his being "with it."

PEOPLE IN MUSIC

Boston Symphony, and Cleveland Orchestra. In 1982 he led the Concertgebouw Orchestra on a transcontinental tour of the U.S.

As a conductor, Haitink does not impose his own personality on a work, but still achieves colorful readings. Especially fine are his performances of the symphonies of ANTON BRUCKNER and GUSTAV MAHLER, but he is equally comfortable conducting the CLASSICAL repertoire. He has received numerous international honors. In 1972 he was named a Chevalier de l'Ordre des Arts et des Lettres of France. He was made an Honorary Knight Commander of the Order of the British Empire by Queen Elizabeth II in 1977.

PEOPLE IN MUSIC

Halévy (born Levy), (Jacques-François-) **Fromental** (-Elie) celebrated French composer; b. Paris, May 27, 1799; d. Nice, March 17, 1862. The family changed its name to Halévy in 1807.

Halévy entered the Paris Conservatory at age 9, where he later studied with CONSTANT LAMBERT (piano), Henri-Montan Berton (harmony), and LUIGI CHERUBINI (COUNTERPOINT). He took second place in the Prix de Rome in 1816 and 1817, finally achieving the Grand Prix de Rome in 1819 with his CANTATA *Herminie.* He became *chef du chant* (choral director) at the Théâtre-Italien in 1826. A year later, his first stage work was performed, the opéra-comique, *L'Artisan,* which had a small success. He gained further notice with his *Clari,* introduced to Paris by the famous Spanish mezzosoprano MARÍA MALIBRAN, in 1828.

In 1829 Halévy's first major success came with *Le Dilettante d'Avignon.* He then was named *chef du chant* at the Paris Opéra, a position he held from 1829 to 1845. He scored his greatest triumph with *La Juive* in 1835, which established his name and was performed throughout Europe and the U.S. His next opera, *L'éclair,* which opened later that year, also enjoyed favorable reception. Among his later operas that have been retained in the repertoire are *La Reine de Chypre* (1841), *Charles VI* (1843), and *La Magicienne* (1858).

Halévy was also active as a teacher at the Paris Conservatory, being made a professor of harmony and accompaniment in 1827, of counterpoint and FUGUE five years later, and of composition in 1840. His students included the composers CHARLES GOUNOD, GEORGES BIZET (who became his son-in-law), and CAMILLE SAINT-SAËNS. He was elected to membership in the Institute in 1836, serving as its secretary from 1854.

Halévy was an extremely talented composer for the stage, winning the admiration of both HECTOR BERLIOZ and RICHARD WAGNER. Yet he could never equal GIACOMO MEYERBEER in popular success. As time went by, only *La Juive* gained a permanent place in the world repertoire.

Haley, Bill (William John Clifton, Jr.), popular American rock 'n' roll singer, guitarist, and bandleader; b. Highland Park, Mich., July 6, 1925; d. Harlingen, Tex., Feb. 9, 1981.

PEOPLE IN MUSIC

◄

Bill Haley and the Comets performing live in 1957. (Hulton-Deutsch Collection/ Corbis)

Haley began to play guitar as a youth, and at the age of 15 embarked on a tour with cowboy-styled groups. He soon formed his own band, the Saddlemen, which, in 1952, was renamed the Comets to broaden their appeal beyond the country audience.

Haley began covering R&B hits with his band, beginning in 1953 with his version of *Crazy Man Crazy*. Next came his hit version of JOE TURNER's *Shake, Rattle and Roll,* which combined elements of blues, country music, and ur-

Haley's fans were surprised when they first saw him on television and in films. He was much older and less "cool" looking than his recordings sounded! Teenagers were not impressed.

PEOPLE IN MUSIC

ban pop. His fame skyrocketed in 1955 with his recording of *Rock Around the Clock.* Immortalized in the motion picture *Blackboard Jungle,* it became the banner of the rising generation of wild, wide-eyed, dance-crazy, rebellious American youth. Some 22 million copies of this song were sold.

But like so many musicians of the period, Haley's fame was short-lived. In 1956, a newcomer on the scene named ELVIS PRESLEY unseated Haley as the King of Rock 'n' Roll. Haley continued to perform on the "oldies circuit," but never again achieved great success on the charts.

Halffter (Escriche), **Ernesto,** important Spanish composer and conductor; b. Madrid, Jan. 16, 1905; d. there, July 5, 1989. Halffter studied composition with the famed composers MANUEL DE FALLA and ADOLFO SALAZAR. He first attracted attention with his *Sinfonietta,* which was included in the program of the Oxford Festival of the I.S.C.M. (International Society for Contemporary Music) in 1931.

In his music, Halffter continued the tradition of Spanish modern nationalism which was pioneered by Falla. He also completed and orchestrated Falla's unfinished scenic cantata, *Atlántida,* which was first performed at La Scala in Milan in 1962. Among his own works are *Fantaisie portugaise* for orchestra (Paris, 1941), and the ballets *Dulcinea* (1940), *Cojo enamorado* (1954), and *Fantasía galaica* (1956). He also composed a Guitar Concerto (1968) and several cantatas.

Halffter's brother Rodolfo (Escriche) (b. Madrid, Oct. 30, 1900; d. Mexico City, Oct. 14, 1987) and his nephew Cristóbal (Jiménez) (b. Madrid, March 24, 1930) were also significant composers.

half-step *See* SEMITONE.

Halka. Opera by STANISLAW MONIUSZKO, 1846–47, produced in its final form in Warsaw, 1858. Considered the national Polish opera, its popularity has never abated in Poland, but it is rarely if ever performed in Western Europe. The story concerns Halka's eternal love for her seducer. She kills herself when he marries another.

Halle, Adam de la. *See* ADAM DE LA HALLE.

Hallelujah (from Heb. *hallel* + *Jah,* praise Jehovah). Religious exhortation from the Old Testament: "Praise ye the Lord!"

Hallelujah, Baby! Musical by JULE STYNE, COMDEN (BETTY), and GREEN (JOHN), 1967. A commentary on the changing social position of African-Americans in the 20th century, by observers who do not age.

Hallelujah Chorus. There are thousands of Hallelujah arias and choruses, but the most famous of all is the triumphant incantation, the *Hallelujah Chorus,* at the end of the second part of GEORGE FRIDERIC HANDEL's *MESSIAH.*

When Handel brought out *Messiah* at its first London performance, King George II rose to his feet (for reasons unknown) at the moment the chorus began, at which point the rest of the audience rose to its feet as was required. Thus was established a tradition of standing up for the chorus, observed in Great Britain and elsewhere to this day.

The *Hallelujah Chorus* was unintentionally debased by the accidental use of its opening notes, in the same rhythm, in the American popular song of the 1920s, *Yes, We Have No Bananas.*

Hallelujah **meter.** A stanza used in a hymn of jubilation, consisting of six lines in iambic measure, with the number of syllables usually in the order of 8, 6, 8, 6, 8, 8.

halling. An animated Norwegian dance in $\frac{2}{4}$ time, usually accompanied by the HARDINGFELE (a traditional Norwegian fiddle).

Hamlet. OPERA by AMBROISE THOMAS, 1868, first produced in Paris. The LIBRETTO faithfully follows Shakespeare's tragedy. The music overflows with melodious and harmonious ARIAS and ensembles. For some reason the opera failed to achieve the success comparable to Thomas's *Mignon.*

Hamlet. Overture-fantasy by PIOTR ILYICH TCHAIKOVSKY, 1888, first performed in St. Petersburg. It follows the principal dramatic points in Shakespeare's tragedy. Over Hamlet's main theme, he even wrote in English, "To be or not to be."

Hamlisch, Marvin (Frederick), American composer of popular music; b. N.Y., June 2, 1944. Hamlisch's father, an accordionist, trained him in music. He then studied piano at the Juilliard School of Music and at Queens College (B.A., 1967).

Hamlisch began writing songs at the age of 15. His first success came in 1974, when he won no less than three Academy Awards for his scores for the films *The Way We Were* and *The Sting.* In 1975, he wrote the score for the musical *A Chorus Line,* which received the Pulitzer Prize for the play and a Tony award for the best musical score. The play ran for over a decade and, at the time of its closure, was the longest-running Broadway musical. The cast album was estimated to have sold over a million copies.

Hamlisch returned to Broadway in 1979 with *They're Playing Our Song,* with lyrics by his ex-lover, CAROLE BAYER SAGER. The plot was loosely based on their relationship. The duo also wrote the best-selling theme for the James Bond film, *The Spy Who Loved Me,* called *Nobody Does It Better* (performed by Carly Simon).

Hamlisch spent most of the '80s and '90s scoring Hollywood films, including 1981's *Pennies from Heaven,* 1982's *Sophie's Choice,* and 1987's *Three Men and a Baby.* He is said to be working on a new Broadway show to open in 1999.

hăhm′mer′klăh-vēr′

Beethoven's piano sonatas opp. 101, 109, and 110 are also marked "Hammerklavier" by Beethoven, but op.106 is the one exclusively with *Hammerklavier* in the title.

Hammerclavier (*Hammerklavier;* Ger.). Name used for the PIANOFORTE in the early 19th century.

Hammerklavier Sonata. This is the title LUDWIG VAN BEETHOVEN gave to his Piano Sonata No. 29 (op.106). In the spirit of rising nationalism in Central Europe, Beethoven pointedly used a German title rather than the Italian PIANOFORTE.

Hammerstein, Oscar, celebrated German-American impresario, grandfather of Oscar (Greeley Clendenning) Hammerstein, II; b. Stettin, May 8, 1846; d. N.Y., Aug. 1, 1919. At the age of 16, Hammerstein ran away from home. He spent some time in England, then went to America, where he worked in a N.Y. cigar factory. Despite

his menial position, he was inspired to design and patent a machine for shaping tobacco leaves by suction. He later edited a tobacco trade journal. At the same time, Hammerstein practiced the violin, learned to compose music, and dabbled in playwriting.

In 1868 Hammerstein produced in N.Y. a comedy in German, and in 1893 he wrote the LIBRETTO and music of an operetta, *The Kohinoor.* His main activity, however, was in management. He built the Harlem Opera House in 1888, the Olympia Music Hall in 1895, and the Republic Theater in 1900, and presented brief seasons of plays and operas in all three.

In 1906 Hammerstein announced plans for the Manhattan Opera House, his crowning achievement. The enterprise was originally planned as a theater for opera in English, but it opened with an Italian company in VINCENZO BELLINI's *I Puritani* that year. Hammerstein entered into bold competition with the Metropolitan Opera, and engaged celebrated singers, among them DAME NELLIE MELBA, LILLIAN NORDICA, LUISA TETRAZZINI, and Mary Garden. Among spectacular events presented by him were the first U.S. performances of five operas by JULES MASSENET, GUSTAVE CHARPENTIER's *Louise,* and CLAUDE DEBUSSY's *Pelléas et Mélisande.* The new venture held its own for four seasons, but in the end Hammerstein was compelled to yield. In April 1910, he sold the Manhattan Opera House to the management of the Metropolitan for $1.2 million, and agreed not to produce grand opera in N.Y. for ten years. He also sold to the Metropolitan (for $100,000) his interests in the Philadelphia Opera House, built by him in 1908.

Defeated in his main ambition in the U.S., Hammerstein transferred his activities to England. There he built the London Opera House, which opened with a lavish production of *Quo Vadis?* by JEAN NOUGUÈS in 1911. However, he failed to establish himself in London, and after a season there, returned to N.Y. Breaking his agreement with the Metropolitan, he announced a season at the newly organized American Opera House in N.Y. The Metropolitan secured an injunction against him, and he was forced to give up his operatic venture.

Hammerstein, Oscar (Greeley Clendenning), **II,** outstanding American lyricist, grandson of OSCAR HAMMERSTEIN, and most famous for his stage collaborations with RICHARD RODGERS; b. N.Y., July 12, 1895; d. Highland Farms, Doylestown, Pa., Aug. 23, 1960. He studied law at Columbia University, graduating in 1917, then became interested in the theater. He collaborated on the LIBRETTOS for RUDOLF FRIML's *Rose-Marie* (1924), SIGMUND ROMBERG's *The Desert Song* (1926), and JEROME KERN's *Show Boat* (1927; including the celebrated song *Ol' Man River*). He continued to work with Kern through the '30s, producing dozens of hit standards, including *The Song Is You* and *All the Things You Are.* The two also worked in Hollywood.

In 1943 composer Richard Rodgers was looking for a lyricist to replace his long-time partner, LORENZ HART, who was becoming increasingly unreliable due to alcoholism. Hammerstein, who had worked with Rodgers before, was the ideal candidate, and together they produced some of the most brilliant and successful musical comedies in the history of the American theater: *Oklahoma!* (1943; Pulitzer Prize), *Carousel* (1945), *Allegro* (1947), *South Pacific* (1949; Pulitzer Prize, 1950), *The King and I* (1951), *Me and Juliet* (1953), *Pipe Dream* (1955), *The Flower Drum Song* (1958), and *The Sound of Music* (1959).

The Rodgers and Hammerstein musicals were noteworthy for their near-perfect wedding of songs and text. Although Hammerstein's lyrics were not as clever as Hart's, he was very skilled at creating songs that perfectly advanced the storyline. This was important in the growth of the classic Broadway musical.

Hammond organ. An electronic keyboard instrument invented by Laurens Hammond in 1933. Its notes are produced by electrical generators. A special mechanism can alter the relative strength of OVERTONES of each KEY, thereby making it possible to produce any desired instrumental TIMBRE.

The Hammond organ is usually constructed in the shape of a SPINET, and it has two manuals and a set of pedals.

Hampson, Thomas, American baritone; b. Elkhart, Ind., June 28, 1955. Hampson studied at Eastern Washington

University (B.A., 1977), Fort Wright College (B.F.A., 1979), the University of Southern California, and the Music Academy of the West at Santa Barbara, where he won the Lotte Lehmann award in 1978. In 1980 he took second prize at the Hertogenbosch International Vocal Competition, and in 1981 first place in the Metropolitan Opera Auditions.

In 1981, Hampson appeared with the Deutsche Oper am Rhein in Dusseldorf, and in 1982 attracted wide notice as Guglielmo in WOLFGANG AMADEUS MOZART's *COSÌ FAN TUTTE* with the Opera Theatre of St. Louis. In subsequent seasons he appeared with opera companies in Santa Fe, Cologne, Lyons, and Zurich. On Oct. 9, 1986, he made his Metropolitan Opera debut in N.Y. as Almaviva in Mozart's *Le nozze di Figaro.* In addition to Mozart, he won success in operas by GIOACCHINO ROSSINI, GAETANO DONIZETTI, GIUSEPPE VERDI, and GIACOMO PUCCINI.

Hampton, Lionel, "Hamp," African-American JAZZ vibraphonist, drummer, pianist, and bandleader; b. Louisville, Ky., April 12, 1913. Hampton was born in Kentucky but raised in Chicago by his grandparents. He was schooled in a Catholic high school, where he learned military drumming. Returning to Chicago, he lived with his uncle, who had many friends in the music business and who bought the young Hampton his first drum kit. He began playing professionally in the mid-1920s, both in clubs and on record.

PEOPLE IN MUSIC

Lionel Hampton, c. 1936. (New York Public Library)

Although initially a drummer, Hampton began playing the VIBRAPHONE as a novelty on stage. He made the first recording of a jazz vibes solo with LOUIS ARMSTRONG in *Memories of You* (1930). He gained nationwide prominence on the vibes as a member of the Benny Goodman Quartet from 1936 to 1940. From then on, he usually led his own bands, most often playing vibes, but occasionally performing on other instruments. Beginning in 1956, he made several successful European tours. From the '60s on, Hampton has continued to tour as a bandleader and perform at various BENNY GOODMAN reunions.

Hancock, Herbie (Herbert Jeffrey), African-American JAZZ pianist and composer; b. Chicago, Apr. 12, 1940. A child prodigy, Hancock began studying piano at age 7, and made an appearance with the Chicago Symphony Orchestra at 11. He later studied engineering at Grinnell (Iowa) College from 1956 to 1960, then took courses at the Manhattan School of Music and the New School for Social Research in N.Y.

While still in school, Hancock led his own band, while also making appearances with such jazz artists as COLEMAN HAWKINS, Donald Byrd, and MILES DAVIS, whose quintet of the mid-'60s made Hancock famous. Hancock also scored a major jazz hit with his composition, *Watermelon Man.* In 1968, Hancock organized a sextet, which later was reduced to a quartet and with which he appeared in pop concerts. In addition to jazz piano he became adept as a player on electric piano. In 1972 he went to Los Angeles, and in 1973 converted to a California brand of Buddhism. That same year, he formed the popular FUNK-jazz band, Headhunters.

Hancock's ability to switch between styles has led to success in several fields. His electric jazz-funk (fusion) has produced several hits, including a re-working of his early hit *Watermelon Man,* and new compositions, including *Chameleon* and *Rockit.*

Among Hancock's most popular albums are *Empyrean Isles* (1964), *Maiden Voyage* (1965), *Speak Like A Child* (1968), *Headhunters* (1973), *V.S.O.P.: The Quintet* (1977), and *Future Shock* (1983). He won an Academy Award for his score to the 1986 film *'Round Midnight,* starring Dexter Gordon.

PEOPLE IN MUSIC

Hancock's 1983 video for "Rockit" featured very clever animation of normally inanimate objects. It was the perfect visual accompaniment to the electronic score. It was one of the most popular videos in the early days of MTV.

Handel (Hendel), **George Frideric** (born Georg Friedrich Händel), outstanding German-born English organist and composer, innovator of the English ORATORIO and a giant of the late BAROQUE; b. Halle, Feb. 23, 1685; d. London, Apr. 14, 1759. Handel's father was a barber-surgeon and personal servant to the Prince of Saxe-Magdeburg. At the age of 61,

he took a second wife, Dorothea Taust, daughter of the local pastor. George Frideric was the second son of this marriage.

As a child, Handel was taken by his father on a visit to Saxe-Weissenfels, where he had a chance to try out the organ of the court chapel. The Duke, Johann Adolf, noticing the young Handel's interest in music, advised that he be sent to Halle for organ lessons with FRIEDRICH WILHELM ZACHOW (1663–1712), the church organist there. Zachow gave Handel instruction in harpsichord and organ and also introduced him to the basics of composition. Handel proved to be a talented student, and substituted for Zachow as organist whenever necessary. He also composed trio sonatas and MOTETs for Sunday church services. After the death of his father in 1697, Handel entered the University of Halle in 1702, where he also served as a second organist at the church.

In 1703 Handel went to Hamburg, where he was engaged as "violino di ripieno" (supplementary or second violinist) by REINHARD KEISER (1674–1739), the famous composer and director of the Hamburg Opera. There he met composer and theorist JOHANN MATTHESON (1681–1764), and in 1703 the two undertook a journey to Lübeck together. They hoped to apply for the post of organist in succession to DIETRICH BUXTEHUDE, who was chief organist there. It was the custom for an incoming organist to marry a

George Frideric Handel. (New York Public Library)

Handel time line

1685	Born
1702	Enters the University of Halle
1703	Travels to Hamburg, where he serves as second violinist at the Hamburg Opera and also meets JOHANN MATTHESON, with whom he travels to Lübeck to meet Dietrich Buxtehude
1705	Operas *Almira* and *Nero* are staged at the Hamburg Opera
1706–09	Visits Italy, where several of his operas are produced
1710	Returns to Germany, where he succeeds AGOSTINO STEFFANI as Kapellmeister to the Elector of Hannover
1711	*Rinaldo* is premiered at the Queen's Theatre in London
1714	Moves to London

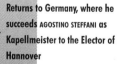

1717–18 Composes *Water Music* for King George I and also becomes resident composer to the Duke of Chandos, for whom he composes the *Chandos Anthems* and the oratorios *Acis and Galatea* and *Esther*

1719 Made Master of Musick of the newly formed Royal Academy of Music

1720 Composes his first collection of *Suites de pieces pour le clavecin (The Lessons)* for Princess Anne

1721–28 Composes more than a dozen operas in London, two of which, *Giulio Cesare* and *Rodelinda,* enter the repertoire

1727 Becomes a British subject and composes four grand anthems for the coronation of King George II and Queen Caroline

1728–31 Becomes associated with the King's Theatre where several revised works are brought out

1734 Sets up his own opera company at Covent Garden

1735–37 *Ariodante, Alcina, Atalanta, Arminio, Giustino,* and *Berenice* are staged at Covent Garden

1739 Presents the oratorio *Saul*

1741 Produces his last opera, *Deidamia,* and also travels to Ireland, where he composes his masterpiece, *Messiah*

1742 *Messiah* is premiered in Dublin

daughter of the incumbent as a condition of appointment, but neither Mattheson nor Handel availed themselves of this opportunity. (JOHANN SEBASTIAN BACH made the same journey in 1704, and also returned without obtaining the succession.)

Handel's first two operas, *Almira* and *Nero,* were staged at the Hamburg Opera in 1705. He was then commissioned to write two more operas, *Florindo* and *Daphne,* originally planned as a single opera combining both subjects. In 1706 he undertook a long voyage to Italy, where he visited Florence, Rome, Naples, and Venice. The first opera he wrote in Italy was *Rodrigo,* which premiered in Florence in 1707. Then followed *Agrippina,* which was staged in Venice two years later with great success, being given 27 performances.

In Rome, Handel composed the SERENATA *Il trionfo del Tempo e del Disinganno,* which was performed there in the spring of 1707. A year later, Handel's first oratorio *La Resurrezione* was given, also in Rome. Later that year, he brought out in Naples his serenata *Aci, Galatea, e Polifemo;* its score was remarkable for a bass solo that required an extraordinary range of two octaves and a fifth.

During his Italian visit, he met ALESSANDRO and DOMENICO SCARLATTI. In 1710 he returned to Germany and was named Kapellmeister to the Elector of Hannover, successor to AGOSTINO STEFFANI. Later that year he visited England, where he produced his opera *Rinaldo* at the Queen's Theatre in London in 1711, which received 15 performances.

After a brief return to Hannover in the summer of 1711, he made another visit to London, where he produced his operas *Il Pastor fido* (1712) and *Teseo* (1713). He also wrote an ode for Queen Anne's birthday, which was presented at Windsor Palace in 1713. It was soon followed by two sacred works, *Te Deum* and *Jubilate,* to celebrate the Peace of Utrecht. These performances won him royal favor and a salary of 200 pounds sterling.

An unpredictable series of events persuaded Handel to remain in London when Queen Anne died in 1714 and Handel's protector, the Elector of Hannover, became King George I. The King bestowed many favors upon the composer and doubled his salary. Handel became a British sub-

ject in 1727. He continued to produce operas, with Italian librettos, for the London stage. In 1716 Handel began to compose *Der für die Sünden der Welt gemarterte und sterbende Jesus,* to the Passion text of the poet Heinrich Brockes.

In 1717 Handel produced one of his most famous works, written expressly for King George I, the *Water Music.* Its first performance occurred on the Thames River, held by royal order. The King's boat was followed by a barge on which an orchestra of 50 musicians played Handel's score, or at least a major portion of it. The final version of the *Water Music* combines two instrumental suites composed at different times: one was written for the barge party, the other was written earlier.

Also in 1717, Handel became resident composer to the Duke of Chandos, for whom he wrote the so-called *Chandos Anthems* (1717–18), 11 in number, the secular oratorio *Acis and Galatea* (1718), and the oratorio *Esther* (1718). He also served as music master to the daughters of the Prince of Wales. For Princess Anne, he composed his first collection of *Suites de pièces pour le clavecin* (1720), also known as *The Lessons.* The famous air with variations nicknamed *The Harmonious Blacksmith* was among these works.

In 1719 Handel was made Master of Musick of a new business venture under the name of the Royal Academy of Music, established for the purpose of presenting opera at the King's Theatre. The first opera he composed for it was *Radamisto* (1720). In the fall of 1720 the Italian composer GIOVANNI BONONCINI (1670–1747) joined the company. A rivalry soon developed between him and Handel that was made famous by the poet John Byrom:

> *Some say, compar'd to Bononcini*
> *That Mynheer Handel's but a ninny.*
> *Others aver that he to Handel*
> *Is scarcely fit to hold a candle.*
> *Strange all this difference should be*
> *Twixt tweedledum and tweedledee.*

Handel won a victory over his rival when Bononcini had the unfortunate idea of submitting to the London Academy of Music a MADRIGAL which he had largely lifted from a

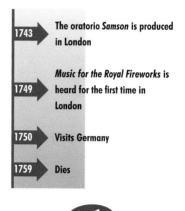

1743	The oratorio *Samson* is produced in London
1749	*Music for the Royal Fireworks* is heard for the first time in London
1750	Visits Germany
1759	Dies

There was apparently a quarrel between Mattheson and Handel at a performance of Mattheson's opera *Cleopatra.* Mattheson asked Handel to yield his place as *maestro al cembalo* (chief keyboardist and orchestral director) for the production. Handel declined, and an altercation ensued, resulting in a duel with swords. The duel was ended when Mattheson broke his sword on a metal button of Handel's coat. Soon thereafter, they were friends again.

One story that has long been told is that Handel overheard a blacksmith whistling a folk tune that attracted his attention. He supposedly adopted this tune to one of the piano pieces written for Anne, and hence it got the nickname *The Harmonious Blacksmith.*

choral piece by the Italian composer ANTONIO LOTTI. Lotti discovered it, and an embarrassing controversy ensued, resulting in Bononcini's disgrace and expulsion from London (he died in obscurity in Vienna, where he had sought refuge). The irony of the whole episode is that Handel was no less guilty of plagiarism. He was known to lift melodies and entire movements from other composers' works when it was necessary to meet a tight deadline!

Between 1721 and 1728 Handel produced over a dozen operas in London, but only two of these, *Giulio Cesare* and *Rodelinda,* became firmly established in the repertoire. In 1727 he composed four grand anthems for the coronation of King George II and Queen Caroline.

In the spring of 1728 the Royal Academy of Music ceased operations, and Handel became associated with the management of the King's Theatre. The following year he went to Italy to recruit singers for a new Royal Academy of Music. Returning to London, he brought out the operas *Lotario, Partenope, Poro, Ezio, Sosarme,* and *Orlando,* but only *Orlando* proved to have any lasting success.

In 1732 Handel gave a special performance of a revised version of his oratorio *Esther* at the King's Theatre. It was followed by the revised version of *Acis and Galatea* (1732) and the oratorio *Deborah* (1733). Later that year, he produced his oratorio *Athalia* at Oxford, where he also appeared as an organist. He was offered an honorary doctor of music degree there, but declined the honor.

Discouraged by the poor reception of his operas at the King's Theatre, Handel decided to open a new season under a different management. But he quarreled with the principal singer, the famous castrato Senesino (FRANCESCO BERNARDI, c.1680–c.1759), who was popular with audiences. Handel lost the support of a substantial number of his subscribers, who then formed a rival opera company called Opera of the Nobility. It engaged the famous Italian composer NICOLA PORPORA (1686–1768) as director, and opened its first season in late 1733. Handel's opera *Arianna in Creta* had its premiere at the King's Theatre in 1734, but in July of that year both Handel's company and the rival group were forced to suspend operations.

Handel set up his own opera company at Covent Garden, inaugurating his new season with a revised version of *Il Pastor fido* in late 1734. This was followed by *Ariodante, Alcina, Atalanta, Arminio, Giustino,* and *Berenice,* all staged between 1735 and 1737, but only *Alcina* sustained a success. In 1736, he presented his ode *Alexander's Feast* at Covent Garden, and in 1737 brought out a revised version of his oratorio *Il trionfo del Tempo e della Verita.* His fortunes improved when he was confirmed by the Queen as music master to the Princesses Amelia and Caroline. He continued to maintain connections with Germany, and traveled to Aachen in 1737.

Upon his return to London, Handel suffered from attacks of gout, a common illness of British society at the time, but he managed to resume work. In 1738 he produced his operas *Faramondo* and *Serse* (an aria from the latter, *Ombra mai fù,* became famous in an anonymous instrumental arrangement under the title *Handel's Celebrated Largo*). There followed a pasticcio, *Giove in Argo* (1739), and *Imeneo* (1740). The following year, he produced his last opera, *Deidamia.*

In retrospect, Handel's failure as an operatic composer was a happy turn of events, because he then directed his energy toward the composition of oratorios, in which he achieved greatness. For inspiration he turned to biblical themes, using English texts. In 1739 he presented the oratorio *Saul* (including the *Dead March*); followed by *Israel in Egypt;* an *Ode for St. Cecilia's Day,* after Dryden; and his great set of 12 Concerti Grossi, op. 6. Milton's *L'Allegro and Il Penseroso* inspired him to write *L'Allegro, il Penseroso, ed il Moderato* in 1740.

In 1741 Handel was invited to visit Ireland, and there he produced his greatest masterpiece, *Messiah.* Working with tremendous concentration, he completed Part I in six days, Part II in nine days, and Part III in six days. The orchestration took him only a few more days, and he signed the score in 1741. The first performance of *Messiah* was given in Dublin in 1742, and its London premiere the following year. If contemporary reports can be trusted, King George II rose to his feet during the *Hallelujah Chorus,* and the entire audience followed suit. Since then, performances of *Messiah* have moved listeners to rise during this celebratory chorus.

Handel's oratorio *Samson,* produced in London in 1743, was also successful. However, his next oratorio, *Semele* in 1744, failed to arouse public admiration. Continuing to work, and alternating between mythological subjects and religious themes, he produced many more oratorios between 1744 and 1752; of these, *Judas Maccabaeus, Solomon,* and *Jephtha* became public favorites.

Besides oratorios, mundane events also occupied Handel's attention. To celebrate the Peace of Aachen, he composed the remarkable *Music for the Royal Fireworks,* which was heard for the first time in London in 1749. In 1750 he revisited Germany. But soon he had to limit his activities on account of failing eyesight, which required the removal of cataracts. The operation proved unsuccessful, but he still continued to appear in performances of his music, with the assistance of his pupil John Christopher Smith. Handel's last appearance in public was at a London performance of *Messiah.* Eight days later, on the Saturday between Good Friday and Easter, he died. He was buried at Westminster Abbey, where a monument marks his grave.

A parallel between the two great German contemporaries, Johann Sebastian Bach and Handel, is often drawn. They were born within a few months of each other, Bach in Eisenach, Handel in Halle, a distance of about 80 miles, but they never met. Bach visited Halle at least twice, but Handel was then away, in London.

But the difference between their lives was profound. Bach was a master of the Baroque organ who produced religious works for church use, a schoolmaster who regarded his instrumental music as a textbook for study. He never composed for the stage, and traveled little. By contrast, Handel was a man of the world who dedicated himself mainly to public performances, and who became a British subject. Bach's life was that of a middle-class German whose genius was inconspicuous. Handel shone in the light of public admiration. Bach was married twice, and survivors among his 20 children became important musicians in their own right. Handel remained unwed, but he was not a recluse. Physically, he tended toward healthy corpulence. He enjoyed the company of friends, but was easily angered. Like Bach, he was deeply religious, and there was no ostentation in his service to his God.

Handel's music possessed grandeur of design, majestic eloquence, and rich harmony. Music lovers did not have to study Handel's style to discover its beauty, while the sublime art of Bach could be fully understood only after careful study of its structure.

Handel bequeathed the bulk of his manuscripts to his student, John Christopher Smith, whose son presented them in turn to King George III. They eventually became a part of the King's Music Library, comprising 32 volumes of operas, 21 volumes of oratorios, seven volumes of odes and serenatas, 12 volumes of sacred music, 11 volumes of cantatas, and five volumes of instrumental music. Seven volumes containing sketches for various works are in the Fitzwilliam Collection at Cambridge.

handle piano. A mechanical PIANOFORTE operating on the same principle as the BARREL ORGAN.

MUSICAL INSTRUMENT

PEOPLE IN MUSIC

Handy, W(illiam) **C**(hristopher), noted African-American pianist, publisher, bandleader, and composer, known as the "father of the BLUES"; b. Florence, Ala., Nov. 16, 1873; d. N.Y., March 28, 1958. Handy's father and grandfather were both ministers. In 1892 he graduated from the Teachers' Agricultural and Mechanical College in Huntsville, Alabama, becoming a schoolteacher and also working in iron mills. He learned to play the CORNET and was a soloist at the Chicago World's Fair in 1893. He also became bandmaster for a traveling show called Mahara's Minstrels. From 1900 to 1902 he taught at the Agricultural and Mechanical College.

Handy led a band on several tours of the South beginning in 1903. The band played the popular music, including classical selections, marches, and songs, that both white and black audiences enjoyed. According to Handy, at one performance in a dance hall in the backwoods of Mississippi, a rag-tag local band asked if they could play during Handy's intermission. He agreed, and was amused to hear what to him was primitive music. But he was even more astonished

Statue of W.C. Handy in Memphis, TN, 1996. (Raymond Gehman/Corbis) ▶

when he saw the audience's positive reaction—and also saw the amount of money they threw on the stage!

This was Handy's first exposure to the blues. Realizing the popularity of the musical form, he began to incorporate some into his repertoire. Handy's famous song *Memphis Blues,* published 1912, was the second piece to be published as a "blues" work and the first blues work to achieve widespread popularity. This song, along with Handy's more celebrated *St. Louis Blues* (1914), introduced both the blues scale (with its flattened thirds and sevenths, the so-called "blue notes") and style into popular music. Handy followed these with more blues: *Yellow Dog, Beale Street, Joe Turner,* the march *Hail to the Spirit of Freedom* (1915), *Ole Miss* for piano (1916), the songs *Aunt Hagar's Children* (1920) and *Loveless Love* (1921), and *Aframerican Hymn* for band and chorus (1916).

Handy also published several collections of songs, including *Blues: An Anthology* (which also appeared as *A Treasury of the Blues*), *Negro Authors and Composers of the U.S.A.* (1935), *Book of Negro Spirituals* (1938), and *Unsung Americans Sung* (1944). His autobiography appeared as *Father of the Blues* (1941). He also was one of the few successful African-American music publishers.

Handy's published blues style foreshadowed the urban style that became popular in the 1920s. Some have accused Handy of taking traditional blues songs and putting his own name on them as their "composer." Others feel he was far more instrumental in transforming the folk blues into a recognizable style. No doubt the truth lies somewhere in the middle, because if Handy was not truly the "father of the blues," he was certainly its greatest early promoter.

Hanna, (Sir) **Roland,** African-American jazz pianist; b. Detroit, Feb. 10, 1932. Hanna began taking piano lessons as a child but soon turned to jazz, commencing his career as a performer in local clubs. During service in the U.S. Army, he played in an army band from 1950 to 1952. After his discharge, he took courses at the Eastman School of Music in Rochester, N.Y., and at the Juilliard School of Music in N.Y. He formed his own trio in 1959. He later was a leading member of the Thad Jones-Mel Lewis Orchestra from 1966 to 1974, then co-founded and played with the N.Y. Jazz Quartet, which began performing in 1971. In 1970 he was knighted by the government of Liberia, from which he draws the title, "Sir Roland Hanna."

In his playing, Hanna reveals not only a refined technique, but a deep knowledge of historical jazz piano playing. He draws on this knowledge to create solos that are appropriate to the piece or general style in which he is playing.

Hanon, Charles-Louis, French pianist, pedagogue, and composer of keyboard exercises; b. Renescure, near Dunkerque, July 2, 1819; d. Boulogne-sur-Mer, March 19, 1900. Next to CARL CZERNY, Hanon was the most illustrious composer of piano exercises. His masterpiece is *Le Pianiste-virtuose* (The virtuoso pianist), which for over a century has been the manual of choice for many millions of diligent piano students all over the face of the musical globe.

Hanon further wrote a collection of 50 instructive piano pieces under the title *Méthode élémentaire de piano* (Elementary method for piano), a useful compilation, *Extraits des chefs-d'oeuvres des grands maîtres* (Extracts from the masterpieces of the great masters), as well as a selection of 50 ecclesiastical chants, *50 cantiques choisis parmi les plus populaires* (50 of the most popular chants).

Hans Heiling. OPERA by HEINRICH MARSCHNER, 1833, first produced in Berlin. Heiling, a hereditary prince of Hell, falls

PEOPLE IN MUSIC

PEOPLE IN MUSIC

Hanon also attempted to instruct uneducated musicians in the art of accompanying PLAINCHANT in a how-to book, *Système nouveau pour apprendre à accompagner tout plainchant sans savoir la musique* (New system for learning to accompany all plainchant without knowing the music).

in love with a mortal woman. However, when she discovers his supernatural essence, she leaves him for a human lover. He plans to slay his rival, but his mother persuades him to desist, and he vanishes.

Hänsel und Gretel. Fairy-tale OPERA by ENGELBERT HUMPERDINCK, 1893, first performed in Weimar and forever forthwith a universal favorite. The subject is from a Grimm fairy tale. A witch lures the siblings Hänsel and Gretel to her gingerbread house which—they discover to their horror—is made out of baked children. Cleverly, the two intended victims push the witch into the burning oven. She explodes and the gingerbread children all return to life. The score is Wagnerian to the core.

PEOPLE IN MUSIC

Hanson, Howard (Harold), important American composer, conductor, and educator; b. Wahoo, Nebr., Oct. 28, 1896; d. Rochester, N.Y., Feb. 26, 1981. Hanson's parents emigrated from Sweden to America and made their home in Nebraska, which had a large population of Scandinavian settlers. Hanson's northern ancestry played an important part in his spiritual outlook and his music. His mother taught him piano, and he began to compose very early in life. He also learned to play the cello.

Hanson attended the Luther College in Wahoo and played piano and organ in local churches. In 1912 he enrolled in the University of Nebraska, and in 1913 went to N.Y., where he took piano lessons and studied composition at the Institute of Musical Art. In 1915 he enrolled at Northwestern University in Evanston, Illinois, furthering his studies in composition.

Hanson progressed rapidly as a composer. His *Symphonic Prelude* was performed by the Chicago Symphony Orchestra, and he also wrote a Piano Quintet and other works. In 1916, at the age of 20, he received an appointment to teach music at the College of the Pacific in San Jose, California. In 1919 he was named its dean. In 1921 he became the first American to win the prestigious Prix de Rome, which enabled him to spend three years at the American Academy there. He composed copiously, the major part of his works reflecting his profound sentiment for his ancestral land, exemplified by his earlier *Scandinavian Suite* for piano (1919).

Hanson believed in music as a function of the natural environment. During his stay in the West, he wrote the score for a *California Forest Play* (1920). The work that gained him admission to Rome was a symphonic poem, *Before the Dawn.* In 1923 he completed a piece for chorus and orchestra entitled *North and West.* All these works clearly indicated his future path as a composer, filled as they are with the spirit of the northern country, inspired by both Scandinavia and the American West.

Next came Hanson's first important work, Symphony No. 1, subtitled *Nordic,* which he conducted at its first performance in Rome in 1923. In it he expressed, "the solemnity, austerity, and grandeur of the North, of its restless surging and strife, and of its somberness and melancholy." Hanson was often described as an American JEAN SIBELIUS, and indeed he professed profound admiration for the great Finnish composer. Like Sibelius, he created flowing melodies accompanied by rich harmonies.

In 1924 Hanson conducted the U.S. premiere of his *Nordic Symphony* in Rochester, N.Y., and also met George Eastman, the inventor of Kodak film. Eastman, who knew next to nothing about music, had nonetheless a keen appreciation of ability among artists and composers, and in 1924 offered Hanson the position of director of the Eastman School of Music. Hanson accepted, not quite 28 years old at the time. Eastman's insight was justified, and Hanson elevated the Eastman School of Music from a provincial conservatory to one of the most important musical institutions in America. He retained his post as director for 40 years.

Apart from his teaching, Hanson inaugurated annual festivals of American music in Rochester. As both director and conductor of these festivals, he programmed not only music that appealed to him, but also modern works in dissonant harmonies. He also maintained a friendly attitude toward his students even when they veered away into the field of musical abstractions. All told, during his tenure in Rochester, Hanson presented works by some 700 composers representing some 1,500 different compositions. He also made numerous recordings with the Eastman School Philharmonic.

In 1925 Hanson completed one of his most significant works, *The Lament for Beowulf* for chorus and orchestra, based on an Anglo-Saxon saga. In 1930 he wrote his Second Symphony, entitled *Romantic,* on commission from SERGE KOUSSEVITZKY and the Boston Symphony Orchestra for its 50th anniversary. Koussevitzky conducted its first performance in 1930. Hanson's Third Symphony (1936–37) glorified the pioneer spirit of Swedish immigrants. It was presented over the NBC Radio network in 1938, with Hanson himself conducting.

In his Symphony No. 4, subtitled *The Requiem* (1943), Hanson paid tribute to the memory of his father. He conducted its first performance with the Boston Symphony Orchestra in 1943, and in 1944 the work received the Pulitzer Prize in music. There followed the Fifth Symphony, *Sinfonia Sacra,* in a single movement (1954), in which Hanson invoked his deep-rooted Christian faith. This work was first performed by the Philadelphia Orchestra in 1955. Hanson wrote his Sixth Symphony to commemorate the 125th anniversary of the N.Y. Philharmonic. Leonard Bernstein conducted its first performance in 1968. Hanson's Seventh Symphony, *A Sea Symphony,* with chorus, derived from Walt Whitman's poem, was first performed in 1977, at the National Music Camp at Interlochen. Whitman's poetry was close to Hanson's creative imagination, and he wrote several other works based on Whitman's poems.

Hanson wrote in other idioms besides symphonies. In 1933 he composed his opera, *Merry Mount,* based on *The Maypole Lovers of Merry Mount* by Nathaniel Hawthorne. Hanson dedicated the work to the memory of Eastman, who had committed suicide two years before. It was one of the few operas by an American composer staged at N.Y.'s Metropolitan Opera, and the production was very successful. Despite this popular reception and favorable critical reviews, however, the opera had only four performances, and was not retained in the repertoire, a fate not unlike that of other American operas produced there. A symphonic suite drawn from the score enjoyed frequent performances at summer symphonic concerts and on the radio.

According to reports, the first performance of *Merry Mount* had a total of 50 curtain calls for Hanson and the singers after its four acts.

In the meantime, Hanson continued an active career as a conductor. In 1932 he led several concerts of American music in major cities of Europe. During 1961–62 he took the Eastman School Philharmonic Orchestra on a grand European tour, under the auspices of the State Department.

As an educator, Hanson enjoyed great prestige. Many talented American composers studied under him. He also received numerous honorary degrees. In 1935 he was elected a member of the National Institute of Arts and Letters, and in 1938 he became a fellow of the Royal Academy of Music in Sweden. He held, at various times, a presidency of the National Association of Schools of Music. He also served as president of the Music Teachers National Association and of the National Music Council. In all he was awarded 19 honorary doctorates in music. In 1945 he received the Ditson Award, and in 1946 was given the George Foster Peabody Award.

With the radical changes in contemporary composition, Hanson's music was increasingly viewed as being hopelessly old-fashioned. The number of performances of his music dwindled, and only occasionally were his symphonies broadcast. Hanson never concealed his bitterness at this loss of appreciation in his country for whose artistic progress he labored so mightily.

Yet Hanson's music has much to recommend it: rich harmonies, powerful rhythms, and beautiful orchestrations. Recently, with a renewed interest in ROMANTIC composition, Hanson's music has enjoyed a modest revival.

Happening. A loosely defined type of collective activity or performance among American theater workers, painters, poets, musicians, and participants in the 1950s and 1960s.

JOHN CAGE's theater piece at North Carolina's Black Mountain College in the early 1950s is usually cited as a model for future Happenings. The "audience" of artists who watched it were also the actors who performed it, so the line between creator, actor, and audience was virtually removed. In 1956, one of the first recognized Happenings was staged by Allan Kaprow in a N.Y. art gallery under the name *18 Happenings in 6 Parts*. The audience was distributed in 14 groups seated in chairs at random, and its participation in the action was encouraged. It included simultaneous performances of light, sound, music, and film, in fragmentary pieces and random order.

In the 1960s, the FLUXUS group and others took up the Happening idea and pushed it in more extreme directions. In the meantime, *Happening* entered the language, penetrating common speech so deeply in the later '60s that everyday events were often described as *Happenings* simply because they had taken place at all.

Happy Birthday to You. This famous greeting song, 1893, was first published as *Good Morning to All* in *Song Stories for the Kindergarten.* The tune is by Mildred Hill.

Happy Days Are Here Again. Song by MILTON AGER, 1930, for the movie musical, *Chasing Rainbows.* It accompanies a scene in which brave soldiers receive news of the Armistice in November 1918. It became the campaign song of Franklin D. Roosevelt in 1932, and of many subsequent Democratic candidates for the Presidency.

happy ending (It. *lieto fine*). In operas and other dramatic works, a morally and emotionally satisfying finale, no matter how improbable or realistic, where virtue triumphs, evil is punished or forgiven, and lovers unite after overcoming insurmountable odds.

Harawi, chant d'amour et de mort. Song cycle by OLIVIER MESSIAEN, 1945, for soprano and piano. It was inspired by the slow lyric song of the Incas.

Harbach (born Hauerbach), **Otto** (Abels), American lyricist and librettist; b. Salt Lake City, Aug. 18, 1873; d. N.Y., Jan. 24, 1963. Harbach studied at Knox College and Columbia University. Originally working as a journalist, he became interested in writing for the musical theater. In 1908 he collaborated with the composer Karl Hoschna on the successful musical *The 3 Twins,* which launched his career. The duo worked together on three other shows until Hoschna's death in 1911. Harbach subsequently wrote more than 40 works for Broadway, often in collaboration with OSCAR HAMMER-

The copyright to this one song is so valuable that a major music publishing company paid $1 million in the late 1980s to continue to exploit it through the year 2013!

PEOPLE IN MUSIC

STEIN II. His musical partners included RUDOLF FRIML, VICTOR YOUMANS, JEROME KERN, and SIGMUND ROMBERG. He also wrote for films.

Harbach's most popular lyrics included *Rose-Marie* and *Indian Love Call* from Friml's *Rose-Marie* (with Hammerstein; 1924), *The Night Was Made for Love* from Kern's *The Cat and the Fiddle* (1931), and *Smoke Gets in Your Eyes* from Kern's *Roberta* (1932).

Harbison, John (Harris), significant American composer; b. Orange, N.J., Dec. 20, 1938. Harbison's father was a professor of history at Princeton University and his mother a magazine writer. Both of them were also amateur musicians.

PEOPLE IN MUSIC

A multi-talented instrumentalist, Harbison studied violin, viola, piano, voice, and tuba at Princeton High School and also took lessons in music theory. In 1956 he entered Harvard University as a composition student of the noted theory teacher WALTER PISTON, receiving a Paine Traveling Fellowship for a season of study with Boris Blacher in Berlin. Returning to the U.S., he studied composition privately with ROGER SESSIONS and with Earl Kim at Princeton University, where he gained a Master of Fine Arts degree in 1963.

From 1963 to 1968, Harbison was a member of the Society of Fellows at Harvard, and from 1969 to 1982 he taught at the Massachusetts Institute of Technology. He was composer-in-residence of the Pittsburgh Symphony Orchestra from 1982 to 1984 and of the Los Angeles Philharmonic from 1985 to 1988. He also made numerous appearances as a conductor, leading the Cantata Singers from 1969 to 1973 and again from 1980 to 1982. In 1977 he held a Guggenheim fellowship, and in 1987 received the Pulitzer Prize in music for his sacred RICERCAR *The Flight Into Egypt,* composed the prior year. In 1989 he received a MacArthur fellowship, and in 1992 he was elected to membership in the American Academy and Institute of Arts and Letters, the same year he returned to Tanglewood as composer-in-residence, later serving as director of its contemporary music festival. In 1998 he won the Heinz Award in arts and humanities.

Harbison freely draws on various modern composition techniques in his own works. In his Shakespearean opera,

The Winter's Tale, he used innovative "dumb shows," acted in pantomime on the stage. In his opera *Full Moon in March,* he made use of the PREPARED PIANO, as well as ready-made recordings for special effects. Other well-known works include the ballet *Ulysses* and the orchestral work *Ulysses' Raft,* both from 1983, and several concertos and symphonies.

Harbison has also written a good deal of chamber music, including *Bermuda Triangle* for tenor saxophone, amplified cello, and electric organ, composed in 1970 and two string quartets. He has also composed numerous vocal works, including *Book of Hours and Seasons* (1975), *The Flower-Fed Buffaloes* for baritone, chorus, and seven instruments (1976), *Mirabai Songs* for soprano and chamber ensemble (1982), *The Natural World* for soprano or mezzosoprano and five instruments (1987), and *Concerning Them Which Are Asleep* for chorus (1994).

Harburg, E(dgar) **Y**(ip) (born Isidore Hochberg), American lyricist; b. N.Y., Apr. 8, 1898; d. Los Angeles, Mar. 5, 1981. Harburg graduated from the City College of N.Y. in 1921, then was co-proprietor of an electrical appliance company, which failed during the Depression. He began to write lyrics for Broadway, and with JAY GORNEY produced the famous song *Brother, Can You Spare a Dime* in 1932. Other early hits were 1933's *It's Only a Paper Moon,* with a melody by BILLY ROSE, and *April in Paris,* with music by VERNON DUKE.

Harburg moved to Hollywood in the mid-1930s, collaborating on several films with HAROLD ARLEN. In 1939, Harburg and Arlen won an Academy Award for their wonderful song *Over the Rainbow* from *The Wizard of Oz.*

Harburg continued to write for films through the mid-'40s. He returned to Broadway in 1947 with the hit musical, *Finian's Rainbow,* for which he wrote the lyrics and cowrote the book with Fred Saidy. The music was written by Burton Lane. Harburg continued to write for Broadway and Hollywood through the '60s, with only occasional success. He died in an automobile accident in 1981.

Harburg was probably the most socially outspoken lyricist in the great age of Broadway and film musicals. His

PEOPLE IN MUSIC

lyrics tended to have a social message as well as serving as entertainment.

hard bop. A jazz style of the 1950s and '60s that returns to the relative simplicities of the blues, resulting in an intensified, more accessible style. Hard bop was a reaction against the complexities and sophistication of BEBOP and COOL JAZZ.

hardingfele (Hardanger fiddle). A traditional Norwegian FIDDLE, named for the Hardanger region in Norway. The instrument features both melody strings (that are fretted) and sympathetic strings (that vibrate when a related tone is played on one of the melody strings). There are at least 20 TUNINGS used. The instrument dates to the middle of the 17th century, and its repertoire includes folk songs, dances (*slåtter*), and bridal marches.

Harlequin (Fr.). The central character in COMMEDIA DELL'ARTE. Harlequin is in the service of a villainous Pantaloon (Pantalone), and adores Columbine (Columbina), who is the object of Pantaloon's lust. In vulgar Latin, Harlequinus was a benign demon, hence, the Italian form *Arlecchino*. The name may also be connected with the Erlkönig (elf-king), leader of the sprites.

harmonic. 1. Pertaining to chords (either CONSONANT or DISSONANT), and to the theory and practice of harmony. 2. HARMONICS. Also *harmonic curve,* the figure described by a vibrating string or other sound source on a spectrograph; *harmonic figuration,* broken chords, ARPEGGIO; *harmonic flute,* harmonic stop; *harmonic mark* (sign, symbol), a degree sign (∘) over a note, indicating a harmonic; *harmonic minor scale,* a natural minor scale with a raised seventh step, producing a LEADING TONE and an augmented second; *harmonic note,* HARMONICS; *harmonic scale:* 1. HARMONIC SERIES. 2. *Harmonic minor scale; harmonic flute, reed, or stop,* organ stop having pipes double the ordinary length, and pierced midway, so that a 16′ pipe yields an 8′ tone; *harmonic tone,* harmonics.

MUSICAL
INSTRUMENT

harmonic series. The natural ascending series of OVERTONES or PARTIALS.

If the FUNDAMENTAL is set at a given note, then the:

2nd harmonic	is an	octave above
3rd harmonic	is a	perfect fifth above the 2nd harmonic
4th harmonic	is a	perfect fourth higher
5th harmonic	is a	major third higher
6th harmonic	is a	minor third higher

and so forth. The first six members of the natural harmonic series form the harmony of the major chord, fundamental to all acoustic phenomena. *See also* HARMONICS.

MUSICAL INSTRUMENT

Harmonica virtuoso Larry Adler, c. 1935. (Hulton-Deutsch Collection/Corbis)

▶

harmonica. Hand-held free-REED instrument in which a set of metal reeds are mounted in a narrow frame. The harmonica is blown by the mouth, and produces different tones on expiration and inspiration. Also called mouth harmonica, mouth organ, or (in U.S. slang) mouth harp.

harmonicon. 1. HARMONICA. 2. ORCHESTRION.

harmonics (overtones, partials). A series of tones naturally produced by a vibrating string or an air column in a pipe.

What we hear as a single tone is actually a set of tones produced by the vibrations of the string or air column as a whole and also as ½, ⅓, ¼, and other subdivisions of the sounding body.

Harmonics determine the TIMBRE (sound quality) of an instrument, depending on their relative strength in the tone complex. The principal harmonics can be produced on a string instrument by lightly touching the string at a chosen point of equal division (a NODE), thus preventing the string from vibrating as a whole. By touching lightly on the node ⅓ of the length of the open violin string e2, the upper b3 an octave and a fifth above will be heard. Since most bugle calls, trumpet flourishes, and fanfares are derived from the natural harmonics, an ingenious experimenter can play a variety of common tunes (and even tunes such as the theme of the last movement of LUDWIG VAN BEETHOVEN's Violin Concerto), sliding one's finger over a string.

The harmonics of string instruments possess a flute-like quality, which explains the French word for harmonics, *flageolet* (from Old Fr. *flageol,* flute). This is also the term used in German and Russian.

Harmonie der Welt, Die (Harmony of the World). Opera by PAUL HINDEMITH, 1957. This opera is based on the life story of astronomer Johannes Kepler (1571–1630).

Harmonies poétiques et religieuses. A piano cycle by FRANZ LISZT, 1849, containing ten pieces, the seventh of which, *Funérailles,* is frequently performed separately.

The cycle is usually assumed to refer to the death of FRÉDÉRIC CHOPIN, Liszt's close friend who died in the seventh month of that year. An alternative theory is that Liszt was mourning the defeat of the Hungarian Revolution of 1848 and the establishment of Austrian rule.

Invocations, the first piece of the cycle, first published in 1834, is written in constantly changing meters ($\frac{8}{4}$, $\frac{9}{4}$, $\frac{10}{4}$, etc.). It bears no key signature, and includes such innovations as an emphasis on the TRITONE (the interval of three whole tones or an augmented fourth). Its ending is marked *trés long silence* ("very long silence"). Fifty years later Liszt returned to the exploration of ATONALITY implied in this piece with his *Bagatelle ohne Tonart* (Bagatelle Without Tonality).

Try these experiments:

Silently depress a key on the piano keyboard, say a low E, and hold it; then strike sharply the e an octave higher and let it go. The upper octave will continue to reverberate on the still-open string of the lower E (the FUNDAMENTAL).

A weaker but still audible reverberation can be produced by striking a fifth above the octave sound (b), and possibly even e1, two octaves above the open string.

Under ideal circumstances on a very-well-tuned and resonant piano, even the fifth natural component of the original string, in this case g♯1, can be detected, thus forming a full major triad.

An acute ear may hear the octave and the twelfth (upper e and b on the fundamental E) by striking the fundamental tone very forcibly and letting it vibrate sonorously.

A real blacksmith who practiced his art in the vicinity of London was buried with his tombstone inscribed with the subject of Handel's air with variations.

MUSICAL INSTRUMENT

Harmonious Blacksmith, The. The nickname for an air with five variations by GEORGE FRIDERIC HANDEL, 1720, from an E-major harpsichord suite.

The origin of the title is told in great detail in many early music histories, but it, however, is entirely false. It is said that Handel heard this air sung by a blacksmith near London while forging iron, or that he was impressed by the steady beat of the artisan's hammer. To lend essence to this story, the alleged anvil of the fictitious harmonious blacksmith was even exhibited in London. The earliest edition of the music under the title of *The Harmonious Blacksmith* was published in England about 1819, 60 years after Handel's death.

harmonium. An organ-like portable instrument on which sound is activated by air pressure generated by a pair of foot pedals and passing through a set of flexible metal FREE REEDS. The harmonium became a popular instrument in the 19th century with special appeal to amateur performers because it could produce a sustained tone and rudimentary dynamics by pressing the pedal. It became a perfect instrument for the home in middle-class culture and in small churches as a substitute for the organ. Also called expressive organ. *See also* REED ORGAN.

harmony. A combination of TONES or CHORDS, CONSONANT or DISSONANT. Also, the CONTRAPUNTAL texture of a HOMOPHONIC piece, as two- or three-part harmony.

The Greek word HARMONIA referred to an ideal music, with an artful coordination between high and low sounds and a balanced rhythmic and melodic arrangement of slow and fast musical phrases. However, for at least the last 1,000 years, the word *harmony* has meant the simultaneous sounding of several melodies, represented in musical notation by vertical position, while melody was linear, notated horizontally. Counterpoint contains both harmonic and melodic elements because it is a harmonious synchronization of linear melodies.

When harmony first emerged as a definite technique, it was entirely consonant, limited to the use of perfect concords, the OCTAVE and the FIFTH. Because a perfect fifth subtracted from an octave formed a perfect fourth, consonant intervals incorporated perfect octaves, fifths, and fourths. The decisive step toward traditional harmony occurred in the late Middle Ages, when thirds and sixths were adopted as acceptable consonant intervals. Originally, the major TRIAD was only implied by the statement of the TONIC and fifth. Curiously, this continued to be the rule until the 16th century, when final triads finally acquired the essential third step of the scale.

With the birth of FAUXBOURDON, FIRST INVERSION of the major chord was introduced. Dissonant passing tones became more and more frequent. FIGURED BASS appeared as harmonic shorthand that opened the way toward the use of triads and seventh chords on all degrees of the scale.

In the 17th century, harmonic composition began to separate itself from COUNTERPOINT. In the next century counterpoint developed into a sublime art in the music of JOHANN SEBASTIAN BACH, but elsewhere harmony gradually became a vertical group of tones with limited independence of its component parts. However, Bach's sons embraced harmonic composition governed by the laws of chord progressions. The melody was emphasized, and the bass became the source of the harmony part.

Four-part harmony emerged at the end of the BAROQUE era, around 1750. The tonic (1st), subdominant (4th), and dominant (5th) triads are the main determinants of tonality, because these three triads contain all seven notes of the diatonic scale. In major keys, these triads are major, and in minor the tonic and subdominant are minor, but the dominant is made major by raising the seventh degree (creating the LEADING TONE), which is the middle tone of the major dominant triad.

Four-part harmony makes it possible to achieve complete sets of seventh chords on all degrees of the scale, as well as the diminished-seventh chord that occurs functionally upon the leading tone in a harmonic minor key. In strict harmony, triads having a diminished or augmented fifth are not allowed. Consequently, a triad built on the seventh degree of either the major or harmonic minor mode cannot be used, nor the SUPERTONIC triad (based on the 2nd scale degree) in minor keys. However, this rule was less strictly enforced in time.

Consecutive intervals, that is, a perfect fifth or octave moving in the same direction to another perfect fifth or octave, particularly between outer voices, are forbidden. Parallel movement of different intervals toward fifths or octaves, known as hidden intervals, is also taboo. A fifth or an octave can be reached only by contrary motion. Any number of examples from Bach's chorales or other well-known sources can be used to discredit this stern code.

In school exercises, the four component parts are named after the voices in a vocal quartet: soprano, alto, tenor, and bass. The most important consideration in four-part harmony is voice-leading. Generally speaking, crossing of voices is not admitted—the soprano must always be the upper voice, the bass must always be the lowest, and the alto may not cross under the tenor. CONTRARY MOTION is recommended, especially between the soprano and bass. Stepwise motion is preferred. Thirds and sixths are favored because they can be used in consecutive motion.

When one voice leaps several scale degrees, the rest of the voices must move stepwise to provide counterbalance and establish proper balance. If the soprano has a melodic leap upward, then the bass ought to move stepwise, preferably in the opposite direction. If in the same direction, the bass must avoid landing on a perfect fifth or octave, which would result in hidden fifths or octaves.

By and large, an ideal exercise in four-part harmony would present an alternation of thirds and sixths between the outer voices, with occasional legitimate parallelisms. The octave is expected in almost every final cadence. The middle voices are less mobile and have less opportunity to move by leaps. Often they are stationary, maintaining the common tone between two successive chords. Each chord can be arranged in six different ways without changing the bass.

The distance between soprano and alto or between alto and tenor must not exceed an octave, but the distance between bass and tenor may be as extensive as a twelfth. When the three upper voices are bunched together within an octave, it is called CLOSE HARMONY. When these upper voices

So deeply ingrained are these rules, particularly in four-part harmony, that a pedantic editor of FRANZ LISZT'S *LIEBE-STRAUM* deleted one of the inner voices in the coda in order to avoid a pair of consecutive fifths.

are dispersed for a total range of more than an octave, the setting is said to be in OPEN HARMONY.

A veritable harmonic revolution occurred with extraordinary suddenness toward the end of the 19th century. In the works of CLAUDE DEBUSSY and his followers the traditional rules of harmony were revised. Naked fifths and octaves moved in parallel lines as they did a thousand years before in organum. Consecutive triads in close harmony became common, disregarding the fact that such progressions necessarily involve consecutive fifths. Parallel formations of major triads were rampant, as were consecutive $^6_4$ chords in major keys (as in, for example, the ending of MAURICE RAVEL's String Quartet).

Up to about 1900 every dissonant combination had to be resolved into a consonance. The 20th century brought about an emancipation of dissonances. Seconds and sevenths acquired musical citizenship and were no longer treated as outcasts. The WHOLE-TONE SCALE erased the distinction between major and minor and established a neutral mode. POLYTONALITY licensed the use of two or more tonal triads simultaneously.

Diatonic harmony has been enriched by PANDIATONICISM, which removes prohibitions of unresolved dissonances within a given tonality. It also encourages the use or two or more triads at the same time. Particularly effective are the simultaneous playing of the dominant triadic formations in close harmony in the middle register with the tonic or subdominant triads in open harmony in the bass register. Pandiatonicism found its most fruitful application in NEOCLASSICAL music, in which the component notes can be used in quartal (four-voiced) harmony. In fact, quartal harmony itself has all but succeeded the tertian (three-voiced) harmony of classical music. Quartads such as E–A–D–G, placed upon the pedal tones F–C, is a typical example.

Finally, ATONALITY and its organized development, 12-tone composition or DODECAPHONY, abolished the concept of triadic tonality altogether. It is replaced with a new concept of integrated melody and harmony wherein harmony becomes a function of the fundamental TONE-ROW.

Subdivisions of the tempered scale in quarter-tone music and even smaller microtones prosper modestly as a monophonic art, but experiments have been made in microtonal harmonies as well. Electronic music has freed harmony of all technical impediments and allows the use of precisely calculated, nontempered intervals as well as microtones.

Further harmonic terminology: *Chromatic harmony* has chromatic tones and modulations; *compound harmony* has 2 or more essential chord-tones doubled; *dispersed* or *extended harmony*, OPEN HARMONY; *dissonant harmony*, see DISSO-NANCE; *essential harmony*, fundamental triads of a key, or the harmonic frame of a composition minus all figuration and ornaments; *false harmony*, the inharmonic relation, or DIS-CORD produced by imperfect preparation or resolution, or by wrong notes or chords; *figured harmony* varies simple chords by figuration of all kinds; *pure harmony*, music performed in pure or just intonation; *spread harmony*, open harmony; *strict harmony*, composition according to strict rules for the preparation and resolution of dissonances; *tempered harmony*, music performed in tempered intonation.

Harnoncourt, Nikolaus, eminent Austrian cellist, conductor, and musicologist; b. Berlin, Dec. 6, 1929. Harnoncourt's father, an engineer, played the piano and composed. The family settled in Graz, where young Nikolaus began to study the cello at the age of nine, later training at the Vienna Academy of Music. He was a cellist in the Vienna Symphony Orchestra from 1952 to 1969.

In 1953 Harnoncourt founded the Vienna Concentus Musicus, which began giving concerts in 1957. The group was dedicated to playing early music on period instruments or modern copies. The group made its first tour of England, the U.S., and Canada in 1966. From the mid-1970s he also appeared internationally as a guest conductor, expanding his repertoire to include music of later eras.

His wife, Alice Harnoncourt (b. Vienna, Sept. 26, 1930), studied violin in Vienna and Paris. She became concertmaster of the Vienna Concentus Musicus at its founding.

Harold in Italy. Symphony with viola OBBLIGATO by HECTOR BERLIOZ, 1834, first performed in Paris. While the original source of inspiration is disputed, the work was ultimately connected to Lord Byron's epic poem *Childe Harold*

PEOPLE IN MUSIC

and his travels. The viola, rarely treated as a concerto soloist, represents Harold. The work gave Berlioz an opportunity to display his brilliant art of rhythmic fluency and colorful orchestration.

harp (Lat., *harpa;* It., *arpa;* Fr., *harpe;* Ger., *Harfe*). A plucked CHORDOPHONE, with several strings running perpendicular to a resonator. The modern Western instrument is supported by a frame and pillar. Harps are often confused with LYRES, which have strings attached to a yoke. However, a lyre's strings run parallel to the resonator, and its construction involves two arms and a crossbar.

The harp is an ancient and in many cultures the most glorified musical instrument. Harps are shown in artwork dating back to Sumeria from the 3rd millennium B.C. on. Harps in the modern sense of the word appeared in Ireland and Wales in the 10th century as a bardic instrument, and were soon adopted by itinerant minstrels. During the RENAISSANCE, the harp became the purveyor of melodious and harmonious music in France, Spain, and Italy. Soon its popularity spread all over the civilized world. The harp was portrayed in Renaissance paintings as the instrument of the angels or beautiful young maidens.

Berlioz was originally commissioned by the virtuoso violinist NICCOLÒ PAGANINI, who was disappointed by the solo part's many silences and relative lack of virtuosity. But he let Berlioz keep the fee, and later approved of the piece he never played.

MUSICAL INSTRUMENT

◀

Concert harp.
(Benson Collection)

The modern orchestral harp has a nearly three-cornered wooden frame, the foot of which is formed by an upright pillar meeting the hollow back (the upperside of which bears the soundboard) in the pedestal. The upper ends of pillar and back are united by the curving neck. The gut strings are 46 (or 47) in number, with a compass of six and a half octaves, from C1 to f4 (or g4).

The range of the modern harp approaches that of the grand piano, and its triangular shape, with a curved neck, is geometrically similar to that of the piano. In fact, if a grand piano were to be dismantled and stood up perpendicularly on the floor, it would make a fairly good substitute for a harp.

The prototype of the modern harp has only seven strings per octave. In order to convert it into an instrument capable of CHROMATICISM and MODULATION, an ingenious "double action" tuning mechanism was patented by the great harp builder Sébastian Érard around 1810. Érard added pedals to the instrument that could be depressed one or two notches. Each notch shortens the corresponding string so that it sounds a semitone higher. Depressing the pedals two notches shortens the string to make it sound another semitone higher.

Thus it becomes possible for each of the seven strings of the octave to be raised a semitone or a whole tone, so the starting scale for the modern harp is tuned in C-flat major. Because each individual string could be raised a semitone or a whole tone, all major and minor scales become available. A chromatic harp was introduced as an experiment in 1845, doing away with the pedals altogether, but like so many simplified devices, it found little favor with harpists.

The harp is plucked with the fingers, never with a plectrum (or pick). Modern harp composers have added a whole arsenal of special effects, such as angelic-sounding harmonics, or demoniacal plucking of strings with a nail, or even tapping on the body of the harp.

The "key signature" used in music notated for the harp may strike a nonharpist as the most curious mixture of sharps and flats. However, these "accidentals" are simply indications as to the tuning, not signposts of tonality, and are usually placed in the middle of the great staff used in harp music.

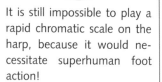

It is still impossible to play a rapid chromatic scale on the harp, because it would necessitate superhuman foot action!

Although WOLFGANG AMADEUS MOZART and LUDWIG VAN BEETHOVEN occasionally wrote for the harp, it never became a Classic orchestra instrument. But it reached a full flowering in the programmatic symphonic poems and operas of the 19th century. The harp was invariably sounded whenever the soul of a female sinner was redeemed in the last act of a Romantic opera. But these overdone effects all but disappeared in the antisentimental 20th century. The harp became a functional instrument, shunning such time-honored devices as sweeping ARPEGGIOS.

IGOR STRAVINSKY had three harps in the original scoring of his early ballet *The Firebird*, but eliminated them in a later revision of the score. This shows how the sentimental use of the harp ended in modern music.

Harp Quartet. Nickname for LUDWIG VAN BEETHOVEN's String Quartet in E-flat major, op.74 (1809). It is, of course, not a quartet of harps, but a quartet that contains some engaging passages in PIZZICATO (plucked) ARPEGGIOS (broken chords) which may suggest to some listeners the sound of a harp.

harpsichord (Fr., *clavecin;* Ger., *Cembalo, Kielflügel;* It., *cembalo*). A KEYBOARD instrument provided with one or two MANUALS (or keyboards). The strings are picked by plectrums.

MUSICAL INSTRUMENT

Earlier instruments closely related to the harpsichord included the SPINET and VIRGINAL. Their ranges varied from three to five octaves, and all were manufactured in a variety of styles and shapes. Italian harpsichords with a single manual and Flemish

◀

Harpsichord makers at work. (Hulton-Deutsch Collection/ Corbis)

harpsichords with two manuals bore a closer resemblance to the modern grand piano. The harpsichord was eventually superseded by the FORTEPIANO in the early 19th century. It is

The harpsichord was an extremely popular domestic instrument, and hundreds of paintings, drawings, and etchings represent women playing them. Early harpsichords were often adorned with curved legs and figures of cupids and mermaids. The lids might have carried inspirational legends in Latin such as "Musica dulce laborum levamen" (Music is a sweet solace from labors) or "Laborum dulce lenimen" (Sweet relief from labors).

interesting to note that the black keys of the piano (sharps and flats) were sometimes white on the harpsichord, while the piano's white keys might be colored black or brown on the harpsichord.

The harpsichord played an all-important role in BAROQUE instrument ensembles, serving as the voice of the BASSO CONTINUO. JOHANN SEBASTIAN BACH and GEORGE FRIDERIC HANDEL presided over the harpsichord when leading their own works, and even FRANZ JOSEPH HAYDN led his ensemble from the harpsichord during his London visits in the 1790s.

The art of harpsichord playing lapsed in the 19th century with the abandonment of the functional use of basso continuo. However, a vigorous revival, along with a number of other period instruments, occurred in the first half of the 20th century when dedicated craftsmen, foremost among them Arnold Dolmetsch (1858–1940), began manufacturing excellent replicas. WANDA LANDOWSKA, master harpsichordist herself, greatly contributed to this revival by teaching harpsichord playing and commissioning contemporary composers (among them MANUEL DE FALLA and FRANCIS POULENC) to write new works for this resurrected Baroque instrument.

PEOPLE IN MUSIC

Harris, Roy (Leroy Ellsworth), significant American composer; b. Chandler, Okla., Feb. 12, 1898; d. Santa Monica, Calif., Oct. 1, 1979. Harris's parents, of Irish and Scottish descent, originally settled in Oklahoma. In 1903 the family moved to California, where Harris had private music lessons. In 1926, he went to Paris, where he studied composition with NADIA BOULANGER. He was able to continue his stay in Paris thanks to two consecutive Guggenheim fellowships, awarded in 1927 and 1928.

Upon his return to the U.S., Harris lived in California and in N.Y., where several of his works were performed and attracted favorable attention. In his compositions, Harris showed a talent of great originality, with a strong melodic and rhythmic speech that is purely American. He also developed a theory of composing using the Greek MODES, assigning to each scale a certain emotional state.

Instrumental music is the genre in which Harris particularly excelled. He never wrote an opera or an oratorio, but made astute use of choral masses in some works. He held many teaching positions, for the longest period at the University of California, Los Angeles, from 1961 to 1973. In 1973 he was appointed composer-in-residence at California State University, Los Angeles, a post he held until his death.

Harris received honorary D.Mus. degrees from Rutgers University and the University of Rochester in N.Y., and in 1942 was awarded the Elizabeth Sprague Coolidge Medal "for eminent services to chamber music." In 1936 he married the pianist Johana Harris (born Beula Duffey; b. Ottawa, Ontario, Jan. 1, 1913; d. Los Angeles, June 5, 1995). She assumed her professional name Johana in honor of JO-HANN SEBASTIAN BACH. After Harris's death, she married, on Dec. 18, 1982, her 21-year-old piano student, John Heggie. They eventually divorced, well before her death in 1995.

Harris wrote 13 symphonies, the best-known and most frequently performed being his Symphony No. 3, which premiered in Boston in 1939. It was the first American symphony to be played in China, during the 1973 tour of the Philadelphia Orchestra under the direction of Eugene Ormandy. Among his other symphonies, the most played are No. 4, *Folksong Symphony,* with chorus (1940), No. 6, *Gettysburg Address* (1944), No. 10, *Abraham Lincoln Symphony* for chorus, brass, two amplified pianos, and percussion (1965), and No. 13, *Bicentennial Symphony 1976,* for chorus and orchestra (1976). He also composed other orchestral, chamber, and choral works.

Harrison, George, English rock singer and guitarist, member of the celebrated group the BEATLES; b. Liverpool, Feb. 25, 1943. Like his co-Beatles, Harrison had no formal musical education, and learned to play the guitar by osmosis and acclimatization. Not as extroverted as JOHN LENNON, not as exhibitionistic as PAUL MCCARTNEY, and not as histrionic as Ringo Starr, he was not as conspicuously projected into public consciousness as his comrades-in-rock. Yet he exercised a distinct influence on the character of the songs that the Beatles sang. In the mid-1960s, he met Indian sitarist RAVI SHANKAR and quickly became his student. Besides absorbing Indian music, he became interested in the Indian culture as a whole, convincing the other Beatles to join him on a re-

PEOPLE IN MUSIC

treat to study with the Mahareshi in 1968. He is the author of the song *Something*, one of the Beatles' greatest successes.

When the group broke up in 1970, Harrison ironically achieved his greatest successes. He brought out the successful albums *All Things Must Pass* (1970) and *The Concert for Bangladesh* (1972). In 1970, he had a hit with *My Sweet Lord;* however, its similarity to the Chiffons' 1963 hit *He's So Fine* led to a lawsuit, with Harrison settling out of court. In 1973 his album *Living in the Material World* (with *Give Me Love*) quickly attained gold status.

For much of the rest of the '70s, Harrison's career slowed. Although inactive musically, he developed a separate interest in producing movies, particularly those made by his friends in the Monty Python comedy troupe.

In 1981 he scored a hit with his single *All Those Years Ago,* written to memorialize John Lennon, who had been tragically murdered at the end of 1980. Another period of inactivity followed, and then Harrison's album *Cloud 9* (with *Got My Mind Set On You,* 1987) was released, again to strong reviews.

In the late '80s, Harrison joined forces with his producer Jeff Lynne and friends BOB DYLAN, TOM PETTY, and ROY ORBISON to form the mock-group, the Traveling Wilburys. Recording and writing together as a lark, the group's first album was a surprise success, leading to a follow-up made without Orbison (who had subsequently died).

Since the early '90s, Harrison again has come in and out of public view. In 1995, he rejoined the remaining living Beatles to help with the filming of a documentary on the group and to complete two recordings that John Lennon had left unfinished at his death.

PEOPLE IN MUSIC

Harrison, Lou, inventive American composer and performer; b. Portland, Oreg., May 14, 1917. From 1934 to 1935, Harrison studied with HENRY COWELL in San Francisco, and then with ARNOLD SCHOENBERG at the University of California, Los Angeles, in 1941. He taught at Mills College in Oakland, California, from 1937 to 1940, and again from 1980 to 1985, and various other West Coast colleges. He also was a music critic for the *New York Herald-Tribune* from 1945 to 1948 during his brief time on the East Coast. He held two Guggenheim fellowships in 1952 and 1954.

Early in his career, Harrison experimented with building different types of keyboard instruments and flutes. He also experimented with electronics, developing a process for direct composing on a phonograph disc, and in 1938 proposed a theory in interval control, and in 1942 supplemented it by a device for rhythm control. He also wrote plays and poems. Harrison was one of the earliest members of an initially small group of American musicians who promoted the music of CHARLES IVES, CHARLES RUGGLES, EDGARD VARÈSE, and Cowell. He prepared for publication Ives's Third Symphony, which he conducted in its first performance in 1946.

Seeking new sources of sound production, Harrison organized a PERCUSSION ensemble of many drums and such homely sound makers as coffee cans and flowerpots. He later composed for the Indonesian GAMELAN, the traditional XY-LOPHONE and gong orchestras of Java and Bali. Many of the instruments were constructed by his longtime associate WILLIAM COLVIG (b. Medford, Oreg., March 13, 1917), including psalteries, harps, flutes, MONOCHORDS (single-string instruments), and several complete gamelans.

Colvig performed on these instruments in many of Harrison's compositions, as well as on traditional instruments in concerts and lectures. His instruments have been used by the San Francisco Symphony and San Francisco Opera Company, among others. He also built the gamelans housed at the University of California, Berkeley, and at Mills College in Oakland.

Among Harrison's more recent compositions are Piano Concerto (N.Y., Oct. 20, 1985), *Last Symphony* (N.Y., Nov. 2, 1990), and *A Parade for M.T.T.* (MICHAEL TILSON THOMAS, conductor of the San Francisco Symphony and a longtime Harrison supporter; San Francisco, Sept. 6, 1995). He also published *About Carl Ruggles* (N.Y., 1946), *Music Primer: Various Items About Music to 1970* (N.Y., 1971), and *Soundings: Ives, Ruggles, Varèse* (with others; Santa Fe, N.M., 1974). Peter Garland edited *A Lou Harrison Reader* (Santa Fe, N.M., 1987).

PEOPLE IN MUSIC

Hart, Lorenz (Milton), outstanding American lyricist, most famous for his stage collaborations with RICHARD RODGERS; b. N.Y., May 2, 1895; d. there, Nov. 22, 1943. Hart began writing poetry as a teenager. He wrote for a number of amateur musical shows while studying journalism at Columbia University from 1914 to 1917. A year after his graduation, he met a teenage composer named Richard Rodgers when they both worked on a Columbia show. They formed an immediate partnership that would last for some 24 years.

In 1925 the pair had their first hits with the songs *Manhattan* and *Sentimental Me,* both written for a Broadway revue. Their first book show, *Dearest Enemy,* was staged on Broadway in that year also. 1927 broke their first major hit, a musical version of Mark Twain's *A Connecticut Yankee in King Arthur's Court,* featuring the hit song *My Heart Stood Still.*

Their Broadway successes slowed in the early 1930s, and for a while the team tried their luck in Hollywood. However, they disliked working for films in which they had little or no control. Returning to Broadway in the later '30s, they scored solid hits with *Babes in Arms* in 1937, *The Boys from Syracuse* a year later, and their last great show, 1940's *Pal Joey.*

By this time, Hart's unreliability—due to his increasing dependence on alcohol—made him a less-than-ideal partner. Rodgers was forced to look elsewhere for a lyricist, turning to OSCAR HAMMERSTEIN II. In reaction to his rejection, Hart became even more addicted to drink, and eventually died of the effects of alcoholism in 1943.

Hartmann, Karl Amadeus, outstanding German composer; b. Munich, Aug. 2, 1905; d. there, Dec. 5, 1963. He studied at the Music Academy in Munich from 1923 to 1927 and later with the well-known conductor HERMANN SCHERCHEN. He began to compose rather late in life, his first major work being a Trumpet Concerto, which was performed in Strasbourg in 1933.

During World War II, Hartmann studied advanced musical composition and analysis with ANTON WEBERN in Vienna from 1941 to 1942. After the war he organized in Mu-

PEOPLE IN MUSIC

nich the society Musica Viva. He received a prize from the city of Munich in 1948, and in 1952 was elected a member of the German Academy of Fine Arts, soon after becoming president of the German section of the I.S.C.M. (International Society for Contemporary Music).

Hartmann kept the forms and structures of classical composition, although he did experiment with CHROMATIC scales and unusual rhythms. He was excessively critical of his early works, and discarded many of them, but some were retrieved and performed after his death. Among his works are the chamber opera, *Des Simplicius Simplicissimus Jugend* (1934–35; Cologne, 1949; a revised version was retitled *Simplicius Simplicissimus,* 1955), nine symphonies, and other orchestral, chamber, and vocal works.

Háry János. OPERA by ZOLTÁN KODÁLY, 1926, first produced in Budapest. János Háry (in Hungarian the family name is first) is an egotistical soldier, a fantastic liar who boasts of singlehandedly defeating Napoleon. The opera opens with a deafening orchestral sneeze which is a protestation of either utter disbelief or total integrity in Hungarian conversational custom.

hasosra. An ancient long silver trumpet of Israel. It is played by priests at ritual occasions; it produces a fierce and fear-inspiring sound.

MUSICAL INSTRUMENT

Hatikva. The national anthem of Israel, originally a Zionist song. The melody is nearly identical with the main theme of BEDŘICH SMETANA's symphonic poem *THE MOLDAU.* Recent research suggests that the melody may have originated in Scandinavia. This is one of the rare national anthems in a minor mode.

Hauptsatz (Ger.). Principal part of a work; EXPOSITION. *Hauptstimme* (main voice), a term first used by ARNOLD SCHOENBERG to indicate the prominent voice in a TONE-ROW.

howpt′zatz

Hausmusik (Ger., home music). *See* GEBRAUCHSMUSIK.

PEOPLE IN MUSIC

Coleman Hawkins, c. 1950.
(Corbis/Bettmann)
▶

Hawkins's first recorded solo was on Henderson's famous recording *The Stampede,* which established the saxophone as a solo instrument.

Hawkins, Coleman (Randolph), "Bean" or "Hawk," outstanding African-American jazz tenor saxophonist; b. St. Joseph, Mo., Nov. 21, 1904; d. N.Y., May 19, 1969. Hawkins began piano lessons when he was five years old, and then learned cello and saxophone when he was nine. He was already working as a teenager, and then attended Washburn College in Topeka, Kansas.

Hawkins joined the Kansas City group the Jazz Hounds (who backed up the famous blues singer MAMIE SMITH) in 1921, for several tours. From 1923 to 1934, he was a member of FLETCHER HENDERSON's band in N.Y. His full tone and heavy VIBRATO became the standard for tenor saxophone, and he was considered the foremost performer on the instrument.

From 1934 to 1939, Hawkins worked in Europe. Upon his return to the U.S. in 1939 he made his most influential recording, *Body and Soul.* This solo became an inspiration to the new generation of jazz musicians and paved the way for the BEBOP of the 1940s. In 1943, he formed a group with young pianist THELONIOUS MONK, and gave Monk his first recording a year later.

Although Hawkins's style fell out of favor in the '50s, he continued to work steadily. He toured Europe in the first half of the decade, and then worked again with Monk and other younger players in the later half. In the '60s, he continued to work with the leading names in jazz, old and new. However, by decade's end he was suffering from depression brought on by alcoholism, and he died from pneumonia in 1969.

Hawkins, Sir John, eminent English music historian; b. London, Mar. 29, 1719; d. there, May 21, 1789. Hawkins studied law while serving as a clerk, and soon was able to act as an attorney. A dedicated fan of music, he entered the musical society of the time and was on friendly terms with GEORGE FRIDERIC HANDEL. He also participated in literary clubs, and knew the leading literary lights of his day, including Samuel Johnson, Oliver Goldsmith, and others. A wealthy marriage in 1753 enabled him to devote his leisure to literature and music. In 1761 he became a magistrate, and in 1763 chairman of the Quarter Sessions. He was knighted in 1772.

The culmination of 16 years of labor was his monumental *A General History of the Science and Practice of Music* (five volumes, published in 1776). The first volume of CHARLES BURNEY's *General History of Music* appeared at the same time. Although Hawkins's complete work came first, the reception to it by the critics was rather hostile, with Burney himself denouncing Hawkins in an unpublished poem. Yet the Hawkins work contained much reliable information, particularly dealing with musical life in London in the 18th century.

Hawkins died of a paralytic stroke and was buried in Westminster Abbey.

Haydn, Franz Joseph (1732–1809), illustrious Austrian composer, the first master of Viennese Classicism and "father of the symphony," brother of (JOHANN) MICHAEL HAYDN; b. Rohrau, Lower Austria, probably March 31, 1732 (baptized, April 1, 1732); d. Vienna, May 31, 1809. Haydn was the second of 12 children born to Mathias Haydn, a wheelwright (someone who repairs carriages and other wheeled vehicles), who also served as village sexton (a church employee who helps maintain the church property, and performs duties varying from ringing the bell for services to digging graves). Haydn's mother, Anna Maria Koller, was daughter of the market inspector and a former cook in the household of Count Harrach, lord of the village.

On Sundays and holidays music was performed at home, the father accompanying the voices on the harp, which he had learned to play by ear. When Haydn was a

PEOPLE IN MUSIC

PEOPLE IN MUSIC

small child, his paternal cousin Johann Mathias Franck, a choral director, took him to Hainburg, where he gave him instruction in reading, writing, arithmetic, and instrumental playing.

When Haydn was eight years old, KARL GEORG REUTTER, Kapellmeister (choral director) at St. Stephen's Cathedral in Vienna, engaged him as a soprano singer in the chorus. After his voice began to break, he was moved to the household of JOHANN MICHAEL SPANGLER, a music teacher. Haydn obtained a loan of 150 florins from Anton Buchholz, a friend of his father's, and was able to rent an attic room where he could use a harpsichord. In the same house lived the famous Italian poet and opera librettist Pietro Metastasio, who recommended Haydn to a resident Spanish family as a music tutor. He was also engaged as accompanist to students of the Italian composer and singing teacher Nicolo Porpora, for whom he performed various menial tasks in exchange for composition lessons.

Haydn soon began to compose. In 1751 he wrote the SINGSPIEL *Der krumme Teufel.* A noblewoman, Countess Thun, engaged him as harpsichordist and singing teacher. He met Karl Joseph von Fürnburg, for whom he wrote his first string quartets. In 1759 Haydn was engaged by Count Ferdinand Maximilian von Morzin as Kapellmeister at his estate in Lukaveč. On Nov. 26, 1760, he married Maria Anna Keller, the eldest daughter of his early benefactor, a Viennese wigmaker.

An important turn in Haydn's life was his meeting with Prince Paul Anton Esterházy. Esterházy had heard one of Haydn's symphonies during a visit to Lukaveč, and engaged him to enter his service as second Kapellmeister at

Franz Joseph Haydn. (New York Public Library)

Haydn time line

1732	Born
1740	Becomes a soprano singer in the chorus of St. Stephen's Cathedral in Vienna
1751	Composes a singspiel, *Der krumme Teufel*
1759	Becomes Kapellmeister to Count Ferdinand Maximilian von Morzin in Lukaveč
1760	Marries Maria Anna Keller
1761	Becomes second Kapellmeister at the estate of Prince Paul Anton Esterházy in Eisenstadt
1766	Is elevated to first Kapellmeister at Esterháza, now under Prince Nikolaus Esterházy, Prince Paul Anton's brother
1772	Symphony No. 49, *La Passione,* No. 44, *Trauersinfonie,* and No. 45, *Abschiedsinfonie,* are performed at Esterháza
1790	The Esterháza estate orchestra disbanded, Haydn takes up permanent residence in Vienna

his estate in Eisenstadt. Haydn signed his contract with Esterházy on May 1, 1761. Prince Paul Anton died in 1762, and his brother, Prince Nikolaus Esterházy, known as the "Magnificent," succeeded him. He took Haydn to his new palace at Esterháza, where Haydn was to provide two weekly operatic performances and two formal concerts. Haydn's service at Esterháza was long-lasting, secure, and fruitful. He composed there music of all descriptions, including most of his known string quartets, about 80 of his 104 symphonies, a number of keyboard works, and nearly all his operas. In 1766 he was elevated to the rank of first Kapellmeister.

Prince Nikolaus Esterházy was a cultural patron of the arts, but he was also a stern taskmaster in his relationship to his employees. His contract with Haydn stipulated that each commissioned work had to be performed without delay, and that such a work should not be copied for use by others. He was also to have his meals with the other musicians and house servants.

Among his other obligations, Haydn had to write pieces that could be performed on the BARYTON, a strange stringed instrument that the Prince played. In consequence, Haydn wrote over 100 trios involving the baryton. He also wrote three sets of six string quartets each (opps. 9, 17, and 20), published in 1771–72. His noteworthy symphonies included No. 49, in F minor, *La passione,* No. 44, in E minor, the *Trauersinfonie,* and No. 45, in F-sharp minor, the famous *Abschiedsinfonie* (Farewell Symphony), performed by Haydn at Esterháza in 1772.

In 1780 Haydn was elected a member of the Modena Philharmonic Society, and in 1784 Prince Henry of Prussia sent him a gold medal. In 1785 he was commissioned to write a "passione istrumentale," *The 7 Last Words of Christ,* for the Cathedral of Cadiz, and in 1787 King Friedrich Wilhelm II gave him a diamond ring. Many other distinctions were conferred upon him. During his visits to Vienna he formed a close friendship with Wolfgang Amadeus Mozart, who was nearly a quarter of a century younger, and for whose genius Haydn had great admiration. If the words of Mozart's father can be taken literally, Haydn told him that Mozart was "the greatest composer known to me either in

1791 Haydn makes his first London concert in the Hanover Square Rooms, and also receives an honorary Doctor of Music degree from Oxford University, for which he composes his Symphony No. 92, *Oxford*

1792 Travels through Bonn and meets Ludwig van Beethoven

1794 Travels again to London, where his 12 "London" Symphonies (also known as "Salomon" Symphonies) are performed

1794 The Eisentstadt orchestra is revived by the newly instated Prince Nikolaus (son of Prince Paul Anton), with Haydn again as Kapellmeister

1796 Composes six important masses for the church at Esterháza, including *Missa in tempore belli,* the *Heiligmesse,* and the *Nelsonmesse*

1796–98 Composes the great oratorio *Die Schöpfung,* first performed at the Schwarzenburg Palace in Vienna on April 29, 1798

1797 Composes *Gott erhalte unser Kaiser* for the national Austrian anthem

1801 His oratorio *Die Jahreszeiten* is performed at the Schwarzenburg Palace

1802 Beset by illness, Haydn resigns his Eisenstadt post

695

1808 Makes his last public appearance at a concert in his honor in the Great Hall of the University of Vienna, Antonio Salieri conducting *Die Schöpfung*

1809 Dies, and is buried at the Hundsturm Cemetery.

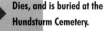

Reinforcing Haydn's status as a servant to the Prince, he had to present himself in the "antichambre" of the palace each morning and afternoon to receive the Prince's orders. He was obliged to wear formal clothes, with white hose and a powdered wig with a pigtail or a hairbag.

person or by name." Mozart reciprocated Haydn's regard for him by dedicating to him a set of six string quartets.

Prince Nikolaus Esterházy died in 1790, and his son Paul Anton (named after his uncle) inherited the estate. After he disbanded the orchestra, he granted Haydn an annuity of 1,000 florins. Although Haydn remained in the service of the new Prince as Kapellmeister, he took up permanent residence in Vienna.

In 1790 Johann Peter Salomon (1745–1815), who produced concerts of music in London, persuaded Haydn to travel there to perform. Haydn accepted the offer, arriving in London on New Year's Day, 1791. On March 11 of that year he appeared in his first London concert in the Hanover Square Rooms, presiding at the keyboard. Haydn was greatly feted by the London nobility, and the King himself expressed his admiration. In 1791 he went to Oxford to receive the honorary degree of Doctor of Music. For this occasion, he submitted his Symphony No. 92, in G major, which became known as the *Oxford* Symphony. He also composed a three-part CANON, *Thy Voice, O Harmony, Is Divine,* as his exercise piece. It was also in England that he wrote his Symphony No. 94, in G major, the *Surprise Symphony.*

On his journey back to Vienna in the summer of 1792 Haydn stopped in Bonn, where young LUDWIG VAN BEETHOVEN showed him some of his works, and Haydn agreed to accept him later as his student in Vienna. In 1794 Haydn went to London once more. His Feb. 10, 1794, concert met with great success. His "London" symphonies, also known as the "Salomon" symphonies because Haydn wrote them at Salomon's request, were 12 in number, and they included No. 99, in E-flat major; No. 100, in G major, known as the *Military Symphony;* No. 101, in D major, nicknamed *The Clock* because of its pendulum-like rhythmic accompanying figure; No. 102, in B-flat major; No. 103, in E-flat major, known as the *Drum Roll Symphony;* and No. 104, in D major, called the *London Symphony.*

Returning to Vienna, Haydn resumed his contact with the Esterházy family. In 1794 Prince Paul Anton died and was succeeded by his son Nikolaus. The new Prince revived the orchestra at Eisenstadt, with Haydn again as Kapellmeister. Conforming to the new requirements of Prince Nikolaus, Haydn turned to works for the church, including six masses:

His Mass in C major was entitled *Missa in tempore belli* (Mass in belligerent times, written in 1796), because it was composed during Napoleon's drive toward Vienna.

The second Mass, in B-flat major, the *Heiligmesse,* also dates from 1796.

In 1798 he composed the third Mass, in D minor, which is often called the *Nelsonmesse,* with reference to Lord Nelson's defeat of Napoleon's army at the Battle of the Nile.

The fourth Mass, in B-flat major (1799), is called the *Theresienmesse,* in honor of the Austrian Empress Maria Theresa.

The fifth Mass, in B-flat major, written in 1801, is known as the *Schöpfungsmesse,* because it contains a theme from the oratorio *Die Schöpfung* (The Creation).

The sixth Mass, in B-flat major (1802), is referred to as the *Harmoniemesse,* for its extensive use of wind instruments (see HARMONIE).

Between 1796 and 1798 Haydn composed his great oratorio *Die Schöpfung* (The Creation), first performed at a private concert for the nobility at the Schwarzenburg Palace in Vienna on April 29, 1798. In 1796 he wrote the Concerto in E-flat major for trumpet (CLARINO), which became a standard piece for trumpet players.

In 1797 Haydn was instructed by the Court to compose a hymn-tune of a solemn nature that could be used as the national Austrian anthem. He succeeded triumphantly in this task with his *Gott erhalte unser Kaiser,* a tune he also made use of as a theme of a set of variations in his String Quartet in C major, op. 76, no. 3, which itself became known as the *Emperor Quartet.*

Between 1799 and 1801 Haydn completed the oratorio *Die Jahreszeiten,* with a text translated into German from

James Thomson's poem *The Seasons.* It was first performed at the Schwarzenburg Palace in Vienna on April 24, 1801. In 1802, beset by illness, Haydn resigned his post.

Haydn made his last public appearance at a concert given in his honor in the Great Hall of the University of Vienna on March 27, 1808, with ANTONIO SALIERI conducting *Die Schöpfung.* When Vienna surrendered to Napoleon, he ordered a guard of honor to be placed at Haydn's residence. Haydn died on May 31, 1809, and was buried at the Hundsturm Cemetery.

Haydn was often called "Papa Haydn" by his intimates because of his good humor. Ironically, he never became a papa in the actual sense of the word. His marriage was unsuccessful—his wife was a veritable tyrant, and indeed, Haydn was separated from her for most of his life. Still, he corresponded with her and sent her money, even though, according to a contemporary report, he never opened her letters.

In schoolbooks Haydn is usually described as "father of the symphony," the creator of the Classic forms of symphony and string quartet. However, the symphonic form was established by JOHANN STAMITZ and his associates at the Mannheim School, having evolved from the Italian sinfonia. The string quartet was developed even earlier. But Haydn certainly did much to build on these forms. In his symphonies, Haydn created a variety of moods, clever and beautiful variations, and more contrast among the movements. String quartets, as conceived by Haydn, were smaller versions of the symphony: both were set in sonata form, consisting in three contrasting movements, *Allegro, Andante, Allegro* (again, taken from the sinfonia), with a *Minuet* inserted between the last two.

Haydn also played a historic role in the evolution of functional HARMONY. He adopted four-part writing as a fundamental principle of composition, particularly in his string quartets.

The precise extent of Haydn's vast output will probably never be known. Many works are lost, while others, listed in various catalogs, may never have existed or were duplications of other works. Some are of doubtful authenticity, and some are definitely not his works. Haydn kept an *Entwurf-Katalog*

Haydn's body was moved from Vienna in 1820 to be reburied at Eisenstadt. Strangely, at this time his skull was separated from his body! It was actually exhibited under glass in the hall of the Gesellschaft der Musikfreunde in Vienna for a number of years. The skull was finally reunited with his body in the Bergkirche in Eisenstadt on June 5, 1954, in a solemn official ceremony.

from 1765 on. Several subsequent catalogues were together, starting in the year after his death. The current definitive catalog was edited by A. van Hoboken (Mainz, 1957–71).

Haydn's authentic symphonies number 104, although Hoboken adds a *Symphonie Concertante* (1792) and three early works to the list. Many of his concertos are lost, although surviving are three for violin, two for cello, one for hunting horn, five for two *lire organizzate* (HURDY-GURDY), five for clavicembalo, and one for violin and clavicembalo. Other works include divertimentos, notturnos, sinfonias, overtures, dances, incidental music, and marches.

Although relatively little attention has been paid to them, Haydn wrote numerous operas for the Esterháza theater, some of which were revived in the last quarter-century. He also wrote between ten and 15 masses, several sacred motets (including the *6 English Psalms*, c.1794–95), oratorios, secular cantatas, Italian orchestral arias, mostly for placement into others' operas, songs in German and English, nearly 400 British folk-song arrangements for voice and trio (1792–1804), vocal duets, trios, and quartets with keyboard accompaniment, and more than 50 canons.

Along with the symphonies, Haydn's compositional development—and therefore the growth of the Classic style—can best be seen in the several sets of string quartets. Other works by Haydn include about 20 string trios, about 30 piano trios, about 40 solo keyboard sonatas, mostly for harpsichord, and music for flute-clock.

Haydn, (Johann) **Michael,** distinguished Austrian composer, brother of (FRANZ) JOSEPH HAYDN; b. Rohrau, Lower Austria (baptized), Sept. 14, 1737; d. Salzburg, Aug. 10, 1806. Haydn went to Vienna about 1745 and became a chorister at St. Stephen's Cathedral. His voice was remarkable for its wide range, extending three octaves. In addition to the academic and musical training he received as a chorister, he also studied composition on his own. He then obtained the post of Kapellmeister to the Bishop of Grosswardein in 1757, and subsequently was named a court musician and Konzertmeister to Archbishop Sigismund Schrattenbach of Salzburg in 1762.

PEOPLE IN MUSIC

In 1768 Haydn married Maria Magdalen Lipp (1745–1827), daughter of the court organist Franz Ignaz Lipp and a soprano in the archbishop's service. Haydn also became principal organist of the Dreifatigkeitskirche in 1777, and was WOLFGANG AMADEUS MOZART's successor as cathedral organist in 1781. Part of his time he devoted to teaching, numbering CARL MARIA VON WEBER and ANTON DIABELLI among his students. When Archbishop Hieronymus Colloredo abdicated in 1800 and the French took control of Salzburg, Haydn lost his positions. Although his last years were made difficult by this change in his fortunes, he turned down the post of Vice-Kapellmeister to Prince Nikolaus Esterházy, his famous brother's patron.

Michael Haydn was a prolific composer of both sacred and secular music, and particularly esteemed for his mastery of church music. His outstanding Requiem in C minor, *Pro defuncto Archiepiscopo Sigismundo,* was composed in memory of his patron in 1771. It was also performed at Franz Joseph Haydn's funeral. Among his numerous Masses, he wrote the fine *Missa sotto il titulo di S. Teresia,* for Maria Theresia (wife of Holy Roman Emperor Franz II), who sang the soprano solos under his direction in Vienna in 1801. He wrote several settings of the Te Deum, Litaniae lauretanae, Salve Regina, Tantum ergo, Regina coeli, and Vespers, as well as nearly 200 sacred motets.

Haydn's secular output included dramatic works, symphonies, minuets, marches, concertos, divertimentos, chamber music, etc. His Symphony in G major (1783) was long attributed to Mozart (who composed an introduction to its first movement) as K.444/425a.

Hayes, Isaac, African-American singer and songwriter of soul and popular music; b. Covington, Tenn., Aug. 6, 1938. Hayes learned to play saxophone and piano, and after singing with local groups went to Memphis as a studio saxophonist and pianist.

Hayes teamed up with lyricist DAVID PORTER in 1964, and subsequently penned such successful songs as *Hold On I'm Coming, Soul Man,* and *B–A–B–Y.* After recording his hits *Walk on By* (1969), *By the Time I Get to Phoenix* (1969), and *Never Can Say Goodbye* (1971), he made waves with his

PEOPLE IN MUSIC

music for the film *Shaft* in 1972, which garnered him an Academy Award, a Golden Globe, and two Grammy Awards. He also won a Grammy Award for his album *Black Moses* released in 1972.

head. 1. Point (of bow). 2. In the VIOLIN family, the part comprising the peg-box and scroll. 3. In the drum, the membrane stretched over one or both ends. 4. In notation, the oval (or square) part of a note that determines its place on the staff. *Go to the head,* DA CAPO; *head tone,* note of the vocal upper register; *head voice,* vocal production of notes in the upper register, giving the illusion of being generated from the top of the head.

MUSICAL INSTRUMENT

health. *See* MIND AND HEALTH.

Hebrides, The. See FINGAL'S CAVE.

heckelphone. A DOUBLE-REED instrument, with a wider conical bore and lower range (A-g2) than the related OBOE, invented by Wilhelm Heckel (1856–1909) in 1904. It is somewhat misleadingly called the baritone oboe. It is used in some modern scores, giving out a rich, somewhat hollow sound. RICHARD STRAUSS used it in *Salome,* and PAUL HINDEMITH wrote a sonata for it.

MUSICAL INSTRUMENT

Heifetz, Jascha, celebrated Russian-born American violinist; b. Vilnius, Feb. 2, 1901; d. Los Angeles, Dec. 10, 1987. His father, Ruben Heifetz, an able musician, taught him the basics of violin playing at a very early age. Heifetz then studied at the Vilnius Music School, and played in public before he was five years old. At the age of six, he played FELIX MENDELSSOHN's Concerto in Kovno. In 1910 his father took him to St. Petersburg and entered him in the Conservatory there. After a few months, he was accepted as a pupil by the well-known Hungarian violinist and teacher, LEOPOLD AUER.

PEOPLE IN MUSIC

Heifetz gave his first public concert in St. Petersburg on April 30, 1911. The following year, with a letter of recommendation from Auer, he went to Berlin. His first concert there in 1912, presented in the large hall of the Hochschule für Musik, attracted great attention. Following his debut, he was engaged to play PIOTR ILYICH TCHAIKOVSKY's Concerto with the Berlin Philharmonic; Heifetz obtained sensational success as a child prodigy of extraordinary gifts. He went on to play in Austria and Scandinavia.

Jascha Heifetz performing at New York's CARNEGIE HALL, *c. 1960. (Corbis-Bettmann)*

▶

MISCHA ELMAN, a great violinist in his own right, and LEOPOLD GODOWSKY, a piano virtuoso, attended Heifetz's American debut in 1917. "It's hot in here," remarked Elman, wiping his brow. "Not for pianists," Godowsky calmly replied.

After the Russian Revolution of 1917, Heifetz went to America, by way of Siberia and the Orient. His debut at CARNEGIE HALL in N.Y. in 1917 won for him the highest expression of enthusiasm from the public and in the press.

Many triumphs followed during Heifetz's tour of the U.S., and soon his fame spread all over the world. He made his first London appearance in 1920, and then toured Australia in 1921, the Orient two years later, Palestine in 1926, and South America. He revisited Russia in 1934, and was welcomed enthusiastically. He became a naturalized American citizen in 1925, and made his home in Beverly Hills, California.

In subsequent years, Heifetz continued to travel as a concert violinist, visiting virtually every country in the world, but from 1974 he ceased to appear in public as a soloist. He taught classes of exceptionally talented pupils at the University of Southern California in Los Angeles from 1962 to 1972.

Heifetz made numerous arrangements for violin of works by JOHANN SEBASTIAN BACH, ANTONIO VIVALDI, and contemporary composers. His most famous transcription is *Hora Staccato* by Grigoras Dinicu, made into a virtuoso piece by adroit ornamentation and rhythmic elaboration. In his desire to promote modern music, he commissioned a number of composers (WILLIAM WALTON, LOUIS GRUENBERG, MARIO CASTELNUOVO-TEDESCO, and others) to write violin concertos for him, several of which he performed.

Heinrich, Anthony Philip (Anton Philipp), American violinist and composer of German-Bohemian birth; b. Schönbüchel, March 11, 1781; d. N.Y., May 3, 1861. As a boy, Heinrich studied the piano and violin, but began adult life as a wholesale merchant and banker. In 1810 he emigrated to America, settling in Philadelphia as a merchant and as unpaid music director of the Southwark Theatre.

After business reverses in 1817, Heinrich moved to the backwoods of Kentucky, first to Bardstown and then to nearby Lexington, where he managed to find enough musicians to conduct a performance of one of LUDWIG VAN BEETHOVEN's symphonies.

Without any knowledge of harmony, Heinrich began to compose in 1818. These first songs and choral and instrumental pieces he published later as op.1, *The Dawning of Music in Kentucky, or The Pleasures of Harmony in the Solitudes of Nature,* and op.2, *The Western Minstrel* (both 1820).

In 1827 Heinrich relocated to London, playing violin in a small orchestra. There he also studied theory, and about 1830 began to write for orchestra. He returned to the U.S. in 1832, and in 1834 again visited England, as well as Germany and Austria a year later. He had some of his works produced at Dresden, Prague, Budapest, and Graz (his symphony *The Combat of the Condor* was performed at Graz in 1836 and also in France). In Vienna he entered a competition with a symphony, but the prize was awarded to another.

Disappointed, he returned to America and settled in N.Y., where he soon gained immense popularity, becoming known as "Father Heinrich." He was a commanding figure in the musical affairs of the U.S., publishing many of his piano pieces and songs. Grand festivals of his works were arranged in N.Y., Philadelphia, and Boston, and critics spoke of him as the "Beethoven of America." But a tour of

Germany in 1857–58 was a dismal failure, and he died in extreme poverty.

Heinrich's works are not among the first-rank of classical music. He wrote for an enormous orchestra, à la HECTOR BERLIOZ, but his musical ideas were not up to the scale of these groups. Nevertheless, he is historically important as the first to employ Native American themes in works of large dimensions and to show decided nationalist aspirations.

In 1917 the Library of Congress acquired Heinrich's memoranda, many published works, and almost all the orchestral scores, numbered in a list made by Heinrich himself in 1857. Among the more striking titles are: *Grand American Chivalrous* Symphony, *The Columbiad, or Migration of American Wild Passenger Pigeons* (1857–58), *The Ornithological Combat of Kings, or The Condor of the Andes and the Eagle of the Cordilleras* (1847), *Pocahontas, the Royal Indian Maid and the Heroine of Virginia, the Pride of the Wilderness* (1837), *The Wild-wood Spirit's Chant or Scintillations of "Yankee Doodle," forming a Grand National Heroic Fantasia Scored for a Powerful Orchestra in 44 Parts* (c.1842), *Manitou Mysteries, or The Voice of the Great Spirit* (before 1845), and *Gran Sinfonia Misteriosa-Indiana* (performed in N.Y., 1975).

heirmos (*hirmos;* Grk., link). A hymnal melody of the Byzantine church written in the 7th century. After the introduction of Christianity into old Russia, heirmos were adapted also in the Russian Orthodox church.

The heirmos usually served as a connection between a Biblical hymn derived from the old Russian and a Christian hymn dedicated to a special saint. A collection of these hymns was called a *heirmologion*.

Heldenbariton (Ger.). Heroic baritone, requiring a powerful voice and stamina for difficult operatic parts, particularly in RICHARD WAGNER's music dramas.

Heldenleben, Ein (A Hero's Life). Symphonic poem by RICHARD STRAUSS, 1899, first performed in Frankfurt. Upon examination, it seems clear that the hero is Strauss himself, because he quotes themes from his earlier tone poems. His critics are depicted by disjointed jabbering of high woodwinds, while the hero reserves for himself an imperturbable violin solo in the noble key of E-flat major.

Heldentenor (Ger.). Heroic tenor, requiring a robust voice and stamina for difficult operatic parts, particularly in RICHARD WAGNER's music dramas.

helicon (Grk., helix, coil). A valved brass instrument, invented in the mid-19th century, used chiefly in military music as a bass. Its tube is bent in a circle, and it is carried over the shoulder. It is similar in shape to the SOUSAPHONE.

MUSICAL INSTRUMENT

Hello, Dolly! Musical by JERRY HERMAN, 1964, based on Thornton Wilder's *The Matchmaker*. In 1890s N.Y., Dolly is a widow turned marriage broker. An especially eligible and well-to-do customer comes along and she manages to corral him for herself.

◄

Carol Channing in Hello, Dolly! *1964. (Dean Conger/Corbis)*

The title song was extremely popular (LOUIS ARMSTRONG had one of his last hits with it), and the 1964 Johnson presidential campaign made it his campaign song as *Hello, Lyndon!* Herman had to endure a plagiarism lawsuit from copyright owners of a forgotten but similar song, *Sunflower,* written in 1948. While the borrowing was undoubtedly unconscious, Herman settled out of court.

PEOPLE IN MUSIC

Hellzapoppin'. Revue by SAMMY FAIN, 1938, on topical subjects.

Helmholtz, Hermann (Ludwig Ferdinand) **von,** celebrated German scientist and acoustician; b. Potsdam, Aug. 31, 1821; d. Berlin, Sept. 8, 1894. Helmholtz studied medicine at the Friedrich Wilhelm Medical Institute in Berlin, where he earned his medical degree in 1843, and also learned to play the piano. He was an assistant at Berlin's Anatomical Museum and professor extraordinary at the Academy of Fine Arts in 1848–49, assistant professor and director of Konigsberg's Physiological Institute from 1849 to 1855, and professor of anatomy and physiology at the University of Bonn from 1855 to 1858 and the University of Heidelberg from 1858 to 1871. He became professor of physics at the University of Berlin in 1871, and from 1888 served as the first director of the Physico-Technical Institute in Berlin. He was ennobled in 1882.

Helmholtz's most important work for music was his *Lehre von den Tonempfindungen als physiologische Grundlage für die Theorie der Musik* (Braunschweig, 1863; English translation by A. Ellis as *On the Sensations of Tone as a Physiological Basis for the Theory of Music,* London, 1875), in which he established a sure physical foundation for the phenomena manifested by musical tones, either single or combined. He successfully described the differences in quality of tone (tone color) in different instruments and voices, analyzing harmonic, differential, and summational tones. He also established the nature and limits of music perception by the human ear. His influence continued into the 20th century, especially on intonational experimental composers like HARRY PARTCH.

Help, Help, the Globolinks! Satirical opera by GIAN CARLO MENOTTI, 1968, to his own LIBRETTO, first performed in Hamburg. The Globolinks are electronic invaders from outer space bent on converting unwary humans into their own kind. But they are vulnerable to the beautiful sounds of traditional music, and are finally routed by schoolchildren led by the exquisite Mme. Euterpova (Euterpe was the Greek musical Muse). The literature teacher Mr. Lavender-Gas escapes, but the school dean, the unmusical Dr. Stone, becomes a Globolink. The score includes passages of mock-electronic music.

hemiola (from Grk. *hemiolios,* the whole and the half; Lat., *sesquialtera*). 1. In notation of the Middle Ages, the use of three notes of equal duration in a measure alternating with two notes of equal duration, in the same measure length, so that the longer notes equal 1 ½ shorter ones. In modern notation, the hemiola is represented by a succession of bars in $\frac{6}{8}$ and $\frac{3}{4}$. JOHANNES BRAHMS used this device often. 2. The same alternation used in a two-measure form as a precadential rhythmic figure. It was very common in the BAROQUE period.

Hen, The (*La Poule*). FRANZ JOSEPH HAYDN's Symphony No. 83, 1785, in the key of G minor. The commonly used French title is explained by the fact that this is the second of Haydn's Paris symphonies.

The title is explained by a supposed imitation of a hen's cluck in the second subject of the first movement.

Henderson, (James) **Fletcher, "Smack,"** African-American jazz pianist, bandleader, and arranger; b. Cuthbert, Ga., Dec. 18, 1897; d. N.Y., Dec. 28, 1952. Henderson studied piano as a child and chemistry as a youth, receiving a degree in chemistry from Atlanta University College. In 1920 he went to N.Y., where he formed the Fletcher Henderson Band, which rapidly advanced into the front ranks of jazzdom. A number of famous jazz figures played in it, including RUSSELL PROCOPE, COLEMAN HAWKINS, JOHN KIRBY, REX STEWART, J.C. HIGGINBOTHAM, LESTER YOUNG, and LOUIS ARMSTRONG. Its principal arranger was DON REDMAN.

PEOPLE IN MUSIC

After Redman left in 1927, Henderson became the principal arranger, with some additional arrangements by BENNY CARTER and others. He was unable to maintain his own band, and by 1939 was working as an arranger for BENNY GOODMAN. From 1941 he led bands and continued to write arrangements. A stroke in 1950 ended his professional career.

Although Henderson never attained the popularity of his peers, his arrangements and his gifted guidance of so many important jazz musicians made his indirect influence extremely significant.

707

PEOPLE IN MUSIC

Henderson (born Brost), **Ray**(mond), American composer of popular songs; b. Buffalo, Dec. 1, 1896; d. Greenwich, Conn., Dec. 31, 1970. After music studies at the University of Southern California in Los Angeles, Henderson played organ in churches and piano in jazz groups in Buffalo. He then went to N.Y. City as a song plugger in TIN PAN ALLEY, and soon began writing songs of his own.

Henderson's first success was *Georgette* from 1922, which was followed by *Sonny Boy,* written for Al Jolson's early talkie *The Singing Fool.* Subsequent hits were *You're the Cream in My Coffee, Button Up Your Overcoat, Alabamy Bound, Hold Everything,* and *Three Cheers,* some written in collaboration with B.G. DeSylva. Unlike most Broadway composers, Henderson could read and write music (he took private lessons with BENJAMIN BRITTEN). His film biography, *The Best Things in Life Are Free,* was made in 1966.

PEOPLE IN MUSIC

Hendricks, Barbara, greatly admired African-American soprano; b. Stephens, Ark., Nov. 20, 1948. Hendricks sang in church and school choirs before majoring in chemistry and mathematics at the University of Nebraska, where she graduated in 1969. During the summer of 1968 she began vocal training with JENNIE TOUREL at the Aspen (Colorado) Music School, continuing under her guidance at the Juilliard School in N.Y. from 1969 to 1971. She also attended MARIA CALLAS's master class there. In 1971, Hendricks won the Geneva International Competition, and in 1972 both the International Concours de Paris and the Kosciuszko Foundation Vocal Competition.

In 1973 Hendricks made her debut in VIRGIL THOMSON's *4 Saints in 3 Acts* in the Mini-Metropolitan Opera production presented at the Lincoln Center Forum Theatre in N.Y. Later that year she made her first concert tour of Europe. In 1974 she appeared as Erisbe in PIER FRANCESCO CAVALLI's *Ormindo* at the San Francisco Spring Opera, and in the title role of Cavalli's *La Calisto* at the Glyndebourne Festival.

In 1975 she made her formal N.Y. debut as Inez in a concert performance of GAETANO DONIZETTI's *La Favorite* at CARNEGIE HALL. In 1976 she sang Amor in WILHELM ARCHIBALD GLUCK's *Orfeo ed Euridice* with the Netherlands

Opera at the Holland Festival. Later that year, she made her N.Y. recital debut at Town Hall. At the Berlin Deutsche Oper in 1978 she appeared as WOLFGANG AMADEUS MOZART's Susanna, a role she quickly made her own. In 1980 she sang Gilda and in 1981 Pamina at the Orange Festival in France. In 1982 she appeared as CHARLES GOUNOD's Juliet at both the Paris Opéra and London's Covent Garden.

In 1986 she made her Metropolitan Opera debut in N.Y. as RICHARD STRAUSS's Sophie. In 1988 she sang at the 70th birthday celebration for LEONARD BERNSTEIN at the Tanglewood Festival, and also starred as Mimi in LUIGI COMENCINI's film version of *LA BOHÈME*. In 1989 she appeared at the Bolshoi Theater in Moscow, in 1991 she sang Manon in Parma, and in 1992 she sang Micaëla in Orange.

In addition to her operatic career, Hendricks has won distinction as a recitalist. Her interpretations of the German and French lieder repertoire, as well as of African-American spirituals, have won praise. In 1986 she was made a Commandeur des Arts et des Lettres of France. Her unswerving commitment to social justice led the High Commissioner for Refugees at the United Nations to name her a goodwill ambassador of the world body in 1987.

Hendrix, Jimi (James Marshall), African-American rock guitarist, singer, and songwriter; b. Seattle, Nov. 27, 1942; d. London, Sept. 18, 1970. Being left-handed, Hendrix taught himself to play the guitar upside down. He played in a high school band before dropping out of school during his senior year to join the U.S. Army paratroopers. Following his discharge in 1961, he worked with groups in Nashville, Vancouver, and Los Angeles.

In 1964 Hendrix went to N.Y., where he joined the Isley Brothers. After working with CURTIS KNIGHT's group in 1964–65, he formed his own outfit, Jimmy James and the Blue Flames. He then went to England, where he organized the Jimi Hendrix Experience in 1966 with bass guitarist NOEL REDDING and drummer MITCH MITCHELL.

After recording his first album, *Are You Experienced?* in 1967, Hendrix made his immensely successful debut in the U.S. with his group at the Monterey (California) Pop Festi-

PEOPLE IN MUSIC

val that same year. In 1968 he recorded the albums *Axis: Bold as Love* and *Electric Ladyland,* followed a year later by a famous appearance at the Woodstock Festival. The last album released during his lifetime was the live *Band of Gypsies,* with BUDDY MILES and Billy Cox (1970). Hendrix died after taking an overdose of drugs in London in 1970. Several albums, beginning with *The Cry of Love* (1971), were released posthumously.

Hendrix played comfortably in many styles (soul, rock, blues), and was beginning to assimilate jazz when he died. He always used his virtuoso technique in the service of musical expression, and was the most important figure in the development of the use of feedback in rock. He was a great showman, playing the guitar behind his back and between his legs, and famously setting the instrument on fire at the end of his set. But he will be best remembered for his incredible technique, both his lightning-fast melodic riffs and his expressive use of distortion and other electronic effects.

Hensel, Fanny (Cäcilie) (Mendelssohn-Bartholdy), German pianist and composer, sister of (Jacob Ludwig) FELIX MENDELSSOHN (-Bartholdy); b. Hamburg, Nov. 14, 1805; d. Berlin, May 14, 1847. Fanny began her musical training with her mother, then studied piano and composition. She subsequently studied with the famous pianist MARIE BIGOT in Paris in 1816. Fanny married the painter W. Hensel on Oct. 3, 1829. From 1843 she oversaw the Sunday morning concerts at Berlin's Elternhaus. Her untimely death in 1847 was a great shock to her brother Felix, who died a few months afterward.

Hensel was a talented composer. Six of her songs were published under her brother's name in his opp. 8 and 9 (*Heimweh, Italien, Suleika und Hatem, Sehnsucht, Verlust,* and *Die Nonne*). Other works published under her own name, some posthumously, include four books of songs, a collection of part-songs entitled *Gärtenlieder* (1829), Oratorio on Biblical Themes (1831), String Quartet in E-flat Major (1834), Piano Quartet in A-flat Major (1822), Piano Trio in D Minor, op.11, and *Das Jahr* (1841) and *Lieder ohne Worte* for piano.

PEOPLE IN MUSIC

Henze, Hans Werner, outstanding German composer of the modern school; b. Gutersloh, Westphalia, July 1, 1926. Henze's early studies at the Braunschweig School of Music from 1942 to 1944 were interrupted by military service, and for a year he was in the German army on the Russian front. In 1946 he took music courses in Heidelberg, while at the same time studying privately with the well-known German composer Wolfgang Fortner.

A musician of restless temperament, Henze joined a radical political group and proclaimed that all music should serve the masses. He lived in Ischia, Italy, from 1953 to 1956, then stayed in Naples and finally settled in Marino. In his vocal works he freely adopted such humanoid effects as screaming, bellowing, and snorting, as well as CIRCULAR BREATHING. Nevertheless, Henze manages to compose music that is feasible for human performance.

But political considerations continued to play a decisive role in Henze's career. In 1967 he withdrew from the membership of the Academy of the Arts of West Berlin, in a gesture of protest against its artistic policies. During his stay in Italy he joined the Italian Communist Party. His political stance did not preclude his acceptance in "bourgeois" musical centers. His works were performed widely in Europe.

Henze held the International Chair of Composition Studies at the Royal Academy of Music in London from 1986. In 1989 he helped found the Munich Biennale, and in 1990 served as the first composer in residence of the Berlin Philharmonic. Among his many dramatic works are *Pollicino,* fairy-tale opera (Montepulciano, Aug. 2, 1980), *Das verratene Meer,* opera (Berlin, May 5, 1990), and *Venus und Adonis,* opera (Munich, Jan. 11, 1997). He also composed many orchestral works, including eight symphonies (1948–93), two piano concertos (1950, 1967), *Allegro brillante* (Dallas, Sept. 14, 989), and *Requiem (9 Spiritual Concertos)* for piano, trumpet, and large chamber orchestra (1990–92), as well as chamber works and vocal pieces, including *The King of Harlem* for mezzosoprano and instrumental ensemble, after García Lorca (Witten, April 20, 1980) and *3 Auden Pieces* for voice and piano (Aldeburgh, June 15, 1983).

PEOPLE IN MUSIC

hep. An antiquated term for "good" or "cool," as in "hep cat." Anyone who uses the term *hep* these days is absolutely not hep.

PEOPLE IN MUSIC

Herbert, Victor (August), famous Irish-born American composer; b. Dublin, Feb. 1, 1859; d. N.Y., May 26, 1924. Herbert was a grandson of Samuel Lover, the Irish novelist. His father died when he was an infant, and his mother married a German physician. The family settled in Stuttgart in 1867, and Victor entered the Stuttgart high school, but he did not graduate.

Herbert's musical ability was already apparent, and he selected the cello as his instrument. He soon was playing with enough skill to take a position as cellist in various orchestras in Germany, France, Italy, and Switzerland, and in 1880 he became a cellist of the EDUARD STRAUSS waltz band in Vienna. In 1881 he returned to Stuttgart, where he joined the court orchestra, and studied composition at the Conservatory.

Herbert's earliest works were for cello with orchestra. He performed his Suite with the Stuttgart Orchestra in 1883, and his first Cello Concerto two years later. In 1886 he married the Viennese opera singer Therese Forster (1861–1927), and in the same year she received an offer to join the Metropolitan Opera in N.Y. Herbert was engaged as an orchestral cellist there, appearing in N.Y. also as a soloist. He played his own Cello Concerto with the N.Y. Philharmonic in 1887.

In his early years in N.Y., Herbert was overshadowed by the celebrity of his wife, but soon he developed a reputation of his own. He formed an entertainment orchestra which he conducted in a repertoire of light music. He also participated in chamber music concerts, and was a soloist with various groups. In 1893 he became bandmaster of the famous Second Regiment Band, one of the most popular military bands of the day.

From 1898 to 1904 Herbert was conductor of the Pittsburgh Symphony Orchestra, presenting some of his own compositions. In 1900 he directed at Madison Square Garden, N.Y., an orchestra of 420 performers for the benefit of the sufferers from the Galveston flood. On April 29, 1906, he led a similar monster concert at the Hippodrome for the victims of the San Francisco earthquake. In 1904 he organized the Victor Herbert N.Y. Orchestra, and gave concerts in N.Y. and neighboring communities.

However, it is as a composer of light operas that Herbert became chiefly known. In the best of these he unites spontaneous melody, sparkling rhythm, and simple but tasteful harmony. Among the more than 40 that he composed, the most successful were *The Serenade* (1897), *The Fortune Teller* (1898), *Cyrano de Bergerac* (1899), *The Singing Girl* (1899), *Babes in Toyland* (1903), *It Happened in Nordland* (1904), *Mlle. Modiste* (1905), *The Red Mill* (1906), *Little Nemo* (1908), *Naughty Marietta* (1910), *Sweethearts* (1913), and *Orange Blossoms* (1922).

In the domain of grand opera, Herbert was not so fortunate. The production of his first grand opera, *Natoma,* in Philadelphia in 1911 aroused great expectations, but the opera failed to sustain lasting interest. Still less effective was his second opera, *Madeleine,* staged by the Metropolitan Opera in N.Y. in 1914.

Herbert was one of the founders of ASCAP in 1914, serving as its vice-president until his death. This organization was at the forefront of protecting composer's rights in their works.

Herman, Jerry (Gerald), American composer and lyricist of POPULAR MUSIC; b. N.Y., July 10, 1933. Herman played piano by ear, and it was only after becoming a professional musician that he took up the study of theory and harmony. He also studied drama at the University of Miami.

Herman worked as a pianist in nightclubs and wrote for television in N.Y. He then composed several REVUES, winning a Tony Award for his Broadway show *Milk and Honey* in 1961. After the failure of *Madame Aphrodite* in 1961, he came roaring back three years later with the smash hit *Hello, Dolly!,* which earned ten Tony Awards. It was followed by another highly successful SCORE, *Mame* in 1966, which also won a Tony.

Herman's 1970s-era shows did not fare too well. But he again won a Tony with his wonderfully eccentric score for the stage adaptation of the film *La Cage aux folles* in 1983.

In 1916 Herbert was among the first to write a special score for a motion picture, *The Fall of a Nation.*

PEOPLE IN MUSIC

A revue based on his many hits songs, staged as *Jerry's Girls,* was a success on Broadway in 1985.

Herman, Woody (Woodrow Charles), noted American clarinetist, saxophonist, and bandleader; b. Milwaukee, May 16, 1913; d. Los Angeles, Oct. 29, 1987. Herman studied at Marquette University. In 1931 he joined a jazz band as a clarinet player, and in 1937 formed his first band.

In the mid-1940s, Herman's was the first prominent big band to make the transition from SWING to a more advanced, BEBOP-influenced style. In 1946, he presented in CARNEGIE HALL in N.Y. the first performance of IGOR STRAVINSKY's *Ebony Concerto,* written specially for him. He also composed popular songs. The instrumental *The Woodchopper's Ball* was his signature tune.

Herman's band was one of the rare large groups that survived over the decades. In the late '60s, he made an attempt to keep up with the popular music of the day—in this case, rock 'n' roll—by recording swinging big-band arrangements of pop hits like *Light My Fire.* By the '80s, however, the group was more or less a nostalgia band, reliving its glory days.

Hérodiade (Daughter of Herodias). Opera by JULES MASSENET, 1881, based on a story from the Bible, first produced in Brussels.

The "daughter of Herodias" is Salome. Her stepfather, Herod, King of Galilee, secretly loves her. However, she rejects him and declares love for the imprisoned John the Baptist. Salome wants to die with her adored holy man. When he is executed alone, she stabs herself to death. Despite the grisly subject, the opera has several melodious arias.

Hérold, (Louis-Joseph) **Louis,** celebrated French composer; b. Paris, Jan. 28, 1791; d. Thernes, near Paris, Jan. 19, 1833. His father, François-Joseph Hérold (b. Seltz, Bas-Rhin, March 18, 1755; d. Paris, Oct. 1, 1802), a piano teacher and composer who had studied with C.P.E. BACH, did not desire his son to become a musician. The young Hérold attended the Hix school, where his aptitude for music was noticed by FRANÇOIS-JOSEPH FÉTIS, then assistant teacher there.

PEOPLE IN MUSIC

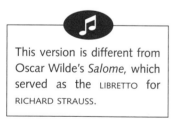

The different groups that Herman led were known as the "Herds." In the late '60s, the band became the "Thundering Herd," in keeping with the high-powered rock sound of the day.

This version is different from Oscar Wilde's *Salome,* which served as the LIBRETTO for RICHARD STRAUSS.

PEOPLE IN MUSIC

After his father's death, Hérold began to study music seriously. In 1806 he entered the Paris Conservatory, taking piano lessons, and winning first prize for piano playing in 1810. He also studied harmony and (from 1811) composition. In 1812, his cantata *Mlle. de la Vallière* won the Prix de Rome.

From Rome, Hérold went to Naples, where he became pianist to Queen Caroline. He produced his first opera, *La gioventu di Enrico Quinto* (1815), there, which was well received. From Naples he went to Vienna, and after a few months' stay returned to Paris. He finished the score of Boieldieu's *Charles de France* there in 1816. The flattering reception of *Charles de France* led to the successful Parisian productions of *Les Rosières* (1817), *La Clochette* (1817), *Le Premier Venu* (1818), *Les Troqueurs* (1819), and *L'Auteur mort et vivant* (1820). The failure of the last-named opera caused him to distrust his natural talent, and to imitate, in several succeeding stage works, the style then in vogue— that of the Italian opera composer Giacomo Rossini.

With the comic opera *Marie,* produced in 1826, Hérold returned, however, to his true element, and won instant and brilliant success. That same year, he was appointed to the staff of the Paris Opéra, for which he wrote several melodious and elegant ballets, including *La Somnambule* (1827) and *La Fille mal gardée* (1828). *La Somnambule* furnished VINCENZO BELLINI with the subject of his popular opera.

Hérold's next grand opera, *Emeline,* staged in 1829, was a failure. However, two years later, his *Zampa* was sensationally successful and placed him in the first rank of French composers. He then collaborated on a number of other works. His last completed work, *Le Pré aux clercs,* from 1832, had a remarkable vogue.

Hérold died of tuberculosis shortly before his 42nd birthday. His unfinished opera *Ludovic* was completed by FROMENTAL HALÉVY and produced posthumously at the Opéra-Comique in 1833. His piano music (55 opus numbers) consists of SONATAS, caprices, RONDOS, DIVERTISSEMENTS, fantasies, VARIATIONS, and POTPOURRIS.

Herrmann, Bernard, American conductor and outstanding composer for films; b. N.Y., June 29, 1911; d. Los Angeles,

PEOPLE IN MUSIC

Dec. 24, 1975. Herrmann won a composition prize at the age of 13, then enrolled at N.Y. University, where he studied with American conductor/composer PHILIP JAMES and Australian-born composer PERCY GRAINGER. He later took courses in composition and conducting at the Juilliard Graduate School of Music.

In 1934 Herrmann was appointed to the staff of CBS radio as a composer of background music and conductor of the CBS Symphony Orchestra summer radio series. From 1942 to 1959 he was chief conductor of the CBS Symphony Orchestra in boldly progressive programs of modern works, including those by Charles Ives.

Herrmann became associated with the actor/director Orson Welles and wrote several scores for the radio broadcasts of Welles's company, the Mercury Theater. His music for Welles's first film, *Citizen Kane* from 1940, is still regarded as a classic of the genre. His use of an electric violin and electric bass in the score for *The Day the Earth Stood Still* in 1951 is an example of early application of electronic technology in film music.

Herrmann subsequently wrote film scores for the thrillers of Alfred Hitchcock, which are filled with eerie atonal devices. Of these, the score for *Psycho* in 1960, for strings only, perfectly described the killer's deranged mental state.

Herrmann scored 61 films in total, being most active in the 1950s and '60s. He spent the last ten years of his life in England, but was in Los Angeles in 1975 to conduct the score for his last film, Martin Scorsese's acclaimed *Taxi Driver*. He died in his sleep shortly after the final recording session for that film.

PEOPLE IN MUSIC

Heseltine, Philip (Arnold), brilliant English composer and writer who used the pen name PETER WARLOCK; b. London, Oct. 30, 1894; d. (suicide) there, Dec. 17, 1930. Heseltine studied in Germany and at Oxford. A meeting with FREDERICK DELIUS in France in 1910 inspired him to pursue a career as a composer.

Heseltine adopted a style that was intimately connected with English traditions of the Elizabethan period and yet revealed IMPRESSIONISTIC undertones in its harmonies. Another influence was the Dutch modern composer BERNARD VAN DIEREN, particularly on Heseltine's use of COUNTERPOINT.

Heseltine was a conscientious objector during World War I. In 1917–18, he was in Ireland, and after the war ended he returned to London. In 1920 he founded the progressive journal of musical opinion *The Sackbut.* He wrote criticism, and made transcriptions of early English music. He also participated in organizing the Delius Festival in 1929. Suffering from depression, he committed suicide by gas in his London apartment in 1930.

Heseltine edited (with P. Wilson) 300 early songs (Elizabethan, Jacobean, and French ayres). He was co-editor of *Oxford Choral Songs* and the *Oxford Orchestral Series,* a collection of early English and Italian dances.

hesitation tango. A tango with a sharper SYNCOPATION than the standard form. SAMUEL BARBER included a hesitation tango in his set for piano four-hands, *Souvenirs.*

hesitation waltz. A type of mildly syncopated WALTZ, similar to the so-called Boston waltz. A slow waltz with jazz-like inflections, it emerged as a popular dance in Europe after World War I. Strangely, despite its nickname, the dance is practically unknown in America and least of all in Boston.

heterophony (from the Grk. *heteros* + *phōnia,* diversity of sound). A single melody played on two or more instruments simultaneously. There may be slight differences in rhythm, attack, or even the melody itself between the various instruments, but not great enough to be heard as distinctively different melodic lines. Heterophony is prominent in accompanied vocal music of the Near East and Asia, and in Asian court music.

Heure espagnole, L'. Opera by MAURICE RAVEL, 1911, first produced in Paris. The action takes place in Toledo, Spain, during the 18th century. The "Spanish hour" of the title is the period of time during which several successive lovers of the wife of a local clockmaker hide themselves in the cabinets of the large clocks in his shop. When he discovers them,

The hesitation waltz's popularity in Europe can be measured by the traffic signs posted in the 1920s in Paris cautioning the pedestrians, "Ne dansez pas la Valse d'hesitation devant les autos" (Do not dance the hesitation waltz in front of the automobiles.)

they all claim to be customers, and the greedy clockmaker accepts the explanations, whereupon they all make merry to the sounds of a HABANERA.

The score is one of the finest examples of Ravel's subtle instrumentation and precise rhythms, for the mastery of which he earned the critical nickname, "the Swiss watchmaker."

This work includes a famous "warning": "I forbid the text to be read out loud during the performance of the music. Failure to conform with these instructions will cause the transgressor to incur my just indignation."

Heures séculaires et instantanées (Secular and Instantaneous Hours). Piano cycle by ERIK SATIE, 1914. Like many of Satie's piano works, it is full of private commentary between composer and pianist.

hexachord. 1. The six tones *ut, re, mi, fa, sol, la* in SOLMIZATION (sight singing). 2. A set of six different pitch classes, usually the first (or last) six of a 12-TONE ROW.

PEOPLE IN MUSIC

Higginbotham, J(ay) **C.,** African-American JAZZ trombonist; b. Social Circle, Ga., May 11, 1906; d. N.Y., May 26, 1973. He acquired mastery of the trombone in his youth, and in 1928 moved to N.Y., where he played with CHICK WEBB, FLETCHER HENDERSON, and BENNY CARTER. He later worked with LOUIS ARMSTRONG from 1937 to 1940 and HENRY "RED" ALLEN from 1940 to 1947, and then subsequently led his own groups.

high fidelity. 1. A trade name developed in the 1950s for a new technique of recording. In this process, the high end was unnaturally boosted, or made more prominent, so that recordings would sound better on the phonographs of the day. 2. In the later '50s and '60s, the term "high fidelity" was used to describe stereophonic records. *See* STEREO.

MUSICAL INSTRUMENT

high hat. In a drum set, a pair of cymbals placed horizontally and facing each other, attached to a floor stand. A foot pedal opens and closes the cymbals, producing a rustling vibration followed by a sharp choke; hence the alternate name, *choke cymbals.*

High Mass. *See* MISSA SOLEMNIS.

Hildegard von Bingen, remarkable German composer, poet, abbess, and mystic; b. Bemersheim, near Alzey, 1098; d. Rupertsberg, near Bingen, Sept. 17, 1179. Hildegard's noble parents, Hildebert and Mechtild, promised to consecrate her to the church as she was their 10th child. Accordingly, she began her religious training as a child, then joined with the reclusive mystic Jutta of Spanheim, who with her followers occupied a cell of the Benedictine monastery of Disibodenberg. At 15 Hildegard took the veil, succeeding Jutta as Mother Superior in 1136. Between 1147 and 1150 she founded a monastery on the Rupertsberg (near Bingen) with 18 sisters. Around 1165 she founded another house at Eibingen (near Rudesheim). She is called "abbess" in letters drawn up by Frederick Barbarossa in 1163.

PEOPLE IN MUSIC

Hildegard conducted extensive correspondence with popes, emperors, kings, and archbishops. She was thus greatly involved in politics and diplomacy. Several fruitless attempts were made to canonize her, but her name is included in the Roman Martyrology, and her feast is celebrated on Sept. 17.

Hildegard is musically important through her MONO-PHONIC chants, several of which were settings of her lyric and dramatic poetry. She collected her poems in the early 1150s under the title *Symphonia armonie celestium revelationum.* This volume survives in two sources, both in early German notation, and comprises 70-odd liturgical poems (the exact number varies, depending on classification). The poetry is rich with imagery, and it shares the apocalyptic language of her visionary writings.

The music is not typical of plainchant, but involves a technique unique to Hildegard. It is made of a number of melodic patterns that repeat in different modal positions. These are used as the basis for melodic variation, as the words dictate. The melodies themselves are rich with ornamentation, so that a single syllable may be accompanied by many notes.

Hildegard also wrote a morality play in dramatic verse, *Ordo virtutum,* which includes 82 melodies that are similarly structured. The lyrics to this work were more closely fit to the melodies, with less ornamentation.

719

Hildegard pointed out that her music is written in a range that is suited to women's voices, contrasting with the formal GREGORIAN MODES, which were written for men. Hildegard was also known for her literary works, which include prophecy, medical and scientific treatises, and religious writings.

Hill, Bertha "Chippie," African-American blues singer; b. Charleston, S.C., March 15, 1905; d. N.Y., May 7, 1950. Hill was born into a large family of 16 children. She made her way to N.Y., where she first appeared as a dancer in Harlem. She then toured as a dancer and singer with MA RAINEY, and subsequently made tours and recordings with LOUIS ARMSTRONG and others. She was active in Chicago as a singer in nightclubs in the 1920s.

Hill retired from music making during the later '20s and '30s, but was then lured out of retirement by the JAZZ revival of the mid-'40s. In 1948 she appeared at Carnegie Hall in N.Y. and at the Paris Jazz Festival. However, two years later, she was killed by a hit-and-run driver.

hillbilly. A once common description for old-time, Appalachian folk song and dance music, as cultivated by white musicians in the 19th and early 20th centuries. The most common instruments were the fiddle, guitar, and banjo, although the double bass and accordion family instruments were also used. Sources include the MINSTREL SHOW, BALLADS from the so-called Anglo-Irish tradition, and African-American folk music.

However, the negative associations with the word "hillbilly" led many musicians to shun its use. Eventually, it was replaced by the more neutral term, COUNTRY MUSIC.

Hiller, Lejaren (Arthur, Jr.), American composer and theorist of computer music; b. N.Y., Feb. 23, 1924; d. Buffalo, Jan. 26, 1994. Hiller studied chemistry at Princeton University, where he earned his Ph.D. in 1947, and music at the University of Illinois, graduating with a master's degree eleven years later. He began his career as a chemist, and served as assistant professor of chemistry at the University of Illinois from 1953 to 1958, where he subsequently taught

PEOPLE IN MUSIC

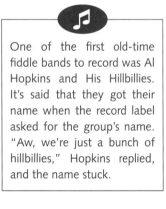

One of the first old-time fiddle bands to record was Al Hopkins and His Hillbillies. It's said that they got their name when the record label asked for the group's name. "Aw, we're just a bunch of hillbillies," Hopkins replied, and the name stuck.

PEOPLE IN MUSIC

music until 1968. He then became Frederick B. Slee Professor of Composition at the State University of N.Y. at Buffalo, and also served as co-director of the Center of the Creative and Performing Arts. In 1980 he was named its Birge-Cary Professor of Music. He retired in 1989.

Hiller published (with L. Isaacson) a manual, *Experimental Music* in 1959, and numerous articles on the application of computers to musical composition. He composed two symphonies (1953, 1960), a Piano Concerto (1949), seven string quartets (1949–79), six piano sonatas (1946–72), and other works.

Hiller achieved fame with his computer composition *Illiac Suite* for string quartet (in collaboration with L. Isaacson; 1957). The name was an abbreviation of Illinois Accumulator, the mainframe computer used to create the SCORE. Encouraged by the publicity, Hiller wrote a *Computer Cantata* for soprano, magnetic tape, and chamber ensemble in 1963.

Other works are *Man with the Oboe* (1962); *Machine Music* for piano, percussion, and tape (1964); *An Avalanche* for pitchmen, prima donna, player piano, percussion, and pre-recorded playback (1968); *HPSCHD* for one to seven harpsichords and one to 51 tapes (1968; in collaboration with JOHN CAGE); *A Preview of Coming Attractions* for Orchestra (1975); *Midnight Carnival* for a principal tape, an indeterminate number of subsidiary tapes, and other events in an urban environment (1976); *Fast and Slow* for saxophone quartet (1984); and *The Fox Trots Again* for chamber ensemble (1985).

Hin und Zurück (Forth and Back). "A sketch with music" by PAUL HINDEMITH, 1927, first performed in the Baden-Baden Festival. A husband kills his cheating wife. Then the action reverses itself, like a film running backward: the adulteress returns to life, her husband pockets the gun, and the situation is restored to normal!

Hindemith, Paul, significant German-born American composer, violist, conductor, pedagogue, and theorist, a leading master of the 20th century; b. Hanau, near Frankfurt am Main, Nov. 16, 1895; d. Frankfurt am Main, Dec. 28,

PEOPLE IN MUSIC

1963. Hindemith began studying violin at the age of nine, and at 14 entered the Hoch Conservatory in Frankfurt, where he studied violin and composition. His father was killed in World War I (in which he also served), and Hindemith was compelled to rely on his own resources to make a living.

Hindemith served as concertmaster of the orchestra of the Frankfurt Opera from 1915 to 1923, and later played viola in ADOLF REBNER's string quartet. From 1922 to 1929 he was violist in the Amar String Quartet, with which he also appeared as a soloist on the viola and viola d'amore. He later was engaged as a conductor, mainly of his own works.

As a composer, Hindemith joined the MODERN MUSIC movement and was an active participant in the contemporary music concerts in Germany. In 1927, he was appointed instructor in composition at the Berlin Hochschule für Musik. With the advent of the Hitler regime in 1933, he experienced increasing difficulties, both artistically and politically. He was married to Gertrud Rottenberg, daughter of the Jewish conductor LUDWIG ROTTENBERG, and he stubbornly refused to cease playing with other Jewish musicians.

Beginning in 1934, Hindemith made three visits to Ankara at the invitation of the Turkish government, and helped to organize the music curriculum at the Ankara Conservatory. He made his first American appearance at the Coolidge Festival at the Library of Congress in Washington, D.C., in a performance of his *Unaccompanied Viola Sonata* in 1937.

After a brief stay in Switzerland, Hindemith emigrated to the U.S., where he was an instructor at the Berkshire Music Center at Tanglewood, Massachusetts (summer 1940). From 1940 to 1953 he was a professor at Yale University, where he led an ensemble dedicated to early music. He was elected a member of the National Institute of Arts and Letters, and during the academic year 1950–51 he was Charles Eliot Norton Lecturer at Harvard University.

Hindemith became an American citizen in 1946. He conducted concerts in the Netherlands, Italy, and England during the summer of 1947. In 1949 he revisited Germany for the first time since the war, and conducted the Berlin Philharmonic in a program of his own works. In 1953 he

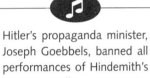

Hitler's propaganda minister, Joseph Goebbels, banned all performances of Hindemith's music. Unwilling to compromise with the barbarous regime, Hindemith accepted engagements abroad.

went to Switzerland, giving courses at the University of Zurich. He also conducted orchestras in Germany and Austria. In 1954 he received the prestigious Sibelius Award of $35,000, offered annually to distinguished composers and scientists by a Finnish shipowner. From 1959 to 1961 he conducted guest appearances in the U.S. In 1963 he visited America for the last time. He then went to Italy, Vienna, and finally Frankfurt, where he died.

Hindemith's early music, such as the opera *Mörder, Hoffnung der Frauen* (op. 12, 1921) and *Suite 1922* for Piano (op. 26), shows him rebelling against CLASSICAL structures. At the same time, he cultivated the techniques of CONSTRUCTIVISM, or music in which the formal structure is emphasized. This is evident in his theatrical sketch *Hin und Zurück* (op. 45a, 1927), in which all the events portrayed on stage are reversed. In a work of a much later period, *Ludus Tonalis* (1943), the postlude is the upside-down version of the prelude.

Hindemith was a strong supporter of HAUSMUSIK ("House music"), to be played or sung by amateurs at home. The score of his *Frau Musica* (as revised in 1944) has an extra part for the audience to sing. A NEOCLASSICAL trend is shown in a series of works, entitled *Kammermusik,* for various instrumental combinations, rich in COUNTERPOINT, and BAROQUE in style. Having made a thorough study of early music, he artfully assimilated its POLYPHONY in his works. His masterpiece of this genre was the opera *Mathis der Maler.*

An exceptionally prolific composer, Hindemith wrote music of all types for all instrumental combinations, including a series of sonatas for each orchestral instrument with piano. Other important works include many operas, ballets—notably *Theme and Variations: The 4 Temperaments* for string orchestra and piano (N.Y. Ballet, 1946) and *Hérodiade,* with recitation, after Mallarmé (produced as *Mirror before Me,* by the Martha Graham Dance Company, 1944)—and orchestral and chamber works. Hindemith also wrote numerous songs and choruses in German, English, and French, as well as many song cycles.

Hines, Earl (Kenneth) **"Fatha,"** remarkable African-American JAZZ pianist; b. Duquesne, Pa., Dec. 28, 1905; d. Oak-

PEOPLE IN MUSIC

land, Calif., April 22, 1983. Hines's father was a professional trumpet player and his mother played piano and organ. Earl took piano lessons as a child, but became interested mainly in jazz.

Hines played in brass bands in his hometown, and then left for Pittsburgh in the late teens. He worked in several jazz bands in that area, before moving on to Chicago in 1923, where he played with groups led by Carroll Dickerson and ERSKINE TATE. He met LOUIS ARMSTRONG in Dickerson's band, and Armstrong invited him to join his Hot Five recording group in 1927. Under Armstrong's influence, Hines evolved a special type of "trumpet piano style" characterized by sharp accents, octave tremolos (trills) in the treble, and insistently repeated melodic notes.

In 1928 Hines organized his own big band in Chicago, playing at the Grand Terrace club. The group toured the U.S, and was among the first black big bands to play in the South. Its theme song, *Deep Forest,* became popular. The band remained together for nearly two decades. Toward the end of its run in the mid-1940s, Hines hired many of the young musicians who were developing BEBOP, including CHARLIE PARKER and DIZZY GILLESPIE. He also hired the up-and-coming SARAH VAUGHAN and BILLY ECKSTINE as vocalists. Nonetheless, the band ended in 1947, due to the great expense in maintaining such a large ensemble.

Hines reunited with Armstrong as a member of the trumpeter's All Stars groups from 1948 to 1951. He then returned to playing as a solo artist, with various accompanists. In 1957, he toured Europe, playing in Berlin in 1965. In 1966 he played in Russia, followed by an appearance in Japan. During his last years he made his residence in San Francisco, where he played his last engagement just a week before his death.

hip-hop. African-American popular dance music of the last two decades of the 20th century, which became the underlying musical basis for RAP.

While inheriting the strong beat of DISCO, hip-hop reemphasized the backbeat of 1960s popular music, and drew upon house music of the late 1970s. Hip-hop developed as SAMPLING technology evolved. Sampling allowed musicians and producers to "sample" or record small excerpts from earlier popular songs. These small pieces were then electronically treated, looped (or repeated), and put one on top of another to form a dense musical texture.

Sampling has been challenged as plagiarism in the courts. For this reason, today most rap artists pay a royalty to the earlier artists who they sample.

Hippolyte et Aricie. Lyric tragedy by JEAN-PHILIPPE RAMEAU, 1733, based on the French playwright Jean Racine's *Fèdre* and the Greek playwright Euripides's *Hippolyte.*

The plot resembles other operas involving Hippolyte, his absent father, the King Theseus, and his amorous stepmother Phaedra. The new element is Alicia, beloved of Hippolyte. Theseus returns, hears false rumors that Hippolyte has attempted to seduce Phaedra, and exiles Hippolyte. Phaedra confesses her guilt and dies, and Hippolyte is reunited with Alicia, thus providing a happier ending than usual for this Greek tragedy.

Hirt, Al(ois Maxwell), popular American trumpeter; b. New Orleans, Nov. 7, 1922; d. there, Apr. 27, 1999. Hirt studied with FRANK SIMON at the Cincinnati Conservatory of Music from 1940 to 1942, then served in the U.S. Army, and played in the 82nd Army Air Force Band.

PEOPLE IN MUSIC

After his discharge from the army in 1946, Hirt played with various bands. In 1956 he formed his own band, and began touring with it in 1960. His first major recording, in 1961, was the album *The Greatest Horn in the World.* A versatile musician, he was equally at ease playing in the country, jazz, and popular music styles.

Histoire du soldat, L' (A Soldier's Story). Ballet with narrative by IGOR STRAVINSKY, 1918, first performed in Lausanne, Switzerland. The score is for seven instruments only. The story concerns a Russian soldier who sells his soul to the devil. Among the dance numbers are a tango, a waltz, and a ragtime number. The use of familiar forms points to Stravinsky's later embracing of NEOCLASSICISM.

Histoires naturelles (Natural history). Song cycle by MAURICE RAVEL, 1907. It depicts mostly birds (peacock, cricket, swan, kingfisher, and guinea hen).

Historische Symphonie (Historical symphony). The Sixth Symphony by LOUIS SPOHR, 1850. The four movements represent the idioms of JOHANN SEBASTIAN BACH, WOLFGANG AMADEUS MOZART, LUDWIG VAN BEETHOVEN, and Spohr, respectively.

History of a Soldier, The. See *HISTOIRE DU SOLDAT, L'.*

Hit the Deck. Musical by VINCENT YOUMANS, 1927. The female owner of a Newport, Rhode Island, coffee shop falls for a sailor customer. She acquires a fortune, but he is not tempted by wealth. Nonetheless, she manages to get pregnant by him, and wills her fortune to the unborn child. Includes *Sometimes I'm Happy* and *Hallelujah!* The latter was arranged by JOHN PHILIP SOUSA and became popular with U.S. Navy bands.

H.M.S. Pinafore, or The Lass Who Loved a Sailor. Comic opera by Gilbert and Sullivan, 1878. A sailor is in love with his captain's daughter. The inequality in rank seems unbridgeable, until a middle-aged baby nurse confesses that she had both the captain and sailor under her care and got them mixed up! This allows the marriage of the two lovers to take place. The sharply satirical LIBRETTO is matched by the musical parody of Italian opera clichés.

hocket (from Lat. *hoquetus,* hiccup; Fr., *hoquet*). A curious device popular in multivoiced medieval music. In hocketing, one voice stops and another comes in, sometimes in the middle of a word, creating the effect of hiccuping.

PEOPLE IN MUSIC

Hodges, Johnny (John Cornelius) **"Rabbit,"** African-American jazz alto and soprano saxophonist; b. Cambridge, Mass., July 25, 1906; d. N.Y., May 11, 1970. After playing drums and piano, Hodges studied saxophone with SIDNEY BECHET. He then played with WILLIE THE LION SMITH, Bechet, and CHICK WEBB, and from 1928 to 1951 was a member of DUKE ELLINGTON's band. He subsequently led his own band and septet for several years before rejoining Ellington in 1955, remaining with him until his death. He published a volume of his own *Sax Originals* (1945; second edition, 1972). He was one of the most gifted saxophonists of the swing era.

hoedown. Community dancing party, originally in the rural American South and West, featuring square dances with calling, accompanied by old-time music. The fourth episode of AARON COPLAND's *Rodeo* ballet suite (1942) is named after and based upon this cultural phenomenon.

Hoffmann, E(rnst) **T**(heodor) **A**(madeus), famous German writer, conductor, and composer; b. Königsberg, Jan. 24, 1776; d. Berlin, June 25, 1822. Hoffmann studied law at the University of Königsberg, but also studied violin, piano, and composition with private teachers.

Hoffman served as music director at the theater in Bamberg, then conducted opera performances in Leipzig and Dresden in 1813–14. In 1814 he settled in Berlin. That year, he began writing music criticism using the pen name of Kapellmeister JOHANNES KREISLER.

As a writer of fantastic tales, Hoffmann made a profound impression on his period, and influenced the entire ROMANTIC school of literature. Indirectly, he was also a formative factor in the evolution of the German school of composition. His own compositions are passable from the technical viewpoint, but strangely enough, for a man of his imaginative power, they lack the inventiveness that characterizes his literary productions. His best-known musical compositions are the operas *Die Lustige Musikanten* (Warsaw, 1805), *Aurora* (1811), and *Undine* (Berlin, 1816).

Of the many adaptations of his novellas and short stories, the most famous are JACQUES OFFENBACH's *Tales of Hoffmann,* LÉO DELIBES's *Coppélia,* PIOTR ILYICH TCHAIKOVSKY's *Nutcracker,* PAUL HINDEMITH's *Cardillac,* and FERRUCCIO BUSONI's *Die Brautwahl.*

Hoffnung, Gerard, German-born English caricaturist, producer, and tubist; born Berlin, March 25, 1925; d., London, September 28, 1959. Hoffnung emigrated with his family to Italy in 1938, then to England a year later with his mother. His lack of interest in school culminated in his expulsion from the Hornsey College of Art in 1943, but this was com-

PEOPLE IN MUSIC

Hoffmann's third Christian name was originally Wilhelm, but he changed it to Amadeus out of love of WOLFGANG AMADEUS MOZART.

PEOPLE IN MUSIC

pensated for by a great drawing ability and a well-developed sense of humor.

While teaching in art schools, Hoffnung published cartoons and caricatures in magazines, drew advertising posters, and designed program covers. In 1950 he gave the first of several radio talks, the success of which led to his being included on radio panel shows with some of Britain's leading humorists of the day. These broadcasts made him nationally famous. He studied the tuba and became good enough to join the Morley College Orchestra.

In 1957 he organized the Hoffnung Music Festival Concert at London's Royal Festival Hall, which featured classical music parody at a level of grandeur not seen or heard before. Its participants included Malcolm Arnold, Dennis Brain (playing hosepipe), Franz Reizenstein, Norman Del Mar, Donald Swann, Humphrey Searle, and Gordon Jacob. Its success led to the 1958 Interplanetary Music Festival, which featured April Cantelo, Lionel Salter, the Dolmetsch Ensemble, Edith Evans, Matyas Seiber, "Bruno Heinz Jaja," P. Racine Fricker, and the immortal *Let's Fake An Opera*.

After Hoffnung's death, a third and final festival, the Astronautical, took place in 1961, with the assistance of Owen Brannigan, John Amis, Forbes Robinson, William Walton, and Joseph Horovitz, composer of the *Horrotorio* (a playful pun on JOHN CAGE's Irish circus, *Roaratorio*). Hoffnung's books of musical caricature remain popular.

Hofmann, Peter, outstanding German tenor; b. Marienbad, Aug. 12, 1944. Hofmann studied at the Hochschule für Musik in Karlsruhe, then made his operatic debut in 1972 in Lübeck as Tamino in WOLFGANG AMADEUS MOZART's *Die Zauberflöte* (The Magic Flute). In 1973, he joined the Württemberg State Theater in Stuttgart.

Hofmann came to prominence with his performance of the role of Siegmund in the centennial Bayreuth productions of RICHARD WAGNER's *Der Ring des Nibelungen* in 1976, and later appeared as Parsifal at Covent Garden, London. He made his U.S. debut as Siegmund with the San Francisco Opera in 1977, then sang Lohengrin with the Metropolitan Opera in N.Y. in 1980. His other roles include Max, Florestan, Alfred in *Die Fledermaus,* Loge, and Bacchus.

PEOPLE IN MUSIC

Hogwood, Christopher (Jarvis Haley), prominent English harpsichordist, conductor, and musicologist; b. Nottingham, Sept. 10, 1941. Hogwood studied classics as well as music at Pembroke College, Cambridge, where he received his bachelor's degree in 1964. He also studied harpsichord with several noted teachers, establishing a lifelong interest in early music.

In 1967 Hogwood joined David Munrow in organizing the Early Music Consort, an ensemble devoted to the performance of medieval music. In 1973 he founded the Academy of Ancient Music with the aim of performing music of the BAROQUE and early CLASSICAL periods on original instruments. He toured widely with the ensemble and made many recordings, including a complete set of WOLFGANG AMADEUS MOZART's symphonies utilizing period instruments. He also served as artistic director of the Handel and Haydn Society of Boston (from 1986) and music director of the St. Paul (Minnesota) Chamber Orchestra (1988–92), subsequently serving as principal guest conductor of the latter (from 1992) and a visiting professor at King's College, London (from 1992). His guest conducting engagements have taken him all over Europe and North America.

In 1989 Hogwood was made a Commander of the Order of the British Empire. He edited works by JOHANN CHRISTIAN BACH, HENRY PURCELL, and WILLIAM CROFT. He was a contributor to *The New Grove Dictionary of Music and Musicians* (1980) and also wrote *Music at Court* (London, 1977), *The Trio Sonata* (London, 1979), and *Handel* (London, 1984).

Holberg Suite (*Aus Holberg's Zeit*). String orchestral work by EDVARD GRIEG, 1884. It was written to commemorate the bicentennial of the Norwegian poet Ludwig Holberg. The suite is in five movements.

Hold Everything. Musical by RAY HENDERSON, 1928. A welterweight prizefighter is torn between a rich socialite and a lower-class but truly loving woman. Being a romantic, he chooses the latter. Includes *You're the Cream in My Coffee.*

PEOPLE IN MUSIC

Billie Holiday, c. 1955.
(Benson Collection)

▶

Holiday, Billie (Eleanora) **"Lady Day,"** outstanding African-American jazz singer; b. Philadelphia, April 7, 1915; d. N.Y., July 17, 1959. Holiday was the illegitimate daughter of a domestic maid, Sadie Fagan, and the jazz guitarist Clarence Holiday. Her father and mother were both teenagers when she was born, and her father soon abandoned his wife and young child. Born in Philadelphia, she was raised in Baltimore by her grandparents until she joined her mother in N.Y. around 1929.

Holiday began singing in Harlem nightclubs when she was 14, and may have also worked as a prostitute. She was "discovered" by the record producer/jazz critic John Hammond, who arranged for her to perform and record with BENNY GOODMAN and his band in 1933. She worked with bands led by TEDDY WILSON in 1935, FLETCHER HENDERSON in 1936, COUNT BASIE in 1937–38, and briefly toured with ARTIE SHAW, also in 1938. She was the first black singer featured with an all-white band, and faced great hostility when the band was on the road, particularly in the South.

Holiday became a star on her own when she appeared at N.Y.'s Café Society in 1939. There, she attracted a wealthy, liberal crowd, who admired her strong personality as much as her music. It was also the first N.Y. club to allow and attract a mixed-race crowd. Her first engagement lasted almost nine months, and during this period she introduced the song, *Strange Fruit.* This daring song addressed the issue of racism in its depiction of the lynching of a southern black man. It was very daring for an African-American vocalist to sing this song, even before a N.Y. audience.

Holiday enjoyed her greatest success in the 1940s. She had a major label record deal with Decca Records, and had many hits with songs that became closely associated with her: *Lover Man, Good Morning Heartache, God Bless the Child,* and *Porgy* (from Porgy and Bess). However, a string of poor choices in romantic attachments and her increasing use of drugs and alcohol began to take their toll on her career in the later 1940s. Compounding this was the death of her mother in 1946, on whom she had depended for emotional support (even though her mother was often more of a problem than a help). Holiday served time for federal narcotics charges in 1946, but made a comeback at N.Y.'s Carnegie Hall in 1948.

The '50s saw more run-ins with the law and increasingly erratic performances. Because of her drug arrests, she lost her "cabaret card" in N.Y., without which she could no longer sing at any N.Y. nightclub, a major financial blow. At the same time, Holiday was still a major star, touring Europe in 1954 and 1958, and recording with many leading jazz musicians. However, her health continued to deteriorate, and by the late '50s her voice was nearly gone.

In May 1959, Holiday was taken to the hospital suffering from heart and liver disease. Once there, in a strange set of circumstances never explained, the police claimed to have found some drugs in her possession, and placed her under arrest in her hospital room! This was the final blow to the once great singer, and she died in July in the hospital.

Holiday rarely sang classic blues *per se.* Her repertoire consisted of the popular tunes of the day, but she gave them a unique interpretation that changed them into deep expressions of sorrow. For her, "blues" was a state of mind and a means of expression. Her unique qualities included her light, subtle, and instrument-like voice, her subtle shadings of intonation, and her commanding sense of rhythm and melodic variation.

Billie Holiday's legacy goes far beyond her music. She has been written about by many major writers, including poems by Frank O'Hara ("The Day Lady Died") and LeRoi Jones (Amiri Baraka), and short stories by Maya Angelou, among many others. Her life story was the subject of a 1972 film, *Lady Sings the Blues,* starring Diana Ross (in her screen debut).

Holidays. A gathering of four symphonic works by CHARLES IVES, 1904–1913, first performed in Minneapolis, April 9, 1954. The constituent works, all published separately, are

Washington's Birthday, Decoration Day, The Fourth of July, and *Thanksgiving and/or Forefather's Day.*

PEOPLE IN MUSIC

Holliger, Heinz, outstanding Swiss oboist, teacher, and composer; b. Langenthal, May 21, 1939. Hollinger began playing recorder at four and piano at six, later studying oboe and composition at the Bern and Paris conservatories. In 1959 he won first prize in the Geneva competition, and then played in the Basel Symphony Orchestra. He also attended the master classes in composition of the famed French composer/conductor PIERRE BOULEZ in Basel from 1961 to 1963. After winning first prize in the Munich competition in 1961, he embarked upon a brilliant international career.

Holliger toured in Europe and the U.S. as soloist with the Lucerne Festival Strings in 1962. He also gave concerts with his wife, harpist URSULA HANGGI, and his own Holliger Ensemble. In addition to giving master classes, he was a professor at the Freiburg im Breisgau Hochschule für Musik from 1965.

Holliger is generally recognized as the foremost oboist of his era, his mastery extending from early music to the commissioned works of such modern composers as KRZYSZTOF PENDERECKI, HANS WERNER HENZE, KARLHEINZ STOCK-HAUSEN, ERNST KRENEK, LUCIANO BERIO, ANDRÉ JOLIVET, and WITOLD LUTOSLAWSKI. In his own works, he is an uncompromising avant-gardist, having composed nontraditional stage works, orchestral, vocal, and chamber works (including many for solo instruments). Many of his works include electronic tape along with the live instruments. Recent compositions include *Gesänge der Frühe* for chorus, orchestra, and tape (1987), *What Where,* chamber opera, after Beckett (1988), Quintet for piano and winds (1989), *Ostinato funèbre* for small orchestra (1991), *(S)irato: Monodie* for orchestra (1993).

PEOPLE IN MUSIC

Holly, Buddy (born Charles Harden Holley), pioneering American rock musician; b. Lubbock, Tex., Sept. 7, 1936; d. Clear Lake, Iowa, Feb. 2, 1959. Holly began playing fiddle, guitar, and piano as a youngster, appearing on stage in a local talent contest with his two brothers when he was just five years old. When he was 13, he formed a duo with another local teen, Bob Montgomery, as Buddy and Bob, and they began performing country music locally. By 1953 they had their own local radio show out of Lubbock.

In 1954 the group had expanded to include a bass player, fiddler, and drummer. They began to get local work opening for major stars, including BILL HALEY and a young ELVIS PRESLEY. Impressed by Presley, Holly began incorporating some of Presley's vocal mannerisms into his own singing—including the "hiccup" sound that would later become Holly's trademark.

In early 1956 Buddy went to Nashville, signed to the Decca label as a country act; by this time, Bob had dropped out of the band. Decca insisted he use professional musicians as backup, and tried to make Holly a country star; the resulting records failed to sell. Discouraged, Holly returned to Texas. He was now fronting a trio, with a bass player and drummer.

In late 1956 Holly began working with a new recording engineer, Norman Petty, who had a small studio in Clovis, New Mexico. After a few rehearsal sessions, Holly recorded in early 1957 his first hit song, *That'll Be the Day.* It became a No. 1 hit that September, both in the U.S. and Great Britain. Meanwhile, the group churned out classic songs, including *Words of Love, Maybe Baby, Not Fade Away, Peggy Sue,* and *Oh Boy,* all during that year.

In early 1958 Holly and the Crickets toured Australia and Great Britain, where they were received enthusiastically. They also issued more hits, including *Rave On.* They returned to the U.S. in March for an immediate cross-country tour. But, Holly was growing weary of being tied to the Crickets' sound, and made some recordings on his own. However, he continued to tour with the band through the fall, although it now featured different musicians than the original lineup.

In October 1958 Holly separated from the Crickets and his manager/producer Norman Petty. He made some recordings in N.Y. with strings that signaled a new style that was more mainstream than his previous hard-rocking recordings. He recorded the beautiful *It Doesn't Matter Anymore* in these sessions, but it went unreleased until after his death.

The deejay at the Lubbock radio station had the colorful name of "Hipockets" Duncan. He became the manager for the teenaged Buddy and Bob act.

In early 1959 Holly assembled a new backup band to participate in a tour promoted as the "Winter Dance Party." Joining him were other stars RITCHIE VALENS (*La Bamba*), The Big Bopper (CHANTILLY LACE), and Dion and the Belmonts. The ill-fated tour was plagued by sub-zero temperatures. The stars toured on an old school bus, often without heat. Many dates were planned that were hundreds of miles apart. Facing more delays, the stars decided to lease a plane to take them from Clear Lake, Iowa, where they performed on February 2, to a date scheduled for the next day in Minnesota. On takeoff the plane crashed, taking the lives of Holly, Valens, and the Bopper.

This terrible accident was immortalized as "The Day the Music Died" in Don McLean's 1972 hit, *American Pie*.

Holly remains one of the most influential of the early rockers. His distinctive vocal style has been much imitated. His sparse backing group style, prominently highlighting his stinging electric guitar lead, has also been copied by generations of rockers. And his many songs continue to be hits for new artists.

PEOPLE IN MUSIC

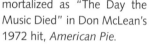

Holst, Gustav(us Theodore von), significant English composer; b. Cheltenham, Sept. 21, 1874; d. London, May 25, 1934. Holst was of Swedish descent, and received his primary musical training from his parents. In 1892 he became organist and choirmaster in a small town in Gloucestershire.

In 1893 Holst entered the Royal College of Music in London, where he studied composition, organ and piano, and also learned to play the trombone. After graduating in 1898, he was a trombonist in the orchestra of the Carl Rosa Opera Company until 1900 and the Scottish Orchestra in Glasgow from 1900 to 1903.

Holst's interest in Hindu philosophy, religion, and music during this period led to the composition of his settings from the Sanskrit of four sets of *Choral Hymns from the Rig Veda,* composed between 1908 and 1912. Meanwhile, from 1903 through the mid-'30s, he supported himself by teaching music at private secondary schools and colleges. Beginning in 1919, he also taught composition at the Royal College of Music.

Deemed unfit for military service in World War I, Holst served as Y.M.C.A. musical organizer among the British troops in the Near East in 1918. After the war, he visited the

U.S. as a lecturer and conductor in 1923 and 1932. However, his deteriorating health limited his activities. His daughter described his mind in these last years as "closed in gray isolation."

Holst's most celebrated work, the large-scale orchestral suite *The Planets,* was composed between 1914 and 1916. It consists of seven movements, each bearing a mythological subtitle:

Mars, the Bringer of War

Venus, the Bringer of Peace

Mercury, the Winged Messenger

Jupiter, the Bringer of Jollity

Saturn, the Bringer of Old Age

Uranus, the Magician

Neptune, the Mystic

The Planets was first performed privately in London in 1918, with the public premiere following in 1920. The melodic and harmonic style of the work is typical of Holst's compositions. Lyrical, dramatic, and triumphant motifs are alternately presented in effective orchestral dress. But *The Planets* was not typical of Holst's musical or philosophical concerns, and its success frightened him. His music in general reflects the influence of English folk songs and the MADRIGAL.

Holst's contributions to British music have been overshadowed by his contemporaries. However, he, like Frank Bridge, BENJAMIN BRITTEN, MICHAEL TIPPETT, and others who began composing in the English pastoral tradition, developed a strong personal style with a variety of languages and moods. Holst's vocal music is particularly fine, whether it be opera (*The Perfect Fool,* 1923, *At the Boar's Head,* 1924, *The Wandering Scholar,* 1930), ballet (*The Lure,* 1921, *The Golden Goose,* 1926, *The Morning of the Year,* 1927), choral music (*The Hymn of Jesus,* 1917, *Ode to Death,* 1919, *First Choral* Symphony, 1924, numerous a cappella works), or songs.

Holst's daughter, Imogen (Clare), b. Richmond, Surrey, April 12, 1907; d. Aldeburgh, March 9, 1984, studied at the Royal College of Music in London. She was a faithful keeper of her father's music and writings. From 1952 to 1964 she was assistant to Benjamin Britten. She also conducted the ensemble of the Purcell Singers from 1953 to 1967 and served as artistic director of the Aldeburgh Festival beginning in 1956. In 1975 she was made a Commander of the Order of the British Empire. She wrote several books on her father and his music.

Home on the Range. Legendary American cowboy song. The words were first published in 1873, and the musical setting was attributed to William Goodwin, under whose name the song was published in 1904 as *An Arizona Home.* David Guion made a standard arrangement of the song in 1930 and claims were made for him as the sole author. William Goodwin instituted a lawsuit for a million dollars in 1934 demanding official recognition of his authorship, but lost for lack of evidence. Several others managed to put in their claim.

In the meantime, *Home on the Range* was proclaimed the official song of the state of Kansas. It joins the honorable company of famous songs, among them *God Save the King, Hail to the Chief,* and *Yankee Doodle,* whose authorship is claimed by many but proved by none.

Home, Sweet Home. Popular song of uncertain origin, written c. 1820. The standard form of this famous song first appeared in the opera *Clari, or The Maid of Milan* by HENRY BISHOP, produced in London, 1823. But—surprise!—the tune first popped up in a collection of songs entitled *Melodies of Various Nations* published in London in 1821, where it was described as a "Sicilian air," and the words were different.

After *Home, Sweet Home* became famous, several musical vultures descended upon it and published it as a folk song in numerous arrangements. Bishop's publishers promptly instituted a suit against the trespassers, claiming that the Sicilian air in question was itself composed by Bishop to fill out the 1821 collection. The contention is at least plausible because no authentic Sicilian or other air has ever been found to match the tune. It appears, therefore, that Bishop plagiarized himself, which is no criminal offense.

Whatever its origin, the magic of *Home, Sweet Home* worked well through the years. When a singer performed it at a concert in an American jail in 1885, the inmates were so moved that seven of them escaped that very night and went directly to their respective homes, where they were apprehended the next day. On the other hand, when an Oklahoma attorney tested its efficacy at a trial in 1935 and sang *Home, Sweet Home* to a jury, pleading for mercy for his client, a bank robber, the jury brought out a verdict of life imprisonment.

hommage (Fr.). A DEDICATION. Also, a piece written in the style of another, intended as a compliment. AARON COPLAND wrote a piano piece entitled *Hommage à Ives,* approximating IVESian harmonies.

homophony (Grk., same sound). 1. A musical texture in which a melody and its accompaniment are clearly distinct. In its modern sense, homophony developed in the late 16th century in Florence and was generally adopted in early BAROQUE operas, as contrasted with the RENAISSANCE's predominantly POLYPHONIC style. In homophonic pieces, the component vocal or instrumental parts are subordinated to the melody and form clear chordal harmonies. Homophonic texture differs from MONOPHONIC, ANTIPHONAL, polyphonic, and HETEROPHONIC textures.

2. A choral music texture that tends toward a single rhythm and a main melodic part, as opposed to the imitative interweavings of polyphonic choral music. An example of homophonic choral music are the CATCHES, GLEES, and HYMNS of English-speaking composers of the 18th century. Even portions of WILLIAM BILLINGS's FUGING tunes are homophonic.

Honegger, Arthur (Oscar), remarkable French composer of Swiss heritage; b. Le Havre, March 10, 1892; d. Paris, Nov. 27, 1955. Honegger studied violin in Paris, and then took courses at the Zurich Conservatory from 1909 to 1911. Returning to France in 1912, he entered the Paris Conserva-

Bishop jealously maintained his claim to the sole and exclusive ownership of the tune. He even sued Gaetano Donizetti when he heard a hint of the piece in Donizetti's opera, *Anna Bolena.*

Among the many French works of this type is the *Hommage à S. Pickwick* by CLAUDE DEBUSSY, from his piano PRÉLUDES, Book II, published in 1913. Debussy pays tribute to the famous character from Dickens's *The Pickwick Papers* in this work. He includes several disguised quotations from *God Save the King,* the British national anthem.

PEOPLE IN MUSIC

737

Arthur Honegger (standing) with an unidentified pianist. (Library of Congress/Corbis)

▶

In 1920 the Paris critic Henri Collet published an article in which he drew a parallel between the "Russian 5" and a group of young French composers whom he designated as "Les Six." These six were Honegger, DARIUS MILHAUD, FRANCIS POULENC, GEORGES AURIC, LOUIS DUREY, and GERMAINE TAILLEFERRE. The label persisted, even though the six composers went their separate ways and rarely gave concerts together. Indeed, only Honegger, Milhaud, and Poulenc became generally known.

tory, and also took lessons with the famous composer Vincent d'Indy. His name first attracted attention when he took part in a concert of Les Nouveaux Jeunes (The New Youth) in Paris in 1918.

In the early years of his career, Honegger embraced the fashionable type of urban music, with emphasis on machine-like rhythms and curt, pert melodies. In 1921 he wrote a sport ballet, *Skating Rink,* and a mock-militaristic ballet, *Sousmarine* (Submarine).

In 1923 Honegger composed the most famous of his machine pieces, *Mouvement symphonique No. 1,* subtitled *Pacific 231.* The score was intended to be a realistic tonal portrayal of a powerful American locomotive, bearing the engine number 231. The music progressed in accelerating rhythmic pulses toward a powerful climax, then gradually slackened its pace until the final abrupt stop. There was a hint of a lyrical song in the middle section of the piece. *Pacific 231* enjoyed great popularity and became in the minds of modern-minded listeners a perfect symbol of the machine age.

Honegger's *Mouvement symphonique No. 2,* composed in 1928, was a musical rendering of the popular British sport rugby. His *Mouvement symphonique No. 3* (1933), however, bore no identifying subtitle. At this time, Honegger was moving away from literal representation and toward music in classical forms, often of historical or religious character. Among his most important works in this genre were *Le Roi David* (King David), composed in 1921, to a biblical subject, and *Jeanne d'Arc au bûcher,* from 1935, glorifying the French patriot saint on the semi-millennium of her martyrdom.

Honegger also composed five symphonies. While the first two lacked descriptive titles, the Third, from 1946, was entitled *Liturgique* with a clear reference to an ecclesiastical ritual. Also composed in 1946, the Fourth was named *Deliciae Basilienses* because it was written to honor the city of Basel. The somewhat mysterious title of the Fifth, *Di tre re* (Of three "res") composed in 1951, signified nothing more strange than the fact that each of its movements ended on the thrice-repeated note D (or "re" in sight-singing syllables).

Honegger spent almost all of his life in France, but he retained dual Swiss citizenship, a fact that has caused some biographers to refer to him as a Swiss composer. In 1926 he married the pianist-composer ANDRÉE VAURABOURG (1894–1980), who often played piano parts in his works. In 1929 he paid a visit to the U.S., returning in 1947 to teach summer classes at the Berkshire Music Center at Tanglewood, Massachusetts. But soon after his arrival he was stricken with a heart ailment and was unable to complete his term. He returned to Paris and remained there until his death.

honky-tonk. 1. A slang expression for a small bar, usually located at the outskirts of town. Often, after a day of work, men would gather at the honky-tonk to drink and gossip, and also to pick up the "loose women" who hoped to attract their attention. Songs about the honky-tonk lifestyle became popular in the late 1940s and early '50s, particularly those performed by country singers like HANK WILLIAMS. 2. Also applied to a ragtime piano style played at small bars.

hook. 1. FLAG. 2. In popular music, a memorable motive or riff, functioning as an identifying repeated figure in the melody or bass.

hopak (*gopak*). Ukrainian popular dance in rapid, slightly SYNCOPATED $\frac{2}{4}$ time. It is usually danced by men only who employ acrobatic movements, sometimes similar to *kozachok*. The word *hopak* comes from the Ukrainian imperative *Hop!* (jump). (The identity of meaning with the English *hop* is accidental.) MODEST MUSSORGSKY, PIOTR ILYICH TCHAI-KOVSKY, and other Russian composers wrote hopaks for their operas.

Hopkins, Sam "Lightnin'," fine African-American blues singer, guitarist, and songwriter; b. Centerville, Tex., March 15, 1912; d. Houston, Jan. 30, 1982. Hopkins worked on a farm where he learned to play the guitar. He accompanied his cousin, the singer TEXAS ALEXANDER, and developed a style of his own. He often played a deep bass note as an accompaniment, followed by fragments of melodies in the treble strings.

After playing in his native Texas for several decades and making a few recordings, Hopkins was "discovered" by blues scholar and record producer Sam Charters in 1959, who recorded his first album. He became a favorite artist in the 1960s–1970s folk and blues revival, recording many albums. Hopkins composed many songs, both traditional blues and songs on topical subjects, including *Happy Blues,* which was written for John Glenn after the astronaut's first space flight.

Hopkins continued to record and perform through the '70s, including making a tour of Europe in 1977. Toward the end of the decade, his health began to fail and he stopped touring. He died in 1982.

Hopkinson, Francis, American statesman, writer, and composer; b. Philadelphia, Sept. 21, 1737; d. there, May 9, 1791. By profession a lawyer, Hopkinson was deeply interested in music. He learned to play the harpsichord, and also studied music theory. He then was a member of an amateur group in Philadelphia who gave public concerts by subscription.

Hopkinson was the composer of the first piece of music written by a native Anglo-American, *Ode to Music* (1754), and of the first original Anglo-American song, *My Days Have Been So Wondrous Free* (1759). He makes this claim in the preface to his *7 [8] Songs for the Harpsichord or Forte Piano,* dated Philadelphia, 1788, and dedicated to George Washington: "I cannot, I believe, be refused the Credit of being the first Native of the United States who has produced a Musical Composition." Other works include *Ode in Mem-*

PEOPLE IN MUSIC

Lightnin' got his nickname when he partnered with pianist "Thunder" Smith in the late 1930s.

PEOPLE IN MUSIC

ory of *James Bremner* (1780), a contrafactum dramatic cantata, *America Independent, or The Temple of Minerva* (1781), and some songs.

Hopkinson's music was written in the conventional English style, modeled after pieces by THOMAS ARNE, but he possessed a genuine melodic gift. He also provided Benjamin Franklin's GLASS HARMONICA with a keyboard, introduced improvements in the quilling of the harpsichord, and invented the bellarmonic, an instrument consisting of a set of steel bells. He was probably the compiler of *A Collection of Psalm Tunes with a Few Anthems, etc.* (1763).

Hopkinson's son, Joseph Hopkinson, wrote the words to *Hail, Columbia.*

hora lunga (*doina;* Rum., long song). Traditional Romanian dance or song genre, in $\frac{6}{8}$ or $\frac{2}{4}$ time, in a leisurely tempo. It may be accompanied by a combination of the shepherd's flute, a leaf held between the lips and used as a reed, a BAGPIPE, and nonnative instruments (violin, panpipes, CIMBALOM, clarinet, etc.). BÉLA BARTÓK discovered this increasingly obscure genre in Maramureš, Transylvania, during one of his many collecting trips.

The hora lunga features long, drawn-out, improvised melodies. The musician may freely stretch or compress its rhythm, and often will highly ornament each note. It is also a very widespread form. With disbelief, then amazement, Bartók studied evidence of or listened to similar music in central Algeria, Ukraine, and Persia. He theorized that one place had to be the common source, and chose Persia. Subsequent research has revealed, however, that similar music is found as far west as Albania and Algeria, and as far east as India, Tibet, western China, and Cambodia.

horn (Fr. *cor;* It. *corno*). 1. FRENCH HORN, also called *valve horn;* distinct from the valveless *natural horn.* 2. Any wind instrument in the shape of a horn. 3. In jazz, any wind instrument, particularly the saxophone and trumpet. Also *horn band,* a band of trumpeters; *Russian horn band,* a band of performers on hunting horns, each of which produces but one tone; *horn call,* fanfare played on the natural horn, thus limited to the harmonics of one fundamental.

JASCHA HEIFETZ transcribed for violin an hora by Romanian composer Grigoraš Dinicu and published it under the title *Hora Staccato.*

MUSICAL INSTRUMENT

horn fifths. A two-part HARMONIC progression, playable on natural horns or trumpets. The harmonic intervals are actually a minor sixth, a perfect fifth, and a major third (in C major):

Horn I	C	D	E
Horn II	E	G	C

The term *horn fifth* is obviously inaccurate, but it has been traditionally accepted. Examples can be found in innumerable works written during the last three centuries, in a variety of rhythmic patterns.

The trumpet calls in GIOACCHINO ROSSINI's overture to *William Tell* is an example of rapid horn fifths. LUDWIG VAN BEETHOVEN's *Les Adieux Sonata* opens with a slow, descending passage of horn fifths, illustrating the postillion horn announcing the departure of a stage coach.

PEOPLE IN MUSIC

Horne, Lena (Calhoun), remarkable African-American singer of popular music; b. N.Y., June 30, 1917. Horne left school at 16 to help support her ailing mother. She began her career as a chorus girl at Harlem's Cotton Club. In the mid to late 1930s, she made a name for herself with such recordings as *Good for Nothing Joe* and *Haunted Town*. In 1941 she sang at CARNEGIE HALL in N.Y.

After finding success as a radio vocalist, Horne went to Hollywood to star in the all-black musical films *Cabin in the Sky* (1943) and *Stormy Weather* (1943), adopting the title song of the latter as her trademark. In subsequent years she pursued a highly successful career in nightclubs and on television. She scored a triumph in N.Y. with her retrospective appearances in *Lena Horne: The Lady and Her Music* (1981–83), which she took on the road to critical acclaim.

Horne's unique renditions of such standards as *Bewitched, Bothered, and Bewildered; Can't Help Lovin' Dat Man; Love Me or Leave Me;* and *Believe in Yourself* placed her in the exalted ranks of the leading vocalists of popular music in her time. In 1947 she married Lennie Hayton.

PEOPLE IN MUSIC

Horne, Marilyn (Bernice), outstanding American mezzo-soprano; b. Bradford, Pa., Jan. 16, 1934. Horne studied with WILLIAM VENNARD at the University of Southern California in Los Angeles, and also attended LOTTE LEHMANN's master classes.

Horne then went to Europe, where she made her professional operatic debut as Giulietta at the Gelsenkirchen Opera in 1957. She remained on its roster until 1960, appearing in such roles as Mimi, Tatiana, Minnie, Fulvia in *Ezio,* and Marie in ALBAN BERG's *Wozzeck,* the role she chose in her U.S. debut at the San Francisco Opera in 1960. She married the African-American conductor HENRY LEWIS that same year, and subsequently made a number of appearances under his direction. They were separated in 1976.

In 1965 Horne made her debut at London's Covent Garden, again as Marie. She appeared at Milan's La Scala in 1969; in 1970 she made her Metropolitan Opera debut in N.Y. as Adalgisa, subsequently becoming one of the Met's principal singers. Her notable performances there included Rosina in *Il Barbiere di Siviglia* (1971), *Carmen* (1972), Fidès in *Le Prophète* (1977), *Rinaldo* (the first Handel opera to be staged there, 1984), Isabella in *L'Italiana in Algeri* (telecast live by PBS, 1986), and Samira in the premiere of JOHN CORIGLIANO's *The Ghosts of Versailles* (Dec. 19, 1991). Acclaimed for her brilliant portrayals in roles by GEORGE FRIDERIC HANDEL, GIOACCHINO ROSSINI, and GIACOMO MEYERBEER, she won equal praise as a concert artist. In 1992 President Bush awarded her the National Medal of Arts, and on Jan. 20, 1993, she sang at the inauguration of President Clinton in Washington, D.C. In 1994 she began teaching at the Music Academy of the West in Santa Barbara, California, where she was artist-in-residence and director of the voice program (from 1995). In 1995 she received a Kennedy Center Honor.

hornpipe. 1. An old English dance in lively tempo, the earlier ones in $\frac{3}{2}$ time, the later in $\frac{4}{4}$. 2. British and Irish traditional dance, associated with sailors, that originated in the 16th century, in various meters ($\frac{3}{2}$, $\frac{2}{4}$, $\frac{4}{4}$). It has a characteristic SYNCOPATION so that the music approaches that of the jig. Its choreography is less refined than other traditional dances, reflecting the energetic gestures and steps of sailors at play, with hand slapping and foot stomping.

MUSICAL
INSTRUMENT

743

Hornpipes, either of folk origin or specially composed dances, have been used frequently in English light operas, as in GILBERT AND SULLIVAN's *H.M.S. Pinafore.*

PEOPLE IN MUSIC

3. A family of reed instruments, with a simple pipe (of wood, cane, and bone), a reed (of wood and cane), and a cowhorn bell. Often two pipes are bound together. The earliest type of hornpipe is the AULOS, one form of which appears in a piece of art from Crete that was created in the 14th century B.C. Subsequent examples are found in Wales, Scotland, the Basque region, Russia, Albania, and Morocco. Many other instruments are equipped with bags and fall into another branch of the pipe family.

Horowitz, Vladimir, Ukrainian-born American pianist of legendary fame; b. Berdichev, Oct. 1, 1903; d. N.Y., Nov. 5, 1989. Reared in a musically inclined Jewish family, Horowitz began playing piano in his early childhood under

Vladimir Horowitz in concert in 1982. (UPI/Corbis-Bettmann)

▶

the direction of his mother, a professional pianist and later an instructor at the Kiev Conservatory. His other teachers were SERGEI TARNOWSKY and Felix Blumenfeld.

Horowitz made his first public appearance in a recital in Kiev in 1920, which marked the opening of a fantastically successful career. Because of the chaos following the Russian revolution, Horowitz left the country. His first performance abroad was in Berlin in 1926. Arriving in Paris in 1928, he took brief instruction with ALFRED CORTOT, and in that same year made his American debut playing PIOTR ILYICH TCHAIKOVSKY's first Piano Concerto with the N.Y. Philharmonic. He subsequently appeared as soloist with several other American orchestras, earning the reputation of a great piano virtuoso. He played for President Hoover at the White House in 1931, and in 1933 married Wanda Toscanini, daughter of the legendary Italian conductor ARTURO TOSCANINI. He became an American citizen in 1942.

Horowitz seemed to possess every gift of public success. He was universally admired, and his concerts sold out whenever and wherever he chose to appear. His natural affinity was with the Russian repertoire, and he formed a sincere friendship with SERGEI RACHMANINOFF, despite the difference in their ages. Rachmaninoff himself regarded Horowitz as the greatest pianist of the century. Horowitz's performance of Rachmaninoff's Third Piano Concerto, which he played numerous times, was his proudest accomplishment. His performances of works by FRÉDÉRIC CHOPIN, FRANZ LISZT, ROBERT SCHUMANN, and Tchaikovsky were equally incomparable.

Yet amid all these successes, Horowitz was plagued by nervous problems. He became subject to irrational fears of failure, and once or twice tried to cancel his engagements at the last minute. It took all the devotion and persuasive powers of his wife for him to overcome his psychological difficulties. Eventually, in 1973, he underwent shock therapy, which appeared to help.

In 1953, the 25th anniversary of his American debut, Horowitz gave a recital performance in CARNEGIE HALL in N.Y. After this recital, he withdrew from the stage, not to return for nearly 12 years. However, he enjoyed making recordings where he was free to play a piece until he was pleased with his performance. He also accepted a few private pupils.

In 1965 Horowitz announced a definite date for his return to performing, a concert in Carnegie Hall. Tickets went on sale two weeks in advance, and a line formed whose excitement and agitation surpassed that of a group of fans waiting to see a ROCK concert or a World Series game. Horowitz himself was so touched by this testimony of devotion that he sent hundreds of cups of coffee to the crowd to make the waiting more endurable on a rainy day.

Despite his agonies over solo performances, Horowitz had no difficulty whatsoever appearing as an accompanist to

During World War II, Horowitz appeared with ARTURO TOSCANINI in numerous patriotic concerts. It was for such a celebration in N.Y.'s Central Park that he made an energetic piano transcription of JOHN PHILIP SOUSA'S *STARS AND STRIPES FOREVER*, allowing him to show off all of his considerable talents. He performed it for years as an encore, to the delight of his audiences.

the famous German baritone DIETRICH FISCHER-DIESKAU. He also played trios with renowned cellist MSTISLAV ROSTROPOVICH and master violinist ISAAC STERN. In 1978, he played at the White House at the invitation of President Carter, a performance that coincided with the 50th anniversary of Horowitz's American debut.

In 1982, at the behest of the Prince of Wales, Horowitz gave a recital in the Royal Festival Hall in London, marking his first appearance in Europe in 31 years. Through his recordings he formed a large following in Japan where he gave a series of concerts in Tokyo and other Japanese cities in 1983.

The climax of Horowitz's career, which became a political event as well, was his decision to accept an invitation to revisit Russia for a series of concerts in 1986. His Steinway grand piano was tuned and cleaned and placed on a special plane to Moscow. Horowitz was accompanied on this trip by his wife, a piano tuner, and his cook. Special foods consisting of fresh sole and other delicacies were shipped to Moscow every day. Horowitz made a short introductory speech in Russian before he played. The Russian music-lovers who filled the hall listened almost tearfully to his playing on his return to Russia after 61 years of absence. His program included works by Rachmaninoff, Tchaikovsky, and ALEXANDER SCRIABIN, and also pieces by DOMENICO SCARLATTI, Chopin, and Schumann.

The Russian trip seemed to give Horowitz a spiritual lift. Returning to N.Y., he resumed his concert and recording career. He was awarded the U.S. Medal of Freedom by President Reagan in 1986, and the National Medal of Arts in 1989. He made his last recording on November 1st of that year. Four days later, in the afternoon, he suddenly collapsed and died of a heart attack. His passing created a universal feeling of loss the world over. His body lay in state in N.Y. and was then flown by his wife to Italy, where it was interred in the Toscanini family plot in Milan.

horse opera. An affectionately derisive name for any television or radio program, or film, dealing with the fantasy world of the Wild West. Like grand opera, the plots have a tendency toward improbability, melodrama, and sentimentality, except that the characters dress differently and ride horses.

The music that accompanies horse operas tends to emphasize galloping rhythms and quasi-Western melodies. One of the most famous borrowings of classical music is the use of the final section of the overture to GIOACCHINO ROSSINI's *William Tell* as the theme of *The Lone Ranger.*

horse trot. An American ballroom dance popular in the early 20th century—along with other "animal dances"— danced to RAGTIME music.

Hörspiel. Literally, *Hörspiel* means a play for hearing: usually it is a short composition for a solo instrument, a small instrumental ensemble, or a choral group.

The term has also been applied to radio drama, particularly as encouraged by Cologne's West German Radio throughout the latter decades of the 20th century. In a purely musical form, it is sometimes called *Funkoper.*

hör′shpēl

Horst, Louis, American dance composer and teacher; b. Kansas City, Mo., Jan. 12, 1884; d. N.Y., Jan. 23, 1964. Horst studied violin and piano in San Francisco, and composition in Vienna and N.Y. From 1915 to 1925 he was music director of the Denishawn Dance Company, and from 1926 to 1948, of Martha Graham's Dance Company, for which he wrote a number of works that played a crucial role in the development of modern dance.

PEOPLE IN MUSIC

Horst wrote extensively on the subject of music and dance. He founded and edited the journal *Dance Observer* (1934) and also wrote the important *Pre-Classic Dance Forms* (1940) and *Modern Dance Forms* (with C. Russell; 1961). He was also active as a teacher at Bennington (Vermont) College from 1934 to 1945, Columbia University Teachers College from 1938 to 1941, and the Juilliard School of Music in N.Y. from 1958 to 1963.

Hot Chocolates. Revue by FATS WALLER, 1929. The cast included CAB CALLOWAY and LOUIS ARMSTRONG at different times, both of whom sang Waller's *Ain't Misbehavin'* in the show.

Hot Time in the Old Town Tonight, A. RAGTIME song by THEODORE METZ, a bandleader, which was published in 1896. There is a story that when he traveled with a minstrel troupe his train stopped in Old Town, Louisiana. He noticed several African-American youth trying to put out a fire, and someone remarked, "There'll be a hot time in Old Town tonight," and he fashioned a song out of it. But his critics claimed that he stole the song from a saloon entertainer in St. Louis.

Hound Dog. Song by Leiber and Stoller, 1952, in the uptempo rhythm-and-blues style that helped usher in rock 'n' roll. Like many American songs recorded in the segregated era, its first recording was by an African-American (WILLIE MAE "BIG MAMA" THORNTON, 1953), which was successful within its black commercial market. It was then covered by a white performer, ELVIS PRESLEY, in 1956, and enjoyed a much larger market.

Housatonic at Stockbridge, The. Song by CHARLES IVES, 1921, to words by Robert Underwood Johnson. The same musical material is used in the last movement of his *3 Places in New England.* The haunting tune is taken from an ANTHEM, *Missionary Chant,* by CHARLES ZEUNER. Its melody also has a similarity with the theme of LUDWIG VAN BEETHOVEN's Fifth Symphony, so beloved by Ives.

PEOPLE IN MUSIC

Houston, Whitney, enormously successful African-American singer of popular music; b. Newark, N.J., Aug. 9, 1963. Houston joined the choir of the local New Hope Baptist Church when she was nine. She received vocal coaching from her mother, the gospel and rhythm-and-blues singer Cissy Houston, with whom she sang in clubs and on recordings.

After graduating from high school, Houston attempted to find a niche as a singer, but it was not until the release of the 1983 album *Paul Jabara and Friends,* on which she sang *Eternal Love,* that her career really began. After several television appearances and the release of her single *All at Once,* which proved enormously popular in Europe, she scored a spectacular success with her album *Whitney Houston* in

1985. One of its singles, *Saving All My Love for You,* won her a Grammy Award as best female pop vocalist of the year.

Houston's career was strongest from the mid-1980s through the mid-'90s. At one point, she broke the Beatles' record for consecutive No. 1 hits. Among her many hits was 1987's *I Want to Dance With Somebody (Who Loves Me),* 1988's *One Moment in Time,* recorded as a tribute to the U.S. Olympics winners, and *I'm Your Baby Tonight,* and her biggest hit, her 1992 cover of DOLLY PARTON's song, *I Will Always Love You,* featured in the film *The Body Guard.* Like many of her contemporaries, Houston's songs were promoted through clever videos, and her natural ease in front of the camera helped in the selling of her hits.

Houston's vocal style has been criticized by some as being overly studied. Nonetheless, she incorporates many of the best elements of gospel and soul singing in her vocals. She is particularly adept at ornamenting individual notes with grace and ease, as well as having great vocal power when needed.

Houston's film career was launched by starring roles in 1993's *The Body Guard* and 1994's *Waiting to Exhale,* although 1996's *The Preacher's Wife* was less successful.

Hovhaness (Hovaness), Alan (born Alan Hovhaness Chakmakjian), prolific and proficient American composer of Armenian-Scottish descent; b. Somerville, Mass., March 8, 1911. Hovhaness took private piano lessons in Boston, then completed his academic studies at Tufts University. In 1932 he enrolled in the New England Conservatory of Music in Boston as a student of the well-known composer and teacher Frederick Converse, then was a scholarship student of the Swiss composer FRANK MARTIN at the Berkshire Music Center at Tanglewood, Massachusetts, in 1942.

PEOPLE IN MUSIC

From his earliest attempts at composition, Hovhaness took great interest in the musical roots of his paternal ancestry, studying the folk songs assembled by the Armenian musician KOMITAS (1869–1935). He gradually came to believe that music must reflect the natural melodies embodied in national songs and ancient church hymns.

After completion of his studies, Hovhaness served on the faculty of the New England Conservatory of Music from

Among Hovhaness's more original compositions is a symphonic score *And God Created Great Whales,* in which the voices of humpback whales recorded on tape were used as a solo with the orchestra. The work was performed to great effect in the campaign to save the whale from destruction by human (and inhuman) predators.

1948 to 1951, then moved to N.Y. He was awarded two Guggenheim fellowships in 1954 and 1958. In 1959 he received a Fulbright fellowship and traveled to India and Japan, where he collected native folk songs and presented his own works, as pianist and conductor. In 1962 he was engaged as composer-in-residence at the University of Hawaii. He then traveled to Korea, subsequently composing several pieces incorporating Korean instruments. He eventually settled in Seattle.

Hovhaness's music has an Eastern quality. He uses modal scales and repeated melodic motives to produce an impressionistic atmosphere. An air of mysticism fills his music, aided by the titles that he often gives to his compositions.

Hovhaness is best known for his over 60 symphonies, among them *Mysterious Mountain* (1955), *St. Vartan* (1950), *All Men Are Brothers* (No. 11, 1960), *Silver Pilgrimage* (No. 15, 1962), *Vishnu* (No. 19, 1966), and *Etchmiadzin* (No. 21, 1970). He has also written several operatic works, and an enormous amount of choral music.

How Much Is That Doggie in the Window? Song by Bob Merrill, 1953, which became a novelty hit.

How to Succeed in Business Without Really Trying. Musical by FRANK LOESSER, 1961, a spoof on climbing the corporate ladder and the "how-to" learning mode popular in postwar America.

A humble but ambitious mail clerk uses a manual on success, his own wits, absolute insincerity, and plain dumb luck to rise to the top. Corporate culture, with its laziness, irresponsibility, unreliability, and lack of integrity, is given full display. Includes *Coffee Break, A Secretary Is Not a Toy,* and *I Believe in You.*

How Sweet It Is (to Be Loved by You). Classic Holland-Dozier-Holland Motown sound, first a hit for MARVIN GAYE in 1965, and subsequently covered by saxophonist JUNIOR WALKER a year later and JAMES TAYLOR in 1975.

PEOPLE IN MUSIC

Hubbard, Freddie (Frederick De Wayne), African-American JAZZ trumpeter, pianist, and bandleader; b. Indianapolis,

Apr. 7, 1938. Hubbard began playing trumpet in school. As a teenager, he was already working at local clubs working with other area musicians, including guitarist Wes Montgomery.

In 1958 Hubbard left for N.Y., where he immediately found work as a session player. In 1961, he began a five-year relationship with ART BLAKELY's Jazz Messengers, a group known for their hard-driving playing in a BEBOP style. Hubbard's reputation was made by his recordings and live performances with Blakely. At the same time, he played on a number of important albums, including ORNETTE COLEMAN's groundbreaking *Free Jazz* album and John Coltrane's *Ascension.*

In 1966 Hubbard formed the first of his own quartets. He reached the height of his popularity as a jazz player when his 1970 album *Straight Life* won a Grammy award. Reflecting the popularity of jazz-ROCK fusion, Hubbard made a series of albums in the mid-'70s that were in a more popular style. However, he never really stopped playing traditional bop. When the MILES DAVIS sidemen HERBIE HANCOCK, WAYNE SHORTER, RON CARTER, and TONY WILLIAMS were looking to re-create Davis's mid-'60s quintet, they hired Hubbard to take Davis's part. The result was a series of concerts and albums dubbed as "V.S.O.P." (Very Special One-time Performance).

Hubbard has continued to be active through the '80s and '90s, as both a touring artist and on record.

huehuetl. A Mexican vertical drum made from a hollowed out log, with animal skin for a head. It is played with sticks or fingers.

Huguenots, Les. Grand opera by GIACOMO MEYERBEER, first produced in Paris, Feb. 29, 1836.

One of the most spectacular of 19th-century operas, it embraces history, religious strife, and family tragedy. The climatic scene occurs on the St. Bartholomew's Day massacre of French Protestants, the Huguenots, in 1572. A Catholic nobleman leads an assault on the house in which the Huguenots make their last stand, realizing too late that his own daughter is among them. She perishes with her Huguenot lover and her father is left to bemoan his fate.

MUSICAL INSTRUMENT

PEOPLE IN MUSIC

Humes, Helen, African-American jazz and blues singer; b. Louisville, Ky., June 23, 1913; d. Santa Monica, Calif., Sept. 13, 1981. Humes's family was musical, and Helen learned to play trumpet and piano as a young girl. She made her first recordings when she was 14 for the Okeh label in St. Louis. She then went to N.Y. where she worked with jazz pianist JAMES P. JOHNSON and various local bands, including briefly with HARRY JAMES.

Humes first gained prominence as a singer with COUNT BASIE's orchestra from 1938 to 1942. Among her most successful renditions were the songs *If Papa Has Outside Lovin',* *Do What You Did Last Night, Everybody Does It Now, Sub-Deb Blues,* and *He May Be Your Man but He Comes to See Me Sometimes.*

After she left Basie, she moved into recording in an early R&B style. Her greatest hit in this new style was *Be-Baba-Leba* from 1945. Her career slowed in the mid-'50s and she retired for nearly 20 years. She re-emerged in 1973 at the Newport Jazz Festival, reuniting with Basie. She was an immediate hit, and returned to the jazz performing circuit, recording and touring until her death in 1981.

PEOPLE IN MUSIC

An entry in the famous London writer Samuel Pepys's diary for Nov. 15, 1667, described Humfrey as being "full of form, and confidence, and vanity" and disparaging "everything, and everybody's skill but his own."

Humfrey, Pelham, English composer; b. 1647; d. Windsor, July 14, 1674. Humfrey was a member of the famous children's choir at the Chapel Royal, and (together with fellow-choristers JOHN BLOW and WILLIAM TURNER) wrote the famous Club Anthem for it.

In 1664 King Charles II sent him to study in France and Italy. Humfrey may have studied under the well-known French composer/musician JEAN-BAPTISTE LULLY, and may also have visited Italy. Whatever the case, he returned to England in 1666 as lutenist of the Chapel Royal, and was appointed Gentleman of the Chapel Royal on Jan. 24, 1667.

On July 14, 1672, Humfrey was appointed Master of the Children of the Chapel Royal. Two years later he died, at the lamentable age of 27. One of his students was the young HENRY PURCELL, whose style clearly shows Humfrey's influence.

humor. Musical humor can be expressed in a variety of ways, from the grossest form to the subtlest reference to some humorous subject by way of musical quotation.

Humor by incongruous quotation is illustrated by the insertion of the thematic LEITMOTIV from RICHARD WAGNER's *Tristan und Isolde* into CLAUDE DEBUSSY's *Golliwog's Cakewalk.* The melody is introduced in the midst of a humorous piece, and its odd harmony and ending (marked with a short rhythmic exclamation) show that the composer is poking fun at Wagner's usual pomposity. The story goes that Debussy intended to play a joke on the pianist Harold Bauer, a great admirer of Wagner, who gave the first performance of this work. Debussy made a bet with Bauer that he would force him to make fun of Wagner. He won his bet when Bauer innocently performed the work without ever noticing the quotation in its derisive musical environment.

A purely musical example of humor is represented by WOLFGANG AMADEUS MOZART's *Musical Joke,* subtitled *Village Musicians.* Mozart ridicules the ineptitude of amateur players by making the fiddles play a figure in a scale of whole tones, and by ending in several different keys.

Imitation of animal sounds, such as the bleating of sheep in the *Don Quixote* of RICHARD STRAUSS, may produce an otherwise unintended comical effect. In JOHN CAGE's *Europeras 1 & 2,* a mechanical bird intones "Verdi! Verdi! Monteverdi!"

Sometimes the title of a piece reveals the humorous intent in the music. Virtually the entire production of ERIK SATIE depends for its humor on incongruous titles such as *Crepuscule matinal* (Morning dusk), *Heures séculaires et instantanées* (Secular and instant hours), etc.

ANNA RUSSELL, GERARD HOFFNUNG, SPIKE JONES, and P.D.Q. BACH all made their careers with musical parody.

humoresque. A light, whimsical instrumental piece, often for piano. The most famous is *Humoresque No. 2* by ANTONÍN DVOŘÁK, which is often parodied. Ragtime pianist ZEZ CONFREY wrote a jazz adaptation playfully called *Humor-restless.*

Humperdinck, Engelbert, famous German composer and pedagogue; b. Siegburg, near Bonn, Sept. 1, 1854; d. Neustrelitz, Sept. 27, 1921. Humperdinck began to study piano at seven, commenced composing at 14, and then studied at the Cologne Conservatory from 1872 to 1876.

Children for decades have sung these lyrics to the melody of Dvořák's *Humoresque:* "Gentlemen will please refrain from using the toilet while the train is waiting at a station…"

PEOPLE IN MUSIC

After winning the Mozart Prize in 1876, he studied COUN-
TERPOINT and fugue at Munich's Royal Music School in
1877. He also studied composition privately there with the
well-known conductor and composer FRANS PAUL LACHNER.

In 1879 Humperdinck won the Mendelssohn Prize of
Berlin for his choral work *Die Wallfahrt nach Kevelaar,* then
went to Italy, where he met RICHARD WAGNER in Naples in
1880. At Wagner's invitation, he worked in Bayreuth
(1881–82). In 1881 he won the Meyerbeer Prize of Berlin,
which enabled him to visit Paris in 1882. He taught at the
Barcelona Conservatory in 1885–86 and the Cologne Conservatory in 1887–88, and then subsequently worked for
the Schott publishing firm in Mainz in 1888–89. After
serving as private teacher to SIEGFRIED WAGNER in
1889–90, he joined the faculty of the Hoch Conservatory
in Frankfurt in 1890. He was made professor there in 1896,
but resigned in 1897. During this period he also was music
critic of the *Frankfurter Zeitung.*

Humperdinck's fame as a composer was assured with the
extraordinary success of his opera HÄNSEL UND GRETEL from
1893, written to a LIBRETTO by his sister ADELHEID WETTE.
This fairy-tale score, with its memorable melodies written in
the style of Wagner, retains its place in the repertoire. Although he continued to write for the stage, his succeeding
works left little impression. He was director of a master class
in composition at Berlin's Akademische Meisterschule from
1900 to 1920. He was also a member of the senate of the
Berlin Academy of Arts.

The noted composer is not to be confused with the pop singer Arnold George Dorsey, b. Madras, India, May 3, 1936, who brazenly adopted the composer's name. The singer enjoyed some success on the charts in the late 1960s, but has since been best known as a Vegas-style lounge singer.

Hungarian Rhapsodies. FRANZ LISZT wrote these works for
piano as a "patriotic anthology of the People of Hungary" in
1851. He wrote 15 of them in three years, and five more
during the last few years of his life. Some have specific sur-
names: No. 3 is the *Héroide funèbre,* No. 9 is *Carnaval de
Pest,* and No. 15 is *Rákóczy March.* The most famous is
No. 2, which opens with a typical Hungarian refrain and
erupts in a wild dancing rhythm in the finale.

Liszt drew the melodic and rhythmic materials for his
Hungarian Rhapsodies mainly from Gypsy bands. This
brought about an embarrassing situation when an obscure
German pianist named Heinrich Ehrlich discovered that the

thematic material of Liszt's famous *Second Hungarian Rhapsody* was lifted in its entirety from his own work, the manuscript of which he had sent to Liszt some years before. Liszt readily acknowledged the borrowing but pointed out that all Hungarian tunes, whether Ehrlich's or anybody else's, derive from the same popular sources. To add to the embarrassment, the manuscript of Ehrlich's score could not be located. Liszt made amends by offering to put the notation in future editions of his *Second Hungarian Rhapsody,* "d'après les thèmes de H. Ehrlich" (after themes by H. Ehrlich), but somehow this never took place.

Hungarian scale. *See* GYPSY SCALE.

Hunnenschlacht. Franz Liszt's symphonic poem, first performed in Weimar on Dec. 29, 1857. It was inspired by a fresco by the painter Kaulbach representing the battle between the Huns and the Christians. The Christians are helped by supernatural spirits hovering over the battlefield. The music alternates between scenes of slaughter (represented by parallel DIMINISHED-SEVENTH chords) and angelic hymnody in MODAL harmonies.

Hunter, Alberta, outstanding African-American blues singer; b. Memphis, Tenn., April 1, 1895; d. N.Y., Oct. 17, 1984. Born in Memphis, Hunter was raised in Chicago, and began singing as a teenager at a local club/"house of ill repute." She moved up to singing in jazz-oriented clubs, eventually working with the noted jazz band led by KING OLIVER in the early 1920s. She was also a talented songwriter, writing *Down Hearted Blues,* a major hit for blues singer BESSIE SMITH in 1923.

Hunter subsequently gained fame as an outstanding blues singer, and also worked in Europe as a singer and actress, appearing with PAUL ROBESON in the London production of *SHOW BOAT* in 1928–29. She made several tours of Europe in the '30s, returning to working in N.Y. in the '40s. She also toured to entertain servicemen during World War II.

Hunter retired in 1956 to pursue a nursing career. After a silence of 21 years, she resumed her career in 1977 and astonished her auditors as one of the last of the great blues

PEOPLE IN MUSIC

singers. She continued to make public appearances in her 89th year.

Hupfeld, Herman, American composer of popular music, singer, pianist, and lyricist; b. Montclair, N.J., Feb. 1, 1894; d. there, June 8, 1951. Hupfeld served in the U.S. Navy in World War I, during which time he wrote and performed his songs to his own words. Possessing a natural flair for sentimental melodies and nostalgic lyrics, he contributed successfully to Broadway shows.

Hupfeld achieved fame with the theme song for the movie *Casablanca* (with Ingrid Bergman and Humphrey Bogart), *As Time Goes By,* a tune that indelibly impinged on the hearts of millions.

PEOPLE IN MUSIC

huqin (*hu-ch'in*). Chinese spike fiddle. A small length of wood is crossed by a handle. The two strings, tuned in fifths, are attached from top to bottom without a fingerboard. The bow is permanently attached between the strings. Also called *erhu* (*erh-hu*).

MUSICAL INSTRUMENT

hurdy-gurdy (Lat. *sambuca rotata;* Fr. *vièle à roue,* wheel viol; It. *ghironda;* Russ. *sharmanka;* Pol. *katarinka*). A once-popular CHORDOPHONE (stringed instrument) with an unique playing mechanism involving two melody strings and between two and four DRONE strings.

By turning a crank, a wooden wheel rotates, rubbing against the strings and setting them into vibration like the bow on a violin. Rather than stopping the melody strings with the fingers, the player presses on a special keyboard that sits above them. The bass drone strings, usually tuned in open fifths, sound whenever the wheel is rotated.

The first form of the instrument occurs in the Middle Ages, where it was known as the *organistrum,* first described around 900 A.D. Although it began life in the monasteries, the hurdy-gurdy came to be used primarily for secular music accompaniment, eventually finding a place in all social classes.

By the 17th century, the instrument and its players were viewed negatively by "educated" musicians. But by the following century, the hurdy-gurdy was used at court, at the

MUSICAL INSTRUMENT

Even when the hurdy-gurdy wasn't used, references to it could be found: in FRANZ SCHUBERT's famous song, *Der Leiermann* (*Die Winterreise*), for example, with its nostalgic image of a hurdy-gurdy player in the lyrics. In the bass accompaniment, open fifths are used in imitation of the characteristic hurdy-gurdy drone strings.

Parisian CONCERT SPIRITUEL, and in the music of the Viennese Classic school and into the early 19th century.

The hurdy-gurdy is not to be confused with the street or barrel organ, which is a piped wind instrument manipulated by a crank.

Hurok, Sol(omon Israelovich), Russian-born American impresario; b. Pogar, April 9, 1888; d. N.Y., March 5, 1974. Fleeing the political oppression of the Jews by the Czarist government of Russia, Hurok's family emigrated to the U.S. in 1906. He became a naturalized citizen in 1914.

In 1913 Hurok began producing a series of weekly concerts announced as "Music for the Masses" at the Hippodrome in N.Y. He then became an exclusive manager for famous Russian artists, among them FEODOR CHALIAPIN, ARTHUR RUBINSTEIN, MISCHA ELMAN, and GREGOR PIATIGORSKY, as well as numerous other opera and ballet celebrities. He negotiated the difficult arrangements with the Soviet government for American appearances of the Bolshoi Ballet, the Ukrainian dance company, and the Leningrad Kirov Ballet, making frequent trips to Russia, helped by his fluency in the language.

Hurok's office became one of the leading presenters of classical performances in the country from the 1930s through his death in the mid-'70s. Ironically, his N.Y. office became the target of a bomb attack by a militant Jewish organization which objected to Hurok's importation of Soviet artists, even though many of the artists were themselves Jewish.

PEOPLE IN MUSIC

Husa, Karel, distinguished Czech-born American composer, conductor, and pedagogue; b. Prague, Aug. 7, 1921. Husa studied violin and piano in his youth, while also taking courses in engineering. In 1941 he entered the Prague Conservatory, studying composition, and in 1945–46 he attended the Academy of Music. In 1946 he was awarded a French government grant to continue his studies in Paris at the École Normale de Musique and the Paris Conservatory, where he studied composition, theory, and conducting.

In 1954 Husa emigrated to the U.S., and joined the music department of Cornell University as teacher of composi-

PEOPLE IN MUSIC

tion and conductor of the student orchestra. He also taught at Ithaca College from 1967 to 1986. He became an American citizen in 1959. He appeared widely as a guest conductor, frequently including his own music in his programs.

In his early works Husa followed the modern Czech school of composition, drawing on folk tunes for his melodies. Later he was influenced by modern composition techniques, while still retaining his love of melody. In 1969 he received the Pulitzer Prize in music for his Third String Quartet. In 1974 he was elected to membership in the Royal Belgian Academy of the Arts and Sciences, and in 1986 he received an honorary Doctor of Music degree from Ithaca College. In 1993 he received the Grawemeyer Award of the University of Louisville for his Cello Concerto (1988), and in 1994 was made a member of the American Academy of Arts and Letters. In 1995 President Vaclav Havel of the Czech Republic bestowed upon him the State Medal Award of Merit, 1st Class.

Hustle, The. A 1975 Van McCoy hit that defined the DISCO era, surviving as the accompaniment to the dance of the same name.

Hüttenbrenner, Anselm, Austrian composer; b. Graz, Oct. 13, 1794; d. Ober-Andritz, near Graz, June 5, 1868. At the age of seven, Huttenbrenner began studying organ. He also studied law at the University of Graz.

In 1815 Hüttenbrenner went to Vienna to study with the famous court composer ANTONIO SALIERI. FRANZ SCHUBERT was his fellow student, and it is their friendship that keeps Hüttenbrenner's name alive. Hüttenbrenner also knew LUDWIG VAN BEETHOVEN intimately, and was present at his death.

Hüttenbrenner was an excellent pianist and a prolific composer. Schubert praised his works, which included six operas, eight symphonies, overtures, ten masses, four Requiems, three funeral marches, chamber pieces, piano works, and some 300 quartets for men's voices and some 200 songs. Hüttenbrenner came into the possession of many Schubert manuscripts after Schubert's death, among them that of the *Unfinished Symphony,* which he held until 1865.

PEOPLE IN MUSIC

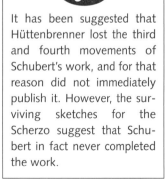

It has been suggested that Hüttenbrenner lost the third and fourth movements of Schubert's work, and for that reason did not immediately publish it. However, the surviving sketches for the Scherzo suggest that Schubert in fact never completed the work.

Hwang, Byung-Ki, Korean composer, virtuoso kayagum performer, and pedagogue; b. Seoul, May 31, 1936. Hwang studied traditional Korean music and the KAYAGUM (a traditional 12-stringed instrument) at the National Classical Music Institute in Seoul from 1951 to 1958. He received first prize at the National Competition of Traditional Music in 1954 and 1956, a National Music Prize in 1965, and the Korean Cinema Music Award in 1973.

From 1974 Hwang was professor of Korean traditional music at the College of Music, Ewha Women's University, in Seoul, and in 1985–86 he was a visiting scholar at Harvard University.

Hwang is noted as the first Korean composer to write modern works for the kayagum. He is also a distinguished kayagum player, and has appeared in recital in the U.S., West Germany, France, and Austria. His U.S. debut took place in N.Y.'s Carnegie Hall in 1986, in a program that included a number of his own compositions.

Hwang's works are elegant in their structures, and IMPRESSIONISTIC in harmonic and melodic design.

PEOPLE IN MUSIC

hydraulic organ. A small kind of organ invented by the Greek musician Ktesibios of Alexandria, who lived c.180 B.C. In this organ, wind pressure was supplied by a combination of water, gravity, and air.

MUSICAL
INSTRUMENT

Hykes, David (Bond), distinctive American composer and vocalist; b. Taos, N. Mex., March 2, 1953. Hykes studied filmmaking at Antioch College in Ohio from 1970 to 1974, and arts administration at Columbia University, where he gained a Master of Fine Arts degree in 1984. He also studied classical Azerbaijani and Armenian music with Zevulon Avshalomov from 1975 to 1977 and North Indian RAGA singing with S. Dahr in 1982.

In 1975 Hykes founded the Harmonic Choir, whose members employ vocal techniques borrowed from Tibetan and Mongolian music. These singers have developed the unique ability to sing more than one note at once, by creating both a FUNDAMENTAL tone and its PARTIALS. From 1979 the ensemble was in residence at the Cathedral of St. John the Divine in N.Y., and from 1980 made tours of the U.S.

PEOPLE IN MUSIC

759

and Europe. In 1981 Hykes traveled to Mongolia under the sponsorship of the Asian Cultural Council.

Hykes' compositions for voice use harmonics to produce rich waves of slowly changing sounds. The result resembles a sort of modernized chant with an ethereal haze of overtones. Among his compositions are *Hearing Solar Winds* (1977–83), *Current Circulation* (1983–84), and *Harmonic Meetings* (1986). Hykes has also recorded solo vocal works, and has composed several film and television scores and a number of instrumental works.

hymn (from Grk., *hymnos;* Fr., *cantique;* It. *inno*). 1. Generic name of religious or sacred songs in praise of a deity. In Greek poetry, a hymn was a chant in honor of a god or hero. In Latin, such pre-Christian hymns are usually translated by the word *carmen.* The Christians, however, accepted the Latinized form *hymnus* in the sense of a poem or a song in praise of the Lord. In established church services, a hymn is usually a metrical poem to be sung by a congregation, thus differing in function and form from PSALMS and CANTICLES.

Hymnody—that is, the doctrine of hymns and the theory of their composition—was generated in the Christian community of Syria about the 4th century. The earliest authenticated Christian hymn, written in Greek notation, was discovered in the town of Oxyrhynchos in Egypt, and is dated approximately 200 A.D. Latin hymns, which are fundamental to the Roman Catholic church, emerged toward the end of the 4th century in the Christian community of Milan, of which St. Ambrose was the bishop.

Hymn tunes of the first millennium A.D. were almost exclusively MONOPHONIC. CONTRAPUNTAL settings were limited to the INTERVALS of the OCTAVE, PERFECT FIFTH, and PERFECT FOURTH. POLYPHONIC hymnody was the fruit of the great school of Notre Dame in Paris in the 11th century, and achieved its flowering with the advent of the so-called Burgundian and Flemish polyphonic systems of composition.

The Roman Catholic church retained the Latin form of hymns, but in Germany, even before the Protestant revolution led by Martin Luther, a trend developed of writing hymns in the German vernacular, or by combining German verses with the Latin ones. A mixture of German and French vernacular with Latin hymns attained a high degree of poetic expression in the so-called *Carmina Burana,* a collection (named after the monastery of Benediktbeuren in Bavaria) that contains texts and melodies notated in rudimentary NEUMES, as they were sung by the GOLIARDS, young clerics and traveling students who wandered over Germany, much in the manner of the TROUBADOURS and TROUVÈRES of France.

Lutheran hymnody absorbed some of the vernacular MODES from popular sources, and the product became the foundation of hymn singing and composing in all Protestant nations. The Anglican Church adopted many Lutheran hymns in the 16th century, among them the most famous hymn believed to have been written by Luther himself, *Ein' feste Burg ist unser Gott* (A Mighty Fortress Is Our God). In England and later in America, Lutheran hymns assumed a metrical form that almost approaches secular song. English and American hymns are invariably set in a chordal style. Occasional canons do not disrupt the prevailing HOMOPHONIC arrangements. A curious departure from this style is the type of hymn called FUGING tunes.

2. A national song of lofty character, like the French *Marseillaise.*

Hymnen. Electronic work by KARLHEINZ STOCKHAUSEN, 1967. It combines the national anthems of many lands as a vision of metaphysical global union. It was first performed in Cologne.

Hyperprism. Extraordinary work for wind instruments and percussion by EDGARD VARÈSE, 1923, first performed in N.Y. It was initially greeted by critics with expressions of dismay and disgust. Comparisons of the work with a zoo where animals are going berserk were made independently by two N.Y. critics. *Hyperprism* has nothing to do with the ZOO, however.

The distinguished *New York Times* music critic Olin Downes described *Hyperprism* as "a catastrophe in a boiler factory."

hypo-. In the system of church modes, the prefix *hypo-* indicates the starting point of a mode a FOURTH below its final (TONIC). So, if the Dorian mode begins on D, then the *Hypodorian* mode will begin on A, a fourth below. A similar relationship exists for the other modes.

I (It.; masc. plural). The.

I Am Woman. HELEN REDDY's 1972 pop hit that became a theme song for the women's liberation movement.

I Can Get It for You Wholesale. Musical by HAROLD ROME, 1962. It depicts life in the N.Y. garment industry, a thicket of double-crossing and profit-taking. The show introduced BARBRA STREISAND as the poor befuddled secretary Miss Marmelstein.

(I Can't Get No) Satisfaction. ROLLING STONES hit of 1965, famous for its guitar riff and, for the time, frank lyrics. Covered by OTIS REDDING in 1966.

I Can't Give You Anything But Love, Baby. Song by JIMMY MCHUGH, with lyrics by DOROTHY FIELDS, 1928. It is one of the most enduring hits of the Great Depression, with its protagonist confessing his financial insolvency, leaving love as his only asset.

I Can't Help Myself. Also known as *Sugar Pie, Honey Bunch.* HOLLAND-DOZIER-HOLLAND composition made famous by the FOUR TOPS in 1965, their first No. 1 pop hit.

I Didn't Raise My Boy to Be a Soldier. Song by PLANTADOSI, 1915, written when America had not yet entered into World War I. As events began to move national sentiment away from absolute neutrality, the same company published another song, *I Don't Want My Boy to Be a Soldier, But I Will Send My Girl to Be a Nurse.* Finally, the company published a song reflecting the entry of the U.S. into World War I: *America, Here Is My Boy!*

I Fall to Pieces. A 1961 country hit for country singer PATSY CLINE.

I Got Rhythm. Song by GEORGE GERSHWIN, 1930, from the musical *Girl Crazy.* This is a very intricate and yet disarmingly simple song. Its rhythmic pattern is formed by an eighth-note rest followed by four dotted-eighth notes and another eighth-note rest, all encompassed within a regular $\frac{4}{4}$ measure. With its success, Gershwin arranged it in a brilliant piano solo. He later wrote a VARIATION set on it for piano and orchestra.

I Got You (I Feel Good). JAMES BROWN funk hit of 1965, his biggest popular hit.

I Have a Dream. CANTATA by ELIE SIEGMEISTER, 1967. It is based on the famous speech by Martin Luther King, Jr., and was first performed in Long Beach, N.Y.

I Heard It Through the Grapevine. Major MOTOWN hit penned by HOLLAND-DOZIER-HOLLAND. It was moderately successful when recorded by GLADYS KNIGHT AND THE PIPS in 1967 but turned into a smash a year later by MARVIN GAYE.

I Left My Heart in San Francisco. A 1962 hit and GRAMMY AWARD winner for Tony Bennett that has since become his theme song. Written by Douglass Cross and George Cory.

I Married an Angel. Musical by RICHARD RODGERS and LORENZ HART, 1938. A nobleman has had so many unhappy experiences with women that he declares he would only marry an angel. Sure enough, a female floats into his room. He is enchanted and marries her. But she proves embarrassing in society because she always tells the truth. It is only when she learns how to deceive, cheat, and be a hypocrite that the hybrid union becomes successful. Includes the title song and *Spring Is Here.*

I Shot the Sheriff. BOB MARLEY-penned REGGAE song popularized by British blues guitarist ERIC CLAPTON in 1974. It helped introduce reggae rhythms to English and American pop music.

I Walk the Line. JOHNNY CASH's first pop hit from 1956, which became the model for his lean, country sound.

I Wanna Be Loved by You. Song by Bert Kalmar, Herbert Stothart, and Harry Ruby, 1928. It was an instant hit in the hands of flapper and "boop-a-doop girl" Helen Kane.

I Want to Be Happy. Song by VINCENT YOUMANS, 1924, from his musical *No, No, Nanette.*

I Want to Hold Your Hand. The Beatles' first U.S. No. 1 pop hit, penned by LENNON and MCCARTNEY.

I Wonder Who's Kissing Her Now. Song by Howard and Orlob, 1909, from the musical *The Prince of the Night.* Joseph Howard was listed as sole author when the song became a huge hit. Therefore, it was quite a shock when one Harold Orlob brought a lawsuit against Howard some 40 years later, with Orlob claiming to have written the song while working for Howard as an arranger. Remarkably, Orlob did not seek damages, only recognition. Howard conceded his claim, and the song was republished under both of their names.

iamb (iambus). In prosody, a metrical foot of two syllables, one short and unaccented followed by one long and accented: ˘ ´– .

Musical phrases following this rhythmic formula may be labeled iambic.

Ibéria. The second movement of the three-part symphonic work *Images* by CLAUDE DEBUSSY, 1910.

Debussy adored Spain, its rhythms, and the very odor of the streets. The three sections of *Ibéria* bear evocative subtitles: *Par les rues et par les chemins* (In the Streets and

By-Ways), *Les Parfums de la nuit* (The Fragrances of the Night), and *Le Matin d'un jour en fête* (The Morning of a Festival Day). In the last section, the violinists are instructed to hold their instruments under their arms and strum them like guitars.

Ibert, Jacques (François Antoine), distinguished French composer; b. Paris, Aug. 15, 1890; d. there, Feb. 5, 1962. Ibert studied at the Paris Conservatory from 1911 to 1914. During World War I he served in the French navy, then returned to the Conservatory after the war ended.

Ibert received the Prix de Rome in 1919 for his cantata *Le Poète et la fée.* While in Rome, he wrote his most successful work, the symphonic suite *Escales* (Ports of Call, 1930), inspired by a Mediterranean cruise he took while serving in the navy. In 1937 he was appointed director of the Academie de France of Rome, and held this post until 1960. He was also administrator of the Réunion des Théâtres Lyriques Nationaux in Paris from 1955 to 1956. In 1956 he was elected a member of the Institut de France.

In his music, Ibert combines the best elements of IM-PRESSIONISM and NEOCLASSICISM. There is an element of humor in his lighter works, such as his popular orchestral *Divertissement* and an even more popular piece, *Le Petit âne blanc* (The Little White Donkey) from the piano suite *Histoires* (1922). Ibert's craftsmanship is excellent. Other works include operas, ballets, and orchestral works.

Ice Cube (Oshea Jackson), rapper, songwriter, and actor; b. Los Angeles, June 15, 1964. Ice Cube initially gained fame as a member of the group N.W.A. (Niggas with Attitude) and as a solo artist, and then as a film actor.

Ice Cube began rapping in the ninth grade, soon meeting a local deejay named Dr. Dre. The duo produced a parody of the popular rap song *Roxanne, Roxanne* that was a local hit in 1984. They next wrote *Boyz 'n the Hood,* a song reflecting life in the ghettos of Compton, California, which was recorded by another rapper friend, Eazy E. The trio then joined with deejay Yella to form N.W.A., but Cube left the group for a while to attend school in Phoenix, Arizona, not returning until 1988.

Listeners and critics were at first bewildered by the sounds of Debussy's imaginary Spain. One suggested that *Ibéria* was so foggy that a letter must have been omitted from the title, i.e., the "S," for *Siberia.* But when a more broad-minded music critic was asked who was the best Spanish composer, he replied, "Debussy!"

PEOPLE IN MUSIC

Ice Cube recorded two albums with N.W.A., the second being 1991's classic *Straight outta Compton,* most of which he wrote, which was a huge bestseller. That same year, he released his first solo album, *Death Certificate,* and gave a critically well-received performance in John Singleton's first feature film, *Boyz 'n the Hood.* His 1992 album, *The Predator,* was the first rap album to debut at No. 1 on both *Billboard*'s pop and R&B album charts. He followed it a year later with another bestseller, *Lethal Injection.* In 1994 he coproduced, cowrote, and starred in the film *Friday,* a comedy about life in Los Angeles that received mixed reviews.

Icelandic Symphony. Symphony No. 16 by HENRY COWELL, 1963, first performed in Reykjavík.

Ice-T (Tracy Marrow), rapper and actor; b. Newark, N.J., c.1958. Ice-T moved to Los Angeles in the seventh grade to live with his aunt. In high school in the Crenshaw area, he became involved with gangs, and he moved out on his own during the 12th grade. He subsequently graduated and joined the Army.

In the early '80s, Ice-T began rapping, recording *The Coldest Rap* in 1982 for a local label. He then went to N.Y., where he worked with several other local rappers, returning to Los Angeles by 1986. He was signed to Sire Records in 1987, forming his own Rhyme Syndicate management company and recording label a year later. He appeared in the film *New Jack City* in 1991, and a year later he formed the speed metal–rap group, Body Count.

ictus (from Lat. *icere,* strike). A separation mark in GREGORIAN CHANT before and after an important note in the melody. This emphasis is given to a special word in the text, rather than following the logic of the melody itself.

I'd Rather Be Right. Musical by RICHARD RODGERS and LORENZ HART, 1937. The plot focuses on a boy unable to marry his best girl on account of lack of money. He has a dream in which he meets President Franklin D. Roosevelt and confides his troubles to him. Roosevelt replies that he cannot help the lovers until he balances the national budget.

PEOPLE IN MUSIC

Body Count's hit song *Cop Killer* attracted the attention of conservative politicians across the land, who condemned its lyrics. The song led Time Warner, the media empire that owned Sire, to drop Ice-T, but his recording and acting careers have continued nonetheless.

Various hilarious situations follow before the dreamer awakens and decides to get married, budget or no budget.

Ideale, Die. Symphonic poem by FRANZ LISZT, 1857, inspired by Schiller's poem by the same name and first performed in Weimar for the unveiling of the dual Schiller–Goethe monument. The music fittingly describes the ideals of both poets.

idée fixe. A term used by HECTOR BERLIOZ to describe the recurrent theme of his *SYMPHONIE FANTASTIQUE,* which occurs in every movement of the work. With it he intended to portray the Shakespearian actress Miss Smithson, with whom he was in love. Actually, he made use of the same theme in a piece composed before he ever beheld Miss Smithson on the stage! *See also* LEITMOTIV.

idiophones (from Grk. *idios* + *phonos,* one's own sound). Instruments whose sound is produced by striking or shaking a metallic, wooden, or other surface directly. Thus, idiophones produce their sound by the substance of the instrument itself (e.g., TRIANGLE, CHIMES, CYMBALS, XYLOPHONE, CASTANETS, RATTLE, GLASS HARMONICA, etc.).

This term—along with CHORDOPHONE, AEROPHONE, and MEMBRANOPHONE—was created by German musicologists ERICH VON HORNBOSTEL and CURT SACHS in their famous classification of world musical instruments.

MUSICAL
INSTRUMENT

Idomeneo, Rè di Creta (Idomeneo, King of Crete). Opera by WOLFGANG AMADEUS MOZART, 1781, first produced in Munich.

Returning from the Trojan War, Idomeneo's ship runs into a storm. To calm the sea god Poseidon, Idomeneo promises to sacrifice the first person who meets his ship at home. It happens to be his son. When Idomeneo tries to evade his pledge, the gods send a monster to ravage the island of Crete. At this point a god descends from the heavens who magnanimously arranges a compromise: Idomeneo sacrifices his throne in favor of his son.

idyl (It. *idillio;* Fr. *idylle;* Ger. *Idylle*). A composition of a pastoral or tenderly romantic nature, without set form.

If I Had a Hammer. A 1948 political-action song by folksingers PETE SEEGER and LEE HAYS. It became a major hit thanks to PETER, PAUL, AND MARY's 1962 recording.

If I Were King (*Si j'étais roi*). Opera by ADOLPHE ADAM, 1852, first produced in Paris.

The action unfolds in the Indian port of Goa in the 16th century, before its capture by Portugal. A fisherman saves a young girl from drowning, not realizing that she is a royal princess of Goa. When he recognizes her on the beach, he tells of his exploits to the king's nephew, who orders him never to mention it again under penalty of death. Aggrieved, the fisherman traces the words on the sand "Si j'étais roi" (If I were king) and falls asleep. The king, touched by this sight, orders the sleeping man transferred to the royal palace and lets him rule Goa for a day. The fisherman discovers that the king's nephew treacherously conducted negotiations with the Portuguese, preparing to surrender the city. The king expels the traitor, and the Portuguese are repelled. The fisherman marries the princess.

The opera is melodious and its overture is often played at popular concerts.

Iglesias (Buga), **Julio,** Spanish singer and songwriter of popular music; b. Madrid, Sept. 23, 1943. Iglesias was 20 before he showed an interest in music, teaching himself to play the guitar. After studying English at Cambridge, he entered the Benidorm Song Festival in 1968 in his native country and carried off all of its prizes.

Iglesias subsequently pursued a successful international career, turning out some 60 albums in six languages, which sold over 100 million copies, and for which his name was entered in the *Guinness Book of World Records.*

Isle de Merlin, L'. Opera by CHRISTOPH WILLIBALD GLUCK, 1758, first performed in Vienna. Two young Frenchmen find themselves on the island of the magician Merlin and fall in love with his two nieces. To gain their object of matrimony, Merlin insists that they play and win a dice game. The Frenchmen lose, but Merlin helps them win their brides nonetheless.

PEOPLE IN MUSIC

Iglesias's biggest English language hit was a duet with country crooner WILLIE NELSON, *To All the Girls I've Loved.*

Isle joyeuse, L'. Piano piece by CLAUDE DEBUSSY, 1904, one of his most brilliant. It paints in luscious IMPRESSIONISTIC harmonies the vision of a "joyous isle."

Illuminations, Les. Song cycle by BENJAMIN BRITTEN, 1940, for voice and string orchestra, first performed in London. The work sets to music ten symbolist poems by the French poet Arthur Rimbaud.

Ilya Muromets. Subtitle of the Third Symphony, 1912, by Reinhold Glière (1875–1956), his most significant work. Its four movements depict the valorous deeds of the legendary Russian knight Ilya Muromets. The music is ROMANTIC with some modernistic touches, such as the employment of WHOLE-TONE SCALES to suggest Ilya's unbounded heroism.

I'm Always Chasing Rainbows. A popular song of 1918, which borrows the melody of the middle part of FRÉDÉRIC CHOPIN's *Fantaisie-Impromptu.*

I'm Forever Blowing Bubbles. Song by John William Kellette, 1918. It sold nearly three million copies of sheet music. This lighthearted song reflected America's mood at the close of World War I, at the dawn of the Roaring Twenties.

I'm in the Mood for Love. Song by JIMMY MCHUGH, 1935. A huge and memorable hit featured in several movie musicals.

I'm Just Wild about Harry. Song by NOBLE SISSLE and EUBIE BLAKE, 1921, introduced in the revue *Shuffle Along.* One of the first post-ragtime songs to gain wide popularity, it served as Harry Truman's presidential campaign song in 1948.

I'm Looking Over a Four-Leaf Clover. Song by Harry Woods, 1927. It is based on the folk belief that a four-leafed clover brings good luck (most clovers only have three leaves).

I'm Walkin'. A 1957 FATS DOMINO hit covered by teen rock star RICKY NELSON, his first charting hit that same year.

Musical humorist SPIKE JONES re-created this song as *I'm in the Nude for Love* ("Funny but . . . who's got a funny butt?").

A common satire of this song begins "I'm looking over my dead dog Rover, who I just ran over before. . . ."

Images. Orchestral suite by CLAUDE DEBUSSY, 1906–12. The first movement is entitled *Gigues.* In the second movement, *IBÉRIA,* Debussy depicts his love of Spain. The third movement, *Rondes de Printemps,* is especially popular. These "dances of spring" are marked by constantly changing rhythms and colorful orchestral timbres.

Debussy also wrote two piano suites entitled *Images I* (1905) and *II* (1907).

Imaginary Landscape. Generic name for four works by JOHN CAGE. Each work makes use of noises and random combinations of sounds produced by various means, including the chance manipulation of a radio receiver. Cage produced the first version in 1939.

em-broh′lyo   **imbroglio** (It., mixture, confusion). 1. The use of rhythmically contrasting sections within a common meter. A simultaneous use of $\frac{3}{4}$ and $\frac{6}{8}$ in Spanish music is an imbroglio. A similar combination of meters is found in WOLFGANG AMADEUS MOZART's opera *DON GIOVANNI* at the end of the first act, and in the street scene in RICHARD WAGNER's *Die Meistersinger.* Much more complex examples of imbroglio are found in the second movement of *Three Places in New England* by CHARLES IVES, and in the Third String Quartet of ELLIOTT CARTER. 2. Literally, "confusion"; a term used to describe scenes in opera where several groups of singers or instrumental ensembles perform together, each serving a different dramatic purpose.

imitation (Ger. *Nachahmung*). The generic term for the repetition of a MOTIVE, PHRASE, or THEME proposed by one part (ANTECEDENT) in another part (CONSEQUENT), with or without modification. It is the most natural and powerful device that lies at the foundation of the CANON and FUGUE. Imitation is found in practically all musical forms since the emergence of the Western art of composition from primitive HOMOPHONY.

Progressing from literal repetition of a musical phrase, imitation evolved into a complex polyphonic art in which themes were inverted, taken at half speed (AUGMENTATION) or double speed (DIMINUTION), and further embellished by a variety of ornamental devices. The minimum requirement of all types of imitation is the preservation of the original theme's rhythmic pattern.

Canonic imitation, strict imitation; *free imitation,* where variants of the antecedent are permitted in the consequent; *strict imitation,* where the consequent answers the antecedent note for note and interval for interval.

imperfection (Lat., *imperfectio*). *See* MENSURAL NOTATION; NOTATION.

Imperial Maryinsky Theater. The great opera house founded in St. Petersburg in 1783, which received the name Maryinsky after an elderly courtier named Marie.

Catherine the Great engaged famous Italian and French musicians and choreographers to direct the theater. Between 1885 and 1915, the Maryinsky enjoyed its greatest success as a home for opera. The czars spent lavishly in supporting it, and many great Russian singers made their homes there. PYOTR ILLICH TCHAIKOVSKY's *Queen of Spades* was premiered there, as was the first Russian production of RICHARD WAGNER's *Ring.*

After the Russian Revolution, the name of the Imperial Theater was changed to the State Academy Theater of Opera and Ballet. In 1935 it was renamed Kirov Theater of Leningrad, to commemorate the Soviet leader Kirov, who was assassinated in 1934. With the transfer of the Russian capital to Moscow after the Revolution, the first place among Russian opera and ballet theaters passed to the Bolshoi Theater in Moscow.

Impériale, L'. Symphony No. 53 in D major, 1779, by FRANZ JOSEPH HAYDN. The 19th-century nickname attests to the majestic sweep of the opening movement.

Impossible Dream, The. Song by MITCH LEIGH, 1965, from the musical *Man of La Mancha.* The dreamer of this dream is Don Quixote, and the song became a popular representation of idealism, however hopeless. Jack Jones had a pop hit with it.

The czars and assorted grand dukes used to pick up ballerinas from the ballet troupe of the Imperial Theater for secret encounters. The last royal mistress, Ksheshinska, who was a favorite of the czar Nicholas II, died in Paris in 1970 at the age of 99. Her name entered history because Lenin made her villa in St. Petersburg his headquarters after the Revolution.

im-prĕh-sah′rē-ōh

impresario (from It. *impresa,* undertaking). The agent or manager of an opera or concert company.

Impresario, The (*Der Schauspieldirektor*). SINGSPIEL by WOLFGANG AMADEUS MOZART, 1786. It tells the amusing story of a producer who has to appease the professional demands of two competing prima donnas.

Impressioni Brasiliane. Orchestral suite by OTTORINO RESPIGHI, 1928. He first conducted it in São Paulo during a South American tour. The work portrays three distinct tropical landscapes.

impressionism. Critical term describing modern French and French-influenced compositions of the early 20th century.

By analogy to the late 19th-century artistic movement, subtle impressions rather than emphatic descriptions are conveyed through the use of MODAL and nondiatonic HARMONIES in free MODULATION and colorful INSTRUMENTATION. CLAUDE DEBUSSY, considered the first impressionist, disliked the term and considered his music closer in spirit to the symbolist literary movement. Perhaps the music of this period synthesizes these two elements. *See also* EXPRESSIONISM.

impromptu (Lat., *in promptu,* in readiness). 1. An IMPROVISATION. 2. INTERLUDES in theatrical plays in the 17th century, as in Molière's *L'Impromptu de Versailles.* 3. A CHARACTER PIECE of varying FORM and little DEVELOPMENT, popular in the 19th century. FRANZ SCHUBERT wrote a number of impromptus for piano, built in a symmetric form in which each main section is subdivided into three subsections and each subsection is subdivided into three further segments, which in turn are split into brief musical phrases in three-part form. It must be noted, however, that the title "impromptu" was not original with Schubert but was appended to the music by his publisher.

FRÉDÉRIC CHOPIN's impromptus for piano are particularly remarkable in their perfect symmetrical design. FRANZ LISZT wrote several piano impromptus on themes by other composers. These impromptus come close to a FANTASIA.

Improperia (Lat., reproaches). The biblical passages chanted during the Roman Catholic Good Friday MASS. It represents the cries of the crucified Jesus to his people, "Popule meus quid feci tibi?" (O my people, what have I done to you?). This is followed by two other passages from the Old Testament.

improvisation (from Lat. *improvisus,* unforeseen; *ex improviso,* without preparation). The art of a completely unrehearsed performance without a preliminary plan; extemporization.

Formerly, improvisation was regarded as integral to the craft of composition. Organists in particular were encouraged to improvise freely on a given hymn tune. Among the greatest improvisers on the organ were GIROLAMO FRESCOBALDI and DIETRICH BUXTEHUDE. JOHANN SEBASTIAN BACH was a master of organ improvisation in the fugal style. As a child, WOLFGANG AMADEUS MOZART included improvisations at his performances at the European courts. LUDWIG VAN BEETHOVEN's improvisations for his musical friends left an overwhelming impression. At his recitals, FRANZ LISZT asked musicians in the audience to give him subjects for free improvisations and amazed them by the spontaneity of his invention. Organ improvisations continued to be the stock-in-trade of organists in the 20th century, but public improvisations by pianists gradually fell into disfavor.

Doubt persists whether supposedly "spontaneous" improvisations were not in fact prepared in advance. Some improvisers prefer to prepare in advance, whether in the classical CADENZA or the JAZZ solo, particularly in the context of larger ensembles.

One group of talented improvisers on the piano and organ were those who accompanied silent movies. While they used a book of standard music for certain scenes, these musicians had to be prepared on a moment's notice to change styles, cover gaps, or invent on the spot. Some of them had a real flair for enhancing the visual image on the screen while producing listenable music.

Jazz has resurrected the art of improvisation to a new height of brilliance, especially in collective improvisations occurring in jam sessions. Depending on the style involved, jazz improvisation is affected by tonality, accompaniment, or length allotted, from a quick "fill" to an essentially unlimited time space.

Jazz saxophonist ORNETTE COLEMAN wished to remove all rules from improvisation. In the early '60s, he experimented with a style he called FREE JAZZ. In it, there were no set chord progressions, rhythms, or melodies. Each musician was instructed to listen to the others and react to them.

In a Little Spanish Town. Song by Mabel Wayne, 1926. At the time, Spanish rhythms and subject matter were popular, so this song took advantage of that popularity.

In a Summer Garden. Symphonic poem by FREDERICK DELIUS, 1908, first performed in London.

In C. Seminal work by TERRY RILEY, inspirational to an entire generation of musical minimalists. The work is scored for variable ensemble, notated in fragments to be played any number of times at will, all within the key of C major, with an occasional F♯ intruding. The composer sets minimal rules: the players cannot go back after they finish playing a segment, and the piece is "over" when all players reach the end (some may finish first). It was premiered in San Francisco on May 21, 1965.

In Memoriam. The Fourth Symphony of GIAN FRANCESCO MALIPIERO, 1948, lamenting lives lost during World War II. Each of its four movements ends in a minor key.

In Nomine. A genre of group instrumental music of the 16th and 17th centuries, with more than 150 examples by many English composers.

The name derives from the musical source, the CHANT *Gloria tibi Trinitas.* The important English religious composer JOHN TAVENER (b. South Lincolnshire, c.1490; d. Boston, England, Oct. 18, 1545) used it as the CANTUS FIRMUS (primary melody) for a MASS in six parts. In the Benedictus, the section with the text "in nomine Domini" is reduced to four voices. Apparently this section was separated from its source and arranged.

By the mid-16th century, instrumental fantasias on In Nomine began to appear. Among the composers who wrote In Nomines are Robert Johnson (I), THOMAS TALLIS, ROBERT WHITE, the FERRABOSCOS (I and II), WILLIAM BYRD, JOHN BULL, THOMAS WEELKES, ORLANDO GIBBONS, THOMAS TOMKINS, WILLIAM LAWES, and HENRY PURCELL. The practice has seen a small revival in the 20th century.

In the Steppes of Central Asia. Symphonic tableau by ALEXANDER BORODIN, 1880, first performed in St. Petersburg. The Russian title is simply *In Central Asia.*

It is a poetic evocation of the Oriental atmosphere of Khiva and Bukhara, the Khanates of central Asia absorbed in the middle of the 19th century by the expansionist Russian empire. Moslem chants are imitated in the score, and there are also spacious PENTATONIC passages to reflect Mongolian folk melodies.

In the Still of the Nite. A 1956 doo-wop hit by the FIVE SATINS, later covered by DION AND THE BELMONTS in 1960. Sometimes referred to as *(I Remember) In the Still of the Nite.*

incarnatus, Et. Part of the CREDO.

incidental music. A set of pieces composed to illustrate selected scenes in a dramatic performance.

Incidental music is distinguished from an orchestral SUITE in its subordination of music to dramatic action. It differs from OPERA because usually there are no vocal parts.

The overture from LUDWIG VAN BEETHOVEN's incidental music to Goethe's *Egmont* is frequently performed as a separate concert piece, as are several numbers from FELIX MENDELSSOHN's score to *A Midsummer Night's Dream*, the *Wedding March* being the most famous. Other examples of incidental music that became popular in concert are *L'Arlésienne* by GEORGES BIZET and *PEER GYNT* by EDVARD GRIEG.

In addition to overtures and marches, interludes, songs, and dances may be provided.

incipit (Lat., it begins). 1. The first word or group of words of a GREGORIAN CHANT, thereby identifying a particular HYMN or a CANTUS FIRMUS. In this sense, REQUIEM, MAGNIFICAT, KYRIE, GLORIA, and other parts of the MASS and CANONICAL HOURS are incipits. In cataloging early manuscripts, the incipit identifies the beginning of the first page. The ending of the manuscript is then indicated by the word *explicit,* meaning "it folds out," that is, it ends. 2. Any short musical example to represent an entire song or work.

The spelling "Nite" was chosen to avoid confusion with the earlier, 1937 Cole Porter ballad *In the Still of the Night.*

Incoronazione di Poppea, L' (The Coronation of Poppea). Opera by CLAUDIO MONTEVERDI, 1642, his last, first performed in Venice. An ambitious Roman woman named Poppea pressures her lover, the emperor Nero, to divorce his wife and install her as empress. He agrees, exiling his wife and his lover's husband, and celebrates with Poppea. The score is noteworthy for its enhanced instrumental sonorities. However, there is some question as to its authenticity.

Incredible Flutist, The. Ballet suite by WALTER PISTON, 1938, one of his few programmatic scores, first performed by the Boston Pops Orchestra. The flutist leads a village circus in a series of dances. He is amazed because everyone in the crowd follows his cues. The score ends with an infectious march.

Indes Galantes, Les. Opera-ballet by JEAN-PHILIPPE RAMEAU, 1735, first produced in Paris. The "gallant Indies" of the title stretch through Turkey, Persia, and South America. The score includes some interesting samples of tonal painting, including a storm represented by a drum roll. There is also a *danse des sauvages* (dance of the savages), in which the actors disport themselves to the rhythm of the French dance CANARY.

indeterminacy. 1. With reference to composition, indeterminancy describes a conventional score produced by CHANCE. With reference to performance, a score which leaves much to be determined by performers. 2. The title of a 1957 recording by JOHN CAGE featuring DAVID TUDOR playing selections of Cage's piano works while Cage reads randomly from his own writings, in one-minute segments.

Indian Love Call. Song by RUDOLF FRIML, 1924, featured in the operetta *ROSE-MARIE*. The melody is hardly Native American, but the song has a certain charm.

Indian Suite. Orchestral suite by EDWARD MACDOWELL, 1895, in five movements, first performed in N.Y. Its thematic materials are derived from Iroquois, Chippewa, Dakota, and Kiowa melodies.

Indianische Fantasie. Movement for piano and orchestra by FERRUCCIO BUSONI, 1914, which he first performed as soloist in Berlin. Original PENTATONIC Indian themes are used as basic material.

Indonesian music. *See* GAMELAN.

Indy, (Paul-Marie-Théodore) **Vincent d',** eminent French composer and pedagogue; b. Paris, March 27, 1851; d. there, Dec. 2, 1931. Owing to the death of his mother at his birth, d'Indy's education was directed entirely by his grandmother, a woman of culture and refinement. From 1862 to 1865 he studied piano, and then studied harmony. In 1869 he made the acquaintance of the noted composer HENRI DUPARC, and with him spent much time studying the masterpieces of JO-

VINCENT D'INDY

Vincent d'Indy.
(Library of Congress/Corbis)

HANN SEBASTIAN BACH, LUDWIG VAN BEETHOVEN, HECTOR BERLIOZ, and RICHARD WAGNER. At that time, he wrote his opp. 1 and 2 and contemplated writing an opera on Victor Hugo's *Les Burgraves du Rhin* (1869–72; unfinished).

During the Franco-Prussian War, d'Indy served in the Garde Mobile. After his discharge, he began to study composition with CÉSAR FRANCK in 1872. A year later, when Franck was appointed professor of organ at the Paris Conservatory, d'Indy joined the class. On his first visit to Germany

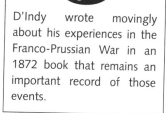

D'Indy wrote movingly about his experiences in the Franco-Prussian War in an 1872 book that remains an important record of those events.

in 1873 he met FRANZ LISZT and Wagner and was introduced to JOHANNES BRAHMS. In 1876 he heard the first performances of Wagner's *Ring* cycle at BAYREUTH, and for several years thereafter made regular trips to Munich to hear all the works of Wagner. He also attended the premiere of *Parsifal* in 1882.

From 1872 to 1876, d'Indy was organist at St. Leu-la-Forêt cathedral, and from 1873 to 1878, chorus master and timpanist with the Colonne Orchestra. For the Paris premiere of *Lohengrin* in 1887, he drilled the chorus and assisted the conductor. In 1871 he joined the Société Nationale de Musique as a junior member and was its secretary and *de facto* leader from 1876 to 1890, when, after Franck's death, he became its president. In 1894 he cofounded the famous SCHOLA CANTORUM, primarily as a school for PLAINCHANT and the PALESTRINA style. Gradually the scope of instruction was enlarged to include all musical disciplines, and the institution became one of the world's foremost music schools.

D'Indy's fame as a composer began with the performance of his dramatic legend *Le Chant de la cloche* (The song of the clock) at a concert in 1886, a work which itself had won the City of Paris Prize the preceding year. As early as 1874, the famous conductor Jules-Étienne Pasdeloup had conducted the overture *Les Piccolomini* (later used as the second part in the *Wallenstein* orchestral trilogy), and in 1882 the one-act opera *Attendez-moi sous l'orme* had been produced at the OPÉRA-COMIQUE. But the prize work attracted general attention, and d'Indy was recognized as one of the most important of modern French masters.

Although d'Indy never held an official position as a conductor, he frequently, and with marked success, appeared in that capacity (chiefly upon invitation to direct his own works). As a conductor, he visited Spain in 1897, Russia in 1903 and 1907, and the U.S. in 1905, when he conducted the BOSTON SYMPHONY ORCHESTRA. In 1892 he was a member of the commission appointed to revise the curriculum of the PARIS CONSERVATORY, but he refused a professorship of composition. But, in 1912, d'Indy accepted an appointment as professor of the ensemble class. Besides his other duties, he was, from 1899, inspector of musical instruction in Paris.

He made his last U.S. visit in 1921. He was made a Chevalier of the Legion of Honor in 1892, and an Officer in 1912.

Both as teacher and creative artist, d'Indy continued the traditions of Franck. Although he used almost every form of composition, his special talent was in the field of larger instrumental forms. Some French critics assign to him a position in French music analogous to that of Brahms in German music. His style rests on Bach and Beethoven. However, his deep study of GREGORIAN CHANT and the early CONTRAPUNTAL style added an element of severity and complexity that makes his approach somewhat difficult and has prompted the charge that his music is lacking in emotional force.

D'Indy wrote numerous articles for various journals, which are remarkable for their critical acumen and literary finish. These include *Cours de Composition musicale* (Course in the composition of music; Book I, 1903; Book II Part 1, 1909, Part 2, 1933), *César Franck* (1906), *Beethoven* (1911), and *Wagner et son influence sur l'art musical français* (Wagner and his influence on French musical art; 1930). His other musical works include operas, orchestral works, songs, choral works, and chamber music.

inégales (*notes inégales;* Fr., unequal). In the performance of French BAROQUE music, the practice of playing a note group of even duration so that the first note of each pair takes time away from the second, producing a dotted effect; e.g., two eighth notes will be played or sung as a dotted eighth and a sixteenth. But there are subtleties of performance. If the syncopation is meant to be gentle, the note is usually marked *louré*. A more incisive syncopation is marked *pointé* or *piqué*.

In addition to the works of French Baroque composers, some editors apply dotting (or even double dotting, which alters two eighth notes to a doubly dotted eighth and a thirty-second) to some works of JOHANN SEBASTIAN BACH and others, inspiring much controversy.

Inextinguishable, The (*Det uudslukkelige*). Symphony No. 4 by CARL NIELSEN, 1916. Nielsen gave the work its name without explanation, but it may reflect an optimistic view towards humanity's prevailing over war, or a repetitive structural feature in the music.

inner parts. Parts in HARMONY or COUNTERPOINT lying between the highest (SOPRANO) and lowest (BASS). *Inner pedal,* a PEDAL POINT in a middle part.

Inscape. Symphonic poem by AARON COPLAND, 1967, first performed in Ann Arbor, Michigan. The title is based on a mystical idea of the English 19th-century cleric-poet Gerard Manley Hopkins.

instrumental motet. A contrapuntal instrumental composition written on the model of the Renaissance MOTET. It is often named with words taken from a specific Latin model, such as the English IN NOMINE.

instrumentation (It. *strumentatura*). The theory and practice of composing, arranging, or adapting music for a body of instruments of different kinds. *See* ORCHESTRATION.

intabulation (from Lat. *tabula,* table; Ger. *Intabulierung;* It. *intavolatura*). The arrangement of a vocal composition for keyboard or stringed instruments, with added ornamentation. The Italian form of the word also refers to collections of TABLATURES.

Intégrales. Chamber work for small orchestra and percussion by EDGARD VARÈSE, 1925. In it, many different sounds not normally associated with musical performance are organized by the composer to form a coherent composition.

The piece was performed for the first time in N.Y. under the auspices of the International Composers Guild with LEOPOLD STOKOWSKI conducting. The critics exercised their literary wits and power of animal metaphors to describe the music as suggesting an intoxicated woodpecker, an injured dog's cry of pain, or a cat's yell of midnight rage. By the 1950s, *Intégrales* was recognized as a classic of modern music.

interference beats. The effect of the simultaneous sounding of two different tones. The result, a pulsing change in amplitude, is called *beating.*

The distinction between CONSONANCE and DISSONANCE in HARMONY depends on the relative number of beats: the more beats generated by the sounding of two or more tones simultaneously, the more dissonant is the resulting combination. The octave, being a perfect consonance, generates no beats. A perfect fifth should also be free of beats, as should be two A CAPPELLA voices or violin strings properly tuned. *See also* ACOUSTICS; JUST INTONATION; TEMPERAMENT.

Beat tones are particularly apparent when two notes are nearly identical but just slightly out of tone. In Balinese GAMELAN music, this effect is desired and is used to create the characteristic shimmering sound of the orchestra.

Because the tuning on a piano is tempered, the fifths are not perfect. On average, the fifth on the piano beats 47 times per minute.

interlude. 1. An Italian INTERMEZZO, French ENTR'ACTE, or German *Zwischenspiel.* 2. An instrumental strain or passage connecting the lines or stanzas of a HYMN, etc. 3. An organ piece played between choral hymns or PSALMS of a church service (interludium).

intermezzo (It., insertion; Fr. *intermède;* Lat. *intermedium*). 1. A theatrical genre that dates back to the liturgical drama in the 13th century, in which they were added between ritual parts of the religious service.

in-ter-med′zōh

Secular intermezzos provided diversions at aristocratic weddings, coronations, and other formal functions. Invariably, they were of a lighter nature than other parts of the occasion, and were not necessarily connected with the action in the drama or religious play into which they were added.

The genre eventually developed into independent musical presentations, leading ultimately to the formation of OPERA BUFFA.

Because intermezzos did not have to be connected with the principal spectacle, their authors strove mainly to please the public by whatever means. These interludes often succeeded in attracting more attention than the stage play itself. Thus, GIOVANNI BATTISTA PERGOLESI inserted an intermezzo *La serva padrona* in a performance of his serious opera *Il prigioniero superbo,* with the result that the intermezzo became extremely popular. Its performances in Paris precipitated the famous GUERRE DES BOUFFONS.

RICHARD STRAUSS wrote an amusing opera of his own in this genre and pointedly entitled it *Intermezzo.* Within operas, intermezzos are instrumental interludes, usually of short duration, between scenes. An intermezzo in PIETRO MASCAGNI's *Cavalleria Rusticana* is often performed as an independent concert piece.

2. A CHARACTER PIECE of instrumental music. "Intermezzo" is taken to mean a piece written at leisure, or between more serious compositions. But it is difficult to justify in this sense the term *intermezzo* that JOHANNES BRAHMS assigned to his highly elaborate ROMANTIC piano pieces. 3. INCIDENTAL MUSIC in modern dramas. 4. A short MOVEMENT connecting the main divisions of a SYMPHONY.

Intermezzo. Opera by RICHARD STRAUSS, 1924, to his own libretto. A composer's wife threatens divorce when a love letter accidentally arrives in his mail. Fortunately, he proves his total innocence, all to uncharacteristically light and harmless music.

intermodulation. Electronic technique of sound manipulation inspired by the interference of two signals. This has been used extensively, in principle, by such modern composers as KARLHEINZ STOCKHAUSEN.

Internationale. A working man's marching hymn written by a wood carver, Pierre Degeyter, in 1871, shortly after the fall of the Paris Commune. The *Internationale* served as the national anthem of the Soviet Union until 1944.

interval. The distance between two NOTES measured in DIATONIC degrees. Intervals are regularly measured from the lower tone to the higher.

The distance between a note and itself is obviously zero, but in determining an interval, this initial note is treated as a prime or unison. The distance between a given note and the next note in the scale is obviously a single unit, but it is called a second, marked with the numerical symbol 2. Thus, the names of the intervals indicate not the distance between two notes, but the numerical order of their positions proceeding up the scale. The interval of a third contains two diatonic units, yet its symbol is 3; and so it goes until the octave (from Lat. *octo*, 8), which contains seven diatonic units.

The naming of intervals is otherwise quite simple: unison, second (2nd), third (3rd), fourth (4th), fifth (5th), sixth (6th), seventh (7th), and octave (8th). Much more solemn and learned are the Latin names of intervals, derived from the Greek: *unisonus, tonus, ditonus, diatessaron, diapente, tonus cum diapente, ditonus cum diapente,* and *diapason.*

Intervals are modified by indications of major, minor, augmented, and diminished. It is most unfortunate that the naming of intervals in English borrows the Latin comparative adjectives MAJOR and MINOR for the size of intervals, and that the same terms are also used to indicate major and minor KEYS. This brings confusion into the minds of students, who are apt to say that the interval E to C is a major sixth, rather than the correct minor sixth, simply because E and C convey to most ears the feeling of a C-major triad, particularly when C is in the melody position.

The unison, fourth, fifth, and octave are perfect intervals, without a subdivision into major and minor, that is, large and small. Furthermore, all intervals can be AUGMENTED or DIMINISHED, and some even doubly augmented or doubly diminished. A fourth can be diminished, augmented, and doubly augmented, as can a fifth. All these possibilities are governed by the intrinsic development of the tonalities of which the intervals are diatonic parts.

Several intervallic pairs are ENHARMONIC EQUIVALENTS, containing identical numbers of SEMITONES. And here we enter a knotted web of problems. A minor third is a CONSONANCE, but its enharmonic equivalent, an augmented second, which sounds exactly the same, is a DISSONANCE, requiring resolution. This seeming contradiction is accounted for by the fact that it is the musical spelling that determines the belonging of an interval or a chord to a particular tonality, and what is consonant in one tonality may be dissonant in another.

An analogy from linguistics may help: the word *four* is a number, but the word *for* is a preposition. *Mother* is the sweetest word in English, dripping in sentimentality, which may well be likened to a perfect consonance. However, the same word, *mother,* is defined in *Webster's New Collegiate Dictionary* as "a slimy membrane composed of yeast and bacterial cells that develops on the surface of alcoholic liq-

Beyond the octave, the intervals are still named by the numerical adjectives in English and in French. They follow Latin forms in German, Italian, Spanish, and Russian.

The French (*majeur, mineur*), Spanish (*mayor, menor*), and Italian (*maggiore, minore*) follow the Latin pattern. Much more convenient is the German terminology in which the adjectives *grosse* and *kleine* are used for major and minor, so that E to C is unmistakably a *kleine Sexte* (small sixth), and the ambiguity is avoided. The Russians follow the German usage.

uids undergoing acetous fermentation and called also a 'mother of vinegar.'"

Augmented interval, wider by a chromatic semitone than major or perfect; *chromatic interval,* augmented or diminished (except augmented fourth, and diminished fifth and seventh); *compound interval,* wider than an octave; *consonant interval,* not requiring resolution; *diatonic interval,* occurring between two notes belonging to the same key (except the augmented second and fifth of the harmonic minor scale); *diminished interval,* chromatic semitone narrower than major or perfect; *dissonant interval,* requiring resolution; *enharmonic interval,* see ENHARMONIC EQUIVALENCE; *extended* or *extreme interval,* augmented; *flat interval,* diminished; *harmonic interval,* both tones sounded together; *imperfect interval,* diminished; *inverted interval,* the higher tone is lowered, or the lower tone raised, by an octave; *major interval,* equal to the standard second, third, sixth, and seventh of the major scale; *melodic interval,* both tones sounded in succession; *minor interval,* a chromatic semitone narrower than major; *parallel* or *consecutive interval* (with an interval preceding), two-dyad progression in the same direction and at the same interval; *perfect* or *perfect major interval,* equal to the standard unison, fourth, fifth, and octave of the major scale; *redundant interval,* augmented; *simple interval,* not wider than an octave; *standard interval,* measured upward from the keynote; *superfluous interval,* augmented.

MUSICAL INSTRUMENT

intonarumori (It., noisemakers). Musical instruments invented c.1913 by Italian FUTURIST LUIGI RUSSOLO, all of which were destroyed in Paris during World War II.

intonation. 1. (Ger. *Tonfall*). The production of TONE, either vocal or instrumental, with an emphasis on proper PITCH. 2. The method of chanting employed in PLAINCHANT. 3. The opening NOTES leading up to the reciting tone of a chant. *Fixed intonation,* see FIXED-TONE INSTRUMENTS; *intoning,* the chanting by the minister, in monotone, of parts of the Anglican church service.

in-trăh'dăh

intrada (It., entry). A short INTRODUCTION or PRELUDE. An opening piece on a festive occasion, most often arranged for trumpets and horns, and with the character of a fanfare in march time.

introduction (It. *introduzione*). 1. An instrumental PRELUDE before an ARIA in an OPERA. 2. In a CONCERTO or similar work, a part for full orchestra before the entry of the soloist. Such an introduction may be very brief, as for instance the cadential chords in the opening bars of SERGEI RACHMANINOFF's Second Piano Concerto, or else it may fill a lengthy section almost qualified to be called an overture, as in the tutti introduction to LUDWIG VAN BEETHOVEN's Violin Concerto. 3. A phrase or division preliminary to and preparatory of a composition or movement. It may be in a parallel minor or major key, as in Beethoven's Fourth Symphony, which opens in B-flat minor in a long preamble before the transition to the principal key in B-flat major. Another example is the opening movement of FRANZ JOSEPH HAYDN's 104th Symphony.

Introduction and Allegro. Chamber piece by MAURICE RAVEL, 1907, for harp, string quartet, flute, and clarinet, first performed in Paris. The music features a modern, IMPRESSIONISTIC treatment of the harp.

introit (*introitus;* Lat., entrance). 1. An opening ANTIPHON sung while the priest is approaching the altar to celebrate the Roman Catholic High MASS. It is responsorial in structure, with a soloist alternating with a chorus, or the chorus divided in two alternating parts. 2. In the modern Anglican church, an ANTHEM or PSALM, sung as the minister approaches the Communion table.

invention (Lat. *inventio*, from *invenire*, find). 1. A musical work that possesses elements of intellectual and artistic discovery. 2. A short piece in free COUNTERPOINT, developing one motive in an impromptu fashion. This form of invention in music reached its highest expressive mark in JOHANN SEBASTIAN BACH's two-part and three-part keyboard inventions, with the three-part works also known as SINFONIAS.

inversion (from Lat. *vertere*, turn). The TRANSPOSITION of the notes of an interval or chord. 1. *Melodic inversion,* in

in-trō′it

J. S. BACH states his aims in the introductory paragraph to his inventions: "A faithful guide, whereby the lovers of the Clavier are presented with a plain method of learning not only how to play clearly in 2 parts, but also to progress toward playing 3 obbligato parts well and accurately; at the same time striving not only to obtain fine inventions, but also to develop them appropriately, and above all to secure a cantabile [singing, vocallike] style of playing so as to create a strong foretaste of the art of composition itself."

which the ascending INTERVALS of the original melody are inverted to become descending intervals and vice versa. In some melodies, an inversion becomes identical with RETROGRADE MOTION, as in a LUDWIG VAN BEETHOVEN contradanza:

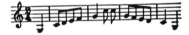

A melodic inversion is said to be TONAL if it follows the TONALITY of the melody. The second subject of the G Major Fugue from Book I of Johann Sebastian Bach's *Well-Tempered Clavier* is such an inversion of the first subject. In tonal inversions, the intervals are not precisely the same. For instance, the C-major scale (IONIAN MODE) when inverted becomes the PHRYGIAN MODE, with the initial interval being a semitone rather than a whole tone. A major TETRACHORD when inverted becomes a minor tetrachord. A broken major TRIAD becomes a broken minor triad when inverted, and vice versa.

Inversions of intervals are obtained by placing the low notes an octave above, or the upper note an octave below. When a major interval is inverted it becomes minor; an AUGMENTED interval becomes DIMINISHED. To obtain the intervallic inversion arithmetically, the original interval must be subtracted from nine. Thus, a second inverted becomes a seventh, a fourth becomes a fifth, and so forth. A perfect interval inverts into another perfect interval, e.g., a perfect fifth inverted becomes a perfect fifth. A consonance inverted becomes another consonance, e.g., thirds become sixths. A dissonance inverted becomes another dissonance, e.g., a second becomes a seventh.

2. *Harmonic inversion,* in which the bass voice is transferred an octave higher and placed on top of the chord. Chord inversions used in traditional harmony are the following: a triad; its first inversion known as the $\frac{6}{3}$ chord, shortened to 6 chord; and the second inversion or $\frac{6}{4}$ chord; the seventh chord and its inversions, the $\frac{6}{5}$ (or $\frac{6}{5}$) chord, $\frac{6}{4}$ (or $\frac{4}{3}$) chord, and $\frac{6}{4}$ (or 2) chord. (The numbers refer to the interval as counted up from the bass note.) 3. INVERTIBLE COUNTERPOINT. 4. An organ point found in some part other than the bass. 5. A standard technique in DODECAPHONIC MUSIC.

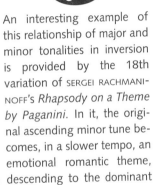

An interesting example of this relationship of major and minor tonalities in inversion is provided by the 18th variation of SERGEI RACHMANINOFF's *Rhapsody on a Theme by Paganini*. In it, the original ascending minor tune becomes, in a slower tempo, an emotional romantic theme, descending to the dominant an octave lower.

invertible counterpoint. A type of POLYPHONIC writing in which contrapuntal parts can be exchanged, say soprano and bass. While the normal interval of invertibility is the octave, other intervals have been used, such as the 10th or 12th. Among great masters of invertible counterpoint were JOHANNES BRAHMS, MAX REGER, and SERGEI TANEYEV. JOHANN SEBASTIAN BACH used them all in his *Art of the Fugue,* a veritable treasure box of scientific inversions. Also called *double counterpoint. See also* COUNTERPOINT.

Invitation to the Dance (*Aufforderung zum Tanz*). Rondo brillant for piano by CARL MARIA VON WEBER, 1819, in D-flat major. A unique composition in its treatment as a concert piece, it became even more famous in HECTOR BERLIOZ's 1841 orchestral arrangement.

invocation. Ode or prayer, particularly in ORATORIO or OPERA.

Iolanthe, or The Peer and the Peri. Comic opera by Gilbert and Sullivan, 1882, first produced in London.

A fairy maiden named Iolanthe is banished from her supernatural domain for having loved a mortal. Their son, who is "a fairy only down to the waist," is in love with a young girl who is a guardian of the court, but several elderly peers also eye her with lust in their hearts. To gain time, she becomes engaged to two earls, one after another. A fairy scandal breaks out when the Lord Chancellor admits that he is Iolanthe's mortal husband. Conscience stricken, he allows his ward to marry his and Iolanthe's son. A final blow to the pride of the House of Lords comes when it turns out that other fairies have also married peers. The Queen of Fairies forgives them all, and the two worlds unite in legitimate domestic felicity.

Ionian mode. *See* AUTHENTIC MODES.

Ionisation. Percussion ensemble work by EDGARD VARÈSE, 1931, first performed in N.Y., 1933. The word *ionisation* is a scientific term that signifies the splitting of atoms into ions. The rhythmic pattern of the score is extremely com-

It is said that a recording of *Ionisation* was regularly played by scientists working on an atom bomb in 1942.

plex, and the balance of instrumental timbres, such as wood and metal, is maintained with extraordinary virtuosity. The work, at first disdained by musicians at large, has become a classic.

Along with the various percussion instruments, the composer scored this work for two sirens.

Iphigénie en Aulide. Opera by CHRISTOPH WILLIBALD GLUCK, 1774, first produced in Paris, after a play by Jean Racine based on Euripides. The Greek fleet is stranded in the port of Aulis and cannot proceed to Troy, for which it is bound. The problem was created when Agamemnon, King of Crete, killed a sacred animal in the temple of Artemis, the virgin huntress and moon divinity. A priest warns that the goddess will not be appeased unless Agamemnon sacrifices his daughter Iphigenia. He is willing to yield, but her bridegroom Achilles voices objections. Finally, the gods are appeased, and Iphigenia is saved.

The overture from the opera is famous as a concert piece.

Iphigénie en Tauride. Opera by CHRISTOPH WILLIBALD GLUCK, 1779, first produced in Paris, based on the play by Euripides. The story is a sequel to the composer's *Iphigénie en Aulide.* The heroine, saved from sacrifice, travels to Tauris (Greek name for the Crimea), where she joins the local Scythians. When her brother Orestes is seized as an invader, she saves him, rejoins the Greeks, and returns to her native land.

Iris. Opera by PIETRO MASCAGNI, 1898, first performed in Rome. The action takes place in modern Japan. Iris, pure and innocent, is abducted by a villainous suitor who places her in a bordello. Her blind father curses her, believing her guilty of prostitution. She throws herself into a sewer, but is lifted by a host of angels to Heaven.

The music uses PENTATONIC progressions to suggest traditional Japanese melodies.

Irma la Douce. Song by MARGUERITE MONMOT, 1956, in French. This ballad was the inspiration for an American film of the same name.

Irmelin. Opera by FREDERICK DELIUS, 1892, to his own libretto, not performed until 1953. Irmelin is a princess in love with a shepherd who fortuitously turns out to be a prince himself. They meet at a brook, and all ends happily. The music is Wagnerian, diversified by sentimental pastoral episodes.

I.S.C.M. (International Society for Contemporary Music). *See* MUSIC FESTIVALS.

Islamey. A popular dance of the Caucasian tribe of the Kabardians. It is accompanied by players on the fiddle and the accordion. The music often features a DRONE on the DOMINANT note of the scale as an accompaniment to the melody. The name is derived from *Islam,* i.e., the Moslem faith.

Islamey. Piano fantasy by MILY BALAKIREV, 1869, long regarded as the most difficult piece ever written for piano.

Isle of the Dead, The. Symphonic poem by SERGEI RACHMANINOFF, 1909, inspired by the famous mortuary painting by Arnold Böcklin. Rachmaninoff conducted its first performance in Moscow. This powerful work is remarkable because of its prevalent meter of $\frac{5}{8}$, unusual for Rachmaninoff's otherwise quite symmetrical musical world.

isorhythm (from Grk. *iso + rhythmos,* same rhythm). A musicological term to indicate melodies, particularly the CANTUS FIRMUS of medieval MOTETS, that are built on the same rhythmic SEQUENCE.

The definition was expanded to include a technique popular in the 14th and 15th centuries, where a contrapuntal line uses a repeated pitch pattern (*color*) and a repeated rhythmic pattern (*talea*). Color and talea do not necessarily coincide, so that the repeated pitches are presented in different rhythms and phrases, eventually returning to the opening pattern.

Israel in Egypt. Oratorio by GEORGE FRIDERIC HANDEL, 1739, based on verses from Exodus and the Psalms, to an

English text. Handel wrote it when he was a resident of London, where it was first performed.

Israel Symphony. Work by ERNEST BLOCH, 1917. Although he was born in Switzerland and lived most of his life in the U.S., Bloch remained faithful to his Jewish heritage. This work is in two movements, portraying the contemplative religious mood of the Jewish people and the contrasting dramatic outcry of the nation deprived of a home. It was first performed in N.Y., 30 years before the formation of the state of Israel.

PEOPLE IN MUSIC

Israel, Brian M., American composer and pianist; b. N.Y., Feb. 5, 1951; d. Syracuse, N.Y., May 8, 1986. Israel studied composition at Lehman College in N.Y. and subsequently on a graduate level at Cornell University. He taught at Cornell from 1972 to 1975 and at Syracuse University from 1975 to 1986.

Israel's compositions form an eclectic mix of BAROQUE contrapuntal devices to SERIALISM, from ironic humor to profound seriousness. His works include chamber and children's operas; orchestral works, including six symphonies; chamber works, including three string quartets; and works for band, choral works, and songs. As a pianist, he was an important supporter of other modern composers. At the time of his death from leukemia, he was at the height of his compositional creativity.

Istar Variations. Orchestral variations by VINCENT D'INDY, 1897. This work was inspired by the Babylonian myth of the goddess Istar who passes through seven gates, gradually shedding her vestments until she is nude. Cleverly, the work begins with the variations and ends with the theme, naked at last. It contains IMPRESSIONISTIC elements of tone painting. It was first performed in Brussels.

It Had to Be You. Amorous ballad by Isham Jones, 1924, which he made famous playing with his band.

It Happened in Nordland. Operetta by VICTOR HERBERT, 1904, first performed in N.Y. The American ambassadress to

Nordland looks very much like the Nordland queen, and is induced to impersonate her when the queen leaves the country to join her lover. There is a happy ending. The most popular numbers are the march *Commanderess-in-Chief* and the waltz *A Knot of Blue.*

It Was a Very Good Year. Popular song by ERVIN DRAKE, 1961. FRANK SINATRA popularized it through his many performances and recordings.

Italian Concerto (*Concerto nach italiänischen Gusto*). Solo harpsichord work by JOHANN SEBASTIAN BACH, by 1735, requiring a two-MANUAL (keyboard) instrument.

Italian overture. *See* OVERTURE.

Italian Serenade. String quartet by HUGO WOLF, 1887, in G major. This is one of very few instrumental works by this composer, and one of his finest.

Italian sixth. A type of AUGMENTED SIXTH CHORD. Its three notes contain the augmented sixth from bottom to top and a major third from bottom to the middle notes, as in A♭, C, and F♯. It resolves most often to the second INVERSION TONIC chord, and occasionally to a DOMINANT chord.

Italian Symphony. The Fourth Symphony of FELIX MENDELSSOHN, 1833, in A major, first performed in London. The Italian element is apparent in the finale, a rapid SALTARELLO, but Mendelssohn himself never authorized the name.

Italiana in Algeri, L'. Opera by GIOACCHINO ROSSINI, 1813, produced in Venice. The Italian woman in the title seeks her beloved, captured by and enslaved by the Bey of Algiers. When after some misadventures she finds him, the wily Bey professes his desire for her. As he relaxes his controls, she frees her lover and escapes with him.

The overture is popular as a concert piece.

Ite missa est. The last sentence of the Roman Catholic MASS: "Go, you [the congregation] are dismissed." While

The *Italian Concerto*'s name is explained by its exploitation of the natural difference between the two manuals, one playing soft and the other loud. This is similar to the Italian instrumental concerto, where a soloist alternates with a louder full orchestra.

considered part of the ORDINARY, few polyphonic Masses set this short passage.

It's De-Lovely. Song by COLE PORTER, 1936, written for the musical *Red, Hot, and Blue.*

It's Not for Me to Say. Song by ROBERT ALLEN, 1957, which became a perennial favorite as recorded by JOHNNY MATHIS.

It's Now or Never. A 1960 pop song based on the melody of *O Sole Mio* by EDUARDO DI CAPUA. It was a hit for ELVIS PRESLEY.

Itsy Bitsy Teenie Weenie Yellow Polkadot Bikini. A 1960 No. 1 novelty hit for Brian Hyland celebrating the joys of the recently introduced two-piece bathing suit.

Ivan Susanin. *See* A LIFE FOR THE CZAR.

Ivanhoe. Grand opera by ARTHUR SULLIVAN, 1891, first produced in London after he separated from his long-time collaborator W. S. GILBERT. Based on the novel by Walter Scott, the opera failed with the public. It was Sullivan's only attempt at a serious opera.

Ives, Charles (Edward), outstanding American composer whose music, extraordinarily original and yet deeply national in its sources of inspiration, profoundly changed the direction of American music; b. Danbury, Conn., Oct. 20, 1874; d. N.Y., May 19, 1954. His father, George Ives, was a bandleader of the first Connecticut Heavy Artillery during the Civil War, and then directed the town band in Danbury. Young Charles's early development was, according to his own testimony, deeply influenced by his father.

At the age of 12, Ives played drums in his father's band and also received from his father basic training in piano and cornet. At the age of 13 he played organ at the Danbury Church. He soon began to improvise freely at the piano. With the encouragement of his father, he began to play in several KEYS at once, partly as a spoof, but eventually as a legitimate alternative to traditional music. At 17 he composed

The bikini is named for the Bikini islands, although there's no proof that it originated there.

PEOPLE IN MUSIC

his *Variations on America* for organ in a polytonal setting. Still earlier he wrote a band piece, *Holiday Quickstep,* which was performed by the Danbury Band in 1888.

Charles Ives.
(Frank Gerratana, New York Public Library)

Ives attended Danbury High School. In 1894 he entered Yale University, where he took regular academic courses and studied organ and composition with the well-known composer and teacher HORATIO PARKER. From Parker he received a fine classical training, and while still in college he composed a full-fledged symphony, written in an entirely traditional manner, demonstrating great skill in formal structure, fluent melodic development, and smooth harmonic modulations.

After his graduation in 1898, Ives joined an insurance company. He also played organ at the Central Presbyterian Church in N.Y. from 1899 to 1902. In 1907 he formed an insurance partnership with Julian Myrick of N.Y. He proved himself an exceptionally able businessman, and the firm of Ives & Myrick prospered. Ives continued to compose music as a hobby. In 1908 he married Harmony Twichell. In 1918 he suffered a massive heart attack, complicated by a diabetic condition, and was compelled to curtail his work both in business and in music because his illness made it difficult to handle a pen. He retired from business in 1930, and by that time had virtually stopped composing.

In 1919 Ives published at his own expense his great masterpiece, the *Concord Sonata* for piano, inspired by the writings of the New England philosophers and authors Ralph Waldo Emerson, Nathaniel Hawthorne, the Alcotts, and Henry David Thoreau. Although written early in the cen-

Ives time line

1874	Born
1886–87	Plays drums in his father's town band and organ at the Danbury Church
1888	His *Holiday Quickstep* is performed by the Danbury Band
1891	Composes his *Variations on America*
1894–98	Attends Yale University
1896	Composes the first of two string quartets, *From the Salvation Army*
1899–1902	Organist at N.Y.'s Central Presbyterian Church
1906	Composes *The Unanswered Question* and *Central Park in the Dark*
1907	Forms an insurance partnership with Julian Myrick as Ives & Myrick
1908	Marries Harmony Twichell
1912–15	Completes work on his *Robert Browning Overture, 3 Places in New England,* and Piano Sonata No. 2, *Concord, Mass., 1840–60*

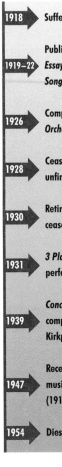

1918 — Suffers a heart attack

1919–22 — Publishes *Concord Sonata, Essays before a Sonata,* and *114 Songs*

1926 — Completes work on his *Third Orchestral Set*

1928 — Ceases work on his ultimately unfinished *Universe Symphony*

1930 — Retires from his business and ceases composing

1931 — *3 Places in New England* is first performed in Boston

1939 — *Concord Sonata* receives its first complete performance by John Kirkpatrick in N.Y.

1947 — Receives the Pulitzer Prize in music for his *Third Symphony* (1911)

1954 — Dies

A curious idiosyncrasy is the frequent QUOTATION of the "fate motive" of Beethoven's Fifth Symphony in many of Ives's works. For some reason, this theme haunted him.

tury, its style is so extraordinary, and its technical difficulties so great, that the work did not receive a performance in its entirety until John Kirkpatrick played it in N.Y. in 1939.

In 1922 Ives brought out, also at his own expense, a volume of *114 Songs,* written between 1888 and 1921 and marked by great diversity of style, ranging from lyrical ROMANTICISM to powerful and dissonant modern styles. Both the *Concord Sonata* and the *114 Songs* were distributed freely by Ives to anyone wishing to receive copies.

His orchestral masterpiece, *3 Places in New England,* also had to wait nearly two decades before its first performance. Of the monumental Fourth Symphony, only the second movement was performed during his lifetime, in 1927, and the first complete performance was given posthumously in 1965. In 1947 Ives received the Pulitzer Prize in music for his Third Symphony, which was written in 1911.

Because of his chronic ailment, and also because of his personal disposition, Ives lived as a recluse, away from the mainstream of American musical life. He almost never went to concerts and did not own a record player or a radio. And while he was well versed in the musical classics and studied the scores of LUDWIG VAN BEETHOVEN, ROBERT SCHUMANN, and JOHANNES BRAHMS, he took little interest in the works of modern composers. Despite this fact, Ives anticipated many of the techniques of modern composition and was far more radical in his use of them than most of his better-known contemporaries.

A unique quality of Ives's music was the combination of simple MOTIFS, often derived from American church hymns and popular ballads, with an extremely complex DISSONANT COUNTERPOINT, which formed the supporting network for the melodic lines. From the Second Symphony onward, quotation of well-known melodies became one of his most-used techniques.

Ives borrowed freely from his own works in creating new ones, and the titles were often changed during the process of composition. In his orchestrations he often indicated interchangeable and optional parts, as in the last movement of the *Concord Sonata,* which has an optional part for flute. Thus he reworked the original score for large orchestra of his *3 Places in New England* for a smaller ensemble to fit the requirements of NICOLAS SLONIMSKY's Chamber Orchestra of Boston, which gave its first performance in N.Y. in 1931. It was in this version that the work was first published and widely performed until the restoration of the large score was made in 1974.

In recent years there has been some dissension over the datings on Ives's manuscripts. He treated some pieces as ongoing works-in-progress and altered them at different times of his life, e.g., the final dissonant chord of the Second Symphony, which replaced a major triad in the original version. Some interpreted this as Ives's attempt to predate his own modernity, while others saw it as a valid approach, comparable to other composers who tinkered with their music for years. Indeed, in his later years, Ives's standard response to his editors posing questions seems to have been, "Do what you think is best."

Ives possessed an uncommon gift for literary expression, and his comments on his works are both humorous and to the point. He published in 1920 *Essays before a Sonata* as a literary companion volume to the *Concord Sonata.* His *Memos,* in the form of a diary, reveal his ability to express himself in short, but apt, phrases. He was acutely conscious of his civic duties as an American and once circulated a proposal to have federal laws enacted by popular referendum.

While during his lifetime he and a small group of devoted friends and admirers had great difficulties in having his works performed, recorded, or published, a veritable Ives cult emerged after his death. Eminent conductors gave repeated performances of his orchestral works, and modern pianists were willing to cope with the forbidding difficulties of his works. In terms of the number of orchestral performances, Ives stood highest among modern composers on American programs to celebrate the bicentennial year of 1976.

All of the Ives manuscripts and his correspondence were given by Mrs. Ives to Yale University, forming a basic Ives archive that John Kirkpatrick organized and catalogued. The Charles Ives Society promotes research and publications. Among Ives's numerous orchestral works are the four numbered symphonies (1896–98; 1900–02; *The Camp Meeting,* 1904; 1909–16); fragments of a *Universe Symphony*

Ives was so popular among American youth in the mid-'70s that his picture appeared on a T-shirt, an honor usually reserved for rock and movie stars.

(1911–28; first performance of a realized version, Los Angeles, Dec. 13, 1984); *3 Places in New England, First Orchestral Set* (1908–14?); *The Unanswered Question* and *Central Park in the Dark* (1906); *Set* for theater or chamber orchestra (1906–11); *Robert Browning Overture* (1908–12); *Holidays,* symphony comprising four independent works: *Washington's Birthday* (1913), *Decoration Day* (1912), *The 4th of July* (1913), and *Thanksgiving and/or Forefathers' Day* (1904); *Second Orchestral Set* (1909–15); *Tone Roads* (1911–15); and *Third Orchestral Set* for small orchestra (1919–26).

His chamber works include two string quartets: No. 1, *From the Salvation Army* (1896), and No. 2 (1907–13); four violin sonatas (1902–08; 1907–10; 1913–14?; *Children's Day at the Camp Meeting,* 1906–16?); Trio for violin, cello, and piano (1904–11); and *In re con moto et al* for string quartet and piano (1913). He wrote a large number of vocal works, including choral works, part songs, and numerous solo songs.

His piano works include two sonatas (No. 1, 1901–09; No. 2, *Concord, Mass., 1840–60,* 1910–15), *3-page Sonata* (1905); and *3 Quarter-tone Pieces* for two pianos (1923–24).

Izeÿl. Opera by EUGÈNE D'ALBERT, 1909, based on pseudo-Hindu lore, first performed in Hamburg. Izeÿl is an Indian princess whose lips are poisonous and who kills her suitors by kissing them. She dies herself when one of the suitors turns out to be immune to her particular brand of poison.

J

jack. In the HARPSICHORD and CLAVICHORD, a thin, upright piece of wood on the rear end of the key lever. On the harpsichord, it holds a bit of crow quill or hard leather set at a right angle so as to pluck or twang the string. On the clavichord, it carries a metallic TANGENT (small piece of metal) to strike the string. 2. In the PIANOFORTE, the ESCAPEMENT lever, or hopper.

Jackson, Mahalia, remarkable African-American GOSPEL singer; b. New Orleans, Oct. 26, 1911; d. Evergreen Park, Ill., Jan. 27, 1972. The daughter of a minister, Jackson sang in her father's church at an early age. At 16 she went to Chicago, where she worked as a maid while singing in the choir of the Greater Salem Baptist Church.

Jackson began touring with the Johnson Gospel Singers in 1932. She revealed an innate talent for expressive hymn singing and soon was in demand for conventions and political meetings. She steadfastly refused to appear in nightclubs. Her 1947 recording *Move On Up a Little Higher* brought her renown as the "Gospel Queen." She appeared in a series of concerts at N.Y.'s CARNEGIE HALL from 1950 to 1956, and in 1952 made her first European tour, which was a triumphant success.

Jackson sang at President Kennedy's inauguration in 1961 and at the civil rights march on Washington, D.C., in 1963. A strong believer in Civil Rights, she sang at many rallies in support of Dr. Martin Luther King, Jr., and gave an emotional performance at his funeral service, following his assassination in 1968. She made her last tour of Europe in 1971. A year later, she died of heart failure.

Jackson, Michael (Joseph), African-American dance-rock superstar; b. Gary, Ind., Aug. 29, 1958. Jackson was raised

PEOPLE IN MUSIC

PEOPLE IN MUSIC

in a musical family and was already singing with his brothers at the age of 4. By the time he was 9, the family group, called the Jackson 5, was signed to Motown Records, and Michael had become the lead singer. They scored hits with the teen-pop songs *A–B–C, I Want You Back,* and *I'll Be There.* The group was so successful among the preteen set that a Saturday morning cartoon show based loosely on their characters was launched.

Michael Jackson, c. 1984.
(UPI/Corbis-Bettmann)

Jackson had a hard transition during his teen years. The Jackson 5 was less successful than before, and eventually left Motown Records. In 1976 they reemerged as the Jacksons but still were in a creative slump. Michael's own solo career had proceeded in fits and starts, with a few early hits but not much more.

Then, in 1977 he appeared in the film version of the Broadway show *The Wiz,* an all-Black version of the Wizard of Oz. Working on the sound track was the talented producer-musician QUINCY JONES. The two became friendly, and Jones became Jackson's producer on his 1979 album *Off the Wall,* which announced a new, more adult sound for the singer. The album produced two hits, including the disco-flavored *Rock with You.*

But it was their second collaboration, 1982's *Thriller,* that made musical history. The album produced a slew of hits—including *Billie Jean, Beat It,* and the title track—which were artfully promoted through clever music videos.

Jackson's talents as a dancer were highlighted, along with his unique fashion sense—his famous sequined glove, aviator sunglasses, and military-style jackets.

Jackson's career reached another high point in 1985 when, in collaboration with Lionel Richie, he penned the song *We Are the World* in support of African famine relief. This song won a Grammy Award in 1985. It also launched a slew of rock-star concerts and recordings supporting charitable causes.

Jackson's follow-up to *Thriller*, 1987's *Bad,* could in no way repeat its amazing success. Nonetheless, it produced seven Top-10 singles, including the title song. Meanwhile, Jackson's unusual personality—his reclusiveness, his increasing use of plastic surgery to alter his appearance, and his Southern California estate complete with its own zoo and amusement park—began to make news and color the public's image of him.

In 1992 Jackson returned with a new album, *Dangerous,* working with producers younger than Quincy Jones. The album was a familiar mix of up-tempo dance numbers and sentimental ballads. To promote it, and in an attempt to give himself a better public image, Jackson gave a highly anticipated interview with Oprah Winfrey. However, in early 1993 he was accused of having sexually molested a young boy. Although the charges went unproved, Jackson went into seclusion at the end of the year, admitting to an addiction to painkillers.

Jackson's behavior became even more strange in the mid-'90s. In 1995 he wed the heir to the Elvis Presley fortune, Elvis's daughter, Lisa Marie, who, for a while at least, was a strong spokesperson for Jackson. He also released the compilation album *HIStory, Parts I and II,* featuring some new material directly attacking the critics of his musical and personal life.

The marriage to Presley failed and Jackson subsequently married a woman who had previously been his nurse. The two have since had two children. Jackson continues to be a strong concert draw, setting new records in 1997. In 1998 he was at work on a new solo album as well as a reunion album with the Jackson 5.

Thriller sold some 30 million copies universe-wide, certified in the *Guinness Book of World Records* in 1984 as the largest sale ever of a single album. It also earned Jackson eight GRAMMY AWARDS.

PEOPLE IN MUSIC

Jackson, Milt(on), "Bags," African-American jazz vibraphonist; b. Detroit, Jan. 1, 1923. Jackson began playing the vibes as a teenager and was already performing locally with saxophonist LUCKY THOMPSON when he was 16. He continued to work Detroit clubs through his teen years, while also attending Michigan State University.

In 1945, DIZZY GILLESPIE heard him while passing through Detoit, and invited him to join his band. After touring the West Coast with Gillespie, Jackson settled in N.Y., where he played with many leading young musicians, including pianist THELONIOUS MONK. In 1949–50 he worked with WOODY HERMAN's big band and then rejoined Gillespie, making his recording debut as a solo artist in 1951.

Also in Gillespie's band in this period were pianist JOHN LEWIS, bassist RAY BROWN, and drummer KENNY CLARKE. When the band took a break, the four members would perform special numbers. This grew into what was originally called the MILT JACKSON QUARTET and then, in 1954, became the MODERN JAZZ QUARTET. Lewis was an artful composer and arranger, and along with Jackson shaped the group's sound, a combination of COOL JAZZ and classical-like compositions and arrangements. The group—now with bassist Percy Heath and drummer Connie Kay—became one of the most successful in jazz and also one of the longest-running of all jazz groups, staying together until 1974.

Jackson meanwhile continued to record on his own and do session work with other musicians. He made some fusion-type recordings in the '70s after the MJQ disbanded, with little success, but then returned to his own style in the '80s. At this time, there were several MJQ reunions, but Jackson continued to record and perform on his own. He continues to be active into the '90s.

Jacquet de la Guerre, Elisabeth, French composer, organist, and clavecinist; b. Paris, 1659; d. there, June 27, 1729. A member of a family of professional musicians and instrument makers, Jacquet de la Guerre showed talent at an exceptionally early age. She was favored by the court of Louis XIV, completing her education under the patronage of

PEOPLE IN MUSIC

Mme. de Montespan. She then married Marin de la Guerre, a church organist.

Her works include an opera, a ballet (lost), keyboard suites, trio and violin sonatas, sacred and secular cantatas, and a Te Deum (lost).

Jagdhorn, Jägerhorn (Ger.). Hunting horn. *Jagdstück,* hunting piece; *Jägerchor,* hunters' chorus.

Jagger, Mick. *See* ROLLING STONES.

Jahreszeiten, Die. *See* SEASONS, THE.

Jakobin, The. Opera by ANTONÍN DVOŘÁK, 1889, first performed in Prague. The action takes place in a small Bohemian town in 1793. Boguś, a young Bohemian, is denounced by his detractors as a radical "Jacobin." (During the French Revolution, the Jacobins were regarded as violent radicals.) Boguś is forced to leave Bohemia for several years, but virtue triumphs in the end, when the true traitors are revealed. The supposed radical returns home with his newly acquired French bride, and he inherits a rich estate.

jaltarang. A set of porcelain cups partially filled with water. Used to perform an Indian RAGA, they are tuned according to the specific SCALE of each piece. They are played with wooden sticks.

jam session (abbrev. of jamboree). An informal get-together in which jazz or popular musicians improvise freely, regardless of professional standing. Sometimes the musicians take turns, while at other times several performers will "blow" at once, producing an effect not unlike the early New Orleans era of jazz (or the extremes of FREE JAZZ).

Jamaican Rumba. Orchestral dance, 1942, by the Australian-British composer ARTHUR BENJAMIN (1893–1960), his most famous composition. It began life as a two-piano work in 1938. The orchestral version was first broadcast from N.Y.

yäht′horn, yä′ger-horn

MUSICAL INSTRUMENT

The name of the dastardly persecutor in *The Jakobin* is Adolf. One line in the libretto, "Wherever brutality reigns, Adolf is there," was loudly applauded at performances during the Nazi occupation of Czechoslovakia, with an obvious reference to Hitler. The Nazi authorities ordered the name be changed to Rudolf, but that didn't help since Rudolf was the name of Hitler's henchman, Rudolf Hess. After several incidents, the opera was banned by the Nazis and not revived until the liberation of Czechoslovakia.

PEOPLE IN MUSIC

James and the band appeared in many B-pictures with colorful names like *Bathing Beauty* and *Two Girls and a Sailor* in the mid-'40s. James also played himself in the film biography of BENNY GOODMAN released in 1956.

PEOPLE IN MUSIC

James, Harry (Haag), popular American jazz trumpeter and bandleader; b. Albany, Ga., March 15, 1916; d. Las Vegas, July 5, 1983. James's father was a trumpeter and his mother a trapeze artist with the Mighty Haag Circus. He took up drums at the age of 4 and trumpet at 8, and became leader of a circus band at 12. He worked as a contortionist until going with his family to Texas, where he played trumpet in local dance bands.

James's break came when he was hired by jazz band leader BEN POLLACK. He played with Pollack's band from 1935 to 1937, and then became a featured member of BENNY GOODMAN's orchestra from 1937 to 1939. He was a soloist on such famous Goodman recordings as *1 O'Clock Jump, Sing, Sing, Sing,* and *Life Goes to a Party.*

James struck out on his own as a bandleader in 1939, producing a sensation with his trumpet version of *You Made Me Love You* in 1941. He subsequently was a leading figure of the BIG-BAND era, bringing out many hit recordings and touring extensively. One of his hit songs, *Ciribiribin,* became his theme song. Several of his albums, including *Wild about Harry,* sold into the millions, even in wartime, when shellac, from which disks were manufactured, was rationed.

In 1943 he married Betty Grable, the pinup girl of the GIs in World War II. She was his second wife out of a total of four, and they were divorced in 1965. Meanwhile, the band continued to record and perform through the '40s and early '50s, with the spotlight always on James's virtuoso trumpet playing.

Although the big-band era was over, James continued to work through the '60s and '70s. Alternating between road jobs and engagements in Las Vegas, the band became one of the most polished of all jazz ensembles, with less emphasis on flashy soloing as James became older. Faithful to the slogan "the show must go on," James, wracked with the pain of terminal cancer, continued to perform in the early '80s. He played his last gig in Los Angeles on June 26, 1983, nine days before his death. He observed, as he was dying, "Let it just be said that I went up to do a one-nighter with Archangel Gabriel."

Janáček, Leoš, greatly significant Czech composer; b. Hukvaldy, Moravia, July 3, 1854; d. Moravská Ostrava, Aug. 12,

1928. Janáček grew up in a musical household, his father being a choirmaster. At the age of 11 he was sent to Brno to serve in the choir of the Augustinian Queen's Monastery. He then attended the German College in Brno from 1869 to 1872.

After college, Janáček held a teaching post and also served as choirmaster of the men's chorus, Svatopluk, from 1873 to 1877, taking the opportunity to study organ at the Prague Organ School. He conducted the Beseda Choral Society in Brno from 1876 to 1888, and also pursued studies at the Leipzig Conservatory, where he took music history and composition courses in 1879 – 80.

In 1880 Janáček continued his composition studies at the Vienna Conservatory. Returning to Brno the next year, he was appointed the first director of the new organ school. His social position in Brno was enhanced by his marriage to Zdenka Schulzová, daughter of the director of the teachers' training college. He also engaged in scholarly activities, editing the music journal *Hudební Listy* (Music bulletins) in the mid-1880s, and also collecting Moravian folk songs.

From 1886 to 1902 Janáček taught music at the Brno Gymnasium. In 1919 he retired from his directorship of the Brno Organ School and then taught master classes in Brno from 1920 to 1925. Throughout these busy years he worked diligently on his compositions, showing particular preference for operas.

Janáček's style of composition underwent numerous changes, from ROMANTIC techniques to bold DISSONANT combinations. He was greatly influenced by the Russian musical nationalism and by the new movement to using natural speech rhythms in composing for the stage. He visited St. Petersburg and Moscow in 1896 and 1902 and published his impressions of the tour in the Brno press.

From 1894 to 1903 Janáček worked on his most important opera, *Její pastorkyňa* (Her foster daughter). It has a highly dramatic libretto. Set in Moravia in the mid-19th century, the plot includes a gruesome murder of a baby. It was difficult to find a producer for the work in Prague because of its grisly subject. However, it was eventually produced on various European stages, mostly in the German text, under the title JENŮFA (1916).

Another opera by Janáček that attracted attention was *Výlet pana Broučka do XV stoleti* (Mr. Brouček's excursion to the 15th century, 1917). It depicts the imaginary travel of a Czech patriot to the time of the religious struggle mounted by the followers of the nationalist leader Jan Hus against the established church. There followed an operatic fairy tale, *Příhody Lišky Bystroušky* (The adventures of the vixen Bystrouška, or The cunning little vixen, 1924), and a mystery play, *Věc Makropulos* (The Makropulos affair, 1926), both enormously successful.

Janáček also composed a symphonic poem, TARAS BULBA (the fictional name of a Ukrainian patriot, after a story by Gogol, written between 1915 and 1918; premiered in Brno in 1921). Like most artists, writers, and composers of Slavic origin, Janáček had a natural interest in the Pan-Slavic movement, which emphasized the common origins of Russian, Czech, Slovak, and other kindred cultures. His *Glagolitic Mass* (Glagolská mše, 1927) to a Latin text translated into Old Slavonic is an example.

Janáček showed great interest in the emerging Soviet school of composition, even though he refrained from any attempt to join that movement. Although influenced by the modern school of composition of IGOR STRAVINSKY and ARNOLD SCHOENBERG, he was never tempted to experiment along their revolutionary lines. He remained faithful to his own well-defined style, and it was as the foremost composer of modern Czech music that he secured his unique place in history.

Janizary music. The military music of the Janizary guards of the Turkish sultans.

In the wake of the Ottoman invasion of Eastern Europe in the 16th century, this type of music—raucous, loud, and enlivened by strong rhythms—captured the imagination of European writers, painters, and musicians. They were impressed by the large Turkish drums, cymbals, and crescent, the last known popularly as JINGLING JOHNNY.

This type of music was adopted by the military bands of Poland, Russia, and Austria in the first half of the 18th century. Big drums, triangles, and cymbals *alla turca* (in the Turkish style) served the purpose of providing exotic color in the "oriental" operas of CHRISTOPH WILLIBALD GLUCK and WOLFGANG AMADEUS MOZART. FRANZ JOSEPH HAYDN used the Janizary rhythms in his *Military Symphony*, which includes triangles, cymbals, and a bass drum in the second movement. The famous rondo finale of Mozart's Piano Sonata in A major, K. 331, is marked "alla turca."

Jankó keyboard. A piano keyboard patented by the Hungarian Paul von Jankó (1856–1919) in 1882. It has six rows of keys so arranged that any given tone can be struck in three different places, that is, on every other row. This permits a smaller stretch of the hand to reach large intervals and complex chords.

Despite a brief flurry of manufacturing at the turn of the century, the Jankó keyboard met the predictable resistance of those who did not want to relearn fingerings and hand positions for their repertory.

Japanese music. The music of Japan, and in East Asia generally, is derived from ancient PENTATONIC (five-note) MODES. The two most common scales are C, D, E, G, A (i.e., a subset of the major scale) or E♭, G♭, A♭, B♭, D♭ (a subset of the minor scale), both free of SEMITONES. But there exists also an authentic Japanese scale of great antiquity that contains semitones, E, F, A, B, C (a subset of the PHRYGIAN MODE).

Japanese FOLK MUSIC is primarily HOMOPHONIC without explicit or implicit harmonic connotations of the Western type, but cultured music of Japan includes concepts of CONSONANCE and DISSONANCE. Like most Oriental music, Japanese music is melodic and rhythmic, with harmonic extension formed by couplings in seconds, fourths, and fifths. Consecutive progressions, particularly in thirds or sixths, are practically nonexistent. Rhythmic patterns possess great variety and in ancient music do not follow any binding METER.

STRING, WIND, and PERCUSSION instruments are represented in Japanese music in original forms, most of them derived from ancient Chinese and Korean instruments imported into Japan in medieval times. The most popular of Japanese string instruments are the KOTO, SHAMISEN (samisen), and BIWA. Also commonly used are bamboo flutes (e.g.,

Some piano manufacturers made special attachments with bells and cymbals for performances of such "Turkish music," and even supplied clappers to strike at the soundboard in imitation of the bass drum.

MUSICAL INSTRUMENT

SHAKUHACHI), small cymbals, bells, and a great variety of drums, especially of the hourglass type.

The most ancient Japanese music still practiced is GAGAKU, the orchestral music of the imperial court originating in the 8th century. It is still performed on imperial and other official occasions. Gagaku can also accompany a dance style called *bugaku.* Both are considered the province of the Japanese upper classes. The most popular of theater forms is KABUKI (from the 17th century), a stylized drama with a large musical ensemble, featuring singing and dancing with male actors, heavily costumed, playing the roles of both sexes. There are also several puppet theater genres categorized as *bunraku,* with a narrator-singer accompanied by a shamisen; and there are numerous songs of varying provenance, usually for solo voice accompanied by a string instrument.

Of the purely instrumental genres, there are large solo repertoires for the pitched instruments. The koto and shakuhachi even have many opposing schools of performance and composition. There is also a great deal of chamber music: one combination, the *sankyoku* from the late 19th century, features a trio of shakuhachi, koto, and shamisen.

The interaction between Western and Japanese music has led to several new trends. Early 20th-century Japanese composers attempted to learn Western music by imitation. KOSAKU YAMADA, educated in Europe, was the first Japanese composer to adopt European methods of composition in opera, symphony, chamber music, and songs.

Later composers sought to mesh the two worlds, or create a new style based solely on Japanese traditional music. Some of the most important Japanese composers later in the century include Yashushi Akutagawa, Kunio Toda, Ikuma Dan, Yoshirō Irino, Yoritsune Matsudaira, Jōji Yuasa, Toshirō Mayuzumi, Yoshio Mamiya, Yuji Takehashi, Akira Miyoshi, and Tōru Takemitsu.

In the U.S., Paul Chihara, an American composer of Japanese descent, employs Japanese modes in an advanced sophisticated manner. Others borrow the musical and theatrical elements of Japanese culture (especially *noh*).

Operas by modern Japanese composers usually follow European models. One of the most interesting Japanese–

Melodramatic operas on Japanese subjects such as GIACOMO PUCCINI'S *MADAMA BUTTERFLY* are unacceptable in Japan as perversions of national culture. *THE MIKADO* by Gilbert and Sullivan was banned in Japan until 1945, when it was performed by the American Army of Occupation. (The ban has since returned.) A more effective synthesis of East and West is found in STEPHEN SONDHEIM'S musical *Pacific Overtures,* about the ending of Japanese isolation by the West in the 19th century.

Western mixes has occurred on the dance stage, in the late 20th-century dance genre *butoh*. It combines traditional Japanese acting styles with modern dance and the use of electronic music as scores.

Jaques-Dalcroze, Émile, Swiss music educator and composer, creator of EURHYTHMICS; b. Vienna (of French parents), July 6, 1865; d. Geneva, July 1, 1950. In 1873 Jacques-Dalcroze's parents moved to Geneva. After completing his courses at the university and conservatory there, he went to Vienna for further study under ROBERT FUCHS and ANTON BRUCKNER. He then went to Paris, where he studied with LÉO DELIBES and GABRIEL FAURÉ. He returned to Geneva as a theory instructor at the conservatory in 1892.

Since he laid special stress on rhythm, he insisted that all his pupils beat time with their hands. This led him, step by step, to devise a series of movements affecting the entire body. With the French psychologist Edouard Claparide, he worked out a special terminology and reduced his practice to a regular system, which he called *eurhythmics*.

When his application to have his method introduced as a regular course at the conservatory was refused, Jacques-Dalcroze resigned, and in 1910 he established his own school at Hellerau, near Dresden. Because of World War I, the school was closed in 1914. He then returned to Geneva and founded the Institute Jaques-Dalcroze. Interest in his system led to the opening of similar schools in London, Berlin, Vienna, Paris, New York, Chicago, and elsewhere.

Aside from his rhythmical innovations, Jaques-Dalcroze also commanded respect as a composer of marked originality and imagination. Many of his works show how thoroughly he had absorbed the spirit of Swiss FOLK MUSIC. Other works have pedagogical purposes, while still others are purely theatrical. He also wrote several textbooks describing his technique of teaching music.

Jarnach, Philipp, German composer and pedagogue of Spanish descent; b. Noisy, France, July 26, 1892; d. Bornsen, near Bergedorf, Dec. 17, 1982. Jarnach was a son of a Spanish sculptor and a Flemish mother. He studied with piano and theory at the Paris Conservatory from 1912 to 1914.

PEOPLE IN MUSIC

Dalcroze Eurythmics is still a popular method used to teach music to young children.

PEOPLE IN MUSIC

At the outbreak of World War I, Jarnach went to Zurich to teach at the Conservatory. There, he met the Italian futurist composer FERRUCCIO BUSONI. This meeting was a decisive influence on his development, and he became an ardent follower of Busoni. After Busoni's death he completed his last opera, *Doktor Faust,* which was premiered in Jarnach's version in Dresden in 1925.

From 1922 to 1927 Jarnach wrote music criticism for the *Berliner Börsencourier.* In 1931 he became a German citizen. From 1927 to 1949 he was professor of composition at the Cologne Conservatory, and from 1949 to 1970 at the Hamburg Conservatory.

Jarnach's music is distinguished by impeccable craftsmanship, but it lacks individuality. He participated in the modern movement in Germany between the two world wars, and many of his works were performed at music festivals during that period. He wrote PROLOG ZU EINEM RITTERSPIEL for orchestra (1917), Sinfonia brevis (1923), *Musik mit Mozart* for orchestra (1935), String Quintet (1920), String Quartet (1924), *Musik zum Gedächtnis des Einsamen* for string quartet (1952; also for orchestra), piano pieces, and songs.

Jarre, Maurice, French composer; b. Lyons, Sept. 13, 1924. Jarre studied electrical engineering in Lyons, then attended courses in composition given by the composer ARTHUR HONEGGER at the Paris Conservatory.

Jarre became best known as a film composer, winning an Academy Award for *Lawrence of Arabia* in 1963 and *Lara's Song* from *Dr. Zhivago* in 1965. His other excellent film scores include *The Year of Living Dangerously* (1983), *Witness* (1985), *The Mosquito Coast* (1986), *Gorillas in the Mist* (1988), and *Dead Poets Society* (1989). He also wrote the orchestral works *Armida* (1953), *Mouvements en relief* (1954), *Passacaille,* in memory of Honegger (Strasbourg Festival, 1956), and *Mobiles* (Strasbourg Festival, 1961).

Jarreau, Al, African-American singer of jazz and popular music; b. Milwaukee, March 12, 1940. Jarreau graduated with a psychology degree from the University of Iowa, then went to San Francisco, where he worked as a rehabilitation counselor. He began singing in local clubs, quickly garnering a following with his flexible vocal technique and warm, sometimes even ecstatic performance style.

Jarreau gained particular attention with his album *We Got By* (1975) and then toured Europe (1976), becoming one of the most popular jazz singers of the day. Other successful albums of this period include *Look to the Rainbow* (1977) and *All Fly Home* (1978). His audience changed substantially in the mid-1980s, when his songs and vocal style became less adventurous owing to an emphasized and often mundane disco beat. Albums dating from this later period include *High Crime* (1984) and *L Is for Lover* (1986).

Jarrett, Keith, versatile American pianist; b. Allentown, Pa., May 8, 1945. After studying at the Berklee School of Music in Boston, Jarrett plunged into the N.Y. jazz scene, coming to prominence as a member of the Charles Lloyd quartet from 1966 to 1970. He also worked with MILES DAVIS from 1969 to 1971 and toured with his own trio and as a solo artist.

PEOPLE IN MUSIC

In 1975 he made a sensationally popular recording of solo improvisations, *The Köln Concert,* which established his reputation as a jazz virtuoso. From the early 1980s he made appearances as a classical pianist, specializing in modern works and especially those of BÉLA BARTÓK. In 1987 he gave a particularly spirited performance in N.Y. of LOU HARRISON's Piano Concerto, a performance he repeated in Tokyo, which served as the basis for the critically acclaimed 1988 recording.

Järvi, Neeme, prominent Estonian conductor; b. Tallinn, June 7, 1937. Järvi graduated with degrees in percussion and choral conducting from the Tallinn Music School, then studied conducting at the Leningrad Conservatory from 1955 to 1960. He pursued postgraduate studies in 1968, and in 1971 captured first prize in the Accademia di Santa Cecilia conducting competition in Rome.

PEOPLE IN MUSIC

Järvi was active in Tallinn as music director of the Estonian State Symphony Orchestra from 1960 to 1980 and of the Estonian Opera Theater from 1964 to 1977. He subsequently served as principal guest conductor of the City of

Birmingham Symphony Orchestra in England from 1981 to 1984. In 1982 he became music director of the Göteborg Symphony Orchestra in Sweden. He also was principal conductor of the Scottish National Orchestra in Glasgow from 1984 to 1988. In 1990 he became music director of the Detroit Symphony Orchestra.

Järvi's guest conducting engagements have taken him to most of the principal music centers of the world. He has won particular notice for his efforts on behalf of such rarely performed composers as Franz Berwald, Niels Gade, Johan Svendsen, Wilhelm Stenhammar, and Eduard Tubin.

jazz. A term covering a wide variety of styles of African-American origin, including New Orleans/DIXIELAND, Chicago, big band/SWING, BEBOP, COOL/THIRD STREAM, FREE JAZZ, jazz-rock/jazz-funk, and neotraditionalism. Most are characterized by improvisation and a "swinging" beat composed of a steady, prominent meter and dotted or SYNCOPATED rhythms.

The word *jazz* appeared for the first time in print in the sports column in *The Bulletin of San Francisco* in 1913. Describing the arrival of a baseball team, writer "Scoop" Gleeson reported: "Everybody has come back to the old town, full of the old 'jazz' and they promise to knock the fans off their feet with their playing." Gleeson then asks himself a rhetorical question: "What is this jazz? Why, it's a little of that 'old life,' the 'gin-i-leer,' the 'pep,' otherwise known as the enthusiasalum." Reminiscing about the occasion in an article published in the same San Francisco newspaper in 1938, Gleeson volunteered that the expression "jazz" had been picked up by the sports editor during a game of craps. According to Gleeson, it was first applied to music when one Art Hickman launched his dance band, but there is no evidence of this in any published source.

The next verified appearance of the word was in *Variety* in 1916, in a brief communication from Chicago reporting a concert of jazz music, with the word spelled *jass.* Another item in *Variety* followed in 1917 in which it was spelled *Jaz.* An engagement of the Dixie Jass Band of New Orleans in a Chicago cabaret was noted in *Variety* that same year. A week later jazz reached N.Y., and it was spelled *jazz* in yet another report in *Variety.*

Jazz (through the 1950s, at least) combines an unlimited variety of rhythmic patterns with fairly standard scales and meters. Jazz melodies, almost without exception, are set in major keys, in $\frac{2}{4}$ or $\frac{4}{4}$ time. Within this framework, the syncopated melody often departs widely from the basic harmony pattern. Typically, the major tonality is modified by the use of BLUE NOTES, the lowered seventh and the lowered third in the melody.

Historically, jazz evolved from RAGTIME, a syncopated type of American music that flourished in the last decade of the 19th century and during the first years of the new 20th. A parallel development is BLUES, a distinctively American ballad form. The blues has a unique rhythmic and harmonic pattern that was adopted in early jazz, and blues singers like BESSIE SMITH were often accompanied by jazz musicians. Other early stylistic contributions to jazz were the work songs and field hollers of rural black America, the street cries of peddlers in urban black America, and the most important influence on orchestration, the New Orleans marching band, notable for its use in funeral processions outside of that city (necessary since burial inside that delta city was banned for health reasons).

The Dixieland/New Orleans jazz style, with its group improvisations and lack of drums, was never recorded, except for a pale imitation, an all-white group called the Original Dixieland Jazz Band, which was formed in 1917. When many New Orleans musicians moved north to Chicago in the 1920s (including LOUIS ARMSTRONG and JELLY ROLL MORTON), the ensembles grew smaller and emphasized star improvisers, while allowing other band members brief solos in a 12-bar (blues) or 16/32-bar (song) structure. The instrumentation solidified, drawn from cornet (later trumpet), trombone, clarinet, piano, guitar, tuba or double bass, and drums. This style was emotionally "hot," much like its predecessor.

A new era of jazz music dawned in the late 1920s with an explosion of swing, which indicated a certain rhythmic manner of performance rather than a structural form. The

An item in the *Victor Record Review* in 1917 reads: "Spell it Jass, Jas, Jab or jazz—nothing can spoil a Jass band. . . . It has sufficient power and penetration to inject new life into a mummy, and will keep ordinary human dancers on their feet till breakfast time. . . ." It was about the same time that the Victor Company issued the first recording bearing the word Jass—*Dixieland Jass One-Step.*

ensemble grew into the big band, averaging between 10 and 15 players, and true composition (and orchestration, or arranging) became an element of jazz. Musicians like DUKE ELLINGTON, COUNT BASIE, FLETCHER HENDERSON, BILLY STRAYHORN, DON REDMAN, and BENNY CARTER created their own recognizable "sounds," shaping their compositions and arrangements with the abilities of individual members of their band in mind (Ellington was especially sensitive to this). The big bands of BENNY GOODMAN and GLENN MILLER emphasized their role as dance bands, while Ellington alternated between the "hot" dance music style and the more reflective "cool" style that sought to portray the African-American experience.

Parallel to these developments, piano jazz evolved from its ragtime beginnings to STRIDE in the 1920s. The oompah bass became more aggressive dynamically and harmonically, while the melody lines grew subtly in syncopation. While this style continued to influence piano playing, the 1930s saw the inauguration of BOOGIE-WOOGIE, which turned the bass line into a "walking" accompaniment, with broken chords (ARPEGGIOS) often following the 12-bar blues harmonic pattern. The melody lines became more bluesy than modal.

A new jazz form, BEBOP (also rebop or bop), appeared in the 1940s. Its tonal and structural underpinnings seemed to return to those of the 1920s, with the emphasis on simple blues progressions or interpretations of popular standards. But the improvisation reached lightning speeds and, in the hands of CHARLIE PARKER and other good musicians, expanded jazz's horizons melodically and harmonically with added notes to chords and melodic CHROMATICISM. Even more important was its unrepressed emotionality, perhaps indicative of the rising black rebellion against segregation, disrespect, and financial desperation.

If bebop had a negative result, it was the dividing of jazz's audience into listener-dancers (who wanted to move) and listener-fans (who were content to sit down). This divide continued in the next decades. In the 1950s, cool jazz, spearheaded by MILES DAVIS, GIL EVANS, JERRY MULLIGAN, CHET BAKER, JOHN LEWIS, and GUNTHER SCHULLER (of the THIRD STREAM), was a listening music. It emphasized com-

In the late 1930s, the SAXO-PHONE, with its brassy yet mellow qualities, capable of raucous exuberance or gentle poetry, went to the fore of the melody instruments in jazz. By the mid-'50s it had virtually replaced the CLARINET.

plete compositions and arrangements, performed in a laid-back manner inappropriate for dancing. Meanwhile, HARD BOP represented a return to a more gospel-influenced, roots music, designed to get the listeners up on their feet.

In the 1960s FREE JAZZ referred both to a highly improvisational style with few if any structural demands and to the freeing of jazz musicians from the need to "belong" to a single style. This had the disadvantage, however, of limiting even further the audience for jazz. Blues and rock and roll had replaced jazz as popular music forms. In an attempt to recapture its audience, *jazz-rock* and JAZZ-FUNK, both of which are examples of the style called *fusion,* combined the instrumentation and relative accessibility of popular music with the extemporaneous freedom and rhythmic complexity of jazz.

In the '80s and '90s, the work of WYNTON MARSALIS and others has emphasized the "classic repertoire" approach to jazz. Marsalis believes jazz can regain a larger audience through emphasizing more traditional jazz styles. He also strongly believes in developing a knowledge of jazz history among today's players and listeners.

Jazz Concerto. Nickname of the Piano Concerto by AARON COPLAND, 1927, which includes elements of jazz. It shocked Boston audiences and critics when Copland performed it for the first time with the Boston Symphony Orchestra.

Jazz Singer, The. The first "talking picture," 1928—actually, only a portion has sound—starring blackface singer AL JOLSON. He sings his signature *My Mammy* on bended knee and with outstretched arms.

jazz-funk (jazz-rock). Jazz styles of the late 1960s and 1970s which merge the electric amplification, instrumentation, and directness of rock with some of the more sophisticated improvisatory, rhythmic, and harmonic features of jazz. A funk-styled bass accompaniment was used as the basis for jazz-styled melodic improvisation.

Jeanie with the Light Brown Hair. Nostalgic ballad by Stephen Foster, 1854, in which the protagonist bemoans his unfortunate separation from his beloved. One of Foster's last compositions, and his last major success.

Jeanne d'Arc au bûcher. Dramatic oratorio by ARTHUR HONEGGER, 1938, first performed in Basel, in concert form. Honegger described the work as a "MIMODRAMA." Joan has a speaking part, and various allegorical figures appear, symbolizing sins and virtues. The music represents a deliberate return to the early type of monodic DRAMMA PER MUSICA.

Jeepers, Creepers. Song by HARRY WARREN and JOHNNY MERCER, 1938, from the movie musical *Going Places*. LOUIS ARMSTRONG made it the theme song of his band. Its infectious rhythm and the tantalizingly nonsensical line "Jeepers, creepers, / Where'd you get those peepers?" made it a perennial favorite.

PEOPLE IN MUSIC

Jefferson Airplane. (Most successful lineup: Vocals/guitar: Paul Kantner, b. San Francisco, March 12, 1942; Vocals: Marty Balin [Martyn Jerel Buchwald], b. Cincinnati, Jan. 30, 1942; Vocals: Grace [Wing] Slick, b. Chicago, Oct. 30, 1939; Lead guitar: Jorma Kaukonen, b. Washington, D.C., Dec. 23, 1940; Bass: Jack Casady, b. Washington, D.C., Apr. 13, 1944; Drums: Spencer Dryden, b. N.Y., Apr. 7, 1943.) San Francisco folk-rock band of the mid-'60s that survived through an amazing number of personnel and name changes.

The band originally formed around folksinger Marty Balin and guitarists Paul Kantner and Jorma Kaukonen, female vocalist Singe Toly, string-bass player Bob Harvey, and drummer Jerry Pelequin (although Alexander "Skip" Spence soon replaced Pelequin). The group gave its first performance in San Francisco on Aug. 13, 1965. Their first album, *Jefferson Airplane Takes Off,* launched the so-called San Francisco sound.

There were inevitable changes in personnel. The vocalist GRACE SLICK joined the group in 1966. She had formerly sung in another Bay Area ensemble, The Great Society. Spencer Dryden replaced drummer Spence, who left that same year to form the psychedelic group, MOBY GRAPE. Slick brought with her a number of songs, including her composition *White Rabbit,* based on Lewis Carroll's *Alice in Wonderland,* and her former husband's ballad *Someone to Love,* both major hits.

The group veered between recording romantic ballads and more politically minded songs, particularly 1969's minor hit *Volunteers* and Kantner's *We Can Be Together.* In 1968 they made a successful European tour, but soon group members were arguing over personal and political differences.

Kaukonen and Casaday formed a side group, Hot Tuna, in 1969 to perform traditional blues, which continued to record and perform through much of the '70s. Kantner began showing an interest in science fiction, producing the theme album *Blows against the Empire* in 1970 featuring members of the group (minus Balin, who was about to leave the band) and many of its peers, including JERRY GARCIA, DAVID CROSBY, and GRAHAM NASH. The group also formed its own vanity label, Grunt, in 1972, releasing various projects. However, from 1972 to 1975 there was no really working version of the group recording or touring.

The group got together again in 1975 under the new name Jefferson Starship, producing the successful album *Red Octopus.* Balin had returned to the group, contributing the hit song *Miracles,* but he soon was gone again. Another European tour in 1978 was marred by Slick's alcoholism, leading her to leave the group to dry out until 1981.

The group reformed with lead singer Mickey Thomas in 1979, and Slick came back two years later for more hits through 1984. Kantner left that year, suing the group, who were forced to rename themselves Starship. Despite the lawsuit, the group went on, with major hits including *We Built This City.*

Slick was gone again by 1988, and a year later the "original" group of Kantner-Balin-Casady-Slick-Kaukonen regrouped for a modest-selling reunion album. More turmoil followed, with Kantner leading various personnel in a group known as Paul Kantner's Jefferson Starship. Balin rejoined Kantner's group in 1993 and Slick did so two years later, to little success. Of late, beyond occasional reunions, the band is no longer working.

PEOPLE IN MUSIC

Jefferson's recordings are difficult to listen to because they were so poorly made. Nonetheless, they have been reissued numerous times since the 1950s, and Jefferson remains one of the most popular of the early blues singers.

Jefferson, "Blind Lemon," African-American blues singer and guitarist; b. near Wortham, Texas, July 1897; d. Chicago, Dec. 1929. Jefferson was afflicted by poor eyesight from childhood. As a youth, he supported himself by singing in the streets. He went to Dallas in 1917, making it the base for occasional trips through the Southwest.

The blues singer LEADBELLY claimed to have worked with Jefferson during this period. Many blind performers hired "lead boys" to help them travel and to discourage thieves who might steal from the money that they collected by playing on street corners. However, there is no evidence that Leadbelly actually ever knew Jefferson, other than hearing his recordings.

Jefferson settled in Chicago in 1925, making a series of historic blues recordings, many of which highlighted his own songs. His *Matchbox Blues* was later covered by numerous artists, including a revised version by CARL PERKINS which was in turn covered by the BEATLES.

Jefferson's records must have been popular, because some 90 titles were recorded by him between 1926 and 1929. His record label even issued a special picture record in celebration of his birthday, a rare honor to a blues artist.

The exact details of Jefferson's death are unknown. Some say he froze to death while sleeping on the streets of Chicago, while others reported that he had a heart attack while being driven to a job.

Jena Symphony. This is a famous example of a work mistakenly ascribed to a great composer through lack of careful scholarship. The manuscript was discovered in the town of Jena in 1910 by the German scholar Fritz Stein, with the name of LUDWIG VAN BEETHOVEN scribbled on some of the orchestral parts. A great deal of excitement was generated, and the *Jena Symphony* was performed as an early work of Beethoven. Eventually the original manuscript was discovered, fully signed with the name of FRIEDRICH WITT (1770–1836), the true composer of this work.

PEOPLE IN MUSIC

Jenkins, Leroy, African-American jazz violinist and composer; b. Chicago, March 11, 1932. Jenkins was mainly self-taught in music, playing violin in a local Baptist church and picking up the basics of theory while teaching in a school in Chicago. He joined the Association for the Advancement of Creative Musicians (AACM), an important Chicago-based group that promoted advanced jazz composition and performance. Jenkins later studied on a scholarship at Florida A&M University.

Jenkins is best known for his improvisations on violin and viola, in a bluesy, romantic style inspired by CHARLIE PARKER. The groups he has led or co-led include the (Paris-based) Creative Construction Company, the Revolutionary Ensemble, and the Leroy Jenkins Trio and Quintet. He has also worked with the rock musician STING.

Among Jenkins's finest recordings, many of which include his own jazz compositions, are *Space Minds, New Worlds, Survival of America, The Legend of Al Glatson, Solo Concert, For Players Only, Manhattan Cycles,* and *Leroy Jenkins' Sting: Urban Blues.*

Jenks, Stephen, American composer and tunebook compiler; b. Glocester, R.I., March 17, 1772; d. Thompson, Ohio, June 5, 1856. Jenks taught in New England and N.Y. singing schools before settling in Ohio in 1829, where he took up farming. He published ten volumes of PSALMODY (1799–1818), which included 127 of his own works and many other compositions by American writers. He was the leading composer of FUGING TUNES of the 19th century.

PEOPLE IN MUSIC

Jennings, Waylon (Arnold), American country music singer, guitarist, and songwriter; b. Littlefield, Texas, June 15, 1937. Taking up the guitar in his youth, Jennings dropped out of school at 14. He played bass in BUDDY HOLLY's band in 1958–59, and then continued to work with the group after Holly died in a plane crash.

Jennings went to Nashville in 1965, where he turned out several albums and starred in the film *Nashville Rebel* in 1966. Disdaining the "Nashville sound," he became a leading figure in "outlaw" country music, also called "redneck rock," with his album *Ladies Love Outlaws* in 1972. He subsequently won a wide following with such albums as *Lonesome, On'ry and Mean* (1973), *Honky Tonk Heroes* (1973), *This*

PEOPLE IN MUSIC

One of Waylon and Willie's biggest hits was the plaintive *Mamas, Don't Let Your Babies Grow Up to Be Cowboys.*

Time (1974), *Waylon, the Ramblin' Man* (1974), *Dreamin' My Dreams* (1975), and *Wanted: The Outlaws* (1976).

In the mid-'70s, Jennings was often paired with WILLIE NELSON, and the two recorded four successful "Waylon and Willie" albums. In the mid-'80s, the two joined with KRIS KRISTOFFERSON and JOHNNY CASH to form the group THE HIGHWAYMEN, working together occasionally over the next decade.

Years of hard living took their toll on Jennings's voice and body. In 1993 he had open heart surgery and temporarily stopped performing. He has continued to record and tour, although he is more popular as a stage performer than on the country charts.

Jenůfa. Opera by LEOŠ JANÁČEK, 1904, first produced in Brno under the name *Její pastorkyňa* (her foster daughter). The subject is grisly, as peasant life in Central Europe often was in the 19th century. Jenůfa is heavy with child by a Moravian farmhand. When the child is born, the moralistic female sexton of the local church drowns it to save Jenůfa from disgrace. The truth is found out, the hideous sexton culprit is taken to prison, and Jenůfa marries a stepbrother of her original seducer.

The work is one of the most remarkable examples of modern Bohemian music drama. The score underwent several revisions, and not until the performance of the final version in Prague, May 26, 1916, was Janáček recognized as an important international composer.

Jephtha. Oratorio by GEORGE FRIDERIC HANDEL, 1752. Jephtha, returning from a victorious campaign, makes a reckless promise to God that he will sacrifice the first thing he encounters when he gets home. Like other antiheroes in this position, he meets his own daughter.

Jeremiah Symphony. Symphony No. 1 by LEONARD BERNSTEIN, 1944, for soprano and orchestra, on a text from the Bible. It is in three sections: *Prophecy, Profanation,* and *Lamentation.* Bernstein conducted its first performance in Pittsburgh.

Jericho trumpets. In Chapter 6 of the Book of Joshua, it is related how the Lord instructed Joshua to destroy the city of Jericho by having seven priests blow seven trumpets made out of ram horns while the people "shouted with a great shout." The noise was such that the walls of Jericho "fell down flat," letting Joshua's people in, and they proceeded to slay "both man and woman, young and old, and ox, and sheep, and ass" (except a local harlot who hid Joshua's spies in her house).

Modern acousticians doubt whether a wall could be brought down by sounding trumpets and shouting. Even rock musicians using electric amplifiers could never do more than frighten peaceful bystanders.

Jerusalem, Siegfried, prominent German tenor; b. Oberhausen, April 17, 1940. Jerusalem began his career as an orchestral bassoonist in 1961 and was a member of the Stuttgart Radio Symphony Orchestra from 1972 to 1977. He began vocal study in Stuttgart in 1972, appearing in minor roles at the Württemberg State Theater from 1975.

PEOPLE IN MUSIC

Jerusalem sang Lohengrin in Darmstadt and Aachen in 1976, and then at the Hamburg State Opera in 1977. That same year he made his debut at the BAYREUTH FESTIVAL as Froh, returning in later seasons as Lohengrin, Walther, Parsifal, and Loge in the Solti-Hall mounting of the *Ring* cycle in 1983.

After making his first appearance at the Berlin Deutsche Oper as Tamino in 1978, Jerusalem became a leading member of the company. He made his U.S. debut with the Metropolitan Opera in N.Y. as Lohengrin in 1980, his British debut at London's Coliseum as Parsifal six years later, and his Covent Garden debut later that year as Erik. He also appeared at the Vienna State Opera, Milan's La Scala, and the Paris Opéra.

Jessonda. This opera by LUDWIG SPOHR, now nearly forgotten, was once a great favorite, particularly in England. It was first performed in Kassel, Germany, where Spohr was court music director, July 28, 1823.

Jessonda is the wife of the rajah of Malabar. He dies, and she must throw herself on his funeral pyre like the good

Brahmin that she is. But lo! Portuguese fanfares are sounded and no less a person than Tristan da Cunha, the explorer for whom a desolate group of islands midway between South America and South Africa was named (one island of the group is called Inaccessible), enters the scene. He recognizes in Jessonda his ideal woman, and she sees in him her ideal man. The chorus of Brahmins urges her to take her rightful place at her husband's funerary mound, but now she wants to live. When the Portuguese marines land in force, the Brahmins desist in their foul superstition, and a happy ending is assured.

The score sounds like any piece of German music of the time, with no attempt to introduce exotic tunes.

Jeu de cartes (The card game). Ballet "in 3 deals" by IGOR STRAVINSKY, 1937, first performed in N.Y. with the composer conducting. Stravinsky, a devotee of poker, portrays in this score a poker game, with the joker constantly intruding to confuse the players. The sequence of dances follows the classical tradition.

Jeu de Robin et de Marion. Medieval play with music by ADAM DE LA HALLE, c.1280. A PASTORALE with dialogue and songs, this is the first surviving secular musical drama. It tells the story of Robin Hood and his beloved Maid Marion.

Jeunehomme Concerto. Nickname for the Piano Concerto No. 9 in E-flat major, K.271 (1777) by WOLFGANG AMADEUS MOZART, written for the French pianist Mlle. Jeunehomme, who played it in Salzburg.

Jeux d'eau. Piano piece by MAURICE RAVEL, 1902. Ravel used the entire range of the piano, from its very lowest note, and emphasized lush harmonies, anticipating the work of CLAUDE DEBUSSY and the other IMPRESSIONISTS. The piece was first performed in Paris.

Jeux d'enfants (Children's games). Suite by GEORGES BIZET, 1871, for piano duet. These 12 pieces describe the carousel, a doll, spinning top, and other appropriate objects. Bizet orchestrated five of the pieces as the *Petite suite* a year later.

Jew's harp. A small instrument with rigid iron frame, having a thin metal tongue. The frame is held against the teeth, and the metallic tongue plucked with the finger (Jew's harp may be a corruption of jaw's harp). Various pitches are attained by changing the shape of the mouth. The instrument has been included in folk ensembles throughout the world, from China to Borneo, from northern Europe to Appalachia.

jig (from Fr., *giguer,* move rapidly to and fro). A lively English dance, similar to the HORNPIPE. The jig is a country dance, with many variations in step and gesture, played rapidly. It was very popular in the 17th century among lower classes.

One writer described the jig as "only fit for Fantastical, and Easie-Light-Headed People." However, jigs penetrated the English court and apparently became favorites with the English aristocracy. The *Fitzwilliam Virginal Book* includes a jig with the unusual title *Nobodyes Gigge.* In the courts, the jig died out at the end of the Elizabethen era and was replaced by the more courtly and dignified French GIGUE.

2. In Irish music, the traditional jig is usually in $\frac{6}{8}$ time. It is written in two 16-bar parts and accompanies Irish step dancing. Slip jigs are written in either $\frac{9}{8}$ or $\frac{12}{8}$.

Jim Crack Corn (Blue Tail Fly). Popular minstrel show song by DANIEL DECATUR EMMETT, 1846. It was a particular favorite of President Lincoln's.

Jim Crow. Blackface minstrel song and dance, c.1829, by THOMAS DARTMOUTH "DADDY" RICE (1808–60). It marked the beginning of the American blackface minstrel show.

Jingle Bells. American Christmas song by JAMES PIERPONT, c.1850, written for a Sunday school entertainment.

jingling johnny (johnnie) (Turkish crescent, Chinese pavilion, Chinese hat; Ger., *Schellenbaum,* ringing tree). An ornate Eastern percussion instrument. It consists of a stick with crossbars in the shape of crescents topped by a hat-like

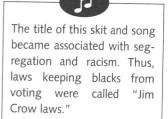

The title of this skit and song became associated with segregation and racism. Thus, laws keeping blacks from voting were called "Jim Crow laws."

A jitterbug revival occurred in the mid-'90s, along with other swing dances.

PEOPLE IN MUSIC

decoration and with bells and jingles. It was popular in Europe during the 18th century.

jitterbug. An American jazz dance of the 1930s and 1940s, notable for its attempt to match the "heat" of the music with appropriate physical gesture and floor movement. Among its components are slow dig steps, quicksteps, and sidesteps (shuffles). The dance was exported to Europe with the American armed forces in World War II.

Job. A masque for dancing by RALPH VAUGHAN WILLIAMS, 1930. The scenario was inspired by William Blake's *Illustrations of the Book of Job.* It was first performed as a concert piece in Norwich.

Joel, Billy (William Martin), American pianist, singer, and songwriter of popular music; b. N.Y., May 9, 1949. As a teenager, Joel joined the rock band the Echoes, which later renamed itself the Hassles. The group made two albums, and then Joel and the drummer, Jon Small, left to form a duo named Attila. They recorded an album, which did not sell.

Joel then organized a band of his own and recorded his first solo album, *Cold Spring Harbor,* in

Billy Joel with his then-wife, Christie Brinkley, c. 1983. (UPI/Corbis-Bettmann)
▶

1972, for the Family Productions label. It did not sell well, and after a family feud with the label, Joel went over to Columbia Records and moved to Los Angeles, where he worked as a barroom pianist.

He composed a ballad called, autobiographically, *Piano Man* (1973), which made a hit. He received a certified platinum award for his song *Just the Way You Are* from the album *The Stranger* in 1978. Other smash albums followed, including *Fifty-second Street,* which captured a GRAMMY AWARD for best album of 1979 and also made him the Grammy Award male pop vocalist of the year. Other hit singles are numerous, including *My Life, Big Shot, Honesty, Say Goodbye to Hollywood,* and *You May Be Right.*

In the 1980s, Joel was prolific, with particularly notable albums of the decade being *The Nylon Curtain, An Innocent Man, The Bridge,* and *Kohupt,* a two-record set of live concerts in Moscow and Leningrad in 1987. In the early '90s, he issued *River of Dreams,* yielding a pleasing music video and some minor hits.

Joel announced in 1998 his retirement from pop song writing, while also making a final tour and issuing a greatest-hits collection. He is now focusing on writing IMPRESSIONISTIC piano music in the style of GEORGE GERSHWIN.

Johansen, Gunnar, remarkable Danish-American pianist, composer, and teacher; b. Copenhagen, Jan. 21, 1906; d. Blue Mounds, Wisc., May 25, 1991. Johansen made his public debut at the age of 12 in Copenhagen, then went to Berlin when he was 14. He met the Italian futurist composer FERRUCCIO BUSONI there, while continuing his piano studies both privately and at the Hochschule für Musik from 1922 to 1924.

From 1924 to 1929 Johansen toured Europe and then settled in the U.S., where he pursued an active concert career. He gained particular distinction for his series of 12 historical piano recitals encompassing works from GIROLAMO FRESCOBALDI to IGOR STRAVINSKY, which he presented in San Francisco, Chicago, and N.Y. in the late 1930s. Beginning in 1939, he held the specially created position of artist-in-residence at the University of Wisconsin at Madison for nearly four decades.

Johansen played and recorded many extremely difficult keyboard works. These included the complete solo piano

Joel created controversy with his mid-'80s hit *Only the Good Die Young*. The song's narrator tries to entice his Catholic girlfriend to sleep with him. The Catholic church was not very happy, to say the least, with the lyrics!

PEOPLE IN MUSIC

works of FRANZ LISZT and Busoni, Busoni's JOHANN SEBAST-IAN BACH transcriptions, as well as Bach's complete solo clavier works. He was also a productive composer, numbering among his compositions three piano concertos (1930, 1970, 1981), 31 piano sonatas (1941–51), and 515 piano sonatas improvised directly on the keyboard and recorded on tape between 1952 and 1982.

John, Elton (born Reginald Kenneth Dwight), phenomenally successful English rock pianist, singer, and songwriter; b. Pinner, Middlesex, March 25, 1947. John took up the piano in early childhood, then won a fellowship to the Royal

PEOPLE IN MUSIC

Elton John receives a star on the Hollywood Walk of Fame in October 1975. (UPI/Corbis-Bettmann)
▶

Academy of Music in London at age 11. After dropping out of school when he was 17, he earned his keep as a jazz pianist in various London clubs and pubs. In 1966 he joined the blues revival band Bluesology as a pianist, remaining with them for about a year.

In 1967 John temporarily gave up performing to try his hand at songwriting. He was hired by Dick James Music, run by the man who owned Northern Songs (the BEATLES' publishing company), where he met a lyricist named Bernie Taupin. The two began working together, while John continued to record (unsuccessfully) through 1969.

Finally, in 1970 John hit it big with his self-titled first album, featuring the ballad *Your Song,* a hit on both sides of the Atlantic. From the early to mid-'70s, John enjoyed his

After leaving the band, Dwight thought he should come up with a more marketable name. From his ex-bandmates vocalist "Long" *John* Baldry and saxophonist *Elton* Dean he came up with his new name, "Elton John."

greatest success with a string of hits: *Rocket Man, Daniel, Crocodile Rock,* and *Candle in the Wind,* written in memory of Marilyn Monroe. Just as he showed he could master a variety of styles, John also became a flamboyant performer, wearing oversized glasses, outrageous clothing, and flashy shoes. John's last major hit of this period was his duet with Kiki Dee in 1976 on *Don't Go Breaking My Heart.*

John and Taupin took a break from working together in 1979 when Taupin moved to Los Angeles. John's career slowed in the early '80s. He made more news for his admitted bisexuality than he did for his music. In 1983 he triumphantly reunited with Taupin for the hit *I'm Still Standing.* At the end of the year, in another surprise twist, he married, although the marriage would only last a little less than three years.

John's career seemed to be on an upturn. In 1985 he appeared at Live Aid, the worldwide concert to support African famine relief, to generally good reviews. However, a year later, he collapsed while touring Australia, and underwent throat surgery in early 1987. Still, he managed to score a hit in 1988, with the R&B-flavored *I Don't Want to Go On with You Like That.* At the end of the year, as a kind of ritual self-cleansing, John auctioned off many of his outrageous stage costumes for charity.

John entered the '90s as a rock elder statesman. In partnership with Tim Rice, the lyricist for *Jesus Christ Superstar,* John wrote the score for Disney's very successful animated film *The Lion King* in 1994, gaining a new generation of fans. John followed this with the critically acclaimed *Made in England* album a year later.

Candle in the Wind was revised after the death of Princess Diana in 1997 as a memorial to her. John sang it at her funeral.

Johnny Johnson. Musical fable by KURT WEILL, 1936, first produced in N.Y. Weill's first American work concerns the fate of a naive soldier who fights Germany in World War I. He tries to end the fighting by introducing laughing gas to the troops, but in the process he loses his girl and is put into an insane asylum. It failed at the box office.

Johnson, "Bunk" (William Geary), African-American jazz trumpeter; b. New Orleans, Dec. 27, 1889?; d. New Iberia, La., July 7, 1949. The early life of Johnson is shrouded in

PEOPLE IN MUSIC

mystery. As a youth he played trumpet with Dixieland bands, touring with minstrel shows, circus troupes, and numerous jazz groups. He claimed to have taught the young LOUIS ARMSTRONG, which is doubtful, as well as working with BUDDY BOLDEN and JELLY ROLL MORTON, which is possible, although there is no evidence to support these claims. Johnson's career was strictly local, in any case, and ended when he lost his front teeth in the late '20s due to disease.

After many years of musical inactivity Johnson was "rediscovered" in 1937, working in sugarcane fields, by two writers on early jazz history. After being fitted with dentures, he resumed his career and enjoyed belated fame in a revival of DIXIELAND music. He made his first recording in 1942 and subsequently performed in N.Y., Boston, and Chicago. Along with clarinetist George Lewis, Johnson was one of the most important musicians in the Dixieland revival.

PEOPLE IN MUSIC

Johnson, Edward, distinguished Canadian-born American tenor and operatic administrator; b. Guelph, Ontario, Aug. 22, 1878; d. there, April 20, 1959. Johnson sang in concert and oratorio performances before going to N.Y. in 1899 to study voice. After appearing in the U.S. premiere of OSCAR STRAUS's *A Waltz Dream* in 1907, he continued his studies in Paris and Florence in 1908–09. He made his operatic debut as Andrea Chenier at the Teatro Verdi in Padua on Jan. 10, 1912, using the stage name Edoardo Di Giovanni. He subsequently appeared in Milan at La Scala, where he sang Parsifal at its first complete stage production in Italy in 1914.

Johnson made his U.S. debut as Loris in *Fedora* at the Chicago Grand Opera on Nov. 20, 1919, remaining on its roster until 1922. He then made his Metropolitan Opera debut in N.Y. as Avito in *L'amore dei tre Re* on Nov. 16, 1922, remaining there until 1935. Johnson became the general manager of the Metropolitan Opera, guiding its fortunes through the difficult years of World War II and the postwar era. He retired in 1950. Although he became an American citizen in 1922, he maintained a close connection with Canada and returned there after his retirement.

Johnson was particularly esteemed for such roles as Romeo, Tannhäuser, Don Jose, Siegfried, Canio, and Pelleas. He also created leading roles in DEEMS TAYLOR's *The King's*

Henchman (1927) and *Peter Ibbetson* (1931) at the Metropolitan.

Johnson, Frank (Francis), black bandmaster and composer; b. probably on the island of Martinique, 1792; d. Philadelphia, April 6, 1844. Johnson settled in Philadelphia around 1809, where he organized his own band and dance orchestra. After touring England in 1837, he led promenade concerts throughout the U.S., highlighting his own works. In Philadelphia, his concerts were often graced by the presence of prominent white artists, an unheard-of practice in his era.

PEOPLE IN MUSIC

Johnson, James P(rice), African-American jazz pianist and composer; b. New Brunswick, N.J., Feb. 1, 1891; d. N.Y., Nov. 17, 1955. Johnson studied piano with his mother. He began his career as a pianist in N.Y. and Atlantic City nightclubs, and later led his own bands and appeared as soloist.

PEOPLE IN MUSIC

Johnson first established himself as a virtuoso on the keyboards with his difficult-to-perform compositions. One of his earliest and most celebrated piano pieces was *Carolina Shout,* written in the early '20s. In 1923, he established a second career as the composer for the musical *Runnin' Wild,* which introduced a new dance, the CHARLESTON.

Johnson was greatly admired by his contemporaries as one of the creators of STRIDE piano. Stride had a lighter, more swinging feel in the left hand than RAGTIME, which emphasized an oompah bass. It also was more demanding melodically and harmonically. Among those who greatly admired Johnson's playing was a young pianist named FATS WALLER. Johnson helped establish Waller's career and showed him many tricks on the keyboard.

Johnson based his Charleston on dances he had seen performed by Southerners who settled in the N.Y. neighborhood where he grew up. The Charleston became the dance most associated with the Roarin' '20s.

In the '30s and '40s, Johnson began writing pieces that combined African-American themes with classical forms. These included *Yamekraw,* scored for piano, *Harlem Symphony, Spirit of America,* written for string quartet, and even an opera, *De Organizer.* Unfortunately, many of these scores have been partially or completely lost.

Johnson continued to record and perform through the late '40s. A paralyzing stroke in 1951 ended his career, and he died four years later.

Johnson, "J. J." (James Louis), outstanding African-American jazz trombonist and accomplished composer; b. Indianapolis, Jan. 22, 1924. Johnson began to play the piano at the age of 9 and the trombone at 14. He toured with Clarence Love and Isaac "Snookum" Russell in 1941–42 before attracting attention as a member of BENNY CARTER's orchestra from 1942 to 1945. After working with COUNT BASIE in N.Y. in 1945–46, he did stints with various artists there. He also made a tour of Korea, Japan, and the South Pacific with a group led by Oscar Pettiford for the U.S.O. in 1951.

After a hiatus from the jazz scene, Johnson resumed his career, touring with Kai Winding in a trombone duo known as Jay and Kai. He then formed his own quintet, which stayed together from 1956 to 1960, with which he toured Europe. After working with MILES DAVIS in 1961–62, he led his own quartet and sextet.

Johnson gave increasing attention to composition, moving to Los Angeles as a composer for film and television in 1970. He returned to Indianapolis in 1988, at which time he was awarded an honorary doctorate by Indiana University.

Johnson is acknowledged as a pioneer figure of the BE-BOP era. Among his works are *Poem* for brass (1956), *Sketch* for trombone and band (1959), *El camino real* (1964), *In Walked Horace* (1966), and *Concepts in Blue* (1980). He is one of the few people who was able to adapt the trombone to the demands of bop's high-energy, melodic improvisation.

Johnson, Robert, influential African-American blues musician; b. Hazlehurt, Miss., c. 1912; d. Greenwood, Miss., Aug. 16, 1938. Relatively little about Johnson's life is known. He played at dance parties, worked with other musicians, and made recordings in Texas during the last two years of his life. He was apparently poisoned by a jealous husband after flirting with the man's wife.

Johnson played guitar and sang within the Delta blues tradition, having been influenced by Son House, Charley Patton, and the jazz guitarist Lonnie Johnson (no relation). But Johnson added other elements to create a unique and powerful style. His vocals were taut and penetrating, his gui-

One legend says that Johnson made "a deal with the Devil" in order to become a great guitarist. Standing at a crossroads at midnight, he sold his soul to the demon in exchange for his unusual musical capabilities.

tar work combined a powerful rhythmic sense with fine, improvised melodic lines, and his songs expressed a deep sense of tragedy and danger. His versatile guitar playing created as full a sound as had yet been heard on an acoustic guitar.

After his death, Chicago blues musicians kept his music and name alive. But the widespread modern revival of his work began in the 1960s, when white blues and rock musicians introduced audiences to Johnson's legacy, including *Crossroads, Hellhound on My Trail, Dust My Broom, Kind Hearted Woman, Terraplane Blues, Love in Vain, Ramblin' On My Mind,* and *If I Had Possession Over Judgment Day.*

Johnston, Ben(jamin Burwell), American composer and teacher; b. Macon, Ga., March 15, 1926. Johnson studied at the College of William and Mary in Williamsburg, Virginia (A.B., 1949), the Cincinnati Conservatory of Music (M.Mus., 1950), and Mills College in Oakland, California (M.A., 1953). In 1959–60 he held a Guggenheim fellowship. He taught at the University of Illinois in Urbana from 1951 to 1983.

PEOPLE IN MUSIC

Johnston worked with the eccentric composer and musical instrument designer HARRY PARTCH in 1949–50. Johnston shared Partch's interest in JUST INTONATION, tuning instruments to the true scale pitches, rather than making the compromises that are inherent in equal temperament. However, Johnston was less rigid in his interest in this tuning system than Partch. He has also written for traditional instruments (most successfully strings and retuned piano), not being inclined to build instruments as Partch did.

In addition to his many fine chamber and vocal works, Johnson's flair for the dramatic and ironic is seen to good advantage in his theater pieces, which include the operas *Gertrude, or Would She Be Pleased to Receive It?* (1965) and *Carmilla* (1970). Among his orchestral works is a Symphony (Rocky Mount, N.C., Oct. 29, 1988), and among his chamber pieces are several string quartets (1964–88), Trio for clarinet, violin, and cello (1982), and *The Demon Lover's Double* for trumpet and microtonal piano (1985). He also composed a cantata, *Night* (1955), and other choral music and songs.

Jolie fille de Perth, La (The pretty girl of Perth). Opera by GEORGES BIZET, 1867, based on a novel by Walter Scott. Like so many operas, the plot involves a betrothed couple, a lecherous Duke, a young Gypsy woman with her own agenda, and an apprentice who can't hold his drink. The whole mess almost ends with a fatal duel, but the Gypsy saves the day, and the couple is reunited in the nick of time.

PEOPLE IN MUSIC

Jolson, Al (Asa Yoelson), popular Lithuanian-born American singer and actor; b. Srednike, Lithuania, May 26, 1886; d. San Francisco, Oct. 23, 1950. Jolson's family emigrated about 1894 to the U.S., settling in Washington, D.C. Jolson's father was a cantor and hoped his son would follow in his footsteps. Instead, Jolson was interested in popular music and began singing on street corners before he was ten years old. He was in N.Y. for a while working as a singing waiter, and then returned to Washington as a young teenager. He began regularly attending vaudeville shows at the local Bijou Theater, where he gained fame by singing from the audience in response to the more popular acts.

Around 1902, Jolson went to N.Y. to form an act with his older brother, Harry. The act gained some success, touring the country's second-level vaudeville houses. In 1905 Harry retired, and Al was stranded in San Francisco. There he gained a strong local following and, it is said, came up with his signature line, "You ain't heard nothin' yet!"

Jolson's San Francisco success brought him to the attention of Lew Dockstader, who ran a touring vaudeville company. He hired Al in 1908, and he became the hit sensation of the company when it played N.Y. in 1909. Jolson was next hired as a leading performer at the Winter Garden in 1911, where he introduced his famous blackface character of Gus in *Whirl of Society* a year later.

Jolson continued to be a major Broadway attraction through the '20s. Most of the shows he appeared in were tailored to his oversized personality. Sometimes, at the intermission, he would ask the audience if they'd like to see the rest of the show or merely hear him sing their favorite songs. More than once he would oblige them with a solo concert instead of the rest of the play!

Jolson starred in the first feature sound film, *THE JAZZ SINGER*, in 1927, winning immortality with his rendition in blackface of the song *My Mammy*. The introduction of speech and singing into film caused an immediate sensation, and it helped make Jolson an even bigger star than before. He appeared in several other films and also returned to Broadway in *The Wonder Bar* in 1931 and *Hold On to Your Hats* in 1940. By this time, however, his style of all-out singing was being replaced by such modern crooners as BING CROSBY and FRANK SINATRA, who sang in a more intimate style.

Jolson entertained the troops in World War II, but his health began to fail, and he had a series of operations on his lungs. During the last few years of his life, Jolson appeared on radio and television. His voice was also used on the sound tracks for the films *The Jolson Story* (1946) and *Jolson Sings Again* (1949).

Jolson popularized many songs, including *Swanee; California, Here I Come; Toot, Toot, Tootsie!; April Showers; Rockaby Your Baby with a Dixie Melody; Let Me Sing and I'm Happy; There's a Rainbow 'round My Shoulder;* and *Sonny Boy*. He was married to the dancer and actress Ruby Keeler from 1928 to 1939.

Jones, George, American country singer; b. Saratoga, Tex., Sept. 12, 1931. Jones began to play guitar when he was nine. He made some appearances locally before serving in the Korean War, then worked as a house painter.

In 1955 he recorded his first hit song, *Why, Baby, Why,* and subsequently gained fame with such songs as *Window Up Above* (1961), *She Thinks I Still Care* (1962), and *We Must Have Been Out of Our Minds* (1963). Jones is comfortable in both honky-tonk and sentimental ballad styles.

Jones was married to the country music star TAMMY WYNETTE from 1969 to 1975, and the two recorded several hit duets together. After their divorce, they continued to record. Eventually he returned to bolstering his image as a heartbroken heavy drinker with *If Drinking Don't Kill Me (Her Memory Will)*. Jones continues to surprise with good recordings, such as *I Don't Need Your Rockin' Chair.*

PEOPLE IN MUSIC

As "Thumper" Jones, George Jones recorded a couple of rockabilly records in the mid-'50s, including *Rock It*. However, he was unsuccessful as a would-be rock star.

PEOPLE IN MUSIC

Jones, Quincy (Delight, Jr.), versatile African-American pianist, trumpeter, bandleader, recording executive, composer, and film producer; b. Chicago, March 14, 1933. Taken to Seattle at the age of 10, Jones took up the trumpet at 14, later studying with Clark Terry in 1950. He also studied arranging and composition at the Berklee College of Music in Boston.

Jones played in LIONEL HAMPTON's band from 1951 to 1953, then was a performer-arranger in DIZZY GILLESPIE's touring band in the Near East in 1956–57. Jones subsequently worked in Europe from 1957 to 1960, which he toured with his own big band. He also wrote arrangements for many leading jazz vocalists, including DINAH WASHINGTON and FRANK SINATRA.

Jones began composing scores for television and films in the late '50s. Among his better-known scores are *In Cold Blood* and *In the Heat of the Night,* both from 1967. He also scored the successful television miniseries *Roots.* Jones also composed in a semiclassical style a number of works, including *Stockholm Sweetnin'* and *Evening in Paris,* both from 1956, *The Quintessence* (1961), *Walking in Space* (1969), *Soundpiece* for string quartet and contralto, and *Soundpiece* for jazz orchestra.

Besides composing, Jones also worked as a record producer and record company executive. He was the first African-American to be the vice president of a leading record label, Mercury Records, a position he took in 1964. In the 1970s and 1980s, he returned to producing, successfully working with a number of artists, most notably MICHAEL JACKSON, for whom he produced the hit album *Thriller* in 1982.

Jones won a number of Grammy Awards, being honored in 1985 as producer of the recording and video productions of *We Are the World,* which raised millions of dollars for famine relief in Africa. He also composed the score for and was coproducer of the film *The Color Purple* (1985).

In the '90s, Jones has expanded into being a general entrepreneur in black music. He runs his own label, Qwest Records, and continues to produce artists. He also has produced films. Jones also cofounded the magazine *Vibe.*

Jones, Sissieretta (born Matilda Sissieretta Joyner), noted African-American soprano, known as the "Black Patti" (with reference to Adelina Patti); b. Portsmouth, Va., Jan. 5, 1868; d. Providence, R.I., June 24, 1933. Jones showed an early talent as a singer and began to study opera, an unusual choice for an African-American singer at that time. She studied at the New England Conservatory of Music in Boston and with leading opera stars in London.

Jones made her debut at a concert at N.Y.'s Steinway Hall in 1888, then began to tour from 1890, giving concerts in the West Indies, North America, and Europe. She gained prominence as a result of her appearances at the Grand Negro Jubilee at N.Y.'s Madison Square Garden and at the White House in a command performance for President Harrison in 1892. The next year, she sang at the Pittsburgh Exposition and the Chicago World's Columbian Exposition. N.Y.'s Metropolitan Opera considered her for African roles in *AIDA* and *L'AFRICAINE,* but racial attitudes and conservative management policies precluded her appearances.

Jones was the principal soprano of the vaudeville troupe known as Black Patti's Troubadours, with which she toured throughout the world between 1896 and 1915. She starred in its operatic "kaleidoscope," in which she sang a medley of arias from operas in staged scenes. She also sang art songs and popular ballads.

Jones, "Spike" (Lindley Armstrong), American bandleader and musical satirist; b. Long Beach, Calif., Dec. 14, 1911; d. Los Angeles, May 1, 1965. He played drums as a boy and led a school band. He formed his own group, the City Slickers, in the mid-'30s and began performing on local radio.

In 1942 Jones made a recording of a satirical song, *Der Führer's Face,* satirizing the rise to power of Adolf Hitler. He then toured the U.S. with his multitalented band, the City Slickers, which included a washboard, a Smith and Wesson pistol, antibug flit guns in E flat, doorbells, anvils, hammers to break glass, and a live goat trained to bleat rhythmically. With this ensemble, he launched what he called a "Musical Depreciation Revue."

PEOPLE IN MUSIC

Jones' great vocal capabilities led critics to compare her to the famous white opera singer ADELINA PATTI. In honoring her, they gave Jones the nickname "The Black Patti," and it stuck.

PEOPLE IN MUSIC

Among his many unusual musical instruments, Jones played the Latrinophone, a toilet seat strung with catgut.

He retired in 1963, when the wave of extravaganza that had carried him to the crest of commercial success subsided. In his heyday he was known as the "King of Corn." Any piece of music was fair game for his slapstick approach. For every Jonesian *William Tell Overture,* there was a *Cocktails for Two* in his own image.

PEOPLE IN MUSIC

Jones, Thad(deus Joseph), African-American jazz trumpeter, cornetist, flugelhornist, bandleader, arranger, and composer; b. Pontiac, Mich., March 28, 1923; d. Copenhagen, Aug. 20, 1986. Jones taught himself to play trumpet when he was about 13 and subsequently appeared professionally with his brother Hank at age 16, and also with saxophonist SONNY STITT.

After working with various dance and show bands, Jones joined his brother Elvin as a member of BILLY MITCHELL's quintet in Detroit from 1950 to 1953. He worked with bass player/composer CHARLES MINGUS in 1954–55 and was a featured soloist and arranger with COUNT BASIE's orchestra from 1954 to 1963. He also appeared with THELONIOUS MONK and JERRY MULLIGAN.

With Mel Lewis, in 1965 Jones formed his own band. The group gained fame through its tours of the U.S. and Europe, including a smashing visit to the Soviet Union in 1972. He left the band in 1979 and settled in Denmark, where he organized his own big band, the Thad Jones Eclipse. He was also active as an arranger and composer with Danish Radio. He returned to the U.S. to briefly take charge of Basie's orchestra in 1985 following the Count's death.

Jones's best-known composition was *A Child Is Born,* which gained the status of a jazz classic.

PEOPLE IN MUSIC

Jones, Tom (real name, Thomas Jones Woodward), Welsh singer and drummer; b. Pontypridd, June 7, 1940. Jones sang as a young boy with a natural feeling for melody. Dropping out of school at 16, he began to play drums and sing in British pubs. He joined the group Tommy Scott and the Senators as lead singer, but the group failed to make it after making a few demo recordings.

Jones returned to Wales and pub singing where he was heard by a fellow Welshman and ex-member of the pop group the Viscounts, GORDON MILLS. Mills signed up as his manager, and changed his name to Tom Jones. Under this new name he began recording in 1965. His second release, *It's Not Unusual,* featuring Jones's big-voiced delivery, was an immediate British hit. He followed a year later with the theme song to the film *What's New, Pussy Cat?,* penned by BURT BACHARACH and HAL DAVID, for a major hit both in Britain and the U.S.

Jones greatest success was the period from 1966 to 1970, when he scored many hits, including *Green Green Grass of Home, Detroit City, I'll Never Fall in Love Again,* and *Help Yourself.* He also starred in his own variety show on television.

In the early '70s, Jones's star began to fade. He became a fixture in Las Vegas, where he was able to perform for months at a time, amassing a large personal fortune, which made it unnecessary for him to record or perform unless he felt moved to do so. He has continued to perform and record on occasion through the '80s and '90s, making a few publicized "comebacks" that have resulted in a couple of hits.

Jones is a talented singer. He combines the bluesy quality of RAY CHARLES with the big-voiced belting of a lounge singer. His sexy demeanor, emphasized by wearing tight pants and low-cut shirts, has made him attractive to generations of female fans.

jongleur (Fr.; from Lat. *joculator,* maker of jokes; Sp. *juglares*). A medieval entertainer employed by royalty and aristocracy to

Jones's female fans became famous for throwing their underwear on stage during his performances.

zhon′glör′

◀

Medieval manuscript illustration of jongleurs and troubadours performing for the emperor of Germany, c.1300. (Gianni Dagli, Orti/Corbis)

provide amusement, including songs and jests. The word itself corresponds to the English *juggler,* suggesting that the jongleur also performed acrobatic acts.

By the 12th century, the jongleurs had become known as *ménestriers,* those who ministered to traveling TROUBADOURS and TROUVÈRES. The term further evolved to *ménestrels* (Eng. *minstrels*). English minstrels were also known as *gleemen.*

Jongleur de Notre Dame, Le. Opera by JULES MASSENET, 1902, first produced in Monte Carlo.

The action takes place in France in the 14th century, focusing on a street juggler who performs for and then collapses in front of a statue of the Holy Virgin. Before he dies, the Virgin silently blesses him, and he becomes, in legend and tradition, "the juggler of Our Lady."

This is one of the few operas ever written that has no human female roles.

Jonny spielt auf (Johnny strikes up). Opera by ERNST KRENEK, 1927, to his own text, first produced in Leipzig. It became sensationally successful as the first opera to make use of the jazz idiom. Jonny (without an "h" and pronounced Yonny) is a black musician who becomes a famous jazz band leader, captivating audiences around the globe. Fox-trot and Charleston rhythms animate the score, but there are also lyric episodes. The work was translated into 18 languages, and a brand of Austrian cigarettes was even named after it.

When the opera was first produced by the Metropolitan Opera in N.Y. (1929), the role of Jonny was changed into that of a blackface musician in order not to offend the segregationist sensitivities of some of the patrons, particularly in scenes when Jonny consorts with white chambermaids.

PEOPLE IN MUSIC

Joplin, Janis (Lyn), plaintive American rock and blues singer; b. Port Arthur, Tex., 1943; d. of an overdose of heroin, Los Angeles, Oct. 4, 1970. Joplin spent an unhappy childhood, running away from home and immersing herself in the bohemian life of San Francisco. After a brief stint in college, she joined the rock group BIG BROTHER AND THE HOLDING COMPANY as lead vocalist in 1966, winning acclaim for her rendition of *Ball and Chain* when she appeared with the group at the Monterey International Pop Festival in

1967. Her passionate, raspy wailing immediately established her as an uninhibited representative of the younger generation.

After recording the album *Cheap Thrills* (1967), she left Big Brother and struck out on her own. She formed her own

Janis Joplin in concert, c.1968. (Ted Streshinsky/Corbis)

backup group, the Kozmic Blues Band, in 1968, with whom she recorded the 1969 album *I Got Dem Ol' Kozmic Blues Again Mama.*

Joplin continued to tour and perform, appearing at the famous Woodstock Festival in the summer of 1969. In early 1970 she revamped her band again, retitling it the Full Tilt Boogie Band. She began recording a new album, which was almost completed when, that October, she died of a heroin overdose. The album, *Pearl,* was released after her death and featured her biggest hit, *Me and Bobby McGee.*

Joplin, Scott, remarkable African-American pianist and composer, best known for his piano rags; b. probably near Marshall, Tex., Nov. 24, 1868; d. N.Y., April 1, 1917. Joplin learned to play the piano at home in Texarkana and later studied with a local German musician. He left home at 17 and went to St. Louis, earning his living by playing piano in local bars and clubs. In 1893 he moved to Chicago (drawn by the prospect of music making and other gaiety of the World's Fair), and in 1896 went to Sedalia, Missouri, where

PEOPLE IN MUSIC

837

Scott Joplin.
(New York Public Library)
▶

The *Maple Leaf Rag* was the first sheet music publication to sell over a million copies.

he took courses at George Smith College, a segregated school for blacks.

Joplin's first music publications appeared in 1895 and were typical sentimental songs and marches of the day. His success as a RAGTIME composer came with the *Maple Leaf Rag,* published in 1899, the most famous of all piano rags, which he named after a local musicians' club, the Maple Leaf Club. The sheet-music edition sold so well that Joplin was able to settle in St. Louis and devote himself exclusively to composition.

Joplin continued to compose rags throughout his career but always had ambitions to create larger-scale works. He composed a ragtime ballet, *The Ragtime Dance,* in 1902, and his first ragtime opera, *A Guest of Honor,* a year later. The later work is lost, and was probably only performed once, at Joplin's expense, in 1903.

In 1907 Joplin went to N.Y., where he continued his career as a composer and teacher. He wrote an opera, *Treemonisha,* to his own LIBRETTO. He completed the score in 1911 and produced it in concert form in 1915 without success. Interest in the opera was revived almost 60 years later: T. J. ANDERSON orchestrated it from the piano score, and it received its first complete performance in Atlanta on Jan. 28, 1972.

Despite Joplin's ambitious attempts to make ragtime "respectable" by applying its principles to European forms, it was with the piano rag that he achieved his greatest artistic success. As a noted historian phrased it, these pieces are "the precise American equivalent, in terms of a native dance music, of MINUETS by Mozart, MAZURKAS by Chopin, or WALTZES by Brahms."

Altogether, Joplin wrote about 50 piano rags, in addition to the two operas and a few songs, waltzes, and marches. The titles of some of these rags reflect his desire to create music on a higher plane: *Sycamore,* "A Concert Rag" (1904), *Chrysanthemum,* "An Afro-American Intermezzo" (1904), *Sugar Cane,* "A Ragtime Classic 2-Step" (1908), *Fig Leaf Rag,* "A High Class Rag" (1908), and *Reflection Rag,* "Syncopated Musings" (1917).

In his last years, Joplin lamented having failed to achieve the recognition he felt his music merited. Suffering from syphilis, he went insane and died shortly afterward in a state hospital. More than 50 years later, an extraordinary sequence of events—new recordings of his music and its use in an award-winning film, *The Sting* (1974)—brought Joplin unprecedented popularity and acclaim. Among pop recordings, *The Entertainer* (1902) was one of the best-selling records for 1974, and among classical recordings, Joplin albums represented 74 percent of the best-sellers of the year. In 1976 he was awarded exceptional posthumous recognition by the Pulitzer Prize Committee.

Jordan, Louis, African-American JAZZ ALTO saxophonist and singer; b. Brinkley, Ark., July 8, 1908; d. Los Angeles, Feb. 4, 1975. Jordan took up the clarinet and the alto saxophone as a teenager. He toured with several black VAUDEVILLE companies, accompanying famed BLUES singers MA RAINEY and BESSIE SMITH.

After moving to N.Y. in the late '20s, Jordan began playing with several local bands, including those led by LOUIS ARMSTRONG and drummer Chick Webb. With Webb, he made his first recordings as a vocalist, revealing his talent as a singer of humorous material.

In 1939 Jordan formed his own band, the Tympany 5, to showcase his talents. Among his biggest hits are *Is You Is or Is You Ain't My Baby?* (1944), *Choo Choo Ch'boogie* (1946), *Ain't Nobody Here But Us Chickens* and *Open the Door Richard* (1947), and *Baby It's Cold Outside* (with ELLA FITZGERALD, 1949).

Jordan's success slowed in the mid-'50s, when his style became outdated and he began to suffer from bouts of ill

Joplin hated pianists who sped up his works in order to impress an audience with their virtuosity. "Ragtime should never be played fast!" he stated on more than one occasion, printing this instruction on many of his scores.

PEOPLE IN MUSIC

health. Because of health concerns, he remained only semi-active for the next two decades, recording and touring whenever possible, visiting England in 1962 and Asia in 1967 and 1968. By the early '70s, his health was failing, and although he continued to work when he could, he eventually had to give up performing. In 1975, he died of a heart attack.

Josquin Desprez (Des Prez). DESPREZ (DES PREZ), JOSQUIN.

hoh′tăh   **jota** (Sp.). A national dance song of northern Spain, dating to the 17th century, in rapid triple time, somewhat like a fast WALTZ. It is usually played on the GUITAR, MANDOLIN, and CASTANETS.

Composers such as MIKHAIL GLINKA (*Jota aragonese*), NIKOLAI RIMSKY-KORSAKOV (*Capriccio Espagnole*), and FRANZ LISZT (*Rhapsodie espagnole,* c.1863) included jotas in their music.

Jubilee. Musical by COLE PORTER and LORENZ HART, 1935. The royal family in an unspecified exotic country is bored stiff by protocol. Taking advantage of a brief student rebellion, they leave the palace and, dropping all inhibitions, mingle with the common people incognito. Includes *Just One of Those Things* and the celebrated *Begin the Beguine*.

jubilus. In Roman Catholic liturgical chant, the last syllable of the word *alleluia* is often highly ornamented and greatly lengthened. This *jubilus* is meant to suggest the happiness one feels over salvation.

Judith. Opera by ALEXANDER SEROV, 1863, first performed in St. Petersburg. The LIBRETTO is drawn from the Apocrypha.

Judith, a patriotic Jewish woman, decides to risk her virtue by entering the tent of the Assyrian chieftain Holofernes, whose army besieges her city. She plies him with wine and, as he sinks into a drunken stupor, she cuts off his head, packs it into a sack, and returns to the city. She holds aloft the richly bearded head of the enemy king at an assembly, and the Jewish people explode in jubilation.

The score contains elements of a monumental ORATORIO style in the manner of HANDEL. It once enjoyed great popularity in Russia.

Judith. Opera by ARTHUR HONEGGER, 1926, first performed in Monte Carlo, on the same subject as ALEXANDER SEROV's work. Originally intended as a biblical drama in 13 scenes, it was eventually made into a full opera.

Judith. Choreographic poem by WILLIAM SCHUMAN, 1950, a "concerto for dancers and orchestra," first performed in Louisville, Kentucky. The subject is the same as that of the ALEXANDER SEROV and ARTHUR HONEGGER works.

jug. An earthen pitcher used in African-American traditional music by blowing into it to produce a low, hollow tone. *Jug band,* a 20th-century African-American traditional ensemble featuring found objects such as jugs, bones, and washboards along with strings, harmonica, kazoo, and winds in various combinations. It is associated with medicine shows and other rural settings.

MUSICAL INSTRUMENT

Juive, La. Grand opera by FROMENTAL HALÉVY, 1835. Underneath the highly melodramatic plot and heavily ROMANTIC music, there is a study of anti-Semitism and its ill-effects on all involved.

Before the opera begins in Constance, a Jew (Éléazar) has rescued the daughter of a magistrate (now Cardinal Brogni), who thought her lost in a war. Éléazar has raised her as Rachel in the Jewish religion. Cardinal Brogni has been persecuting the Jews of the city for years. Rachel has a lover, Prince Léopold, who pretends to be a Jew named Samuel and, unknown to her, is already married. Eventually, he has to reveal his true status.

When the shattered and betrayed Rachel denounces him to the court both are condemned to death, along with Éléazar. Rachel changes her story to save Léopold's life, but Éléazar refuses to save his and her lives by converting. The Jew hints to the Cardinal of the survival of his long-lost daughter, but the two are still burned at the stake. As the flames rise, Brogni asks one more time if his daughter is alive. When Éléazar says yes, the Cardinal pleads to know where she is. "There!," says Éléazar, pointing to Rachel. The two die as the curtain falls.

Julien. Opera by GUSTAVE CHARPENTIER, 1913, a failed sequel to the highly successful *Louise,* composed in 1900.

Julien, a painter who figured in the earlier opera, is visited by the deceased Louise's spirit in a vision to encourage him to continue working on his art. Eventually, he follows her to the land of death.

Julius Caesar. *See GIULIO CESARE IN EGITTO.*

PEOPLE IN MUSIC

Jullien, Louis (George Maurice Adolphe Roch Albert Abel Antonio Alexandre Noé Jean Lucien Daniel Eugène Joseph-le-brun Joseph-Barême Thomas Thomas Thomas-Thomas Pierre Arbon Pierre-Maurel Barthélemi Artus Alphonse Bertrand Dieudonné Emanuel Josué Vincent Luc Michel Jules-de-la-plane Jules-Bazin Julio César), famous eccentric French conductor and composer; b. Sisteron, April 23, 1812; d. Paris, March 14, 1860. The son of a bandmaster, Jullien went to Paris in 1833 and studied composition with the noted teachers Adolphe-Clair Le Carpentier and Fromental Halévy. However, he was a poor student who never completed his exercises. Instead, he began to compose light dances. Of these, the waltz *Rosita* attained enormous popularity in Paris.

Jullien left the Conservatory in 1836, and became engaged as conductor of dance music at the Jardin Turc. He also attempted to launch a musical journal. However, he was compelled to leave France in 1838 when a number of creditors sought payment on loans they had made to him. He went to London, where he conducted concerts at the Drury Lane Theatre in 1840–41. He then opened a series of "society concerts," at which he presented large choral works, such as GIOACCHINO ROSSINI's Stabat Mater, as well as movements from LUDWIG VAN BEETHOVEN's symphonies.

In 1847 Jullien engaged HECTOR BERLIOZ to conduct at the Drury Lane Theatre, which he had leased. He went bankrupt in 1848 but attempted to recoup his fortune by organizing a "concert monstre" with 400 players, three choruses, and three military bands. He succeeded in giving three such concerts in London in 1849.

Jullien then attempted the composition of an opera, *Pietro il Grande,* which he produced at his own expense at

Covent Garden in 1852. In 1853 he was engaged by P. T. Barnum for a series of concerts in the U.S. For his exhibition at the Crystal Palace in N.Y. in 1854, attended by a great crowd, he staged a huge, simulated fire for his *Fireman's Quadrille.*

Despite his eccentricities, Jullien possessed a true interest in musical progress. At his American concerts he made a point of including several works by American composers, including *Santa Claus Symphony* by WILLIAM HENRY FRY and some chamber music by GEORGE FREDERICK BRISTOW.

In 1854 Jullien returned to London, but his managerial ventures resulted in another failure. In 1859 he went to Paris, but was promptly arrested for debt and spent several weeks in prison. He died a few months later in an insane asylum to which he had been confined.

Jumbo. Musical by RICHARD RODGERS and LORENZ HART, 1935. Two circus managers are locked in fierce business rivalry. The daughter of one is in love with the son of the other. The financial rivalry is settled when the press agent of the girl's father arranges for arson and collects a large amount of money in insurance. The couple can then get married. Includes *My Romance, Little Girl Blue,* and *The Most Beautiful Girl in the World.*

Junge Lord, Der. Opera by HANS WERNER HENZE, 1965, first performed in Berlin. In a typical Henze musical critique of middle-class snobbery, a well-dressed ape arrives with his master in a small German town. The snobbish residents take the ape's simian grunts as the laconic utterances of a British lord. Naturally, the locals get their comeuppance.

Jupiter Symphony. WOLFGANG AMADEUS MOZART wrote many symphonies in the key of C major, but the greatest of all is his last, No. 41, K.551, *Jupiter.* Who gave this name to this work is unknown. The finale is a model of fugal construction with the main subject based on the simple progression of four notes: C–D–F–E.

just intonation. A system of tuning based on the precise relationships between string lengths, expressed in ratios.

Jullien used the pseudonym Roch Albert for his spectacular pieces, such as *Destruction of Pompeii.* He published some dance music (*Royal Irish Quadrille,* etc.) under his own name.

843

Unaccompanied voices or open strings will usually follow just (or pure) intonation. Other instruments can either be refingered, retuned, adapted, or newly built to play just relationships. Like other intonations, just intonation affects both the horizontal (melodic) and vertical (harmonic) elements of pitch. It has its unique qualities (e.g., true CONSONANCE and the expansion of consonance beyond the TRIAD) and limitations (finding instruments to play the unlimited possibility of ratios, to permit key changes).

Ancient Greek theory operated in just intonation, and it seems possible that this approach persisted into the second millennium A.D. There were a few attempts to accommodate just intonation over the centuries, but only in the 20th century did musicians appear who were willing to challenge the established 12-note equally tempered scale by building or adapting instruments, and then devising the theory and notation, to compose in just tuning. These included HARRY PARTCH, BEN JOHNSTON, LOU HARRISON, and many West Coast composers. *See also* ACOUSTICS.

K

Kabalevsky, Dmitri (Borisovich), noted Russian composer; b. St. Petersburg, Dec. 30, 1904; d. Moscow, Feb. 14, 1987. When he was 14, Kabalevsky's family moved to Moscow, where he received his primary musical education at the Scriabin Music School from 1919 to 1925. He also studied music theory privately, and in 1925 he entered the Moscow Conservatory in composition and piano. In 1932 he was appointed instructor in composition there, and in 1939 a full professor. Through his long career, Kabalevsky developed many methods of music education that became widely adopted in the Soviet Union, and he served on several government committees on music education.

As a pianist, composer, and conductor, Kabalevsky made guest appearances in Europe and the U.S. His music is typical of the Russian school of composition in its Soviet period. His melodic writing is marked by broad DIATONIC melodies invigorated by an energetic rhythmic pulse. While adhering to basic tonality, his harmony is apt to be rich in euphonious DISSONANCES.

A prolific composer, Kabalevsky wrote in all musical genres. In his operas he successfully reflected both the lyrical and the dramatic aspects of the librettos. Typical of the period, several of these operas were based on Soviet subjects that were acceptable to the government. His instrumental writing was functional, taking into consideration the capacities of the instruments.

In addition to his operas, Kabalevsky's compositions include orchestral works, including four symphonies (1932; 1934; 1934; 1956, *The Comedians*); two string quartets (1928, 1945), many piano works, including children's pieces; vocal works including numerous school songs and choruses; a requiem for voices and orchestra (Moscow, 1963); an oratorio, *A Letter to the 30th Century* (1970); incidental music for plays; and film scores.

Kaddish. Symphony No. 3 by LEONARD BERNSTEIN, 1963, for female speaker, mixed chorus, soprano solo, boys' choir, and orchestra. It was first performed in Tel Aviv, with Bernstein conducting. The Kaddish is a Hebrew lamentation for the dead, and Bernstein dedicated his score to the memory of President John Kennedy. The text is partly in Hebrew and partly in Aramaic, the language spoken by Jesus Christ.

Kagel, Mauricio, remarkable Argentine composer; b. Buenos Aires, Dec. 24, 1931. Kagel studied with the well-known Argentine composers JUAN CARLOS PAZ and ALFREDO SCHIUMA, and also took courses in philosophy and literature at the University of Buenos Aires.

PEOPLE IN MUSIC

In 1949 Kagel became associated with the Agrupación Nueva Música (New Music Group). From 1949 to 1956 he was choral director at the Teatro Colón. In 1957 he obtained a stipend for the Academic Cultural Exchange with West Germany and went to Cologne, which he made his permanent home. In 1961 and 1963 he gave lectures and demonstrations of modern music in the U.S., and in 1964–65 he taught composition at the State University of New York at Buffalo. In 1969 he became director of the Institute of New Music at the Rheinische Musikschule in Cologne. In 1974 he was made professor at the Cologne Hochschule für Musik. In 1977 he became a member of the Akademie der Künste in Berlin. He was awarded the Mozart Medal of Frankfurt am Main in 1983 and was made a Commandeur de L'Ordre des Arts et des Lettres of France in 1985. In 1989 he was composer-in-residence at the Cologne Philharmonie. He is the author of *Worte über Musik: Gespräche, Aufsätze, Reden, Hörspiele* (Munich, 1991).

As a composer, Kagel evolved an extremely complex method. He used complex, SERIAL organization of NOTES, INTERVALS, and DURATIONS, supplemented by ALEATORY (chance) techniques. In his musical works, he tries to unite all elements of human expression, aiming at the creation of a universe of theatrical arts in their visual, aural, and social aspects. Among his many dramatic works are *Aus Deutschland,* lieder opera (1977–80), *Der Tribun* for political orator, marching band, and loudspeaker (1978–79), *. . . nach einer Lektüre von Orwell,* theater picture or scenic environment (1982–83), and *Zwei Akte* for two actors, saxophone, and harp (1988–89). His orchestral works include *Les idées fixes* (1988–89), *Die Stücke der Windrose* for salon orchestra (1988–89), *Op.1.991* (1990), and *Konzertstück* for kettledrum and orchestra (1990–92). He also composed numerous chamber works, vocal pieces, and tape and electronic scores.

Kaiserquartett. EMPEROR QUARTET.

Kalevala. The great national epic of Finland, compiled by the Finnish scholar Elias Lönnrot (1802–84). The source material, medieval epic songs, had survived primarily in oral tradition. Its verses contain numerous references to the healing properties of music. In several passages, the wounds of heroes are healed by chanting the story of how the wounds were inflicted.

kalimba. *See* LAMELLAPHONES.

Kalomiris, Manolis, distinguished Greek composer and pedagogue; b. Smyrna, Dec. 26, 1883; d. Athens, April 3, 1962. Kalomiris studied composition and music history at the Conservatory of the Gesellschaft der Musikfreunde in Vienna from 1901 to 1906. He then went to Russia, where he taught piano at a private school in Kharkov.

In 1911 Kalomiris settled in Athens, where he taught at the Conservatory until 1919. He was founder-director of the Hellenic Conservatory from 1919 to 1926 and of the National Conservatory from 1926 to 1948. He was greatly esteemed as a teacher. He published several textbooks on HARMONY, COUNTERPOINT, and ORCHESTRATION, and also wrote music criticism.

Kalomiris promoted Greek nationalism in his music. Almost all his works are based on Greek folk-song melodies or SCALES, and many are inspired by Hellenic subjects. In his harmonies and instrumentation he followed the Russian school of composition, with the added influence of RICHARD

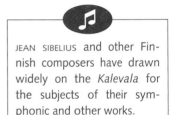

JEAN SIBELIUS and other Finnish composers have drawn widely on the *Kalevala* for the subjects of their symphonic and other works.

PEOPLE IN MUSIC

WAGNER, which was felt in his lush, bass-heavy accompaniments. His compositions include operas, orchestral works, chamber music, piano pieces, choruses, and songs.

kamānja (from Pers., *kamān,* bow; Arab., *kamānja*). Persian spike FIDDLE, dating from the end of the first millennium A.D. It has a round or heart-shaped body, long neck and long spike, and two or four strings tuned (singly or in pairs) a PERFECT FOURTH apart.

Kamarinskaya. Symphonic fantasy by MIKHAIL GLINKA, 1850. It is based on two Russian songs: a wedding march and the Russian peasant dance of the same name.

kammer (Ger.). Chamber; court. *Kammermusik,* chamber music; *Kammermusiker,* court musician; *Kammerkantate,* chamber cantata; *Kammerton* (chamber tone), tuning fork.

Kammersymphonie (Chamber symphony). Work by ARNOLD SCHOENBERG, 1906, first performed in Vienna seven years later. The one-movement *Kammersymphonie* joins sonata form and symphonic structure. It is a transitional work in Schoenberg's career, moving toward his mature use of ATONAL MUSIC in its use of the WHOLE TONE SCALE and harmonies based on PERFECT FOURTHS, instead of the more common thirds.

Kander, John (Harold), American composer of popular music; b. Kansas City, Mo., Mar. 18, 1927. Kander studied piano privately, then took courses at Columbia University in N.Y. In 1962, he tried his hand at a Broadway musical, *The Family Affair,* but was unsuccessful. That same year he teamed up with the lyricist Fred Ebb (b. N.Y., April 8, 1932), with whom he produced the hit songs *My Coloring Book* and *I Don't Care Much.*

Encouraged by their success, Kander and Ebb wrote the musical *Flora, the Red Menace* in 1965 as a vehicle for Liza Minnelli. It was followed a year later by their smash hit *Cabaret,* which won the Tony and Drama Critics awards and was made into a film in 1972. Among their subsequent shows were *Zorba* (1968), *Chicago* (1975), *Woman of the*

MUSICAL
INSTRUMENT

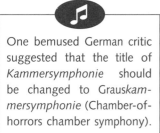

PIOTR ILYICH TCHAIKOVSKY considered that the entire Russian symphonic school was expressed in this work, as an oak in an acorn.

kähm′mer

One bemused German critic suggested that the title of *Kammersymphonie* should be changed to Graus*kammersymphonie* (Chamber-of-horrors chamber symphony).

PEOPLE IN MUSIC

Year (1981), *The Rink* (1984), and *Kiss of the Spiderwoman* (1990).

kantele. A PSALTERY dating from at least the 11th century. It is the national instrument of Finland and mentioned in the *KALEVALA*. The instrument has a trapezoidal shape. Originally the four horsehair strings were tuned to the scale G–A–B♭–C–D, but the instrument was later fitted with a variable number of metal strings. The kantele is held in the lap and played with bare fingers.

There are numerous related instrument in Eastern Europe, such as the Russian GUSLI, Estonian *kannel,* Latvian *kokle,* and Lithuanian *kanklės.*

Kantner, Paul. *See* JEFFERSON AIRPLANE.

Karajan, Herbert von, preeminent Austrian conductor in the grand Germanic tradition; b. Salzburg, April 5, 1908; d. Anif, near Salzburg, July 16, 1989. Karajan was a son of a

MUSICAL
INSTRUMENT

PEOPLE IN MUSIC

◄

Herbert von Karajan, c. 1960. (Hulton-Deutsch Collection/ Corbis)

cultured family of Greek–Macedonian extraction whose original name was Karajannis. His father was a medical officer who played the clarinet, and his brother was a professional organist.

Karajan began his musical training as a pianist, taking lessons at the Salzburg Mozarteum. Eventually he went to Vienna, where he pursued academic training at a technical college while continuing to take piano lessons. He then entered the Vienna Academy of Music as a conducting student.

In 1928 Karajan made his conducting debut with a student orchestra at the Vienna Academy of Music. Shortly afterward, in early 1929, he made his professional debut with the Salzburg Orchestra. He then received an engagement as conductor of the Ulm Stadttheater from 1929 to 1934. From Ulm he went to Aachen in 1935, where he was made conductor of the Stadttheater and subsequently served as Generalmusikdirektor until 1942.

In 1938 Karajan conducted his first performance with the Berlin Philharmonic, the orchestra he would lead for more than three decades. Later that year, he conducted LUDWIG VAN BEETHOVEN's *Fidelio* at his debut with the Berlin Staatsoper. After his performance of RICHARD WAGNER's *Tristan und Isolde* soon thereafter, he was hailed by the *Berliner Tageblatt* as "das Wunder Karajan" ("the wonder[ful] Karajan").

Karajan's growing fame as a master of both opera and symphony led to engagements elsewhere in Europe. In 1938 he conducted opera at La Scala in Milan and also made guest appearances in Belgium, the Netherlands, and Scandinavia. In 1939 he became conductor of the symphony concerts of the Berlin Staatsoper Orchestra.

There was a dark side to Karajan's character. He became fascinated by the powerful and ruthless National Socialist (Nazi) party, and in 1933 he registered in the Salzburg office of the Austrian Nazi party. Barely a month later, he joined the German Nazi party in Ulm. He lived to regret these actions after the collapse of the Nazi empire.

Karajan's personal affairs also began to interfere with his career. He married the operetta singer Elmy Holgerloef in 1938, but divorced her in 1942 to marry Anita Gütermann.

In 1947 Karajan was officially forgiven for his Nazi sympathies by the Allied army of occupation.

Trouble came when suspicious Nazi officials discovered that she was one-quarter Jewish and suggested divorce. But World War II was soon to end, and so was the Nazis' power. Karajan divorced Gütermann in 1958 to marry the French fashion model Eliette Mouret.

Karajan was characteristically self-assertive and demanding in his personal relationships and in his numerous conflicts with managers and players. Although he began a close relationship with the Vienna Symphony Orchestra in 1948, he left it in 1958. His association as conductor of the Philharmonia Orchestra of London from 1948 to 1954 did more than anything to reestablish his career after World War II, but in later years he ended his relationship with that ensemble.

When WILHELM FURTWÄNGLER, longtime conductor of the Berlin Philharmonic, died in 1954, Karajan was chosen to lead the orchestra on its first tour of the U.S. However, he insisted that he would lead the tour only on the condition that he be duly elected Furtwängler's successor. Protesters were in evidence for his appearance at N.Y.'s CARNEGIE HALL with the orchestra in 1955, but his Nazi past did not prevent the musicians of the orchestra from electing him their conductor during their visit to Pittsburgh on March 3. After their return to Germany, the West Berlin Senate ratified the musicians' vote on April 5, 1955.

Karajan soon came to dominate the musical life of Europe as no other conductor had ever done. In addition to his prestigious Berlin post, he served as artistic director of the Vienna Staatsoper from 1956 until he resigned in a bitter dispute with its general manager in 1964. He concurrently was artistic director of the Salzburg Festival from 1957 to 1960, and thereafter he remained closely associated with it. From 1969 to 1971 he held the title of artistic adviser of the Orchestre de Paris.

In the meantime, Karajan consolidated his positions in Berlin and Salzburg. In 1963 he conducted the Berlin Philharmonic in a performance of Beethoven's Ninth Symphony at the gala concert inaugurating the orchestra's magnificent new concert hall, the Philharmonie. In 1967 he organized his own Salzburg Easter Festival, which became one of the world's leading musical events. In 1967 he renegotiated his

Karajan became a world-renowned artist. He went on frequent tours of Europe and Japan with the Berlin Philharmonic, and also took the orchestra to the Soviet Union in 1969 and China a decade later.

contract and was named conductor-for-life of the Berlin Philharmonic. He made a belated Metropolitan Opera debut in N.Y. that same year, conducting Wagner's DIE WALKÜRE.

In 1982 Karajan again made news when he personally selected the 23-year-old clarinetist Sabine Meyer to be a member of the Berlin Philharmonic (any romantic reasons for his insistence were not apparent). The musicians of the orchestra rejected her because of their standing rule to exclude women, but also because the majority of the musicians had less appreciation of Fräulein Meyer as an artist than Karajan himself did. A compromise was reached, however, and in 1983 she was allowed to join the orchestra on probation. She resigned in 1984 after a year of uneasy coexistence.

In 1985 Karajan celebrated his 30th anniversary as conductor of the Berlin Philharmonic, and in 1988 his 60th anniversary as a conductor. In 1987 he conducted the New Year's Day Concert of the Vienna Philharmonic, which was televised to millions on both sides of the Atlantic. In early 1989 he made his last appearance in the U.S., conducting the Vienna Philharmonic at N.Y.'s Carnegie Hall. Soon thereafter he announced his retirement from his Berlin post, citing failing health. Shortly before his death, he dictated an autobiographical book to Franz Endler, which was published in an English translation in 1989.

Karajan amassed a huge personal fortune during his career. His records were among the best-selling of all classical artists, and he is said to have made over 800 records and videotapes. He had many lavish vacation homes and participated in many sports, including mountain climbing and skiing, as well as piloting his own plane.

Karajan was also a devotee of assorted physical and spiritual fads. He practiced yoga and aerobics, and for a while embraced Zen Buddhism. Moreover, he was known to believe in the transmigration of souls, and he expressed a hope of being reborn as an eagle soaring above the Alps, his favorite mountain range. As an alternative, he investigated cryogenics (the freezing of a dead body), hoping that his body could be thawed a century or so later to enable him to enjoy yet another physical incarnation. None of these actions prevented him from being overcome by a sudden heart attack in his home in the Austrian Alps. A helicopter with a medical staff was quickly summoned to fly him to a hospital, but it arrived too late.

karatāli. Indian circular wooden clappers, with short handles. Each clapper is held in one hand and clicked together. The instrument is known throughout many different Indian cultures and language groups.

Kashchei, the Immortal. Opera by NIKOLAI RIMSKY-KORSAKOV, 1902, first performed in Moscow, 1902. Kashchei's daughter has magical powers that she inherited from her grandfather. By means of a magic potion, she causes Prince Ivan to forget his beloved bride. This done, she sharpens a sword with which she plans to kill him, but at the crucial moment a tempest clears the air and awakens the prince. He returns to his beloved and Kashchei's evil domain is blown away.

This opera is rarely performed, even in Russia, but it is an important work that influenced a whole generation of Russian compo-sers. IGOR STRAVIN-SKY's symphonic poem *THE FIRE-BIRD* (which features a dance of Kashchei's pagan hordes) was influenced by the harmonic and rhythmic innovations introduced by Rimsky-Korsakov in this opera.

Káta Kabanová. Opera by LEOŠ JANÁČEK, 1921, first produced in Brno. The libretto is based on the

Scene from Káta Kabanová. (Robbie Jack, Corbis)

853

tragedy *The Storm* by the Russian playwright Alexander Ostrovsky (1823–86). Káta carries on clandestinely with a friend of her husband's. Internal guilt and external condemnation drive her to suicide, which she accomplished by diving into the Volga during a storm.

katabasis (Grk., retreat, descent). As explained in the DOCTRINE OF AFFECTS, descending melodic passages that illustrate states of mind such as depression and humiliation. The settings of texts relating to falls from grace and descents into hell are examples.

Katerina Izmailova. See LADY MACBETH OF THE MTZENSK DISTRICT.

Kavafian, Ani, gifted Turkish-born American violinist of Armenian descent, sister of Ida Kavafian; b. Istanbul, May 10, 1948. In 1956 Kavafian went with her family to the U.S., where she took violin lessons in Detroit. She then entered the Juilliard School of Music in N.Y., where she received instruction in violin and in chamber music performance from members of the Juilliard Quartet, earning a Master of Arts degree in 1972.

PEOPLE IN MUSIC

In 1969 Kavafian made her debut at Carnegie Recital Hall in N.Y. Her European debut followed in Paris in 1973. She appeared as soloist with leading orchestras and also played chamber music concerts, serving as an artist-member of the Chamber Music Society of Lincoln Center from 1980. She likewise gave duo performances with her sister.

Beginning in 1982, Kavafian taught at the Mannes College of Music, and at the Manhattan School of Music and Queens College of the City University of N.Y., beginning a year later. On Sept. 24, 1993, she was soloist in the premiere of TOD MACHOVER's *Forever and Ever,* a concerto for hyperviolin and chamber orchestra, with Hugh Wolff and the St. Paul (Minnesota) Chamber Orchestra.

PEOPLE IN MUSIC

Kavafian, Ida, talented Turkish-born American violinist of Armenian descent, sister of ANI KAVAFIAN; b. Istanbul, Oct. 29, 1952. In 1956 Kavafian went with her family to the U.S., where she took up violin studies in Detroit at the age of six. She entered the Juilliard School in N.Y. in 1969, where she continued her training, earning a Master of Arts degree in 1975.

Kavafian won the Vianna da Motta International Violin Competition in Lisbon in 1973 and the silver medal at the International Violin Competition of Indianapolis in 1982. She helped to found the chamber group Tashi in 1973, and subsequently toured with it. She made her N.Y. recital debut in 1978 and her European debut in London in 1982. She frequently played in duo concerts with her sister, Ani. In 1988 she was awarded the Avery Fisher Career Grant, and in 1993 she became a member of the Beaux Arts Trio.

Kay, Ulysses Simpson, eminent African-American composer, nephew of Joseph "King" Oliver; b. Tucson, Ariz., Jan. 7, 1917; d. Englewood, N.J., May 20, 1995. Kay received early training at home. On the advice of his uncle, the famous jazz cornetist Joe "King" Oliver, he studied piano.

In 1934 Kay enrolled at the University of Arizona at Tucson, earning a Bachelor of Music degree in 1938. He then went to study at the Eastman School of Music in Rochester, N.Y., where he earned his Masters degree two years later. In 1941–42 he attended the classes of German composer PAUL HINDEMITH at the Berkshire Music Center in Tanglewood, Massachusetts.

Kay served in the U.S. Navy from 1942 to 1945, then studied composition with the well-known experimental composer OTTO LUENING at Columbia University from 1946 to 1949. He went to Rome as winner of the American Rome Prize, and was attached there to the American Academy until 1952. From 1953 to 1968 he was employed as a consultant by Broadcast Music Inc. (BMI) in N.Y.

Kay was on the faculty of Boston University in 1965 and that of the University of California, Los Angeles in 1966–67. In 1968, he was appointed professor of music at the Herbert H. Lehman College in N.Y., where he was made Distinguished Professor in 1972, retiring in 1988. He received honorary doctorates from several American universities.

Kay's music is distinctly American, particularly in its rhythmic intensity. In HARMONY and COUNTERPOINT, he

PEOPLE IN MUSIC

pursues a moderately advanced style, introducing DISSO-NANCES when appropriate. His instrumentation is masterly. His compositions include operas, a ballet score, orchestral works, chamber and solo works, band music, choral pieces, songs, and film scores, including *The Quiet One* from 1948.

kayagum. Korean 12-stringed ZITHER with moveable bridges, dating from the turn of the 7th century.

Kaye, Sammy, American bandleader; b. Lakewood, Ohio, March 13, 1910; d. Ridgewood, N.J., June 2, 1987. He graduated from Ohio University. Having learned to play the CLARINET and alto SAXOPHONE, he organized his own band, which gained notice in a coast-to-coast radio broadcast in 1935. He scored his first hit with a recording of the title song from the film *Rosalie* in 1937.

After appearing in N.Y. in 1938, he became one of the most popular bandleaders of the SWING era, as millions were enticed to "Swing and Sway with Sammy Kaye." He was host of the *Sunday Serenade* radio show and later made appearances on television. During a career of some 50 years, he made more than 100 recordings. Among the most popular were *The Old Lamp-Lighter, Harbor Lights, Remember Pearl Harbor, I Left My Heart at the Stage Door Canteen,* and *Walkin' to Missouri.*

kazoo. A toy instrument consisting of a short tube with a membrane at one end, into which the player hums, producing a curiously nasal tone. Also known as MIRLITON, and, in the 17th century, a *flûte-eunuque* (eunuch flute).

Kempff, Wilhelm (Walter Friedrich), distinguished German pianist; b. Juterbog, Nov. 25, 1895; d. Positano, Italy, May 23, 1991. He studied piano with his father, also named Wilhelm Kempff. At the age of nine he entered the Berlin Hochschule für Musik, where he studied composition and piano. He also attended the University of Berlin.

Kempff began his concert career in 1916, and, two years later, he made the first of many appearances with the Berlin Philharmonic. From that time he toured throughout Europe, South America, and Japan, featuring improvisation as

MUSICAL
INSTRUMENT

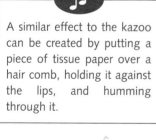

PEOPLE IN MUSIC

A similar effect to the kazoo can be created by putting a piece of tissue paper over a hair comb, holding it against the lips, and humming through it.

PEOPLE IN MUSIC

part of his programs. From 1924 to 1929 he was director of the Stuttgart Hochschule für Musik. From 1957 he gave annual courses in Positano, Italy. He made his London debut in 1951 and his American debut in N.Y. in 1964. He continued to appear in concerts well past his 80th year.

Kempff represented the classic tradition of German pianism. He avoided adding extra ornamentation or effects to his performances of WOLFGANG AMADEUS MOZART, LUDWIG VAN BEETHOVEN, FRANZ SCHUBERT, and other masters.

Kennedy, Nigel (Paul), versatile English violinist; b. Brighton, Dec. 28, 1956. Kennedy was born into a family of cellists, and in 1972 became a student of the well-known violin teacher Dorothy DeLay at the Juilliard School in N.Y.

In 1977, Kennedy made his London debut as soloist with the Philharmonia Orchestra and subsequently performed throughout his homeland and on the Continent. In 1985 he made his first tour of the U.S. His interests range over the field of serious, JAZZ, ROCK, and POP music. He has been closely associated with the jazz violinist STÉPHANE GRAPPELLI and has led his own rock group. Kennedy's repertoire extends from JOHANN SEBASTIAN BACH to DUKE ELLINGTON. He also played WILLIAM WALTON's Viola Concerto.

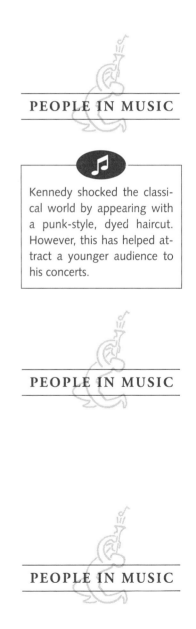

PEOPLE IN MUSIC

Kennedy shocked the classical world by appearing with a punk-style, dyed haircut. However, this has helped attract a younger audience to his concerts.

Keppard, Freddie, African-American jazz cornetist; b. New Orleans, Feb. 15, 1889; d. Chicago, July 15, 1933. Keppard learned to play the MANDOLIN, VIOLIN, and ACCORDION before mastering the CORNET. In 1906 he organized his own group, the Olympia Orchestra, and in 1912 became coleader of the Original Creole Orchestra, playing with it in Los Angeles, Chicago, and N.Y.

After moving to Chicago, Keppard played with "King" Oliver, Jimmie Noone, and others. Although forgotten in the last years of his life, he was a pioneer jazz figure. He had few equals as a cornetist in his time.

PEOPLE IN MUSIC

Kern, Jerome (David), famous American composer for stage and screen; b. N.Y., Jan. 27, 1885; d. there, Nov. 11, 1945. Kern was educated in N.Y. public schools, studying music with his mother, then at the N.Y. College of Music in

PEOPLE IN MUSIC

1902–03. He subsequently spent a year studying theory and composition in Heidelberg, Germany.

Jerome Kern, c. 1938. (Hulton-Deutsch Collection/ Corbis)

Kern then returned to N.Y., where he became pianist and salesman for a publishing firm in 1905. That same year, he published his first song, *How'd You Like to Spoon with Me,* which became famous. In 1906 he was in London, where he was connected with a theatrical production.

Kern gained his first success as a composer for the stage with his musical comedy *The Red Petticoat,* which opened in N.Y. in 1912. He continued to write for the stage through the '40s, as well as for films beginning in the '30s.

Kern's greatest success was SHOW BOAT, which premiered in Washington, D.C., in 1927. A most remarkable score, and one of the finest of its kind in the genre, it contains the famous song *Ol' Man River.* It has been widely proclaimed a classic of American musical theater and has been revived by opera companies as well.

In addition to *Show Boat,* Kern composed over 40 stage musicals, including *Very Good Eddie* (1915), *Roberta* (1933), and *Very Warm for May* (1939). Among the films he scored were *Swing Time* (1936) and *Cover Girl* (1944). He also wrote songs that were added into other musicals and films, including *The Last Time I Saw Paris* for *Lady Be Good* from 1941. Among the lyricists he worked with were Oscar Hammerstein II, Dorothy Fields, Johnny Mercer, and IRA GERSHWIN.

Kern's orchestral works include *Scenario* (based on themes from *Show Boat;* 1941) and *Mark Twain Suite* (1942).

kettledrum. *See* TIMPANI.

key. 1. (Fr. *tonalité;* Ger. *Tonalität, Tonart;* It. *tonalità;* Sp. *tonalidad*). The series of TONES forming any given MAJOR or MINOR SCALE, with reference to their harmonic relations, particularly the relation of the other tones to the TONIC or keynote.

Chromatic key, one having SHARPS or FLATS in the signature; *extreme key,* a remote key; *major key,* one having a major THIRD and SIXTH; *minor key,* one having a minor third and sixth; *natural key,* one with neither sharps nor flats in the signature; *parallel key,* either a minor key with the same keynote as a given major key, or vice versa; *remote key,* an indirectly related key.

2. (Lat. *clavis;* Fr. *touche;* Ger. *Taste;* It. *tasto;* Sp. *tecla;* Russ. *klavisha*). A finger lever in the keyboard of a PIANO or ORGAN, traditionally covered with ivory. Also, a pedal or foot key in the organ or pedal piano. 3. (Fr., *clef;* Ger., *Klappe;* It., *chiave;* Sp., *llave*). A flat padded disk attached to a lever worked by the finger or thumb, closing the sound holes of various wind instruments. 4. A tuning wrench.

key action. In the keyboard of a PIANO or ORGAN, the keys and the entire mechanism connected with and set in action by them.

key harp (keyed harp; It. *clavi-arpa*). A frame HARP controlled by a keyboard. The strings are plucked by the piano-like mechanism. The instrument is first reported in the 17th century.

key signature. The ACCIDENTALS at the beginning of a composition (and each succeeding staff) which indicate the overall key of a piece. There are 12 different MAJOR keys and 12 MINOR, identified by the number of sharps or flats in the key signature.

Changes of key signature in the course of a composition are common, but they are not made for each passing MODULATION. Even the extensive exposition of the second SUBJECT in a SONATA FORM movement, usually in the DOMINANT key, never warrants a change of key signature. However, in works

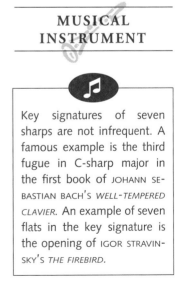

MUSICAL INSTRUMENT

Key signatures of seven sharps are not infrequent. A famous example is the third fugue in C-sharp major in the first book of JOHANN SEBASTIAN BACH'S *WELL-TEMPERED CLAVIER*. An example of seven flats in the key signature is the opening of IGOR STRAVINSKY'S *THE FIREBIRD*.

not bound by a strict key relationship, in which tonalities range far and wide, composers often prefer to signalize a modulation by changing the key signature. The score of GUSTAV MAHLER's Sixth Symphony includes episodes in every major and minor key, each carrying an appropriate key signature.

Relative major and minor keys are those having the same key signature. The customary raised seventh (leading tone) in a minor key is marked by an accidental, as a G♯ in the key of A minor, or an F double-sharp in the key of G-sharp minor. In key signatures loaded with flats, the raised seventh in a minor key is the cancellation of the corresponding flat, becoming a natural, e.g., D♮ in E-flat minor. Attempts have been made by modern composers, among them BÉLA BARTÓK, to add accidentals in the key signature. A piece in G minor would then carry the mandatory two flats but also the extra F♯.

Key signatures are meaningless in 20th century ATONAL music. But as the atonal movement has waned, the key signature has made a strong comeback.

key stop. A key attached to the fingerboard of a VIOLIN so as to replace the fingers in stopping the strings. The instrument is called a key-stop (keyed-stop) violin.

key(ed) trumpet. A natural TRUMPET provided with keys, usually five, that function much as woodwind instrument keys do. The instrument was first made in Germany in the late 18th century. It had a softer tone than its predecessor, and thus never became popular as a solo instrument. By the mid-19th century, it had been replaced by the (modern) valve trumpet.

MUSICAL
INSTRUMENT

keyboard (Ger. *Klaviatur, Tastatur, Klavier;* Fr. *clavier;* It. *tastiera, tastatura*). A set of depressible keys or levers, usually laid out in horizontal MANUALS, that activates the sound-inducing mechanism on PIANOS, ORGANS, HARPSICHORDS, and other instruments of similar construction.

A large organ may have as many as five manuals, a harpsichord either one or two. A special feature on the organ is the pedal keyboard, arranged in rows of large white and black keys, that are operated by the feet. (Pedal pianos and pedal harpsichords have also been built.)

MUSICAL
INSTRUMENT

Through the centuries the arrangement of the 12 CHRO-MATIC NOTES within the octave has been formed with seven white keys on the lower level of the keyboard and five shorter black keys on the slightly raised level. The row of white keys forms a DIATONIC scale, and the row of black keys represents the PENTATONIC.

The opposition of the white and the black keys is standard on all piano keyboards, but the harpsichord, CLAVI-CHORD, and SPINET may possess a different coloring of these rows. There are antique harpsichords in which the color scheme is reversed, the diatonic keys being black and the pentatonic keys white. There are also instruments using red keys in either of the rows, much as in some chess games with chess pieces being red and white instead of the standard black and white.

The dimensions of the keys on all keyboard instruments are adjusted to the normal relaxed position of the five fingers of a human player resting on the five consecutive white keys.

Numerous attempts have been made to make the keyboard more handy, to adapt it for playing scales without a constant change of fingering. The JANKÓ KEYBOARD has six different but aligned rows of keys, one slightly above the other. A system of levers makes it possible to play the chromatic scale with the greatest of ease by letting the fingers walk from one row to another. The narrower Jankó keys made it possible for a pianist to reach the interval of a 14th with one hand. This makes it possible to play some unbridgeable intervals such as those found in ROBERT SCHU-MANN's *Symphonic Études.*

The Clutsam keyboard was in the form of a fan arc, with the radius of an arm's length. A pianist playing it must presumably be placed in the center of the circle, using outstretched arms at all times. Finally, the Fokker organ with 31 equal-tuned scale notes uses three colors and four sequential keyboards at a diagonal to allow the performance of the extra notes per octave.

None of these alternatives have replaced the original keyboard in the hearts and minds of pianists.

keynote. The first note of a KEY or SCALE; TONIC.

Some early organs had massive keyboards. They were so wide that the monks who used them had to play their church hymns with clenched fists, and even elbows, in order to depress the keys sufficiently to activate the pipes.

Khachaturian, Aram (Ilich), brilliant Russian composer of Armenian descent; b. Tiflis, June 6, 1903; d. Moscow, May 1, 1978. His father was a bookbinder. Khachaturian played TUBA in the school band, and also studied biology.

In 1922 Khachaturian went to Moscow and entered the Gnessin Music School, where he was a student for four years. He then studied composition privately with the school's founder, the composer Mikhail Gnessin, until 1929. That year, he entered the Moscow Conservatory, taking an undergraduate degree in 1934 and then finishing his postgraduate studies three years later. In 1933 he married the composer NINA MAKAROVA.

Khachaturian began composing at the age of 21 and soon progressed to the first rank of Soviet composers of his generation. He drew on Russian folk melodies, particularly the characteristic SCALE progressions of traditional Caucasian tunes, without quoting actual folk songs. His *Sabre Dance* from his ballet *Gayane* became popular all over the world.

In 1948 Khachaturian was severely criticized by the Central Committee of the Communist party, along with SERGEI PROKOFIEV, DMITRI SHOSTAKOVICH, and others, for writing music in a modern style. Although he admitted his deviations in this respect, he continued to compose essentially in his typical manner. Nonetheless, he was made a People's Artist of the USSR in 1954.

Beginning in the early '50s, Khachaturian began appearing in major world cities as the conductor of his own works. He made his American debut in Washington, D.C., in 1968, conducting the National Symphony Orchestra. Later that year, he conducted in N.Y. to a rousing audience reception.

Khachaturian's works include the ballets *Shchastye* (Happiness; premiered in 1939) and *Gayane,* including the *Sabre Dance* (premiered 1942; revised 1952 and 1957), as well as orchestral and other vocal works, mostly in praise of Soviet leaders and ideology. He also composed film music, marches for band, chamber music, and piano pieces.

Khachaturian's nephew, Karen (Surenovich) Khachaturian (b. Moscow, Sept. 19, 1920), is a composer and teacher.

Khan, (Ustad) **Ali Akbar,** Indian SAROD player, composer, and, with RAVI SHANKAR, one of the leading exponents of bringing Indian music to an international audience; b. Shibpur, Bengal (now Bangladesh), Apr. 14, 1922. Ali Akbar Khan was the son of the master musician and teacher (Ustad) Alauddin Khan (b. Bengal, c.1865; d. Bengal, Sept. 6, 1972). His father taught him (and Ravi Shankar) traditional Indian music. Khan's first performances took place in 1936. He later became a court musician in Jodhpur.

Khan's first U.S. performance took place in N.Y. in 1955, and the interest aroused led to many return visits. In 1956 he founded a college of music in Calcutta and, in 1967, a similar institution in Marin County, California.

Khan has become a world-renowned performer of Indian music, and continues to record and tour. Unlike Shankar, whom some Indian musicians criticize for "selling out" to the West, Khan is admired in his homeland for maintaining the pure, traditional style of performance and composition.

Traditionally, sarod players have a public repertoire of pieces and a secret repertoire that they only teach to their most-cherished students. Because Khan could not find a disciple worthy of learning his father's secret repertoire, in the mid-'80s he decided to record it so it would not be lost.

khorovod (Russ., *khor* + *vod*, leading chorus). Russian round dance of ancient origin. A scene featuring an adaptation of it is included in Igor Stravinsky's *Firebird*.

Khovanshchina. Music drama by MODEST MUSSORGSKY, 1886, posthumously produced in St. Petersburg. The title means "Khovanskyism," a contemptuous name used by young Peter the Great for the rebellious activity of the followers of Prince Khovansky, the leader of the "Old Believers." Surrounded by Peter's loyal troops, they throw themselves in a funeral fire rather than give up their cause.

The score, left unfinished by Mussorgsky, was completed by NIKOLAI RIMSKY-KORSAKOV. He provided the orchestration, and also smoothed out some of its more unusual harmonies and fixed some awkward melodic progressions.

Killing Me Softly With His Song. A 1973 No. 1 pop hit by Charles Fox and Norman Gimbel, and popularized by Roberta Flack. The song's subject is supposedly the singer-songwriter Don Maclean; apparently, one of his songs was upsetting to this song's composers! It was revived by the rap/pop group the Fugees in 1996.

This powerful quartet of tragic songs was prophetic of Mahler's own personal loss when his eldest daughter died of scarlet fever in 1907.

PEOPLE IN MUSIC

B. B. King, c. 1979. (Hulton-Deutsch Collection/ Corbis)

▶

Kindertotenlieder (Songs on the death of children). Song cycle by GUSTAV MAHLER, 1905, based on poems by Rückert.

King and I, The. Musical by RICHARD RODGERS and OSCAR HAMMERSTEIN II, 1951.

A Victorian widow is engaged by the king of Siam as a governess to his multiple offspring. She attempts to introduce him and his family to Western culture and ideas, which he initially resists. Naturally, they fall in love.

Rodgers did not use any "Eastern" elements in his score, perhaps wisely feeling he could at best only approximate the sound of traditional Siamese music. The show contains many hit songs, including *Getting to Know You, We Kiss in the Shadow, I Have Dreamed, I Whistle a Happy Tune, Hello Young Lovers,* and *Shall We Dance.*

King, "B. B." (Riley B.), important African-American BLUES singer and guitarist; b. Itta Bena, Miss., Sept. 16, 1925. While working on a farm, King learned to play GUITAR. By his teen years, he was working as a street singer.

When he was about 20 years old, he moved to Memphis, where he continued to play on street corners. He also shared a room with his second cousin, the blues guitarist Bukka White. He then worked as a disc jockey for a Memphis radio station under the name "Blues Boy," which became "B. B." His radio exposure led to a recording contract with the local Bullet label in 1949.

In 1950 King scored his first hit with his recording of *3 O'Clock Blues.* Through the '50s, King recorded and toured with a large band, building a large following in the Black community. In 1960 he signed with the major record label ABC, who hoped to duplicate with him the success that they had with RAY CHARLES. However, his audience remained within the blues community.

Then, in the mid-'60s, several British musicians staged a "blues revival." Electric guitarists like ERIC CLAPTON praised King, and he found a new audience among the large white rock audience. In 1968 he appeared at the popular rock concert hall the Fillmore West. He also scored a major R&B and pop hit that year with *The Thrill Is Gone,* which became one of his theme songs. A year later, King made his first tour of Europe. He then headed an all-blues concert at CARNEGIE HALL in N.Y. in 1970.

King has continued to perform and record prolifically through the '70s, '80s, and '90s. He won a GRAMMY AWARD in 1981 for his album *There Must Be a Better World Somewhere.* In 1989 he collaborated with the Irish rock band U2 on the blues-rock hit *When Love Comes to Town.*

Playing an electric guitar (nicknamed Lucille), B. B. King is one of the most innovative and soulful blues artists of our time. His single-note electric guitar leads are played cleanly and show great musical imagination. His vocals are emotion soaked and powerful.

King (born Klein), **Carole,** American pop singer and songwriter; b. N.Y., Feb. 9, 1941. King took piano lessons as a child. As a high school student, she started a female singing group called the Co-Sines.

At 17, King met the lyricist Gerry Goffin, whom she soon married. She recorded a couple of their songs, achieving a minor success with *Oh Neil,* an answer record to NEIL SEDAKA's 1959 hit *Oh Carol.* This attracted the attention of music publisher and record producer Don Kirshner, who hired the duo to write pop songs for his artists. Their first hit was for the SHIRELLES, who scored big in 1960

King's guitar gained its famous nickname of Lucille early in his career. He says that he was playing in a bar when a fight broke out over a woman named Lucille. The bar caught fire, and B. B. barely escaped with his life. He figured any woman who was worth dying over must be pretty special!

PEOPLE IN MUSIC

with their *Will You (Still) Love Me Tomorrow?*. Several other hits followed, among them *Some Kind of Wonderful, When My Little Girl Is Smiling, Up on the Roof, One Fine Day, I'm into Something Good, Take Good Care of My Baby, Do the Loco-Motion,* and *Goin' Back.* The duo ended their partnership and marriage in 1967.

King then moved to Los Angeles, where she formed a short-lived ROCK group, City, with guitarist Danny Kortchmar, who introduced her to his friend, singer-songwriter James Taylor. King played piano on Taylor's breakthrough album *Sweet Baby James,* in 1970. He returned the favor, appearing on her smash 1971 album *Tapestry,* which featured the hits *You've Got a Friend* (covered by Taylor in 1972), *I Feel the Earth Move,* and *So Far Away.*

King was never able to equal *Tapestry's* enormous success. Nonetheless, she has continued to record and perform through the '90s.

Tapestry sold over 10 million copies, a record for a female artist at that time.

King Lear. Concert overture by HECTOR BERLIOZ, 1834, first performed in Paris, with the composer conducting. Berlioz was extremely fond of Shakespeare, although he could not read the Bard in English. This orchestral work is a typical act of homage.

King of the Road. A 1965 ROGER MILLER country smash that also ranked high on the pop charts. One of the first odes to the life of the trucker, it inspired numerous parodies, including *Queen of the Road.*

King Priam. Opera by MICHAEL TIPPETT, 1962, to his own libretto based on the *Iliad,* premiered in Coventry.

Paris, son of Priam of Troy, kidnaps Helen (wife of the Greek king, Menelaus), starting the Trojan War. The opera focuses on Priam and the Greek hero Achilles. Priam's son Hector mistakenly kills Patroclus, who fought in disguise for Achilles. Achilles is roused from his tent and kills Hector in revenge. Priam comes to gather the body of his son in Achilles' tent. The old King and the young hero find a moment of understanding among enemies. By the end, Achilles is dead, and his son kills Priam as he kneels in prayer, while Troy falls.

King's Henchman, The. Opera by DEEMS TAYLOR, first performed at the Metropolitan Opera in N.Y., Feb. 17, 1927, one of the few American operas given by that institution. It had 14 performances and then sank into oblivion. The LIBRETTO was not American.

Its hero was the messenger of the King of England who was sent to fetch the royal bride from overseas. Instead, he takes her for himself, but commits suicide when his treachery is revealed. The SCORE is in the style of RICHARD WAGNER, as is the subject.

Kipnis, Alexander, eminent Russian-born American bass, father of IGOR KIPNIS; b. Zhitomir, Feb. 13, 1891; d. Westport, Conn., May 14, 1978. Kipnis studied conducting at the Warsaw Conservatory, graduating in 1912, and later took voice lessons at Berlin's Klindworth-Scharwenka Conservatory.

PEOPLE IN MUSIC

In 1913 Kipnis sang at Monti's Operetten Theater and in 1914 at the Filmzauber operetta theater. At the outbreak of World War I he was interned by the German government as an enemy alien, but he was soon released and made his operatic debut as the hermit in *Der Freischütz* at the Hamburg Opera in 1915. He sang there until 1917, then was a member of the Wiesbaden Opera until 1922.

Kipnis made his U.S. debut as Pogner in RICHARD WAGNER's *Die Meistersinger von Nürnberg* with the visiting German Opera Company in Baltimore in 1923. He then was a member of the Chicago Civic Opera from 1923 to 1932. He also sang regularly at the Berlin Städtische Oper during this same period, the Berlin State Opera from 1932 to 1935, and the Vienna State Opera from 1935 to 1938.

Kipnis became an American citizen in 1931. He subsequently made guest appearances at the Bayreuth, Salzburg, and Glyndebourne festivals, as well as at Covent Garden in London and the Teatro Colón in Buenos Aires. In 1940 he made his belated Metropolitan Opera debut in N.Y. as Gurnemanz in Wagner's *PARSIFAL.* He remained a member of the Metropolitan Opera company until 1946. He then devoted himself mainly to teaching. Through the years he appeared as a soloist with RICHARD STRAUSS, SIEGFRIED WAGNER, and ARTURO TOSCANINI.

PEOPLE IN MUSIC

Kipnis, Igor, distinguished American harpsichordist and fortepianist, son of ALEXANDER KIPNIS; b. Berlin, Sept. 27, 1930. In 1938 the family moved to the U.S., where Kipnis took piano lessons with his maternal grandfather, Heniot Lévy, a well-known pianist and teacher. After attending the Westport, Connecticut, School of Music, he studied at Harvard University, where he earned his bachelor's degree in 1952. He also took HARPSICHORD lessons with the noted musician and teacher Fernando Valenti.

After graduation, Kipnis served abroad in the Signal Corps of the U.S. Army. Returning to the U.S., he eked out his living as a bookstore salesman in N.Y. He later was employed as an editorial adviser to Westminster Records Co. He made his concert debut as a harpsichordist in a N.Y. radio broadcast in 1959, and his formal concert debut followed there in 1962. He taught at the Berkshire Music Center in Tanglewood, Massachusetts, during the summers of 1964–67.

In 1967 Kipnis made his first European tour, and subsequently appeared throughout the world. He served as an associate professor of fine arts from 1971 to 1975 and artist-in-residence from 1975 to 1977 at Fairfield University in Connecticut. He also taught and played at the Festival Music Society concerts in Indianapolis and taught at its Early Music Institute. In 1981 he made his debut as a FORTEPIANIST in Indianapolis, doing much to revive the instrument. In 1982 he became a visiting tutor at the Royal College of Music in Manchester, England. From 1983 to 1995 he also served as vice president and co-artistic director of the Connecticut Early Music Festival.

Kipnis also promoted interest in modern music. Such contemporary composers as NED ROREM, GEORGE ROCHBERG, Richard Rodney Bennett, Barbara Kolb, and John McCabe, wrote works for him. From 1995 he was active in a piano duo with Karen Kushner.

Kirchner, Leon, significant American composer; b. N.Y., Jan. 24, 1919. In 1928 the family went to Los Angeles, where Kirchner studied piano with the well-known pianist and teacher Richard Buhlig. In 1938 he entered the University of California, Berkeley, where he took courses in theory,

PEOPLE IN MUSIC

earning his Bachelor of Music degree in 1940 and a master's degree in music in 1949. He also took lessons with Swiss-born composer ERNEST BLOCH in San Francisco.

In 1942 Kirchner returned to N.Y., where he had fruitful private sessions with the modern composer ROGER SESSIONS. In 1943 he entered military service in the U.S. Army. After demobilization in 1946, he was appointed to the faculty of the San Francisco Conservatory, concurrently teaching at the University of California, Berkeley. In 1948 he received a Guggenheim fellowship, and from 1950 to 1954, he served as associate professor at the University of Southern California in Los Angeles.

Kirchner subsequently taught at Mills College in Oakland, California, from 1954 to 1961, and in 1961 was named professor of music at Harvard University, where he remained until his retirement in 1989. He also conducted the Harvard Chamber Players (from 1973) and the Harvard Chamber Orchestra (from 1978), and was engaged as a guest conductor and as a pianist with orchestras in the U.S. and overseas. He was elected a member of the National Institute of Arts and Letters and the American Academy of Arts and Sciences in 1962, and in 1994 he received a Kennedy Center Friedheim Award. In 1967 he was awarded the Pulitzer Prize in music for his Third String Quartet.

In his music, Kirchner takes a middle course. He is clearly a modern composer, but he does not follow any one school or technique. Through his natural inclination toward CLASSICAL order, he prefers formal types of composition, often following the established BAROQUE style. His finely crafted scores are also notable for their linear CHROMATICISM, asymmetric rhythms, and lyricism. Among his works are the opera *Lily* (1973–76; N.Y., April 14, 1977, composer conducting), various orchestral works, including *Music* for flute and orchestra (Indianapolis, Oct. 20, 1978) and *Music II* for orchestra (1990); and chamber works, including *Illuminations,* fanfare for nine instruments for the 350th anniversary of Harvard University (1986).

Kirk, (Rahsaan) **Roland,** African-American jazz instrumentalist, composer, and activist; b. Columbus, Ohio, Aug. 7, 1936; d. Bloomington, Ind., Dec. 5, 1977. Kirk lost his

PEOPLE IN MUSIC

Kirk was born Ronald Kirk, but changed his name to Roland and added the first name Rahsaan. He said that spirits came to him in a dream vision and told him to make these changes.

sight in infancy and was raised at the Ohio State School for the Blind. He began playing TRUMPET in the school band, but a doctor felt that the hard blowing the instrument demanded was putting too great a strain on his eyes. Around 1948 Kirk took up CLARINET and FLUTE instead.

By his mid-teen years, Kirk was already leading bands and performing in the Columbus area. While rummaging in the basement of a local music store, he discovered two strange SAXOPHONE-like instruments: the manzello (an alto saxlike instrument with a large bell) and the strich (something like a soprano saxophone, but larger). Kirk developed the capability to play these instruments, and an ordinary saxophone, all at the same time!

Pianist Ramsey Lewis heard Kirk play while passing through Columbus and recommended him to his record label, Cadet Records. They issued Kirk's first solo album in 1960. He then briefly recorded and toured with bassist CHARLES MINGUS's band in 1961. Kirk made his first trip to England in 1963, achieving great success in jazz clubs there.

From the mid-'60s, Kirk appeared with his own bands, under various names, including The Vibration Society. He toured Europe, Australia, and New Zealand. He composed many songs of the pop variety, including *Serenade to a Cuckoo; Here Comes the Whistleman; I Talk with the Spirits; Rip, Rig and Panic;* and *Funk Underneath.*

In the 1970s Kirk led the Jazz and People's Movement, which protested the lack of African-American music and musicians in U.S. mainstream broadcast culture. Even after suffering a stroke in 1975, he could still play with one hand. A second stroke, in 1977, took his life.

Kirk had a unique style. His playing combined the power of GOSPEL and R&B with the manic energy of BEBOP. His use of CIRCULAR BREATHING enabled him to play long melodic runs, far longer than most players could handle. And his pure showmanship was unrivaled: the figure of Kirk on stage wearing dark glasses and a crumpled hat, with three saxophones strapped around his neck, was unusual and riveting.

PEOPLE IN MUSIC

Kirkby, Emma, English soprano; b. Camberley, Feb. 26, 1949. Kirkby studied classics at Oxford, then made her debut in London in 1974. She specialized in early music. She was a member of the Academy of Ancient Music, the London Baroque, and the Consort of Musicke. In 1978 she toured the U.S., then gave concerts in the Middle East with the lutenist Anthony Rooley (1980–83). She made her operatic debut as Mother Nature in *Cupid and Death* by Gibbons and Locke in Bruges in 1983. Her U.S. opera debut followed in 1989 when she sang Dorinda in GEORGE FRIDERIC HANDEL's *Orlando.*

Kirkby's repertoire ranges from the Italian quattrocento to arias by Handel, WOLFGANG AMADEUS MOZART, and FRANZ JOSEPH HAYDN. She sang at a London Promenade Concert in works by CHARPENTIER and MONTEVERDI, and in 1996 at the Purcell Celebration at the London Barbican. Her careful attention to purity of intonation free from intrusive vibrato has been praised.

Kirnberger, Johann Philipp, noted German music theorist and pedagogue; b. Saalfeld (baptized), April 24, 1721; d. Berlin, July 26 or 27, 1783. Kirnberger studied VIOLIN and HARPSICHORD at home, then took ORGAN lessons in Grafenroda and in Sondershausen, where he also studied violin.

PEOPLE IN MUSIC

After completing his studies with Johann Sebastian Bach in Leipzig from 1739 to 1741, Kirnberger traveled in Poland during the 1740s as a tutor in various noble Polish families. From 1751 to 1754 he was violinist to Frederick the Great in Berlin and from 1754 to 1758 to Prince Heinrich of Prussia, and from 1758 to 1783 he was Kapellmeister to Princess Anna Amalie.

Kirnberger was greatly renowned as a teacher, numbering among his pupils J. A. P. Schulz, C. P. E. BACH, the Graun brothers, and J. F. Agricola. As a theoretical writer, he was regarded as one of the greatest authorities of his time, even though his presentations were often disorganized to such an extent that he had to call upon others to edit or even rewrite his publications. In his compositions he displayed a command of COUNTERPOINT and seriously strove to establish a scientific method of writing according to basic rules.

Kismet. A musical extravaganza, 1953, put together by George Forrest and Robert Wright, based on the music of ALEXANDER BORODIN.

The authors had previously borrowed music from EDVARD GRIEG for their 1944 Broadway hit *Song of Norway*.

The play tells the story of the ambitious wife of the Baghdad chief of police who drowns her husband in a fountain in order to marry the young caliph. The slow section from Borodin's *POLOVTZIAN DANCES* (*PRINCE IGOR*) is used as the basis for the song *Stranger in Paradise*. Another hit, *This Is My Beloved,* is taken from a Borodin string quartet.

Kismet was a major success on Broadway and in London. It was made into a film in 1955. An all-black version of the show renamed *Timbuktu* was staged on Broadway in 1978.

Kiss Me Kate. Musical by COLE PORTER, 1948. The plot concerns a group of actors performing Shakespeare's *The Taming of the Shrew* in Baltimore. The actors portraying Petruchio and Kate, the famous battling lovers, are themselves in love. And, like the Shakespearian characters, they are always fighting! There is the inevitable happy ending in both play and life. It includes the songs *Always True to You, Brush Up Your Shakespeare, Another Op'nin' Another Show, So in Love,* and *Wunderbar.*

Kiss, The (Hubička). Opera by BEDŘICH SMETANA, 1876. A widower is engaged to a young woman in his village, but she won't seal their betrothal with the traditional kiss for fear of arousing his dead wife's jealousy. Angered, the widower brings a girl from out of the tavern and kisses her. The bride-to-be is outraged and runs into the ever-dangerous woods. He finally tracks her down and forces a kiss.

Kissin, Evgeny, amazingly precocious Russian pianist; b. Moscow, Oct. 10, 1971. Kissin enrolled at the Gnessin Music School for Gifted Children in Moscow at the incredible (but verified) age of 6 as a student of Anna Kantor, who remained his only teacher.

At the age of 12 he gave performances of both FRÉDÉRIC CHOPIN piano concertos with the Moscow Philharmonic. International reputation came to him when he was engaged in 1987 to perform PIOTR ILYICH TCHAIKOVSKY's First Piano Concerto with HERBERT VON KARAJAN and the Berlin Philharmonic. In 1990 he made his U.S. debut playing Chopin's First Piano Concerto with the N.Y. Philharmonic, conducted by ZUBIN MEHTA. Ten days later there followed his

PEOPLE IN MUSIC

first appearance at Carnegie Hall, which astonished even the most seasoned listeners. He subsequently pursued a remarkably brilliant career as a soloist with the foremost orchestras of the world, as a recitalist, and as a chamber music artist. He made his first tour of the U.S. in 1991, and in 1997 he appeared at the Royal Festival Hall in London.

kit. A small, three-stringed VIOLIN, about 16 inches long, and tuned c_1–g_1–d_2. From the BAROQUE period through the 19th century, traveling dance teachers carried kits with them to accompany their lessons.

kithara (*cithara;* Grk.). National instrument of ancient Greece, a member of the LYRE family. It consists of a square sound box made of wood, with between 3 and 11 strings stretched from one side to the other, connected by a crossbar. Ancient sculpture and paintings show that similar instruments existed in Mesopotamia. The first Greek examples are depicted on vases from the 7th century B.C.

Kitt, Eartha, African-American singer of popular music and actress; b. North, S.C., Jan. 26, 1928. Kitt was taken to N.Y. as a child, where she sang in church, received PIANO training, and studied dance at the High School for Performing Arts.

Kitt won a scholarship to study dance with noted dancer and choreographer Katherine Dunham in 1944, and then traveled with her troupe in South America and Europe until 1950. She subsequently concentrated her career upon singing and acting, appearing in nightclubs, theaters, and films, and on recordings, radio, and television.

Kitt excelled particularly in earthy, passion-laden songs delivered in a low-key monotone. Her throaty growl also became a trademark. She has toured with her one-woman nightclub act for decades, with little change in her basic style (or looks!).

Klagende Lied, Das (The song of lament). Cantata by GUS-TAV MAHLER, 1880, with a text by the composer. The original version consisted of three parts: *Waldmärchen, Der Spielmann,* and *Hochzeitsstück.* In a subsequent revision, the first part was separated from the cantata.

MUSICAL INSTRUMENT

Some kits were cleverly built into walking sticks, for easy portability; hence the nickname walking-stick fiddle.

MUSICAL INSTRUMENT

PEOPLE IN MUSIC

The English pop group Bronski Beat collaborated with Eartha Kitt on their 1989 hit *Cha Cha Heels.*

klăng^{k′}far-bĕ

Klangfarbe (Ger., tone color). In the 20th century, *Klangfarbe* has come to refer to a special dimension of musical sound.

"It must be possible," ARNOLD SCHOENBERG states in his *Harmonielehre* (1911), "to form a succession of Klangfarben possessing a mutual relationship of a logical type equivalent to that of the melody formed by a succession of different tones." This melody of tone colors is exemplified in the movement originally entitled *The Changing Chord* in his *Fünf Orchesterstücke,* op.16, composed in 1909.

ANTON WEBERN developed the idea in the direction of serialism, in which the fundamental Klangfarbe series is formed by the successive sounding of 12 different notes by 12 different instruments.

klăng^k-fahr-bĕn-mel′oh-dē

Klangfarbenmelodie (Ger., a melody of tone colors). This description was first used by ARNOLD SCHOENBERG in his *Harmonielehre* (1911), in which he proposed to regard the change of instrumental color as a melodic change. Thus a tone color melody can be created by playing the same note successively on different instruments. Schoenberg himself never carried out the idea, but his disciples ALBAN BERG and ANTON WEBERN developed it more fully. It received its complete development with their avant-garde followers, in serial and electronic music.

klăh-vēr′

MUSICAL INSTRUMENT

Klavier (Ger.). 1. KEYBOARD. 2. A keyboard stringed instrument. In the 18th century, a CLAVICHORD or HARPSICHORD; now, a PIANOFORTE of any kind. *Klavierauszug,* piano arrangement, or vocal score, particularly a reduction from a full score; *Klavierstück,* piano piece, usually brief; *Klaviertrio,* chamber work for piano, VIOLIN, and CELLO; *Klavierquartett,* work for (usually) piano, violin, VIOLA, and cello; *Klavierquintett,* work for (usually) piano and string quartet.

PEOPLE IN MUSIC

Kleiber, Carlos, outstanding German-born Austrian conductor, son of ERICH KLEIBER; b. Berlin, July 3, 1930. Kleiber left Nazi Germany with his parents in 1935, eventually settling in South America in 1940. He showed an early interest in music, but his father opposed it as a career. After studying chemistry in Zurich in 1949–50, he turned decisively to music and completed his training in Buenos Aires.

From 1952 to 1968 Kleiber served as a theater or opera conductor in a number of European cities, including Potsdam, the Deutsche Oper am Rhein in Dusseldorf, the Zurich Opera, and at the Wurttemberg State Theater in Stuttgart. From 1968 to 1978, Kleiber conducted at the Bavarian State Opera in Munich.

In 1966 Kleiber made his British debut conducting AL- BAN BERG's *Wozzeck* at the Edinburgh Festival. He led performances of RICHARD WAGNER's *TRISTAN UND ISOLDE* for his first appearances at the Vienna State Opera in 1973 and at the Bayreuth Festival in 1974. Also in 1974, he made his first appearances at London's Covent Garden and Milan's La Scala with RICHARD STRAUSS's *DER ROSENKAVALIER*.

In 1977 Kleiber made his U.S. debut conducting GIUSEPPE VERDI's *OTELLO* at the San Francisco Opera. A year later, he made his first appearance with à U.S. orchestra, when he led the Chicago Symphony Orchestra. In 1979 he conducted the Vienna Philharmonic, and in 1982 the Berlin Philharmonic. In 1988 he made his Metropolitan Opera debut in N.Y. conducting GIACOMO PUCCINI's *LA BOHÈME*. In 1989 and 1992 he conducted the New Year's Day Concert of the Vienna Philharmonic. He became a naturalized Austrian citizen in 1980.

Kleiber has been accorded accolades from critics, audiences, and his peers. His brilliant performances reflect an unreserved commitment to the score at hand, his authority, and his mastery of technique. His infrequent appearances, combined with his passion for perfection, have made him a legendary figure among the world's contemporary conductors.

Kleiber, Erich, eminent Austrian conductor, father of CARLOS KLEIBER; b. Vienna, Aug. 5, 1890; d. Zurich, Jan. 27, 1956. Kleiber studied at the Prague Conservatory and the University of Prague. After making his debut at the Prague National Theater in 1911, he conducted opera in Darmstadt (1912–19), Barmen-Elberfeld (1919–21), Düsseldorf (1921–22), and Mannheim (1922–23).

PEOPLE IN MUSIC

In 1923 Kleiber was appointed Generalmusikdirektor (General Music Director) of the Berlin State Opera. His tenure was outstanding, both for the brilliant performances of the standard repertoire and for the exciting programming of contemporary works. He conducted the world premiere of ALBAN BERG's *WOZZECK* (Dec. 14, 1925). In 1934, in protest against the German National Socialist government, he resigned his post and emigrated to South America. He conducted regularly at the Teatro Colón in Buenos Aires from 1936 to 1949.

Having first conducted at London's Covent Garden in 1937, Kleiber returned there from 1950 to 1953. He then was appointed Generalmusikdirektor once more of the Berlin State Opera in 1954, but resigned in March 1955, before the opening of the season, because of difficulties with the East German Communist regime.

Kleiber was renowned for his performances of the music of WOLFGANG AMADEUS MOZART and LUDWIG VAN BEETHOVEN. He also composed, numbering among his works a Violin Concerto, a Piano Concerto, orchestral variations, Capriccio for orchestra, numerous chamber music works, piano pieces, and songs.

Klemperer, Otto, celebrated German conductor; b. Breslau, May 14, 1885; d. Zurich, July 6, 1973. After early training from his mother, Klemperer entered the Hoch Conservatory in Frankfurt in 1901, where he studied piano and theory.

PEOPLE IN MUSIC

Klemperer made his debut conducting Max Reinhardt's production of *Orpheus in the Underworld* in Berlin in 1906. On GUSTAV MAHLER's recommendation, he then was appointed chorus master and subsequently conductor of the German Theater in Prague. He also assisted MAHLER in the preparations for the Munich premiere of Mahler's Eighth Symphony in 1910. He became a conductor at the Hamburg Opera in 1910, but was obliged to leave in 1912 as the result of a scandalous affair with the recently married soprano ELISABETH SCHUMANN.

Klemperer next held minor positions at Barmen (1913–14) and Strasbourg (1914–17), where he worked as assistant to the well-known composer and conductor HANS PFITZNER, with whom he also studied. In 1917 Klemperer was appointed music director of the Cologne Opera. While in Cologne, he conducted the German premiere of Leoš Janáček's *KÁTA KABANOVÁ*. In 1924 he was named music director of the Wiesbaden Opera.

Klemperer made his U.S. debut as guest conductor with the N.Y. Symphony Orchestra in 1926. In 1927 he became music director of Berlin's Kroll Opera, which was dedicated to the performance of new works. He conducted the world premiere of PAUL HINDEMITH's *NEUES VOM TAGE* (1929), as well as the first Berlin performances of Hindemith's *CARDIL-LAC*, IGOR STRAVINSKY's *OEDIPUS REX,* and ARNOLD SCHOEN-BERG's *Die glück-*

liche Hand. He also conducted the premiere per-formance of Schoenberg's *Be-gleitungsmusik* as part of the Kroll concerts.

When politi-cal and economic pressures forced the Kroll Opera to close in 1931, Klemperer be-came a conductor at the Berlin State Opera. When the Nazis came to power in 1933, he was compelled to emigrate to the U.S. That same

Otto Klemperer.
(Library of Congress/Corbis)

year he became music director of the Los Angeles Philhar-monic. He also appeared as a guest conductor in N.Y., Philadelphia, and Pittsburgh. His career was disrupted in 1939 when he underwent an operation for a brain tumor.

After World War II, in 1947, Klemperer was engaged as conductor at the Budapest State Opera, where he remained until 1950. He made his first appearance as a guest conductor with the Philharmonia Orchestra of London in 1951. He was appointed its principal conductor in 1959, spending most of the balance of his career in England.

Before the war, Klemperer had been noted for his energetic and hard-driven interpretations. However, during his later London years he won great renown for his measured performances of the Viennese classics. He particularly distinguished himself by conducting a memorable series of LUDWIG VAN BEETHOVEN's symphonies at the Royal Festival Hall. In the early 1960s he conducted new productions of *FIDELIO, DIE ZAUBERFLÖTE,* and *LOHENGRIN* at Covent Garden. His serious and unsentimental readings of Mahler's symphonies were largely responsible for the modern critical and popular interest shown in that composer's music. In 1970 he conducted in Jerusalem and accepted Israeli citizenship. He retired in 1972.

Klemperer was also a composer. He studied with Schoenberg during the latter's American sojourn, but his compositional style had more in common with that of Pfitzner. He wrote an opera, *Das Ziel* (1915; rev. 1970), a Missa sacra (1916), six symphonies (from 1960), 17 pieces for voice and orchestra (1967–70), nine string quartets (1968–70), and about 100 songs.

Kluge, Die (The wise one). Opera by CARL ORFF, 1943, based on a Grimm fable, first performed in Frankfurt.

A king marries a peasant woman who is far superior to him in intelligence. This annoys him so much that he decides to divorce her, but gives her unqualified permission to take from the palace one thing she values above all else. Thereupon the wise woman carries him to her modest little house. When he awakens and realizes what has occurred, he restores her to royal status and they live happily ever after.

Knickerbocker Holiday. Musical by KURT WEILL and Maxwell Anderson, 1938, based on Washington Irving's *Father Knickerbocker's History of New York.*

The scene is set in 17th-century N.Y., when it was a Dutch colony named New Amsterdam. Governor Peter Stuyvesant (a historical figure) is represented as a protofascist. The antifascist spirit is represented by a young

Dutchman, who is also the governor's rival in love. The show was a relative failure, but it includes *September Song,* which became a perennial favorite.

Knight, Gladys, American RHYTHM AND BLUES singer and group leader, b. Atlanta, Ga., May 28, 1944. Knight performed for over 40 years as the leader of the family-based group the Pips, and as a solo artist. A child prodigy, she began singing with a GOSPEL group at age four, and three years later was a winner on TV's *Ted Mack's Original Amateur Hour.*

PEOPLE IN MUSIC

Knight began singing with her brother Merald "Bubba" (b. Sept. 4, 1942) and cousin William Guest (b. June 2, 1941), among other family members, when she was 8. By the time she was 13, the group was on the road opening for JACKIE WILSON and SAM COOKE.

Initial recordings for Brunswick and other small labels were less than successful until 1961, when they had a major rhythm and blues hit with *Every Beat of My Heart* on Vee Jay. After recording for other small labels, the group finally hooked up with BERRY GORDY's Soul label (a subsidiary of his Motown empire) in 1965, beginning eight years of major rhythm and blues and pop hit making. By this time, the group lineup had settled around the two Knights, their cousin Guest, and Edward Patten (b. Aug. 2, 1939), another cousin. Major hits included *The End of the Road, Friendship Train, If I Were Your Woman, Neither One of Us (Wants to Be the First to Say Goodbye),* and *Daddy Could Swear, I Declare.*

The Pips left Motown in 1973 to join Buddah, where they had one of their biggest hits with *Midnight Train to Georgia.* In 1978 Gladys signed a solo deal with Columbia, and the Pips began recording on their own, but neither had much success. By the mid-'80s they were back together, scoring a smash hit in 1987 with *Love Overboard.* Most recently, Knight has performed as a solo artist and on occasion with the Pips.

Gladys Knight and the Pips were inducted into the Rock and Roll Hall of Fame in 1996.

Knoxville: Summer of 1915. Work by SAMUEL BARBER, 1948, for soprano and orchestra. It was inspired by a passage in the novel/memoir *A Death in the Family* by James Agee, reminiscing of the time he was a child in Tennessee. It was first performed in Boston.

PEOPLE IN MUSIC

Knussen, (Stuart) **Oliver,** English composer; b. Glasgow, June 12, 1952. Remarkably precocious, Knussen began playing piano as a small boy. In the mid-1960s he studied theory with the British conductor and composer Constant Lambert while also attending the Central Tutorial School for Young Musicians.

In 1968 Knussen made musical headlines when, at the age of 15, he conducted the London Symphony Orchestra in the premiere performance of his own First Symphony. It was written in an eclectic, but astoundingly effective, modern style. He was awarded fellowships for advanced study with GUNTHER SCHULLER at the Berkshire Music Center in Tanglewood, Massachusetts, from 1970 to 1973, where he later was coordinator of its contemporary music activities (1986–93).

Beginning in 1983, Knussen served as an artistic director of the Aldeburgh Festivals. In 1994 he was made a Commander of the Order of the British Empire. Among his compositions are the opera *Where the Wild Things Are* (1979–81) and *Higglety Pigglety Pop!* (1983–84), three symphonies (1966–67; 1970–71, with soprano; 1973–76), chamber pieces, and various works utilizing voice, including *Vocalise with Songs of Winnie-the-Pooh* for soprano and six instruments (1970).

Koanga. Opera by FREDERICK DELIUS, 1904, first performed in Elberfeld, Germany. A beautiful young mulatto slave on a Mississippi plantation loves the handsome African prince Koanga, but her owner lusts after her himself. The lovers organize a vodun ritual to defeat their white foes. Eventually Koanga dies, and his beloved stabs herself with his spear.

Delius incorporated into the score folk melodies he had heard during his stay in Florida, as well as melodies he believed were based on traditional African song.

Kodály, Zoltan, renowned Hungarian composer, ethnomusicologist, and music educator; b. Kecskemét, Dec. 16, 1882; d. Budapest, March 6, 1967. Kodály was brought up in a musical family, receiving his general education at the Archiepiscopal Grammar School in Nagyszombat. At the same time he took lessons in PIANO, VIOLIN, VIOLA, and

PEOPLE IN MUSIC

Zoltán Kodály, c. 1960.
(Hulton-Deutsch Collection/
Corbis)

CELLO. He soon began to compose, producing an overture when he was 15, which was performed in Nagyszombat in 1898.

In 1900 Kodály went to Budapest, where he entered the University as a student of Hungarian and German. He also studied composition with Hans Koessler at Budapest's Royal Academy of Music (diplomas in composition, 1904, and teaching, 1905; Ph.D., 1906, with a dissertation on the structure of Hungarian folk song). He also worked with BÉLA BARTÓK, collecting, organizing, and editing a vast wealth of national folk songs, which he later made use of in his own compositions.

In 1906 Kodály went to Berlin, and in 1907 proceeded to Paris, where he took some lessons with the organist CHARLES-MARIE WIDOR. But it was the music of CLAUDE DE-BUSSY that most profoundly influenced him in his subsequent development as a composer. Returning to Budapest, he was appointed a professor at the Royal Academy of Music in 1907. In collaboration with Bartók, he prepared the detailed paper *Az uj egyetemes nepdalgyujtemeny tervezete* (A project for a new universal collection of folk songs) in 1913. They continued their collecting expeditions until World War I intervened.

Kodály wrote music criticism for several newspapers in Budapest from 1917 to 1919. In 1919 he was appointed deputy director of the Budapest Academy of Music, but lost his position that same year for political reasons. However, he resumed his teaching there in 1922. In 1923 he was commissioned to write a commemorative work in celebration of the half-century anniversary of the union of Buda, Pest, and Obuda into Budapest. The resulting work, the oratorio *Psalmus hungaricus* (1923), brought him wide recognition. The initial performance in Budapest was followed by productions all over Europe and in America.

Another major success was his opera *Háry János* (1926). The orchestral suite from this work became highly popular in Hungary and throughout the world. His orchestral works *Marosszéki táncok* (Dances of Marosszek, 1930, based on a piano work) and *Galántai táncok* (Dances of Galánta, for the 80th anniversary of the Budapest Philharmonic Society, 1933) were also successful. His reputation as one of the most significant national composers was firmly established with repeated performances of these works. Among his most important subsequent works were the orchestral pieces *Variations on a Hungarian Folk Song "Felszállott a páva"* (Peacock variations, for the 50th anniversary of the Amsterdam Concertgebouw Orchestra, 1939) and the Concerto for Orchestra (for the 50th anniversary of the Chicago Symphony Orchestra, 1941).

Kodály's great interest in music education is reflected in his numerous choral works, which he wrote for both adults and children during the last 30 years of his life. He also pursued his studies of traditional Hungarian music, and from 1940 was associated with the Hungarian Academy of Sciences, serving as its president from 1946 to 1949. He continued to teach at the Academy of Music until 1940, and then gave instruction in Hungarian folk music until 1942. Even after his retirement, he taught the latter course there. Kodály toured as a conductor of his own music in England, the U.S., and the Soviet Union in 1946–47, then throughout Western Europe.

In succeeding years, Kodály held a foremost place in the musical life of his country, receiving many honors, including three Kossuth Prizes in 1948, 1952, and 1957. He also received foreign honors, being made an honorary member of the Moscow Conservatory and the American Academy of Arts and Sciences, both in 1963. In 1967 he was awarded the Gold Medal of the Royal Philharmonic Society of London. An International Kodály Society was organized in Budapest in 1975.

As a composer, Kodály's style was not as radical as that of Bartók. He never departed from basic TONALITY, nor did his experiments in rhythm reach the raw power of Bartók's percussive style. He preferred a ROMANTIC treatment of his melodic and harmonic materials, with the addition of IMPRESSIONISTIC elements. All the same, Kodály succeeded in producing a substantial body of music of notable distinction.

Koechlin, Charles (Louis Eugène), noted French composer, pedagogue, and writer on music; b. Paris, Nov. 27, 1867; d. Le Canadel, Var, Dec. 31, 1950. Koechlin prepared for a military career but was compelled to change his plans when stricken with tuberculosis. While recuperating in Algeria, he took up serious music studies. In 1890 he entered the Paris Conservatory, where he studied with André Gédalge, JULES MASSENET, and GABRIEL FAURÉ, graduating in 1897.

PEOPLE IN MUSIC

Koechlin lived mostly in Paris, where he was active as a composer, teacher, and lecturer. With MAURICE RAVEL and Florent Schmitt, he organized the Societé Musicale Indépendante in 1909 to advance the cause of contemporary music. With ERIK SATIE, ALBERT ROUSSEL, DARIUS MILHAUD, and others, he was a member of the group Les Nouveaux Jeunes (The New Young [Musicians], 1918–20), which influenced the formation of LES SIX ("The Six," a group of six French modern composers).

Although Koechlin composed prolifically in all genres, he became best known as a writer on music and as a lecturer. He made three lecture tours of the U.S. in 1918, 1928, and 1937. His pro-Communist leanings caused him to promote music for the working class during the 1930s, including a number of works "for the people" and also film scores. In spite of the fact that such works as his *Symphonie d'hymnes* (Prix Cressent, 1936) and Symphony No. 1 (Prix Halphan, 1937) won honors, his music made no real impact.

Taking Fauré as his model, he strove to preserve the best elements in the French CLASSICAL tradition. A skillful craftsman, he produced works of clarity and taste. At the same time, he showed an advanced understanding of modern HARMONY and COUNTERPOINT.

As an educator and critic, Koechlin wrote treatises on counterpoint, harmony, FUGUE, and ORCHESTRATION. He also wrote monographs on Debussy, Fauré, choir school, Pierre Maurice (a Swiss composer who, like Koechlin, synthesized German and French elements), and WIND INSTRUMENTS.

Kogan, Leonid (Borisovich), outstanding Russian violinist; b. Dnepropetrovsk, Nov. 14, 1924; d. Dec. 17, 1982. Kogan's father was a photographer who played the violin. When Kogan was ten the family moved to Moscow, where he became a pupil of Abram Yampolsky, first at the Central Music School and later at the Conservatory from 1943 to 1948.

Kogan was obviously a child prodigy on the instrument, but his parents and teachers carefully sheltered him from overexposure. In 1947 he was a cowinner of the first prize at the World Festival of Democratic Youth in Prague. He then won first prize in the Queen Elisabeth of Belgium Competition in 1951. His career was instantly assured, and he played recitals in Europe to unanimous acclaim.

Kogan made an auspicious American debut, playing the JOHANNES BRAHMS Violin Concerto with the Boston Symphony Orchestra in 1958. In 1952 he joined the faculty of the Moscow Conservatory, where he was named professor in 1963 and head of the violin department in 1969. In 1965 he received the Lenin Prize.

Kogan's playing showed the finest qualities of the Russian School: an emotionally ROMANTIC spirit and a fine melodic style, without sacrificing technical skill. In addition to the standard repertoire, in which he excelled, he also played modern works, particularly those by Soviet composers. Kogan died while traveling on a train in 1982.

PEOPLE IN MUSIC

Kogan was married to Elizabeta Gilels. Apparently his violin genes were strong, because their two children were also musical: a girl played the piano, and a boy, Pavel Kogan (b. Moscow, June 6, 1952), was so talented on the violin that in 1970 he won the Sibelius contest in Finland. In 1975 Pavel was soloist with the Philadelphia Orchestra. In the late '80s, Pavel was active as a conductor at Moscow's Bolshoi Theater, the Zagreb Philharmonic, and the Moscow Symphony Orchestra.

Kokkonen, Joonas, prominent Finnish composer; b. Iisalmi, Nov. 13, 1921; d. Järvenpää, Oct. 4, 1966. Kokkonen studied at the Sibelius Academy in Helsinki, earning his diploma in 1949. He also studied musicology at the University of Helsinki, taking a Master of Arts degree in 1948.

Kokkonen taught at the Sibelius Academy from 1950, serving as a professor of composition from 1959 to 1963 and chairman of the composition department from 1965 to 1970. In 1963 he was elected to membership in the Finnish Academy, and in 1973 he was awarded the Sibelius Prize.

Like all composers of his generation in Finland, Kokkonen experienced the inevitable influence of Jean Sibelius. However, he soon abandoned the characteristic sound of Finnish folk music and formed an individual style of composition. His mature compositions are rich with COUNTERPOINT, influenced by the BAROQUE composers, particularly JOHANN SEBASTIAN BACH. His harmonies are freely dissonant but maintain clearly identifiable TONAL centers, showing the influence of BÉLA BARTÓK. The structures of his works are determined by the material itself, so that form serves the needs of musical content.

Kokkonen's international fame reached its height with the opera *Viimeiset Kiusaukset* (The last temptations), concerning the life of a 19th-century Finnish evangelist, which premiered in Helsinki in 1975.

Kol Nidrei (Hebr., "all vows"). A very early Jewish religious song, sung on the eve of Yom Kippur, the Day of Atonement. It is set in an expressive minor mode and marked by profound religious sentiment.

The Kogan family shunned politics. Leonid resolutely declined to participate in any protests, domestic or foreign, against the presumed anti-Semitism in Russian politics, even though he himself was Jewish.

PEOPLE IN MUSIC

Kol Nidrei for cello and orchestra, by MAX BRUCH, which is based on this early religious melody, is his most popular work. He wrote it in 1880 for the Jewish community of Liverpool, although he himself was Protestant.

Königskinder (The royal children). Opera by ENGELBERT HUMPERDINCK, 1910, first produced in N.Y. The libretto reverses the course of events of Humperdinck's famous children's opera, *HÄNSEL UND GRETEL*. Here the malevolent witch feeds poisonous candy to the young prince and the girl whom he loves, and both die. The opera is an expanded version of his incidental music for a play *Königskinder*, produced in 1897, notable for its use of SPRECHSTIMME long before ARNOLD SCHOENBERG. It is similar to other Humperdinck works in its Wagnerian ethos.

Kontakion (Russ., *kondak*). A portion of the Byzantine liturgical Hours, sung as an ode in the kanñ. It is a morality poem, containing a narrative recited by a soloist, followed by a choral refrain.

The kontakion was eventually limited to the Orthodox Matins, but it remained a major influence on ecclesiastical poetry and music. It was eventually superseded by the Byzantine canon. After the conversion of Russia to Christianity in the 10th century, it was used in Russian church singing.

Kontakte (Contacts). Work by KARLHEINZ STOCKHAUSEN, 1960, for piano, percussion, and electronic sounds, first performed in Cologne. The "contacts" of the title signifies the meeting of electronic and traditional acoustic instruments. It is one of the most significant, if not the earliest, experiments in ELECTRONIC MUSIC.

Kontarsky. Family of German musicians.

1. **Alfons,** German pianist; b. Iserlohn, Westphalia, Oct. 9, 1932. Alfons studied piano at the Cologne Hochschule für Musik from 1953 to 1955 and with Eduard Erdmann in Hamburg from 1955 to 1957. With his brother Aloys, Alfons won first prize for duo-piano playing in the Bavarian

Legend has it that the Kontakion was given to a 6th-century Byzantine poet known as Roman the Melodious (Melode Romanous) by the Blessed Virgin.

PEOPLE IN MUSIC

Radio Competition in Munich in 1955. They subsequently toured throughout the world, giving performances of many modern scores. They have also recorded works by PIERRE BOULEZ, KARLHEINZ STOCKHAUSEN, BÉLA BARTÓK, IGOR STRAVINSKY, BERND ALOIS ZIMMERMANN, and MAURICE RAVEL. Alfons taught at the Cologne Hochschule für Musik from 1967.

2. **Aloys,** German pianist; b. Iserlohn, Westphalia, May 14, 1931. Aloys's training and career follow that of his brother, Alfons.

3. **Bernhard,** German pianist and conductor; b. Iserlohn, Westphalia, April 26, 1937. Bernard studied at the Cologne Hochschule für Musik and at the University of Cologne. In 1964 he received the Mendelssohn Prize in Chamber Music. He was a conductor at the Württemberg State Theater in Stuttgart. He also appeared as a pianist, both as a soloist and in ensemble with his brothers.

Konzert (Ger.). 1. CONCERTO. 2. CONCERT. *Konzertmeister,* CONCERTMASTER; *Konzertsaal,* concert hall; *Konzertstück* (It., concertino): 1. A concert piece. 2. A short concerto with orchestra in one movement and free form.

kōhn′tsârt′

Examples of *konzertstück* include FRÉDÉRIC CHOPIN's *Allegro de concert,* FELIX MENDELSSOHN's *Capriccio brillant,* ROBERT SCHUMANN's *Concertstück* for four horns, and IGOR STRAVINSKY's unfinished work for piano that was incorporated into PETROUCHKA.

Koopman, Ton, remarkable Dutch organist, harpsichordist, and conductor; b. Zwolle, Oct. 12, 1944. Koopman studied ORGAN and HARPSICHORD in Amsterdam, and also took courses in musicology. In the early '70s, Koopman took doctoral degrees in both instruments and won several prizes for his performance.

After serving as director of Musica Antiqua and as a teacher at the Sweelinck Conservatory in Amsterdam, Koopman founded the Amsterdam Baroque Orchestra in 1979. He toured widely in subsequent years as a conductor, organist, and harpsichordist, excelling in early music performances. In 1992 he founded the Amsterdam Baroque Choir, and in 1994 he became co-principal conductor (with Peter Eötvös) of the Netherlands Radio Chamber Orchestra in Hilversum. He has recorded works by JOHANN SEBASTIAN BACH, GIROLAMO FRESCOBALDI, GEORG PHILIPP TELEMANN, John Stanley, and DIETRICH BUXTEHUDE.

MUSICAL
INSTRUMENT

kora. A plucked HARP-LUTE of West Africa, associated with the Mandinka and Maninka peoples.

The standard instrument has 21 nylon (formerly gut) strings, attached with tuning pins at the top of a long wooden neck, which passes through a large gourd resonator. The strings are attached at the bottom by an iron anchor ring. The gourd is covered with a head made of antelope skin or cowhide.

The professional performer (*jali*), who sits on the ground, faces the head of the resonator, called the sound board, and holds the instrument with the attached wooden

Kora player. (Eliot Elisofon, Smithsonian Institution)

▶

handles. The strings are divided into two rows, running perpendicular to the soundboard. They pass over a single, notched bridge.

The range of the kora covers three OCTAVES. There are numerous tunings, each of which is usually used for only a few pieces. The *jali*'s repertoire centers on praise songs, honoring a family or clan. The complex accompaniment blends melodies and harmonies in a mostly steady rhythm. There are several playing techniques, including flicking a nail against the instrument to fill in a rhythmic interruption. The instrument's tone is sometimes enriched by a jingle (or small metal bell) attached to the bridge with wire loops.

The first Western report of the instrument dates from 1799. The family of kora-like instruments includes the *ekorro, seron, bolon, mvet, Fan harp,* and so on.

Korean temple blocks. Rounded and hollowed WOOD-BLOCKS, struck with a drumstick. Usually grouped in five instruments, whose pitches approximate the PENTATONIC (five-note) folk scale.

Korngold, Erich Wolfgang, remarkable Austrian-born American composer; b. Brunn (Brno), May 29, 1897; d. Los Angeles, Nov. 29, 1957. Korngold received his earliest musical education from his father, the noted Viennese music critic Julius Korngold (b. Brunn [Brno], Dec. 24, 1860; d. Los Angeles, Sept. 25, 1945), then studied privately with many leading teachers in Vienna.

Korngold's progress was astounding. At the age of 12 he composed a Piano Trio, which was soon published, revealing a competent technique and an ability to write in a style strongly influenced by RICHARD STRAUSS. About the same time he wrote (in piano score) a pantomime, *Der Schnee-mann,* which was orchestrated and performed at the Vienna Court Opera in 1910, creating a sensation. In 1911 Arthur Nikisch conducted Korngold's *Schauspiel-Ouvertüre* with the Leipzig Gewandhaus Orchestra, the same year the youthful composer gave a concert of his works in Berlin, appearing also as a pianist. His *Sinfonietta* was conducted by FELIX WEINGARTNER and the Vienna Philharmonic in 1913.

Korngold was not quite 19 when his two short operas, *Der Ring des Polykrates* and *Violanta,* were produced in Munich. His first lasting success came with the simultaneous premiere in Hamburg and Cologne of his opera *Die tote Stadt* in 1920.

In 1929 Korngold began a fruitful collaboration with the stage director Max Reinhardt, noted for his spectacular and lavish productions. In 1934 he went to Hollywood to arrange FELIX MENDELSSOHN's music for Reinhardt's film version of *A Midsummer Night's Dream.* He taught at the Vienna Academy of Music from 1930 to 1934 before settling in Hollywood, where he wrote some of the best ROMANTIC

MUSICAL INSTRUMENT

PEOPLE IN MUSIC

When GUSTAV MAHLER heard Korngold play some of his music as a young boy, he kept repeating, "Ein Genie! Ein Genie!" (A genius! A genius!)

film scores of the era. He became a naturalized U.S. citizen in 1943.

Korngold's music represents the last breath of the Romantic spirit of Vienna. It is marvelously consistent with the melodic, rhythmic, and harmonic style of the judicious modernity of the early 20th century.

After the early outbursts by critics declaring Korngold as a new Mozart, his star began to sink rapidly. His operas and other "serious" works have long been forgotten. Ironically, his film scores, in the form of orchestrated suites, continue to have great popularity.

MUSICAL
INSTRUMENT

koto. National Japanese instrument of the long ZITHER type. It has a rectangular body made of strong wood planks that is laid on the floor. It has seven to 13 silk strings that are plucked with fingers, fingernails, or a plectrum. Some modern kotos may have as many as 17 strings.

The koto was originally used to accompany the Japanese GAGAKU or musical drama. In subsequent centuries, schools of solo performance emerged, and music was written down (including the timeless *Variations on Rokudan*).

In the 20th century the koto evolved into a virtuoso instrument. Several Japanese composers have written music for the instrument. HENRY COWELL, among other Americans, wrote concertos for koto and orchestra.

PEOPLE IN MUSIC

Koussevitzky (Kussevitsky), **Serge** (Alexandrovich), celebrated Russian-born American conductor and DOUBLE-BASS virtuoso; b. Vishny-Volochok, July 26, 1874; d. Boston, June 4, 1951. Koussevitzky's father and three brothers were all amateur musicians. Koussevitzky learned to play the trumpet and took part, with his brothers, in a small wind ensemble, numbering eight members in all. They earned their living by playing at balls and weddings and occasionally at village fairs.

At the age of 14, Koussevitzky went to Moscow. Because Jews were not allowed to live there, he was quickly baptized. He then received a fellowship with free tuition at the Musico-Dramatic Institute of the Moscow Philharmonic Society, where he studied double bass.

In 1894 Koussevitzky joined the orchestra of the Bolshoi Theater, becoming principal double-bass player in 1901, and retaining that post until 1905. In the meantime, he became known as a soloist of the first rank, making his public debut in Moscow in 1901. In 1903 he gained great attention with a double-bass recital in Berlin.

To supplement the meager repertoire for his instrument, Koussevitzky arranged various works for it and also wrote several pieces. With aid from RHEINHOLD GLIÈRE, he wrote a Double-bass Concerto, which he performed for the first time in Moscow in 1905. Later that year, he married Natalie Ushkov, daughter of a wealthy tea merchant family. He soon resigned from the orchestra of the Bolshoi Theater. In an open letter to the Russian publication *Musical Gazette,* he explained the reason for his resignation as the economic and artistic difficulties in the orchestra. He then went to Germany, where he continued to give double-bass recitals. He also played the First Cello Concerto by Camille Saint-Saëns on the double bass.

In 1907 Koussevitzky conducted a student orchestra at the Berlin Hochschule für Musik. His first public appearance as a conductor took place in 1908, with the Berlin Philharmonic. In 1909 he established a publishing house, Editions Russes de Musique (Editions of Russian Music). Among composers with whom he signed contracts were

◄

Serge Koussevitzky. (Library of Congress/Corbis)

ALEXANDER SCRIABIN, IGOR STRAVINSKY, SERGEI PROKOFIEV, NICOLAI MEDTNER, and SERGEI RACHMANINOFF. The association with Scriabin was particularly fruitful, as in subsequent years Koussevitzky became his greatest champion.

Returning to Moscow in 1909, Koussevitzky organized his own symphony orchestra there, featuring works by Russian composers but also including classical masterpieces. He played many Russian works for the first time, among them Scriabin's *Promethée*. In the summer of 1910 he took his orchestra to towns along the Volga River in a specially chartered steamboat. He repeated the Volga tour in 1912 and 1914.

The outbreak of World War I in 1914 made it necessary for Koussevitzky to curtail his activities. However, he continued to give concerts in Moscow, and in 1915 he presented a memorial Scriabin program. After the 1917 Revolution he was offered the directorship of the State Symphony Orchestra in Petrograd, which he conducted until 1920.

In 1920 Koussevitzky left Russia because of the poor economic situation for musicians following the Revolution. He went first to Berlin, then to Rome, and finally to Paris, where he organized the Concerts Koussevitzky with a specially assembled orchestra. He presented many new scores by French and Russian composers, among them MAURICE RAVEL's orchestration of MODEST MUSSORGSKY's *Pictures at an Exhibition,* ARTHUR HONEGGER's *Pacific 231,* and several works by Prokofiev and Stravinsky.

In 1924 Koussevitzky was appointed conductor of the Boston Symphony Orchestra, a position he held with great eminence until 1949. Just as in Russia he championed Russian composers, and in France the French, so in the U.S. he encouraged American composers. Symphonic compositions by AARON COPLAND, ROY HARRIS, WALTER PISTON, SAMUEL BARBER, HOWARD HANSON, WILLIAM SCHUMAN, and others were given premiere performances by Koussevitzky. For the 50th anniversary of the Boston Symphony Orchestra in 1931, he commissioned works from Stravinsky (*Symphony of Psalms*), PAUL HINDEMITH, Honegger, Prokofiev, ALBERT ROUSSEL, Ravel (Piano Concerto), Copland, GEORGE GERSHWIN, and others.

A highly important development in Koussevitzky's American career was the establishment of the Berkshire Music Center at Tanglewood, Massachusetts. Koussevitzky and the Boston Symphony Orchestra presented summer concerts at the Berkshire Festival in 1935 for the first time. Since then, the concerts have become an annual institution. The Berkshire Music Center was opened on July 8, 1940, with Koussevitzky as director and Copland as assistant director. Among distinguished guest instructors were Hindemith, Honegger, and OLIVIER MESSIAEN. Koussevitzky himself taught conducting, being succeeded after his death by his former student LEONARD BERNSTEIN.

Koussevitzky held honorary degrees from many educational institutions, as well as many awards. He became a naturalized American citizen on April 16, 1941. When his wife died in 1942, he established the Koussevitzky Foundation as a memorial to her, the funds to be used for commissioning works by composers of all nationalities. He married Olga Naoumoff (1901–78), a niece of Natalie Koussevitzky, on Aug. 15, 1947.

As a conductor, Koussevitzky possessed extraordinary emotional power. In Russian music, and particularly in PIOTR ILYICH TCHAIKOVSKY's symphonies, he was unexcelled. He was capable of achieving the subtlest nuances in the works of the French school, his interpretations of CLAUDE DEBUSSY being particularly notable. As a champion of modern music, Koussevitzky had few equals in his time. His commitment to present unfamiliar music before new audiences helped win over both the critics and new listeners.

Koven, Regnald de. DE KOVEN, REGINALD.

koza (Pol., goat). Polish bellows-blown BAGPIPE, with a goatskin bag. The chanter (or melody pipe) usually has eight fingerholes, and the DRONE pipe is bent at a 90° angle. Both the chanter and drone end in an upturned bell of horn or metal.

krakowiak (Pol.; Fr. *cracovienne*; Ger. *Krakauer Tanz*). Fast syncopated Polish dance in $\frac{2}{4}$ time, developed in the region of Kraków.

Examples date back to tablatures and songbooks of the 16th century, where it was called *chorea polonica* or *volta*

Koussevitzky was sometimes criticized for the liberties he allowed himself in the treatment of classical masterpieces. Undoubtedly his performances of Johann Sebastian Bach, Ludwig van Beethoven, Johannes Brahms, and Franz Schubert were untraditional, but nonetheless they were motivated by a sincere attempt to interpret this music for a new generation.

MUSICAL INSTRUMENT

polonica. It is sometimes considered the Polish national dance, although the POLONAISE predates it. The krakowiak became an important part of the musical stage. FRÉDÉRIC CHOPIN wrote a *Krakowiak* rondo for piano and orchestra, op.14 (1828), and another for the finale of his First Piano Concerto, op.11 (1830).

Kraus (Trujillo), **Alfredo,** distinguished Spanish TENOR of Austrian descent; b. Las Palmas, Canary Islands, Sept. 24, 1927. Kraus had vocal training with Gali Markoff in Barcelona and Francisco Andres in Valencia, then completed his studies with Mercedes Llopart in Milan in 1955.

In 1956 Kraus won first prize in the Geneva Competition and made his operatic debut as the Duke of Mantua in Cairo. That same year he also made his European debut in Venice as Alfredo Germont, a role he repeated for his British debut at London's Stoll Theatre in 1957 and at Lisbon's Teatro São Carlo in 1958. In 1959 he appeared at London's Covent Garden for the first time, as Edgardo in LUCIA DI LAMMERMOOR. His U.S. debut followed at the Chicago Lyric Opera, as Nemorino in L'ELISIR D'AMORE in 1962. Four years later, he made his Metropolitan Opera debut in N.Y. as the Duke of Mantua. He also toured as a recitalist. In 1996 he celebrated his 40th anniversary on the concert stage.

A consummate artist with a voice of remarkable beauty, Kraus was particularly noted for his portrayals of Rossini's Count Almaviva, Don Ottavio, Ernesto in DON PASQUALE, Des Grieux in MANON, Nadir in LES PÊCHEURS DE PERLES, and Werther.

Kreisler, Fritz (Friedrich), great Austrian-born American violinist; b. Vienna, Feb. 2, 1875; d. N.Y., Jan. 29, 1962. Kreisler began playing the VIOLIN when he was only 4, with the guidance of his father. He made such progress that at age 6 he was accepted as a pupil of Jacob Dont. He also studied with Jacques Auber until, at age 7, he entered the Vienna Conservatory, where his principal teachers were Joseph Hellmesberger, Jr. (violin), and ANTON BRUCKNER (theory). He gave his first performance there when he was 9 and was awarded its gold medal at 10.

Kreisler subsequently studied with LAMBERT MASSART (violin) and LÉO DELIBES (composition) at the Paris Conservatory, sharing the premier prix in violin with four other students in 1887. He made his U.S. debut in Boston in 1888, then toured the country during the 1889-90 season with the pianist Moriz Rosenthal.

Fritz Kreisler, c. 1913.
(Library of Congress/Corbis)

Returning to Europe, Kreisler abandoned music to study medicine in Vienna and art in Rome and Paris. He then served as an officer in the Austrian army in 1895–96. Resuming his concert career, he appeared as a soloist with Hans Richter and the Vienna Philharmonic in 1898. The following year, his appearance as a soloist with Arthur Nikisch and the Berlin Philharmonic launched his international career.

From 1900 to 1901, on his second tour of the U.S., both as a soloist and as a recitalist with JOSEF HOFMANN and JEAN GÉRARDY, Kreisler carried his audiences by storm. In 1902 he made his London debut as a soloist with the Philharmonic Society orchestra, and he was awarded its Gold Medal in 1904. EDWARD ELGAR composed his Violin Concerto for him, which Kreisler premiered under the composer's direction in London in 1910.

At the outbreak of World War I in 1914, Kreisler joined his former regiment, but he was discharged almost immediately after being wounded in battle. He then returned to the U.S. to pursue his career. After the U.S. entered the war in

1917, Kreisler withdrew from public appearances. After the war ended, he once again performed in N.Y. and once again resumed his tours.

From 1924 to 1934 Kreisler made his home in Berlin, but in 1938 he went to France and became a naturalized citizen. In 1939 he settled in the U.S., becoming a naturalized citizen in 1943. In 1941 he suffered a near-fatal accident when he was struck by a truck in N.Y. However, he recovered and continued to give concerts until 1950.

Kreisler was one of the greatest violin masters. His brilliant technique was ably matched by his remarkable tone, both of which he always placed in the service of the composer. He was the owner of the great Guarneri "del Gesù" violin of 1733 and of instruments by other masters. He gathered a rich collection of invaluable manuscripts. In 1949 he donated the original scores of JOHANNES BRAHMS's Violin Concerto and ERNEST CHAUSSON's *Poème* for violin and orchestra to the Library of Congress.

Kreisler also excelled as a composer. He wrote some of the most popular violin pieces in the world, among them *Caprice viennois, Tambourin chinois, Schön Rosmarin,* and *Liebesfreud.* He also published a number of pieces in the classical vein, which he attributed to various composers (ANTONIO VIVALDI, GAETANO PUGNANI, FRANÇOIS COUPERIN, PADRE MARTINI, KARL DITTERS VON DITTERSDORF, FRANÇOIS FRANCOEUR, JOHANN STAMITZ, and others). In 1935 he reluctantly admitted that these pieces were his own, with the exception of the first eight bars from the "Couperin" *Chanson Louis XIII,* taken from a traditional melody. He explained his motive in doing so as the necessity of building up well-rounded programs for his concerts that would contain virtuoso pieces by established composers, rather than a series of compositions under his own, as yet unknown, name!

Kreisler also wrote the operettas *Apple Blossoms* in 1919 and *Sissy* in 1932, published numerous arrangements of early and modern music (ARCANGELO CORELLI's *La Folia,* GIUSEPPE TARTINI's *The Devil's Trill,* ANTONÍN DVOŘÁK's *SLAVONIC DANCES, DANZA ESPAÑOLA* by GRANADOS, *TANGO* by ISAAC ALBÉNIZ, etc.), and prepared CADENZAS (elaborate solos for the violinist to play) for the Beethoven and Brahms violin concertos.

Kremer, Gidon, brilliant Latvian violinist; b. Riga, Feb. 27, 1947. Kremer's parents were violinists in the Riga Symphony Orchestra. He studied the violin with his father and grandfather, then continued professional studies at the Moscow Conservatory.

Kremer took part in several competitions, culminating in first prizes at the Paganini Competition in Genoa in 1968 and the Tchaikovsky Competition in Moscow in 1970. He made a well-received N.Y. debut at Avery Fisher Hall in 1977. In subsequent years he appeared as soloist with major orchestras of the world, gave recitals, and performed in chamber music settings. He has won special commendation for his efforts to broaden the repertoire for his instrument.

Kremer's great contribution to modern music has been the consistent presentation of new violin works, particularly those of Soviet composers, among them ALFRED SCHNITTKE and SOFIA GUBAIDULINA. He has also given particularly beautiful performances of the works of Estonian composer ARVO PÄRT. In 1997 he was soloist in the premiere of Aribert Reimann's Violin Concerto in Chicago.

PEOPLE IN MUSIC

Krenek (born Křenek), **Ernst,** remarkable Austrian-born American composer and teacher; b. Vienna, Aug. 23, 1900; d. Palm Springs, Calif., Dec. 23, 1991. Krenek studied with the conductor-composer Franz Schreker in Vienna from 1916, and at the Berlin Academy of Music from 1920 to 1923. He then was a conductor and composer at the operas in Kassel and Wiesbaden from 1925 to 1927. He returned to Vienna in 1928. He was a writer for the *Frankfurter Zeitung* from 1930 to 1933, and also traveled widely in Europe as a lecturer and an accompanist in programs of his own songs.

In 1938, escaping the Nazi occupation of Vienna, Krenek settled in the U.S. He became a naturalized American citizen in 1945. He was a professor of music at Vassar College from 1939 to 1942, then head of the music department at Hamline University in St. Paul, Minnesota, from 1942 to 1947. He subsequently made his home in California. He married GUSTAV MAHLER's daughter, Anna, in 1923. After their divorce in 1925, he married Berta Hermann. He later married Gladys Nordenstrom in 1950.

PEOPLE IN MUSIC

Krenek's evolution as a composer mirrors the development of modern music in general. The tradition of Mahler, strengthened by the domestic ties of Krenek's first marriage, was the dominant influence of his early life in music. He then became associated with modern groups in Vienna, particularly ARNOLD SCHOENBERG, ALBAN BERG, and ANTON WEBERN. In Germany he was associated with PAUL HINDEMITH as a creator of modern opera in a satiric manner.

Krenek's first international success came at the age of 26, with the production of his "jazz" opera *JONNY SPIELT AUF*, which premiered in Leipzig in 1927 and two years later was presented at the Metropolitan Opera in N.Y.

In 1933 Krenek adopted a modified 12-TONE method of composition. His historical opera *Karl V* was written in this way. Its scheduled premiere in Vienna was cancelled, however. The Nazis had recently taken control of the city, and they opposed any works written in a modern style.

Deprived of all means of subsistence, Krenek went to the U.S. A few performances of his works by American orchestras followed. Still, his modern style upset some American music lovers. A Boston Symphony Orchestra dowager was heard to say after a performance of Krenek's Piano Concerto, "Conditions must be terrible in Europe!"

Strangely, there have been fewer performances of Krenek's works in the U.S., where he made his home, than in Europe. IGOR STRAVINSKY, who admired him as an intellectual and as a composer, predicted in 1963 that Krenek will one day be honored in both America and Europe. Stravinsky's prediction came at least partially true when the liberated Austrian government awarded Krenek the Grand State Prize of 1963.

A number of festivals and other celebrations were timed for Krenek's 90th birthday in 1990. These included the world premiere in Vienna of his oratorio *Opus sine nomine* and three short operas, *Der Diktator, Das geheime Königreich,* and *Schwergewicht, oder die Ehre der Nation.* The Salzburg Festival presented a selection of Krenek's orchestral music, and a revival of *Jonny spielt auf* took place at the Leipzig Opera. These honors concluded with the Stuttgart Krenek Festival, held from Nov. 16 to 23, 1990. Krenek died a year after these festivities.

The Nazis published an infamous collection of what they called "Entartete Musik" (degenerate music). Among the composers depicted in this brochure were Mahler, Schoenberg, and Krenek. Krenek's photograph was retouched to make him appear even more evil!

Kreutzer Sonata. The common name for LUDWIG VAN BEETHOVEN's most famous violin sonata, op. 47.

Although it bears the name of his contemporary Rodolphe Kreutzer, the famous French violinist, pedagogue, and composer (1766 to 1831), the violinist never performed it. The first performance was given on May 24, 1803, in Vienna, with Beethoven himself playing the piano part and George Polgreen Bridgetower (c.1779–1860), the original dedicatee, on the violin.

Krupa, Gene, successful American JAZZ drummer; b. Chicago, Jan. 15, 1909; d. Yonkers, N.Y., Oct. 16, 1973. Krupa joined a jazz band when still in his adolescence, then studied percussion with Al Silverman, Ed Straight, and Roy Knapp in 1925. After working for a time with local musicians, he went to N.Y. in 1929, where he performed in bands led by Red Nichols and Irving Aaronson, among others.

In 1934 Krupa became a featured member of BENNY GOODMAN's band, winning acclaim for his brilliant playing in the recording of *Sing, Sing, Sing.* He left Goodman in 1938, forming his own band (featuring singer Anita O'Day), which toured Europe and the Orient and became internationally famous. He was again a member of Goodman's band in 1943, and then of TOMMY DORSEY's in 1943–44.

After World War II, Krupa led his own band until 1951, later touring with Jazz at the Philharmonic and with his own trios and quartets. He and Cozy Cole cofounded a school of percussion in N.Y.

Possessed with a phenomenal technique and despite a tendency to play to the audience, Krupa popularized the drums with extended, virtuosic solos. He recorded the sound track for the largely fictional film *The Gene Krupa Story* in 1959.

Kubelík, Jan, famous Czech-born Hungarian violinist, father of RAFAEL KUBELÍK; b. Michle, near Prague, July 5, 1880; d. Prague, Dec. 5, 1940. Kubelík began violin training with his father, then studied violin and composition at the Prague Conservatory from 1892 to 1898. He continued his studies in Vienna, where he performed for the first time on Nov. 26, 1898.

Tolstoy took it as the title of his famous moralistic novella *The Kreutzer Sonata,* in which a middle-class Russian woman rehearses the sonata with a dashing violinist and eventually falls in love with him. Technically the novel is flawed because the difficulties of Beethoven's work would deter any music amateur from tackling it. Their attempts to perform it would have so frustrated the players that they would have probably ended up hating each other!

PEOPLE IN MUSIC

Jan Kubelík, c. 1935. (Hulton-Deutsch Collection/ Corbis)

▶

In 1900 Kubelík made his London debut, and thereafter made a series of triumphant tours of Europe and the U.S. He was awarded the Gold Medal of the Philharmonic Society of London in 1902. In 1903 he married a Hungarian countess and became a naturalized Hungarian citizen. He continued his active career for over four decades, giving a series of farewell concerts in 1939–40. In 1940 he gave his last concert in Prague, after his beloved homeland had been dismembered by the Nazis.

Kubelík also composed, numbering among his work six violin concertos, as well as a Symphony and some chamber music. He also prepared CADENZAS (showy solo passages to be performed at the end of a work) for the violin concertos of LUDWIG VAN BEETHOVEN, JOHANNES BRAHMS, and PIOTR ILYICH TCHAIKOVSKY.

PEOPLE IN MUSIC

Kubelík, (Jeronym) **Rafael,** eminent Czech-born Swiss conductor, son of JAN KUBELÍK; b. Bychory, near Kolin, June 29, 1914; d. Lucerne, Aug. 11, 1996. Kubelík studied violin with his father and then continued his musical training at the Prague Conservatory. In 1934 he made his conducting debut with the Czech Philharmonic in Prague, and then was conductor at the National Theater in Brno from 1939 to 1941.

Kubelík was chief conductor of the Czech Philharmonic from 1942 to 1948, one of the most difficult periods in the history of the orchestra and the Czech nation. He refused to collaborate with the Nazi occupation authorities, and when the Communists took control of the government in 1948, he left the country for the West, vowing not to return until the political situation changed.

Kubelík appeared as a guest conductor in England and Western Europe, then made his U.S. debut with the Chicago Symphony Orchestra in 1949. His success led to his appointment as the orchestra's music director in 1950. However, his inclusion of many contemporary works in his programs alienated some of his audience, including members of the Chicago press, causing him to resign his post in 1953. He subsequently was music director at the Royal Opera House at Covent Garden in London from 1955 to 1958. His tenure there was notable for important productions of LES TROYENS, BORIS GODUNOV (in the original version), and JENŮFA. He then was chief conductor of the Bavarian Radio Symphony Orchestra in Munich from 1961 to 1979.

Kubelík made his Metropolitan Opera debut in N.Y. as its first music director in 1973, conducting *Les Troyens*. However, he again attracted controversy and soon submitted his resignation. In spite of these problems, his artistic integrity remained intact. He continued to appear widely as a guest conductor in Western Europe and the U.S. In light of his controversial tenure in Chicago, it was ironic that he became an honored guest conductor with that orchestra in later years.

Kubelík retired in 1985. He returned to Czechoslovakia after the fall of the Communists in 1990, after an absence of 42 years. He symbolically conducted the Czech Philharmonic in two performances of BEDŘICH SMETANA's symphonic cycle *Má Vlast* (My Land) during the opening of the Prague Spring Festival, despite his increasingly ill health.

Kubelík was the foremost Czech conductor of his generation. He was greatly esteemed for his distinguished interpretations of the standard repertoire, which were marked by a pristine musicianship, unfettered by self-indulgence. He naturally was also known for his interpretations of the music of his homeland.

Kubelík became a Swiss citizen in 1966. His second wife was the Australian soprano ELSIE MORISON. He also composed several operas, including *Veronika* (1947) and *Cor-*

nelia Faroli (1972), a number of orchestral and choral works, six string quartets and other chamber music works, and songs.

MUSICAL INSTRUMENT

kulintang. Gong-chime of the Philippines, consisting of between eight and 12 gongs placed open-face down in two rows. The gongs are suspended and isolated by taut strings. It is played with a pair of padded sticks. Similar instruments are found in Malaysia and many parts of Indonesia. It is a member of the Indonesian GAMELAN.

MUSICAL INSTRUMENT

kultrún (*cultrún*). Rattle drum of the Araucano people of Chile. It has a calabash body with a horseskin head. Inside the gourd, there are pebbles that create a rattling sound when the head is struck by a drumstick.

Kunc, Božidar. *See* MILANOV, ZINKA.

Greek writers compared the sound of the kymbala to galloping horse hooves.

kymbala (Grk.). Ancient CYMBALS, either plate-like or bulbous in shape. When struck together, they produce a dull, percussive sound. Not the same as *antique cymbals* (CROTALES).

kü′rē-ĕh

Kyrie (Grk., Lord). The first section of the ORDINARY in the Roman Catholic MASS, sung after the INTROIT. The brief text is divided into three sentences, with repetitions: *Kyrie eleison* (Lord, have mercy), *Christe eleison* (Christ, have mercy), and *Kyrie eleison.*

L. (Ger. *links*). Left, as in *l.h.*, left hand.

La. The sixth DIATONIC degree of the SCALE. It is also used in the system of MOVABLE DO, where it is also called *Lah*.

La Bamba. Latin-American folk song popularized by Ritchie Valens in 1959. It was also featured in the 1987 film made about his life, where it is performed by the Mexican-American band Los Lobos.

La Barbara, Joan (Linda Lotz), American composer and outstanding experimental vocalist; b. Philadelphia, June 8, 1947. La Barbara learned piano from her grandfather, later singing in church, school choirs, and a folk music group. She studied voice with Helen Boatwright at the Syracuse University School of Music between 1965 and 1968, and music education at N.Y. University, earning her B.A. degree in 1970. She also studied voice with Phyllis Curtin at the Berkshire Music Center at Tanglewood in 1967–68.

In 1971 La Barbara made her debut as a vocalist at N.Y.'s Town Hall with STEVE REICH and Musicians, with whom she continued to perform until 1974. She also worked with PHILIP GLASS between 1973 and 1976. She toured in the U.S. and Europe, and in 1979 was composer-in-residence in West Berlin. Beginning in 1981, she taught voice and composition for five years at the California Institute of the Arts in Valencia. In 1979 she married the American composer MORTON SUBOTNICK.

A champion of contemporary music, La Barbara developed her performing talents to a high degree. Her vocal techniques include MULTIPHONICS (producing more than one tone at once) and CIRCULAR BREATHING, with unique throat clicks and a high flutter to match. Many contempo-

La was the sixth note in medieval musician GUIDO D'AREZZO'S HEXACHORD, or six-note scale, which he developed to teach sight singing. It is based on the last line of the *Hymn to St. John*, "*Labii reatum.*"

PEOPLE IN MUSIC

rary composers have written works for her to perform; in fact, it is hard to imagine anyone else being capable of performing these very demanding works.

La Barbara has won numerous awards and fellowships, including six NEA grants, and grants from ASCAP and the ISCM. In 1993 she appeared in the N.Y. premiere of Subotnick's opera, *Jacob's Room,* and in 1994 in the premiere of Robert Ashley's quartet of operas *Now Eleanor's Idea.* Her own compositions, many involving electronics, effectively exploit her vocal abilities.

La Guerre, Élisabeth Jacquet de. *See* JACQUET DE LA GUERRE, ÉLISABETH.

La, La, Lucille. Musical by GEORGE GERSHWIN, 1919. The first musical composed entirely by Gershwin, it features the song *Nobody but You.*

A puritanical matron wills her considerable fortune to her nephew on condition that he divorce his wife, a chorus girl. He decides to comply with the terms, divorce his wife, get the legacy, and then remarry her. A Philadelphia hotel employee named Lucille arranges for him to be surprised in the company of a woman not his wife. (At that time, divorces were only granted for adultery or on similar grounds.) He registers at the hotel as John Smith, only to discover that there are 38 other John Smiths already registered there! Much merriment and many mistaken identities follow, until all is brought right in the end.

PEOPLE IN MUSIC

Labèque, Katia (b. Hendaye, March 3, 1950) and **Marielle** (b. Hendaye, March 6, 1952), French duo-pianists. The sisters began piano study in early childhood with their mother, a pupil of the great French pianist Marguerite Long (1874–1966). They made their formal debut in Bayonne in 1961.

After completing their studies with Jean-Bernard Pommier at the Paris Conservatory (first prize at graduation, 1968), the Labèques embarked upon a remarkable career as duo-pianists, touring widely in Europe, North America, and the Middle and Far East, giving numerous recitals and appearing with leading orchestras of the world. Their repertoire is wide, ranging from the masterworks of the past to contemporary scores by OLIVIER MESSIAEN, PIERRE BOULEZ, LUCIANO BERIO, and others. They play popular works as well, from SCOTT JOPLIN to GEORGE GERSHWIN. They championed Gershwin's duo-piano versions of *Rhapsody in Blue, Concerto in F,* and *An American in Paris.*

Lacrimosa (Lat.). A part of the REQUIEM MASS. *Lacrimoso,* tearfully.

Lady, Be Good! Musical by GEORGE GERSHWIN, 1924. A brother-and-sister dance team (originally played by Adele and Fred Astaire) encounter an heiress who falls in love with the brother. He at first feels he cannot return her affections, but after a series of comic episodes, the pair is united.

One of Gershwin's best known songs, *The Man I Love,* was dropped from the show just before its N.Y. opening (it resurfaced in *Strike Up the Band,* 1927). The song *Fascinating Rhythm,* which survived the cuts, remains a rare example of POLYMETER (more than one meter expressed at the same time) in American popular song.

Lady in the Dark. Musical by KURT WEILL and IRA GERSHWIN, 1941. The title character is the editor of a women's magazine who undergoes a strenuous program of psychoanalysis. This gives a clue to three extended dream episodes as she recounts them to the analyst. The dreams plainly indicate that she should marry the magazine's managing editor, and so she does. Includes *Tchaikovsky,* a tongue-twisting tour de force originally written for the comedian Danny Kaye, who must recite the names of 50 Russian composers at a very fast pace.

Lady Is a Tramp, The. Song by RICHARD RODGERS and LORENZ HART, 1937, from the musical *Babes in Arms.* It was later interpolated in the 1957 film of their musical *Pal Joey.*

Lady Macbeth of the Mtzensk District (**Katerina Izmailova**)**.** Opera by DMITRI SHOSTAKOVICH, 1934, first performed in Leningrad. The story depicts adultery and murder in Russia in the middle of the 19th century. The protagonist conspires with her lover to murder her husband. The cul-

The Labèques have broken the rule that all classical performers must dress conservatively. They have exploited their good looks, dressing in contemporary clothing, and are not afraid to play to the audience.

In this opera, the lover's adultery is underscored by the sound of a slide trombone—the downward slide indicating his fall into sin!

prits are convicted and sent to Siberia. When her lover takes another mistress there, she kills her rival and then commits suicide.

Unexpectedly, *Pravda,* the official newspaper of the Soviet Communist Party, attacked the opera as a product of bourgeois decadence and damned it for its modern style of HARMONY. Shostakovich apologized for his musical sins and stopped writing operas for a number of years. The opera was eventually revived in a sanitized version under the title *Katerina Izmailova,* 1963, the name of the heroine.

lai (Fr. lay). Chansons of the French TROUVÈRES and late medieval composers. Like most French song forms of the period, the texts are STROPHIC.

In the case of the lai, there are nearly as many poetic (and thus musical) forms as there are examples. The lai could also be a poem without music. GUILLAUME DE MACHAUT wrote several of both types.

The term *lai* may refer to one of several related genres: *descort, Leich, estampie, ductia, ensalada,* and even the liturgical SEQUENCE.

Lakmé. Opera by LÉO DELIBES, 1883, first performed in Paris. Lakmé, the daughter of a priest of Brahma, is loved by a British officer. He inadvertently profanes the Buddhist temple by entering it with his shoes on and is denounced by the priest. In the end, Lakmé realizes the futility of her love, plucks a poisonous flower, and dies.

The score is permeated with attractive pseudo-oriental melodies and rhythms. Lakmé's *Bell Song* is a perennial favorite with COLORATURA SOPRANOS.

Lalo, Édouard (-Victoire-Antoine), distinguished French composer of Spanish descent; b. Lille, Jan. 27, 1823; d. Paris, April 22, 1892. Lalo studied violin and cello at the Lille Conservatory. After his father objected to his pursuing a career as a professional musician, he left home at age 16 to study VIOLIN at the Paris Conservatory. He also studied composition privately with Erwin Schulhoff.

Between 1848 and 1860, Lalo made a precarious living as a violinist and teacher, and also began to compose, pro-

PEOPLE IN MUSIC

ducing some songs and chamber music. He became a founding member of the Armingaud Quartet in 1855, serving first as a violist and subsequently as second violinist. Lalo nearly abandoned composing after 1860 because his own works had failed to find an audience. However, his 1865 marriage to the CONTRALTO Bernier de Maligny, who sang many of his songs, prompted him to resume composing.

Lalo wrote an opera, *Fiesque,* and submitted it to a competition sponsored by the Théâtre-Lyrique in Paris in 1867. It was refused production, a rebuke that left him deeply bitter. However, he was so convinced of the value of the score that he subsequently reworked parts of it into various other works, including the first *Aubade* for small orchestra, the Divertissement, and the Symphony in G minor.

The Divertissement was introduced at the Concert Populaire in 1872 and was Lalo's first popular success. Then, the talented violinist PABLO DE SARASATE gave the premiere performance of Lalo's Violin Concerto in 1874, and, a year later, of Lalo's *Symphonie espagnole* for violin and orchestra.

While producing orchestral works, Lalo continued to write for the stage. In 1875 he began work on the opera *Le Roi d'Ys.* The major portion of the score was finished by 1881, and extracts were performed in concerts. However, no theater was interested in mounting a full production. He then accepted a commission from the Opéra to write a ballet. Although the resulting work, *Namouna* (1882), failed to make an impression, he drew a series of orchestral suites from it, which became quite popular. In 1888, Lalo finally succeeded in persuading the Paris Opéra-Comique to produce *Le Roi d'Ys.* Its premiere was an enormous success. Lalo was rewarded by being made an Officer of the Legion of Honor.

While *Le Roi d'Ys* is considered Lalo's masterpiece by his countrymen, his instrumental music is of particular importance in assessing his achievement as a composer. His craftsmanship, combined with his originality, places him among the most important French composers of his time.

Lalo's son, Pierre (b. Puteaux, Sept. 6, 1866; d. Paris, June 9, 1943), was a music critic who became well known for his writings attacking the modern works of CLAUDE DEBUSSY.

Lalo's *Symphonie espagnole,* a brilliant virtuoso piece with vibrant Spanish rhythms, brought him international fame. It remains his best-known composition outside his native country.

PEOPLE IN MUSIC

Lamb wrote rags in the classical style of SCOTT JOPLIN. He was thrilled when he had a chance to meet Joplin after the composer had moved to N.Y. Joplin praised Lamb highly, saying his works were "real colored rags." To Lamb, that was the highest compliment.

PEOPLE IN MUSIC

Lamb, Joseph F(rancis)**,** remarkable American ragtime pianist and composer; b. Montclair, N.J., Dec. 6, 1887; d. N.Y., Sept. 3, 1960. Although he had no formal musical training and spent most of his life in the textile import business, Lamb was one of the most important composers of piano rags during the heyday of RAGTIME. He also wrote a number of songs for TIN PAN ALLEY. After almost 30 years, he was rediscovered in 1949; he began composing rags again and also appeared as a ragtime pianist.

Lamb's most notable rags were *Sensation* (1908), *Ethiopia Rag* (1909), *Excelsior Rag* (1909), *Champagne Rag* (1910), *American Beauty Rag* (1913), *Cleopatra Rag* (1915), *Contentment Rag* (1915), *The Ragtime Nightingale* (1915), *Reindeer* (1915), *Patricia Rag* (1916), *Top Liner Rag* (1916), and *Bohemia Rag* (1919).

Lambert, (Leonard) **Constant,** remarkable English conductor, composer, and writer on music; b. London, Aug. 23, 1905; d. there, Aug. 21, 1951. Lambert won a scholarship to the Royal College of Music in London, where he studied with the composer and teachers R.O. Morris and RALPH VAUGHAN WILLIAMS from 1915 to 1922.

Lambert's first major score, the 1926 ballet *Romeo and Juliet,* was commissioned by the great dance producer Serge Diaghilev. This early association with the dance proved decisive, for he spent most of his life as a conductor and composer of ballets. His interest in jazz resulted in such fine scores as *Elegiac Blues* for orchestra and *The Rio Grande* for piano, chorus, and orchestra, both composed in 1927; and the Concerto for piano and nine performers, written in 1930–31. Of his many ballets, the most striking in craftsmanship was his *Horoscope* in 1937. In the meantime, he became conductor of London's Camargo Society for the presentation of ballets beginning in 1930.

Lambert was made music director of the Vic-Wells Ballet in 1931, remaining in that capacity after it became the Sadler's Wells Ballet and the Royal Ballet. After resigning in 1947, he was made one of its artistic directors in 1948 and conducted it on its first visit to the U.S. a year later. He also appeared at London's Covent Garden (1937, 1939, 1946–47). Lambert was associate conductor of the London

Promenade Concerts in 1945–46, and frequently conducted broadcast performances over the BBC. Lambert also wrote on music for several British journals.

Lambert was one of the most gifted musicians of his generation. However, his demanding work as a conductor and his excessive consumption of alcohol prevented him from fully asserting himself as a composer in his later years.

Lambert, Michel. *See* LULLY, JEAN-BAPTISTE.

lamellaphones. Hand-held musical instruments native to sub-Saharan Africa whose sound is produced by the vibration of thin tongues of metal or wood plucked by the thumbs. The tongues are attached to a rectangular wooden or metal resonator. Some feature small strips of metal twisted around the tongues, in order to add a buzzing or humming sound to the tone.

Among the best known lamellaphones are the *sanza* (sansa), *mbira, likembe,* and *kalimba* (thumb pianos).

lament. Dirges chanted upon the death of an important person or a beloved friend.

Surviving examples date back to the death of Charlemagne in 814. In France laments bore the names of *déploration, plainte,* and TOMBEAU. JOHANNES OCKEGHEM wrote a lament on the death of Gilles Binchois and was in turn musically lamented by JOSQUIN DES PREZ, who was upon his own death lamented by NICOLAS GOMBERT. FRANÇOIS COUPERIN LE GRAND wrote an apotheosis for JEAN-BAPTISTE LULLY, but he himself had to wait for nearly two centuries to be musically commemorated with comparable grandeur by MAURICE RAVEL in his *Le Tombeau de Couperin.*

Other types of laments are the DIRGE, ELEGY, and THRENODY.

lamento (It., lamentation, complaint). A common regular type of ARIA in Italian opera in which a character expresses unquenchable sorrow. *Lamento d'Arianna,* the only surviving segment from CLAUDIO MONTEVERDI's opera *Arianna* (1608), in which Ariadne laments her painful abandonment by the treacherous Theseus, is an outstanding example.

MUSICAL
INSTRUMENT

Dating back as far as ancient Egypt, professional women lamenters have been hired to shed tears at funerals, at military conscriptions when young men are taken to war, and at peasant weddings when the fate of a youthful bride was deplored with great wailings.

PEOPLE IN MUSIC

Landini, Francesco (Franciscus Landino, Magister Franciscus de Florentia, Francesco degli orghany, Magister Franciscus Cecus Horghanista de Florentia, Cechus de Florentia), important Italian composer; b. probably in Florence, c.1325; d. there, Sept. 2, 1397. Francesco's father was the painter Jacopo Del Casentino (d. 1349), cofounder of Florence's guild of painters in 1339.

After being blinded by smallpox as a child, Francesco turned to music. He learned to play the ORGAN and other instruments and also sang. He became well known as an organist, organ builder, organ tuner, and instrument maker, and was also active as a poet. He was organist at the monastery of S. Trinita in 1361. He was *cappellanus* at the church of S. Lorenzo from 1365 until his death.

Francesco's output is particularly significant because it represents about one quarter of the surviving Italian 14th-century music. Some 154 works have been identified as his. These include 90 ballate for two voices, 42 for three voices, and eight in both two- and three-part versions; nine madrigali (of the Trecento, not RENAISSANCE type) for two or three voices; one French VIRELAI; and one CACCIA.

lent′ler   **Ländler** (Ger.; Fr. *Tyrolienne*). A slow folk dance of the German-speaking areas of Europe in $\frac{3}{4}$ or $\frac{6}{4}$ time, a precursor of the 19th-century WALTZ.

The Ländler dates from the 17th century and has been known under numerous names, including the German dances (DEUTSCHER TANZ) written by FRANZ JOSEPH HAYDN and WOLFGANG AMADEUS MOZART and intended for courtly dancers. In its original form, it was an outdoor dance, with hopping, stamping, and passing under while the couple holds each other by the waist. Songs associated with this music might include YODELING.

The Ländler survived into the 19th century, but it evolved into a faster, more refined, and lighter dance. By the early 20th century, the music of the Ländler held great nostalgic value for Austrian composers such as GUSTAV MAHLER and ALBAN BERG.

PEOPLE IN MUSIC

Landowska, Wanda (Alexandra), celebrated Polish-born French harpsichordist, pianist, and pedagogue.; b. Warsaw,

July 5, 1879; d. Lakeville, Conn., Aug. 16, 1959. She studied PIANO at the Warsaw Conservatory and in Berlin with the well-known Polish-born pianist MORITZ MOSZKOWSKI.

In 1900 Landowska went to Paris, where she married Henry Lew, a writer. She traveled widely in Europe as a pianist, and as a harpsichordist from 1903. Subsequently, she devoted her efforts principally to reviving the art of HARPSICHORD playing. In 1912 she commissioned the Pleyel firm of Paris to construct a harpsichord for her. This was the first of the many keyboard instruments built for her in subsequent years. In 1913 she was invited to give a special harpsichord course at the Berlin Hochschule für Musik.

The outbreak of World War I in 1914 found Landowska in Germany, where she was interned until the war ended. In 1918 her husband was killed in an automobile accident in Berlin. In 1919 she gave master classes in harpsichord at the Basel Conservatory, then returned to Paris. In 1925 she bought a villa in St.-Leu-la-Forêt, near Paris, and established there a school for the study of early music. A concert hall was built there in 1927, where she presented regular concerts of early music and gave lessons on the subject. She also assembled a large collection of harpsichords. Her school attracted students from all over the world.

Landowska also commissioned new music for the harpsichord. MANUEL DE FALLA wrote for her a chamber concerto for harpsichord. She played the solo part in its first performance in Barcelona in 1926. Another commission was FRANCIS POULENC's *Concert champêtre* for harpsichord and small orchestra in 1929. She appeared for the first time in America as soloist with the Philadelphia Orchestra, under LEOPOLD STOKOWSKI, in 1923.

When the Germans invaded France in 1940, Landowska fled to Switzerland, abandoning her villa, library, and instruments. In 1941 she reached N.Y. She presented a concert of harpsichord music there in 1942, and then devoted herself mainly to teaching and making recordings. She settled in Lakeville, Connecticut, where she died in 1959.

Landowska was one of the greatest harpsichord performers. Her interpretations of BAROQUE music were notable in their balance between CLASSICAL precision and freedom from rigidity, particularly in the treatment of ORNAMENTATION.

Landowska toured Russia in 1909, where she played for the great Russian author Tolstoy. He showed great interest in her ideas on classical music.

Landowska also wrote several books on music and composed CADENZAS for WOLFGANG AMADEUS MOZART's concertos.

PEOPLE IN MUSIC

Lane, Burton (born Morris Hyman Kushner), American composer of popular music; b. N.Y., Feb. 2, 1912; d. there, Jan. 5, 1997. Lane studied piano as a child and played strings in the school band. Showing early talent in music, he composed some pieces for the band while still a teenager.

After leaving high school, Lane was hired by Remick Music, a N.Y.-based publishing firm, where he met GEORGE GERSHWIN, who encouraged him to continue composing. Lane's first Broadway songs appeared in the 1929 revue *Three's a Crowd,* with lyrics by Harold Dietz. Two years later, he placed some songs in *Earl Carroll Vanities of 1931.*

With Broadway work drying up because of the Depression, Lane moved to Hollywood. He wrote for some 40 films between the early '30s and the mid-'50s, including *St. Louis Blues, Babes on Broadway* (including *How About You?*), *Ship Ahoy,* and *Royal Wedding* (including *Too Late Now*). Among the lyricists who worked with him were IRA GERSHWIN, FRANK LOESSER, E.Y. HARBURG, and ALAN JAY LERNER.

In the '40s, Lane returned to Broadway with a series of hit shows, including *Hold On to Your Hats* (1940), *Laffing Room Only* (1944), and the classic *Finian's Rainbow.* After a period of inactivity, he returned with the smash 1965 hit *On a Clear Day You Can See Forever,* with lyrics by Alan Jay Lerner. Sadly, his last show, 1978's *Carmelina,* also with lyrics by Lerner, died soon after it opened.

Some of Lane's memorable songs from *Finian's Rainbow* include *Something Sort of Grandish, Old Devil Moon,* and *How Are Things in Glocca Morra?*

Lane was a member of the Theatre Hall of Fame and the Songwriters Hall of Fame. In the early '90s, he accompanied popular singer Michael Feinstein on a two-CD set of his songs.

Langridge, Philip (Gordon), esteemed English tenor; b. Hawkhurst, Kent, Dec. 16, 1939. Langridge studied violin at the Royal Academy of Music in London and took voice lessons with Bruce Boyce and Celia Bizony. He was active as a violinist but also began to make appearances as a singer from 1962.

Langridge first sang at the Glyndebourne Festival in 1964, making regular appearances there from 1977. He also

PEOPLE IN MUSIC

sang at the Edinburgh Festivals from 1970. He appeared at Milan's La Scala in 1979, then sang for the first time at London's Covent Garden as the Fisherman in IGOR STRAVINSKY's *The Nightingale* in 1983. He made his Metropolitan Opera debut in N.Y. as Ferrando in *Così fan tutte* on Jan. 5, 1985. He was chosen to create the role of Orpheus in HARRISON BIRTWISTLE's opera *The Mask of Orpheus* at London's English National Opera in 1986. In 1992 he appeared as Igor Stravinsky's Oedipus Rex at the inaugural operatic production at the Saito Kinen Festival in Matsumoto. He was made a Commander of the Order of the British Empire in 1994.

Admired as both an operatic and a concert singer, Langridge maintains an extensive repertoire ranging from the BAROQUE masters to contemporary works. He is married to the singer Ann Murray.

Lanner, Joseph (Franz Karl), historically significant Austrian violinist, conductor, and composer; b. Vienna, April 12, 1801; d. Oberdobling, near Vienna, April 14, 1843. A self-taught violinist and composer, Lanner joined Pamer's dance orchestra, a popular Viennese group, when he was 12. In 1818 he formed a trio, which, a year later, became a quartet when JOHANN STRAUSS, SR., joined. The group grew in size, and, by 1824, it was a full-sized classical orchestra that performed in coffeehouses, in taverns, and at balls. The orchestra was subsequently divided into two ensembles, with Lanner leading one and Strauss the other. Strauss went his own way in 1825.

PEOPLE IN MUSIC

With Strauss, Lanner is acknowledged as the creator of the 19th-century Viennese WALTZ. His output totals 209 popular pieces, including 112 waltzes, 25 LÄNDLER, ten QUADRILLES, three POLKAS, 28 GALOPS, and six MARCHES. He also composed an overture to the fairy tale *Der Preis einer Lebensstunde,* the *Banquet-Polonaise,* a TARANTELLA, and a BOLERO.

His son August (Joseph) Lanner (1834–55) was a short-lived but talented violinist, dance composer, and conductor.

Lanza, Mario (born Alfredo Arnold Cocozza), American tenor and actor; b. Philadelphia, Jan. 31, 1921; d. Rome, Oct. 7, 1959. Lanza's parents were Italian immigrants who

PEOPLE IN MUSIC

settled in Philadelphia. He studied singing with various local teachers and signed as a teenager with a major classical management firm. At this time, he took his stage name, a variation of his mother's maiden name, Maria Lanza.

However, before Lanza could begin a career as a professional singer, he was drafted into the Army. Appearing in several army shows and billed as the "Service Caruso," Lanza began to gain attention for his strong voice. He settled in N.Y. after the war, recording and appearing on radio shows. The head of MGM studios heard one of his recordings and signed him to a film contract in 1947.

Lanza's first film, *That Midnight Kiss* from 1949, set the pattern for all his Hollywood work. The score mixed sentimental popular hits with familiar operatic selections, giving Lanza a chance to show off his voice without loading the film down with too much high-toned music. The film was an immediate hit.

Lanza's next film, *The Toast of New Orleans,* included his most popular song, *Be My Love,* a million-selling hit. In 1951 Lanza had the opportunity to portray his idol, ENRICO CARUSO, in the Hollywood-version of the famed tenor's life, entitled *The Great Caruso.* Besides the obligatory arias, the film introduced *It's the Loveliest Night of the Year,* which gave Lanza another million-seller.

However, from this point, Lanza's career began to suffer. Extremely high-strung, Lanza began to balk at the quality of the projects MGM offered him. Meanwhile, tales of his binge eating were sweeping through Hollywood, and the already rotund star was beginning to burst out of the seams of his clothing. He also became dependent on tranquilizers and alcohol.

Lanza completed two further films for MGM, although in his final picture for the studio, an adaptation of the popular operetta *The Student Prince,* he only sang on the soundtrack. He then retired from performing for a year, returning in 1956 in the film *Serenade.* Despite the abuse to his body, Lanza was still in good voice and had a hit with the film's title song.

Nevertheless, Lanza was tired of the Hollywood scene, and in 1957 moved to Italy. There he appeared in the film *The Seven Hills of Rome* in 1958, introducing the ever-popular

MGM producer Joe Pasternak said of Lanza, "[He had] the most beautiful voice I had ever heard—but his bushy hair made him look like a caveman!"

song, *Arriverderci, Roma.* He then toured England and continental Europe, appearing in good shape and singing well.

However, in autumn 1959 Lanza checked into a clinic in Rome. A week later, he was dead of an apparent heart attack.

Lanza's legacy is still much debated. Some opera fans and stars consider him to be "America's Caruso," one of the great voices of our century. Others feel he catered to a pop audience by performing the most well-worn parts of the opera repertoire.

Lark Ascending, The. Work for violin and orchestra by RALPH VAUGHAN WILLIAMS, 1921, first performed in London. It was inspired by the George Meredith poem.

Lark Quartet (*Lerchenquartett*). String Quartet, op.64, no. 5, in D major (1790–92) by FRANZ JOSEPH HAYDN. The opening tune in the high violin has been described as imitating a lark's song.

Larrocha (y de la Calle), **Alicia de,** brilliant Spanish pianist; b. Barcelona, May 23, 1923. Larrocha studied piano with Frank Marshall and theory with Ricardo Lamote de Grignon. She made her first public appearance at the age of five and was soloist with the Orquesta Sinfónica of Madrid at the age of 11.

In 1940 Larrocha launched her career in earnest. She began making major tours of Europe in 1947 and appeared in the U.S. for the first time in 1955. In 1986 she was soloist at the London Promenade Concerts, and in 1989 she gave a recital at London's Barbican Hall. In 1995 she appeared at the Edinburgh Festival. She also served as director of the Marshall Academy in Barcelona from 1959.

Larrocha's interpretations of Spanish music have been widely praised for their authentic quality. She has also been praised for her excellent taste and exquisitely polished technique in classical works, particularly those of WOLFGANG AMADEUS MOZART.

Lasso, Orlando di, great Franco-Flemish composer, known in Latin as Orlandus Lassus and in French as Roland de Las-

One rumor that circulated at the time of Lanza's death was that he was killed by the Mafia because he refused to sing for the famous mobster Lucky Luciano.

PEOPLE IN MUSIC

PEOPLE IN MUSIC

sus; b. Mons, 1532; d. Munich, June 14, 1594. Lasso entered the service of the nobleman Ferrante Gonzaga when he was about 12 years old, and subsequently traveled with him. He then was placed in the service of Constantino Castrioto of Naples at the age of 18. He later proceeded to Rome and entered the service of Antonio Altoviti, Archbishop of Florence, after which he was maestro di cappella (musical director for the chapel) at St. John Lateran in 1553–54.

In 1555 Lasso went to Antwerp, where he enjoyed a fine reputation both socially and artistically. His first works were published that year in Venice, containing 22 madrigals set to poems of Petrarch. He also brought out a collection of madrigals and motets set to texts in Italian, French, and Latin in Antwerp.

In 1556 Lasso became a singer at the Munich court chapel of Duke Albrecht of Bavaria. He took Regina Wechinger (Wackinger), an aristocratic woman, in marriage in 1558. In 1563 he was made maestro di cappella of the Munich court chapel, a position he held with great eminence until his death. He made occasional trips, including two trips to Italy and France. In 1570 he received from the Emperor Maximilian a hereditary rank of nobility.

Lasso's compositions represent the highest achievement of the great era of Franco-Flemish POLYPHONY. His total mastery in sacred as well as secular music made him one of the most versatile composers of his time. He was equally capable of writing in the most elevated style and in the popular idiom. He wrote Italian MADRIGALS, German LIEDER, French CHANSONS, and Latin MOTETS.

The sheer scope of his production is amazing: more than 2,000 works in various genres. The *Patrocinium Musices* (12 volumes, Munich, 1573–98) contains seven volumes of Lasso's works. Other important collections published during his lifetime include books of madrigals; part chansons; Lieder; *sacrae cantiones; Psalms of David* (1584).

After Lasso's death, collections published include the *Lagrime di S Pietro* (1595) and *Prophetiae Sibyllarum* (1600). Lasso's sons published 516 of his motets under the title *Magnum opus musicum* (1604). Eitner published *Chronologisches Verzeichnis der Druckwerke des Orlando di Lassus*

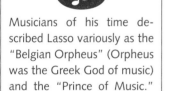

Musicians of his time described Lasso variously as the "Belgian Orpheus" (Orpheus was the Greek God of music) and the "Prince of Music."

(Berlin, 1874). W. Boetticher published a complete catalogue of Lasso's works in Berlin in 1956.

Last Savage, The (*Le dernier sauvage*). OPERA BUFFA by GIAN CARLO MENOTTI, 1963, to his own LIBRETTO. Originally in Italian, it was first performed in French at the Paris Opéra-Comique.

The plot is typical of the fanciful stories Menotti likes to score. An eccentric Chicago millionairess goes to India in quest of the Abominable Snowman. Scheming individuals produce a tall human whom they declare to be the Snowman. Delighted, the heiress imports him to America, but he is appalled by modern life and abominates the snows of Chicago. When he hears a concert of modern music, he decides to quit, and goes back to the Himalayas.

Last Time I Saw Paris, The. Ballad by JEROME KERN, 1940, a lament on the fate of the city under Nazi occupation. It was sung by KATE SMITH. The song was added into the film *Lady Be Good* of 1941.

lauda (It.; plural, *laude, laudi*). HYMN of praise. These hymns were particularly popular with wandering religious orders.

During the Middle Ages, groups of penitents would travel from town to town, repenting their sins. As they traveled, they'd sing these songs. They'd also pick up local popular melodies—including many unrelated dance forms, such as the FROTTOLA and BALLATA—which they added to the lauda.

The laude influenced the development of the ORATORIO in the early 17th century.

Laudi spirituali, medieval songs of devotion.

Laudamus te (Lat., we praise Thee). Part of the GLORIA of the MASS.

launeddas. A triple pipe from the Island of Sardinia (off of Italy). Each pipe has a single reed. The melodic pipes are on the outside, the DRONE in the center. The right pipe is

MUSICAL
INSTRUMENT

shorter than the left, and all three are blown by mouth. The instrument may be of Phoenician origin.

Laura. Popular song by DAVID RAKSIN, 1944, originally wordless. It served as the theme song for the film of the same name. JOHNNY MERCER's words were added later, and in this form, the song sold millions of disks.

Lavignac, (Alexandre Jean) **Albert,** eminent French musicologist and teacher; b. Paris, Jan. 21, 1846; d. there, May 28, 1916. He studied piano, harmony, and composition at the Paris Conservatory, winning several prizes between 1857 and 1865. In 1871 he was appointed assistant professor of SOLFÈGE (sightsinging) there, becoming a full professor in 1875 and then professor of harmony in 1891.

Lavignac's *Cours complet theorique et pratique de dictée musicale* (Complete theoretical and practical course in music dictation; 6 volumes, Paris and Brussels, 1882) attracted considerable attention. It was followed by several educational texts. His magnum opus was the famous *Encyclopédie de la musique et Dictionnaire du Conservatoire* (Encyclopedia of music and dictionary of the conservatory; Paris, three volumes, 1920–31), which he edited from 1913 until his death.

Law, Andrew, American singing teacher and composer; b. Milford, Conn., March 21, 1749; d. Cheshire, Conn., July 13, 1821. Law graduated from Rhode Island College, receiving his Master of Arts degree in 1778. He then studied theology and was ordained in Hartford in 1787. He subsequently was active as a preacher in Philadelphia and Baltimore.

Later in his career, Law became a pioneer singing teacher in New England. He invented a new system of notation, patented in 1802, which employed four (later seven) different shapes of notes without the staff. It was not successful and was used in only a few of his own books. A second innovation (at least as far as American usage was concerned) was his setting of the melody in the SOPRANO voice instead of in the TENOR. In 1786 he received an honorary M.A. degree

PEOPLE IN MUSIC

Lavignac's emphasis on the importance of students learning the skill of musical dictation led to its introduction as a regular subject in all the important European conservatories.

PEOPLE IN MUSIC

from Yale University, and in 1821 an LL.D. from Allegheny College in Meadville, Pennsylvania.

Law compiled and/or wrote several collections of hymns and instructional books on music. Only one of his hymn tunes, *Archdale,* acquired popularity, but his teaching books, quaintly but clearly written, contributed considerably to early music education in America.

Laws, Hubert, African-American flutist; b. Houston, Nov. 10, 1939. Laws learned to play saxophone, piano, and guitar as well as flute. He played saxophone with the Jazz Crusaders from 1954 to 1960 while pursuing classical music studies. From 1967 he played with the N.Y. Jazz Sextet, and he was a member of other groups before joining the Metropolitan Opera Orchestra in N.Y. as a flutist. He also appeared as a soloist with the N.Y. Philharmonic while continuing to appear in JAZZ settings.

Laws achieved his greatest success in the mid-'70s when he recorded a series of albums in a jazz-fusion style. His version of IGOR STRAVINSKY'S *RITE OF SPRING* was particularly popular and inspired a series of jazz-pop versions of classical themes.

His brother Ronnie Laws (b. Houston, Oct. 3, 1950) is a tenor saxophonist and bandleader. In addition to their solo work, the two have performed together in various settings since the early '70s.

PEOPLE IN MUSIC

Le Caine, Hugh, Canadian physicist, acoustician, and innovative creator of electronic musical instruments; b. Port Arthur, Ontario, May 27, 1914; d. Ottawa, July 3, 1977. Although Le Caine's childhood training combined music and science, he emphasized science in his formal studies, receiving B.S. (1938) and M.S. (1939) degrees from Queen's University in Kingston, Ontario. He obtained his Ph.D. in nuclear physics from the University of Birmingham in 1952. He also studied piano briefly at the Royal Conservatory of Music of Toronto and privately with Viggo Kihl.

His childhood dream was to one day apply scientific techniques to the development and invention of new musical instruments. He went on to develop ground-breaking

PEOPLE IN MUSIC

electronic instruments which ultimately formed the basis of pioneering electronic music studios at the University of Toronto, founded in 1959, and McGill University in Montreal in 1964. He exhibited electronic instruments at Expo '67 in Montreal and contributed numerous articles on his findings in scholarly journals.

While Le Caine saw himself as a designer of instruments that assisted others in creative work, he himself created a number of striking electronic compositions in the course of his development. These include the now-classic *Dripsody* (1959), which used only the sound of a single drop of water falling. Other compositions were *Alchemy* (1964) and *Perpetual Motion for Data Systems Computer* (1970).

His instruments revolutionized musical composition. His Sackbut SYNTHESIZER (perfected in 1973), for example, is recognized as the first voltage-controlled synthesizer. Among his other instruments are the Spectrogram (1959–62; designed to facilitate the use of complex sine tones in composition), the Alleatone (c.1962; "a controlled chance device selecting one of 16 channels with weighted probabilities"), the Sonde (1968–70; it can generate 200 sine waves simultaneously), and the Polyphone (1970; a polyphonic synthesizer operated by a keyboard with touch-sensitive keys).

lead. 1. The giving-out or proposition of a THEME by one part. 2. A CUE.

lead sheet. A special form of musical score that includes the melody (on a staff) and its harmony, marked in shorthand (e.g., C$_7$ or G min) above or below the melody. The first verse of the text may be placed below the melody line, the additional verses at the bottom of the page.

Leadbelly (Lead Belly; born Huddie Ledbetter), influential African-American folksinger, guitarist, and songwriter; b. Mooringsport, La., Jan. 21, 1885; d. N.Y., Dec. 6, 1949. Leadbelly had no formal music education but possessed a genuine talent for guitar playing and songwriting.

After mastering the 12-string guitar, Leadbelly claimed to have worked as accompanist to Blind Lemon Jefferson in Dallas. However, there is evidence to suggest that the two may never have met. In any case, while in Texas, he was jailed for murder, serving a prison term between 1918 and 1925. He served another term, for attempted homicide, at the Louisiana State Penitentiary between 1930 and 1934. There he was discovered by folk researchers John and ALAN LOMAX, who recorded him in prison and helped obtain his release.

Leadbelly then settled in N.Y., where he made a series of historically significant recordings for the Library of Congress between 1935 and 1940. He served another term for assault in 1939–40. He spent his last years playing in nightclubs.

After his death, many of Leadbelly's songs and arrangements became popular. He adapted a turn-of-the-century popular song, *Goodnight, Irene,* into a unique personal version. The folk group the Weavers took this song to the top of the charts in 1950. Other songs associated with Leadbelly are *On a Monday, I Ain't Goin' Down to the Well No More,* and *Rock Island Line.* His career was made the subject of the film *Leadbelly* in 1975, and a biography by Charles Wolfe and Kip Lornell was published in 1995.

Leadbelly played a 12-string guitar, emphasizing the bass notes by playing "walking bass" (broken chord) accompaniments. His bass-playing style showed the influence of BOOGIE WOOGIE pianists.

leading. 1. (*noun*) The melodic progression or conduct of any part. 2. (*adjective*) Principal, chief; guiding, directing. *Leading chord,* the dominant seventh chord; *leading melody,* principal melody or theme; *leading motive, see* LEITMOTIV; *leading note, tone,* the seventh degree of the DIATONIC scale which resolves into the tonic, a semitone upward. In MINOR keys, the seventh degree in the natural scale is raised to provide the necessary leading tone (producing the HARMONIC MINOR SCALE).

Lear. Opera, 1978, by Aribert Reimann (b. 1936), first performed in Munich, based on Shakespeare's *King Lear.* The lead role was created by DIETRICH FISCHER-DIESKAU. The musical style is highly ATONAL and EXPRESSIONIST.

lectionary (from Lat. *legere,* read). A calendar of liturgical readings for the church year. In a secular sense, a collection of readings (from *lectio,* the act of reading) as opposed to a collection of speakings (from *dictio,* the act of speaking).

Ledbetter, Huddie. *See* LEADBELLY.

ledger lines (leger lines). Extra horizontal lines placed above or below the regular STAFF to accommodate notes either too high or too low in a given range.

In early music, composers made use of a great number of CLEFS for this purpose, thus avoiding the clutter of too many ledger lines. In modern notation, only two clefs, the treble and the bass, are used in piano music. When the notes rise to stratospheric altitudes, then the sign [8va—], meaning to be played an octave higher, is placed above them. When the notes sink too deeply into the infernal region below the bass staff, the sign [8va—] or the words OCTAVE BASSA are used. For very high notes, the symbol [15va—], meaning two octaves higher, is occasionally employed.

Ledger space, a space bounded on either side or both sides by a ledger line.

Led Zeppelin. (Vocal: Robert Plant, b. West Bromwich, U.K., Aug. 20, 1948; Guitar: Jimmy Page, b. London, Jan. 9, 1944; Bass/keyboards: John Paul Jones [John Baldwin], b. Sidcup, U.K., Jan. 3, 1946; Drums: John Bonham, b. Birmingham, U.K., May 31, 1947; d. Windsor, U.K., Sept. 25, 1980.) Exceptional heavy-metal group of the '70s.

PEOPLE IN MUSIC

Led Zeppelin's equipment setup for a concert, 1975. (Neal Preston/Corbis)

Born out of the ashes of the blues-rock band the Yard-birds, the band was a massive success from their first album in 1968. This was followed by an immensely successful U.S. tour, and the band's heavy metal sound soon spread far and wide. The band enjoyed their greatest success in 1971 with the FM-radio hit *Stairway to Heaven,* still a rock favorite.

The band continued to record and tour through the '70s, with a mid-decade break for over a year while lead singer Plant recovered from an automobile accident. The group was already winding down when drummer Bonham died in classic rock 'n' roll style from inhaling his own vomit following heavy drinking and drug use.

The group reunited twice in the '80s, for the Live Aid concert and again for Atlantic Records' 40th anniversary party. In 1995 Page and Plant reunited for an *MTV Unledded* show, which led to a follow-up tour. A year later, the group was inducted into the Rock and Roll Hall of Fame. Plant and Page have continued to record and tour through the late '90s.

Lee, Peggy (born Norma Dolores Egstrom), popular American singer, songwriter, and actress; b. Jamestown, N.D., May 26, 1920. Lee was born to a family of Scandinavian immigrants. Her mother died when she was four, and her father became an alcoholic. Lee was already working locally as a singer when she was a teenager.

After graduating from high school, she sang on a radio station in Fargo, where she was given her stage name of Peggy Lee. In the late '30s she traveled to California and then to Chicago, where she joined the vocal group The Four Of Us. BENNY GOODMAN's manager heard her perform in a club and recommended her to the bandleader.

In 1941 Goodman chose her as vocalist with his band, to replace Helen Forest. She gained her first success with Goodman on the song *Why Don't You Do Right?* In 1943 she left Goodman and launched a solo career. With her first husband, guitarist Dave Barbour, she collaborated on such hits as *Mañana, Golden Earrings,* and *I Don't Know Enough about You,* which she interpreted with great skill. She was equally successful with her sophisticated renditions of *Lover, Fever,*

PEOPLE IN MUSIC

and particularly *Is That All There Is?*, which became her theme song.

Lee was a solid hitmaker through the '50s. She also appeared in a few films, and scored some others. But her best-remembered film work was for Walt Disney's 1955 animated feature *The Lady and the Tramp*. Lee supplied the voice for the Siamese cat, Peg, and for several other characters in the film, as well as composing and performing the song *He's a Tramp* and five others.

Lee's career suffered in the late '50s because of poor health. Although she continued to perform over the next few decades, her health increasingly limited her appearances. With composer Paul Horner and playwright William Luce, she wrote the autobiographical musical *Peg* (1983), but it was unsuccessful. Into the '90s she continued to sing, often appearing in a wheelchair.

left-hand music. Either through accident, war, or illness, some pianists have lost the use of one arm. They have sought out composers to write special music that can be performed with one hand.

The Austrian pianist Paul Wittgenstein lost his right arm fighting on the Eastern Front during the World War I. He developed a startling virtuosity with his left hand. Taking advantage of his family wealth, Wittgenstein commissioned a number of important, and some unimportant, composers, among them MAURICE RAVEL, RICHARD STRAUSS, SERGEI PROKOFIEV, ERICH KORNGOLD, BENJAMIN BRITTEN, and FRANZ SCHMIDT to write for him concertos for piano left hand and orchestra.

When the Hungarian nobleman and amateur musician Count Zichy lost his right arm in a hunting accident, he decided to compose piano pieces for the left hand, which he performed at social occasions in Budapest. He also made arrangements for three hands. He even played the arrangement of a patriotic Hungarian march with FRANZ LISZT, supplying the bass line with his left hand.

ALEXANDER SCRIABIN was so eager to become a piano virtuoso in a grand style that he strained his right hand while a conservatory student in Moscow, trying to compete with his classmate JOSEF LHÉVINNE. But while Lhévinne was physi-

The American pianist Gary Graffman, a victim of the sometimes crippling carpal-tunnel syndrome, made a specialty of playing most of these left-handed concertos.

cally robust, Scriabin was rather frail and could never rival him on the concert platform. So he bandaged his ailing right hand and as a consolation prize wrote a charming group of piano pieces for left hand alone. Even pianists with both hands in perfect order like to play these pieces in public.

legato (*legate;* It., connected). A direction to perform the passage in a smooth and connected manner, with no break between the tones; also indicated by the legato mark, a curving line under or over notes to be so executed.

lĕh-gah′tōh

The opposite is STACCATO.

legend (Lat., *legenda,* item to be read; Ger. *Legende;* Fr. *légende*). A vocal or instrumental composition depicting the course of a short tale of legendary character. A narrative romantic BALLAD.

Legend of the Invisible City of Kitezh and the Maiden Fevronia, The. A mystical opera by NIKOLAI RIMSKY-KORSAKOV, 1907, first produced in St. Petersburg. Because of a sustained devotional character and the hymn-like quality of its theme, it was often described as "the Russian *Parsifal.*"

The action takes place at the time of the Tatar invasion of Russia. Fevronia, the bride of the Prince of Kitezh, prays that the city of Kitezh be made invisible so as to be saved from the invaders. Her prayer is answered. As the city vanishes, only the pealing of the church bells reveals its existence.

A symphonic interlude, depicting the battle between the Russians and the Tatars, is based on a SCALE of alternating WHOLE-TONES and SEMITONES. This is known in Russia as the Rimsky-Korsakov scale and elsewhere as the OCTATONIC SCALE.

Legende von der heiligen Elisabeth, Die. Oratorio by FRANZ LISZT, 1857. He conducted its first performance in Budapest in 1865. The subject was suggested to Liszt by the frescoes of Moritz Schwind in Wartburg.

St. Elisabeth was the Hungarian wife of a German crusader who perished during the holy wars. She was expelled by her German mother-in-law, took refuge in a nearby cave, and became a saint.

leger lines. *See* LEDGER LINES.

Legge, Walter. *See* SCHWARZKOPF, (OLGA MARIA) ELIZABETH (FRIEDERIKE).

Leginska (born Liggins), **Ethel,** English-born American pianist, teacher, and composer; b. Hull, April 13, 1886; d. Los Angeles, Feb. 26, 1970. She showed a natural talent for music at an early age.

Leginska studied piano at the Hoch Conservatory in Frankfurt, and later in Vienna with the Polish pianist and teacher, Theodor Leschetizky. After making her London debut in 1907, she toured Europe. She married the composer Emerson Whithorne (born Whittern, 1884–1958) in 1907, but they divorced in 1916. In 1913 she appeared for the first time in America, at a recital in N.Y.

Leginska's playing was described as having masculine vigor, dashing brilliance, and a great variety of tonal color. However, criticism was voiced against her individualistic treatment of CLASSICAL works. In the midst of her career as a pianist, she developed a great interest in conducting. She organized the Boston Philharmonic Orchestra with 100 players, and later the Women's Symphony Orchestra of Boston. She also appeared as a guest conductor with various orchestras in America and in Europe. In 1939 she settled in Los Angeles as a piano teacher.

Leginska wrote music in various genres, distinguished by rhythmic display and a certain measure of modernism. She also composed two operas, various works for orchestra, piano pieces, and songs.

Legrand, Michel, French composer of popular music; b. Paris, Feb. 24, 1932. Legrand came from a musical family; his father led a popular orchestra and wrote scores for films. Legrand entered the Paris Conservatory at the age of 11, and while still a student began making professional jazz arrangements. He wrote for radio, television, and the cinema.

In the late '50s, Legrand settled in N.Y., where he wrote jazz arrangements for leading players including MILES DAVIS and JOHN COLTRANE.

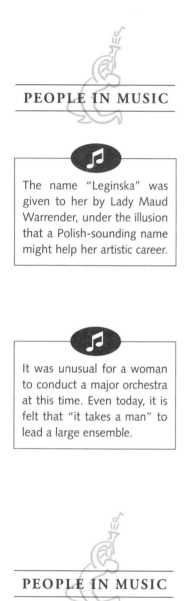

PEOPLE IN MUSIC

The name "Leginska" was given to her by Lady Maud Warrender, under the illusion that a Polish-sounding name might help her artistic career.

It was unusual for a woman to conduct a major orchestra at this time. Even today, it is felt that "it takes a man" to lead a large ensemble.

PEOPLE IN MUSIC

However, Legrand is best known for his motion picture scores. His inventive score for the motion picture *Les Parapluies de Cherbourg* (The umbrellas of Cherbourg; 1965), in which the characters sang throughout, received great praise. He won the Academy Award for this film, which spawned the hit pop song *I Will Wait for You.* Among his other soundtracks are *Picasso Summer, Summer of '42, Brian's Song, Beat Friends,* and *The Thomas Crown Affair.*

Lehár, Franz (Ferenc), celebrated Austrian operetta composer of Hungarian descent; b. Komorn, Hungary, April 30, 1870; d. Bad Ischl, Oct. 24, 1948. Lehár began his training with his father, Franz Lehár (1838–98), a military bandmaster. He then entered the Prague Conservatory at age 12 and studied violin and theory.

PEOPLE IN MUSIC

In 1885 Lehár was brought to the attention of the Czech composer Zdeněk Fibich, who gave him private lessons in composition. In 1887 Lehár submitted two piano sonatas to ANTONÍN DVOŘÁK, who encouraged him in his musical career.

In 1888 Lehár became a violinist in a theater orchestra in Elberfeld. In 1889 he entered his father's band (50th Infantry) in Vienna, and assisted him as conductor. From 1890 to 1902 Lehár led military bands in Pola, Trieste, Budapest, and Vienna.

Although his early stage works were unsuccessful, Lehár gained some success with his marches and waltzes. With *Wiener Frauen* (Viennese women), which premiered in Vienna in 1902, he established himself as a composer for the theater. His most celebrated operetta, *Die lustige Witwe* (The Merry Widow), was first performed in Vienna in 1905. It subsequently received innumerable performances throughout the world. From then on Vienna played host to most of his finest scores, including *Der Graf von Luxemburg* (The Count of Luxembourg; 1909), *Zigeunerliebe* (Gypsy Love; 1910), and *Paganini* (1925). For Berlin, he wrote *Der Zarewitsch* (The czarevich [heir apparent]; 1927), *Friederike* (1928), and *Das Land des Lächelns* (The land of smiles; 1929).

Lehár's last years were made difficult by his marriage to a Jewish woman, which made him suspect to the Nazis. Ironi-

In Alfred Hitchcock's 1943 film *Shadow of a Doubt,* starring Joseph Cotton, the Merry Widow Waltz melody is associated with the murderous Uncle Charley. He is called the Merry Widow murderer because he marries rich dowagers and then kills them for the inheritance. The tune also affects him psychologically, so when he hears it he goes into a murderous rage.

Franz Léhar.
(Hulton-Deutsch Collection/
Corbis)

▶

cally, *Die lustige Witwe* was one of Hitler's favorite stage works. After World War II, Lehár went to Zurich in 1946. He returned to Bad Ischl shortly before his death two years later.

Lehár's music displays the spirit of gaiety and frivolity that was the mark of Vienna early in the 20th century. His gift for melody and infectious rhythms is combined with genuine wit and irony. A blend of nostalgia and sophisticated humor, undiminished by the upheavals of wars and revolutions, made a lasting appeal to audiences.

In addition to his stage works, Lehár also wrote a number of orchestral pieces, including several symphonic poems, two violin concertos, about 65 waltzes (the most famous being *Gold und Silber,* 1899), more than 50 marches, various works for piano (including sonatas), and over 90 songs.

PEOPLE IN MUSIC

Lehmann, Lotte, celebrated German-born American soprano; b. Perleberg, Feb. 27, 1888; d. Santa Barbara, Calif., Aug. 26, 1976. Lehmann studied singing privately in Berlin. She made her debut in 1910 as the second Boy in WOLFGANG AMADEUS MOZART's *DIE ZAUBERFLÖTE* at the Hamburg Opera, but soon was given important parts in RICHARD WAGNER's operas, establishing herself as one of the finest Wagnerian singers.

In 1914 Lehmann made her first appearance in London, as Sophie in RICHARD STRAUSS's *DER ROSENKLAVIER* at Drury

Lane. In 1916 she was engaged at the Vienna Opera. In 1916, Strauss selected her to sing the Composer in the revised version of ARIADNE AUF NAXOS when it was first performed in Vienna. She then appeared as Octavian, and later as the Marschallin, both roles in Strauss's *Der Rosenklavier;* the Marschallin became one of her most famous roles. In 1922 she toured in South America. In 1924 she made her first appearance at London's Covent Garden as the Marschallin, continuing to sing there regularly with great success until 1935 and again in 1938.

In 1930 she made her U.S. debut as Sieglinde in Wagner's DIE WALKÜRE with the Chicago Opera. Four years later, she sang the same role at her Metropolitan Opera debut in N.Y., where she continued to appear, with mounting success, in the roles of Elisabeth in TANNHÄUSER, Tosca, and the Marschallin, until her farewell performance as the Marschallin in 1945. In 1946 she appeared as the Marschallin for the last time in San Francisco. In 1945 she became a naturalized American citizen. She gave her last recital in Santa Barbara, California, in 1951, and thereafter devoted herself to teaching.

Lehmann was universally recognized as one of the greatest singers of the century. The beauty of her voice, combined with her rare musicianship, made her a compelling artist. In addition to her unforgettable Strauss roles, she excelled as Mozart's Countess and Donna Elvira, Beethoven's Leonore, and Wagner's Elisabeth, Elsa, and Eva, among others. She published a novel, *Orplid mein Land* (1937), and several books on music.

Lehrstück. Teaching piece, cultivated in Germany after World War I, designed as an exercise for amateur performers which would raise political and/or artistic consciousness.

The problems of writing music in a modern idiom adaptable for educational purposes for workers and young people preoccupied a number of German composers in the 1920s. The idea of a Lehrstück for accompanied chorus with the additional use of half-spoken, half-sung passages, or SPRECHSTIMME, arose in Germany about that time. The playwright Bertolt Brecht was especially interested in

Lehrstück, and collaborated with composers KURT WEILL, PAUL HINDEMITH, HANS EISLER, ERNST TOCH, and others to create this type of composition.

Leigh, Mitch (real name, Irwin Mitchnick), American composer, arranger, and conductor of popular music; b. N.Y., Jan. 30, 1928. He studied with the German-born modern composer PAUL HINDEMITH at Yale University. Upon graduation, he entered the field of commercial music, founding Music Makers, Inc.

Leigh's most successful work was the Broadway musical *Man of La Mancha,* which premiered in 1965. It included the hit song *The Impossible Dream.* However, Leigh's other Broadway works were all dismal failures.

Leinsdorf (real name, Landauer), **Erich,** eminent Austrian-born American conductor; b. Vienna, Feb. 4, 1912; d. Zurich, Sept. 11, 1993. Leinsdorf entered a local music school when he was five, and began piano studies with the wife of the composer Paul Pisk at age eight. From 1923 to 1928 he continued his piano studies with Paul Emerich, and subsequently studied theory and composition with Pisk.

In the early '30s, Leinsdorf continued his studies in Vienna. He made his premiere as a conductor in 1933. A year later, he went to Salzburg, where he had a successful audition with the well-known conductors BRUNO WALTER and ARTURO TOSCANINI at the Salzburg Festivals and was appointed their assistant.

In 1937 Leinsdorf was engaged as a conductor of the Metropolitan Opera in N.Y., where he made his American debut conducting DIE WALKÜRE on Jan. 21, 1938, with notable success. He then conducted other Wagner operas, ultimately succeeding Artur Bodanzky as head of the German repertoire at the Met in 1939. In 1942 he became an American citizen.

In 1943 Leinsdorf was appointed music director of the Cleveland Orchestra. However, his induction into the U.S. Army that December interrupted his term there. After his discharge in 1944, he once again conducted at the Metropolitan for a year. He also conducted concerts with the

Cleveland Orchestra during this period and made appearances in Europe.

From 1947 to 1955 Leinsdorf was music director of the Rochester (N.Y.) Philharmonic Orchestra. In the fall of 1956 he was briefly music director of the N.Y. City Opera. He then returned to the Metropolitan as a conductor and musical consultant in 1957. He also appeared as a guest conductor in the U.S. and Europe.

In 1962 Leinsdorf received the prestigious appointment of music director of the Boston Symphony Orchestra, a post he retained until 1969. He then conducted opera and symphony concerts in major music centers of America and in Europe. From 1978 to 1980 he held the post of principal conductor of the (West) Berlin Radio Symphony Orchestra. From 1981 he held various guest conducting engagements. He published the semiautobiographical book *Cadenza: A Musical Career* (Boston, 1976), as well as *The Composer's Advocate: A Radical Orthodoxy for Musicians* (New Haven, 1981).

leitmotiv (*leitmotif;* Eng.; from Ger. *leiten,* lead). Any striking musical MOTIVE (THEME, PHRASE) associated with or accompanying one of the characters in a musical drama. Also, some particular idea, emotion, or situation therein.

The concept of the leitmotiv is commonly associated with RICHARD WAGNER'S MUSIC DRAMAS, but the term was first used in an annotated catalogue of works by CARL MARIA VON WEBER, published in 1871, in which it was described as a "strong delineation of each individual character in an opera."

The main purpose in Wagner's application of leading motives in his operas was to musically identify characters, emotions, objects, and important ideas. By employing them in combinations, and by varying the rhythm and sometimes the actual notes of these motives, Wagner intended to establish "a new form of dramatic music, which possesses the unity of a symphonic movement." This unity can be achieved, Wagner believed, "in a network of basic themes permeating the entire work, analogously to the themes in a symphony. They are contrasted with each other, supplement

līt′mōh-tēf

Wagner himself never used the term *leitmotiv*, but described the identifying themes in his operas as "melodic moments," "thematic motives," "fundamental themes," "idea motives," or "remembrance motives."

each other, assume new shapes, separate and coalesce . . . according to dramatic action."

However, Wagner's use of leading motives is not limited to the characters on the stage. He carefully tabulates the motives of material objects, such as the ring and the sword in *DER RING DES NIBELUNGEN,* and abstract concepts such as the Covenant, Conflict, Transformation, Love, and many others.

Wagner was, of course, not the first to introduce identifying themes in opera. Papageno's appearances in WOLFGANG AMADEUS MOZART's *ZAUBERFLÖTE* (Magic flute) are announced by a scale on his magic bell. And there are definite leading motives in Weber's *Der Freischütz.* GIUSEPPE VERDI used leading motives in several of his operas. PIOTR ILYICH TCHAIKOVSKY can hardly be called a Wagnerian, but the presence of identifying motives in his operas is easily recognized.

However, Wagner's influence in the use of leading motives was enormous. Hardly a single opera written since Wagner escaped this unifying concept. Faithful Wagnerians compiled catalogues of leading motives in his music dramas, including melodic fragments that were merely transitional passages. Among composers who absorbed the Wagnerian gospel was RICHARD STRAUSS, who introduced the leading motives into his symphonic works as well as his operas. ENGELBERT HUMPERDINCK, LEOŠ JANÁČEK, and to some extent even CLAUDE DEBUSSY, all experienced Wagnerian influences.

In the modern era, ALBAN BERG consciously outlined the significance of leading motives in his opera *WOZZECK,* a doctrine which enables the composer "by means of leading motives, to achieve the connections and relationships and thereby attain again a unity." ARNOLD SCHOENBERG's 12-tone themes as applied in his operas, particularly in the score of *Moses und Aron,* are logical developments of the leading motive.

Leningrad Symphony. The commonly accepted name of the Seventh Symphony of DMITRI SHOSTAKOVICH, 1942. He dedicated it to the heroes of the siege of Leningrad in 1941 during World War II.

It was first performed in the town of Kuibyshev (formerly Samara). The Finale prophesies the victorious end of the Great Patriotic War, as the anti-Nazi war was known in

Before Wagner, HECTOR BERLIOZ used the *IDÉE FIXE,* a device related to the leitmotiv, in his *Symphonie fantastique.*

A more obvious exploitation of identifying motives is represented by commercial jingles in advertising. A cleverly selected tune is designed to form a lasting association with the advertised product, thus (in theory) promoting its sales.

Russia. It reaffirmed Shostakovich's status in the Soviet Union and made him sufficiently famous to appear on the cover of *Time* in the U.S.

Lennon, John (Winston), English rock singer, guitarist, songwriter, and poet, member of the fantastically popular rock group the Beatles; b. Liverpool, Oct. 9, 1940, during a German air raid on the city; d. N.Y., Dec. 8, 1980. *See* THE BEATLES for Lennon's early life and career.

In 1968, as the Beatles were coming apart, Lennon began performing on his own, often accompanied by his paramour (and later wife) Yoko Ono. The two made two albums of "electronic" music, really MUSIQUE CONCRÈTE, *Two Virgins* (1968, with its famous cover photo in which they appear fully nude) and *Life with the Lions* a year later. *Wedding Album* (1969) documented their marriage.

Holding several "bed-ins for peace" to celebrate their nuptials, Lennon and Ono recorded in a Montreal hotel room the song *Give Peace a Chance,* credited to "the Plastic Ono Band," and featuring the assembled reporters and friends on the chorus (including LSD guru Timothy Leary and satirist Tommy Smothers).

◀

Mourners at a vigil following John Lennon's murder. (Lynn Goldsmith/© Corbis)

Lennon's first true "solo" album was *John Lennon/ Plastic Ono Band* in 1970. An extremely sparse recording, the songs were influenced by Lennon's and Ono's participation in primal scream therapy under the guidance of a Calif. therapist named Dr. Janov. The album had several powerful songs, including *Mother* and *God.* More successful was its follow-up, *Imagine* in 1971, with the hit title cut. Lennon and Ono then embarked on a political partnership with N.Y.-based radicals including Abbie Hoffman, resulting in an album of wretched topical songs, *Some Time in New York* in 1972.

Lennon returned to singer-songwriter material on his next two albums, producing minor hits with *#9 Dream* and a No. 1 hit with *Whatever Gets You through the Night.* An ill-conceived album of oldies followed, and then Lennon went into self-imposed retirement, becoming a "house husband" to care for his newly born son, Sean.

Lennon came out of retirement in 1980 with the album *Double Fantasy,* featuring tracks by both him and Ono. The album produced several hits, including the 1950's style opening track, *(Just Like) Starting Over.* Sadly, just as he was making this career comeback, Lennon was gunned down by a crazed assailant, Mark David Chapman, on his way home from a recording session in December 1980. Subsequently, several unfinished tracks were issued on various albums.

In 1996 the remaining ex-Beatles regrouped to finish two of Lennon's last songs, *Free as a Bird* and *Real Love.*

Lentz, Daniel (Kirkland), significant American composer; b. Latrobe, Pa., March 10, 1941. Lentz studied music and philosophy at St. Vincent College (B.A., 1962), music history and composition at Ohio State University (M.A., 1965), and composition with Arthur Berger, ALVIN LUCIER, and Harold Shapero at Brandeis University (1965–67). He also studied composition with ROGER SESSIONS and GEORGE ROCHBERG at the Berkshire Music Center at Tanglewood, Massachusetts, in the summer of 1966, and electronic music in Stockholm on a Fulbright grant in 1967–68. He was a visiting lecturer at the University of California, Santa Barbara, from 1968 to 1970 and at Antioch College in Yellow Springs, Ohio, in 1973.

In 1969 Lentz formed the group California Time Machine, with which he performed until 1973. He then formed San Andreas Fault in 1974, playing with them until 1976, and finally, in 1982, LENTZ, whose personnel includes multiple vocalists, keyboards, and occasional percus-

PEOPLE IN MUSIC

sion. In 1991 he became an associate professor at Arizona State University West in Phoenix, and in 1992 was a visiting professor at the University of California, Los Angeles. He held numerous NEA grants between 1973 and 1993, as well as a grant from the Deutscher Akademischer Austauschdienst in Berlin in 1979.

Many of Lentz's early works were quite provocative. His *Love and Conception* (1968–69), in which a male pianist and his female page-turner ultimately engage in mock sexual intercourse, led to his dismissal from his position at the University of California, Santa Barbara, where it was premiered. Their performance, at first accompanied by two tandem AM radio broadcasts of fictional reviews of the piece, is finally replaced by live, synchronous FM broadcasts of the piece itself, which frees them to waltz about the stage, fall into each other's arms and, overcome with passion, into the piano.

While retaining its freshness and, at times, almost exquisite beauty, Lentz's music throughout the 1980s was heavily reliant upon electronic equipment. This placed great demands not only on the ensemble performers but on Lentz himself, who often functioned simultaneously as composer, producer, editor, sound mixer, and recording engineer in live performances. Much of his work from 1989 has tended toward acoustic media. His *b.e. cummings* (1991) was his last piece utilizing MULTI-TRACK recording.

Since his move to the Sonoran Desert in 1991, Lentz has collaborated often with the minimalist American composer HAROLD BUDD, resulting in such recordings as *Music for Pianos* in 1992 and *Walk into My Voice* in 1995. Many of his works, such as the orchestral *An American in L.A.* in 1989, emphasize rich sounds and rhythms. His text settings can challenge the ear. Frequently, short syllables are introduced at the start, which, through gradual interlocking of parts, form audible words (occasionally sentences) only at the very end.

Among other noteworthy late compositions are *A Crack in the Bell* for vocal soloist, three keyboards, and optional chamber orchestra (1986); *Apache Wine* for chamber orchestra (1989); *Cathedral of Ecstasy* for vocalists, electric keyboards, and percussion (1990); *Night Breaker* for four pianos (1990); and *Talk Radio* for vocalist and chamber ensemble (1990–91). Lentz's 1996 concert-length *Apologetica,* scored for mixed choir, string choir, two MIDI keyboards, and two MIDI percussion, was highly praised.

Lenya, Lotte (born Karoline Wilhelmine Blamauer), sultry Austrian-American singer and actress; b. Vienna, Oct. 18, 1898; d. N.Y., Nov. 27, 1981. Lenya began her stage career as a dancer in Zurich, where she went at the outbreak of World War I in 1914.

In 1920 Lenya went to Berlin, where she met the composer KURT WEILL, whom she married six years later. In 1927 she made her debut as a singer in the Brecht-Weill scenic CANTATA *Kleine Mahagonny* in Baden-Baden. The next year, she created the role of Jenny in the premiere of the Brecht-Weill *DIE DREIGROSCHENOPER* (Threepenny opera) in Berlin. She later created the role of the singing Anna in the duo's *The Seven Deadly Sins* in 1933.

When the Nazis came to power in 1933, Lenya and Weill fled Berlin, and, after a couple of years in Paris and London, went to America. Not a singer of professional caliber, Lenya could ably adapt herself to the peculiar type of half-spoken, half-sung style appropriate to Weill's works. She created the roles of Miriam in his *The Eternal Road* in 1937 and the Duchess in his *The Firebrand of Florence* in 1945.

After Weill's death in 1950, Lenya devoted herself to reviving his works for the American stage, especially the work that came to be known as *The Threepenny Opera* in 1954. She also performed in other music theater works, notably JOHN KANDER and Fred Ebb's *CABARET*.

Leoncavallo, Ruggero, noted Italian opera composer; b. Naples, April 23, 1857; d. Montecatini, Aug. 9, 1919. From 1866 to 1876, Leoncavallo studied piano and composition at the Naples Conservatory. When he was 16, he toured as a piano soloist.

Leoncavallo earned his living as a young man by playing piano in cafés, a life he continued for many years, traveling through Egypt, Greece, Turkey, Germany, Belgium, and the Netherlands before settling in Paris. There, he composed CHANSONETTES and other popular songs, as well as an OPERA, *Songe d'une nuit d'été* (after Shakespeare's *Midsummer Night's Dream*), which was privately sung in a salon.

Leoncavallo began to study RICHARD WAGNER's scores, and became an ardent Wagnerian. He resolved to emulate the master by producing a trilogy, *Crepusculum,* depicting the Italian RENAISSANCE. The separate parts were based on the lives of key figures in the period: *I Medici, Girolamo Savonarola,* and *Cesare Borgia.* Leoncavallo spent six years on basic historical research. Having completed the first part, and with the scenario of the entire trilogy sketched, he returned in 1887 to Italy, where the publisher Ricordi became interested in the project, but kept delaying the publication and production of the work.

Annoyed, Leoncavallo turned to Sonzogno, the publisher of PIETRO MASCAGNI, whose opera *CAVALLERIA RUSTICANA* had just been tremendously successful. Leoncavallo submitted a short opera in a similarly realistic vein. He wrote his own libretto based on a factual story of passion and murder in a Calabrian village and named it *PAGLIACCI.* The opera was given with sensational success at the Teatro dal Verme in Milan under the direction of ARTURO TOSCANINI in 1892 and rapidly took possession of operatic stages throughout the world.

The enormous success of *Pagliacci* did not deter Leoncavallo from carrying on more ambitious projects. The first part of his unfinished trilogy, *I Medici,* was finally brought out in Milan in 1893, but its reception was so poor that he turned to other subjects. The same fate befell his youthful *Tommaso Chatterton* at its production in Rome in 1896.

Leoncavallo's next opera, *La Bohème,* which premiered in 1897, won considerable success. However, it had the ill fortune of coming a year after GIACOMO PUCCINI's masterpiece on the same story, and it was dwarfed by comparison. There followed a light opera, *Zazà* in 1900, which was fairly successful and was produced repeatedly on world stages.

In 1894 Leoncavallo was commissioned by the German Emperor Wilhelm II to write an opera for Berlin, *Der Roland von Berlin,* on a German historic theme. It was produced in Berlin in late 1904, but, despite the royal patronage, it proved a fiasco.

In 1906 Leoncavallo made a tour of the U.S. and Canada, conducting his *Pagliacci* and a new operetta, *La Jeunesse de Figaro,* specially written for his American tour.

Leoncavallo's *Pagliacci* is often played on the same evening with Mascagni's *Cavalleria rusticana,* both works being of brief duration. Historically, these two operas signalized the important development of Italian operatic VERISMO—or operas with realistic plots sung and performed in a natural style—which influenced composers of other countries as well.

However, this new work was so unsuccessful that he never attempted to stage it in Europe. Back in Italy he resumed his industrious production. However, he was never able to repeat the success of his *Pagliacci,* no matter how many works he produced.

Leoncavallo visited England in 1912 and made another trip to the U.S. in 1913. Other than that, he remained in Italy until his death in 1919. He was so prolific that he left many finished and unfinished works which were staged through the '20s, although again none achieved lasting success. Of Leoncavallo's many songs, the most famous is *Mattinata* (1904).

Leonius (Leonin, Magister Leoninus, Magister Leonini, Magister Leo, Magister Leonis), celebrated French composer and poet, master of the Notre Dame School of Paris; b. Paris, c.1135; d. there, c.1201. Leonius most likely received his initial education at the Notre Dame Cathedral schools in Paris. He was active at the collegiate church of St. Benoit in Paris by the mid-1150s, eventually serving as a canon (a member of the clerical staff) there for some 20 years. He was also a member of the clergy of Notre Dame by reason of his position at St. Benoit. He had earned the academic degree of master by 1179, probably in Paris. He later became a canon at Notre Dame, where he was a priest by 1192, and was also a member of the congregation of St. Victor by 1187.

Leonius's great achievement was the creation of OR-GANUM (a second accompanying part to the main MELODY, scored in parallel FOURTHS or FIFTHS) to augment the divine service. It is also possible that he prepared many of the revisions and variant versions of the organa, preceding the work of PEROTIN.

Leonius wrote a famous theoretical tract explaining his method of arranging church music. It does not survive in its original version, but is known to us in early (13th- and 14th-century) copies.

PEOPLE IN MUSIC

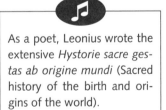

As a poet, Leonius wrote the extensive *Hystorie sacre gestas ab origine mundi* (Sacred history of the birth and origins of the world).

Leonore Overtures. LUDWIG VAN BEETHOVEN wrote four overtures for his opera *FIDELIO.* The first three are each called *Leonore Overture,* after the opera's heroine and its original name. The fourth is the *Fidelio Overture* proper, first used for the 1814 revival of the opera. *Leonore No. 3* is the one most often performed as a concert piece, and it is sometimes played before the dungeon scene.

Leppard, Raymond (John), eminent English conductor; b. London, Aug. 11, 1927. He studied HARPSICHORD and VIOLA at Trinity College, Cambridge (M.A., 1952), where he also was active as a choral conductor and served as music director of the Cambridge Philharmonic Society. In 1952 he made his London debut as a conductor, and then conducted his own Leppard Ensemble. He became closely associated with the Goldsbrough orchestra, which became the English Chamber Orchestra in 1960. He also gave recitals as a harpsichordist, and he was a Fellow of Trinity College and a lecturer on music at his alma mater (1958–68). His interest in early music prompted him to prepare several realizations of scores from that period. While his editions provoked controversy, they had great value in introducing early operatic masterpieces to the general public. His first realization, CLAUDIO MONTEVERDI's *L'INCORONAZIONE DI POPPEA,* was presented at the Glyndebourne Festival under his direction in 1962. He subsequently prepared performing editions of Monteverdi's *ORFEO* (1965) and *IL RITORNO D'ULISSE IN PATRIA* (1972), and of PIER FRANCESCO CAVALLI's *Messa concertata* (1966), *L'Ormindo* (1967), *La Calisto* (1969), *L'Egisto* (1974), and *L'Orione* (1967). On Nov. 4, 1969, he made his U.S. debut conducting the Westminster Choir and N.Y. Philharmonic, at which occasion he also appeared as soloist in the FRANZ JOSEPH HAYDN D-major Harpsichord Concerto. In 1973 he became principal conductor of the BBC Northern Symphony Orchestra in Manchester, a position he retained until 1980. He made his U.S. debut as an opera conductor leading a performance of his edition of *L'Egisto* at the Santa Fe Opera in 1974.

Settling in the U.S. in 1976, Leppard appeared as a guest conductor with major U.S. orchestras and opera houses. On Sept. 19, 1978, he made his Metropolitan Opera debut in N.Y. conducting *BILLY BUDD.* He was principal guest conductor of the St. Louis Symphony Orch. (1984–90). From 1987 to 1991 he was music director of the Indianapolis Symphony Orchestra, thereafter its first conductor laureate.

PEOPLE IN MUSIC

At the invitation of the Prince of Wales, Leppard conducted his edition of HENRY PURCELL's *DIDO AND AENEAS* at London's Buckingham palace in 1988. He returned there in 1990 to conduct the 90th-birthday concert of the Queen Mother. On Jan. 27, 1991, he conducted a special concert of WOLFGANG AMADEUS MOZART's works with members of the N.Y. Philharmonic and the Juilliard Orchestra at N.Y.'s Avery Fisher Hall at Lincoln Center, which was telecast live to millions via PBS. It re-created a concert given by Mozart himself in Vienna on March 23, 1783, and celebrated his 235th birthday and the launching of Lincoln Center's commemoration of the 200th anniversary of his death. In 1993 he conducted the Indianapolis Symphony Orchestra on a major tour of Europe, and in 1994 he was named artist-in-residence at the University of Indianapolis.

Leppard was made a Commander of the Order of the British Empire in 1983. As a composer, he produced film scores for *Lord of the Flies* (1963), *Alfred the Great* (1969), *Laughter in the Dark* (1969), *Perfect Friday* (1970), and *Hotel New Hampshire* (1985). He also orchestrated FRANZ SCHUBERT's *Grand Duo* Sonata and conducted its first performance with the Indianapolis Symphony Orchestra (Nov. 8, 1990).

Although long associated with early music, Leppard has acquired mastery of a truly catholic repertory, ranging from Mozart to BENJAMIN BRITTEN. His thoughtful views on performance practice are set forth in his book *The Real Authenticity* (London, 1988). T. Lewis edited *Raymond Leppard on Music* (White Plains, N.Y., 1993), an anthology of critical and personal writings, with a biographical chronology and discography.

Lerner, Alan Jay, distinguished American lyricist and playwright, most famous for his collaborations with FREDERICK LOEWE; b. N.Y., Aug. 31, 1918; d. there, June 14, 1986. Lerner was educated at Harvard University and also attended the Juilliard School of Music in N.Y. during the summers of 1936 and 1937.

Lerner met the composer FREDERICK LOEWE in 1942. They collaborated on their first musical, *What's Up?*, a year later, but it was a modest success at best. A second work, *The Day before Spring* from 1945, fared better but was still no hit. Two

PEOPLE IN MUSIC

years later, their collaborative efforts paid off when they produced the outstanding BRIGADOON, producing numerous hits for the pair, including *Almost Like Being in Love.*

The duo took a break in 1948, when Lerner went to Hollywood. There he collaborated with KURT WEILL on *Love Life,* and contributed songs to the Fred Astaire film *Royal Wedding,* which opened in 1951. Also that year, Lerner wrote the screenplay for *An American in Paris,* inspired by the songs of George and Ira Gershwin.

Lerner and Loewe reunited for more successful productions in the '50s. Their first hit of the decade came in 1951 with the popular show *Paint Your Wagon,* producing many pop hits including *I Talk to the Trees* and *They Call the Wind Maria.* Five years later, they wrote the smashing success *My Fair Lady,* after George Bernard Shaw's play *Pygmalion.* The play launched the stage career of JULIE ANDREWS and was one of the most popular Broadway musicals of all time. There followed their film score *Gigi* (1958; after Colette's story), which gathered many Academy Awards. It featured the perennial favorite *Thank Heavens for Little Girls.*

Lerner and Loewe returned to the Broadway stage with the enormously successful musical *Camelot* in 1960. The show became closely associated with the presidency of John Kennedy. It represented a new era in American politics, and the musical seemed to reflect that sunny optimism.

Long wishing to retire, Loewe finally quit after the success of *Camelot.* Lerner continued to write musicals, never equaling his previous successes. His most popular of these later works was *On a Clear Day You Can See Forever* from 1965, written in collaboration with BURTON LANE. A film version appeared in 1970. Lerner and Loewe collaborated on one more film score, *The Little Prince,* in 1974.

Lerner's career slowed in the '70s. Suffering from various ailments and addicted to drugs, he seemed to have lost his touch as a lyricist. He had a spectacular failure in 1976 with the much-anticipated musical play *1600 Pennsylvania Avenue,* with music by LEONARD BERNSTEIN. The play told the stories of the American presidency, but it was heavy-handed at best and quickly closed.

Lerner's last Broadway work was *Dance a Little Closer* in 1983. He died of lung cancer three years later.

lesson (Fr. *leçon;* Ger. *Übung*). English and (less commonly) French instrumental pieces of the BAROQUE period, composed mostly for the HARPSICHORD or ORGAN.

Lessons first appeared in mid-16th century LUTE collections. THOMAS MORLEY published his first *Booke of Consort Lessons* in 1599, and WILLIAM BYRD included one *Lesson or Voluntarie* in his manuscript *My Ladye Nevells Booke* in 1591. Thereafter, Matthew Locke, William Babell, Johann Philipp Krieger, GEORGE FRIDERIC HANDEL, JEAN PHILIPPE RAMEAU, and JOHANN SEBASTIAN BACH wrote or published lessons or similar works.

Sometimes the term has alternative meanings, e.g., FRANÇOIS COUPERIN's *Leçons de ténèbres,* where it refers to the liturgical reading. The ambiguous "lesson" eventually evolved into the less ambiguous "study" (ÉTUDE).

Let 'Em Eat Cake. Musical by GEORGE GERSHWIN, 1933, a sequel to the Pulitzer Prize-winning *Of Thee I Sing.* This was the last musical Gershwin wrote for Broadway. Sadly, it was a great failure.

Let's Make an Opera. An "entertainment for young people" by BENJAMIN BRITTEN, 1949, with optional audience participation, first produced at the Aldeburgh Festival, England.

The organizers of the opera discuss on stage the music, production, and story. Then the opera, supposedly planned in front of an audience, is actually produced, entitled *The Little Sweep.* The story recounts the inhumane practice of sweeping the chimneys in Victorian England by lowering children from roofs into fireplaces to clean the soot with their little bodies.

Levine, James (Lawrence), brilliant American pianist and conductor; b. Cincinnati, June 23, 1943. Levine's maternal grandfather was a cantor in a synagogue, and his father was a violinist who led a dance band. His mother was an actress. He began playing the piano as a small child.

At the age of ten, Levine was soloist in FELIX MENDELSSOHN's Second Piano Concerto at a youth concert of the Cincinnati Symphony Orchestra. He then studied theory

PEOPLE IN MUSIC

with Walter Levin, first violinist in the La Salle Quartet, and in 1956 took piano lessons with RUDOLF SERKIN at the Marlboro School of Music. In 1957 he began piano studies at the Aspen Music School. In 1961 he entered the Juilliard School of Music in N.Y., taking courses in conducting.

In 1964 Levine graduated from the Juilliard School and joined the American Conductors Project connected with the Baltimore Symphony Orchestra. In 1964–65 he served as an apprentice to George Szell with the Cleveland Orchestra, then became a regular assistant conductor with it until 1970. In 1966 he organized the University Circle orchestra of the Cleveland Institute of Music. He also led the student orchestra of the summer music institute of Oakland University in Meadow Brook, Michigan, from 1967 to 1969.

In 1970 Levine made a successful appearance as guest conductor with the Philadelphia Orchestra at its summer home at Robin Hood Dell. He subsequently appeared with other American orchestras, and in 1970 conducted the Welsh National Opera and the San Francisco Opera. He made his Metropolitan Opera debut in N.Y. in 1971 in a festival performance of *TOSCA*. His success led to further appearances and to his appointment as its principal conductor in 1973. He then was its music director from 1975 until becoming its artistic director in 1986.

In 1973 Levine also became music director of the Ravinia Festival, the summer home of the Chicago Symphony Orchestra, and served in that capacity with the Cincinnati May Festival until 1978. In 1975 he began to conduct at the Salzburg Festivals, and in 1982 he conducted at the Bayreuth Festival for the first time. In 1995 he conducted his first *RING* cycle there. In 1997 he received the national Medal of Arts. From 1999 he was also music director of the Munich Philharmonic.

In addition to his conducting career, Levine continued to make appearances as a pianist, playing chamber music with impeccable technical precision. But it is as a conductor and a planner of the seasons at the Metropolitan Opera that he inspired respect.

Lewis, Jerry Lee, rollicking American rock 'n' roll and country music pianist and singer; b. Ferriday, La., Sept. 29,

Levine has helped broaden the often stuffy programming at the Metropolitan, introducing modern works by LEOŠ JANÁČEK, ARNOLD SCHOENBERG, and JOHN CORIGLIANO, and important revivals, along with the more predictable favorites.

PEOPLE IN MUSIC

Lewis, like LITTLE RICHARD, developed a manic stage personality. He would stand up and pound the piano keys, sweeping his hands up and down the keyboard. He dressed in (for the day) very flashy clothing and wore his long hair in a slicked-back pompadour.

PEOPLE IN MUSIC

1935. Lewis began playing piano as a child, making appearances in the Ferriday area by his teenage years.

Lewis came to Memphis, Tennessee, in early 1956, after hearing the first recordings made by ELVIS PRESLEY for the Sun label there. He approached the label and made some demo recordings. He was signed by mid-1956 to the label, issuing his first single, *Crazy Arms,* later that year, which was a minor country hit. However, it was his next release, 1957's *Whole Lotta Shakin' Goin' On,* that made him a rock 'n' roll star. By year's end, Lewis issued the classic *Great Balls of Fire,* which became his theme song.

However, just as quickly as Lewis became a star, his career came to a dramatic halt in 1958. He was touring England when it was revealed that he was traveling with a 13-year-old girl, who he said was his first cousin and also child wife. Even his records were shelved at radio stations, and he was reduced to playing at village fairs and roadhouses.

It was not until 1968 that Lewis returned to public favor, this time as a country singer. He had hits with records such as *Another Place, Another Time* and *What's Made Milwaukee Famous (Has Made a Loser Out of Me).* In 1977 he recorded an autobiographical single, *Middle-Age Crazy.*

The '80s saw Lewis both recording and touring in ROCK and country styles. Meanwhile, he began to enter the pantheon of aging rock stars. He was among the first inductees into the Rock and Roll Hall of Fame in 1986, and three years later was the subject of an autobiographical film, *Great Balls of Fire,* starring Dennis Quaid as the "Ferriday Fireball."

In the '90s, Lewis kept on keeping on. He briefly opened his own nightclub in Memphis. In a bizarre turn, he also opened his home to tourists, in an attempt to finally settle a decades-long unpaid tax bill with the I.R.S. He also recorded a new album in 1995, *Young Blood,* although it failed to make much of an impression on the charts.

Lewis, John (Aaron), esteemed African-American jazz pianist and composer; b. La Grange, Ill., May 3, 1920. Lewis studied anthropology and music at the University of New Mexico, completing his studies at the Manhattan School of Music, earning a masters degree in 1953.

In 1952, Lewis and Milt Jackson founded the Modern Jazz Quartet (piano, vibraphone, drums, double bass), a group that for 22 years was one of the focal points of both COOL JAZZ and classical jazz, a merger known as THIRD STREAM. He composed and arranged works that, while leaving room for improvisation, also included such formal devices as fugal COUNTERPOINT. He also composed extended pieces requiring the additional forces of string quartet or orchestra, several movie scores (*Odds against Tomorrow, No Sun in Venice, A Milanese Story*), and a ballet, *Original Sin* (San Francisco Ballet, March 1961). Significantly, the Modern Jazz Quartet (MJQ) abandoned the usual nightclub habitat in favor of concert halls.

The Modern Jazz Quartet disbanded in 1974, but in later years its members reunited for occasional tours. Lewis has also led his own sextet.

Lewis, Meade (Anderson) **"Lux,"** African-American jazz pianist; b. Chicago, Sept. 4, 1905; d. Minneapolis, June 7, 1964. Lewis was nicknamed "The Duke of Luxembourg" as a child, hence the contraction "Lux." He studied violin and piano, and played in nightclubs and bars in Chicago. However, Lewis was not terribly successful as a musician in his early career, despite making an early recording in the BOOGIE-WOOGIE style, *Honky Tonk Train Blues,* in 1927. Instead, he and fellow pianist Albert Ammons made a living operating a taxicab service together.

All that changed in the early '30s when jazz producer John Hammond, Jr., heard Lewis's recording and sought him out. He brought Lewis, Ammons, and fellow boogie pianist Pete Johnson to N.Y., where they gave a memorable performance at his *From Spirituals to Swing* concert in 1939. This led to club engagements and additional recordings for the trio.

Lewis spent the post-World War II years in Los Angeles. He took up the CELESTE and began playing in a much more delicate style than his earlier performances. He appeared with a celeste quartet and made several recordings, although they failed to find a large audience.

Sadly, Lewis died following a hit-and-run accident in 1964.

PEOPLE IN MUSIC

Lhévinne, Josef, celebrated Russian pianist and pedagogue,; b. Orel, Dec. 13, 1874; d. N.Y., Dec. 2, 1944. After preliminary study in his native town, Lhévinne was taken to Moscow and entered Vasili Safonov's piano class at the Conservatory in 1885. At the age of 15, he played the Emperor Concerto, with ANTON RUBINSTEIN conducting. He graduated in 1891 and won the Rubinstein Prize in 1895.

In 1900 Lhévinne traveled to the Caucasus and taught piano at the Tiflis Conservatory. From 1902 to 1906 he taught at the Moscow Conservatory. In 1906 he went to the U.S., where he made his American debut in N.Y. with the Russian Symphony Orchestra. Afterward he made numerous concert tours in America.

Lhévinne lived mostly in Berlin from 1907 to 1919. He was interned during World War I, but was able to continue his professional activities. In 1919 he returned to the U.S., appearing in recitals and with major American orchestras. He also taught at his own studio from 1919 and at the Juilliard Graduate School in N.Y. from 1922. He published *Basic Principles in Pianoforte Playing* in 1924.

Lhévinne's playing was distinguished not only by its virtuoso quality, but by an intimate understanding of music, impeccable phrasing, and fine gradations of singing tone. He was at his best in the works of the ROMANTIC school. His performances of the concertos of FRÉDÉRIC CHOPIN and PIOTR ILYICH TCHAIKOVSKY were particularly notable.

Lhévinne's wife, Rosina Bessie (b. Kiev, March 28, 1880; d. Glendale, Calif., Nov. 9, 1976), was also a distinguished pianist and pedagogue. She graduated from the Moscow Conservatory in 1898, winning the gold medal, the same year she and Lhévinne were married. She appeared as a soloist in Vienna in 1910, St. Petersburg in 1911, and Berlin in 1912. She remained in Berlin with her husband through World War I, and in 1919 they went to the U.S., where they opened a music studio. She also taught at the Juilliard Graduate School in N.Y. from 1922, and later privately. Among her famous students were VAN CLIBURN, MISCHA DICHTER, JOHN BROWNING, and GARRICK OHLSSON.

Liberace (born Wladziu Valentino Liberace), flamboyant American pianist and showman; b. West Allis, Wis.,

May 16, 1919; d. Palm Springs, Calif., Feb. 4, 1987. Liberace received training from his father, a HORN player. He then studied piano, exhibiting so natural a talent that no less a master than IGNACY PADEREWSKI encouraged him to attempt a concert career. Liberace made his concert debut at age 11 and was fronting major symphonies as a teenager. However, he was sidetracked from serious music by jobs at silent-movie houses and nightclubs.

In 1940 Liberace moved to N.Y. and soon evolved a repertoire of semiclassical works, such as a synthetic arrangement of the first movement of LUDWIG VAN BEETHOVEN's *Moonlight Sonata* and SERGEI RACHMANINOFF's Prelude in C-sharp minor. During the '50s, he became a popular performer on television and also made numerous recordings and toured extensively overseas.

Liberace built himself a house in California, complete with a piano-shaped swimming pool. Inspired by a popular movie on Chopin, he placed a candelabrum on the piano at his public appearances. This decorative object identified him as a ROMANTIC musician, an impression enhanced by his dress suit of white silk mohair and a wardrobe of glittering cloaks, which he removed with theatrical flair before performing.

A favorite in Las Vegas, Liberace became a model for the kitschy-but-lovable piano star. His use of elaborate sets—including the famous "dancing waters" that accompanied his flamboyant playing style—also influenced rock and other popular classical acts. Musicians as diverse as rock pianist ELTON JOHN and classical violinist NIGEL KENNEDY owe much to Liberace for their stage work. Fittingly, the Liberace Museum remains one of the biggest tourist attractions in Las Vegas.

Liberace died in 1987, officially of a "kidney complaint." It was widely acknowledged, however, that he died of AIDS.

Early in his career, before he came up with his catchy one-name stage name, Liberace went by the colorful name of "Walter Busterkeys."

libretto (It., little book; plural, *librettos, libretti*). The book containing the text or play of an OPERA. Also, the text or play itself, distributed to the audience to acquaint them with the subject of the opera.

In the 19th century it was common to supply a translation into the language of the country in which the opera was

lē-bret′tōh

Some librettos also included a *protesta*, a protestation by the author of the libretto that his use of names of pagan deities should not be understood as a lack of Christian faith!

performed. Italian librettos usually carried an *argomento* (not an argument, but a summary), listing the acts and scenes, the cast of characters. One of the greatest of all librettists was PIETRO METASTASIO, whose librettos were set to music by some fifty composers, accounting for over 1,000 different Italian operas.

Some librettos have independent literary value, such as Boito's rendering of Shakespeare for GIUSEPPE VERDI, or Hofmannsthal's thoughtful texts for RICHARD STRAUSS. Then there were GILBERT AND SULLIVAN, in whose comic operas the merit is distributed equally between literature and music. In a class by itself is the composer-librettist, of whom RICHARD WAGNER was supreme. In modern times GIAN CARLO MENOTTI has written the librettos for his own operas, as well as two for SAMUEL BARBER.

The plots of most operas before the 20th century are based on standard formulas. Many, especially in the BAROQUE period, were drawn from Greek mythology and drama. In other plots, mistaken identities abound. Rigoletto hires assassins to kill the seducer of his daughter. In the darkness of the night they kill the daughter instead and deliver her body to her father in a sack. A most unlikely story, but plausibility is not a virtue among most librettists.

A very common theme may be described as seduction followed by abandonment (or love gone wrong), which is at the heart of *FAUST, LA BOHÈME, LA TRAVIATA,* and, on a lighter note, *ARIADNE AUF NAXOS.* Suicides are common, with female self-destruction outnumbering male. Examples are the seduced granddaughter of *THE QUEEN OF SPADES,* the murderess in *LADY MACBETH OF THE MTZENSK DISTRICT,* and the heroine of *LAKMÉ.* Lodoletta in PIETRO MASCAGNI's opera of that name does not commit suicide but dies in the snow outside her lover's Paris house.

Cross-dressing is another common device in opera plots, usually as a means of advancing the plot. In BEETHOVEN's *FIDELIO,* the faithful Leonora dresses as a boy, assumes the symbolic name of Fidelio ("the faithful one"), and penetrates the prison in which her beloved is unjustly held. The motive of the rescue is so common in opera that a subgenre of "rescue operas" has developed. In WOLFGANG AMADEUS MOZART's *LE NOZZE DI FIGARO,* Cherubino, a young lad, disguises himself as a maid to avoid serving the infantry. (To make it even more confusing, Cherubino is played by a female singer!)

Religious fanaticism, particularly in the Inquisition, is a convenient dramatic feature in many operas. Thus in LA JUIVE the fanatical cardinal has a girl burned at the stake moments before he finds out that she is his natural daughter. Superstition plays a helpful role in libretti of all kinds, as in IL TROVATORE. Operatic murders, particularly by stabbing, are too numerous to number. Insanity should not be overlooked. Mad scenes in opera are most effective recourses. Fortunately, most of the victims, a majority of them female, recover their sanity as soon as the dramatic situation is favorable for such a development.

Sometimes stories of operas are changed for political or social reasons. MIKHAIL GLINKA's opera A LIFE FOR THE CZAR could not very well be staged in Russia after the Revolution, and the Soviet authorities changed the title to *Ivan Susanin,* the self-sacrificing peasant hero of the opera. And instead of saving the Czar, he is made to save a patriotic Russian officer! Attempts were made in Soviet Russia to rewrite other librettos in order to make them revolutionary. Thus TOSCA became *The Commune,* and THE HUGUENOTS became *The Decembrists* (the revolutionary Russian group of December 1825 who rebelled against Czar Nicholas I).

Some operas cannot be performed in certain countries. THE MIKADO is forbidden in Japan because the Japanese Emperor is portrayed in an undignified manner. GOUNOD's FAUST was renamed *Gretchen* in Germany because the sentimental treatment of Goethe's great poem in the libretto was considered an affront to German literature. The libretto of VERDI's UN BALLO IN MASCHERA was based on a historical event, the assassination of the King of Sweden. The opera was forbidden in Italy because of the rash of attempted assassinations in Europe at the time. Accordingly, the libretto was changed, and the mythical "Governor of Boston" substituted for the Swedish King.

Sometimes religious restrictions make it impossible to have an opera performed under any circumstances. For instance, SAMSON AND DELILAH by CAMILLE SAINT-SAËNS could not be performed for nearly a century on the British stage because of a regulation whereby biblical personages could not be represented in the theater. The restriction, however, did not apply to ORATORIOS or CANTATAS!

In Czarist Russia there was a rule against representation of a member of the reigning dynasty on the stage. So, when Catherine the Great was to make her entrance in Tchaikovsky's *The Queen of Spades,* the Imperial March announcing her presence was played, but the Empress herself did not appear. No restrictions were applied to Russian Czars before the Romanov dynasty. In MODEST MUSSORGSKY's opera *BORIS GODUNOV,* Czar Boris is a child murderer. Ivan the Terrible is treated by NIKOLAI RIMSKY-KORSAKOV in his opera *THE MAID OF PSKOV* as the brute that he was. Ironically, Stalin decreed rehabilitation of the historic Ivan, perhaps because he felt an affinity with his remote precursor. SERGEI PROKOFIEV had trouble in his scenic oratorio *Ivan the Terrible,* trying to conform with the new official attitude. The Imperial censors demanded minor changes to Pushkin's verses as used by Rimsky-Korsakov in his opera *LE COQ D'OR,* to avoid embarrassing similarities between the bumbling Czar of the opera and the last Czar, Nicholas II, who was not very bright. The composer refused, and it was not until after his death that the work was performed.

It is very easy to ridicule opera, but the difficulty is to suggest a rational and sensible substitute. Here Coleridge's injunction regarding the poetic approach as being a "willing suspension of disbelief" is particularly helpful. An opera goer must leave his skepticism with his hat in the cloakroom.

But Tolstoy, great writer that he was, felt insulted by the nonsense depicted on the stage when he attended a rehearsal of the opera *Feramors* by ANTON RUBINSTEIN. Tolstoy's humorless account of that occasion in his extraordinary tract *What Is Art* (in which he also attacks music, ballet, painting, and Shakespeare) is worth quoting:

> The procession began with a recitative of a person dressed up in Turkish costume who with a mouth open at an unnatural angle sings: 'I accompany the bri-i-i-i-de.' After singing this he waves his arm, naked of course, under his mantle. The procession opens, but here the French horn accompanying the recitative does something wrong, and

Sometimes adjustments of the texts of some operas have to be made for unusual reasons when they are performed in a different country. The name of Pinkerton in *MADAMA BUTTERfly* had to be changed in German productions to Linkerton because *pinkeln* means to urinate in colloquial German!

the conductor suddenly startled as if a disaster had happened, taps on the music stand with his stick, and the whole thing starts all over again.

The libretto of the opera is one of the greatest absurdities imaginable. An Indian king wants to marry; a bride is presented to him, and he changes his attire to that of a minstrel. The bride falls in love with the supposed minstrel, and becomes desperate at this development. Fortunately, she soon finds out that the minstrel is the King, and everyone is well content. That such Indians never existed, that the personages in the opera do not resemble any Indians or indeed any people, except those in other operas, can be in no doubt whatsoever; that nobody talks in recitative, that no group of four people place themselves at measured distances from one another to perform a quartet, constantly waving their arms to express their emotions; that nobody, except on the stage, walks in pairs carrying halberds made of foil and wearing slippers instead of shoes; that no one ever becomes angry or tender as in the theater, no one laughs or cries like that, and that no one can possibly be moved by such a spectacle, is obvious.

lick. In jazz and popular music, a brief solo passage; a "hot lick" is a particularly intriguing and stimulating one.

Licks are usually created by one musician and then repeated by many others. Sometimes a certain type of lick becomes associated with one style of music, such as a "blues lick," or with a particular instrument, such as a "guitar lick."

The lick is set off from its surroundings by its range or a rest coming before or after it. Similar but not identical to RIFF.

Lidice Memorial. Symphonic elegy by BOHUSLAV MARTINŮ 1943, commemorating the Nazi obliteration of the Czech community of Lidice in June, 1942. Its first performance took place in N.Y.

Liebesfuss (Ger., love foot; Fr. *pavillon d'amour*). The bulbous opening at the end of the ENGLISH HORN, which has the effect of dampening the sound. The same type of exten-

MUSICAL
INSTRUMENT

sion was characteristic of the manufacture of a clarinetto d'amore, flauto d'amore, oboe d'amore, and other "amorous" instruments, now largely obsolete.

Liebestraum. Characteristic piano genre by FRANZ LISZT, 1850. The title usually remains untranslated, to avoid the relatively pedestrian "Dream of Love" or "Love's Dream."

Liszt wrote three *Liebesträume* in 1850, originally for voice and piano; No. 3 in A-flat major for piano is the one that is most often performed. Each bore a subtitle *Notturno,* and each was provided with an epigraph from German poetry. The first praised exalted love, the second was a meditation on saintly death, and the third sang of earthly love.

leed   **Lied** (Ger.; Eng. *song;* Fr. *chanson;* plural, *Lieder*). An art (classical) song in German for voice and piano, "composed" as distinguished from "spontaneous" song of folk origin.

The standard form of the lied is for a single voice with piano accompaniment. The structure is most often STROPHIC, requiring only a single musical setting for each repeated stanza of the poem. German poems most suitable to be set to music in this form are rhymed verses containing the same number of syllables in each line. This symmetry of design in the poem corresponds to the symmetry of the musical setting.

Music historians ascribe the creation of the lied to FRANZ SCHUBERT who, in 1814, when he was only 16 years old, wrote his first, *Gretchen am Spinnrade* (Gretchen at the Spinning Wheel). However, Schubert did have predecessors, notably CARL FRIEDRICH ZELTER and JOHANN FRIEDRICH REICHARDT, but also C.P.E. BACH and LUDWIG VAN BEETHOVEN. All four wrote songs to German texts in a manner distinguished by a fluid singing line, lyricism of expression, and symmetry of rhythmical design.

Besides the great Schubert, other 19th-century composers of lieder were FELIX MENDELSSOHN, ROBERT SCHUMANN, FRANZ LISZT, JOHANNES BRAHMS, RICHARD WAGNER, CARL LOEWE, and HUGO WOLF. Wolf expanded the piano accompaniment into an integral part of the lied as an art form. He furthermore introduced a chromatic harmony that earned him the sobriquet "the Wagner of the lied."

GUSTAV MAHLER, RICHARD STRAUSS, and MAX REGER, although not primarily composers of lieder, also have contributed to the art.

Toward the end of the 19th century, the German lied went into decline. Most songs of this period were THROUGH-COMPOSED, with each stanza written anew. In the 20th century, ARNOLD SCHOENBERG created a novel type of lied in his 15 settings of poems by Stefan George, *Das Buch der hängenden Garten,* by introducing a songful narrative, SPRECH-STIMME, in which the text is recited in rising and falling speech-like inflections. While the ROMANTIC German lied cultivated poems of love, sorrow, and death, the modern German lied addressed topical issues, often contemporary social problems, as in the songs of HANS EISLER and KURT WEILL.

Going back in time, we find a proliferation of the so-called *Generalbasslied,* that is, songs provided with BASSO CONTINUO, which indicated the harmonies. To the same category belong the HOMOPHONIC ARIAS of the early opera and ORATORIO, closely related to Italian forms of accompanied song.

Another variation on the lied is the *volkstümliches Lied,* a song in the folk manner, also known as *Lieder im Volkston.* German composers have always been talented at taking the elements of folk melodies and rhythms and incorporating them into new songs. Anthologies of German "folk songs" are filled with Lieder whose composers are perfectly identifiable.

What can be more folk-flavored than *Lorelei,* to words by Heinrich Heine? Yet, it is not a folk song! It was written by a lesser Lied composer named Friedrich Silcher.

Lied von der Erde, Das (Song of the earth). Symphony by GUSTAV MAHLER, 1911, in six parts, for TENOR, CONTRALTO, and orchestra. The text is a group of Chinese poems in German translation. Despite the source of the text, the music has no Oriental elements. Rather, the work is a series of ROMANTIC impressions of the poems themselves.

The work was first performed posthumously in Munich. Mahler superstitiously chose not to number the work (it would have been No. 9) because of earlier composers who didn't write more than nine symphonies (primarily LUDWIG VAN BEETHOVEN and ANTON BRUCKNER). He did write a No. 9, but died before he could finish No. 10!

Lieder ohne Worte. Characteristic piano pieces by FELIX MENDELSSOHN, 1829–45, published in eight sets. These "songs without words" are aptly named, because they present their moods and pictures in the style of a lied. A few other composers have followed in Mendelssohn's footsteps.

The original Liedertafel was organized in imitation of the legendary King Arthur's Round Table. The singers, like the knights of yore, were expected to be loyal to their group in serving the cause of music.

Liedertafel (Ger., song table). A male choral society organized in Berlin in 1809. Numerous branches of the society sprang up in many other cities of Germany and among German musical groups in America.

lieto fine (It.). *See* HAPPY ENDING.

Life for the Czar, A. Opera by MIKHAIL GLINKA, 1936, first produced in St. Petersburg. The Czar of the opera is young Michael Romanov, elected in 1612 to rule Russia after a long period of social unrest. The Poles, intermittently warring with Russia, send a group of soldiers to kill him. Losing their way, they ask the peasant Ivan Susanin to guide them to the Czar's house, but he instead leads them into an impenetrable forest. The invaders kill him, but the Czar is saved.

The opera could not be performed after the Russian Revolution under its original title. Accordingly, the LIBRETTO was renamed after the heroic peasant, *Ivan Susanin*. The words in the finale chorus, which contain the glorification of the Czar, were altered to extol the greatness of Russia itself.

The opera is regarded as the first theatrical work in a national Russian style, even though it follows the Italian model. It includes genuine Russian folk songs and a remarkable chorus in $\frac{5}{4}$ time.

Life Is Just a Bowl of Cherries. Song by RAY HENDERSON, 1931, and popularized by BING CROSBY and ETHEL MERMAN. Its light-hearted message appealed strongly to listeners in the Depression years, when life was anything but a "bowl of cherries."

ligature (from Lat. *ligare,* bind, tie). 1. In MENSURAL NOTATION, a fusion of two or more melodic notes into one notational symbol. The component parts of a ligature indicate not only the relative PITCH, but also the rhythmic values, following an elaborate set of rules.

2. A tie of two or more notes, sometimes resulting in a SYNCOPATION. 3. A group or series of notes to be executed in one breath, to one syllable, or as a LEGATO phrase.

Ligeti, György (Sándor), eminent Hungarian-born Austrian composer and teacher; b. Dicsöszentmárton, Transylvania, May 28, 1923. The original surname of the family was Auer, and Ligeti's great-uncle was the celebrated violinist LEOPOLD AUER.

PEOPLE IN MUSIC

Ligeti studied composition at the Kolozsvar Conservatory from 1941 to 1943 and privately with the composer-pianist Pál Kadosa in Budapest. He continued his training at the Budapest Academy of Music from 1945 to 1949, where he subsequently was a professor, beginning in 1950. After the Hungarian revolution was crushed by the Soviet Union in 1956, Ligeti fled his homeland. In 1967 he became a naturalized Austrian citizen.

Ligeti worked at the electronic music studio of the West German Radio in Cologne in 1957–58. From 1959 to 1972 he lectured at the Darmstadt summer courses in new music, and from 1961 to 1971 he also was a visiting professor at the Royal Stockholm Academy of Music. In 1972 he served as composer-in-residence at Stanford University, and in 1973 he taught at the Berkshire Music Center at Tanglewood, Massachusetts. In 1973 he became a professor of composition at the Hamburg Hochschule für Musik.

Ligeti has won numerous awards and honors. In 1964 he was made a member of the Royal Swedish Academy in Stockholm, in 1968 a member of the Akademie der Künste in Berlin, and in 1984 an honorary member of the American Academy and Institute of Arts and Letters. In 1986 he received the lucrative Grawemeyer Award of the University of Louisville, and in 1988 he was made a Commandeur in the Ordre National des Arts et Lettres in Paris. In 1990 he was awarded the Austrian State Prize, and in 1991 he received the Praemium Imperiale of Japan. In 1993 he won the Ernst von Siemens Music Prize.

Ligeti tries to bring together sounds and visual elements in his works, alternating rapidly changing groups of sounds with static chordal masses and shifting dynamic colors. He describes his orchestral style as micropolyphony. The Kyrie from his *Requiem* for SOPRANO, MEZZOSOPRANO, two choruses, and orchestra (Stockholm, March 14, 1965) was used in the film SCORE for *2001: A Space Odyssey.* Other works include the opera LE GRAND MACABRE (Stockholm, April 12,

1978), various orchestral pieces, including a Piano Concerto (1985–88), *Macabre Collage* (1991; arranged from the opera *Le Grand Macabre*), and Violin Concerto (in two versions: 1990, 1992), numerous chamber pieces, including a Sonata for Solo Viola (1991–94) and works for a variety of keyboard instruments, and many vocal compositions. Early in his career, Ligeti also wrote works for electronic instruments, as well as a *Poème symphonique* for 100 metronomes (1962; Hilversum, Sept. 13, 1963).

Light My Fire. A 1967 No. 1 hit for the DOORS that introduced lead singer Jim Morrison to a large audience. It was covered a year later successfully by blind guitarist JOSÉ FELICIANO.

The group issued two versions of the song: a short version for AM radio and the long, album-only version, which became a favorite on FM radio.

Like a Prayer. Hit MADONNA single from 1987. The video for the song, featuring a black Christ figure and Madonna dancing in front of burning crosses, angered many people in the church. Because of the controversy, Madonna was dropped as a spokesperson for Pepsi Cola, even though she had only just been signed to the company. Nonetheless, she kept the million-dollar signing fee!

In 1997 the ROLLING STONES covered *Like a Rolling Stone* in an homage to BOB DYLAN.

Like a Rolling Stone. A No. 3 smash for BOB DYLAN in 1965, his first "electric" number, with rambling, poetic lyrics. The title comes from blues guitarist MUDDY WATERS, not the British rock group.

Like a Virgin. MADONNA's first No. 1 song, in which she played off her good girl/bad girl image.

Lin, Cho-Liang, outstanding Chinese-born American violinist; b. Hsin-Chu, Taiwan, Jan. 29, 1960. Lin began to study the VIOLIN as a child and won the Taiwan National Youth Violin Competition at age ten. When he was 12 he entered the New South Wales State Conservatorium of Music in Sydney, Australia, and at 15 he went to the U.S.,

PEOPLE IN MUSIC

where he enrolled at the Juilliard School in N.Y. as a scholarship student, graduating in 1981.

Lin won wide notice when he was chosen to play at the inaugural concert for President Jimmy Carter in 1977, the same year that he won first prize in the Queen Sofia International Competition in Madrid. In subsequent years he pursued a highly rewarding career as a virtuoso, touring throughout the world. He appeared as a soloist with virtually every major orchestra, and also was active as a recitalist and chamber music player. In 1993–94 he made an extensive tour of Europe, North America, and the Far East. In 1988 he became a naturalized U.S. citizen.

Lin's extensive repertoire ranges from the standard literature to specially commissioned works. In his performances, he combines effortless technique with a beguiling luminosity of tone.

Lincoln Portrait. Ode for narrator and orchestra by AARON COPLAND, 1942, one of his most celebrated works. The text is selected from Lincoln's own speeches, and there are modified quotations from folk BALLADS of the time. It was first performed in Cincinnati, with the poet Carl Sandberg narrating and Andre Kostelanetz conducting.

Lind, Jenny (Johanna Maria) celebrated Swedish soprano, b. Stockholm, Oct. 6, 1820; d. Wynds Point, Herefordshire, Nov. 2, 1887. Lind made her first stage appearance in Stockholm at the age of ten. That same year she entered the Royal Opera School there. During this period, she also sang in many comedies and melodramas.

Lind made her formal operatic debut at the Royal Opera in Stockholm in 1838 and continued to appear in various roles there through 1842. In 1840 she was appointed a regular member of the Royal Swedish Academy of Music and was also given the rank of court singer. However, she felt the need to improve weaknesses in her voice, and went to Paris to study with Manuel García in 1841–42.

Returning to Stockholm in late 1842, Lind continued to perform there, while also making appearances in Germany and Copenhagen, Denmark. In 1846 she made her Vienna

PEOPLE IN MUSIC

Because of the quality of her voice, Lind was nicknamed the "Swedish Nightingale."

debut as Norma at the Theater an der Wien. She again sang throughout Germany, returning to Vienna as Marie in 1847 and creating a sensation. Later that year, Lind made a phenomenally successful London debut as Alice in ROBERT LE DIABLE. Her appearances in LA SONNAMBULA and LA FILLE DU RÉGIMENT were acclaimed. She then created the role of Amalia in GIUSEPPE VERDI's I MASNADIERI there.

After touring the English provinces, Lind retired from the operatic stage, making her farewell appearance as Norma in Stockholm in 1848 and as Alice at London's Her Majesty's Theatre a year later.

If her success in Europe was great, her U.S. concert tour exceeded all expectations. Sponsored by P.T. Barnum, she was billed as a natural phenomenon rather than an artist. Nonetheless, her outstanding musicality made a deep impression upon the musical public. She made her N.Y. debut in 1850, subsequently giving 93 concerts in all, her final one in Philadelphia in 1851.

In 1852 Lind married her accompanist, Otto Goldschmidt, in Boston. They returned to Europe, settling in England in 1858. She continued to appear in concert and ORATORIO performances until her retirement in 1883, when she became professor of singing at London's Royal College of Music. She also devoted much time to charitable causes.

Lind possessed an extraordinary COLORATURA voice, with a compass reaching high G (g3), although her middle register remained veiled from overuse in her early career. Despite this, she was, without question, one of the greatest vocal artists of her era.

Lindy hop. An exuberant American jazz dance, first created c.1927, in syncopated $\frac{2}{4}$ time. It was named after Charles Linbergh's solo air flight to Paris. The dancers take two slow steps, then two quicksteps, with occasional sidesteps (shuffles) and other variants.

linear counterpoint. A modern term describing a type of COUNTERPOINT in which individual lines are emphasized over harmonic patterns.

lining out. *See* DEACONING.

Linus. A mythological Greek hero who tried to teach music to Hercules. He was slain by his pupil with his own lyre when he corrected an error Hercules made during a lesson. A *Song of Linus* was sung each year at harvest time in Homer's day to commemorate his tragic death.

Linz Symphony. Symphony No. 36 by WOLFGANG AMADEUS MOZART in C major, 1783 (K. 425). It was written to honor a music patron in the Austrian city of Linz.

lion's roar (Ger. *Löwenebrull;* It. *rugghio di leone;* Fr. *tambour à cordes*). A MEMBRANOPHONE of the frictional type, consisting of a bucket covered with a membrane through which a rosined cord is passed. When the cord is pulled vigorously, a sound resembling the roar of a lion is produced.

Its generic English name is *friction drum,* and it is found in various forms throughout the Americas, Europe, India, and Japan. EDGARD VARÈSE wrote a part for it in his *Ionisation.*

See also BULL-ROARER.

Lion Sleeps Tonight, The. Adaptation of the traditional South African folk song *Wimoweh,* which became a No. 1 hit for the Tokens in 1961. The rock group R.E.M. used this song as the basis for their 1987 song, *The Sidewinder Sleeps Tonite.* In 1995 it was revived in the popular Disney film *The Lion King.*

Lipatti, Dinu (actually, Constantin), outstanding Rumanian pianist and composer; b. Bucharest, April 1, 1917; d. Chene-Bourg, near Geneva, Dec. 2, 1950. Lipatti's father was a violinist who had studied with the Spanish violinist PABLO SARASATE, and his mother was a pianist. His godfather was the Rumanian violinist-composer GEORGES ENESCO.

Lipatti received early training from his parents, then studied at the Bucharest Conservatory from 1928 to 1932. He received a second prize at the International Competition at Vienna in 1934, a judgment which prompted the French pianist ALFRED CORTOT to quit the jury in protest! (He thought Lipatti should have been the grand prize winner.)

Lipatti then studied piano, with Cortot, as well as conducting and composition in Paris from 1934 to 1939. He

PEOPLE IN MUSIC

gave concerts in Germany and Italy, returning to Rumania at the outbreak of World War II. After escaping from Rumania in 1943, he settled in Geneva as a teacher at the Conservatory. After the war, he resumed his career, playing in England four times between 1946 and 1948. Lipatti's remarkable career was tragically cut short by cancer, and he died in 1950.

Lipatti was generally regarded as one of the most sensitive interpreters of FRÉDÉRIC CHOPIN, and was also praised for his deep understanding of the BAROQUE masters. He was also a fine composer. His compositions include works for solo piano, piano duo, and piano trio, as well as *Aubade* for wind quartet, the symphonic poem *Satrarii,* and songs. He was married to the pianist and teacher Madeleine Cantacuzene.

lira (Grk., lyra). Bowed string instrument of modern Greece, Bulgaria, and Dalmatia. It has a pear-shaped wooden body and a disc-shaped peghead that holds the lateral pegs for three (occasionally four) strings. The strings are fingered on their sides, eliminating the need for a fingerboard. The earliest references to the lira are found in the late first millennium A.D. It should not be confused with the LYRE.

lira da braccio (It., lyre of the arm). A bowed CHORDOPHONE, probably an outgrowth of the medieval FIDDLE, but held against the player's body. There were two sizes, the smaller held against the shoulder, the larger (sometimes known as the *lirone da gambe*) held lower. The instrument normally had five playing strings and two drones. Most sources indicate that the fingerboard was fretted. Its popularity dates from the late 1400s to the early BAROQUE.

lira organizzata ("organized" lyre; It.; Fr. *vielle organisée;* Ger. *Orgelleier*). A HURDY-GURDY in which the sound is enhanced by organ pipeworks and bellows, powered by a rotating wheel. Thus the term *organized* refers to the instrument, not the way someone keeps her or his business files. The instrument is usually built in a guitar-like shape.

lirone (*archi viola;* It., large lira). *Lira da gamba,* a VIOLA DA GAMBA-like bowed CHORDOPHONE with a wide fretted neck.

It has two drone strings and from 9 to 14 melody strings, held between the knees. Its popularity was brief: from the mid-16th to the mid-17th centuries.

Listen to the Mockingbird. Song by Septimus Winner, 1855, described on the published edition's cover as "a sentimental Ethiopian ballad." This was one of the most successful songs of this type, selling 20 million copies of sheet music.

Liszt, Franz (Ferenc; baptized Franciscus), greatly celebrated Hungarian pianist and composer, creator of the modern form of the symphonic poem, and innovating genius of modern piano technique; b. Raiding, near Odenburg, Oct. 22, 1811; d. Bayreuth, July 31, 1886. Liszt's father was an amateur musician who devoted his energies to the education of his son. At the age of nine, young Liszt was able to play a difficult PIANO CONCERTO by noted German pianist-composer FERDINAND RIES.

Franz Liszt, c. 1880.
(Library of Congress/Corbis)

A group of Hungarian music-lovers provided funds to finance Liszt's musical education. In 1822 the family traveled to Vienna. LUDWIG VAN BEETHOVEN was still living, and Liszt's father made every effort to persuade him to attend young Liszt's Vienna concert in 1823. Legend has it that Beethoven did come and was so impressed that he ascended the podium and kissed the boy on the brow.

However that might be, Liszt's appearance in Vienna created a sensation. He was hailed by the press as "child Hercules." The link with Beethoven was maintained through

An "Ethiopian ballad" was the common, polite name for a song written in imitation of a traditional African-American folk song. This type of song was performed by white musicians in blackface as part of a minstrel show.

Liszt himself perpetuated the legend and often showed the spot on his forehead where Beethoven was supposed to have implanted the famous kiss.

Liszt's own teachers: CARL CZERNY, who was Beethoven's student and friend and with whom Liszt took piano lessons, and the great ANTONIO SALIERI, who was Beethoven's early teacher and who at the end of his life became Liszt's teacher in composition.

In 1823 Liszt gave a concert in Pest. The announcement of the concert was made in the florid manner characteristic of the period: "Esteemed Gentlemen! High born nobility, valorous army officers, dear audience! I am a Hungarian, and before traveling to France and England, I am happy now to present to my dear Fatherland the first fruits of my training and education." Salieri appealed to Prince Esterházy for financial help so as to enable Liszt to move to Vienna, where Salieri made his residence. "I recently heard a young boy, Francesco Liszt, improvise on the piano," Salieri wrote, "and it produced such a profound impression on me that I thought it was a dream." Apparently Esterházy was sufficiently impressed with Salieri's plea to contribute support.

Under the guidance of his ambitious father, Liszt applied for an entrance examination at the Paris Conservatory, but its powerful director, LUIGI CHERUBINI, declined to accept him, because he was a foreigner (Cherubini himself was a foreigner, but had become a French citizen). Liszt settled for private lessons in COUNTERPOINT from Antoine Reicha, a Czech musician who instilled in Liszt the importance of folklore. Liszt's father died in 1837.

Liszt soon joined the brilliant company of Parisian men and women of the arts. NICCOLÒ PAGANINI's spectacular performances on the violin in particular inspired Liszt to emulate him in creating a piano technique of great difficulty and brilliance, utilizing all possible sonorities of the instrument. To emphasize the narrative ROMANTIC quality of his musical ideas, he accepted the suggestion of his London manager, Frederick Beale, to use the word "recital" to describe his concerts.

In his own compositions, Liszt often wrote PROGRAM MUSIC. He liked to attach descriptive titles to his works, such as "fantasy," "reminiscence," and "illustration." The RHAPSODY was also made popular by Liszt, but he was not its originator. It was used for the first time in piano pieces by the Czech composer and teacher Wendel Johann Tomaschek.

Today, almost all solo concerts are called "recitals." In Liszt's day, however, this was a new term, drawn from the idea of an author reciting a poem.

A true Romantic, Liszt conceived himself as an actor playing the part of his own life, in which he was a child of the MUSES. He was fascinated by Étienne Pivert de Senancour's popular novel *Obermann* (1804) that depicted a fictional traveler. He wrote a suite of piano pieces under the general title *Années de pélerinage,* in which he followed in music Obermann's imaginary progressions.

Handsome, artistic, a brilliant conversationalist, Liszt was sought after in society. His first lasting attachment was with an aristocratic married woman, the Comtesse Marie d'Agoult (1805–1876). They had three daughters, one of whom, Cosima, married Liszt's friend HANS VON BÜLOW before abandoning him for RICHARD WAGNER. D'Agoult was fluent in several languages and had considerable literary talents, which she exercised under the *nom de plume* Daniel Stern. Liszt was 22 when he began his relationship with her, while she was 28.

D'Agoult confided her impressions of Liszt in her diary: "He was tall and rather slender with a pale visage and green eyes, the color of seawater, which suddenly came to life with sparks of excitement. He talked very fast, exposing his ideas with a strange passion. The spark of his looks, his gesticulation, his conversational manner, his smile, all these traits were full of depth and infinite tenderness."

The growing intimacy between Liszt and d'Agoult soon became the gossip of Paris. Fellow composer HECTOR BERLIOZ warned Liszt not to let himself become too deeply involved with her. "She possesses a calculated attraction," he told Liszt. "She has a lively spirit, but she lacks true friendship." D'Agoult rapidly established herself as a salon hostess in Paris. She also encouraged Liszt's friendship with fellow composer-performer FRÉDÉRIC CHOPIN. Indeed, the Chopin biography published under Liszt's name just after the Polish composer's death was largely written by d'Agoult.

Liszt's second and final lasting attachment was with another married woman, Princess Carolyne von Sayn-Wittgenstein, who was separated from her husband. Her devotion to Liszt exceeded all limits, even in a Romantic age. "I am at your feet, beloved," she wrote him. "I prostrate myself under your footprints." Liszt tried to marry her, but encountered resistance from the Roman Catholic church, to which they

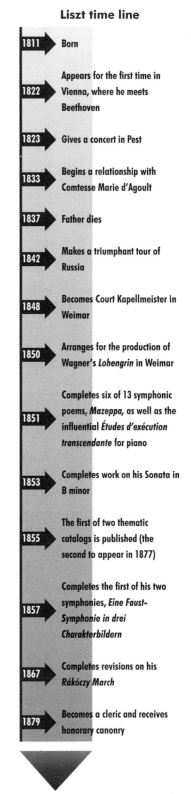

Liszt time line

1811 Born

1822 Appears for the first time in Vienna, where he meets Beethoven

1823 Gives a concert in Pest

1833 Begins a relationship with Comtesse Marie d'Agoult

1837 Father dies

1842 Makes a triumphant tour of Russia

1848 Becomes Court Kapellmeister in Weimar

1850 Arranges for the production of Wagner's *Lohengrin* in Weimar

1851 Completes six of 13 symphonic poems, *Mazeppa,* as well as the influential *Études d'exécution transcendante* for piano

1853 Completes work on his Sonata in B minor

1855 The first of two thematic catalogs is published (the second to appear in 1877)

1857 Completes the first of his two symphonies, *Eine Faust-Symphonie in drei Charakterbildern*

1867 Completes revisions on his *Rákóczy March*

1879 Becomes a cleric and receives honorary canonry

1885 Completes his *19 Hungarian Rhapsodies*, begun some 40 years earlier

1886 Dies at the age of 74 of double pneumonia, during a visit to Bayreuth

When Liszt met an attractive woman in Rome, he said to her, "Under this priestly cloak there beats the passionate heart of a man."

both belonged. The church refused to annul her marriage, and, after her husband's death, the church still refused to allow them to marry, because she had previously been divorced. After more than 15 years of trying, Liszt gave up, and set up a separate residence. Thus, Liszt, the great lover of women, never married.

Liszt became known informally as "abbé," thanks to four minor orders conferred upon him by Pope Pius IX in 1865, but his religious affiliations were not limited to the Catholic church. He was also a member of the order of Freemasons and served as a lay member of the Order of St. Francis. In 1879 he was formally made a cleric and given an honorary canonry. But he was never ordained a priest, and thus was free to marry an appropriate woman if he so wished.

Liszt's romantic infatuations did not interfere with his brilliant virtuoso career. One of his greatest successes was his triumphant tour in Russia in 1842. Russian musicians and music critics exhausted their flowery vocabulary to praise Liszt as the miracle of the age. "How fortunate we are that we live in the year 1842 and so are able to witness the living appearance in our own country of such a great genius!" wrote the music critic Stasov. His Majesty Czar Nicholas I himself attended a concert given by Liszt in St. Petersburg and expressed his appreciation by sending him a pair of trained Russian bears. Liszt acknowledged the imperial honor but did not venture to take the animals with him on his European tour (they remained in Russia).

Liszt was a consummate showman. In Russia, as elsewhere, he had two grand pianos installed on the stage at right angles, so that the keyboards were visible from the right and the left, respectively and he could alternate his playing on both. He appeared on the stage wearing a long cloak and white gloves, discarding both with a spectacular gesture. Normally he needed eyeglasses, but he was too vain to wear them in public.

It is not clear why, after all his triumphs in Russia and elsewhere in Europe, Liszt decided to abandon his career as a piano virtuoso and devote his entire efforts to composition. He became associated with Wagner, his son-in-law, as a prophet of "music of the future." Indeed, Liszt anticipated Wagner's advanced CHROMATIC HARMONY in his works.

Inevitably, Liszt and Wagner were attacked by conservative music critics. An extraordinary caricature entitled "Music of the Future," distributed in N.Y. in 1867, represented Liszt with arms and legs flailing, leading a huge orchestra that had not only human players but also goats, donkeys, and a cat placed in a cage with an operator pulling its tail. At Liszt's feet there was placed a score marked "Wagner, not to be played much till 1995."

In 1848 Liszt accepted the position of Court Kapellmeister in Weimar. When Wagner was exiled from Saxony, Liszt arranged for the production of LOHENGRIN in Weimar on Aug. 28, 1850. He was also instrumental in supervising performances there of DER FLIEGENDE HOLLÄNDER and TANN-HÄUSER, as well as music by Berlioz and a number of operas by other composers.

Liszt also established a teaching series at his home. A vivid description of these classes was compiled by one of his students, August Göllerich. Liszt was invariably kind to his students. Occasionally he would doze off, but would always wake up when a student finished playing and say "Schön" (beautiful). When one of his American students called to his attention that the date was July 4, Liszt asked if someone would play variations on *Yankee Doodle* for him, because, as he said, "Today we are all Americans."

Apparently Liszt did not charge his students. He was also generous to colleagues and often lent them money. Wagner, constantly in financial straits, often asked Liszt for loans (which were seldom, if ever, returned). He was also hospitable to his colleagues. During his Weimar years, for instance, young JOHANNES BRAHMS stayed in his home for three weeks.

Liszt was very much interested in the progress of Russian music. In Weimar he received young ALEXANDER GLAZUNOV, who brought with him his First Symphony. He played host to ALEXANDER BORODIN and CÉSAR CUI, and was lavish in his appreciation of their works. He also expressed admiration for NIKOLAI RIMSKY-KORSAKOV and MODEST MUSSORGSKY, although they never paid a visit. When Rimsky-Korsakov asked him to contribute a variation to a Russian collection based on CHOPSTICKS (then a waltz), Liszt obliged with his own contribution, adding, "There is nothing wittier than your variations. Here you have at last a condensed manual of harmony and counterpoint. I would gladly recommend this album to conservatory professors as an aid to teaching composition."

In his Weimar years, Liszt aged rapidly. Gone were the classical features that had so fascinated his contemporaries, especially women, during his virtuoso career. Photographs taken in Weimar show him with snow-white hair descending upon his shoulders. He walked with difficulty, dragging his feet. He suffered attacks of phlebitis in his legs and had constant intestinal difficulties. He neglected his physical state, and finally developed double pneumonia and died during a visit to Bayreuth at the age of 74.

While Liszt is usually thought of as a great Hungarian composer, he was actually brought up in the atmosphere of German culture. He spoke German at home, with French as a second language. His women companions conversed with him in French, and most of Liszt's own correspondence was in that language. It was not until middle age that he decided to take lessons in Hungarian, but he never acquired fluency. He used to refer to himself humorously as "half Gypsy and half Franciscan monk."

In his secular works Liszt was deeply conscious of his Hungarian heritage, but he gathered his material mainly from Gypsy dance bands that played in Budapest, not from actual folk musicians. He borrowed a theme for one of the most famous of his *Hungarian Rhapsodies* from an unpublished work by an obscure Austrian musician named Heinrich Ehrlich, who had sent him a manuscript for possible inclusion in one of Liszt's recitals. He explained this as an accidental oversight.

As a composer, Liszt made every effort to expand the technical possibilities of piano technique. In his two piano concertos, and particularly in his *Études d'exécution transcendante* (1851) he made use of the GRAND PIANO, which expanded the keyboard in both the bass and the treble. He also extended the field of piano literature with his brilliant transcriptions of operatic excerpts from works by Mozart, Verdi, Wagner, Donizetti, Gounod, Rossini, and Beethoven. These transcriptions were particularly useful at the

When it was suggested after his death in Bayreuth that his body be transferred to Budapest, the prime minister of Hungary objected, because Liszt never regarded himself as a purely Hungarian musician.

time when the piano was the basic instrument at home (and the phonograph still a dream of the future).

Liszt was a great musical technician. He organized his compositions with deliberate intent to create music that is essentially new. Thus he abandons the traditional succession of two principal themes in the SONATA form. In his symphonic poem *Les Préludes,* one melody dominates the entire work. In his popular third *Liebestraum* for piano, the passionate melody modulates by thirds rather than by the traditional (and accepted) fifths and fourths. The great *Faust Symphony* (1854–57) is more a literary essay on Goethe's great poem than a didactic composition.

Liszt's two piano concertos are free from the contrasts of the established CLASSICAL school. The CHROMATIC opening of the First Concerto led von Bülow to improvise an insulting line to accompany the theme, "Sie sind alle ganz verrückt" (They are all completely crazy). Later in the same work, the introduction of the TRIANGLE solo aroused derisive whoops from the press. Liszt was indifferent to such outbursts.

Liszt's numerous works fall into nearly every genre, and a selective list must be well short of comprehensiveness. Many of his orchestral works were orchestrated by Raff or Conradi (although Liszt often redid the orchestrations later). Among the pieces that he is best remembered for are two symphonies (1854–57; 1855–56), 13 symphonic poems (1848–82, including *Mazeppa,* 1851, orchestrated by Raff, first performed in Weimar, Apr. 16, 1854), four piano concertos (1832–85), and hundreds of piano works, including the *Rákóczy March* (1865; rev. 1867), *19 Hungarian Rhapsodies* (1846–85, including No. 15 in A minor), and the Sonata in B minor (in one movement, perhaps his most influential and groundbreaking work; 1851–53). He also wrote numerous arrangements and transcriptions.

Liszt also wrote many vocal works, including sacred and choral works and numerous solo songs (in several languages), and various ORGAN and chamber pieces. Liszt published two thematic catalogues of his works (1855; 1877). A complete thematic catalogue is found in L. Friwitzer, "Chronologisch-systematisches Verzeichnis samtlicher Tonwerke Franz Liszts," *Musikalische Chronik* V (Vienna, 1887).

litany. A song of supplication imploring God, the Blessed Virgin, and assorted saints with a promise to repent in exchange for divine intercession.

A litany is chanted by the priest in a MONOTONE with the choir or congregation responding. These are usually performed during the period of Rogation Days (from Lat. *rogare,* beg). The unrelenting repetitiousness of a litany gives it its cumulative power to move both the listeners and the saints whom they are hoping to reach.

Litanies of the Anglican Church are less impressive, and the words often have a somewhat colloquial inflection (e.g, "Spare us, Good Lord").

Among modern works in this style is JOHN CAGE's vocalization for two equal voices, *Litany for the Whale* (1980).

Little Drummer Boy, The. Annoying Christmas song written by Harry Simeone and Henry Onorati. It was a chart hit (every Christmas) for Simeone in 1958, 1959, 1960, 1961, and 1962. It has since been revived in many versions, all equally sentimental.

Little Nemo. *See* WHIFFENPOOF SONG, THE.

Little Night Music, A. Musical by STEPHEN SONDHEIM, 1973, based on the Ingmar Bergman film *Smiles of a Summer Night.* Its most memorable song is *Send in the Clowns,* winner of a GRAMMY AWARD in JUDY COLLINS's 1976 rendition. Other numbers include *Now-Soon-Later, Every Day a Little Death, It Would Have Been Wonderful,* and *Liasons.*

Little Russian Symphony. PIOTR ILYICH TCHAIKOVSKY's Second Symphony, 1873, in C minor, first performed in Moscow.

The title, as it commonly appears in English, is misleading: it is not a student's or beginner's symphony, but a symphony of Little Russia, a common nickname in Czarist Russia for the Ukraine. Ukrainian songs are used as themes in the work.

Little Richard. *See* PENNIMAN, RICHARD WAYNE.

Little Sweep, The. See *LET'S MAKE AN OPERA.*

liturgical drama. Medieval plays in Latin containing action, dialogue, and occasional singing episodes. While liturgical drama makes use of biblical subjects, it never became part of the Roman Catholic liturgy itself, but remained a TROPE (or optional addition).

One of the most popular types of liturgical drama is the genre of MIRACLE PLAYS. These tell the stories of the saints, of whom St. Nicholas was a favorite. During the Renaissance, liturgical drama developed into mystery plays (a contraction of their original name, *ministerial plays,* from the Latin word *ministerium,* a service). Gradually these plays assumed a secular theatrical role while still following biblical subjects. Incidental music such as dances, trumpet flourishes, processions—even folk songs—was used.

In Italy these dramas with music became known as *sacre rappresentazioni,* and as *autos* (acts) in Spain and Portugal. These performances were true predecessors of scenic ORATORIOS.

Liturgical Symphony (*Symphonie liturgique*). The Third Symphony of ARTHUR HONEGGER, 1946, first performed in Zurich. The three movements are *Dies Irae, De Profundis,* and *Dona nobis pacem.*

liturgy (Old Grk., *leōs + ergon,* people work). The most comprehensive term for the official service of the established Christian Church. In the Byzantine ritual, the liturgy is synonymous with the MASS.

lituus (Lat.). 1. A hooked bronze TRUMPET, originally Etruscan, taken up by the ancient Romans. 2. CORNET. 3. Instrument called for by JOHANN SEBASTIAN BACH in his motet *O Jesu Christ, mein Lebens Licht* (BWV 118). Musicological opinion is that Bach intended the cornet or trumpet.

MUSICAL INSTRUMENT

live electronic music. Music that requires electronic music in its performance beyond simple tape playback or amplification of sound. When a singer or acoustic instrumentalist performs through electronic or computer equipment so that the final sound has been processed, the output is called *electroacoustic music.*

llamada (Sp., fanfare). Generic term for works of a proclamatory nature.

PEOPLE IN MUSIC

Lloyd Webber, Andrew, tremendously successful English composer, brother of Julian Lloyd Webber; b. London, March 22, 1948. His father, William Southcombe Lloyd Webber (1914–82), was a composer and the director of the London College of Music, and his mother was a piano teacher. As a child, Lloyd Webber learned to play piano, violin, and horn, and soon began to improvise music, mostly in the style of American musicals. He attended Westminster School in London, then went to Magdalen College, Oxford, the Guildhall School of Music, and the Royal College of Music.

Scene from Jesus Christ, Superstar, *1996 revival.*
(Robbie Jack/Corbis)

▶

In college he wrote his first musical, *The Likes of Us,* dealing with a philanthropist.

In 1967 Lloyd Webber composed the theatrical show *Joseph and the Amazing Technicolor Dreamcoat,* with lyrics by Tim Rice, which was performed at St. Paul's Junior School in London in 1968. It was later expanded to a full-scale production, and achieved considerable success for its amalgam of biblical subject with ROCK music, French CHANSONNETTES, and COUNTRY songs. In 1970 it was produced in America and in 1972 was televised.

Lloyd Webber and Rice achieved their first major commercial success with *Jesus Christ, Superstar.* It premiered in

London in 1972 and ran for 3,357 performances. It was as successful in America. Interestingly enough, this "rock opera" was first released as a record album, which eventually sold three million copies. *Jesus Christ, Superstar* opened on Broadway in 1971, even before the London production. The musical closed on Broadway on June 30, 1973, after 720 performances and after receiving seven Tony awards. In 1981 the recording of *Jesus Christ, Superstar* was given the GRAMMY award for best cast show album of the year.

After *Jesus Christ, Superstar,* Lloyd Webber and Rice ended their partnership. Lloyd Webber next produced a musical with a chief character totally different from Jesus. *Evita* gives a semifictional account of the career of the first wife of Argentine dictator Juan Perón. It was staged in London on June 21, 1978, followed by a N.Y. run, with splendid success.

But perhaps Lloyd Webber's most spectacular production was *Cats,* inspired by T.S. Eliot's *Old Possum's Book of Practical Cats.* It was produced in London in 1981, and was brought out in N.Y. in 1982 with fantastic success. *Evita* and *Joseph and the Amazing Technicolor Dreamcoat* were still playing on Broadway, so that Lloyd Webber had the satisfaction of having three of his shows running at the same time. *Cats* continued to run on Broadway, achieving the status of longest-running musical in 1998.

After two less-successful productions—*Song and Dance* (1983) and *Starlight Express* (London, 1984)—Lloyd Webber reached another blockbuster success with his version of the Victor Hugo romance *The Phantom of the Opera* (London, 1986; N.Y., 1988). In 1989, his musical *Aspects of Love,* which was only a minor hit, opened in London. He then adapted the famous film *Sunset Boulevard* for the stage, premiering in London in 1993 and a year later on Broadway. This was somewhat more successful, but still not as long running as his previous big hits.

Apart from popular shows, Lloyd Webber wrote a mini-opera, *Tell Me on a Sunday,* about an English girl living in N.Y., produced by BBC Television in 1980. Quite different in style and intent were the Variations for cello and jazz ensemble (1978), written for his brother, and the *Requiem* (N.Y., 1985).

Various religious groups protested against *Jesus Christ, Superstar.* Some found setting a biblical story to rock music distasteful, while others were shocked by the portrayal of a romantic relationship between Jesus and Mary Magdalen. Still others were offended by the implication that the Jews allowed Christ to be killed.

Lloyd Webber was knighted in 1992 and made a Lord in 1996.

Lloyd Webber, Julian, talented English cellist, brother of ANDREW LLOYD WEBBER; b. London, April 14, 1951. Lloyd Webber studied with Douglas Cameron from 1964 to 1967 and then at the Royal College of Music in London until 1971. He also studied with Pierre Fournier in Geneva.

Lloyd Webber made his concert debut at London's Queen Elizabeth Hall in 1972, subsequently playing many engagements as a soloist with English orchestras. He made his American debut in N.Y. in 1980. In 1978 he became professor of cello at the Guildhall School of Music in London. He edited *Song of the Birds: Sayings, Stories and Impressions of Pablo Casals* (London, 1985).

Locrian mode. *See* AUTHENTIC MODES.

Loeffler, Charles Martin (born Martin Karl Löffler), outstanding American composer, violinist, and violist of German descent; b. Berlin, Jan. 30, 1861; d. Medfield, Mass., May 19, 1935. Loeffler's father was a writer who moved the family to Russia, where he was engaged in government work in the Kiev district. Later they lived in Switzerland, and finally moved to Berlin.

In 1875 Martin Karl began taking violin lessons in Berlin with Eduard Rappoldi, who prepared him for study with JOSEPH JOACHIM. He also studied theory at the Berlin Hochschule für Musik between 1874 and 1877. Sometime between 1875 and 1878, his father was arrested on political grounds. He died in 1884 after suffering a stroke. This was the pivotal event of his son's life. Young Loeffler developed such a hatred toward the German empire that he changed his name (removing the umlaut). He also created a new life story for himself. He declared he was born in Alsace, a northeastern province of France bordering Germany, and adopted French culture for his own. (His wife and sister were the only people he told the story to until his death.)

Loeffler then went to Paris, where he continued his musical education. He was engaged briefly as a violinist in the Pasdeloup orchestra, then was a member of the private orchestra of the Russian Baron Paul von Derwies at his grand homes near Lugano and in Nice from 1879 to 1881. When Derwies died in 1881, Loeffler went to the U.S., with letters of recommendation from Joachim. He became a naturalized citizen in 1887. He played in the orchestra of LEOPOLD DAMROSCH in N.Y. in 1881–82. In 1882 he became second concertmaster of the newly organized Boston Symphony Orchestra, but was able to accept other engagements during late spring and summer months.

In the spring of 1883, Loeffler traveled with an orchestra led by the German-American conductor THEODORE THOMAS on a transcontinental tour. In the summers of both 1883 and 1884 he traveled to Paris, where he took violin lessons with Hubert Leonard. He resigned from the Boston Symphony Orchestra in 1903 and devoted himself to composition and farming in Medfield. In 1910 he was married to Elise Burnett Fay. Among his many awards and honors, Loeffler was an officer of the

Charles Martin Loeffler.
(Library of Congress/Corbis)

French Academy (1906), a Chevalier in the French Legion of Honor (1919), and a member of the American Academy of Arts and Letters. He received an honorary doctorate from Yale University in 1926.

Loeffler's position in American music is unique, brought up as he was under many different national influences: French, German, Russian, and Ukrainian. One of his most vivid scores, *Memories of My Childhood,* composed in 1924, reflects the modal feeling of Russian and Ukrainian folk songs. But his musical style was entirely French, with

Loeffler's most enduring work, *A Pagan Poem* from 1907, reflects this interest in Medieval and early-music forms.

PEOPLE IN MUSIC

definite leanings toward IMPRESSIONISM. His use of quaint styles and pseudo-Medieval forms, was also typical of the French school.

Loeffler was a master of colorful orchestration, and his harmonies are rich without becoming overbearing. His rhapsodic forms are peculiarly suited to the evocative moods of his music. His only excursion into the American idiom was the use of jazz rhythms in a few of his lesser pieces. He is best known for his instrumental music, especially those involving the viola and VIOLA D'AMORE.

Loesser, Arthur, esteemed American pianist, teacher, and writer on music, half-brother of FRANK (HENRY) LOESSER; b. N.Y., Aug. 26, 1894; d. Cleveland, Jan. 4, 1969. Loesser studied at the Institute of Musical Art in N.Y.

In 1913 Loesser made his debut in Berlin, and three years later in N.Y. After touring the Orient and Australia in 1920–21, he appeared widely in the U.S. In 1926 he was appointed a professor of piano at the Cleveland Institute of Music. In 1943 he was commissioned in the U.S. Army as an officer in the Japanese intelligence department. He mastered the language and, after the war, gave lectures in Japanese in Tokyo. He was the first American musician in uniform to play for a Japanese audience in 1946.

Loesser was also a music historian and writer. He published *Humor in American Song* in 1943 and an entertaining volume, *Men, Women and Pianos: A Social History,* in 1954.

Loesser, Frank (Henry), talented American composer and lyricist, half-brother of ARTHUR LOESSER; b. N.Y., June 29, 1910; d. there, July 28, 1969. Loesser was educated at City College in N.Y., where he began writing songs for college activities. He subsequently was active as a reporter, singer, and vaudeville performer. In 1931 he settled in Hollywood and devoted himself mainly to writing musical comedies. During World War II he was in the U.S. Army and wrote several Army songs, including *Praise the Lord and Pass the Ammunition* in 1942 and *Roger Young* in 1945.

After World War II, Loesser found his greatest success in producing shows for Broadway, which included *Where's*

PEOPLE IN MUSIC

Charley? (1948), *Guys and Dolls* (1950), *The Most Happy Fella* (1956), and *How to Succeed in Business without Really Trying* (1961), which won a Pulitzer Prize and ran for 1,416 performances. His last musical was *Pleasures and Palaces,* which opened (and closed) in Detroit in 1965.

Loewe, (Johann) **Carl** (Gottfried), outstanding German LIEDER composer; b. Lobejun, near Halle, Nov. 30, 1796; d. Kiel, April 20, 1869. Loewe's father, a schoolmaster and cantor, taught him the rudiments of music. When he was 12 he was sent to the Francke Institute in Halle. There, his attractive manner, excellent high voice, and ability to improvise brought him to the attention of Jerome Bonaparte, who granted him a stipend of 300 thalers annually until 1813. His teacher was Daniel Gottlob Türk, the head of the Institute. After Türk's death in 1813, Loewe joined the Halle Singakademie. He also studied theology at the University of Halle, but soon devoted himself entirely to music.

PEOPLE IN MUSIC

Loewe had begun to compose as a boy. Under the influence of German composer and teacher CARL FRIEDRICH ZELTER, Loewe wrote German BALLADES. His works combined great dramatic impact with fine lyrical melodies. Loewe was regarded by many musicians as the greatest song composer between FRANZ SCHUBERT and JOHANNES BRAHMS. His setting of Goethe's poem *Erlkönig* (1818), which came just after Schubert wrote his great setting, is one of Loewe's finest creations. Other songs that rank among his best are *Edward, Der Wirthin Töchterlein, Der Nock, Archibald Douglas, Tom der Reimer, Heinrich der Vogler, Oluf,* and *Die verfallene Mühle.*

Loewe was personally acquainted with Goethe and also met CARL MARIA VON WEBER. In 1820 he became a schoolmaster at Stettin, and in 1821 music director there and organist at St. Jacobus Cathedral. He lived in Stettin, except for frequent travels, including trips to Vienna (1844), London (1847), Sweden and Norway (1851), and Paris (1857), among other places. In 1866 he settled in Kiel.

Loewe was himself an excellent vocalist and was able to perform his ballades in public. He published several textbooks on singing and composition. In addition to his 368 ballades, Loewe wrote six operas, ORATORIOS, CANTATAS, symphonies, piano CONCERTOS, string quartets, piano SONATAS, and a piano trio.

PEOPLE IN MUSIC

Loewe, Frederick, remarkable Austrian-American composer of popular music; b. Vienna, June 10, 1901; d. Palm Springs, Calif., Feb. 14, 1988. Loewe studied piano in Berlin with FERRUCCIO BUSONI and Eugène D'Albert and composition with Emil Nikolaus von Reznicek. He emigrated to the U.S. in 1924 and, after a period as a concert pianist, devoted himself to composing popular music. Adapting himself quickly to American popular styles, he became one of the most successful writers of musical comedies.

Loewe had a number of minor hits in the mid-'30s and early '40s, working with a variety of lyricists. Then, in 1942 he met the lyricist and playwright ALAN JAY LERNER, which led to their collaboration on the unsuccessful musical *What's Up?,* in 1943. Two years later, their next effort, *The Day before Spring,* received a respectable hearing, but it was with *BRIGADOON* in 1947 that they achieved broad success.

After *Paint Your Wagon* in 1951, Lerner and Loewe took Broadway by storm with *My Fair Lady,* which opened in 1956 and enjoyed 2,717 performances. It was based on George Bernard Shaw's *Pygmalion.* They then brought out the film score *Gigi* in 1958, after a story by Colette, which won nine Academy Awards. Their final Broadway collaboration was the highly acclaimed musical *Camelot,* which opened in 1960.

Older than Lerner and less interested in a long career, Loewe retired on the income from these major hits. After Lerner unsuccessfully collaborated with other composers, he lured the elder composer out of retirement in 1974 to provide the score for the film *The Little Prince.* However, after that, Loewe happily retired from composing for the stage.

See also LERNER, ALAN JAY.

When *Lohengrin* premiered, Wagner was in exile in Switzerland as a fugitive from Saxony. He was being sought by the authorities for his rather small role in the 1848 Revolution against the Saxon leadership.

Lohengrin. Opera by RICHARD WAGNER, 1850, to his own libretto, first performed in Weimar. FRANZ LISZT conducted the premiere in Wagner's absence. It was Wagner's first great masterpiece.

Scene from Lohengrin, *1997 production.*
(Robbie Jack/Corbis)

In *Lohengrin,* as always, Wagner shows his fascination with Nordic legends. Elsa of Brabant has a mystic dream of a noble knight who could defend her from the terrible accusation of murdering her own brother. Her dream knight arrives in a boat drawn by a swan. She marries him to the strains of the famous bridal chorus (which has sanctified millions of ordinary marriages in Europe and America). Although he warns her never to ask his name and origin, she does, and he reveals that he is Lohengrin, the Knight of the Holy Grail, son of Parsifal; his swan is Elsa's brother, believed to be dead. The swan's human shape is restored, but Lohengrin must leave now that his identity is known. Swanless, he summons a dove to draw the boat away.

Lomax, Alan, important American ethnomusicologist, b. Austin, Tex., Jan. 31, 1915. He acquired his interest in folk music from his father, John Avery Lomax (b. Goodman, Miss., Sept. 23, 1867; d. Greenville, Miss., Jan. 26, 1948). He then studied at the University of Texas in Austin (B.A., 1936) and at Columbia University (1939).

Lomax joined his father as a researcher in 1933. With him he collected folk songs in the Southwestern and Midwestern regions of the U.S. They supervised field recordings of rural and prison songs, discovering the African-American blues guitarist and songwriter LEADBELLY. They also rediscovered JELLY ROLL MORTON and recorded interviews with

PEOPLE IN MUSIC

him at the Library of Congress in Washington, D.C., in 1938. Lomax also collected folk songs in Europe.

In 1963 Lomax was made director of the Bureau of Applied Social Research and, at Columbia University, director of the project on *cantometrics.* This was a theory that Lomax developed himself, that showed relationships among different cultures based on elements of their musical performances. He has written numerous books, both alone and with his father, drawing on his collecting activities.

Lombardi alla prima Crociata, I (The Lombards at the First Crusade). Opera by GIUSEPPE VERDI, 1843. It deals with two crusading brothers from Lombardy who are rivals in love. The more ambitious one plans to kill the other, but slays their father by mistake. To expiate his sin, he goes to Jerusalem and becomes a hermit. His niece is captured by the infidels, but falls in love with her captor's son. Her lover is wounded, but is baptized by the hermit just in time to save his expiring heathen soul. As the battle rages, the brothers are reunited; the hermit is forgiven by his brother and dies in peace.

The opera was first performed in Milan. It was then staged in London in 1846 and in N.Y. in 1847. In France, Germany, Poland, and Russia it played under the title *Jerusalem,* but it returned to Italy's La Scala as *Gerusalemme.*

London Bridge Is Falling Down. A nursery rhyme that became popular in England and the U.S. during the last quarter of the 19th century.

London Symphonies. A group of 12 symphonies by FRANZ JOSEPH HAYDN, beginning with No. 93 and ending with his last symphony, No. 104. He wrote them for the London violinist and impresario JOSEPH SALOMON, who arranged for Haydn's London tours in 1791–92 and again in 1794–95.

London Symphony, A. RALPH VAUGHAN WILLIAMS's Symphony No. 2, 1914, one of his most popular, first performed in London. Within its four movements are realistic recreations of the noises of London streets, with the chimes of Big Ben heard throughout. However, Vaughan Williams did not wish this piece to be considered PROGRAM MUSIC; instead, he hoped the additional sounds would add to the enjoyment of the work as a whole.

Londonderry Aire (Air). Famous Irish melody, perhaps an authentic folk song, first published in 1855. In 1913 Frederick Weatherly wrote a set of lyrics to the tune, entitled *Danny Boy.*

Long Christmas Dinner, The. Opera by PAUL HINDEMITH, 1961, to an English libretto by him and Thornton Wilder, based on Wilder's play. It was first performed in Mannheim (in German). The dinner is indeed long, lasting a century, with one generation following another for a meal.

Long Tall Sally. LITTLE RICHARD's first major crossover hit, from June 1956. Two months later it was shamelessly covered by white-bread teen heartthrob Pat Boone. Seven years later, it was covered by the mop-topped Liverpudlians, the BEATLES.

longevity. Cursory reading of actuarial tables seems to indicate that musicians as a class of people live on the average about 12 years longer than nonmusicians under similar social and geographical conditions.

The greatest conductor of modern times, ARTURO TOSCANINI, continued to lead an orchestra well into his 80s and resigned only after he suffered an embarrassing lapse of memory at a concert. LEOPOLD STOKOWSKI conducted concerts and made recordings after he turned 91. PIERRE MONTEUX had already arranged a program he expected to conduct with the Boston Symphony Orchestra on his 90th birthday, but unfortunately predeceased the date by a few months.

Organists usually live longer than symphony conductors. The celebrated French organist CHARLES-MARIE WIDOR lived to be 93. There are several cases on record of church organists who died at the console. Among them was the blind French organist Louis Vierne, who died while playing one of his new compositions at the organ of Notre Dame de Paris in 1937. However, he was only 66 at the time.

> When an aging symphony conductor showed a desperate reluctance to quit, an unfeeling music critic remarked: "Conductors rarely die and never resign."

979

The record of longevity for pianists is not as impressive as that of organists. The American pianist Henry Holden Huss, who was also a composer of sorts, made a point of playing a program of his works on his 90th birthday. ARTUR RUBINSTEIN continued to give concerts even after he became blind, and he died at the age of 95.

Violinists and cellists usually stop playing in public after 70, but the greatest cellist of the 20th century, PABLO CASALS, continued to play publicly until shortly before his death at 97. Among singers, Manuel García lived to be 101, but he abandoned his professional singing career long before and remained active mainly as a teacher. Marie Olenine D'Alheim terminated her career as a concert singer in her middle age to enter radical politics. She joined the French Communist party and went to Moscow, where she died at the round age of 100.

One has to cite less universally known names to find nonagenarians and centenarians among composers. Havergal Brian reached the age of 96. Henri Büsser died at the age of 101, but he was little known outside of France. CARL RUGGLES lived to be 95, and he was fortunate in acquiring a solid reputation before he died. EUBIE BLAKE, the African-American RAGTIME virtuoso, performed and recorded into his late 90s. He died a few days after reaching his 100th anniversary.

A most spectacular case of a composer's longevity is that of the American composer Margaret Ruthven Lang, who reached the age of 104 before she finally died. Descending further into the depths of obscurity we find the name of Victor Kuzdo, a Hungarian-American violinist and composer whose vital enzymes sustained him in Glendale, California, until his death at the age of 106. This all-time record in the annals of musical biography is being currently challenged by Leo Ornstein, who, at 106, is very much alive.

Statistically, mediocre musicians live much longer than men of genius. Among truly great composers, only GIUSEPPE VERDI lived well into his 80s. RICHARD WAGNER did not even reach the biblically sanctioned age of three-score and ten (70 years old). LUDWIG VAN BEETHOVEN, CLAUDE DEBUSSY, MAURICE RAVEL, and PIOTR ILYICH TCHAIKOVSKY died before their 60th birthdays. And FRÉDÉRIC CHOPIN, FRANZ SCHUBERT,

ROBERT SCHUMANN, FELIX MENDELSSOHN, not to mention WOLFGANG AMADEUS MOZART, died in their 30s or 40s, at the height of their genius. Is it that angels are eager to carry away the best musicians for heavenly concerts?

longhair. A derogatory characterization of a person interested in CLASSICAL music; synonymous with HIGHBROW. It comes from the conventional portraiture of older musicians sporting a luxuriant head of long hair. FRANZ LISZT in his last photograph appears thus uncropped.

long-playing records (recordings). PHONOGRAPH discs intended to rotate at 33-⅓ revolutions per minute (rpm), introduced by Columbia Records in 1947. This makes it possible to place 25 minutes (more or less) on a single side of a disc, as opposed to 4½ minutes on a single side of the 78-rpm disc. This result was accomplished by having more circular grooves in combination with a slower speed of recording.

Long-playing records inaugurated a new era in phonograph recordings, enabling phonograph companies to record a whole act of an opera or a whole symphony on a single disc. Long-playing records are often called LPs for short. CDs (COMPACT DISCS), introduced in the early '80s, have since replaced LPs among home listeners.

Look For the Silver Lining. Song by JEROME KERN, 1920, included in the musical *Sally.* It provided the sentimental theme for the biographical film on Kern, *Till the Clouds Roll By.* It has also been revived by Garrison Keillor on his "Prairie Home Companion" broadcasts.

Loriod, Yvonne, distinguished French pianist and teacher; b. Houilles, Seine-et-Oise, Jan. 20, 1924. Loriod studied at the Paris Conservatory, winning no fewer than seven *premiers prix.*

In 1943 Loriod began collaborating with composer OLIVIER MESSIAEN on the premiere of his *Visions de l'Amen* for two pianos. She would later play the first performances of all of his PIANO parts. After World War II, she toured extensively. She made her U.S. debut in the premiere of Messiaen's *Turan-*

PEOPLE IN MUSIC

galîla-Symphonie with the Boston Symphony Orchestra in 1949. She taught at the Paris Conservatory from 1967 to 1989.

A foremost champion of the music of Messiaen, she married him in 1961. She also excelled in performances of the music of BÉLA BARTÓK, ARNOLD SCHOENBERG, Jean Barraqué, and PIERRE BOULEZ.

PEOPLE IN MUSIC

Lortzing, (Gustav) **Albert,** celebrated German opera composer; b. Berlin, Oct. 23, 1801; d. there, Jan. 21, 1851. Lortzing's parents were actors, and the family wandered from town to town. He learned acting from his father and music from his mother at an early age. After some lessons in PIANO and theory in Berlin, Lortzing continued to study on his own and soon began to compose. In 1823, he married the actress Rosina Regina Ahles in Cologne. In their long marriage they had 11 children.

In 1824 Lortzing wrote his first stage work, the SINGSPIEL *Ali Pascha von Janina, oder Die Französen in Albanien* (Ali Pasha from Janina, or the French in Albania), which, however, was not produced until four years later. In 1832, he brought out the LIEDERSPIEL *Der Pole und sein Kind, oder Der Feldwebel vom IV. Regiment* (The Pole and his child, or the sergeant of the Fourth Regiment) and the singspiel *Szenen aus Mozarts Leben* (Scenes from Mozart's life), which were well-received on several German stages.

From 1833 to 1844 Lortzing was engaged at the Municipal Theater of Leipzig as a tenor. There, he launched a light opera, *Die beiden Schützen* (The two sharpshooters) in 1837, which became instantly popular. That same year, he also produced there his undoubted masterpiece, *Zar und Zimmermann, oder Die zwei Peter* (The Czar and the carpenter, or the two Peters). It was performed with enormous success in Berlin in 1839, and then in other European music centers.

Lortzing's next three operas were failures. In 1842 *Der Wildschütz, oder Die Stimme der Natur* (The gamekeeper, or the voice of nature) was produced, a comic opera that was in many respects the best that Lortzing wrote. Its success, although impressive, never equaled that of *Zar und Zimmermann*. At about the same time, Lortzing attempted still another career, that of opera producer, but it was short-lived, as was his brief conductorship at the Leipzig Opera in 1844 – 45.

Composing remained his chief occupation. He produced *Undine* (Ondine) in Magdeburg (1845) and *Der Waffenschmied* (The blacksmith) in Vienna (1846). He then went to Vienna as conductor at the Theater an der Wien, but soon returned to Leipzig, where he produced the light opera *Zum Grossadmiral* (For the great admiral; 1847).

The revolutionary events of 1848 seriously affected his position in both Leipzig and Vienna. After the political situation settled, he produced in Leipzig a ROMANTIC opera, *Rolands Knappen, oder Das ersehnte Gluck* (Roland's need, or the longed-for happiness, 1849). Although at least four of his operas were played at various German theaters, Lortzing received no income from these works, because of a flaw in the regulations protecting the rights of composers. He was forced to travel again as an actor, but he could not earn enough to support his large family, left behind in Vienna.

In the spring of 1850 Lortzing obtained the post of conductor at Berlin's nondescript Friedrich-Wilhelmstadt Theater. His last score, the comic opera *Die Opernprobe, oder Die vornehmen Dilettanten* (The opera rehearsal, or the distinguished amateurs) was produced in Frankfurt am Main, while he was on his deathbed in Berlin. He died the next day. Lortzing also wrote an ORATORIO, *Die Himmelfahrt Jesu Christi* (The ascension of Jesus Christ, 1828), some incidental music to plays, choral works, and songs.

Zar und Zimmermann was based on the true story of a carpenter who stood in for Czar Peter the Great, in order to save the Czar from a murder plot.

It is as a composer of characteristically German Romantic operas that Lortzing holds a distinguished, if minor, place in the history of dramatic music. He was a follower of CARL MARIA VON WEBER, but lacked Weber's imagination. In his lighter works, he approached the type of French operetta. In his best creations he exhibited a fine sense of facile melody and infectious rhythm. His harmonies, though unassuming, were always proper and pleasing, and his orchestration was both competent and effective.

Lost Chord, The. Organ piece by ARTHUR SULLIVAN, 1877, composed during the eventually fatal illness of his beloved brother Fred. The "lost chord" is the second INVERSION of the DOMINANT SEVENTH CHORD. It is played against a DRONE bass note (or PEDAL POINT) and forms a painful DISSONANCE.

Lost in the Stars. Musical tragedy by KURT WEILL, 1949, based on Alan Paton's novel *Cry, the Beloved Country.*

A young black South African takes part in a robbery and kills a white man. He is caught and sentenced to hang. The father of the slain white man goes to see the murderer's father, and the two find a way to mend their racial differences in mutual sorrow.

The score approaches a type of scenic ORATORIO, with ARIAS and choruses bearing a religious character. Outstanding among them are the title song and the lament *Cry, the Beloved Country.*

Lott, Felicity (Ann), English soprano; b. Cheltenham, May 8, 1947. Lott studied in London at Royal Holloway College, University of London, and at the Royal Academy of Music. In 1976 she sang at Covent Garden in the world premiere of HANS WERNER HENZE's *We Come to the River.* She also appeared there as Anne Trulove in *THE RAKE'S PROGRESS,* and in other roles. She appeared in Paris for the first time in 1976. She made her Vienna debut in 1982 singing the *Vier Letze Lieder* of RICHARD STRAUSS.

In 1984 Lott was engaged as soloist with the Chicago Symphony Orchestra. In 1986 she sang at the wedding of the Duke and the Duchess of York at Westminster Abbey. In 1990 she was made a Commander of the Order of the

PEOPLE IN MUSIC

British Empire. On Sept. 4, 1990, she made her Metropolitan Opera debut in N.Y. as the Marschallin, the role she chose for her San Francisco Opera debut in 1993. Among her other fine roles are Pamina, Countess Almaviva, Donna Elvira, and Arabella.

loud pedal. The far-right pedal of the piano. When depressed, it releases (lifts) all DAMPERS normally resting on the strings, allowing the strings that have been struck to continue vibrating (i.e., sound). This makes it necessary to change the pedaling quickly when the harmony changes, to avoid unwelcome CACOPHONY.

The handling (or more accurately, the footing) of the loud pedal must be considered with great care on general musical grounds rather than narrowly pianistic grounds. One of the natural safety impulses among beginning pianists is to step on the right pedal to create a wash of sound in which the annoying wrong notes may be conveniently drowned out.

When a composer writes for piano orchestrally, requiring sustained tones across changing harmonies, a compromise must be sought using the skill of subtle half-pedaling. An outstanding example is a variation in ROBERT SCHUMANN's *Études Symphoniques* in which the theme occurs in the bass while the harmony changes above.

Louie Louie. Rhythm and blues singer and composer Richard Berry's ode to a Caribbean sailor and his lost love. This song became popular in the U.S. northwest in the early '60s, where it was covered by Paul Revere and the Raiders (unsuccessfully) and the Kingsmen. The later version shot up the charts in 1963. Since then, a favorite of garage bands everywhere and a rock classic.

Louise. "Roman musical" by GUSTAVE CHARPENTIER, 1900, to his own libretto. The work was an immediate success, with nearly 1,000 performances during the first half of the century. It is a counterpart of the Italian OPERA VERISMO and even includes imitated cries of vegetable vendors on Parisian streets.

Louise is a poor seamstress who yields to the passion of Julien, a young Paris artist. Her fate is uncertain at the end of the opera. In its sequel, *Julien,* she is spoken of as dead.

MUSICAL INSTRUMENT

The F.B.I. was worried by the popularity of *Louie Louie* on American college campuses. Believing the lyrics to be obscene, they tried desperately to understand them on the basis of the Kingsmen's very poorly recorded single. They were unsuccessful!

Louisiana Story. Film score by VIRGIL THOMSON, 1948, composed for a documentary film, for which he won the Pulitzer Prize. Thomson drew a suite from it, *Acadian Songs and Dances,* which premiered in Philadelphia in 1951.

loor **loure.** A dance in $\frac{6}{4}$ or $\frac{3}{2}$ time and slow tempo, the DOWN-BEAT strongly marked, with a syncopated melody. It is often included in the BAROQUE instrumental suite as well as in French BALLETS and OVERTURES of the ROCOCO period.

Love for Three Oranges. Opera by SERGEI PROKOFIEV, 1921, first produced in Chicago, with the composer conducting. The composer's libretto is based on a Gozzi COMMEDIA DELL'ARTE play. "Spectators" observe the goings-on from a gallery and participate in the action.

A witch (Fata Morgana) decrees that the young Prince of Clubs, who laughed when she suffered an embarrassing fall, be doomed to wander in search of three oranges. In the desert, the Prince meets Tchelio, the court magician, who warns him not to open the oranges unless they are near water. The Prince steals the large oranges from a castle cook, and he and his companion Truffaldino rest in the desert with them.

While the Prince sleeps, the thirsty Truffaldino slices open an orange, out of which a princess steps, begs for water, and dies. Truffaldino repeats his tragic mistake, and runs away. The Prince awakens and opens the last orange. This time Princess Ninetta steps out, but she is saved from death by the Spectators, who rush in with a bucket of water. The Princess is then changed into a rat. She and the Prince undergo more trials, but are eventually victorious. The rat returns to human form, and, as Fata Morgana is led away to prison, the royal couple celebrate.

The suite from the opera is popular, especially the *March.*

Love Life. Musical by KURT WEILL, 1948. An American couple married in 1791 are still together a century and a half later. Although there are no signs that death will soon do them part, they neither love nor cherish each other anymore. Their longevity provides a basis for a musical history of the U.S., from glee singers to crooners. Includes *Green-Up Time* and *Mr. Right.*

Love Me Tender. Theme from ELVIS PRESLEY's first film, and a No. 1 hit. It was adapted from the traditional folk song *Aura Lee.*

luce (It., light). A proposed *color organ* marked by ALEXANDER SCRIABIN in the score of his last symphonic work, *Promethée.* According to Scriabin's unfulfilled hopes, the luce would have bathed the concert hall in shimmering hues that changed along with the work's harmonies.

Lucia di Lammermoor. Opera by GAETANO DONIZETTI, 1835, first produced in Naples. The libretto is based on Walter Scott's novel *The Bride of Lammermoor.*

Edgar loves Lucia, but her ambitious brother wants her to marry a British Lord. When Edgar goes to war, Lucia is told that he was unfaithful to her. When Edgar returns, he finds her engaged to the Lord. He pronounces a curse on the whole family, after taking part in a famous sextet, the other five singers being Lucia, her brother, Lucia's husband, his chaplain, and Lucia's lady-in-waiting. On her wedding night Lucia murders her husband and goes insane. In this celebrated "mad scene" she imagines herself married to Edgar; she then swoons and dies. Vowing to join her in eternity, Edgar stabs himself to death.

For all its overheated narrative, *Lucia di Lammermoor* is one of the most melodious products of the Italian art of BEL CANTO.

Lucier, Alvin (Augustus, Jr.), important American composer of the experimental school; b. Nashua, N.H., May 14, 1931. Lucier studied at Yale University from 1950 to 1954 and then continued his training at Brandeis University from 1958 to 1960. He also studied composition with LUKAS FOSS and orchestration with AARON COPLAND at the Berkshire Music Center in Tanglewood, Massachusetts, during the summers of 1958 and 1959, and in Rome on a Fulbright scholarship from 1960 to 1962. He was on the faculty of Brandeis University from 1962 to 1970, where he served as choral director.

With ROBERT ASHLEY, David Behrman, and Gordon Mumma, Lucier founded the Sonic Arts Union in 1966, an

PEOPLE IN MUSIC

ELECTRONIC MUSIC performing group with which he toured the U.S. and Europe. He joined the faculty of Wesleyan University in 1970. From 1972 to 1977 he was music director of the Viola Farber Dance Company.

Lucier contributed many articles to music journals and other publications. With D. Simon, he published *Chambers* in 1980. In 1990 he was in Berlin on a Deutscher Akademischer Austauschdienst fellowship.

Lucier's works exploit virtually all known musical and nonmusical sources available to the creative artist and redefine the term "music" in radical terms. He uses everything from brain-wave scanners and pulse generators to found objects like glass oven dishes or pieces of fabric to make his music. Many of these items have been incorporated into SOUND INSTALLATIONS.

Among Lucier's better-known works are *I am sitting in a room* for voice and electromagnetic surfaces, strewn material, and closed-circuit television system, from 1972; 1974's *Still and Moving Lines of Silence in Families of Hyperbolas* for singers, players, dancers, and unattended percussion, and *Music on a Long Thin Wire* for audio oscillators and electronic monochord, composed in 1977. Among later works are *Fideliotrio* for viola, cello, and piano (1988), *Silver Streetcar for the Orchestra* for triangle (1988), *Carbon Copies* for piano, saxophone, and percussion (1988), *Amplifier and Reflector I* for open umbrella, ticking clock, and glass oven dish (1991), and *Navigations* for string quartet (Frankfurt am Main, Oct. 11, 1991).

Mozart was only 16 when he wrote *Lucio Silla.*

Lucio Silla. Opera by WOLFGANG AMADEUS MOZART, 1772, first performed in Milan, Dec. 26, 1772.

Silla was the Roman general who reached the highest power after he was elected consul in 81 B.C. and then proclaimed himself dictator of Rome. In Mozart's opera he renounces his power and returns it to the people.

Lucrezia Borgia. Opera by GAETANO DONIZETTI, 1833, first produced in Milan.

Lucrezia, the most infamous of the historical Borgia family in 16th-century Italy, shelters her illegitimate son in the Borgia castle and helps him elude arrest by her husband's henchmen. While handing our cups of poisoned wine to some, she unwittingly passes poison to her son.

Supposedly, the LIBRETTO was drawn from a tragedy by Victor Hugo, but he was outraged when the opera was produced and demanded a total revision. This was done. Lucrezia turned Turkish, and the title was changed to *La Rinnegata* (The renegade).

ludi spirituales (Lat., spiritual plays). Medieval sacred MYSTERY PLAYS on biblical subjects.

Ludus Tonalis. Piano cycle by PAUL HINDEMITH, 1944, subtitled *Studies on Counterpoint, Tonal Organization, and Piano Playing.* The body of the work consists of twelve FUGUES with intervening INTERLUDES. The work was first performed in Chicago.

Ludwig, Christa, remarkable German soprano; b. Berlin, March 16, 1924. Ludwig was reared in a musical family (both parents were singers). She studied at the Hochschule für Musik in Frankfurt.

In 1946 she made her operatic debut in Frankfurt in the role of Orlofsky in *DIE FLEDERMAUS.* In 1954 she sang the roles of Cherubino and Octavian at the Salzburg Festival, and in 1955 she was engaged by the Vienna State Opera. She made her Metropolitan Opera debut in N.Y. as Cherubino in 1959.

In subsequent years, Ludwig made considerable impact as a Wagnerian singer, being equally successful in such disparate roles as Kundry, Fricka, Venus, and Magdalene in *DIE MEISTERSINGER VON NÜRNBERG.* She also obtained brilliant success as the Marschallin and other roles in operas by RICHARD STRAUSS. She also sang the female leads in both of ALBAN BERG's operas. In the Italian repertoire, she gave fine interpretations of the roles of Amneris, Rosina, and Lady Macbeth. On March 20, 1993, she gave her last N.Y. recital at Carnegie Hall, and on April 3, 1993, she made her farewell appearance at the Metropolitan Opera singing Fricka in *DIE WALKÜRE.* Her career closed with concert and operatic farewells in Vienna in 1994.

Cleverly, the introductory praeludium is converted into the final postludium by turning the page upside down. Its music is then read backward, with some allowances for ACCIDENTALS.

PEOPLE IN MUSIC

Music critics in Europe and America praised Ludwig as a superb singer not only in opera but also in the art of German LIEDER. She has received numerous international arts and governmental honors and awards, including the Golden Ring of the Vienna State Opera (1980) and the Silver Rose of the Vienna Philharmonic (1980). She was honored by the French government as a Chevalier of the Légion d'honneur and as a Commandeur de l'ordre des arts et des lettres in 1989. Her autobiography was published as *"... und ich wäre so gern Primadonna geworden"* (Berlin, 1994).

In 1957 Ludwig married Walter Berry, the Austrian baritone, with whom she frequently appeared in opera. They separated and in 1970 were divorced, but they continued to appear together in both opera and concert settings. In 1972 she married the French actor Paul Deiber.

Luening, Otto (Clarence), multifaceted American composer, teacher, flutist, and conductor; b. Milwaukee, June 15, 1900; d. N.Y., Sept. 2, 1996. Luening was of deeply rooted German ancestry, traceable to one Manfried von Luninck, who flourished in 1350. One of Luening's maternal ancestors was said to be a descendant of Martin Luther's sister. Luening's great-grandfather emigrated to the U.S. in 1839 and settled in Wisconsin; he made the first barley beer in Milwaukee. Luening's paternal grandfather was American- born. He became active in bilingual culture in Wisconsin and was an organizer of the German-English Academy.

Luening's father was an educated musician who received his training at the Leipzig Conservatory. He had met RICHARD WAGNER and sang in performances of LUDWIG VAN BEETHOVEN's Ninth Symphony, with Wagner conducting. Returning to Milwaukee, he became active in German-American music. He kept his cultural associations with Germany, however, and in 1912 took his family to Munich. There the young Luening enrolled in the Akademie der Tonkunst, where he studied flute, piano, and composition. He gave his first concert as a flutist in Munich in 1916.

When America entered World War I in 1917, Luening went to Switzerland, where he studied at the Zurich Conservatory until 1920. He also took private lessons with the Italian modern composer FERRUCCIO BUSONI. Pursuing sci-

PEOPLE IN MUSIC

entific interests, he attended a seminar in abnormal psychology at the University of Zurich. He also appeared as an actor in the English Players Company. It was during this period that he began to compose. His first violin SONATA and a sextet were performed at the Zurich Conservatory.

Luening returned to the U.S. in 1920, where he earned a living as a flutist and conductor in theater orchestras. In 1925 he moved to Rochester, N.Y., where he served as coach and executive director of the opera department at the Eastman School of Music. In 1928 he went to Cologne, and upon his return to America, from 1932 to 1934, he was on the faculty of the University of Arizona in Tucson. In 1934 he became chairman of the music department at Bennington College in Vermont, holding this position until 1944.

After teaching at Barnard College in N.Y. from 1944 to 1947, Luening joined the philosophy faculty at Columbia University from 1949 to 1968, where he also was codirector of the Columbia-Princeton Electronic Music Center from 1959 to 1980 and music chairman of the School of the Arts from 1966 to 1970. He likewise taught composition at the Juilliard School from 1971 to 1973.

An important development in Luening's career as a composer took place in 1952, when he began to experiment with the resources of magnetic tape. He composed a strikingly novel piece, *Fantasy in Space,* in which he played the flute with its accompaniment electronically transmuted on tape. LEOPOLD STOKOWSKI featured it on a program in N.Y. in 1952, along with Luening's two other electronic pieces, *Low Speed* and *Invention.*

Luening found a partner in composer VLADIMIR USSACHEVSKY, who was also interested in electronics. Together, they produced the first work that combined real sounds with an electronic background, *Rhapsodic Variations* for tape recorder and orchestra, performed by the Louisville Orchestra on March 20, 1954. Its performance anticipated by a few months the production of EDGARD VARÈSE's similarly constructed work, *Déserts.* Another electronic work by Luening and Ussachevsky, *A Poem in Cycles and Bells* for tape recorder and orchestra, was played by the Los Angeles Philharmonic later that year. LEONARD BERNSTEIN conducted the first performance of still another collaborative composition by Luening and Ussachevsky, *Concerted Piece* for tape recorder and orchestra, with the N.Y. Philharmonic in 1960.

From that point on, Luening devoted a major part of his creative effort to integrating electronic sound into the fabric of a traditional orchestra, without abandoning fundamental scales and intervals. Most, but not all, of these works were in collaboration with Ussachevsky. He also wrote straightforward pieces without electronics, of which the most important is *A Wisconsin Symphony*, a sort of musical memoir of a Wisconsin-born composer, which premiered in his home state in 1976.

In addition to many other honors, he also held three Guggenheim fellowships in 1930–31, 1931–32, and 1974–75. In 1952 he was elected to membership in the National Institute of Arts and Letters, and he served as composer-in-residence at the American Academy in Rome in 1958, 1961, and 1965. His long and distinguished career is recounted in his autobiography, *The Odyssey of an American Composer* (N.Y., 1980).

Luftpause (Ger., breathing rest). A break between melody NOTES, and particularly at the end of a phrase. Originally, the luftpause was inserted into a melody to add to its expressiveness. However, ROMANTIC performers, particularly violinists, have abused the effect.

Lugubre Gondole, Le. Piano piece by FRANZ LISZT, 1883, composed in Venice a few weeks before RICHARD WAGNER died there.

Mystically inclined admirers of Wagner saw in this "lugubrious gondola" a premonition of death. However, Liszt wrote a *Pensée des Morts* as a youth nearly 50 years earlier and no death among his close friends followed its composition. Liszt did write a memorial piece upon learning of Wagner's death in Venice, entitled *Richard Wagner: Venezia.* Contrary to expectations, there are no quotations from Wagner's own music, except for the ostentatious use of AUGMENTED TRIADS, vaguely reminiscent of *The Ride of the Valkyries.*

Luisa Miller. Opera by GIUSEPPE VERDI, 1849, first produced in Naples. The gruesome libretto is derived from the

German poet Friederich von Schiller's tragedy *Kabale und Liebe.*

Luisa loves Rodolfo, but his father wants him to marry a duchess. The evil parent forces Luisa to write Rodolfo a letter renouncing her love. Rodolfo poisons her and himself, but Luisa has just enough singing breath remaining to tell him of his father's treachery. With his dying strength, he kills the henchman of his father who forced her to denounce her love.

lullaby. *See* BERCEUSE.

Lullaby of Broadway. Song by Harry Warren, from the musical *Gold Diggers of 1935.*

Lully, Jean-Baptiste (originally, Giovanni Battista Lulli), celebrated Italian-born French composer; b. Florence, Nov. 28, 1632; d. Paris, March 22, 1687. The son of a poor Florentine miller, Lully learned to play guitar at an early age.

Lully's talent for singing brought him to the attention of Roger de Lorraine, Chevalier de Guise. Lully was taken to Paris in 1646 as a page to Mlle. de Montpensier, a young cousin of Louis XIV. He quickly adapted to the manner of the French court. While he was serving in Mlle. de Montpensier's court in the Tuileries, Lully perfected his violin technique. He also had the opportunity to hear the 24 VIOLONS DU ROI (the King's 24 violinists, also known as the "great [large] orchestra"), and he was present at performances of LUIGI ROSSI's *Orfeo* at the Louvre in 1647.

When Mlle. de Montpensier suffered political disgrace in 1652 and was forced to leave Paris, Lully was released from her service. Early in 1653, he danced with the young Louis XIV in the ballet *La Nuit.* Shortly thereafter, he was made *compositeur de la musique instrumentale du Roi* (composer of the King's instrumental music) with joint responsibility for the instrumental music in court ballets.

At some time before 1656, Lully became conductor of Les Petits Violons du Roi, a smaller offshoot of the large orchestra. This ensemble was heard for the first time in 1656 in *La Galanterie du temps.* Thanks to Lully's strict discipline with regard to organization and interpretation, Les Petits Vi-

PEOPLE IN MUSIC

Although Lully mastered the French language, he never lost his Italian accent.

olons soon came to rival the parent ensemble. The two groups were combined in 1664.

Lully became a naturalized French citizen in 1661, the same year in which he was appointed *surintendant de la musique et compositeur de la musique de la chambre* (director of music and composer of the music for the chamber). He also became *maître de la musique de la famille royale* (master of the royal family's music) in 1662.

In 1664 Lully began his association with the famous French actor and playwright Jean-Baptiste Molière. He provided Molière with the music for a series of *comédies-ballets*, culminating with *Le Bourgeois gentilhomme* in 1670.

Lully acquired the sole right to form an Académie Royale de Musique (Royal Academy of Music) in 1672, and thus gained the power to forbid performances of stage works by any other composer. From then until his death he produced a series of *tragédies lyriques*, most of which were composed to texts by the librettist Philippe Quinault. The subject matter for several of these works was suggested by the King, who was extravagantly praised and idealized in their prologues. Lully took great pains in perfecting these texts, but he was often content to leave the writing of the non-melodic parts to his pupils.

Lully's monopoly of French musical life created many enemies for him. In 1674 Henri Guichard attempted to establish an Académie Royale des Spectacles (Royal Academy of Spectacles or Plays). Their rivalry resulted in Lully accusing Guichard of trying to murder him by mixing arsenic with his snuff. Lully won the court case that followed, but the decision was reversed on appeal.

A further setback for Lully occurred when his collaborator Quinault was thought to have slandered the King's mistress in his text of *Isis* in 1677. Quinault was compelled to end his partnership with Lully in disgrace for some time. The King continued to support Lully, however, in spite of the fact that the composer's homosexuality (a capital offense at the time) had become a public scandal. Lully's acquisition of titles culminated in 1681, when noble rank was conferred upon him with the title Secretaire du Roi (Secretary to the King).

In his last years Lully turned increasingly to sacred music. It was while he was conducting his *Te Deum* in 1687 that he accidentally struck his foot with a pointed cane that he was using to pound out the beat. Gangrene set in, and he died of blood poisoning two months later.

Lully's historical importance rests primarily upon his music for the theater. He developed what became known as the French OVERTURE, with its three contrasting slow-fast-slow movements. He further replaced the Italian recitativo SECCO style with accompanied French RECITATIVE. Thus, through the Italian-born Lully, French opera came of age.

Some of Lully's best-known stage works include *Cadmus et Hermione* (1673), *Alceste, ou Le Triomphe d'Alcide* (1674), and *Acis et Galatée, pastorale héroïque* (heroic pastoral; 1686). He also scored numerous ballets and theatrical works. His sacred and choral works include a *Te Deum* (1677), *De profundis* (1683), *Motets à deux pour la chapelle du Roi* (Paris, 1684), six *grands motets* for two choirs and orchestra (1685), and 14 *petits* (small) *motets*. Lully also wrote a variety of instrumental pieces, including overtures, suites, dances, and organ pieces. A complete catalog of his works was edited by H. Schneider (Tutzing, 1981).

Lulu. Opera by ALBAN BERG, 1928–35, produced posthumously in Zurich, 1937. Berg, a slow worker, was only able to complete two of its three acts. One section of the third act was included in the *Lulu Suite* that was premiered in 1934. The libretto is drawn from two dramas of the German playwright Wedekind (*Pandora's Box* and *Earth Spirit*).

Lulu is a vixen who attracts both young and old, and men and women. Directly or otherwise, she leads many of them to death. She meets her own doom when, reduced to prostitution, she is disemboweled by Jack the Ripper in London.

The score is a tour de force of Berg's personal use of 12-TONE composition. It preserves the structure of a classical SUITE while creating a dramatic arch (many of the characters of Act I return transformed in Act III), and relies on a Wagnerian use of LEITMOTIVS.

In a true tale of musical mystery, Berg in fact had virtually finished a short score of the third act, and a vocal score had been drawn up. But Berg's widow banned its publication. Unknown to her, the Austrian composer FRIEDRICH CERHA was secretly orchestrating the third act under the auspices of Berg's publisher. After years of work, Cerha completed the third act. Five years later, after Berg's widow's death, the premiere of the complete version took place at the Paris Opéra.

Lupu, Radu, outstanding Romanian pianist; b. Galai, Nov. 30, 1945. Lupu began his piano studies at the age of six, making his recital debut when he was 12. In 1963 he was awarded a scholarship at the Moscow Conservatory, where he studied until 1969. In quick succession he won first prize in the Van Cliburn (1966), Enesco (1967), and Leeds (1969) competitions.

In 1972 Lupu made his American debut as soloist with the Cleveland Orchestra, and he subsequently played with the Chicago, Los Angeles, N.Y., and Boston orchestras. In Europe he made successful appearances in Berlin, Paris, Amsterdam, London, Vienna, and other cities in varied programs ranging from CLASSICAL to modern works. In 1996 he was a soloist with the Berlin Philharmonic at the London Promenade Concerts.

lur (Dan.). A late Nordic Bronze Age brass instrument of Scandinavia. It includes a conical tube, three to six feet in length and twisted into a loose "S"; a cupped, lip-vibrated mouthpiece; and a disc ornamented with geometric figures instead of a bell.

Lustige Witwe, Die. *See* MERRY WIDOW, THE.

lute (It. *lauto, liuto;* Fr. *luth,* Ger. *Laute*). A generic name for a variety of plucked string instruments, most popular from the 16th through 18th centuries.

The body of the lute is shaped like a half of a pear, with its neck turned back at a right angle. The FINGERBOARD has embossed FRETS indicating the positions of the notes of the scale. The lute usually has five sets of double strings, plus a single string for the highest sound, and they are plucked with the fingers. The tuning is in perfect fourths, with a

PEOPLE IN MUSIC

MUSICAL
INSTRUMENT

MUSICAL
INSTRUMENT

third in the middle, the lowest string being G or A, and with a range of two octaves.

The lute was the favorite instrument of the aristocracy during its golden age in the 16th and 17th centuries. About the middle of the 18th century it inexplicably lost its popularity and joined the honorable company of obsolete instruments. It has become a major component of the early music revival.

Lute-like instruments existed in Mesopotamia in great antiquity, but they had only two or three strings, and there is no evidence that the familiar lute of the RENAISSANCE actually descended by way of imitation or import of these earlier instruments. Long-necked lutes existed in Persia and Arabia in the Middle Ages. Their European variety was called *colascione,* which usually had five strings. A small variety of the Arabian lute was called ʼUD. Another lute-like instrument of Arabian provenance was the *tanbur.* The Russian *domra* was popular at the same time as the European lute. When it went out of fashion, it was superseded by the *balalaika.*

The MANDOLIN is of the lute family, and it managed to retain its popularity through the 20th century. Other types of lutes are the mandora, a large variety of the mandolin, and PANDORA. Two very large lutes are the THEORBO and chitarrone. None of these instruments, however, have the unique characteristic of a turned neck.

A whole musical literature was created for the lute at the time of its greatest popularity. A large number of collections of music written specially for the lute (most in TABLATURE) was published in the 16th and 17th centuries. It is from these books that music historians are able to trace the formal development of European dances, instrumental works, and vocal compositions.

Lutenists enjoyed great renown in the Renaissance period, particularly in England. The English-born lutenist JOHN DOWLAND, a contemporary of Shakespeare, commanded salaries equalling those of high officials. The Italian court lutenist Rizzio, who was brought to Scotland by Mary Stuart, assumed such power at the Scottish court that Mary's antagonists arranged for his assassination. Portraits of lutenists, both men and women, were favorites with the great painters of the Renaissance. There are numerous refer-

Any stringed instrument with a neck attached to a sound body, where the strings run parallel to the neck, is generically called a "lute." This would include, for example, the GUITAR.

ences to lute players in English literature beginning with Chaucer.

A maker of lutes, or of stringed instruments in general, is called a luthier.

MUSICAL INSTRUMENT

lutheal. A mechanical attachment invented in 1919 by the Belgian piano manufacturer Georges Cloetens. It was to be placed on the metal framework inside the grand piano, imparting to it the sound of a CLAVECIN.

MAURICE RAVEL was quite fascinated by the potential of the lutheal and made use of it in the piano part of his violin piece *Tzigane.* But the lutheal failed to prove attractive to the public or the music critics. Accordingly, Ravel made another version of *Tzigane* for violin and piano, and still another version for VIOLIN with orchestral accompaniment. He further made use of the lutheal in the original setting of *L'Enfant et les sortilèges,* but in the final version reproduced the effects of the lutheal by various orchestral timbres.

PEOPLE IN MUSIC

Luther, Martin, great German religious reformer; b. Eisleben, Nov. 10, 1483; d. there, Feb. 18, 1546. As part of the changes that led to Protestantism and the Reformation, Luther wrote pamphlets on a new German LITURGY.

The first MASS in German was sung in Wittenberg in 1524. Johann Walter (1496–1570), who aided Luther in organizing the music for the Mass, transcribed melodies that Luther played on the flute. Together they created new hymns with lyrics in German. Many hymns are attributed to Luther. It seems that while some are fully his, others were German translations or adaptations of Latin hymns.

PEOPLE IN MUSIC

Lutoslawski, Witold, outstanding Polish composer; b. Warsaw, Jan. 25, 1913; d. there, Feb. 7, 1994. Lutoslawski learned to play the piano as a child, then studied VIOLIN and theory and composition as a teenager. He also studied mathematics at the University of Warsaw from 1931 to 1933.

Lutoslawski entered the Warsaw Conservatory in 1932, where he continued composition studies and also studied piano, graduating as a pianist in 1936 and as a composer a year later. He served in the Polish Army in 1937–38. He was mobilized in the summer of 1939 and taken prisoner of war by the invading Nazi armies at the outbreak of World War II. He managed to escape to Warsaw, where he earned a living playing piano in cafés and also participated in secret concerts in private homes.

After the war, Lutoslawski worked briefly for the Polish Radio, then devoted himself to composition. When his works reached the outside world, he obtained prestigious engagements as a lecturer and instructor in England, West Germany, Denmark, and Sweden. From the '60s forward, numerous honorary degrees and awards were conferred on him by European countries and in the U.S.

Lutoslawski's early works are marked by a NEOCLASSICAL tendency, drawing on national Polish melodies. Gradually he turned to a more structural type of composition in which melodic and rhythmic elements are organized into a strong unifying network. He was also extraordinarily open-minded. He was attracted by the music of JOHN CAGE, finding useful applications in the operations of chance. The influence of BÉLA BARTÓK is felt in the constantly changing colors, angular melodies, and nonsymmetrical rhythms. Lutoslawski's *Musique funèbre* for string orchestra (Katowice, March 26, 1958), dedicated to the memory of Bartók, shows the strongest tendency in this direction. He freely applied a full sound palette in building orchestral COLORS.

Although possessing a masterful technique of composition, it took Lutoslawski fully ten years to achieve the desired balance of structural contents to complete his Third Symphony (1972–83; Chicago, Sept. 29, 1983). His list of works is not large, but each composition, whatever its length, is an accomplished masterpiece. Among later works are various orchestral compositions, including *Fanfare for Louisville* (1986), Piano Concerto (1988), *Partita* for violin and orchestra (1988), and *Interludium* for chamber orchestra (1989); the chamber pieces *Slides* for eight instruments and string quartet (1988) and *Subito* for violin and piano (1992), and *Chantefleurs et Chantefables* for soprano and chamber orchestra (1990).

Lydian mode. *See* AUTHENTIC MODES.

PEOPLE IN MUSIC

Lynn, Loretta (Webb), American country-music singer, guitarist, and songwriter; b. Butcher Hollow, Ky., April 14, 1932. A coal miner's daughter, Lynn taught herself the basics of GUITAR playing. She was attracted to COUNTRY music by hearing singers like Molly O'Day over the radio.

At age 13, she wed a serviceman, Oliver Vanetta Lynn, whose nickname was "Mooney." They moved to Washington State, where she quickly had four children (and suffered several miscarriages) over the next five years. Meanwhile, recognizing her talents, Mooney encouraged her to sing in local clubs. She was heard by a promoter named Don Grashey, who owned a small label called Zero records. She recorded four songs for the company in 1960. Her husband relentlessly promoted her single, *Honky Tonk Girl,* and it eventually reached No. 14 on the country charts. This led to her being hired by the GRAND OLE OPRY radio program and the family's relocating to Nashville.

In Nashville, Lynn was befriended by PATSY CLINE, who became a role model for the singer in the last year of Cline's life (Cline died in an airline crash in 1961). Lynn began touring with the Wilburn Brothers' road show, and she was signed to Decca Records in 1962. It was unusual for a female singer to write her own material in the mid-'60s; it was even more unusual for it to be so outspoken. Nonetheless, Lynn had hits with her own songs about the problems in wedded life, including *You Ain't Woman Enough (To Take My Man), Don't Come Home A-Drinkin' (With Lovin' On Your Mind),* and *Your Squaw Is on the Warpath.* In 1970, she scored her biggest hit with the autobiographical song, *Coal Miner's Daughter.*

Lynn continued to enjoy success in the '70s, always following her own muse. In 1975 she wrote the first (and perhaps only) country song to address birth control, *The Pill,* which was a major hit. She also recorded many successful duets in this period with country singer and songwriter CONWAY TWITTY, including *After the Fire Is Gone* and the humorous *You're the Reason Our Kids Are Ugly.*

Lynn continued to record and tour through the '80s and early '90s, although her songwriting output slowed. She stopped touring in the mid-'90s when her husband was hos-

Lynn's life was the subject of the film biography *Coal Miner's Daughter* in 1980, starring Sissy Spacek, who won an Academy Award for her performance in the title role.

pitalized and subsequently died of cancer. She has since returned to occasional performing, mostly on television.

Her twin daughters, Peggy and Patsy (b. 1956), have formed a duet group called The Lynns that has had moderate success in the mid to late '90s.

lyre. 1. An ancient Greek stringed instrument, the body made of wood or tortoise shell, from which rose two curving arms joined above by a crossbar. The strings, from three to ten in number, were stretched from this crossbar to or over a BRIDGE set on the SOUNDBOARD and were plucked with a PLECTRUM. It is related to the KITHARA, and both were associated with Apollo and are often reproduced in sculptures and drawings of the Greek god of beauty. 2. In military bands, a mallet instrument consisting of loosely suspended steel bars tuned to the scale and struck with a hammer.

lyric (lyrical; It. *lirico*). Literally, pertaining to or proper for the LYRE, or for accompaniment by the lyre; by extension, that which is appropriate for singing or for expression in song. The lyric mode is opposed to epic (narrative) and dramatic (scenic, accompanied by action).

Lyric drama (Fr., *drame lyrique*), opera; *lyric opera,* one that emphasizes the lyric mode; *lyric stage,* the operatic stage.

Lyric Suite (*Lyrische Suite*). Work for string quartet by ALBAN BERG, 1927, first performed in Vienna. Its six movements are set in the technique of 12-TONE composition, with lyric sentiment emphatically expressed by a quotation from the prelude to RICHARD WAGNER's *TRISTAN UND ISOLDE*. Fifty years later, it was discovered that the melodic line of the finale was a setting of a hitherto secret text, celebrating Berg's love for Hanna Fuchs-Robettin. The work was first performed in this version in N.Y. in 1979.

lyrics (lyric). The text of a popular song, including show tunes. *Lyricist,* the author of verses for such songs.

MUSICAL INSTRUMENT

M

Ma, Yo-Yo, brilliant Chinese cellist; b. Paris, Oct. 7, 1955. Ma was born into a musical family active in Paris, his father a violinist, and his mother a MEZZOSOPRANO. He began to study violin as a young child, then graduated to the VIOLA, and finally the CELLO.

Ma was taken to N.Y. when he was seven. When he was nine he enrolled at the Juilliard School of Music, where his principal teachers were Leonard Rose and Janos Scholz. He subsequently received additional training at Harvard University. He quickly established a reputation as a master of the cello in his appearances with the great orchestras of the world, as a recitalist, and as a chamber music player. He has been deservedly acclaimed for his unostentatious musicianship, his superlative technical resources, and the remarkable tone of his melodious lyricism. He was awarded the Avery Fisher Prize in 1978.

In order to extend his repertoire, he made a number of effective transcriptions for his instrument. He also promoted contemporary works and was the soloist in the premieres of the cello concertos of Christopher Rouse (Los Angeles, Jan. 23, 1994) and JOHN WILLIAMS (Tanglewood, Mass., July 7, 1994).

Ma Mère L'Oye (Mother Goose). Suite of five children's pieces by MAURICE RAVEL, 1910, for piano four-hands, which he later orchestrated. The subjects are taken from the famous book of fairy tales by Charles Perrault. Ravel composed these pieces for two Parisian girls, one age 10 and the other only six. They gave the work its first performance at a concert in Paris.

Má vlast (My Country). Symphonic cycle by BEDŘICH SMETANA, 1874–79, in six movements:

Vyšehrad (the old citadel of Prague)

Moldau (Vltava, the river on which Prague was built)

Šárka (a legendary warrior woman)

Z Českych luhů a hájů (From Bohemia's Meadows and Groves)

Tábor (an ancient city; it includes the Hussite war song)

Blaník (a Bohemian hill on which the Hussites congregated)

Maazel, Lorin (Varencove), American conductor; b. Neuilly, France (of American parents), March 6, 1930. Maazel's parents took him to Los Angeles when he was an infant. At a very early age he showed innate musical ability, including PERFECT PITCH. He began to study violin at age five, then piano at age seven.

Fascinated by the art of conducting, Maazel went to symphony concerts and soon began to take lessons with Vladimir Bakaleinikov, who was an associate conductor of the Los Angeles Philharmonic. In 1938 he conducted a performance of FRANZ SCHUBERT's *Unfinished* Symphony with the visiting University of Idaho Orchestra.

In 1938 Bakaleinikov was appointed assistant conductor of the Pittsburgh Symphony Orchestra, and the Maazel family followed him to Pittsburgh. From Bakaleinikov, Maazel quickly learned to speak Russian. In 1939 the young conductor made a sensational appearance in N.Y., leading the National Music Camp Orchestra of Interlochen at the World's Fair. Maazel was only 11 when he conducted the NBC Symphony Orchestra in 1941 and 12 when he led an entire program with the N.Y. Philharmonic in 1942. He survived these exhibitions and took academic courses at the University of Pittsburgh.

In 1948 Maazel joined the Pittsburgh Symphony Orchestra as a violinist, and at the same time was appointed its apprentice conductor. In 1951 he received a Fulbright fellowship for travel in Italy, where he undertook a serious study of BAROQUE music. He also made his adult debut as a conductor in Catania in 1953. This was followed over the balance of the decade by appearances at various European festivals. In 1960 he became the first American to conduct at

Maazel's young age inevitably drew comments from music critics and journalists. One critic compared him to a trained seal! Nonetheless, all were amazed by his technique and skill.

the Bayreuth Festival, where he led performances of RICH-ARD WAGNER's opera *LOHENGRIN*.

In 1962 Maazel toured the U.S. with the Orchestre National de France, the same year in which he made his Metropolitan Opera debut in N.Y. conducting WOLFGANG AMADEUS MOZART's *DON GIOVANNI*. In the summer of 1963 he made a tour of Russia, conducting concerts in Moscow and Leningrad. From 1965 to 1971, Maazel was artistic director of the Deutsche Oper in West Berlin. From 1965 to 1975, he also served as chief conductor of the (West) Berlin Radio Symphony Orchestra. Also in this period, he was associate principal conductor of the New Philharmonia Orchestra of London from 1970 to 1972, and its principal guest conductor from 1976 to 1980.

In 1972 Maazel became music director of the Cleveland Orchestra, a position he held with great distinction until 1982, when he was made conductor emeritus. He led the Cleveland Orchestra on 10 major tours abroad and maintained its stature as one of the world's foremost orchestras. He was also chief conductor of the Orchestre National de France from 1977 to 1982, then its principal guest conductor until 1988, and finally its music director until 1991.

In 1980 Maazel became conductor of the famous Vienna Philharmonic New Year's Day Concerts, a position he retained until 1986. In 1982 he assumed the positions of artistic director and general manager of the Vienna State Opera, the first American to be so honored. However, he resigned these positions in the middle of his four-year contract in 1984 after a conflict over artistic policies with the Ministry of Culture. He then served as music consultant to the Pittsburgh Symphony Orchestra from 1984 to 1986, becoming its music advisor, music director, and principal guest conductor in 1986. In 1993 he also assumed the post of chief conductor of the Bavarian Radio Symphony Orchestra in Munich. In 1994 he again conducted the Vienna Philharmonic's New Year's Day Concert. In 1996 he stepped down as music director of the Pittsburgh Symphony Orchestra.

Maazel is equally able to conduct operatic or symphonic scores. He is blessed with a phenomenal memory and possesses an extraordinary baton technique. He also maintains an avid interest in nonmusical pursuits. He is fluent in

French, German, Italian, Spanish, Portuguese, and Russian. He was married twice: first in 1952 to the Brazilian-American pianist Miriam Sandbank, and, after their divorce in 1969, to the Israeli pianist Israela Margalit (from whom he also was later divorced). Maazel has received many international awards and honors.

Macbeth. Opera by GIUSEPPE VERDI, 1847, first performed in Florence. The Italian LIBRETTO follows faithfully the main events of Shakespeare's play, but the opera itself is not one of Verdi's best.

Macbeth. Opera by ERNST BLOCH, 1910, first performed in Paris. The score bristles with unorthodox harmonies and asymmetric rhythms and was judged severely by conservative Paris critics.

Macbeth. Symphonic poem by RICHARD STRAUSS, 1890, after Shakespeare, first performed in Weimar. This is the first of seven remarkable works in this genre, each based on an explicit story or a literary work.

MacDowell, Edward (Alexander), greatly significant American composer; b. N.Y., Dec. 18, 1860; d. there, Jan. 23, 1908. MacDowell's father was a Scotch-Irish tradesman, his mother an artistically inclined woman who encouraged his musical studies. He took piano lessons privately with several keyboard virtuosi, including supplementary work with Teresa Carreño, who later championed his works.

In 1876, after traveling in Europe with his mother, MacDowell enrolled as an auditor in the elementary class at the Paris Conservatory. In 1877 he was admitted as a regular student. He also studied piano with the well-known French teacher A.-F. Marmontel and SOLFÈGE with Marmontel's son, Antonin. Somewhat disappointed with his progress, he withdrew from the conservatory in 1878 and went to Wiesbaden for further study with the German composer/music critic Louis Ehlert.

In 1879 MacDowell enrolled at the newly founded but already prestigious Hoch Conservatory in Frankfurt, studying piano, composition, and COUNTERPOINT and FUGUE.

One critic writing in his review of the premiere of Bloch's *Macbeth* stated, "This music is an indecipherable puzzle. . . . It is simply noise for the sake of noise."

PEOPLE IN MUSIC

During MacDowell's stay there, his composition class was visited by FRANZ LISZT. MacDowell performed the piano part in ROBERT SCHUMANN's Quintet, op.44, in Liszt's presence. At another visit, MacDowell played Liszt's *Hungarian Rhapsody* No. 14 for him.

Two years later, MacDowell visited Liszt in Weimar and played his own first piano Concerto for him, accompanied by Eugène d'Albert at the second piano. Encouraged by Liszt's interest, MacDowell sent him the manuscript of his *Modern Suite,* op.10, for piano solo. Liszt recommended the piece for performance at the meeting of the Allgemeiner Deutscher Musikverein in Zurich in 1882. He also recommended Mac-Dowell to the publishers Breitkopf & Härtel, who subsequently brought out the first works of MacDowell to appear in print, the *Modern Suites* for piano, opp. 10 and 14.

Edward MacDowell, c. 1895.
(Library of Congress/Corbis) ▶

Despite his youth, MacDowell was given a teaching position at the Darmstadt Conservatory. He also accepted private pupils, among them Marian Nevins of Connecticut, to whom he was secretly married on July 9, 1884, in N.Y., followed by a public ceremony in Waterford, Connecticut, on July 21. During the early years of their marriage, the MacDowells made their second home in Wiesbaden, where MacDowell composed industriously. His works were performed in neighboring communities, and Carreño put several of his piano pieces on her concert programs. There were also performances in the U.S.

However, the MacDowells were beset by financial difficulties. His mother proposed that he and his wife live on the family property, but MacDowell declined. He also declined an offer to teach at the National Conservatory in N.Y. at the at-the-time generous fee of $5 an hour. Similarly, he rejected an offer to take a clerical position at the U.S. consulate in Krefeld, Germany.

In 1888 MacDowell finally returned to the U.S., where he was welcomed in artistic circles as a famous composer and pianist. Musical America at the time was virtually a German colony, and MacDowell's German training was a certificate of his worth. The Boston Symphony Orchestra conductors Wilhelm Gericke, Arthur Nikisch, and Emil Paur, all Austro-Germans, played his works. In late 1888 MacDowell made his U.S. debut as a composer and pianist at a Boston concert of the Kneisel String Quartet, featuring his *Modern Suite,* op.10. In 1889 he was soloist in the premiere performance of his second piano Concerto with the N.Y. Philharmonic, under the direction of Theodore Thomas. Frank van der Stücken invited MacDowell to play his concerto at the spectacular Paris Exposition in 1889.

In 1896 Columbia University invited MacDowell to become its first professor of music, "to elevate the standard of musical instruction in the U.S., and to afford the most favorable opportunity for acquiring instruction of the highest order." MacDowell interpreted this statement to its fullest. By 1899 two assistants had been employed, but students received no credit for the courses. At the same time, MacDowell continued to compose and to teach piano privately. He also conducted the Mendelssohn Glee Club from 1896 to 1898 and served as president of the Society of American Musicians and Composers in 1899–1900.

In the academic year 1902–03, MacDowell took a sabbatical. He played concerts throughout the U.S. and in Europe, giving a performance of his second piano Concerto in London in 1903. During his sabbatical, Columbia University replaced its president, Seth Low, with Nicholas Murray Butler, whose ideas about the role of music in the university were diametrically opposed to those of MacDowell. MacDowell resigned in 1904, creating a scandal in the music world. It was not until some time later that the Robert Cen-

MacDowell had no difficulty having his works published, although for some reason he preferred that his early piano pieces, opp. 1–7, be printed under the pseudonym Edgar Thorn.

ter Chair that MacDowell had held at Columbia University was renamed the Edward MacDowell Chair of Music to honor its first recipient.

Through the combination of the trauma resulting from this episode, an accident with a hansom cab, and the development of what appears to have been syphilis, MacDowell rapidly deteriorated mentally. He showed signs of depression, extreme irritability, and a gradual loss of vital functions. He eventually lapsed into total insanity and spent the last two years of his life in a childlike state, unaware of his surroundings. In 1906 a public appeal was launched to raise funds for his care. MacDowell was only 47 years old when he died.

The sum of $50,000 was raised for the organization of the MacDowell Memorial Association. Marian MacDowell, who outlived her husband by nearly half a century (she died in Los Angeles in 1956, at the age of 98), deeded to the association her husband's summer residence at Peterborough, N.H. This property became an artists' retreat under the name of the MacDowell Colony, for American composers and writers, who could spend summers working undisturbed in separate cottages, paying a minimum rent for lodging and food.

During the summer of 1910, Mrs. MacDowell arranged an elaborate pageant with music from MacDowell's works. The success of this project led to the establishment of a series of MacDowell Festivals in Peterborough, N.H.

MacDowell received several awards during his lifetime, including two honorary doctorates (Princeton University, 1896, and University of Pennsylvania, 1902) and election into the American Academy of Arts and Letters (1904). In 1940 a five-cent U.S. postage stamp with his likeness was issued. In 1960 he was the second composer elected to the Hall of Fame at New York University, where, in 1964, a bust was unveiled.

Among American composers, MacDowell occupies a historically important place as the first American whose works were accepted as comparable in quality and technique with those of the average German composers of his time. His music adhered to the prevalent representative ROMANTIC art. Virtually all of his works bear titles borrowed from mythical history, literature, or painting. Even his piano sonatas, set in classical forms, carry descriptive titles, indicative of the mood of melodic resources, or as an ethnic reference.

Because MacDowell lived in Germany during his formative years, German musical culture was decisive in shaping his development. Even the American rhythms and melodies in his music seem to be European reflections of an exotic art. Some critics have drawn a parallel to the works of EDVARD GRIEG, because Grieg was also a regional composer trained in Germany. But Grieg possessed a much more vigorous personality and succeeded in communicating the true spirit of Norwegian song modalities in his works.

A lack of musical strength and originality accounts for MacDowell's gradual decline in the estimation of succeeding generations. The frequency of performance of his works in concert (he never wrote for the stage) declined in the decades following his death, and his influence on succeeding generations of American composers receded to a faint recognition.

Machaut (Machault, Machau, Mauchault), **Guillaume de** (Guillelmus de Mascaudio), French composer and poet; b. probably in Machaut, Champagne, c.1300; d. probably in Rheims, April 13?, 1377. Machaut entered the service of John of Luxembourg, King of Bohemia, about 1323, serving as his secretary until the king's death in 1346. He was granted a canonry in Verdun in 1330, another in Arras two years later, and yet another in Rheims in 1333, retaining the first two until 1335. He settled in Rheims permanently about 1340. From 1346 Machaut was in the service of the French nobility, including the future king Charles V.

Machaut's fame is illustrated by the number of surviving presentation manuscripts dedicated solely to his music. His *Messe de Nostre Dame* for four voices is the first POLYPHONIC setting of the MASS attributable to one composer. He also wrote 42 BALLADES, 33 VIRELAIS, 23 MOTETS, 22 RONDEAUX, 19 LAIS, a double HOCKET (*Hoquetus David*), a COMPLAINTE, and a CHANSON ROYAL. His poem *Remede de Fortune,* considered an early work, contains songs in almost every genre in which he composed. Other poems without music are *La Louanges des dames* and *Le Livre du voir dit,* a work of the

PEOPLE IN MUSIC

1360s that tells the story of Machaut's love for a 19-year-old woman, Péronne d'Armentières.

machine music. The modern machine became an object of artistic inspiration early in the 20th century.

The Italian FUTURISTS made a cult of automobiles and airplanes. George Antheil's *Ballet mécanique* shocked concert audiences by its use of propellers and other mechanical noisemakers. Max Brand (1896–1980) produced the first machine opera in *Machinist Hopkins* in 1929. ARTHUR HONEGGER made a declaration of love for powerful American locomotives in his symphonic movement *Pacific 231.* Frederick Converse (1871–1940) glorified the Ford car in his *Flivver 10,000,000* from 1927.

But locomotives, automobiles, and airplanes soon lost their glamour and became public nuisances. By mid-century the machine as a positive subject for artistic creation was obsolete.

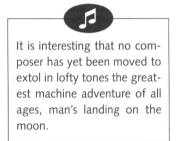

It is interesting that no composer has yet been moved to extol in lofty tones the greatest machine adventure of all ages, man's landing on the moon.

PEOPLE IN MUSIC

Machover, Tod, American cellist, conductor, and composer; b. N.Y., Nov. 24, 1953. Machover studied composition at the University of California, Santa Cruz (1971–73), Columbia University (1973–74), and the Juilliard School in N.Y., where he earned his bachelor's degree in music in 1975, and his master's two years later. Among his teachers were noted modern composers LUIGI DALLAPICCOLA, ROGER SESSIONS, and ELLIOTT CARTER. Machover also studied computer music at the Massachusetts Institute of Technology and at Stanford University.

Machover was first cellist in the orchestra of the National Opera of Canada in Toronto in 1975–76. He then moved to Paris, where he worked at PIERRE BOULEZ's center for electronic composition, IRCAM, serving as guest composer in 1978–79 and director of musical research from 1980 to 1984. In 1985 he joined the electronic-music faculty at the Massachusetts Institute of Technology, where he also was director of its Experimental Media Facility from 1986. Among his honors were the Koussevitzky Prize in 1984 and the Friedheim Award in 1987. He edited the books *Le Compositeur et l'ordinateur* (Paris, 1981) and *Musical Thought at IRCAM* (London, 1984) and was the author of *Quoi, quand, comment? La Recherche musicale* (Paris, 1985; English translation, 1988, as *The Concept of Musical Research*) and *Microcomputers and Music* (N.Y., 1988).

While he has written for purely acoustic sound sources, Machover is primarily associated with electroacoustical experiments and live interactive installations. His best-known work is the opera *Valis*, based on a Philip K. Dick novel, which premiered in Paris in 1987. He has also written several orchestral works, solo acoustic works, and piano pieces, as well as many pieces for electronic instruments and recording tape.

Mack the Knife, The Ballad of *(Die Morität von Mackie Messer).* Song by KURT WEILL and BERTOLT BRECHT, 1928, from the ballad opera *DIE DREIGROSCHENOPER* (The Threepenny Opera). The German name translates as "The Murderous Deeds of Mackie Messer," "Mackie Messer" being the nickname of Macheath, the notorious gangster at the center of the opera's story.

When he translated *Die Dreigroschenoper* for its American premiere in 1954, MARC BLITZSTEIN translated Macheath's nickname literally. *The Ballad of Mack the Knife* is, not surprisingly, ironic in the extreme.

♫

Both teen pop singer Bobby Darin and jazz trumpeter LOUIS ARMSTRONG had major hits in the late '50s with *Mack the Knife.*

Madama Butterfly. Opera by GIACOMO PUCCINI, 1904, based on the David Belasco play. It was first produced in Milan.

Pinkerton, a lieutenant in the U.S. Navy on a visit to Nagasaki, becomes enraptured with a local 15-year-old Japanese girl nicknamed Cio-Cio (butterfly). She is also formally referred to as Cio-Cio-San, the last word corresponding to *madame*. She and Pinkerton go through a Japanese marriage ceremony, which he knows is not legally binding. He then sails to the U.S., leaving her pregnant. But she has faith in him, expressing her feelings in an aria (*Un bel di vedremo*), based on a five-note (PENTATONIC) theme, which has become a favorite of the soprano repertory. A son is born to Cio-Cio-San. When Pinkerton returns, he brings with him his American wife. Cio-Cio-San yields to the American Mrs. Pinkerton's entreaties to let her have the child. After the Pinkertons leave, she then commits a ritual suicide.

The story of *Madame Butterfly* has inspired many other stage works and films. *M Butterfly*, the Broadway hit, played on the idea of cross-cultural (and cross-sexual) identities. The hit Michael Douglas–Glenn Close film *Fatal Attraction*, telling of an adulterous affair between two coworkers, features the music from the opera throughout in drawing a parallel between the mistress and the tragic heroine.

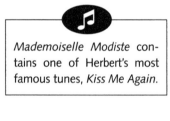

Mademoiselle Modiste contains one of Herbert's most famous tunes, *Kiss Me Again*.

PEOPLE IN MUSIC

The SCORE is remarkable in its bold innovations, making use of consecutive TRIADS, unresolved DISCORDS, and percussive orchestral effects. The notes of *THE STAR-SPANGLED BANNER* are heard in the background, and there is also a fair amount of pseudo-Japanese melodies.

After an opening-night fiasco, Puccini revised the work for a second premiere, this time successful. Recent revivals of the original version have divided the critics as to the relative merits of the two.

Mademoiselle Modiste. Comic opera by VICTOR HERBERT, 1905, first performed in N.Y.

A modest young clerk in a Paris hat shop is loved simultaneously by a French nobleman (whose snobbish family rejects her) and an American millionaire. As a preliminary step to conquest, the American sponsors her career as a singer, and she becomes a PRIMA DONNA under an Italian stage name. When she sings at a charity bazaar at her French suitor's castle, the two recognize that the old flame has been rekindled. This time his family is only too happy to allow the match.

Maderna, Bruno, Italian-born German conductor and composer; b. Venice, April 21, 1920; d. Darmstadt, Nov. 13, 1973. Maderna commenced musical studies at the age of four, and soon took violin lessons. He began touring as a violinist and conductor when he was only seven, appearing under the name "Brunetto Maderna" in Italy and abroad.

Maderna studied at the Verdi Conservatory in Milan, the Rome Conservatory, where he earned a diploma in composition, in 1940, and at the Venice Conservatory. He then served in the Italian army during World War II, eventually joining the partisan forces against the Fascists. After the war, he studied conducting in Darmstadt. He taught composition at the Venice Conservatory from 1947 to 1950, and then made his formal conducting debut in Munich in 1950.

Maderna subsequently became a great champion of the AVANT-GARDE. With LUCIANO BERIO, he helped to form the Studio di Fonologia in Milan in 1954. Also with Berio he was conductor of the Italian radio's Incontri Musicali from 1956 to 1960. In 1963 he became a naturalized German citizen.

Maderna taught conducting and composition in various venues in Europe and the U.S. from the mid-'50s through the early '70s. He was chief conductor of the RAI (Italian Radio Orchestra) in Milan from 1971. Stricken with cancer in the early '70s, he continued to conduct concerts as long as it was physically possible.

Maderna was held in great esteem by composers of the international avant-garde, several of whom wrote special works for him. Maderna's compositions follow the trends of new European music of the period, including the overlayering of two or more separate works to create a new one. After a period of neglect, his music has undergone a revival in recent years. His works include operatic and stage works, orchestral and chamber works, vocal works, and many electronic pieces.

Madonna (born Madonna Louise Veronica Ciccone), fabulously popular and audacious American rock singer and actress; b. Bay City, Mich., Aug. 16, 1958. Madonna took up acting and dancing while attending junior high school in Pontiac, Michigan. After private dance lessons from 1972 to 1976, she studied on scholarship at the University of Michigan from 1976 to 1978.

Making her way to N.Y., Madonna eked out a living by modeling and acting in an underground film. She worked with Alvin Ailey's dance group and studied choreography with Pearl Lang. She then studied drums and guitar with Dan Gilroy. After working with the disco star Patrick Hernandez in Paris, she returned to N.Y., appearing as a drummer and singer with Gilroy's Breakfast Club rock group. In 1982 she organized her own band and in 1983 brought out her first album, *Madonna,* with the hits *Borderline* and *Lucky Star.* With her album *Like a Virgin* (1984), she achieved massive success, which led to her first coast-to-coast tour.

Madonna made a career out of changing her look and provoking critics and admirers alike by her "daring" use of her own image in videos and on tour. Meanwhile, she continued to churn out the hits through the mid-'80s, including the controversial single, *Papa Don't Preach,* which seemed to endorse out-of-wedlock pregnancy.

PEOPLE IN MUSIC

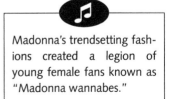

Madonna's trendsetting fashions created a legion of young female fans known as "Madonna wannabes."

At the same time, Madonna pursued a film career. In 1985 she appeared in the critically acclaimed film *Desperately Seeking Susan*. She also acted in *Who's That Girl?* two years later, a box-office bomb, although the title song was a hit. The popular movie *Dick Tracy* in 1990 featured Madonna as a slinky, sequined, torch singer/gun moll. Her most successful screen role was 1996's *Evita*, in which she showed herself capable of singing a demanding score by Andrew Lloyd Webber.

Meanwhile, her pop career continued. Her album *Like a Prayer* continued the Madonna controversies. The title song, with a video showing Madonna dancing in front of burning crosses and romancing a black Jesus figure, naturally upset some Christians. She followed it with a 1991 documentary, *Truth or Dare*, a warts-and-all glimpse of her 1990 tour.

In the early '90s, Madonna seemed obsessed by her own sexuality. In 1992 she released the graphic picture book *Sex*, showing her "fantasies" of sexual relationships, including disturbing images of violent sexual behavior. The book was an immediate hit, despite the controversy over its content. The accompanying album, *Erotica*, was less of a success. This was followed by 1994's *Bedtime Stories*, which included the song *Human Nature*, which had a particularly effective, tightly choreographed music video. It was followed in 1995 by a rather lukewarm collection, *Something to Remember*.

After a few years out of the limelight and the top of the charts, Madonna bore a child (a daughter, whom she named Lourdes) in 1996. This was followed by a new look and a new album, *Ray of Light*, released in 1998. Madonna, now a follower of the Jewish mystical book the Kabalah, proclaimed herself remade by motherhood. The album, combining techno-pop backings with Madonna's emotional lyrics, was a critical success, although not as successful commercially as her earlier releases.

madrigal. A secular POLYPHONIC composition of Italian parentage that achieved its flowering during the RENAISSANCE. It survived in other forms in the BAROQUE period, but lapsed into obsolescence in the 19th century. The derivation of the word is uncertain.

There are really two types of Italian *madrigale,* although the poetic form for both arose in the 14th century and was marked by a fairly definite scheme in iambic pentameter. The first type, composed by Francesco Landini and his contemporaries, is written for two or three texted voices, with the lower vocal part commonly doubled instrumentally. The second type arose during the RENAISSANCE, when strict formality of the verses and tunes was abandoned in favor of a more relaxed, imaginative, and individual style. These polyphonic settings increased to four, five, and six parts, rarely with instrumental doubling.

By the beginning of the 17th century, the role of the melodic line became more and more pronounced. The polyphonic style gave way to HOMOPHONY (a single melody line accompanied by a harmony part), forming a natural bridge to OPERA. A dramatic genre of madrigal cycle developed into the MADRIGAL COMEDY. Early examples of MONODY (recited song texts) were still called madrigals (e.g., Monteverdi's *Madrigali guerrieri e amorosi,* 1638), but the term soon disappeared. Its form survived in the lightweight GLEES of BAROQUE and Classical-era England and America.

Among great (and not necessarily Italian) madrigal composers are Jacob Arcadelt, Andrea Gabrieli, Orlando di Lasso, Luca Marenzio, Carlo Gesualdo, and CLAUDIO MONTEVERDI. GIOVANNI PIERLUIGI DA PALESTRINA was the greatest writer of spiritual madrigals, as opposed to the more common secular type.

Elizabethan composers in England, among them William Byrd, eagerly followed the Italian model. A great impetus to the development of the English madrigal school was the publication in England of a collection of Italian madrigals in translation, *Musica transalpina,* in 1588.

madrigal comedy, madrigal opera. A chain of MADRIGALS united in content and forming a dramatic sequence. A contemporary of the early DRAMMA PER MUSICA. The best-known composers of madrigal comedy are Orfeo Vecchi and Adriano Banchieri. A distant relative of the COMMEDIA DELL'ARTE, its origins may be found in RENAISSANCE madrigal collections with a common theme, often found in courtly weddings.

Madrigali guerrieri e amorosi. A famous book of MADRI-
GALS by CLAUDIO MONTEVERDI, published in 1638. These
"madrigals of war and love" for voices and instruments are
written in the STILE CONCITATO (agitated or energetic style),
combining love with "warlike expression."

Maelzel, Johann Nepomuk. *See* METRONOME.

măh-ĕh′strōh   **maestro** (It., master). An honorary name accorded, often
without merit, to composers, conductors, and teachers, and
even to lower species of musical eminences. In Italian, the
word conveys little more than a common term for a teacher,
but when used by the English, Americans, or Russians in addressing a musical celebrity, it sounds lofty and deferential.

Maestro al cembalo, a BAROQUE harpsichordist who functions as ensemble leader and sets the tempo; *maestro di cappella,* originally, the director of a court chapel, but now a
choirmaster or conductor.

Magaloff, Nikita. *See* SZIGETI, JOSEPH.

Magic Flute, The. SINGSPIEL by WOLFGANG AMADEUS MO-
ZART, 1791. It was produced in Vienna less than 10 weeks
before his death. The German LIBRETTO is by Emanuel Schikaneder, an impresario and actor, and its mazelike entangle-
ments are many. The gorgeous music absorbs the listener entirely, letting the plot proceed on its irrational course.

An earnest youth (Tamino) falls in love with the portrait
of the daughter (Pamina) of the Queen of the Night. He is
given a magic flute to enable him to penetrate the fortress in
which she is held in captivity somewhere in Egypt. His companion is a comical birdcatcher (Papageno) who owns a set
of magic bells (in the score, an *instrumento d'acciacio*), capable of paralyzing any foe. After a series of perilous adventures and tests, Tamino and Pamina are united under the
guidance of Sarastro, the father of Pamina, who serves as the
light to the queen's darkness. The queen and her forces are
defeated, and Tamino and Pamina sing a hymn to the sun
symbolizing the conquest of love and art over the powers of
darkness. Even Papageno finds himself a wife, Papagena.

The Magic Flute is not only the favorite opera of many Mozart aficionados but perhaps the most complex, both musically and dramatically. A partial clue to the story may lie in its heavy pseudo-Oriental symbolism, such as was followed in the Masonic Order, of which both Mozart and Schikaneder were members. At the beginning, Tamino is pursued by a serpent, which is killed by the female messengers of the protective Queen of the Night. The multi-headed serpent was a well-known Masonic symbol. The lovers undergo an initiation similar to that of the Masonic Order, and give a vow of silence, commonly administered in the French Order of Masons in the 18th century. The Egyptian pyramid, which is the locale of one of the scenes, is a famous Masonic symbol (reproduced on the reverse side of The Great Seal of the U.S. and on the $1 bill).

The similarity between the symbols used in the libretto and the Masonic ritual may have angered members of Mozart and Schikaneder's lodge. However, the legend that the Masons resolved to put Mozart to death because he revealed their secrets is pure fantasy.

◀

Handbill for the first performance of Mozart's Magic Flute. *(Austrian Archives/Corbis)*

magic square. An arrangement of numbers placed in such a way that each of its horizontal or vertical rows equals the same sum, e.g.:

1	2	3
2	3	1
3	1	2

This arrangement is used as a model by 12-TONE composers for developing their SETS.

măhg-nē′fē-kăht

Magnificat (Lat.). The most important HYMN of the VESPERS service in the Roman Catholic LITURGY, namely, the CANTICLE of the Blessed Virgin Mary. Its opening words are "Magnificat anima mea Dominum," its text taken from Luke 1:46–55.

Many pious composers wrote Magnificats as separate choral works. In the Anglican church service the Magnificat is a part of Evensong, using the English words, "My soul doth magnify the Lord."

Mahler, Gustav, Austrian composer and conductor in the late ROMANTIC tradition; b. Kalischt, Bohemia, July 7, 1860; d. Vienna, May 18, 1911. Mahler attended school in Iglau, and in 1875 entered the Vienna Conservatory, where he studied piano, harmony, and composition. He also took courses in history and philosophy at the University of Vienna from 1877 to 1880.

In the summer of 1880, Mahler received his first engagement as a conductor, at the operetta theater in the town of Hall in Upper Austria. He subsequently held posts as theater conductor in various German and Austrian cities through 1885. In 1885 he served as second KAPELLMEISTER (conductor) at the Prague Opera, where he gave several performances of RICHARD WAGNER's operas. From 1886 to 1888 he was assistant to the well-known conductor Arthur Nikisch in Leipzig, and in 1888 he received the important appointment of music director of the Royal Opera in Budapest.

In 1891 Mahler was engaged as conductor at the Hamburg Opera. During his tenure there, he developed his mature conducting technique. In 1897 he received a tentative offer as music director of the Vienna Court Opera, but there was an obstacle to overcome: Mahler was Jewish, and although there was no overt anti-Semitism in the Austrian government, an imperial appointment could not be given to a Jew. Mahler was never orthodox in his religion and had no difficulty in converting to Catholicism, Austria's prevailing faith. He held this position at the Vienna Court Opera for

PEOPLE IN MUSIC

Mahler time line

1860 ▶ Born

1885 ▶ Becomes second Kapellmeister at the Prague Opera

1886–88 ▶ Serves as Arthur Nikisch's assistant in Leipzig

1888 ▶ Becomes music director of the Royal Opera in Budapest and completes his first symphony, *Titan*

1891 ▶ Becomes conductor at the Hamburg Opera

1894 ▶ Completes his second symphony, *Resurrection*

1896 ▶ Completes his third symphony, *Ein Sommermorgentraum*

10 years. Under his guidance, it reached the highest standards of artistic excellence.

In 1898 Mahler was engaged to succeed Hans Richter as conductor of the Vienna Philharmonic. Here, as in his direction of opera, he proved a great interpreter, but he also allowed himself considerable freedom in rearranging the orchestration of CLASSICAL scores when he felt it was called for. He also aroused antagonism among the players by his autocratic behavior. He resigned from the Vienna Philharmonic in 1901, and in 1907 he also resigned from the Vienna Court Opera.

In the meantime, Mahler worked as a composer, confining himself exclusively to composition of symphonic music, sometimes with vocal parts. Because of his busy schedule as conductor, he could compose only in the summer months, in a villa on the Worthersee in Carinthia. In 1902 he married Alma Schindler (*see* WERFEL, ALMA MAHLER). She had studied music with Alexander von Zemlinsky, ARNOLD SCHOENBERG's brother-in-law, but was forced to give up composition after her marriage by her autocratic husband. They had two daughters, the younger of whom, Anna, was briefly married to Ernst Krenek. The elder, Maria, died of scarlet fever in 1907. While in mourning, Mahler discovered his own heart condition, which he understood would eventually kill him.

Having exhausted his opportunities in Vienna, Mahler accepted the post of principal conductor of the Metropolitan Opera in N.Y. in 1907. He made his American debut there on Jan. 1, 1908, conducting Wagner's *TRISTAN UND ISOLDE*. In 1909 he was appointed conductor of the N.Y. Philharmonic. His performances both at the Metropolitan and with the N.Y. Philharmonic were enormously successful with audiences and N.Y. music critics, but inevitably he had conflicts with the board of trustees of both organizations, which were mostly commanded by rich women. The N.Y. newspapers published lurid accounts of his struggle for artistic command with the two governing committees.

Mahler resigned from the Metropolitan Opera, and on Feb. 21, 1911, he conducted his last concert with the N.Y. Philharmonic. He then returned to Vienna, where he died of

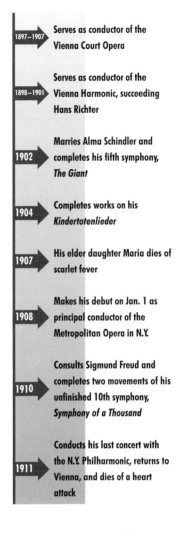

1897–1907 Serves as conductor of the Vienna Court Opera

1898–1901 Serves as conductor of the Vienna Harmonic, succeeding Hans Richter

1902 Marries Alma Schindler and completes his fifth symphony, *The Giant*

1904 Completes works on his *Kindertotenlieder*

1907 His elder daughter Maria dies of scarlet fever

1908 Makes his debut on Jan. 1 as principal conductor of the Metropolitan Opera in N.Y.

1910 Consults Sigmund Freud and completes two movements of his unfinished 10th symphony, *Symphony of a Thousand*

1911 Conducts his last concert with the N.Y. Philharmonic, returns to Vienna, and dies of a heart attack

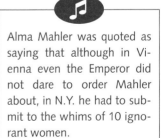

Alma Mahler was quoted as saying that although in Vienna even the Emperor did not dare to order Mahler about, in N.Y. he had to submit to the whims of 10 ignorant women.

a heart attack brought on by a bacterial infection, at the age of 50. The newspaper editorials mourned Mahler's death, sadly noting that his N.Y. tenure had been a failure.

As to Mahler's own compositions, the *New York Tribune* said bluntly, "We cannot see how any of his music can long survive him." His symphonies were sharply condemned in the press as being too long, too loud, and too discordant. It was not until the second half of the 20th century that Mahler became fully recognized as the last great ROMANTIC symphonist.

Mahler's symphonies were drawn on the grandest scale, and the technical means employed for their realization were correspondingly elaborate. The sources of his inspiration were twofold: the lofty concepts of universal art, akin to those of ANTON BRUCKNER, and ultimately stemming from Wagner, and the simple folk melodies of the Austrian countryside, in pastoral moods recalling intimate episodes in LUDWIG VAN BEETHOVEN's symphonies.

True to his ROMANTIC nature, Mahler at first attached descriptive titles to his symphonies. The first was named the *Titan* (after Jean Paul; 1883–88; Budapest, Nov. 20, 1889), the second, *Resurrection* (1887–94; Berlin, Dec. 13, 1895), the third, *Ein Sommermorgentraum* (A Summer's Morning Dream; 1893–96; Krefeld, Oct. 9, 1902), and the fifth, *The Giant* (1901–02; Oct. 18, 1904). The great Eighth Symphony became known as the *Symphony of a Thousand* because it required about 1,000 instrumentalists, vocalists, and soloists for performance. However, this nickname was the inspiration of Mahler's agent, not of Mahler himself. Mahler completed two movements of his work in 1909–10, *Adagio* and *Purgatorio,* which were not performed in Vienna until Oct. 12, 1924, Fritz Schalk conducting. Later in life Mahler tried to disassociate his works from their programmatic titles. He even claimed that he never used them in the first place, contradicting evidence of the manuscripts, in which the titles appear in Mahler's own hand.

Mahler was not an innovator in his harmonic writing. Rather, he brought the ROMANTIC era to its highest achievement by virtue of the expansiveness of his emotional expression and the grand design of his musical structures.

Morbid by nature, Mahler brooded upon the inevitability of death. One of his most poignant compositions was the song cycle for voice and orchestra, *Kindertotenlieder* (Songs on the Death of Children). He wrote it during the period 1901–04, a few years before his daughter Maria's death, and he blamed himself superstitiously for this anticipation of his personal tragedy (Alma may have contributed to this feeling).

Mahler's importance to the evolution of modern music is great. The early works of Schoenberg and ALBAN BERG show the influence of Mahler's concepts. A society was formed in the U.S. in 1941 "to develop in the public an appreciation of the music of Bruckner, Mahler and other moderns." The International Gustav Mahler Society was formed in Vienna in 1955, with Bruno Walter as honorary president. On Mahler's centennial, the government of Austria issued a memorial postage stamp with Mahler's portrait.

Mahler destroyed the manuscripts of several of his early works, among them a piano quartet, which was performed in Vienna in 1878 with the composer at the piano (one movement survives), and three projected or unfinished operas. Mahler also made controversial performing editions or arrangements of symphonies by many CLASSICAL and RO-MANTIC composers.

In 1910 Mahler briefly consulted the founding father of psychoanalysis, Sigmund Freud. However, the treatment apparently did not help Mahler resolve his psychological problems completely.

Maid of Orleans, The. Opera by PIOTR ILYICH TCHAI-KOVSKY, 1881, first performed in St. Petersburg. It is loosely based on German playwright Friedrich von Schiller's romantic play.

Joan of Arc, the Maid of Orleans, hears mysterious voices urging her to save France from the English, who are approaching the city of Orleans. Joan helps the French king Charles VII to win the battle, but she is accused of consorting with the devil. She is turned over to the authorities, who sentence her to be burned at the stake as a heretic.

The LIBRETTO follows history a little more closely than GIUSEPPE VERDI's *Giovanni d'Arco,* but like the Verdi opera, love scenes are added for Joan and Charles. In reality, Joan was condemned for, among other things, cutting her hair short and wearing masculine attire, not for her romantic behavior. Tchaikovsky's heroine does get to sing a beautiful aria bidding farewell to the fields and hills of her native farmland.

Maid of Pskov, The. Opera by NIKOLAI RIMSKY-KORSAKOV, 1873, first produced in St. Petersburg. The action takes place in Pskov in 1570, where Ivan the Terrible, accompanied by his dreaded henchmen, enters the city to subdue a growing rebellion. He discovers that a girl betrothed to a rebel is his natural daughter Olga, born to Vera Sheloga. As his soldiers are about to lay Pskov to waste, Ivan orders them to desist to spare Olga, but she runs out into the streets and is slain.

In 1898 Rimsky-Korsakov wrote a one-act opera called *Boyarina Vera Sheloga,* depicting the original affair between Vera and Ivan.

Mairzy Doats. Nonsense song by Milton Drake, Al Hoffman, and Jerry Livingston, 1943. It caught the imagination of the nation in wartime, in need of a break in the somber mood.

The story is that the incomprehensible words were actually imitations of a small person talking very rapidly and seeming to make sense with words that seem to make none. One plausible possibility:

> *Mares eat oats and does eat oats,*
> *And little lambs eat ivy.*
> *A kid'll eat ivy, too,*
> *Wouldn't you?*

major (Lat.; Fr. *majeur*). Greater; opposed to MINOR (lesser). *See* INTERVAL, CADENCE, CHORD, TRIAD, and SCALE.

major-minor syndrome. In BAROQUE music, most minor-key works end on a MAJOR TRIAD. Such a closing MAJOR THIRD acquired the name PICARDY THIRD (*tierce de Picardie*), introduced by Jean-Jacques Rousseau in his music dictionary (although the origin of the expression is unknown).

In the practice of modern composers, a major third is often superimposed on a minor third. ALEXANDER SCRIABIN employed such a major-minor syndrome in his last opus numbers, but he spread the harmony widely, so that the frictional DISSONANCE of a semitone was avoided. It was IGOR STRAVINSKY who cultivated a true major-minor syndrome in placing both the minor and the major third within a triad. He made use of it as a motto in his choral work *Le Roi des étoiles* (The King of the Stars, 1912), and it occurs also in *Le Sacre du printemps* (The Rite of Spring). Most importantly, Stravinsky breaks up the combined chord, with both the major and the minor third assuming thematic significance.

Makeba, Miriam, black South African singer; b. Prospect, near Johannesburg, March 4, 1932. Makeba sang in a church choir in Pretoria, then joined a traveling show. She first attracted attention when she sang the leading part in the African opera *King Kong* in Johannesburg in 1959. That same year, she went to the U.S., where she appeared in N.Y. nightclubs and on television.

Makeba had several hit records in the '60s, including *Pata Pata.* She testified at the United Nations on the racist policies of South Africa. She made a successful tour of Europe, and also traveled to Ethiopia and Kenya as a representative of black art. She was married to the African-American activist Stokely Carmichael from 1968 to 1978.

In 1986 and 1987 Makeba joined PAUL SIMON's *Graceland* tour of the U.S., Europe, and South Africa, celebrating his album inspired by the music of her homeland.

malagueña (Sp.). An old Spanish dance originating in the provinces of Malaga and Murcia, in rapid TRIPLE time.

măh-lă-gay′nyăh

A popular song of the same name was derived from Ernesto Lecuona's suite *Andalucia* in 1930, with English words by Marian Banks. It was a big hit on popular radio and remained in the pop-song repertoire for decades.

Malibran, María (Felicità García), famous Spanish MEZ-ZOSOPRANO, b. Paris, March 24, 1808; d. Manchester, Sept. 23, 1836. She was the daughter of Manuel (del Popolo Vicente Rodríguez) García (b. Seville, Jan. 21, 1775; d. Paris, June 9, 1832), one of the great TENORS and singing teachers of his era. María was taken to Naples, where she sang a child's part in Paer's *Agnese* in 1814. She studied voice with her father from the age of 15, and also studied solfège with the French vocal teacher Auguste-Mathieu Panseron.

Malibran made her debut as Rosina at the King's Theatre in London in 1825, then went to N.Y., where she sang in the same opera in her family's season at the Park Theatre, which began that fall. She became a popular favorite, singing in *Otello, Tancredi, La Cenerentola, Don Giovanni,* and the two operas written for her by her father, *L'Amante astuto* and *La Figlia dell'aria.* She married the French merchant François Malibran, but he soon became bankrupt, and she returned to Europe without him in 1827.

Malibran made her Paris debut as Semiramide at the Théâtre-Italien in 1828. She then alternated her appearances in Paris and London during the 1829–32 seasons. She subsequently went to Italy, singing in Bologna in 1832 and Naples a year later, making her debut at Milan's La Scala as Norma in 1836.

Malibran met the violinist Charles de Bériot in 1829, with whom she lived until her previous marriage was annulled in 1836. They then were married that same year. However, soon after, Malibran suffered serious injuries when thrown from her horse. Since she was pregnant, complications developed and she died.

Malibran's voice was of extraordinary compass, but the medium REGISTER had several "dead" tones. She was also a good pianist and composed numerous NOCTURNES, ROMANCES, and chansonnettes, published in album form as *Dernières pensées* (Last thoughts).

PEOPLE IN MUSIC

Malipiero, Gian Francesco, Italian composer and conductor; b. Venice, March 18, 1882; d. Treviso, near Venice, Aug. 1, 1973. His grandfather, Francesco (b. Rovigio, Jan. 9, 1824; d. Venice, May 12, 1887), was a well-known composer of operas. Francesco was best remembered for *Giovanna di Napoli,* which was produced with great success when the composer was 18 (GIOACCHINO ROSSINI even praised it). Other operas by his grandfather were *Attila* (1845; renamed *Ildegonda di Borgogna*), *Alberigo da Romano* (1846; his best), and *Fernando Cortez* (1851). Gian Francesco's father, Luigi, was a pianist and conductor.

In 1898 Gian Francesco enrolled at the Vienna Conservatory as a violin student. In 1899 he returned to Venice, where he studied at the Liceo Musicale Benedetto Marcello with the composer Marco Bossi. He followed Bossi to Bologna in 1904 and took a diploma in composition at the Liceo Musicale G. B. Martini that same year. He subsequently worked as an assistant to the noted Italian composer Antonio Smareglia, gaining valuable experience in orchestration.

In 1912–13 Malipiero gained fame by submitting five works to a Roman competition, each under a different pseudonym, and winning four out of five of its prizes. Malipiero went to Paris in 1913, where he absorbed the techniques of musical IMPRESSIONISM. However, his own style of composition was more strongly determined by the POLYPHONIC practices of the Italian BAROQUE.

In 1921 Malipiero returned to Italy, where he was a professor of composition at the Parma Conservatory until 1923. Afterward he lived mostly in Asolo, near Venice. He was made professor of composition at the Liceo Musicale Benedetto Marcello in Venice in 1932, continuing there when it became the conservatory eight years later. From 1939 to 1952 he was also its director.

Malipiero's work reflects many 20th-century styles. An extremely prolific composer, he wrote 35 operas, six ballets, 18 works for voice/s and orchestra, 17 sinfonias, 11 concertos, many other orchestral works, numerous vocal pieces, chamber and instrumental works, and piano music. However, Malipiero's work is notably uneven in quality. But he is considered one of the best 20th-century Italian composers, comparable to LUIGI DALLAPICCOLA and ALFREDO CASELLA.

Malipiero was also an active writer and editor. He edited a complete edition of the works of CLAUDIO MONTEVERDI (16 volumes, Bologna and Vienna, 1926–42) and many works by ANTONIO VIVALDI, as well as other Italian composers. He also wrote many other scholarly books in his long career. He was made a member of the National Institute of Arts and Letters in N.Y. in 1949, the Royal Flemish Academy in Brussels in 1952, the Institut de France in 1954, and the Akademie der Künste in West Berlin in 1967.

Malipiero's s nephew, Riccardo Malipiero (b. Milan, July 24, 1914), is also a composer who studied with his uncle at the Liceo Musicale Benedetto Marcello in Venice, 1937–39.

mambo. A ballroom dance derived from the RUMBA. It appeared in Cuba during the 1940s, and was made popular in the U.S. particularly by Perez Prado and his band. The mambo had spread to non-Hispanic audiences by the 1950s.

This couple dance, in $\frac{4}{4}$ time, uses forward and backward steps, beginning on the upbeat, to percussive POLYRHYTHMIC accompaniment. The mambo was a major influence on the CHA-CHA.

The title song of *Mame* became a hit, particularly as sung by LOUIS ARMSTRONG.

Mame. Musical by JERRY HERMAN, 1966. Mame is a totally uninhibited woman who lives it up in N.Y. At the same time, she has to raise her young orphaned nephew. He is shocked by the scandalous behavior of his "Auntie Mame" but manages to retain his sanity through it all, marries a nice woman, and has a son. At the end of the comedy, Mame takes her great-nephew on a trip around the world, determined to educate him by her own rule: "Life is a banquet."

Mamelles de Tiresias, Les (The Breasts of Tiresias). OPERA BUFFA by FRANCES POULENC, 1947, first produced in Paris.

Tiresias is weary of being a woman, so she ignites her bulging breasts, which rise and pop like balloons. Her husband, on the other hand, wants to be a woman. He succeeds brilliantly and gives birth to 40,000 children. In the end, they return to their original genders and appeal to the audience to breed energetically in order to repopulate the French countryside devastated by war. The score is glorified slapstick, recalling the sonorous world of LES SIX.

Man I Love, The. Song by GEORGE GERSHWIN, 1924, originally intended for the musical *Lady, Be Good!* but cut just before its Broadway opening. It has since become a standard in the pop-song repertoire. The melody is enhanced by the use of BLUE NOTES.

Man of La Mancha. Musical by Mitch Leigh, 1965, first performed in N.Y. It is based on Spanish author Miguel de Cervantes's parody epic *Don Quixote.*

The play opens in a Seville prison cell, where Cervantes wrote his famous book. It then moves through a retelling of several of his famous character's adventures. The major characters are a common woman whom Don Quixote idolizes as Dulcinea, the windmill that he believes is a monster, the mule drivers whom he fights, and his faithful sidekick, Sancho Panza. Includes the title song and the immensely popular *Impossible Dream.*

Man on the Flying Trapeze, The. A VAUDEVILLE waltz song of unknown origin, first popular in the 1870s. Its second line was used by William Saroyan as the title of his novel *The Daring Young Man on the Flying Trapeze.*

Mancini, Henry, highly successful American composer, arranger, pianist, and conductor of popular music; b. Cleveland, April 16, 1924; d. Los Angeles, June 14, 1994. Mancini studied flute and piano in childhood and later attended the Juilliard Graduate School in N.Y. in 1942. He worked as a pianist and arranger with Tex Beneke's popular dance band from 1945 to 1947, and also studied composition with the modern composers Mario Castelnuovo-Tedesco, Ernst Krenek, and Albert Sendrey in Los Angeles.

Mancini joined the music staff of Universal-International film studios in 1952. He wrote many scores for the studio, and also wrote for television, gaining success with his music for the *Peter Gunn* series in 1958. Thanks to its success, that same year he was able to leave the studio's employ and begin freelancing.

Mancini's scores for the films *Breakfast at Tiffany's* in 1961, which included the hit song *Moon River,* and *The Days of Wine and Roses,* from a year later, both won him Academy and Grammy awards. Other scores included *Touch of Evil, Experiment in Terror, Hatari, Charade, The Pink Panther, Two for the Road, The Molly Maguires, Sometimes a Great Notion, The Silver Streak, Victor/Victoria,* and television soundtracks such as *Mr. Lucky* and *The Thorn Birds.* In later years he appeared widely as a guest conductor in concerts of popular fare with American orchestras. He published *Sounds and Scores* (1962), a guide to orchestration.

mandolin (U.K., Fr. *mandoline;* Ger. *Mandoline;* It. *mandolino*). A smaller member of the LUTE family, originating in

PEOPLE IN MUSIC

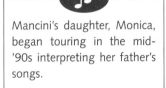

Mancini's daughter, Monica, began touring in the mid-'90s interpreting her father's songs.

MUSICAL
INSTRUMENT

Italy in the 17th century. The name itself is the diminutive of *mandola*.

The instrument is shaped like a pear half and has a fretted FINGERBOARD with four pairs of strings, tuned like those of the VIOLIN (G, D, A, E). Flat-backed mandolins were introduced in the late 19th century as being more convenient to hold against the body. The mandolin is played with a PLECTRUM (or pick). Progressively larger sizes of the mandolin are the mandola, the mandoloncello, and the mandolone or mandocello. An ensemble consisting of mandolins, combined with guitars, is popularly known as a Neapolitan orchestra.

Although the mandolin is generally regarded as a popular or traditional instrument, WOLFGANG AMADEUS MOZART and LUDWIG VAN BEETHOVEN wrote for it. The mandolin is also included in GUSTAV MAHLER's Seventh Symphony, in ARNOLD SCHOENBERG's Serenade, op.24, and in ANTON WEBERN's *Fünf Stücke für Orchester.*

Among folk and traditional performers, BILL MONROE is most closely associated with the mandolin. David Grisman is the most prominent contemporary player, who plays both in traditional BLUEGRASS style and his own compositions with a quartet, including two mandolins in a jazz-swing style.

Manfred Symphony. Orchestral work by PIOTR ILYICH TCHAIKOVSKY, 1886, first performed in Moscow. The program of the work is inspired by Lord Byron's famous poem depicting Manfred wandering in the Alps in search of oblivion. The score is in four movements and is sometimes listed by literal-minded musicologists as Tchaikovsky's Seventh Symphony. Although brilliant and dramatic, *Manfred* is musically inferior to Tchaikovsky's full-fledged symphonies.

mannerism. A generic term descriptive of an overwrought work of art. In painting, mannerism refers to the 16th- and early 17th-century Italian painting that used exaggeration of scale and color contrast to impart a heightened reality to the works. Parmigianino and Caravaggio are among the Mannerists.

Applying this term to music has proven controversial. For different critics, it has meant late BAROQUE and ROCOCO

The Gibson company, a pioneering firm in mandolin design and manufacture in the U.S., sponsored many mandolin orchestras in the early 20th century. For these groups, the company built a large mandobass, featuring a mandolin-shaped body tuned as a bass. It was held upright like a regular acoustic bass.

schools, whose music is marked by ornate designs and great ornamentation. It is also used to describe the work of MADRI-GAL and MOTET composers of the late RENAISSANCE, embodied in the highly CHROMATIC music of Carlo Gesualdo.

Mannheim school. A group of musicians active at the court of the German city of Mannheim in the middle of the 18th century who developed a method of composition and performance that marked a radical departure from the normal style of the BAROQUE period.

Their leader was the Bohemian master Johann Stamitz, who proposed that the melody should dictate the overall shape of a composition, and that standard forms should be used to organize larger works. Most importantly, he felt that the SONATA form should be used as a guide for composing symphonies. Harmony, too, underwent a decided change in the works of the Mannheim school, away from the rigid dependence on BASSO CONTINUO.

In performance, the Mannheim group introduced novel dynamic usages, the most important of which was the effect of continuous CRESCENDO and corresponding DIMINUENDO. Previously, Baroque music had alternated loud and soft passages, in call-and-response forms. Among other innovations were arpeggiated chords (in ascending melodic form, known as the "rocket theme"), extensive TREMOLOS, abrupt general pauses, pyrotechnical ACCENTS, simulated sighs, and various emotional devices, almost ROMANTIC in nature. With regard to the orchestra, the Mannhein musicians gave greater independence to the wind instruments.

The achievements of the Mannheim school soon became known in Paris and London and had considerable influence on the evolution of symphonic and chamber music. On the other hand, there was a great deal of opposition on the part of traditional and academic musicians who dubbed the innovations of the Mannheim school Mannerist. The fact that most of the Mannheim musicians came from Bohemia (modern-day Czechoslovakia) rather than from the main centers of German musical culture gave occasion for narrow nationalistic disdain.

But there was no denying the power of the Mannheim dynamic characteristics. A musician who heard the Mann-

In a letter to WOLFGANG AMADEUS MOZART, his father, Leopold, referred to the "over-mannered Mannheim taste."

heimers play reports that "their crescendo makes the listeners rise involuntarily from their seats, and gradually sink back out of breath with the corresponding diminuendo."

PEOPLE IN MUSIC

Manning, Jane (Marian), English soprano; b. Norwich, Sept. 20, 1938. Manning studied at the Royal Academy of Music in London. In 1964 she made her debut in London in a program of contemporary music, and subsequently established herself as a leading interpreter of modern music in England. From 1965 she sang regularly on the BBC and also toured extensively around the globe. In all, she sang in more than 300 premieres of contemporary scores. In 1988 she founded her own Jane's Minstrels in London, an ensemble devoted to the furtherance of contemporary music. She was active as a lecturer, serving as a visiting professor at Mills College in Oakland, California (1982–86) and as a lecturer at the University of York (1987). In 1995 she became a visiting professor at the Royal College of Music in London, and from 1996 to 1999 served as honorary professor at the University of Keele. She married the composer Anthony Payne in 1966. She published *New Vocal Repertory: An Introduction* (in two volumes, 1986, 1997). In 1990 she was made a member of the Order of the British Empire.

Manon. Opera by JULES MASSENET, 1884, first produced in Paris. Manon intends to become a nun but is diverted from her purpose by a dashing cavalier, who carries her off to Paris. His father urges him to renounce the ways of the world and join the priesthood. Manon is arrested on suspicion of loose morals. Although her lover secures her freedom by bribing the authorities, she has no more strength to live and wastes away.

In *Manon,* Massenet is at his sentimental best. Its libretto differs from that of GIACOMO PUCCINI's opera *Manon Lescaut,* but both are drawn from Antoine-François Prévost's novel of the same name.

Manon Lescaut. Opera by GIACOMO PUCCINI, 1893, first produced in Turin. A beautiful French girl intends to enter a convent, but a traveling companion induces her to join him in Paris. She becomes debauched by city life but agrees to take a ship to America with her lover. They make the voyage safely, but she dies in New Orleans.

The libretto differs from that of JULES MASSENET's opera *Manon.*

maqām (Arab.; Turk. *makam;* Azeri. *mugam;* Centr. Asia *makom*). 1. General term for the modal systems of Western Asia, based on a MICROTONAL PITCH range (usually treated as quarter tones). Each system has several MODAL SCALES, with a set group of pitches, upon which both melodies and improvisations are built. Performers must incorporate and develop melodic figures associated with each scale. Modalities are not necessarily transposable at the octave, because the pitches may differ. 2. A vocal or instrumental composition in cyclic form.

maracas. Latin American rattles, usually a pair of gourds filled with dry seeds and shaken vigorously to rhythmically accompany traditional and popular dances. In the 20th century, maracas began to be used as percussion instruments in modern scores, quite independently from their ethnic content. Thus, SERGEI PROKOFIEV uses a pair in his patriotic oratorio *Alexander Nevsky.* EDGARD VARÈSE has a part for maracas in his famous percussion work *Ionisation.*

MUSICAL INSTRUMENT

PEOPLE IN MUSIC

Marais, Marin, great French viola da gambist and composer; b. Paris, May 31, 1656; d. there, Aug. 15, 1728. Marais studied bass viol with Sainte-Colombe and composition with the famous composer/bandleader JEAN-BAPTISTE LULLY, becoming a member of the royal orchestra in 1676. He was made *Ordinaire de la chambre du Roi* in 1679 and retired in 1725.

Marais possessed matchless skill as a virtuoso on the VIOLA DA GAMBA and set a new standard of excellence by enhancing the sound quality of the instrument. He also established a new method of fingering, which was widely adopted by other players.

As a composer, Marais was an outstanding master of bass viol music, producing five extensive collections between 1686 and 1725, numbering some 550 works in all. In his dramatic music, he followed Lully's French manner. His

RECITATIVES follow the rhythm and inflection of French verse. The purely instrumental parts in his operas were quite extensive. In his *Alcione* (1706), he introduced a "tempeste," which is one of the earliest attempts at stage realism in operatic music. His other operas are *Alcide* (1693), *Ariane et Bacchus* (1696), and *Sémélé* (1709). He also published trios (or symphonies) for violin, flute, and viola da gamba (1692), and a book of trios for violin, viola da gamba, and harpsichord under the title *La Gamme* (1723).

Marais was married in 1676 and had 19 children. His son Roland became a talented viola da gambist who published two books of pieces for his instrument with basso continuo in Paris in 1735 and 1738, and a *Nouvelle méthode de musique pour servir d'introduction aux acteurs modernes* (New method to introduce music for modern players; 1711).

If humans had three legs instead of two, they would march in waltz time.

march (from Lat. *marcare,* mark; Sp. *marcha;* Fr. *marche;* It. *marcia,* Ger. *Marsch*). A composition of strongly marked rhythm, suitable for timing the steps of a body of persons proceeding at a walking pace. The march is a universal step corresponding to the natural alternation of the right and left foot in walking. Because uniform steps are essential in military practice, the march has become the chosen rhythm of armies all over the world.

While the time signature for a march is commonly $\frac{4}{4}$ or ALLA BREVE, there are marches in $\frac{6}{8}$ or $\frac{12}{8}$, a type known as *Reiter-Marsch* (rider march), for binary time with rapid subdivisions in triplets suggesting a galloping horse. FRANZ SCHUBERT's song *Erlkönig* is a rider march, descriptive of the desperate ride of a father with a dying son in his arms.

The most immediate function of the march is military, and indeed a military march, or *marche militaire* in French, is a distinctive musical form. A perfect example of a military march is the one in *Faust.*

Edward Elgar wrote five military marches under the general title POMP AND CIRCUMSTANCE, of which No. 1 is celebrated. Its slow section, set to the words "Land of Hope and Glory," is widely used as a commencement march in American schools. JOHN PHILIP SOUSA, the American "March King," composed more than 100 military marches, of which *Stars and Stripes Forever* is one of the most rousing.

March time also can be adopted to a variety of functions: a solemn religious march as exemplified by the *March of the Priests* in AIDA, a wedding march in FELIX MENDELSSOHN's music for *A MIDSUMMER NIGHT'S DREAM* and in RICHARD WAGNER's *Lohengrin*, or a children's march in HECTOR BERLIOZ's *Carmen*.

A category by itself is the funeral march. The slow movement in LUDWIG VAN BEETHOVEN's *Eroica Symphony* is an example, although the march from FRÉDÉRIC CHOPIN's Piano Sonata in B-flat minor is the one customarily performed at funerals. There are also funeral marches with ironic intent, such as CHARLES GOUNOD's *MARCHE FUNÈBRE D'UNE MARIONETTE* (Funeral march for a marionette). An example of a funeral march gone beserk is a set of *Three Funeral Marches* by Lord Berners: *For a Statesman, For a Canary,* and *For a Rich Aunt,* the last naturally full of gaiety in anticipation of a lucrative inheritance.

Patriotic marches abound. Of these the grandest is *LA MARSEILLAISE*. However, some national anthems avoid the march scheme. *THE STAR-SPANGLED BANNER* is in slow waltz time, as is the British national anthem, *God Save the Queen.*

Alla marcia, in march style; *march form,* a structure found in American and British marches with an introduction; one or two sections in the TONIC key in 16- or 32-bar phrases; a trio section in the DOMINANT or SUBDOMINANT key and often the implied lighter texture; and a concluding section in the tonic, either a repetition of the previous tonic sections or a new section. All but the last section have internal repeats.

The usual tempo of a marching tune in England and America is 80 steps per minute, which corresponds to the normal human heart rate.

Marche funèbre d'une marionette. Orchestral piece by CHARLES GOUNOD, 1873, humorously intended. The melody acquired popularity in the 1950s when Alfred Hitchcock, British director of morbid horror films, selected it as his television program's signature tune.

Marche slave. Orchestral work by PIOTR ILYICH TCHAIKOVSKY, 1876, to celebrate the liberation of Serbia from the Ottoman empire, first performed in Moscow. Its thematic materials combine Serbian and Russian elements, with the Russian czarist anthem emerging victorious. Although

Tchaikovsky regarded it as a patriotic gesture of no musical significance, *Marche Slave* became a regular repertory piece in Russia and elsewhere.

Marching Through Georgia. Song by Henry Clay Work, 1865. It was written to celebrate General William Tecumseh Sherman's scorched-earth campaign against the Confederates toward the end of the Civil War, especially the 1864 march "From Atlanta to the Sea." A popular SQUARE DANCE was adopted to this tune in the 20th century.

Maria Stuarda. Opera by GAETANO DONIZETTI, 1835, concerning the ill-fated Queen of Scotland. The popularity of this work is a result of the post–World War II BEL CANTO revival.

Maria Theresia. FRANZ JOSEPH HAYDN's Symphony No. 48 from 1769, composed in the sunny key of C major. It was so nicknamed because the Austrian empress Maria Theresia paid a visit at Esterházy's country estate where Haydn was employed and liked the symphony that Haydn played for her.

mariachi. An ensemble music of Mexico, featured in festivities and cafe and nightclub entertainment. Mariachi bands consist of violins, *guitarrón* (large guitar), guitars, trumpets, and Mexican PERCUSSION instruments, particularly the MARIMBA. The songs are typically sung in parallel thirds and use the subject matter of the Mexican CANCIÓN or CORRIDA.

The origin of the word itself is obscure, but it is suggested that it represents a corruption of the French word *mariage,* and that it was first used at the time of the Emperor Maximilian (19th century).

AARON COPLAND made use of typical mariachi tunes in his symphonic work *El Salón México,* named after a once popular nightclub in Mexico City.

Marienleben, Das (The Life of Mary). Song cycle by PAUL HINDEMITH, 1923, to 15 poems by German poet Rainer Maria Rilke, depicting the life of the Virgin Mary. Hindemith revised the cycle in 1941, with the purpose of bringing out the voice part as the dominant factor in the contra-puntal structure.

marimba. Family of African and Latin American xylo-phones with tuned resonators placed underneath the wooden bars to produce a richer sound. In traditional in-struments, gourds are used as resonators.

MUSICAL INSTRUMENT

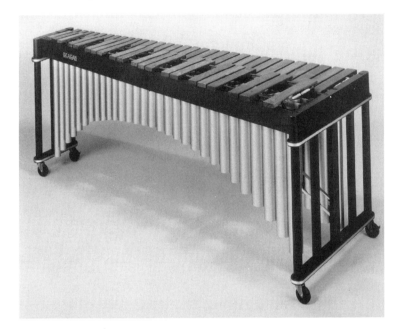

◀ *Marimba. (Slingerland Drum Co.)*

While the marimba is of ancient origin, its modern form was created in Guatemala early in the 20th century. From there it spread to the U.S. and later to Europe. Its range, at first limited, has been gradually expanded to six octaves.

marimbaphone. Trade name of the American MARIMBA, patented in Chicago in 1915. The resonators are wooden blocks carefully tuned to provide the most full resonance possible. In some modern versions, electric amplification is used.

MUSICAL INSTRUMENT

Marines' Hymn, The. A popular march song and the an-them of the U.S. Marine Corps. The famous lyrics refer to the entry of the Marines into Mexico City in 1847 ("the halls of Montezuma") and the Marine landing in North Africa in the war against the Barbary pirates in 1805 ("the shores of Tripoli"). The tune is taken from an operetta by JACQUES OFFENBACH, *Geneviève de Brabant,* published in 1868, but it seems that Offenbach himself picked it up from a folk source.

The uncopyrighted sheet music edition of the U.S. Marine Corps Publicity Bureau in 1918 attributed the text to an unidentified Marine officer during the war with Mexico. How the words came to be attached to an Offenbach air is a puzzle.

PEOPLE IN MUSIC

Marley, Bob (Robert Nesta), Jamaican reggae singer and composer; b. Rhoden Hall, Feb. 6, 1945; d. Miami, May 11, 1981. Marley was taken to Kingston, Jamaica's capital, as a child and worked as an electrical welder. He picked up popular tunes in the streets and from the radio, opened a small record shop, then began recording his own tunes, a mixture of CALYPSO and SOUL music.

Marley helped found a group, the Wailers, which became the most popular purveyors of REGGAE. Marley later went solo and produced highly successful records that reached an international audience and influenced rock musicians profoundly from the 1970s. In 1974 rock superstar ERIC CLAPTON covered Marley's song, *I Shot the Sheriff,* achieving a major rock hit and introducing reggae style into the mainstream. This helped launch Marley's career in Europe and America.

Marley joined the Rastafarian religious group, followers of Haile Selassie of Ethiopia (whose original name was Ras Tafari). In 1976 he became embroiled in politics, supporting the Jamaican People's National Party. As he was preparing to sing at a band concert in late 1976, he was shot and wounded. After that episode, he went to Europe, scoring an unusual popular success, particularly in England, Sweden, the Netherlands, and West Germany. In 1977 he made a tour of the U.S., where his fame had preceded him via his record albums.

His songs, in Jamaican dialect, preached revolution. Typical of these were *Rebel Music, Everywhere Be War,* and *Death to the Downpressors.* But his 1974 album *Natty Dread* (a pun on the Rasta hair style) mixes politics (*Them Belly Full, Revolution*), religion (*So Jah Seh*), self-image (*Lively Up*

Yourself), and relationships (*No Woman No Cry*), with subtle arrangement and rhythmic COUNTERPOINT.

Marley died of cancer in 1981.

Marriage of Figaro, The *(Le Nozze di Figaro).* Comic opera by WOLFGANG AMADEUS MOZART, 1786, first produced in Vienna. The libretto is the first one that Da Ponte wrote for Mozart, based on Beaumarchais's sequel to *The Barber of Seville.*

Count Almaviva is now married to Rosina. Figaro, formerly a cunning barber, is now the count's valet. He wants to marry the countess's maid Susannah, but the count himself longs for her. The countess laments her husband's flighty ways (*Dove sono*), and Figaro stages complex schemes to arouse the count's jealousy, so he will pay more attention to his wife. The youthful page Cherubino is used by Figaro to play the suitor of the countess. As the count enters the house, the page puts on a maid's dress to hide his sex.

The complications increase as the opera continues. The plot reaches the height of its absurdity when an elderly female housekeeper whom Figaro has promised to marry is revealed as his own mother. But the more absurd the situations are, the more beautiful the music.

Marriner, (Sir) Neville, English conductor; b. Lincoln, April 15, 1924. Marriner studied violin with his father, subsequently entering the Royal College of Music in London when he was 13. His studies were interrupted by military service during World War II, but after resuming his training there, he completed his violin studies in Paris.

Marriner was active as a violinist in chamber music ensembles and was a professor of violin at the Royal College of Music from 1949 to 1959. In 1952 he joined the Philharmonia Orchestra of London as a violinist, and from 1956 to 1958 was principal second violinist of the London Symphony Orchestra. His interest in conducting was encouraged by PIERRE MONTEUX, who gave him lessons at his summer school in Hancock, Maine, in 1959.

In 1958 he founded the Academy of St.-Martin-in-the-Fields. He served as its director until 1978, establishing an international reputation through recordings and tours. From

PEOPLE IN MUSIC

1968 to 1978 he also served as music director of the Los Angeles Chamber Orchestra. He then was music director of the Minnesota Orchestra in Minneapolis from 1978 to 1986. In 1981 he became principal guest conductor of the Stuttgart Radio Symphony Orchestra, serving as its chief conductor from 1983 to 1989. He appeared as a guest conductor with the world's leading orchestras. On Sept. 29, 1994, he opened the 1994–95 season of N.Y.'s Carnegie Hall conducting the Academy of St.-Martin-in-the-Fields in a program featuring Cecilia Bartoli as the soloist of the evening. The concert was subsequently telecast throughout the U.S. by PBS.

Marriner has proved himself one of the most remarkable conductors of his day, his extensive activities serving as an invaluable foundation for his career as a symphony conductor of the first rank. His enormous repertoire encompasses works from the BAROQUE era to the great masterworks of the 20th century. In his performances he demonstrates authority, mastery of detail, and impeccable taste. In 1979 he was made a Commander of the Order of the British Empire. He was knighted in 1985.

PEOPLE IN MUSIC

Marsalis, Wynton, outstanding African-American trumpet virtuoso; b. New Orleans, Oct. 18, 1961. He was born into a cultured musical family. His father, Ellis Marsalis, is a jazz pianist who insisted that his sons receive professional training. Wynton's younger brother, Delfeayo, is a trombonist, while his older brother Branford (b. Breaux Bridge, La., 1960) is a saxophonist of considerable talent who has played with MILES DAVIS, ART BLAKEY, DIZZY GILLESPIE, and the English rock musician Sting, in addition to leading his own groups. In 1974 Ellis Marsalis founded the jazz program for the nascent New Orleans Center for the Creative Arts, which nurtured important new talent.

Wynton took up the trumpet at age six, later studying privately and at his father's school. He appeared as soloist in the FRANZ JOSEPH HAYDN Trumpet Concerto with the New Orleans Philharmonic when he was 14, while at the same time performing with local groups in classical, jazz, and rock settings. He won the Harvey Shapiro Award as the most gifted brass player at the Berkshire Music Center at Tangle-wood at age 17, then attended the Juilliard School in N.Y. from 1979 to 1981.

Marsalis joined ART BLAKEY's Jazz Messengers in 1980, appearing with them at the jazz festival at Montreux, Switzerland, that year. In 1981 he began touring with his own quintet, which included his brother Branford.

Through the mid-'80s and '90s, Marsalis has been a widely applauded, if controversial, figure in jazz. He is credited with leading a jazz revival that has brought forward many young musicians of great talent. However, some feel he is too conservative. He has faced even more criticism since becoming the founding director of Jazz at Lincoln Center in 1987. Some feel he has championed African-American composers and musicians at the expense of their white counterparts. Nonetheless, the program has been very successful. Marsalis has led a large orchestra on world tours, performing both classic jazz works and his own compositions.

In 1984 Marsalis achieved unprecedented success when he won Grammy awards in both the jazz and classical categories for his recordings. In all, he won a grand total of eight Grammy awards. On Oct. 30, 1990, he hosted a benefit concert for Graham-Windham (a private child care agency), the Austin Society of America, and the Immunohematology Research Foundation at Alice Tully Hall in N.Y. Featured were the musical members of his family. In 1993 Wynton was invited to perform at the White House in Washington, D.C., for President Bill Clinton. He published the book *Sweet Swing Blues on the Road* (N.Y., 1994) and the companion volume to the PBS series *Marsalis on Music* (N.Y., 1995). He won the Pulitzer Prize for his composition *Blood on the Fields* in 1997.

Marschner, Heinrich (August), important German opera composer; b. Zittau, Saxony, Aug. 16, 1795; d. Hannover, Dec. 14, 1861. Marschner sang in the school choir and also studied music privately. In 1813 he went to Leipzig, where he studied law at the university. Encouraged by the cantor (choir leader) of the Thomasschule, J. C. Schicht, he turned

PEOPLE IN MUSIC

to music as his main vocation. In 1816 he became a music tutor in Count Zichy's household in Pressburg, and also served as KAPELLMEISTER (choral director) to Prince Krasatkowitz. In leisure hours he began to compose light operas. His first, *Titus* (1816), did not achieve a performance, but soon he had written two more and a SINGSPIEL produced in Dresden. A year later, he had the opportunity to meet LUDWIG VAN BEETHOVEN.

Marschner's first success was the historical opera *Heinrich IV und d'Aubigne* (Henry IVth and d'Aubigne), which was accepted for production in 1820 by CARL MARIA VON WEBER, then music director at the Dresden Court Opera. In 1821 Marschner moved to Dresden and had his SINGSPIEL *Der Holzdieb* (The Wood Thief) staged at the Court Opera four years later. He expected to succeed Weber as music director at the Court Opera after Weber died in London, but failed to obtain the post.

Marschner went to Leipzig, where he became kapellmeister of the Stadttheater (State Theater). He wrote for it two ROMANTIC operas, in the manner of Weber: *Der Vampyr* (The Vampire, 1828) and *Der Templer und die Jüdin* (The Knight and the Jewess), based on *Ivanhoe* by Walter Scott (1829). In 1830 he received the position of kapellmeister of the Hannover Hoftheater.

His most successful opera, *Hans Heiling*, produced in Berlin in 1833, exhibited the most attractive Romantic traits of his music: flowing melody, sonorous harmony, and nervous rhythmic pulse. The opera formed a natural transition to the exotic melodrama of GIACOMO MEYERBEER's great stage epics and to RICHARD WAGNER's early lyrical music dramas. Historically important was his use of a continuous dramatic development, without the conventional type of distinct ARIAS separated by RECITATIVE. In this respect he was the heir of Weber and a precursor of Wagner.

Marschner's later operas were not successful. He died in 1861.

Marseillaise, La. The French national ANTHEM, one of the most beautiful of all, both in patriotic text and rousing melody.

World music has become very popular today, as American listeners have discovered the richness and variety of music making that can be heard in other cultures. Music making is one of the oldest and most widespread human activities. Only a century ago, few people had the chance to hear the Indian SITAR or African KORA; today, through performances, recordings, and videos, we can experience these musical instruments and dozens more.

When early explorers first discovered "primitive" people, they were immediately astounded by the variety of musical instruments and melodies that they heard played on them. Illustrators quickly traveled to exotic lands to portray these people. Sometimes they had a good knowledge of music; other times, not. Yet these early prints are often the only evidence of what kind of music was played by native musicians before they were exposed to European instruments and styles. This print was made by the French artist Grasset de St. Sauveur in 1796 and portrays two musicians from Senegal. On the left, the standing musician blows on a simple HORN, probably made from an animal's horn. At the same time, he strikes an elaborately decorated cylindrical DRUM. The other musician plays a typical African XYLOPHONE, or wooden–keyed percussion instrument. Gourd-like RESONATORS can be seen below some of the keys; these helped project the sound of the instrument. Instruments like these are still played among traditional African musicians today. (*Corbis/Gianni Dagli Orti*)

The Japanese have a rich and long musical tradition that dates back at least 1,000 years. They developed a court music that was performed by professional musicians for the entertainment of the nobility featuring a wide variety of stringed and percussion instruments. In this 18th century woodblock print by Suzuki Harnuobu, two courtly women pose besides a KOTO, a traditional ZITHER that features long strings that run from one end of the instrument to the other. It is played by plucking the strings with the fingers. The NOTES can also be changed by fretting or STOPPING the strings, or by bending them or lightly pressing them. (*Corbis/Bettman*)

Japan opened to the West in the late 19th century, and soon Japanese scenes were popular in Western newspapers and magazines. This group of young girls playing traditional instruments is a hand–colored photograph, the kind that would be reproduced in the popular photo sections of weekly magazines. The girl on the left plays a simple frame DRUM, using a pair of MALLETS. In the middle, we see an a different type of drum. It has an hourglass–shaped body, and is held on the shoulder. The HEAD is struck with the palm of the hand, like the Indian TABLA drums. The musician on the right plays a SAMISEN, a stringed LUTE. Like the American BANJO, it has an animal skin stretched across its head. (*Corbis/Hulton-Deutsch Collection*)

The MANDOLIN has been popular among FOLK MUSICIANS in several different cultures. Here we see a musician from Budapest, Hungary dressed in a traditional costume playing the 8–string instrument. The instrument, a relative of the GUITAR or LUTE, was first popular in RENAISSANCE Italy, but spread rapidly through Europe. In America, it is most closely associated with BLUEGRASS music. (*Corbis/Barry Lewis*)

The great Indian musician RAVI SHANKAR is probably the most famous performer on the SITAR. The sitar features two different sets of strings; one set runs under the NECK of the instrument and is not fretted by the player; instead they vibrate "in sympathy" with the other strings that are strummed and fretted by the musician. Note the heavy metal FRETS on the instrument's FINGERBOARD or neck; these can be moved for playing in different SCALES or MODES. Also note the large tuning KEYS that are placed on the side of the neck. This photograph was taken in 1971 at the famous "Concert for Bangaladesh" held at New York's Madison Square Garden to raise money for the victims of a terrible storm that ravaged that tiny country. (*Corbis/Henry Diltz*)

The LUTE is an instrument with many relatives found all through the world. Many musicologists believe that the instrument originated in Northern Africa among the Moorish people who live in what is modern-day Morocco. Here is a traditional Moroccan musician holding an 'UD, which is the traditional name for this lute–like instrument. Note that the instrument has a pear-shaped body and the distinctive headstock, holding the tuning KEYS, that is placed at a 90 degree angle to the NECK. These design features are both found in the RENAISSANCE lute that was popular throughout Europe. (*Corbis/Wolfgang Kaehler*)

Indian music has a much more elaborate system of RHYTHMS than European classical music. Just like there are various SCALES or MODES that are used in Indian music, Indian musicians have developed various TALA or rhythmic patterns. These patterns are played by a drummer on a pair of tuned drums called TABLA. This recent photograph shows the master drummer Zakir Hussain playing the tabla. The larger drum is seen in the foreground of the photograph; it has a gourd-shaped body. The smaller drum cannot be seen. (Corbis/Neal Preston)

One of the most venerable and ancient instruments is the PANPIPES. It is made up of a group of thin reeds, tied together, each of a different length and thus producing a different NOTE. The player blows across the top of the reed, setting the air into vibration and producing the musical TONE. We know that the instrument was played in Ancient Greece through the paintings on vases and other objects that remain from that time. Today, the instrument is mostly heard in South American music. Here, a traditional Peruvian musician is shown playing the instrument. (*Corbis/Nik Wheeler*)

The hurdy–gurdy is one of the most unusual of the traditional European folk instruments. Like the BAGPIPES, it is capable of playing both a MELODY and a DRONE. However, unlike the bagpipe that is a wind instrument, the hurdy–gurdy has strings like a VIOLIN or GUITAR. The player turns a small crank with his right hand, which turns a wheel that rubs against the strings, setting them into vibration. Like the sitar, one set of strings runs under the instrument's NECK and is not fretted but only vibrate when the other set are played. The other set is fretted by means of a small KEYBOARD; the player presses down on a small lever, which STOPS the string at the appropriate point to sound a NOTE. This traditional hurdy–gurdy player was photographed recently at a streetfair in France. (*Corbis/Michael St. Maur Shiel*)

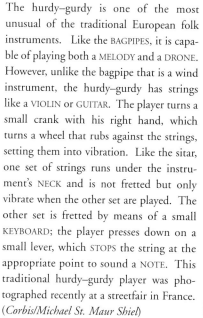

The islands of Java and Bali are famous for their elaborate orchestras featuring GONGS, XYLOPHONES, and DRUMS known as GAMELAN. These orchestras were used for ceremonial purposes in the royal courts and to accompany the famous shadow-puppet plays that were produced every year. This photograph shows a Balinese gamelan. In the foreground, we see a player playing on a row of gongs that are tuned to different notes. He uses a pair of wooden MALLETS to strike them individually to play a MELODY. Behind him and to his left is the drummer, who is playing on a large, cylindrical drum with two heads. The drummer serves as the conductor of the orchestra. On the far right and right rear of the picture, we see a trio of xylophone players, who play with small hammer–like mallets. These traditional orchestras continue to flourish in different communities on the islands today. (*Corbis/Roman Soumar*)

Another instrument found in the GAMELAN is a long FLUTE. Notice that, unlike the Western flute, this flute has no MOUTHPIECE; instead the player blows directly into one end. A gold, tasseled cap hangs off the mouthpiece. This traditional Balinese musician is a member of one of the most famous gamelan orchestras. (*Corbis/Buddy May*)

There are many rich folk traditions in the United States that can be still heard today. In Southern Louisiana, the music of French immigrants, Native Americans, and African–Americans mixed together to form what is known as Cajun (when performed by white musicians) or Zydeco (when performed by black musicians) traditions. Lawrence Ardoin is a master Zydeco ACCORDION player. He is shown here playing with his group which includes FIDDLE and ELECTRIC GUITAR at a folk festival in Lafayette, Louisiana, the center of Cajun country. (*Corbis/Philip Gould*)

Another popular American FOLK MUSIC tradition is BLUEGRASS music. The late Kentucky–born MAN-
DOLIN player BILL MONROE, shown here playing at Nashville's "Grand Ole Opry" radio program in the
late 1980s, is generally credited with creating this musical form. It features high–energy music played on
MANDOLIN, BANJO, FIDDLE, GUITAR, and BASS, with rich vocal harmonies. Monroe wrote many classic
bluegrass instrumentals and songs, including "Blue Moon of Kentucky" and the instrumental "Rawhide."
(*Corbis/David G. Houser*)

DID YOU KNOW???

- Bill Monroe was called "The Father of Bluegrass music."
- His song "Blue Moon of Kentucky" was popularized by Elvis Presley.
- He was a member of "The Grand Ole Opry" for over 50 years.

It was composed, or rather improvised, on the spur of the moment by Rouget de Lisle, a French Army officer in Strasbourg, on the night of April 24–25, 1792. It was published almost immediately under the title *Chant de Guerre pour l'Armée du Rhin* (War Song for the Army on the Rhine). It was then widely sung as a patriotic song during the war with Austria. The title *La Marseillaise* was adopted later by a revolutionary volunteer group from Marseilles during the final phase of the French Revolution.

The song was prominently featured as a sign of French solidarity in the World War II movie *Casablanca*, starring Humphrey Bogart and Ingrid Bergman.

Marteau sans Maître, Le (The Hammer Without a Master). Work by PIERRE BOULEZ, 1955, for soprano and chamber ensemble. It is based on surrealist poems by René Char. It was first performed in Baden-Baden.

Martenot, Maurice (Louis Eugène), French inventor of an electronic instrument named the Ondes musicales, better known as the ONDES MARTENOT. b. Paris, Oct. 14, 1898; d. there, Oct. 10, 1980. Martenot studied composition at the Paris Conservatory.

Martenot began to work on the construction of an electronic musical instrument with a keyboard, which he called the Ondes musicales. He gave its first demonstration in Paris in the spring of 1928, and, later that year, the first musical work for the instrument, *Poème symphonique pour solo d'Ondes musicales et orchestre,* by Dimitri Levidis (c.1885–1951), was presented in Paris. Martenot published *Methode pour l'enseignement des Ondes musicales* (Method for teaching the Ondes musicales) in 1931.

The instrument became popular, especially among French composers. It is included in the scores of

Arthur Honegger's *Jeanne d'Arc au bûcher* (1935)

Charles Koechlin's *Le Buisson ardent,* part one (1938)

Jean Martinon's Second Symphony, *Hymne à la vie* (1944)

Olivier Messiaen's *Turangalîla-Symphonie* (1946–48).

It was used as a solo instrument in

PEOPLE IN MUSIC

Koechlin's *Hymne* (1929)

André Jolivet's Concerto (1947)

Wanda Landowski's Concerto (1954)

Jacques Bondon's *Kaleidoscope* (1957)

Jacques Charpentier's *Concertino alla francese* (1961)

Many other composers were attracted to it as well.

Of all the early electronic instruments—Ondes Martenot, TRAUTONIUM, and THEREMIN—only Martenot's has proved viable. When EDGARD VARÈSE's *Ecuatorial,* written in 1934 for a brass ensemble and including a Theremin, was published in 1961, the score substituted an Ondes Martenot for the obsolescent Theremin.

Martenot's sister, Ginette (b. Paris, Jan. 27, 1902; d. Neuilly-sur-Seine, Sept. 6, 1996), became the chief exponent of the Ondes Martenot in concert performances in Europe and the U.S.

Martha. Opera by FRIEDRICH FLOTOW, 1847, produced in Vienna. Queen Anne is ruling England as the action takes place in Richmond, England.

The queen's maid of honor decides to go to the town marketplace dressed as a country girl named Martha. She hires herself as a servant to a young farmer, not realizing that the paper she signed is a legal contract. Her maid signs a similar obligation. Martha sings *The Last Rose of Summer,* and at night both girls return to the palace.

Now back to her usual identity as Lady Harriet, "Martha" refuses to recognize the farmer, but he is now hopelessly in love with her. As operatic luck would have it, he is revealed to be a hereditary earl. But it is now his turn to rebuke Lady Harriet when she begins to feel the pangs of love. To bring him back, she reproduces the marketplace in her garden, puts on her rustic clothes, and waits for her lover to return, which he does not fail to do. There is a doubly happy ending, since Lady Harriet's maid marries the earl's foster brother.

This work's score is one of the most melodious in opera, and flows along quite charmingly. The overture is popular at summer concerts, but the opera itself is rarely heard.

Martin, Dean (Dino Paul Crocetti), American singer, actor, and entertainer; b. Steubenville, Ohio, June 7, 1917; d. Hollywood, Calif., Dec. 25, 1995. Martin had a rough-and-tumble childhood. He left school in the middle of the 10th grade and worked as a shoeshine boy, among other part-time jobs.

In 1941 he got his first job singing with a dance band, taking the stage name of Dino Martini, which was soon shortened to Dean Martin. Soon after, he made some recordings for a number of small record labels. In 1946 he first worked with comedian Jerry Lewis. The two became popular television and radio performers, as a sort of poor man's Bing Crosby–Bob Hope duo. In 1948 Martin signed with Capitol Records, beginning a decade-long run of hit recordings, including his signature song, *That's Amore,* his No. 1 hit *Memories Are Made of This,* and *Volare.*

In 1956 Martin broke up with Lewis. His film career, however, continued unabated. Meanwhile, he became a member of the notorious "Rat Pack," led by FRANK SINATRA. This group of entertainers frequented Las Vegas, where they enjoyed gambling, drinking, and entertaining women.

Sinatra signed Martin to his new record label, Reprise, in 1961. Three years later, Martin had his biggest career hit, *Everybody Loves Somebody Sometime,* which replaced the Beatles' *A Hard Day's Night* at the top of the charts. Martin also began a successful variety show on television, which projected his easygoing image of a comedian, singer, and bon vivant.

Martin spent most of the '70s and '80s as a favorite Las Vegas lounge act. In 1987 he appeared successfully at the London Palladium, and also did a reunion tour with old friends Sinatra and Sammy Davis, Jr. However, he had to cut short his participation in the tour due to kidney problems.

In 1993 it was announced that Martin was suffering from lung cancer. He died two years later.

Martin, Frank, renowned Swiss composer, b. Geneva, Sept. 15, 1890; d. Naarden, the Netherlands, Nov. 21, 1974. Martin was the last of 10 children of a Calvinist minister, a descendant of the Huguenots. His musical training

PEOPLE IN MUSIC

Martin was a welterweight boxer for a while, using the name "Kid Crochet."

PEOPLE IN MUSIC

Frank Martin, 1960. (Hulton-Deutsch Collection/Corbis) ▶

emphasized the conservative foundations of the religious and cultural traditions of the Swiss establishment. However, Martin soon went beyond this strict training, encouraged in this development by Ernest Ansermet, then conductor of the Orchestre de la Suisse Romande in Geneva.

In 1918 Martin went to Zurich and, in 1921, to Rome. He finally settled in Paris in 1923, then the center of modern music. He returned to Geneva in 1926 as a pianist and harpsichordist, where he taught at the Institute Jacques-Dalcroze from 1927 to 1938. He also was founder and director of the Technicum Moderne de Musique from 1933 to 1939, and served as president of the Association of Swiss Musicians from 1942 to 1946. He moved to the Netherlands in 1946. From 1950 to 1957 he taught composition at the Cologne Hochschule für Musik.

Martin was one of Switzerland's few international figures in composition. His early music showed the influence of CÉSAR FRANCK and French IMPRESSIONISTS, but soon he succeeded in creating a distinctive style. He showed a mastery of COUNTERPOINT and formal structure, while still communicating a depth of emotion in his works. Still later he became fascinated by the logic and self-consistency of ARNOLD SCHOENBERG's method of composition with 12 tones and adopted it in a modified form in several of his works. He also demonstrated an ability to adopt folk-song materials using modern techniques.

In his music, Martin followed the religious and moral precepts of his faith. In 1944 the director of Radio Geneva asked him to compose an ORATORIO to be broadcast immediately upon the conclusion of World War II. He responded with *In terra pax* (A world at peace) for five soli, double chorus, and orchestra, which was given its broadcast premiere from Geneva on May 7, 1945. The first public performance followed in Geneva 24 days later.

Among Martin's many fine works are two operas, *Der Sturm* (The Tempest) after Shakespeare (1952–54), and *Monsieur de Pourceaugnac* after Molière (1960–62), many orchestral and vocal works, including oratorios and requia, and incidental music for the stage.

Martin, Mary (Virginia), American singer, dancer, and actress; b. Weatherford, Tex., Dec. 1, 1913; d. Rancho Mirage, Calif., Nov. 3, 1990. The daughter of a lawyer and a violinist, Martin first established a dance school in her hometown. She studied at the Ward-Belmont School in Nashville.

PEOPLE IN MUSIC

In 1938 Martin went to N.Y. where, although totally unknown to the general public, she stopped the show with her rendition of the song *My Heart Belongs to Daddy* in COLE PORTER's musical comedy *Leave It to Me.* Her N.Y. success brought her a film contract with Paramount studios in Hollywood, which was short-lived, because she preferred the theater.

On the stage she scored a series of hits, beginning with a starring role in RICHARD RODGERS and OSCAR HAMMERSTEIN's *SOUTH PACIFIC* in 1949 and a decade later in *THE SOUND OF MUSIC,* two of the longest-running musicals in Broadway history. She became best known for her 1954 creation of the lead character in the musical *Peter Pan,* in which she was made to fly through the air.

In 1969 Martin retired to Brazil with her husband. A decade later, after his death, she resumed her career. In 1989

Martin was honored by the Kennedy Center of the Performing Arts in Washington, D.C., for her achievements in the theater. She died a year later.

Her son, Larry Hagman, is a veteran television actor whose fame was assured when he was cast as the villainous J. R. Ewing in the nighttime soap series *Dallas.*

Martinů, Bohuslav (Jan), Czech composer; b. Policka, Dec. 8, 1890; d. Liestal, near Basel, Aug. 28, 1959. Martinů was born in the bell tower of a church in the village where his father was a watchman. He studied violin with the local tailor when he was seven, and from 1906 to 1909 he was enrolled at the Prague Conservatory. He then entered the Prague Organ School in 1909, where he studied organ and theory, but was expelled in 1910 because he failed to take his studies seriously.

In 1913–14 Martinů played in the second violin section in the Czech Philharmonic in Prague, returning to his hometown during World War I to avoid service in the Austrian army. After the war, he reentered the Prague Conservatory but again failed to graduate. He also played again in the Czech Philharmonic from 1918 to 1923.

In 1923 Martinů went to Paris, taking private lessons with ALBERT ROUSSEL. He met many composers and performers of modern music and was greatly influenced by their ideas. In a relatively short time his name became known in Europe through increasingly frequent performances of his chamber works, ballets, and symphonic pieces. Several of his works were performed at the festivals of the ISCM (International Society for Contemporary Music).

Martinů remained in Paris until June 1940, when he fled the German invasion and went to Portugal. He finally reached the U.S. in 1941 and settled in N.Y. Personal difficulties prevented him from accepting an offer to teach at the Prague Conservatory after the liberation of Czechoslovakia in 1945. Later on he was a visiting professor of music at Princeton University from 1948 to 1951.

In 1953 Martinů returned to Europe, spending the last two years of his life in Switzerland. On Aug. 27, 1979, his remains were taken from Schonenberg, Switzerland, to Policka, Czechoslovakia, where they were placed in the family mau-

PEOPLE IN MUSIC

In 1932 Martinů's String Sextet won the Elizabeth Sprague Coolidge Award for best new modern work.

soleum. Martinů's centennial was celebrated in 1990 all over Czechoslovakia.

Although Martinů spent most of his life away from his homeland, he remained spiritually and musically faithful to his native country. He composed a poignant tribute to the martyred village of Lidice when, in 1943, the Nazi authorities ordered the execution of all men and boys over the age of 16 to avenge the assassination of a local party official. Martinů immortalized the victims in a heartfelt lyric work entitled *Memorial to Lidice.*

As a musician and stylist, Martinů belonged to the European tradition of musical nationalism. He avoided literal exploitation of Czech or Slovak musical materials, but his music is nonetheless characterized by a strong feeling for Bohemian melodies and rhythms. His stylizations of Czech dances are set in a modern idiom without losing their authenticity or simplicity.

In large works he followed the NEOCLASSICAL trend, with some IMPRESSIONISTIC elements. His mastery of modern COUNTERPOINT was extraordinary. His sense of operatic comedy was very strong, and he was also capable of sensitive lyricism.

Martirano, Salvatore, American composer of the modern school; b. Yonkers, N.Y., Jan. 12, 1927; d. Urbana, Ill., Nov. 17, 1995. Martirano studied piano and composition at the Oberlin Conservatory of Music, graduating in 1951, then spent a year studying composition at the Eastman School of Music in Rochester, N.Y., with Bernard Rogers.

PEOPLE IN MUSIC

From 1952 to 1954, Martirano took courses with LUIGI DALLAPICCOLA at the Cherubini Conservatory in Florence, Italy. He served in the U.S. Marine Corps and played clarinet and cornet with the Parris Island Marine Band. From 1956 to 1959 he held a fellowship to the American Academy in Rome, and in 1960 he received a Guggenheim fellowship and the American Academy of Arts and Letters Award. In 1963 he joined the faculty of the University of Illinois at Urbana.

Martirano wrote in a progressive AVANT-GARDE idiom. His work is free from inhibitions, and often uses MULTIMEDIA and ELECTRONIC means. His works include *The Magic*

Stones, a chamber opera based on *Decameron* (1952); *O, O, O, O, That Shakespeherian Rag* for mixed chorus and instrumental ensemble (1958); *Underworld* for four actors, four percussion instruments, two double basses, tenor saxophone, and tape (1965; video version 1982); *Ballad* for amplified nightclub singer and instrumental ensemble (1966); *L's.G.A.* for a gas-masked politico, helium bomb, three 16mm movie projectors, and tape (1968); *Sal-Mar Construction I–VII* for tape (1971–75); *Look at the Back of my Head for a While,* video piece (1984); *Sampler: Everything Goes When the Whistle Blows* for violin and synthetic orchestra (1985; revised 1988); *Phleu* for amplified flute and synthetic orchestra (1988); and *LON/dons* for chamber orchestra (1989).

PEOPLE IN MUSIC

Marton, Eva, Hungarian soprano; b. Budapest, June 18, 1943. Marton studied at the Franz Liszt Academy of Music in Budapest. She made her formal operatic debut as the Queen of Shemakha in *Le Coq d'or* at the Hungarian State Opera there in 1968. She remained on its roster until joining the Frankfurt Opera in 1971, then became a member of the Hamburg State Opera in 1977.

In 1975 Marton made her U.S. debut in N.Y. as a soloist in the world premiere of ALAN HOVHANESS's folk ORATORIO *The Way of Jesus.* She then made her first appearance at the Metropolitan Opera as Eva in RICHARD WAGNER's *Die Meistersinger von Nürnberg* on Nov. 3, 1976. Five years later, she scored a notable success as the Empress in *Die Frau ohne Schatten* there. She thereafter was one of the Metropolitan's most important artists, appearing in numerous key roles through 1988. She first sang Turandot at the Vienna State Opera in 1983, appearing as Elektra there in 1989. In 1987 she made her debut at London's Covent Garden as Turandot, and in 1990 she returned there as Elektra. In 1992 she appeared as Turandot in Chicago and as the Dyer's Wife at the Salzburg Festival. Her appearances as an oratorio and lieder artist were also well received.

Martyrs, Les. See POLIUTO.

Mary Had a Little Lamb. A nursery rhyme whose tune is identical with the second section of the song *Good Night*

Ladies, to the words "Merrily we roll along." The melody was composed by the American bandmaster E. P. Christy in 1847.

The story of little Mary who took her lamb to school is purportedly factual. The words have been subject to numerous parodies.

Maryland, My Maryland. Song based on the German Christmas tune *O Tannenbaum.* The words, written in 1861, were fitted to the German melody. Maryland adopted it as its state song in 1939. It is also played at the horse races at Pimlico.

Masaniello. *See MUETTE DE PORTICI, LA.*

Mascagni, Pietro, Italian opera composer; b. Livorno, Dec. 7, 1863; d. Rome, Aug. 2, 1945. Mascagni's father was a baker who wished him to continue in that trade, but yielded to his son's determination to study music. He took lessons in his native town until he was enabled, by the aid of an uncle, to attend the Milan Conservatory, where he studied from 1882 to 1884. However, he became impatient with school discipline and was dismissed. He then conducted operetta troupes and taught music in Cerignola.

Mascagni composed industriously. In 1888 he sent the manuscript of his one-act opera CAVALLERIA RUSTICANA to the music publisher Giulio Cesare Sonzogno for a competition, winning first prize. The opera was performed at the Teatro Costanzi in Rome on May 17, 1890, with sensational success. The dramatic story of village passion, and Mascagni's emotional score, combined to produce an extraordinary appeal to opera lovers. The short opera made the tour of the world stages with amazing rapidity, productions being staged all over Europe and America with never-failing success. The opera was usually presented in two parts, separated by an *intermezzo sinfonico* (which became a popular orchestral number performed separately). *Cavalleria rusticana* marked the advent of the operatic style known as VERISMO.

Ironically, Mascagni could never remotely approach the success of his first production, although opera houses all over the world were only too eager to stage his successive op-

PEOPLE IN MUSIC

When, two years later, another "realistic" opera, RUGGERO LEONCAVALLO'S *PAGLIACCI,* was taken by Sonzogno, the two operas became twin attractions on a single bill. They are often referred to as "Cav and Pav."

eras. Thus, his opera *LE MASCHERE* was produced in 1901, at six important Italian opera houses simultaneously. Mascagni himself conducted the premiere in Rome, but the opera failed to fire the imagination of the public. It was produced in a revised form in Turin 15 years later but was not established in the repertoire, even in Italy.

Pietro Mascagni, c. 1900. (Library of Congress/Corbis) ▶

In 1902 Mascagni made a tour of the U.S., conducting his *Cavalleria rusticana* and other operas. However, owing to mismanagement, the visit proved a fiasco. A South American tour in 1911 was more successful. He also appeared frequently as a conductor of symphony concerts. In 1890 he was made a Knight of the Crown of Italy, and in 1929 he was elected a member of the Academy. At various times he also was engaged in teaching, and from 1895 to 1902 he was director of the Rossini Conservatory in Pesaro.

Mascagni's last years were darkened by the inglorious role that he had played as an ardent supporter of the Italian Fascist regime, so that he was rejected by many of his old friends. It was only after his death that his errors of moral judgment were forgiven, and his centennial was widely celebrated in Italy.

Maschere, Le (The Masks). Opera by PIETRO MASCAGNI, 1901, with the familiar characters of the COMMEDIA DELL'-ARTE engaged in traditional encounters. So great were the auguries of success for *Le Maschere* that the opera was premiered on the same day in six Italian cities. But this simultaneous exhibition was a humiliating disaster. In Genoa, the audience hissed and booed so vehemently that the management had to lower the curtain without completing the performance.

Mason, Daniel Gregory, American composer and educator, grandson of LOWELL and nephew of WILLIAM MASON; b. Brookline, Mass., Nov. 20, 1873; d. Greenwich, Conn., Dec. 4, 1953. Mason came from a famous family of American musicians, his father, Henry Mason, being a co-founder of the piano manufacturing firm Mason & Hamlin.

Mason entered Harvard University, where he took his bachelor of arts degree in 1895. He continued his musical studies privately in Boston after graduation. However, still feeling the necessity for improvement of his technique, he went to Paris, where he took courses with the composer Vincent d'Indy. Returning to America, he became active as a teacher and composer. In 1905 he became a member of the faculty of Columbia University, where, in 1929, he was appointed MacDowell Professor of Music. He was chairman of the music department until 1940 and continued to teach for two more years until he retired.

As a teacher, Mason developed a high degree of technical ability in his students. As a composer, he represented a conservative trend in American music. While an adherent to the idea of an American national style, he took a narrow view of what constituted native music, accepting only the music of Anglo-Saxon New England and the "old South." He was an outspoken opponent of the "corrupting" and "foreign" influences of 20th-century Afro-American and Jewish-American music.

Mason's ideals were the German masters of the ROMANTIC school, but there is an addition of IMPRESSIONISTIC colors in his orchestration. His harmonies are full and opulent, and his melodic writing expressive and songful. The lack of strong individuality, however, has resulted in the virtual disappearance of his music from the active repertoire, with the exception of the festival overture *Chanticleer* (1928) and the Clarinet Sonata (1912–15). He also composed three symphonies, chamber works, and vocal works. He also wrote several books on music education and philosophy.

Not totally seriously, Mascagni dedicated the opera "to my distinguished self."

PEOPLE IN MUSIC

Mason, Lowell, distinguished American organist, conductor, music educator, and composer, grandfather of DANIEL GREGORY and father of WILLIAM MASON; b. Medfield, Mass., Jan. 8, 1792; d. Orange, N.J., Aug. 11, 1872. As a youth Mason studied singing, and at age 16 he directed the church choir at Medfield. In 1812 he went to Savannah, Georgia, where he studied harmony and composition with Frederick Abel. He taught singing in schools from 1813 to 1824 and became principal of the singers in 1815 and organist in 1820 of the Independent Presbyterian Church.

In 1827 Mason went to Boston and was president of the Handel and Haydn Society until 1832. He began teaching music privately from 1829 and in the public schools from 1837. He founded the Boston Academy of Music in 1833 with George J. Webb. He was superintendent of music in the Boston public schools from 1837 to 1845, remaining active as a teacher until 1851. He also made two trips to Europe, to study modern music education methods, in 1837 and then from 1851 to 1853.

In 1854 Mason settled in Orange, N.J. He received an honorary doctorate in music from N.Y. University the next year, only the second such conferring of that degree in the U.S.

Mason became wealthy through the sale of his many collections of music, including *Handel and Haydn Society's Collection of Church Music* (1822; 16 later editions), *Lyra Sacra* (1832), *Boston Academy Collection of Church Music* (1836), *The Psaltery* (1845), *Cantica Laudis* (1850), *New Carmina Sacra* (1852), and *Song Garden* (three parts; 1864–65). Many of his own hymn tunes, including *Missionary Hymn* (From Greenland's Icy Mountains), *Olivet, Boylston, Bethany, Hebron,* and *Olmutz,* are still found in hymnals.

Mason's valuable library, including 830 manuscripts and 700 volumes of hymnology, was given to Yale College after his death.

Mason, Luther Whiting, American music educator; b. Turner, Maine, April 3, 1828; d. Buckfield, Maine, July 4, 1896. Mason studied with LOWELL MASON at the Boston Academy of Music and may have been a distant relative.

In 1853 he became a music teacher in Louisville schools. Three years later, he relocated to Cincinnati, where he in-

vented the National System of music charts and books, which had instant success and made him famous. He settled in Boston in 1864 and reformed music instruction in the primary schools. In 1880 he was invited by the Japanese government to supervise music in the schools of Japan, where he labored three years with notable results (school music in Japan was termed "Mason-song"). He spent some time in Germany perfecting his principal work, *The National Music-Course.*

Mason, William, American pianist, teacher, and composer, son of LOWELL and uncle of DANIEL GREGORY MASON; b. Boston, Jan. 24, 1829; d. N.Y., July 14, 1908. Mason studied with several distinguished teachers, including Ignaz Moscheles and FRANZ LISZT, in 1853–54. His *Memories of a Musical Life* provide an anecdotal overview of his travels.

PEOPLE IN MUSIC

A fine pianist, Mason preferred teaching to performing and became a leading N.Y. teacher. In 1855 he established a chamber music series with noted conductor Theodore Thomas that introduced new ROMANTIC music to audiences through 1868. He wrote many piano pieces.

masque. An English spectacle or a social assembly during the 16th and 17th centuries that featured a variety of artistic presentations, including poetry, drama, dance, and music.

The subjects of such masques were usually taken from Greek mythology, and members of the aristocracy were themselves often engaged to perform the parts of shepherds and shepherdesses, benevolent gods and goddesses, etc. Among poets whose masques were produced at the English court were Ben Jonson and John Milton.

A curious byproduct of the masque was the 17th-century *antimasque,* a comic or grotesque interlude between the allegorical scenes, analogous to the *kyōgen* interludes of the medieval Japanese *noh* drama.

When OPERA was introduced into England, masques became integrated with it and disappeared as an independent form.

Masques et bergamasques. Orchestral suite by GABRIEL FAURÉ, 1919, first performed in Monte Carlo as incidental music. The title is taken from Paul Verlaine's poem *Clair de lune.* A bergamasque is a RENAISSANCE dance that originated in the northern Italian town of Bergamo.

Mass (Lat. *missa,* dismissed). The primary and most solemn service of the Roman Catholic church, which includes recitation of the sacred texts, singing, and playing on the organ.

The Mass is the most significant manifestation of religious music. Its theory and practice through the centuries determined the development of POLYPHONIC MUSIC in all parts of Europe before the Reformation. Virtually every composer in the musically productive countries—Italy, Germany, France, and Spain—wrote Masses. As a distinct musical form, the Mass reached its greatest flowering during the RENAISSANCE period, when great masters of the Netherlands and Italy applied themselves to the composition of large religious works.

The most eloquent and devout Mass is the *Missa solemnis,* the High Mass, also known as *Missa cantata,* that is, "sung Mass." A lesser Mass is *Missa lecta,* the "read Mass," or Low Mass, which has no purely musical parts. The Ordinary of the Mass (*ordinarium Missae*) contains chants that are included in every service and therefore in most Masses written by composers through the centuries that are performed not only in church but in concert. The divisions of the Ordinary are KYRIE, GLORIA, CREDO (the Nicene Creed, also known as *Symbolum apostolicum*), SANCTUS, AGNUS DEI, and Ite, missa est (or the *Benedicamus Domino*). The Kyrie is the only division of the Mass that is in the Greek language, the rest being in Latin.

Besides the Ordinary of the Mass, there exists a group of divisions with texts to be sung on particular days. The totality of these items is known as the Proper of the Mass (*proprium Missae*). They consist of the INTROIT (*psalmus ad introitum*), which precedes the Kyrie, the GRADUAL, the ALLELUIA (or TRACT, on solemn occasions), and the SEQUENCE, which are sung between the Gloria and Credo. The Credo is followed by the offertory. The conclusion of the Proper of the Mass is the *Communion (psalmus ad communionem),* after which the congregation is dismissed.

Both the Ordinary and Proper are interwoven with recitations and readings: in the Ordinary, the *Canon,* in the Proper, the *Collect, Epistle, Gospel, Secret, Preface,* and *Post-Communion.* Although the Latin texts of the Mass are traditional, the melodies are not. There are hundreds of different settings of individual numbers of the Mass.

An extremely important and musically fruitful extension of the Mass is the REQUIEM (or *Missa pro defunctis*), so named because it opens with the Introit *Requiem aeternam dona eis Domine* (Peace eternal give them, Lord).

Although the Mass is the most solemn religious service, it could not separate itself entirely from the world outside the church. As a result, the songs of the common people began to intrude on the holy precincts of the Mass. This produced some extremely original musical forms, among them the CANTUS FIRMUS Mass and, later in the RENAISSANCE, the parody Mass and paraphrase Mass. The cantus firmus Mass involves a use of fragments of Gregorian PLAINCHANT, usually in a hidden middle voice. The parody Mass does not imply the modern meaning of imitative caricature, but preserves the original Greek meaning of *para-ode* (near-song). The parody Mass reached its peak during the Renaissance, its principal feature being a use of religious POLYPHONY, secular MADRIGALS, and even folk songs. Sometimes an entire MOTET or other choral composition is incorporated. The paraphrase Mass is the free use of material, chant or polyphony.

Of such additions to the Mass, the most famous was the medieval popular song *L'Homme arme* (The Armed Man), which glorified the soldier. In this respect, a Mass using pre-existing material is a compound or synthetic work. It is not to be derogated for that, because most great composers wrote Masses based on nonecclesiastical melodies. The practice so shocked the orthodox that a council of the Roman church, held at Trent in the middle of the 16th century, issued a prohibition against using secular melodies as the cantus firmus in the Mass.

By the BAROQUE period, Masses were generally freely written. In the late Baroque, JOHANN SEBASTIAN BACH wrote his great B Minor Mass, and nearly another century later LUDWIG VAN BEETHOVEN composed his glorious *Missa*

Even the great GIOVANNI PIER-LUIGI DA PALESTRINA wrote a parody Mass based on *L'Homme arme.*

Solemnis. FRANZ SCHUBERT, CARL MARIA VON WEBER, FRANZ LISZT, CÉSAR FRANCK, CHARLES GOUNOD, and ANTON BRUCKNER wrote Masses marked by a grandeur of design that befits the subject.

While the great Masses from Palestrina to Beethoven are POLYPHONIC in structure, HOMOPHONIC Masses were produced in the less-devout 19th century. The Lutheran church retains most of the divisions of the Mass, as does the Anglican church. But such Masses are designed not for the great Gothic cathedrals but for the humble surroundings of a parochial chapel.

Sometimes separate items of the Mass, particularly the Gloria, attract a modern composer with the aim of stylization rather than reconstruction of the ancient model. Requiem Masses that contain the dramatic section DIES IRAE somehow respond to the state of mind of the Romantic composer. WOLFGANG AMADEUS MOZART, HECTOR BERLIOZ, GIUSEPPE VERDI, and JOHANNES BRAHMS wrote Requiem Masses, and BENJAMIN BRITTEN contributed a moving *War Requiem,* interweaving settings of the soldier-poet Wilfred Owen with the Latin liturgy. LEONARD BERNSTEIN wrote *Mass* which he described as a theater piece to the texts of the Roman liturgy and a libretto by Stephen Schwartz (*Godspell*).

The Latin version of the Mass became liturgical history in the 1950s when the Roman Catholic church mandated that the Mass be sung and spoken in the language of each country.

Mass in a Time of War *(Missa in tempore belli).* MASS in C major by FRANZ JOSEPH HAYDN, 1796. The score is nicknamed *Paukenmesse* (timpani Mass) because of the prominence given to those instruments.

Mass of Life, A. CANTATA by FREDERICK DELIUS, 1909, inspired by German philosopher Friedrich Nietzsche's *Also sprach Zarathustra.* It was first performed in London.

Massa's in the Cold Ground. Song by STEPHEN FOSTER, 1852. It is typical of the MINSTREL SONGS in its use of exaggerated dialect and sentimental subject matter. Here, incredibly, a slave mourns the loss of his owner.

Massenet, Jules (-Emile-Frédéric), French composer; b. Montaud, near St.-Etienne, Loire, May 12, 1842; d. Paris, Aug. 13, 1912. At the age of nine, Massenet was admitted to the Paris Conservatory, where he studied piano, harmony, and composition. After taking first prize for piano in 1859, he carried off the Grand Prix de Rome with the cantata *David Rizzio* four years later.

In 1878 Massenet was appointed professor of composition at the Paris Conservatory, and at the same time was elected a member of the Académie des Beaux-Arts. He continued to teach at the conservatory until 1896, numbering among his students Alfred Bruneau, Gabriel Piérne, and Gustave Charpentier. As a teacher, he exercised a profound influence on French opera.

After CHARLES GOUNOD, Massenet was the most popular French opera composer. He possessed a natural sense of graceful melody in a distinctive French style. His best operas, MANON (1884), *Werther* (1892), and *Thaïs* (1894), enjoy tremendous popularity in France. The celebrated *Méditation* for violin and orchestra from *Thaïs* is a regular repertoire number among violinists.

In addition to many operas, Massenet composed incidental music, ORATORIOS, secular works, and CANTATAS, some 200 songs, orchestral works, and piano pieces, both for

PEOPLE IN MUSIC

◀

Jules Massenet shown on the cover of the journal L'Illustration, *1884. (Gianni Dagli Orti/ Corbis)*

two- and four-hands. He completed and orchestrated LÉO DELIBES's opera *Kassya* in 1893.

Mastersinger (Ger., *Meistersinger;* Fr. *maître-chanteur*). In Germany, the artisan successors to the aristocratic MINNESINGER.

The Guild of Mastersingers emerged in Germany after the end of the Crusades and the concurrent decline of the Minnesingers. Socially they differed from the Minnesingers, who were mainly knights. The Mastersingers were men of the people who had common trades, such as shoemaking and carpentry, and at the same time were devoted to music, organized communal singing, and cultivated folk arts. The founder of the Mastersingers is reputed to be one Frauenlob (praise of women), who was also regarded as the last of the Minnesingers. If this is true, then the birth of the Mastersingers can be dated to the early decades of the 14th century.

The Mastersingers proved to be a very durable society, which was carried well into the 19th century before finally dissolving under the pressure of modern professionalism. RICHARD WAGNER's opera *DIE MEISTERSINGER VON NÜRNBERG* reflects the atmosphere of the social and professional activities in the German townships of the 16th century with remarkable accuracy. Most of the characters in Wagner's music drama are historical, and Wagner makes use of actual melodies of the guild.

Masur, Kurt, German conductor; b. Brieg, Silesia, July 18, 1927. Masur received training in piano and cello at the Breslau Music School from 1942 to 1944, then studied conducting privately and took courses in piano and composition at the Leipzig Hochschule für Musik from 1946 to 1948.

In 1948 Masur began his career with appointments as répétiteur (rehearsal pianist) and conductor at the Halle Landestheater. He conducted several theater and opera orchestras in Germany through the mid-'60s. His most prominent appointment was as conductor of the Dresden Philharmonic, a position he held from 1955 to 1958, and again from 1967 to 1972.

In 1970 Masur assumed the time-honored position of Gewandhauskapellmeister of Leipzig, where he would serve

PEOPLE IN MUSIC

as music director of the Gewandhaus Orchestra with notable distinction for over 25 years. He also made extensive tours with his orchestra in Europe and abroad. In 1973 he made his British debut as a guest conductor with the New Philharmonia Orchestra of London. His U.S. debut followed in 1974 as a guest conductor with the Cleveland Orchestra. In 1981 he conducted LUDWIG VAN BEETHOVEN's Ninth Symphony at the gala opening of the new Gewandhaus in Leipzig. In 1988 he was named principal guest conductor of the London Philharmonic.

In the autumn of 1989, during the period of political upheaval in East Germany, Masur played a major role as peacemaker in Leipzig. His name was even mentioned as a possible candidate for president of Germany in 1993, but he said he had no interest in politics.

Masur gained great prominence in the U.S. when, in 1990, he was appointed music director of the N.Y. Philharmonic, to commence with the 1991–92 season. In 1995 Masur announced he was stepping down from his conducting position in Leipzig at the end of the 1998 season. Just before stepping down from this post, he was named honorary conductor of the Gewandhaus Orchestra, and also was made a Commander of the Legion of Honor.

Masur's tenure with the N.Y. Philharmonic has had its share of controversy. In 1997 he refused to agree to a plan by the orchestra's board to leave his post in 2000, so a search for a new conductor could begin. Instead, his contract was extended to 2002. In 1998 it was announced that he would serve as the principal conductor of the London Philharmonic Orchestra, beginning in 2000, for a five-year period, while continuing to hold his position in N.Y.

While Masur has earned a reputation as a faithful guardian of the classical and ROMANTIC Austro-German repertoire, he frequently programs contemporary scores.

Matchiche, La. Popular VAUDEVILLE song, 1903, by Charles Borel-Clerc (1879–1959), published under various titles. This is a French version of the name of the Brazilian dance *maxixe,* which dates to the 1870s and is related to the polka. GEORGE GERSHWIN quoted it as a typical Parisian song in his orchestral sketch *An American in Paris.*

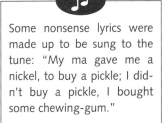

Some nonsense lyrics were made up to be sung to the tune: "My ma gave me a nickel, to buy a pickle; I didn't buy a pickle, I bought some chewing-gum."

Matelots, Les (The Sailors). Ballet by GEORGES AURIC, 1925, first performed in Paris. A sailor is engaged to a woman of Marseilles. To test her loyalty, he, in the company of two of his friends, assumes a disguise. When she resists the advances of the other sailors, he is satisfied that she is faithful. The ballet is a typical product of post–World War I French culture.

Materna. Hymn tune by Samuel Augustus Ward, 1888, originally for the text *O Mother Dear Jerusalem.* It was later adapted to the words *America the Beautiful* by Katherine Lee Bates.

Mathis der Maler (Mathis the Painter). Opera by PAUL HINDEMITH, 1938, to his own libretto. This work was inspired by the Colmar triptych of the painter known as Matthias Grünewald (who flourished in the first half of the 16th century).

In the opera, the artistic career of Mathis is interrupted by a peasant uprising of 1542. Although Mathis is not political and is employed by the religious authorities, he hides two fleeing rebels and gradually comes to join the rebel cause. Realizing that both camps are guilty of wrongdoing, however, he withdraws from the political world and dedicates himself to art.

The score echoes the spirit of the German RENAISSANCE in its choral-like structure. Although modern in style, the work is rich with POLYPHONY and TONAL HARMONIES.

Despite the originality of the score and its ideological acceptability to the Nazis, Hitler's ministry put obstacles in the way of its production: not only was Hindemith a relatively AVANT-GARDE composer and modern music festival organizer, but he was married to a woman who was partly Jewish. The work was premiered in Zurich, Switzerland, rather than Germany, for these reasons.

Four years before the opera's premiere, Hindemith assembled a symphony from three extended orchestral excerpts, which retains a place in the classical repertoire.

PEOPLE IN MUSIC

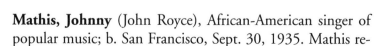

Mathis, Johnny (John Royce), African-American singer of popular music; b. San Francisco, Sept. 30, 1935. Mathis received classical vocal training before deciding upon a career as a popular vocalist. He was signed to Columbia Records in 1956, initially as a jazz singer. However, he immediately scored a hit with the soft-ballad *Wonderful, Wonderful.* It was followed through the '50s with scores of soft-ballad hits, including *Misty, Chances Are,* and *The 12th of Never.* Mathis appeared in nightclubs and subsequently made tours of the U.S., Europe, Africa, and the Far East.

Mathis's position as a top-of-the-chart pop singer ended in the '60s with the beginnings of rock 'n' roll. Nonetheless, he has continued to tour and record. He has even occasionally scored a surprise hit, such as his 1987 duet with Deniece Williams on *Too Much, Too Late,* which became his first No. 1 single in 30 years.

Matin, Le. FRANZ JOSEPH HAYDN's Symphony No. 6 (1761), in the key of D major. Some sense of the mists of early morning is conveyed by the ADAGIO opening.

matins. The music sung at morning prayer, the first of the CANONICAL HOURS.

Matrimonio segreto, Il (The Secret Marriage). Opera by Domenico Cimarosa, 1792, based on Colman and Garrick's comedy *The Clandestine Marriage.* It was first performed in Vienna and was so successful that Emperor Leopold II ordered an immediate encore of the entire opera.

A rich man of Bologna tries to arrange a marriage of his older daughter to a titled Britisher, named Count Robinson. But Robinson likes the younger sister better. However, she is already married secretly to a young lawyer. They hope to run away together. Meanwhile, the bride's aunt is infatuated with the count. Identities are switched, and assorted lovers experience unintended encounters in bedrooms. In the end the situation is clarified, and the *matrimonio segreto* is finally revealed not to be a secret after all.

Matthews, Artie, African-American RAGTIME composer; b. Braidwood, Ill., Nov. 15, 1888; d. Cincinnati, Oct. 25, 1958. Matthews spent his formative years in Springfield, Illinois, learning ragtime from the pianists Banty Morgan and

PEOPLE IN MUSIC

Having retired from ragtime performance, Matthews was surprised when, in the early '50s, jazz scholars approached him to discuss his earlier work. No longer able to play his rags, he offered to play them selections by JOHANN SEBASTIAN BACH instead.

Art Dillingham. After working in the tenderloin district of St. Louis (c.1908), he took lessons in piano, organ, and theory. He was active as a composer and arranger for local theaters. During this period, he composed an outstanding series of piano rags, the famous *Five Pastime Rags* (two in 1913, 1916, 1918, 1920). He also wrote a jazz classic for piano, *Weary Blues* (1915), and several songs.

In 1915 Matthews went to Chicago as a church organist, and after World War I he settled in Cincinnati. He obtained a degree from the Metropolitan College of Music and Dramatic Arts in 1918. Together with his wife, Anna Matthews, he founded the Cosmopolitan School of Music for classical training of black musicians in 1921.

PEOPLE IN MUSIC

Mauceri, John (Francis), American conductor; b. N.Y., Sept. 12, 1945. Mauceri studied at Yale University (B.A., 1967; M.Phil., 1972) and with the well-known conductors BRUNO MADERNA, COLIN DAVIS, SEIJI OZAWA, and LEONARD BERNSTEIN at the Berkshire Music Center at Tanglewood, Massachusetts in 1971. He conducted the Yale University Symphony Orchestra from 1968 to 1974, then appeared widely as a guest conductor of opera, musical theater, and orchestras.

Mauceri was music director of the Washington (D.C.) Opera from 1980 to 1982, the American Symphony Orchestra in N.Y. from 1984 to 1987, and the Scottish Opera in Glasgow from 1987. He was hired as the conductor of the Hollywood Bowl Orchestra in 1990, where he has spent the entire decade. His specialty there has been film music and other popular-classical mixes.

PEOPLE IN MUSIC

Maxwell Davies, Peter. *See* DAVIES, PETER MAXWELL.

Mayall, John, English blues singer and harmonica player; b. Manchester, Nov. 29, 1933. An ardent promoter of African-American blues, he formed a group called the Bluesbreakers in the early 1960s. At one time or another, the group employed the leading British blues players, including ERIC CLAPTON, Peter Green, John McVie, Mick Taylor, Aynsley Dunbar, and Mick Fleetwood.

PEOPLE IN MUSIC

In the mid-'60s, the Bluesbreakers released a number of successful albums, among them *A Hard Road* and *The Turning Point* (with no drummer), and the first classic of British blues, under the title *Bluesbreakers with Eric Clapton.* Another album, *U.S. Union,* produced a workable wedding of jazz and blues.

In the late '60s, Mayall emigrated to America, settling in California. He continued to record for a while through the mid-'70s with various accompanists. Since then, he has been less active, although he occasionally records and performs.

Maytime. OPERETTA by SIGMUND ROMBERG, 1917, first produced in N.Y. The story takes place over three generations. A couple in love, doomed to separation in the mid-19th century, bury the deed to the family home in N.Y. in the hope that their descendants will discover it and make a fortune. The suitor's grandson falls in love with the granddaughter of the girl his grandfather once loved, and they discover the valuable document. The money realized from it helps to rebuild and redecorate her dress shop. Among memorable songs in the score is the waltz *Will You Remember?*

Mayuzumi, Toshirō, Japanese composer; b. Yokohama, Feb. 20, 1929; d. Kawasaki, April 10, 1997. Mayuzumi studied at the National University of Fine Arts and Music in Tokyo from 1945 to 1951, then took courses at the Paris Conservatory for a year.

Returning to Japan in 1952, Mayuzumi organized the modern group Ars Nova Japonica and also worked at the ELECTRONIC MUSIC studio in Tokyo. His style of composition combines the sounds of traditional Japanese music, SERIAL techniques, and electronic sounds, all amalgamated in a remarkably effective manner. He was also a successful composer of film scores, including that for *The Bible.*

PEOPLE IN MUSIC

Mazeppa. The fourth of the *Twelve Transcendental Etudes* by FRANZ LISZT, 1851, after the poem by Victor Hugo. It portrays the adventurous life of the Cossack chieftain who defied Peter the Great and lost. The galloping horses are represented by the harmonies of the DIMINISHED SEVENTH chords, while the warlike mood is portrayed by TRIADIC leaps and bounds. Lyrical sections feature melodies richly accompanied by harmonious ARPEGGIOS.

The work was later orchestrated by Joachim Raff and first performed, under the same title, in Weimar.

mazurka (Polish). A moderately lively Polish national dance in triple time. As the name indicates, it originated from the Mazur district in northern Poland. Its main characteristic is an off-beat ACCENT and a SYNCOPATED first beat.

KUJAWIAK and OBEREK are distinctive varieties.

The mazurka's popularity as an art form is owed mainly to FRÉDÉRIC CHOPIN. He skillfully added chromatic runs and ornaments to the basic rhythmic design to turn it into a virtuoso piano piece.

MUSICAL INSTRUMENT

PEOPLE IN MUSIC

mbira. *See* LAMELLAPHONES.

McCartney, Sir (John) **Paul,** English rock singer, songwriter, and guitarist, member of the fantastically popular rock group the BEATLES; b. Liverpool, June 18, 1942. McCartney picked out chords on a family piano (his father was an amateur ragtime player), and at puberty he began playing a left-handed guitar. He was the only Beatle who attended college, studying English literature. Fascinated by Elvis Presley, he tried to emulate the spirit of American rock 'n' roll (and rhythm and blues). With fellow Liverpudlians John Lennon, George Harrison, and Stuart Sutcliffe, he formed the group known as the Silver Beatles, which later took the name the Beatles. (*See* separate entry on the BEATLES for the remainder of the group's history.)

In 1969 McCartney married rock photographer Linda Eastman, who would collaborate with him as a backup singer and keyboardist through most of his solo career. In 1970 McCartney went to court to end the Beatles' partnership with Apple Records. He subsequently was active as a solo act and with his own group, Wings. McCartney proved to be an adept writer of pop songs. Through the '70s he had many major hits, including *My Love* (1972), *Band on the Run* (1975), and *Silly Love Songs* (1976).

Wings more or less broke up in the early '80s. McCartney resumed his solo career, also issuing duets with STEVIE WONDER (*Ebony and Ivory*) and MICHAEL JACKSON (*The Girl Is Mine*) during this period. His career slowed in the mid-'80s but picked up steam again at the decade's end. He formed a new recording and touring band, and also collaborated with punk-rocker Elvis Costello on a number of songs for the 1989 album *Flowers in the Dirt.* A series of successful tours followed of the U.S. and Europe through the early '90s.

McCartney and the two other surviving ex-Beatles reunited in 1996 for the hugely successful *Anthology* television documentary and CD sets. A year later, he issued his first new solo album in four years, *Flaming Pie,* which failed to win either critical or commercial success. In 1998 his wife and longtime collaborator, Linda, died of cancer.

In addition to his rock compositions, McCartney has put his hand into classical composing, including *The Liverpool Oratorio* (1994) and an orchestral piece, *Standing Stone* (1997; revised 1998).

McFerrin, Bobby (Robert), gifted African-American popular vocalist and conductor; b. N.Y., March 11, 1950. His father, Robert Ferrin (b. Marianna, Ariz., March 19, 1921), was a significant baritone who, in 1949, appeared in the first productions of KURT WEILL's *Lost in the Stars* and William Grant Still's *Troubled Island.* He won the Metropolitan Auditions of the Air in 1953 and became the first black male to join the company, making his debut in 1955, as Amonasro in *AIDA.* He sang the role of Porgy (played by Sidney Poitier) in the film version of *PORGY AND BESS* in 1959.

Bobby studied theory from the age of six and played piano in high school, forming a quartet that copied the styles of HENRY MANCINI and Sergio Mendes. In 1970 he heard MILES DAVIS's jazz-rock fusion album *Bitches Brew* and completely changed his musical direction. He studied music at Sacramento State University and at Cerritos College, then played piano professionally until 1977, when he began to develop his voice. He toured in 1980 with jazz vocalist Jon Hendricks and debuted a solo act in 1982.

His recordings include *Bobby McFerrin* (1982), *The Voice* (1984), *Spontaneous Improvisation* (1986), *Simple Pleasures* (1988; arranged as overdubbed a cappella; includes the song *Don't Worry, Be Happy,* which made him a household name), and *Medicine Music* (1991).

McFerrin also made several music videos and sang with HERBIE HANCOCK, YO-YO MA, Manhattan Transfer, and others. In 1989 he established the 11-voice ensemble Voicestra,

PEOPLE IN MUSIC

with which he created the sound track for *Common Threads,* a 1989 documentary on the AIDS quilt. The group's first concert tour, in 1990, received critical acclaim. McFerrin began studying conducting in 1989, making his debut with a performance of LUDWIG VAN BEETHOVEN's Symphony No. 7 with the San Francisco Symphony in 1990.

McFerrin is a virtuoso, using a remarkable range of voices with sophisticated control and accompanying them with body percussion, breath, and other self-generated sounds. Aesthetically, he fuses a number of musical styles, including jazz, rock, gospel, and New Age, in a brilliant palette. His solo and ensemble shows are based on various improvisatory structures through which he produces highly polished, expertly burnished works.

McGhee, Brownie (Walter Brown), African-American blues guitarist, singer, and songwriter; b. Knoxville, Tenn., Nov. 30, 1915; d. Oakland, Calif., Feb. 16, 1996. He was known for his deft guitar playing and singing in partnership with Sonny Terry (b. Greensboro, N.C., Oct. 24, 1911; d. N.Y., March 12, 1986), the blues harmonica player. Terry wailed vocally and instrumentally, and McGhee melded this into a smooth, closely integrated blend.

During their 40-year association (1939–79), Terry and McGhee appeared in concert and at blues and folk music festivals throughout the U.S., Europe, New Zealand, and Australia. They also recorded some 30 albums, many of which featured McGhee's songs: *Life Is a Gamble, Tell Me Why, Blues Had a Baby (And They Called It Rock and Roll), Walk On, Hole in the Wall, I Couldn't Believe My Eyes, My Father's Words, Watch Your Close Friend,* and *Rainy Day.* The duo broke up in 1979, and McGhee continued to perform on his own until he was stricken by cancer in 1996.

His brother, Granville "Sticks" McGhee (b. Knoxville, Tenn., March 23, 1918; d. N.Y., Aug. 15, 1961), had a hit in 1948 with *Drinkin' Wine Spo-Dee-O-Dee.* He also performed with his brother and Terry in the '50s.

McPartland, Jimmy (James), American jazz trumpeter and bandleader; b. Chicago, March 15, 1907; d. Port Washington, N.Y., March 13, 1991. McPartland studied violin, then

From 1994 to 1996 McFerrin held the Creative Chair of the St. Paul (Minnesota) Chamber Orchestra.

PEOPLE IN MUSIC

PEOPLE IN MUSIC

took up the cornet. At the age of 16, he organized a band with his brother, and subsequently played with Bix Beiderbecke, Ben Pollack, and Jack Teagarden.

After military service in World War II, he resumed his career by organizing his own quartet in Chicago. He later led his own band on tours. He married MARIAN MCPARTLAND in 1945.

McPartland, Marian (Margaret Turner), English-born American jazz pianist and composer; b. Windsor, March 20, 1918. McPartland first played violin, then won a scholarship to the Guildhall School of Music in London, where she studied piano.

She began her career as a jazz pianist in joint appearances with the jazz pianist Billy Mayerl. In 1945 she married JIMMY MCPARTLAND, and in 1946 they went to America and played in a combo. In 1951 she organized her own trio, and worked through most of the decade in small clubs. She wrote a number of songs in the popular vein, including the successful *There'll Be Other Times*. In the '60s she focused more on education, although she continued to perform.

McPartland became a successful soloist and recording star beginning in the '70s. She gained great exposure thanks to her radio program, *Piano Jazz*, broadcast over National Public Radio, on which she interviewed many leading jazz players. She continued to perform and record through the '80s and '90s.

PEOPLE IN MUSIC

McPhee, Colin (Carhart), American composer and ethnomusicologist; b. Montreal, Canada, March 15, 1900; d. Los Angeles, Jan. 7, 1964. McPhee studied piano and composition at the Peabody Conservatory in Baltimore, graduating in 1921. From 1921 to 1924 he lived in Toronto, where he took lessons with the German pianist and teacher Arthur Friedheim. He continued his studies in Paris from 1924 to 1926.

Returning to the U.S. in 1926, McPhee joined the modern movement in N.Y. and was briefly a student of EDGARD VARÈSE. He wrote scores for the experimental films H_2O and *Mechanical Principles* in 1931. Then he became interested in the GAMELAN music of Java and Bali. He moved to Indonesia

PEOPLE IN MUSIC

in 1931 and, except for brief interruptions, remained there until 1939. His *Tabuh-Tabuhan* for two pianos, orchestra, and exotic percussion, composed and premiered during an interlude in Mexico City in 1936, is the quintessential work in his Bali-influenced style.

McPhee then returned to the U.S. and was a consultant to the Office of War Information during World War II. Later he was active with the Institute of Ethnomusicology at the University of California, Los Angeles, from 1958 to 1964.

Among McPhee's compositions are three symphonies, *Transitions* for orchestra (1954), *Nocturne* for chamber orchestra (1958), Concerto for wind orchestra (1960), Concerto for piano and wind octet (1928), and piano works, including *Four Piano Sketches* (1916), *Kinesis* (1930), and *Balinese Ceremonial Music* for two pianos (1934–38).

McPhee wrote the memoirs *A House in Bali* (1946) and *A Club of Small Men* (1948), along with the textbook *Music in Bali* (1966).

McRae, Carmen, African-American jazz vocalist and pianist; b. N.Y., April 8, 1922; d. Beverly Hills, Calif., November 10, 1994. McRae began singing as a child, as well as writing songs. When she was 16, her song *Dream of Life* was recorded by her idol, BILLIE HOLIDAY.

In 1944 McRae joined BENNY CARTER's band. She subsequently sang with the bands of COUNT BASIE, Mercer Ellington, and others. In the early '50s, she worked as a pianist at Harlem's Minton Playhouse, the famous club that was a gathering place for BEBOP musicians. In the early '60s, she was briefly married to the drummer Kenny "Klook" Clarke (b. Pittsburgh, Jan. 9, 1914; d. Montreuil-sous-Bois, Paris, Jan. 26, 1985) and recorded several songs as Carmen Clarke.

Through the '60s, '70s, and '80s, she toured the U.S. and Europe as an interpreter of the jazz vocal repertoire. She was one of the few singers to maintain her style in the face of pressures to adopt to changing popular tastes.

McShann, Jay "Hootie" (James Columbus), African-American jazz pianist, blues singer, and bandleader; b. Muskogee, Okla., Jan. 12, 1909 (some sources give his birth year as 1916). McShann took up the piano at an early age. He first played professionally with saxophonist Don Byas, then studied briefly at the Tuskegee Institute. He was back in the Tulsa area by 1935.

PEOPLE IN MUSIC

In 1936, McShann moved to Kansas City, where he formed his first band. Among his hits were *Hootie Blues* (from which he got his nickname), *Confessin' the Blues,* and *Swingmatism.* The legendary jazz figure CHARLIE PARKER was a member of McShann's band from 1937 to 1941.

After a stint in the U.S. Army (1943 – 45), McShann resumed his career, working mainly in California. He continued to be active well into old age. In 1974 he toured Europe with the show *The Musical Life of Charlie Parker.* He also appeared in the beautiful 1979 film *The Last of the Blue Devils.* He continued to record and perform through the '80s.

Me and Juliet. Musical by RICHARD RODGERS and OSCAR HAMMERSTEIN, II, 1953. A theatrical love triangle involves an assistant manager, the chorus girl he loves, and the electrician who longs for her so strongly that he's willing to kill them both. Fortunately, love triumphs in the end.

Although *Me and Juliet* fell far short of the successes enjoyed by OKLAHOMA! and SOUTH PACIFIC, the score has its merits. One of the best numbers, *No Other Love,* was used by Rodgers in his score for the television documentary *Victory at Sea.*

Me and My Shadow. Song by Billy Rose and AL JOLSON, 1927. The song's hero is so lonely that he only has "his shadow" to keep him company as he "walks down the avenue."

meantone temperament. *See* TEMPERAMENT.

measure. The NOTES and RESTS contained within two vertical lines. The metrical unit in composition, with regular accentuation, familiarly called a BAR.

Measure note, a note shown by the time signature to be an even divisor of a measure; *measure rest, see* REST.

mechanical instruments. Instruments that are played mechanically, rather than by a human musician, such as the player piano (PIANOLA) or MUSIC(AL) BOX.

Meck, Nadezhda von. *See* TCHAIKOVSKY, PIOTR ILYICH.

MUSICAL INSTRUMENT

Medea's Meditation and Dance of Vengeance. Symphonic scene by SAMUEL BARBER, 1956. It is the fourth version of a ballet that began life as *The Serpent Heart,* choreographed by Martha Graham in 1946 and revised and performed the following year as *Cave of the Heart.* That same year, Barber created a ballet suite, using the title *Medea.*

Médecin malgré lui, Le (The Doctor in Spite of Himself). Opera by CHARLES GOUNOD, 1858, first produced in Paris, based on a Molière play.

A maltreated wife intends to get even with her husband by spreading the rumor that he is a miracle worker in medicine. When he fails to cure the daughter of a wealthy citizen, he is beaten by the servants. The daughter, however, is not sick at all, and only pretends illness in order to elope with her lover. Eventually the lovers inherit a fortune, the girl's father is reconciled to her marriage, and the maltreated wife of the hapless "doctor" forgives him.

Medée. Tragédie lyrique by MARC-ANTOINE CHARPENTIER, 1693, first produced in Paris. The libretto is derived from the ancient Greek myth of Medea, wife of Jason, who is enraged by his plan to take a younger wife. She wreaks vengeance by arranging the bride-to-be's death and by murdering her (Medea) and Jason's two sons.

Medée. Opera by LUIGI CHERUBINI, 1797, based on the Greek myth. It is considered his masterpiece, but it fell into relative obscurity. A century and a half later, the postwar BEL CANTO revival led to the revival of this opera in its Italian form, *Medea.* MARIA CALLAS has popularized the part. The EARLY MUSIC movement has led to recent performances in its original French version.

mediant. The third degree of the scale.

medieval music. In the history of Western music, the period from about 500 to around 1450.

Very little SECULAR MUSIC survives from this period, because little of it was notated. Therefore, surviving works dating from the 12th century are those composed for the church, both MONOPHONIC (with one vocal or melody line) and POLYPHONIC (with more than one vocal/melody line). In the first category belong PLAINCHANT (plainsong), which consisted of voices singing in unison. The melodies were based upon MODES. In the second category, dating from the ninth century, belong ORGANUM, the earliest attempts at polyphonic or harmonic writing.

Examples of music from the 12th and 13th centuries, a period known as ARS ANTIQUA, is far more plentiful. In addition to organum, there are the polyphonic CLAUSULA, CONDUCTUS, and the early MOTET. From this period also come the rich supply of monophonic songs created and disseminated by the TROUBADOURS, TROUVÈRES, and MINNESINGERS.

In the early 13th century, music became more expressive in its melodies and more complicated in its rhythms. This period is known as ARS NOVA, and to it belong a wealth of new polyphonic forms, wherein compositions were constructed by the successive layering of sometimes quite contrasting melodic lines. For the great French composers (e.g., GUILLAUME DE MACHAUT) there is the BALLADE, the RONDEAU, the VIRELAI, and the motet. For the Italians (e.g., FRANCESCO LANDINI) there is the BALLATA, the CACCIA, and the early MADRIGAL.

Settings from these and other composers can sound quite strange to even the most modern ears.

In the first half of the 15th century, composers began to create works that looked ahead to the lush, CONSONANT, chordal style of the RENAISSANCE. The English composer JOHN DUNSTABLE was a leader in this movement, followed closely by GUILLAUME DUFAY and GILLES BINCHOIS. Polyphony applied to sacred music was no longer taboo, and many composers devoted themselves to complete and quite elaborate settings of the ORDINARY of the MASS.

As to purely instrumental works, much that survives falls into the categories of dance music, such as the ESTAMPIE and the SALTARELLO. Among the instruments used were various strings (bowed, plucked, and hammered), winds, and percussion devices, as well as several ORGANS (PORTATIVE, POSITIVE, and early church) and the earliest of CLAVICHORDS.

meditation (Lat., *meditari*). An ELEGY. *Méditation* for solo violin in the opera *Thaïs* by JULES MASSENET is a favorite concert number. The coaxingly viscid *Ave Maria* by CHARLES

GOUNOD, superimposed on the First Prelude in C Major of JOHANN SEBASTIAN BACH's first book of the *WELL-TEMPERED CLAVIER,* is subtitled *Méditation.*

Medium, The. Tragedy by GIAN CARLO MENOTTI, 1946, to his own English libretto, first produced in N.Y. on Broadway (the first of his "Broadway operas").

The medium Madame Flora arranges for ghosts to speak to bereaved relatives through a hidden microphone. So realistic are the voices, produced by her daughter, that the medium begins to believe in their reality. In a panic, she shoots and kills her deaf-mute helper whom she finds in the closet.

The Medium is one of the composer's most successful works. Its dramatic impact is considerable.

medley. *See* POTPOURRI.

PEOPLE IN MUSIC

Medtner, Nicolai (Nikolai Karlovich), notable Russian pianist and composer of German descent; b. Moscow, Jan. 5, 1880; d. London, Nov. 13, 1951. Medtner first studied piano with his mother, then with his uncle. In 1892 he entered the Moscow Conservatory, where he studied piano and composition. He graduated in 1900, winning the gold medal, the same year that he won the Rubinstein Prize in Vienna.

For the next two years, Medtner appeared with much success as a pianist in the European capitals. Returning to Russia, he taught at the Moscow Conservatory from 1902 to 1921, then lived in Berlin and Paris. He eventually settled in London in 1935. He made tours of the U.S. in 1924–25, and again in 1929–30, and the Soviet Union in 1927.

In Russian music, Medtner was a solitary figure. He never followed the nationalist trend, but endeavored to create a new type of composition, rooted in both CLASSIC and ROMANTIC traditions. His sets of fairy tales in sonata form are unique examples of his favorite genre. He wrote his best compositions before he left Russia. Although he continued to compose during his residence abroad, his late music lacks the verve and romantic sincerity of his earlier works. He wrote almost exclusively for the piano and for the voice.

A revival of Medtner's music was begun in Russia after his death, and a complete edition of his works appeared in Moscow (12 volumes, 1959–63). His works include three piano concertos, a piano quintet, three violin sonatas, and 107 songs. He also published a collection of essays as *Muza i moda* (The Muse and Fashion; 1935).

Meeresstille und glückliche Fahrt (Calm Sea and Happy Voyage). Concert overture by FELIX MENDELSSOHN, 1828. Despite its reassuring title, the music becomes quite turbulent, but the voyage ends happily. It was first performed in Berlin and may be regarded as a companion piece to his *Fingal's Cave*, written about the same time.

Meet Me in St. Louis, Louis. Song by Kerry Mills, 1904, written to celebrate the St. Louis World's Exposition. Despite its silly name and trivial tune, the song remained popular for decades.

The song provided the inspiration and title for a 1944 MGM musical comedy starring Judy Garland. It was adapted as a Broadway play in 1989, although with far less success than the film.

Mefistofèle. Opera by Arrigo Boito, 1868, first produced in Milan. Boito's libretto drew from both parts of Goethe's great philosophical poem *Faust*, unlike CHARLES GOUNOD's opera, which ends with the death of Marguerite. Boito adds the encounter with Helen of Troy, and ends with the redemption of Faust. The role of the devil is one of the great operatic bass roles.

Mefistofèle has excellent musical and literary qualities, but it has never attained the success enjoyed by Gounod's *FAUST*.

PEOPLE IN MUSIC

Mehta, Mehli, Indian violinist and conductor, father of ZU-BIN MEHTA; b. Bombay, Sept. 25, 1908. Mehta studied at the University of Bombay and at Trinity College of Music in London (licentiate, 1929). He founded the Bombay Symphony Orchestra in 1935, serving as its concertmaster until 1945, then conductor until 1955. Subsequently, he was assistant concertmaster of the Halle Orchestra in Manchester from 1955 to 1959.

In 1959 Mehta settled in the U.S., where he played in the Curtis String Quartet in Philadelphia until 1964. He then went to Los Angeles, where he founded the American

The Mehta family belonged to the historic tribe of Parsi nobles, the fire-worshiping followers of Zarathustra. They fled en masse from the turbulence of Persia 13 centuries before Zubin Mehta's birth, settling in India.

Youth Symphony Orchestra. He also taught at the University of California there until 1976, serving as conductor of its symphony and chamber orchestras.

Mehta, Zubin, exuberant, effulgent, and eloquent Indian conductor, son of MEHLI MEHTA; b. Bombay, April 29, 1936. Zubin was tutored by his father. He learned to play violin and piano, and at age 16 he successfully conducted a rehearsal of the Bombay Symphony Orchestra.

PEOPLE IN MUSIC

Zubin Mehta, c. 1980. (David Rentas) ▶

Before deciding on a musical career, he took a course in medicine at St. Xavier College in Bombay. However, he soon gave up medicine and went to Vienna, where he studied double bass at the Academy of Music and took conducting lessons. During the summers of 1956 and 1957 he attended conducting classes at the Accademia Chigiana in Siena. In 1957 he graduated from the Vienna Academy of Music and made his professional debut conducting the Tonkünstler Orchestra in the Musikverein.

In 1958 he married the Canadian singer Carmen Lasky, with whom he had two children. After their divorce in

1964, she married Zubin Mehta's brother Zarin in 1966, thus making Zubin an uncle by marriage of his own children. In 1969 he married the actress Nancy Kovack in a dual ceremony, Methodist and Zoroastrian.

In the meantime, Mehta's career progressed by great strides. He won the competition of the Royal Liverpool Philharmonic in 1958 and conducted it for a season as an assistant. Later he obtained guest engagements in Austria and Yugoslavia. In 1959 he competed in a conducting contest in Tanglewood, where he won second prize. In 1960 he received a bona fide engagement to conduct the Vienna Symphony Orchestra. That same year he also made a highly successful appearance as a guest conductor with the Philadelphia Orchestra.

Later in 1960, Mehta conducted two concerts of the Montreal Symphony Orchestra. He produced such a fine impression that he was appointed its music director. In 1962 Mehta took the Montreal Symphony Orchestra to Russia, where he gave eight concerts. He then conducted two concerts with it in Paris and one in Vienna, where he took 14 bows in response to a thunderous ovation.

In the meantime, Mehta received a contract to conduct the Los Angeles Philharmonic, becoming its associate conductor in 1961 and its music director in 1962. He was thus the holder of two major conducting jobs, the youngest conductor to function in this dual capacity. His career was assuming the allure of a gallop, aided by his ability—rare among conductors—to maintain self-control under trying circumstances.

Mehta made his debut at the Metropolitan Opera in N.Y. in 1965, conducting AIDA. His performances of CARMEN and TURANDOT were highly praised. In 1967 he resigned his post in Montreal, and in 1968 was named music advisor of the Israel Philharmonic, becoming its music director in 1977. In 1978 he left the Los Angeles Philharmonic after being offered the musical directorship of the N.Y. Philharmonic, with which he toured Europe in 1980. He remained with the N.Y. Philharmonic for over a decade.

On July 7, 1990, Mehta served as conductor of the three tenors extravaganza in Rome with JOSÉ CARRERAS, PLACIDO DOMINGO, and LUCIANO PAVAROTTI in a concert telecast live to the world. In 1991 he left his post with the N.Y. Philharmonic, although he returned on Dec. 7, 1992, for its 150th anniversary concert, conducting a performance of RICHARD STRAUSS'S *TILL EULENSPIEGELS LUSTIGE STREICH.*

Mehta's association with the Israel Philharmonic was particularly affectionate. He conducted it during the Six-Day War and at the 25th anniversary of Israel's independence. In 1974 he was given an honorary Ph.D. by Tel Aviv University. No Jew could be more Israeli than the Parsi Mehta!

In 1995 Mehta was appointed Generalmusikdirektor of the Bavarian State Opera in Munich, which post was assumed in 1998. In 1997 he received the Great Silver Medal of Austria.

Professionally, Mehta maintains an almost infallible reliability. He conducts all of his scores, even the most mind-boggling modern scores, and operas as well, from memory. He is also an eloquent speaker in English and Hindi and fluent in German, French, and Spanish. He even speaks understandable Russian.

Meistersinger (Ger.). *See* MASTERSINGER.

Meistersinger von Nürnberg, Die. Opera by RICHARD WAGNER, 1868. It was produced in Munich, 1868, with Hans von Bülow conducting. As in all Wagner's operas, the text is his own. It is his first work to include comic moments.

The action takes place in Nuremberg in the 16th century. A singing contest is organized by the Guild of Mastersingers under the guidance of the cobbler Hans Sachs (a historical figure who played an important role in organizing singing societies in Germany in the 16th century). The first prize is the hand of Eva, daughter of the local goldsmith. Von Stolzing, in love with Eva, sings a supremely beautiful song, but the pedantic clerk Beckmesser faults him for violation of the rules. After the prize is given to Walter, Sachs explains the principles underlying the art of German song.

The opera is interesting for its many realistic details. For instance, Eva, Beckmesser, and others call on the cobbler-mastersinger to have their shoes repaired. The contrapuntal texture of the music is glorious. Unhampered by the LEITMOTIFS, the music flows with rhapsodic freedom.

Beckmesser was modeled after the famous Viennese music critic Eduard Hanslick, a persistent opponent of Wagner. In the early sketches of *Die Meistersinger,* Wagner used the name Hans Lick for Beckmesser.

Melba, (Dame) Nellie (real name Helen Porter Mitchell Armstrong), famous Australian soprano; b. Burnley, near Richmond, England, May 19, 1861; d. Sydney, Australia, Feb. 23, 1931. Melba's father, who had decided objections to anything connected with the stage, was nevertheless fond of music and proud of his daughter's talent. When she was only

Nellie Melba with her pet birds, 1927. (Hulton-Deutsch Collection/Corbis)

six years old, he allowed her to sing at a concert in the Melbourne Town Hall, but would not consent to her having singing lessons. Instead, she was taught piano, violin, and harp, as well as instruction in harmony and composition. As she grew older, she frequently played the organ in a local church and was known among her friends as an excellent pianist.

Not until after her marriage in 1882 to Captain Charles Armstrong was Melba able to gratify her ambition to sing, when she began to study with a local teacher. Her first public appearance was in 1884, in a benefit concert in Melbourne. The next year her father received a government appointment in London, and she accompanied him, determined to begin an operatic career. She then studied with Mathilde Marchesi in Paris.

Melba gave her first concert in London in 1886. A year later, her debut as Gilda at the Théâtre Royal de la Monnaie in Brussels created a sensation. The famous impresario Augustus Harris immediately engaged her for the spring season at London's Covent Garden, where she appeared in 1888, as Lucia, to only a half-full house. However, she scored a major success at the Paris Opéra as Ophelia in Ambroise Thomas's *Hamlet* in 1889. She then sang with great success in St. Petersburg in 1891, Milan (where she enjoyed an immense triumph over a carefully planned opposition), Stockholm, Copenhagen, and N.Y., all in 1893, and Melbourne in 1902. From her first appearance at Covent Garden she sang there off and on until 1914.

Besides being one of the most brilliant stars of several seasons at the Metropolitan Opera in N.Y., where she first sang in 1893, Melba also sang with Walter Damrosch's Opera Company in 1898 and at OSCAR HAMMERSTEIN's Manhattan Opera in 1906 – 07 and 1908 – 09. She also made several transcontinental concert tours of the U.S. In 1915 she began teaching at the Albert Street Conservatory in Melbourne. In 1918 she was made a Dame Commander of the Order of the British Empire. She returned to Covent Garden for appearances in 1919 and 1923, making her farewell appearance there in 1926. Then she returned to Australia and retired from the stage.

Melba was by nature gifted with a voice of extraordinary beauty and bell-like purity. Through her art she made this fine instrument perfectly even throughout its entire compass (B♭–f³) and wonderfully flexible, so that she executed the most difficult FIORITURE (embellishment) without the least effort.

However, as an actress Melba did not rise above the conventional. For this reason, she was at her best in parts demanding brilliant COLORATURA (Gilda, Lucia, Violetta, Rosina, Lakme, etc.). On a single occasion she attempted the dramatic role of Brünnhilde in *Siegfried* (Metropolitan Opera, N.Y., 1896) and met with disaster.

Melchior, Lauritz (born Lebrecht Hommel), celebrated Danish-born American tenor; b. Copenhagen, March 20, 1890; d. Santa Monica, Calif., March 18, 1973. He studied at the Royal Opera School in Copenhagen, making his operatic debut in the baritone role of Silvio at the Royal Theater

As a measure of Melba's universal popularity, her name was attached to a delicious dessert, Peach Melba, and also to Melba Toast, patented in 1929 by Bert Weil. A motion picture based on her life was produced in 1953 starring Patrice Munsel.

PEOPLE IN MUSIC

there in 1913. Five years later, he made his tenor debut there as Tannhäuser.

In 1921 Melchior went to London to continue his training, and also studied in Berlin and Munich. In 1924 he made his Covent Garden debut in London as Siegmund, returning there regularly from 1926 to 1939. He was in Bayreuth in 1924 to study, and made his first appearance at the Festspielhaus there that year as Siegfried. He continued to make appearances there until 1931.

In 1926 Melchior made his Metropolitan Opera debut in N.Y. as Tannhäuser, and quickly established himself as one of its principal artists. With the exception of the 1927–28 season, he sang there regularly until his farewell performance as Lohengrin in 1950. In 1947 he became a naturalized U.S. citizen.

After the close of his operatic career, Melchior appeared on Broadway and in films. He also continued to give concerts. He was considered one of the greatest interpreters of RICHARD WAGNER's works of his era.

melodeon. 1. A type of REED ORGAN. Technically, the keyboard melodeon works by blowing air through the reeds. Thus, as the pressure on the bellows changes, the volume is made louder or softer. A true reed organ, on the other hand, has two sets of bellows to create a vacuum effect, sucking the air through the reeds. Thus, changing the pressure on the bellows does not make the notes louder or softer. 2. A type of button ACCORDION. A melodeon usually has one row of buttons and plays a different note on the pull or draw of the bellows.

MUSICAL INSTRUMENT

melodic. 1. In the style of a melody; progressing by single tones. 2. Vocal, singable; as a melodic interval.

melodic minor scale. A minor scale that eliminates the interval of an AUGMENTED SECOND between the sixth and seventh degrees of the HARMONIC MINOR SCALE, thereby providing smoother melodic progression. When ascending, the sixth and seventh degrees are raised (C–D–E♭–F–G–A♮–B♮–C); when descending, these notes are unaltered (C–B♭–A♭–G–F–E♭–D–C).

MUSICAL
INSTRUMENT

MUSICAL
INSTRUMENT

melodion. Friction-bar keyboard instrument, invented by J. C. Dietz in the early 19th century. Steel bars are pressed against a revolving cylinder in place of strings.

melodium. 1. American portable HARMONIUM of the mid-19th century. 2. Monophonic ELECTROPHONE, invented in Germany during World War II.

melodrama. 1. Originally, any musical drama. 2. A form of recitation with musical accompaniment, ranging from piano to full orchestra. 3. A romantic and sensational drama in which music plays a subordinate part.

In 17th-century Italy, melodrama was another name for DRAMMA PER MUSICA, that is, OPERA. The first melodrama, so named, was *Il Tito* by Antonio Cesti, produced in 1666. In the early years of opera, the terms *melodramma,* TRAGEDIA LIRICA, and DRAMMA LIRICO were used interchangeably. This practice continued through the 19th century in France, with operas often described as DRAME LYRIQUE or TRAGÉDIE LYRIQUE.

In the meantime the term *melodrama* gradually acquired the meaning of a recitation or theatrical performance in which lines were spoken with musical accompaniment, which can range from a piano to a full orchestra; many melodramas were staged. The first melodrama of this last type was probably *Ariadne auf Naxos* by Georg Anton Benda (1722–1795), produced in 1775, which greatly impressed WOLFGANG AMADEUS MOZART, who heard it three years later. Zdeněk Fibich wrote a trilogy of melodramas, *Hippodamia,* that enjoyed numerous performances in Prague. ENGELBERT HUMPERDINCK enhanced the genre with his opera *Königskinder,* produced in 1897, by indicating the inflection of the spoken voice in written notes, marking the approximate level of pitch in each syllable. ARNOLD SCHOENBERG elevated melodrama to high art in his *PIERROT LUNAIRE,* which is specifically described as a melodrama in the score. In it Schoenberg introduced SPRECHSTIMME, inflected speech-voice, midway between speaking and singing.

Parallel to these developments there emerged a more mundane and, by the same token, more popular type of melodrama. It incorporated the simultaneous use of recitation and music, as distinguished from SINGSPIEL and OPÉRA COMIQUE, in which spoken dialogue and singing alternate. ROBERT SCHUMANN and FRANZ LISZT wrote these kinds of melodramas. SERGEI PROKOFIEV in *Peter and the Wolf* and WILLIAM WALTON in *Façade* made use of this technique. The genre was particularly popular in Russia, where it became known under the more proper title *melodeclamation.*

In the 19th century, melodrama as we commonly call it today came into being. This type of melodrama usually did not include music at all. Instead, it was an overblown, popular theatrical style featuring tear-jerking stories, full of love affairs gone wrong, tragic reversals of fortune, murder, mayhem, and insanity.

Popular television programs like *Beverly Hills 90210* or *Melrose Place* are modern equivalents of melodramas. They feature steamy love affairs, twisted plot lines, heightened and often overblown emotions, and "shocking" revelations.

mélodrame (Fr.). In opera, an orchestral INTERLUDE between scenes.

melody (from Grk. *melos + aeidein,* sung music; Fr. *mélodie;* It., Lat., *melodia;* Ger. *Melodie*). 1. The progression of single tones in time, as contrasted with HARMONY, the sounding of several tones at once. 2. The leading part (usually the soprano). 3. An air or tune.

In modern usage, melody is a tonal line propelled by rhythmic beat. The main body of the melody resides in the middle register, its center of gravity. Ideally, in classical music theory, a perfect melody would feature an equal amount of notes in the upper and lower registers, balanced around its center. Similarly, descending and ascending passages would be balanced. This does not mean, of course, that the melody must, like the king of France in the nursery rhyme, march up the hill with 40,000 men and then come back down again. Rhythmic values must also be taken into consideration, so that in an ideal melody a long high note would be counterbalanced by a long low note, or by a succession of short low notes.

Most memorable melodies move within the range of an OCTAVE between two DOMINANTS (FIFTHS) in a MAJOR KEY, with the important points on the TONIC (ROOT), the MEDIANT (MAJOR THIRD), and the upper dominant. These key notes within the octave are derived from the natural HAR-MONIC SERIES. Some famous melodies featuring these notes include:

GEORGE M. COHAN's World War I song *Over There*

The first and last movements of WOLFGANG AMADEUS MOZART's *Eine kleine Nachtmusik*

The finale of FRANZ JOSEPH HAYDN's *Military Symphony* (no. 100)

By adding the SUPERTONIC (second) and SUBDOMINANT (fourth), you get a major PENTACHORD, with the dominant duplicated below the tonic. The number of melodies so constructed number in the thousands, if not millions. All are in a major key, and many of them begin with an ascending leap from the dominant to the tonic. Famous examples are:

LA MARSEILLAISE

The last movement of LUDWIG VAN BEETHOVEN's Violin Concerto

The overture to GIOACCHINO ROSSINI's *William Tell*

The *"Waltz of the Flowers"* from PIOTR ILYICH TCHAI-KOVSKY's *Nutcracker* Suite

The *Wedding March* from RICHARD WAGNER's *Lohengrin*

This type of melody is not as numerous in minor keys as in major, but they still comprise a respectable inventory. Examples are the theme of the second movement of Tchaikovsky's violin concerto and that of *Moldau* from BEDŘICH SMETANA's orchestral suite *MÁ VLAST*.

While most melodies are contained within the octave from the dominant to the dominant, continuous melodic lines extending over an octave are not rare. A remarkable example is the auxiliary theme in the last movement of Beethoven's *Choral Symphony,* which begins on the tonic, rises to the sixth in the octave above, and ends on the tonic in that higher octave, with all melodic notes of equal rhythmic value.

But while such an enlarged range is acceptable for instrumental passages, it becomes almost impossible for the human voice. The range of *THE STAR-SPANGLED BANNER* is an octave and a fifth, which makes it difficult for most to sing. Futile attempts have been made to arrange it so that the second half could be transposed to a lower key.

The organized atonal systems, particularly the dodecaphonic (12-tone) techniques, follow their own rules. There are no major/minor triads in an atonal melody, and therefore no link with the harmonic series. But even in dodecaphonic melodies, the center of gravity is present as the arithmetical mean of high and low notes.

It should also be noted that the principles underlying the melodic structure of much non-Western music differ widely from those of Western MELOS. There are few harmonic implications in much of this music. The scales themselves are formed from sets of intervals not necessarily contained within an octave. The study of non-Western melodies, therefore, must take place within a special discipline in ethnomusicology, acoustics, or theory.

melograph. Mechanical devices for recording music played on a piano.

melopée, melopoeia (Grk. *melos* + *poein,* create song). An ancient Greek term denoting all types of musical composition and performance.

In Plato's *Symposion,* melopeia is described as the art of musical forms, while Aristotle defines it as the science of melody. The Aristotelian meaning was revived in the RENAISSANCE in the theories of the HARMONY OF THE SPHERES. A rather circular definition of the term is given by Marin Mersenne: "Melopoeia nil aliud est quam ars melodiae" (Melopeia is nothing but the art of melody).

melos (Grk., song). The name bestowed by RICHARD WAGNER on the style of RECITATIVE employed in his later MUSIC DRAMAS.

membi. Indigenous vertical FLUTE found in Paraguay and southern Brazil.

RICHARD WAGNER introduced the notion of *unendliche Melodie* (endless melody), a romantically exaggerated description of a melody that naturally flows into the beginning of the next motive with an avoidance of perfect cadences, analogous to a circle or any other closed curve.

mā′lŏhs

MUSICAL INSTRUMENT

MUSICAL INSTRUMENT

PEOPLE IN MUSIC

membranophones. A class of instruments (drums) whose playing area is made of stretched animal skin (membranes). At present, many of these instruments (especially in the Western classical orchestra) use plastic heads instead of skin.

Memphis Blues, The. Song by W. C. HANDY, 1912, which launched the BLUES as a national genre.

Handy originally wrote the tune as a campaign song for a candidate for mayor of Memphis, Tennessee. He published the song in 1912 as a piano solo, and the lyrics were added in 1913. *The Memphis Blues* is considered the first published blues, but its most important effect was to combine popular music and country blues (which predates the 20th century) to invent the more sophisticated urban blues.

Handy lived long enough to enjoy its merited fame. In 1941 a movie musical, *The Birth of the Blues,* added to his glory, and after his death a postage stamp with his picture was issued by the U.S. Post Office.

Men and Mountains. Orchestral suite by CARL RUGGLES, 1924, first performed in N.Y. Its title was inspired by William Blake's line "Great things are done when men and mountains meet." The score is set in DISSONANT COUNTERPOINT, but it maintains a curiously lyric musical feeling.

Mendelssohn (-Bartholdy), (Jacob Ludwig) **Felix,** famous German composer, pianist, and conductor; b. Hamburg, Feb. 3, 1809; d. Leipzig, Nov. 4, 1847. He was a grandson of the philosopher Moses Mendelssohn and the son of the banker Abraham Mendelssohn. His mother was Lea Salomon. The family was Jewish, but upon its settlement in Berlin the father decided to become a Protestant and added Bartholdy to his surname.

Mendelssohn received his first piano lessons from his mother. Subsequently he studied piano with Ludwig Berger and violin with Carl Wilhelm Henning and Eduard Rietz. He also had regular lessons in foreign languages and in painting (he showed considerable talent in drawing with pastels), as well as piano lessons with Marie Bigot in Paris, where he went with his father for a brief stay in 1816.

His most important teacher in his early youth was Carl Friedrich Zelter, a well-known German composer in his own right, who recognized the size of Mendelssohn's talent. Zelter arranged for Mendelssohn to become a member of the Singakademie in Berlin

in 1819 as an alto singer. In that year, Mendelssohn's 19th Psalm was performed by the Akademie. In 1821 Zelter took him to Weimar and introduced him to Goethe, who took considerable interest in the boy after hearing him play. In 1825 Mendelssohn's father took him again to Paris to consult the Italian composer/teacher LUIGI CHERUBINI on Mendelssohn's prospects in music. However, he returned to Berlin, where he had better opportunities for development.

Mendelssohn was a precocious musician, both in performing and in composition. What is perhaps without parallel in music history is the extraordinary perfection of his works written during adolescence. He played in public for the first time at the age of nine in Berlin in 1818, performing the piano part of a trio by Joseph Wölffl. He wrote a remarkable octet at the age of 16, and at 17 composed the overture for the incidental music to Shakespeare's *A MIDSUMMER NIGHT'S DREAM*, showing a mastery of form equal to that of the remaining numbers of the work, which were composed 15 years later.

Mendelssohn proved his great musicianship when he conducted JOHANN SEBASTIAN BACH'S *ST. MATTHEW PASSION* in the Berlin Singakademie in 1829, an event that inspired the revival of Bach's vocal music. In that spring Mendelssohn made his first journey to England, where he conducted his Symphony No. 1 in C Minor (seated, in the fashion of the

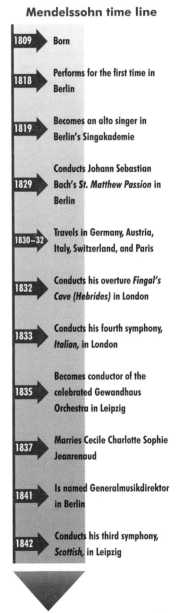

Mendelssohn time line

1809	Born
1818	Performs for the first time in Berlin
1819	Becomes an alto singer in Berlin's Singakademie
1829	Conducts Johann Sebastian Bach's *St. Matthew Passion* in Berlin
1830–32	Travels in Germany, Austria, Italy, Switzerland, and Paris
1832	Conducts his overture *Fingal's Cave (Hebrides)* in London
1833	Conducts his fourth symphony, *Italian,* in London
1835	Becomes conductor of the celebrated Gewandhaus Orchestra in Leipzig
1837	Marries Cecile Charlotte Sophie Jeanrenaud
1841	Is named Generalmusikdirektor in Berlin
1842	Conducts his third symphony, *Scottish,* in Leipzig

1843	The famous Leipzig Conservatory, organized by Mendelssohn, officially opens in April
1844	Makes his eighth visit to London, conducting the Philharmonic Concerts
1846	Conducting the first performance of his oratorio *Elijah* in Birmingham
1847	Shortly after his tenth and final visit to England, and the death of his favorite sister, Fanny Mendelssohn Hensel, Mendelssohn dies

Mendelssohn became a favorite of the English public, numbering Queen Victoria among his most fervent admirers. Altogether he made 10 trips to England as a pianist, conductor, and composer.

It was in England that the *Wedding March* from Mendelssohn's music to A MID-SUMMER NIGHT'S DREAM began to be used to accompany bridal processions. It became particularly fashionable when it was played at the wedding of the Princess Royal in 1858.

time, at the keyboard). He later performed in London the solo part in LUDWIG VAN BEETHOVEN's *Emperor* Concerto. He then traveled through Scotland, where he found inspiration for the composition of his overture *Fingal's Cave (Hebrides),* which he conducted for the first time during his second visit to London in 1832. Ten days later he played in London the solo part of his G minor Concerto and his *Capriccio brillante.*

From 1830 to 1832 Mendelssohn traveled in Germany, Austria, Italy, Switzerland, and Paris. In May 1833 he led the Lower-Rhine Music Festival in Düsseldorf, and in June 1835 he conducted at Cologne. He was still a very young man when, in 1835, he was offered the conductorship of the celebrated Gewandhaus Orchestra in Leipzig. He engaged the violin virtuoso Ferdinand David (1810–73) as concertmaster of the orchestra, which soon became the most prestigious symphonic organization in Germany.

In 1837 Mendelssohn married Cecile Charlotte Sophie Jeanrenaud of Frankfurt, the daughter of a French Protestant clergyman. Five children (Carl, Marie, Paul, Felix, and Elisabeth) were born to them, and their marriage was exceptionally happy.

At the invitation of King Friedrich Wilhelm IV, Mendelssohn went in 1841 to Berlin to take charge of the music of the court and in the cathedral. He received the title of Royal Generalmusikdirektor, but residence in Berlin was not required. Returning to Leipzig in 1842, he organized the famous Conservatory. Its splendid faculty comprised, besides Mendelssohn (who taught piano, ensemble playing, and later composition), ROBERT SCHUMANN (who taught piano and composition), Moritz Hauptmann (who taught music theory), Johann Nepomuk David (who taught violin), and Louis Plaidy and Ernst Ferdinand Wenzel (who taught piano). The Conservatory was officially opened in April 1843.

In the summer of 1844 Mendelssohn conducted the Philharmonic Concerts in London, his eighth visit to England. During his ninth visit he conducted the first performance of his oratorio *Elijah* in Birmingham in 1846. He made his tenth and last visit to England in the spring of 1847, a profoundly painful period of his life, for his favorite sister, Fanny Mendelssohn Hensel, died in May 1847. Mendelssohn's own health began almost immediately to deteriorate, and he died at the age of 38.

The exact cause of Mendelssohn's early death was not determined. He suffered from severe migraines and chills before he died, but no evidence could be produced by the resident physicians for either a stroke or heart failure. The effect of Fanny's death on her brother has been the subject of much armchair speculation.

The news of Mendelssohn's death produced a profound shock in the world of music, not only in Germany and England, where he was personally known and beloved, but in distant America and Russia as well. Mendelssohn societies were formed all over the world, including America, where the Mendelssohn Quintette Club was founded in 1849. A Mendelssohn Scholarship was established in England in 1856, its first recipient being Arthur Sullivan.

Of all musicians known to history, Mendelssohn possessed the instinct of music in its purest form. Not even WOLFGANG AMADEUS MOZART had his genius developed to a perfection found in Mendelssohn's earliest works. A number of his string symphonies, written during his adolescent years, later came to light, revealing an extraordinary mastery of musical technique. This is not to say that the quality of Mendelssohn's music is comparable to Mozart's. Rather, his art was an example of perfection that appears to be attained without gradual learning.

Mendelssohn's music personified his romantic spirit. There were no tempestuous outbursts of drama or tragedy in his symphonies, chamber music, piano compositions, or songs. His works could serve as a manual of proper composition of his time. His melodies were born on the wings of song, his COUNTERPOINT was never obtrusive, and his orchestration was euphonious. The very perfection of Mendelssohn's musical canon was the cause of the gradual decline of his popularity among musicians of the succeeding decades.

Mendelssohn did not create disciples of his imitators. But in performance by orchestras and instrumentalists his music is ever alive. His symphonies, notably the *Scottish,* op.56 (1830–42; Leipzig, March 3, 1842, composer conducting) and *Italian,* op.90 (London, May 13, 1833, composer conducting), maintain their smiling flow, and his

Songs Without Words are favorites of amateur and professional pianists alike. The popularity of his Violin Concerto remains undiminished among students and virtuosos. His trios and other chamber music are radiant in their communal cohesion.

Prolific throughout his career, Mendelssohn composed 13 string symphonies, five orchestral symphonies, and many concertos, including ones for violin, piano, violin and piano, and two pianos. He also composed other orchestral works including the well-known overture for Shakespeare's *A MIDSUMMER NIGHT'S DREAM,* op.21 (1826–27) and *Die Hebriden or Fingals Hohle* (The Hebrides or Fingal's Cave), overture, op.26 (1830).

Mendelssohn also composed numerous chamber pieces in various arrangements as well as piano works, including SONATAS, variations, preludes and FUGUES, characteristic pieces—including the famous *Lieder ohne Worte* (Songs Without Words), in eight books—and organ music.

Among Mendelssohn's ORATORIOS are *St. Paul,* op.36 (1834–36), and *Elijah,* op.70 (1846). His other sacred music includes psalms, hymns, CANTATAS, MOTETS, MASS movements, and ANTHEMS. He also composed secular cantatas and choral songs, and many individual songs, several of which were composed by his sister Fanny but published under his name.

Mengelberg, (Josef) **Willem,** celebrated Dutch conductor; b. Utrecht, March 28, 1871; d. Chur, Switzerland, March 21, 1951. Mengelberg studied at the Utrecht and Cologne conservatories. He was appointed municipal music director in Lucerne in 1891. His work there attracted so much attention that in 1895 he was placed at the head of the Concertgebouw Orchestra in Amsterdam, holding this post for 50 years (resigning in 1945), a record tenure for any conductor. During his directorship, he elevated that orchestra to a lofty position.

In addition to his primary post, Mengelberg was director of the Museumgesellschaft concerts in Frankfurt from 1908 to 1921. He became conductor of the Toonkunst choral society in Amsterdam in 1898. He appeared frequently as guest conductor in all the European countries, including

PEOPLE IN MUSIC

England, where he was an annual visitor from 1913 until World War II.

Mengelberg first appeared with the N.Y. Philharmonic in 1905, then conducted it regularly from 1922 to 1930, with ARTURO TOSCANINI serving as associate conductor in 1929–30. In 1928 he received the degree of Mus.Doc. at Columbia University (honoris causa), and in 1933 he was appointed professor of music at Utrecht University. During the occupation of the Netherlands by the Germans, Mengelberg openly expressed his sympathies with the Nazi cause, thereby losing the high respect and admiration that his compatriots had felt for him. After the country's liberation (1945), he was barred from professional activities there, the ban to be continued until 1951, but he died in that year in exile in Switzerland.

Mengelberg was an outstanding representative of the RO-MANTIC tradition. His performances of LUDWIG VAN BEE-THOVEN's symphonies were notable for their dramatic sweep and power. He was a great champion of many major composers of his era, including GUSTAV MAHLER and RICHARD STRAUSS, both of whom appeared as guest conductors of the Concertgebouw Orchestra and became Mengelberg's friends. Mahler dedicated his Fifth and Eighth Symphonies to Mengelberg and the Concertgebouw Orchestra, as did Strauss his *Ein Heldenleben*. Mengelberg was the first to lead a major cycle of Mahler's works, in Amsterdam in 1920.

His nephew Karel (Willem Joseph) Mengelberg (b. Utrecht, July 18, 1902; d. Amsterdam, July 11, 1984) was a composer and conductor. Another nephew, Kurt Rudolf Mengelberg (b. Krefeld, Feb. 1, 1892; d. Beausoleil, near Monte Carlo, Oct. 13, 1959), was a musicologist and composer. A great-nephew, Misha Mengelberg (b. Kiev, June 5, 1935), is a composer.

Mennin (born Mennini), **Peter,** American composer and music educator; b. Erie, Pa., May 17, 1923; d. N.Y., June 17, 1983. Mennin's family went to the U.S. from Italy. His early environment was filled with music, mostly from phonograph recordings.

Mennin studied piano privately. In 1940 he enrolled in the Oberlin Conservatory in Ohio, where he took courses in

PEOPLE IN MUSIC

harmony. He quickly learned the basics of composition, and at the age of 18 he wrote a symphony and a string quartet. In 1942 he enlisted in the U.S. Army Air Force. After his discharge in 1943, he resumed his studies at the Eastman School of Music in Rochester, N.Y.

Mennin worked productively, writing another symphony in 1944. A year later, a movement from it, *Symphonic Allegro,* was performed by the N.Y. Philharmonic, with LEONARD BERNSTEIN conducting. Mennin's Third Symphony was performed by Walter Hendl with the N.Y. Philharmonic in 1947. Mennin progressed academically as well, obtaining his Ph.D. from the Eastman School of Music in 1947. He received two Guggenheim fellowships (1948, 1956).

From 1947 to 1958 Mennin taught composition at the Juilliard School of Music in N.Y. In 1958 he assumed the post of director of the Peabody Conservatory in Baltimore. In 1962 he received his most prestigious appointment, that of president of the Juilliard School of Music, serving in that capacity until his death.

Despite his academic work, Mennin continued to compose prolifically. He diversified his symphonies by adding descriptive titles. Thus his Fourth Symphony (1949), scored for chorus and orchestra, was subtitled *The Cycle,* while his Seventh Symphony (1964) was called *Variation* Symphony. The four movements of his Eighth Symphony (1974) bore biblical titles. Increasingly also, he began attaching descriptive titles to other works. His Concertato for orchestra was named *Moby Dick* (1952), followed by a *Canto* for orchestra (1963), a *Cantata de Virtute* (1969), *Reflections of Emily,* to texts by Emily Dickinson (1976), and *Voices* (1976).

Mennin's musical mind was directed toward pure structural forms. His music is characterized by an integrity of purpose and clear development of thematic materials, despite the bold use of DISSONANT harmonies in CONTRAPUNTAL passages.

His brother Louis (Alfred) Mennini (b. Erie, Penn., Nov. 18, 1920) is a composer and educator.

PEOPLE IN MUSIC

Menotti, Gian Carlo, prolific Italian composer and librettist; b. Cadegliano, July 7, 1911. Menotti was the sixth of 10 children. He learned the rudiments of music from his

Gian Carlo Menotti (pointing) *on a movie set, 1950. (UPI/ Corbis-Bettmann)*

mother and began to compose as a child, making his first attempt at an opera, *The Death of Pierrot,* at the age of 10.

From 1924 to 1927 Menotti studied at the Milan Conservatory, then went to the U.S. He entered the Curtis Institute of Music in Philadelphia, where he studied until 1933. He subsequently taught composition there, traveling often to Europe. He made his home in Mt. Kisco, N.Y. Although Menotti associated himself with the cause of American music and spent much of his time in the U.S., he retained his Italian citizenship.

Menotti is the first composer to create American opera possessing such an appeal to audiences that it has become a part of the permanent repertoire. Inheriting the natural Italian gift for operatic drama and an expressive singing line, he adapted these qualities to the requirements of the American stage and to the changing fashions of the period. His serious operas have a strong dramatic content in the realistic style stemming from the Italian VERISMO. He wrote his own librettos, marked by an extraordinary flair for drama and for the communicative power of English. With this is combined a fine, though subdued, sense of musical humor.

Menotti used modern techniques—such as introducing dissonant harmonies to underscore the final dramatic moments of a work—when appropriate. But he was also willing to draw on the successful formulas developed by GIU-

SEPPE VERDI and GIACOMO PUCCINI. The influence of MODEST MUSSORGSKY's realistic language is also in evidence, particularly in recitative.

Menotti's first successful stage work was *Amelia Goes to the Ball,* an OPERA BUFFA in one act (originally to an Italian libretto by the composer, as *Amelia al ballo*), staged at the Academy of Music, Philadelphia, in 1937. This was followed by another comic opera, *The Old Maid and the Thief,* commissioned by NBC, first performed on the radio in 1939, then two years later on the stage, by the Philadelphia Opera Company.

Menotti's next operatic work was *The Island God,* produced by the Metropolitan Opera, N.Y. in 1942, with indifferent success. But with the production there of *THE MEDIUM* in 1946, Menotti established himself as the foremost composer-librettist of modern opera. The imaginative libretto, dealing with a fraudulent spiritualist who falls victim to her own practices, suited Menotti's musical talent to perfection. This opera had a long and successful run in N.Y., an unprecedented occurrence in the history of the American lyric theater.

A short humorous opera, *The Telephone,* was first produced by the N.Y. Ballet Society in 1947, on the same bill with *The Medium.* These two contrasting works were subsequently staged all over the U.S. and in Europe, often on the same evening. Menotti then produced *The Consul* in 1950, his best tragic work. *The Consul* exceeded Menotti's previous operas in popular success. It had a long run in N.Y. and received the Pulitzer Prize in music.

Menotti's next opera was *The Saint of Bleecker Street,* set in a N.Y. locale. It won the Drama Critics' Circle Award for the best musical play of 1954 and the Pulitzer Prize in music for 1955. A MADRIGAL ballet, *The Unicorn, the Gorgon and the Manticore,* commissioned by the Elizabeth Sprague Coolidge Foundation, was first presented at the Library of Congress, Washington, D.C., in 1956. His opera *Maria Golovin,* was written in 1958 expressly for that year's International Exposition in Brussels.

In 1958 Menotti organized the Festival of Two Worlds in Spoleto, Italy, staging old and new works. In 1977 he in-

On Christmas Eve, 1951, NBC presented Menotti's television opera AMAHL AND THE NIGHT VISITORS, a Christmas story of undeniable poetry and appeal that became an annual television production every Christmas in subsequent years.

augurated an American counterpart of the festival in Charleston, South Carolina. In many of the festival productions, Menotti acted also as stage director. In the meantime he continued to compose. He prolifically wrote operas through the '60s, '70s, and '80s, including *The Boy Who Grew Too Fast* (1982), *The Wedding* (1988), and *Singing Child* (1993).

Menotti's last years were plagued with disputes over his role as an artistic director. In 1991 a major dispute arose between the composer and the director of the Spoleto Festival USA in Charleston, but ultimately Menotti retained control. However, in 1993 he announced that he was taking the festival away from Charleston, but the city's mayor intervened and Menotti lost control of his festival. That same year he was named artistic director of the Rome Opera, but again conflicts over artistic policy between the composer and the superintendent led to Menotti's dismissal in 1994.

Among Menotti's nonoperatic works are the ballets *Sebastian* (1944) and *Errand into the Maze* (1947); two Piano Concertos (No. 1, 1945; No. 2, 1982); *Apocalypse,* symphonic poem (1951); Violin Concerto (1952, Efrem Zimbalist soloist); *Triple Concerto à Tre,* in three movements (1970); *Landscapes and Remembrances,* cantata to his own autobiographical words (1976); First Symphony, *The Halcyon* (1976); Double Bass Concerto (1983); and *For the Death of Orpheus* for tenor, chorus, and orchestra (1990).

Menotti is also the author of librettos for SAMUEL BARBER's operas *Vanessa* (1958), *A Hand of Bridge* (1959), and the revised *Antony and Cleopatra* (1975). He also wrote a play without music, *The Leper* (1970).

mensural notation, mensuration. A type of rhythmic notation and system, in use from the 13th to the 17th centuries. It was originally developed by Franco of Cologne c.1250, but various versions and variations developed over the centuries.

This system used LIGATURES, a type of musical symbol derived from the medieval NEUMES that combined several notes into one sign. The time value given to each ligature was dependent on how they were grouped together.

PEOPLE IN MUSIC

Yehudi Menuhin performing as a child prodigy, c. 1927. (Corbis-Bettmann) ▶

Menuhin, (Sir) Yehudi, celebrated American violinist; b. N.Y., April 22, 1916; d. Berlin, March 12, 1999. Menuhin was born of Russian-Jewish parents (the family surname was originally Mnuhin). As a child, he was taken to San Francisco, where he began to study violin. In 1923 he began taking lessons with Louis Persinger, who was then concertmaster of the San Francisco Symphony Orchestra. In 1924, at the age of seven, Menuhin made his public debut in Oakland playing Charles Bériot's *Scène de ballet.* On Jan. 17, 1926, when he was nine, he played a recital in N.Y. A year later, he made his European debut in Paris, where he also began to study with the well-known Romanian violinist GEORGES ENESCU, who became his most influential teacher and who guided his future career.

Returning to the U.S. in 1927, Menuhin played LUDWIG VAN BEETHOVEN's Violin Concerto in D with the N.Y. Symphony Orchestra, winning unanimous acclaim from the public and the press. He subsequently made tours throughout the U.S. and Europe. In 1929 he appeared with Bruno Walter and the Berlin Philharmonic, playing concertos by JOHANN SEBASTIAN BACH, Beethoven, and JOHANNES BRAHMS on the same program. Later that year, he made his London debut. He continued to pursue his studies with Enescu, and also received additional instruction from Adolf Busch. In 1935 Menuhin completed his first world tour, giving concerts in 73 cities in 13 countries, including Australia.

Menuhin also became active in organizing music festivals. In 1956 he established the Gstaad Festival in Switzerland. In 1959 he made his home in London and founded the Bath Festival, which he directed until 1968. He also founded the Windsor Festival and directed it from 1969 to 1972. He devoted much time to conducting and musical education. In 1963 he founded his own boarding school for musically gifted children at Stoke d'Abernon, Surrey.

In 1971 Menuhin succeeded John Barbirolli as president of Trinity College of Music in London. In 1976 he was awarded an honorary doctorate by the Sorbonne of Paris, the first musician to be so honored. In September 1981 he celebrated the 50th anniversary of his first appearance in Leipzig by performing the Brahms Concerto with KURT MASUR and the Gewandhaus Orchestra. In 1985 he was granted honorary British citizenship, thereby formally becoming Sir Yehudi. In 1986 President François Mitterand made him a Grand Officer of France's Legion of Honor. In 1987 he was made a member of the Order of Merit. He was created a life peer as Lord Menuhin of Stoke d'Abernon in 1993. Menuhin died at the age of 82 in 1999.

Apart from Menuhin's musical activities, he became deeply interested in art, politics, and above all, education and philosophy. He embraced the cause of Asian religions and practiced yoga. In 1963 he appeared on the BBC in London in a discussion entitled *Yehudi Menuhin and His Guru*. Menuhin published a collection of essays under the title *Theme and Variations* (London, 1972), an autobiography, *Unfinished Journey* (N.Y., 1977), with Curtis W. Davis, *The Music of Man* (London, 1980), based on the television series of the same title, and *Life Class* (London, 1986).

Mephisto Waltz. Four piano pieces by FRANZ LISZT, published individually, the first of which, from 1859, is the most famous. Its initial cumulative chord, formed by a series of PERFECT FIFTHS separated by a MINOR SIXTH, was a great innovation at the time. Liszt was berated by stern academic critics for taking such harmonic liberties.

Liszt's Mephisto is based on a demonic spirit from *Faust* by the German poet Lenau, not the more familiar text by

Goethe. Originally Liszt wrote his first *Mephisto Waltz* for orchestra as the second movement, entitled *Der Tanz in der Dorfschenke* (The Dance in the Village Tavern), to his score *Two Episodes from Lenau's "Faust."* The second *Mephisto Waltz* was written in 1881, originally for orchestra and later transcribed for piano. The third *Waltz* was a piano piece Liszt wrote in 1883. The fourth, for piano written in 1885, was not published until many years after his death.

Mer, La. Symphonic SUITE by CLAUDE DEBUSSY, 1905, first performed in Paris. The three sketches of this sea poem are impressions in instrumental colors of three aspects or events: *De l'aube à midi sur la mer* (From the Dawn to Noon on the Sea), *Jeux de vagues* (Play of the Waves), and *Dialogue du vent et de la mer* (Dialogue of the Wind and the Sea). The character of the music seems to justify the label of *impressionism* attached to *La Mer,* although Debussy himself downplayed this cliché borrowed from painting.

Traditionally minded critics damned the work as formless. One critic cleverly suggested that Debussy retitle it *Le mal de mer* (seasickness). When ERIK SATIE was asked which movement of *La Mer* he liked best, he said the first, *From Dawn to Noon,* and more specifically, "about a quarter of eleven."

Although *La Mer* is a song of the sea, Debussy was not too fond of sea travels. He traveled by boat as little as possible, suffering from seasickness the few times he went to England.

PEOPLE IN MUSIC

Mercer, Johnny (John Herndon), American lyricist and composer of popular music; b. Savannah, Ga., Nov. 18, 1909; d. Los Angeles, June 25, 1976. As a youth, Mercer went to N.Y., where he attracted the attention of jazz band leader Paul Whiteman. He subsequently wrote songs for him, as well as for BENNY GOODMAN and Bob Crosby.

Mercer's first success as a lyric writer was *Lazybones,* with music by HOAGY CARMICHAEL. Other notable hits of the '30s included *I'm an Old Cowhand, Hooray for Hollywood,* and *Jeepers Creepers.* Seeing that he was making most of his living by selling to the movies, Mercer relocated to the West Coast in 1940.

Out west, Mercer immediately found success performing his songs on radio and became involved in music publishing. In 1942 he co-founded Capitol Records as an outlet for his music. The label had immediate success with his songs *Ac-Cent-Tchu-Ate the Positive, G. I. Jive,* and *Glow Worm.*

Mercer continued to score hits through the '50s. He scored the Broadway revue *Top Banana,* a showcase for the comedian Phil Silvers, in 1951. Meanwhile, he continued to contribute individual songs and full scores to Hollywood films, most notably the wonderful lyrics for 1954's *Seven Brides for Seven Brothers.*

In 1961 Mercer scored one of his greatest career successes with the lyrics for HENRY MANCINI's *Moon River,* followed a year later by the equally successful theme from *The Days of Wine and Roses.* His career slowed thereafter, although he continued to work. In 1974 he did his last major work, contributing the lyrics for the musical *The Good Companions* scored by André Previn, which premiered in London. Two years later, Mercer died.

Mercer, Mabel, English-born American singer; b. Burton upon Trent, Staffordshire, Feb. 3, 1900; d. Pittsfield, Mass., April 20, 1984. Mercer's father, an African-American, died before she was born. Her mother was a white British vaudeville singer. She became a stage performer in her early adolescence, appearing as a dancer in a music hall in London. After World War I, Mercer went to Paris, where she made a success as a nightclub singer.

In 1938 Mercer went to the U.S. and settled in N.Y. She con-

PEOPLE IN MUSIC

◀

Mabel Mercer receiving an ASCAP award, 1981. (UPI/ Corbis-Bettmann)

tinued her career as a nightclub singer but also gave regular recitals of popular songs. In 1983 she received the Medal of Freedom from President Ronald Reagan. She was briefly married to jazz musician Kelsey Pharr.

Mercury Symphony. Symphony No. 43 in E Flat Major by FRANZ JOSEPH HAYDN, composed in 1772. The reason for this name, and who decided to give it to this work, remains unknown. It is clear, however, that the Mercury referred to here is the winged messenger of the gods, not the smallest planet of the solar system or the liquid metal.

merengue, meringue. Characteristic Afro-Cubanesque song dance of Venezuela, Haiti, and the Dominican Republic. It uses four-line stanzas and refrain verse forms. Responsorial singing, POLYRHYTHMS, and $\frac{5}{8}$ effects are layered over the basic $\frac{2}{4}$ beat.

PEOPLE IN MUSIC

Merman, Ethel (born Ethel Agnes Zimmerman), popular American singer and Broadway star; b. N.Y., Jan. 16, 1908; d. there, Feb. 14, 1984. Merman was of German-Scottish extraction. She took a commercial course in high school and held several jobs as a secretary while trying to satisfy her desire to be a singing actress. She never took vocal lessons but developed her booming powerful voice naturally.

Merman obtained some bookings at Long Island night spots and soon attracted the attention of Broadway managers. She auditioned for GEORGE GERSHWIN, who engaged her to sing in his musical *Girl Crazy* in 1930. She brought the house down with the hit song *I GOT RHYTHM,* holding a high C for 16 bars in the coda while the orchestra played the melodic line.

Merman's distinct personality and talents as a singer appealed to many composers, who created roles to suit her. Her first association with COLE PORTER was *ANYTHING GOES* (1934), the first of five musicals he wrote for her; she also appeared in the film version two years later. Merman would continue to appear in both movies and on the Broadway stage throughout her career.

Merman's longest-running and most famous role was in IRVING BERLIN'S *ANNIE GET YOUR GUN* from 1946, another part created for her. Its success led to a second collaboration with Berlin, CALL ME MADAM (1950). Merman's last great original role came in 1959 with Jule Styne's *Gypsy*. The brash role of the stage mother of Gypsy Rose Lee perfectly suited Merman's character.

In the '50s and '60s, Merman appeared regularly on television variety programs and recorded several individual hits as well as cast albums and soundtracks. She also developed her skills as a comic actress with parts in the comedic films *It's a Mad Mad Mad Mad Mad World* from 1963 and the movie satire *Airplane!* in 1980. A brief revival of *Annie Get Your Gun* with Merman was staged in 1966 on Broadway.

Merman's private life was tempestuous. She married and divorced four times, and her daughter (from the second marriage) committed suicide. In 1983 she underwent surgery to remove a brain tumor; she died soon after in early 1984. When the news of her death was announced, Broadway theaters observed a minute of silence to honor her memory.

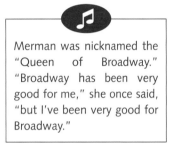

Merman was nicknamed the "Queen of Broadway." "Broadway has been very good for me," she once said, "but I've been very good for Broadway."

Merry Mount. Opera by HOWARD HANSON, 1934, first produced in N.Y., based on Hawthorne's *The Maypole of Merry Mount*. The action takes place in New England in 1625, where Satan is a living presence in the troubled minds of the inhabitants. A Puritan cleric is induced by a woman of free morals to take part in pagan games on Merry Mount. When he becomes horrified by these evil forces, he enters a church set aflame by Indians and perishes in the inferno, together with his seductress.

Merry Widow, The (*Die lüstige Witwe*). OPERETTA by FRANZ LEHÁR, 1905, first produced in Vienna. A rich Austrian widow is the object of courtship on the part of a Slavic fortune seeker, who finally wins her love in Paris. *The Merry Widow* is probably the most popular Viennese operetta of the century.

Lehár inserted a song praising Maxim's restaurant in Paris as a token of gratitude to its chef who allowed him to have free meals there during his days as a starving artist.

Merry Wives of Windsor, The. Opera by OTTO NICOLAI, 1849, first produced in Berlin. The libretto follows Shakespeare faithfully, with Falstaff remaining the principal, pathetically comic character. The opera became tremendously popular in Germany, and its sprightly overture remains a standard piece at summer concerts.

Messe de requiem. Sacred work by GABRIEL FAURÉ, 1887, one of the most beautiful choral works. Its peculiarity is the omission of the DIES IRAE. Fauré preferred to express faith, charity, and hope in his music rather than the vengeful drama of Judgment Day.

Messiaen, Olivier (Eugène Prosper Charles), French composer and teacher; b. Avignon, Dec. 10, 1908. A son of an intellectual family (his father was a translator of English literature; his mother, Cécile Sauvage, a poet), Messiaen absorbed the atmosphere of culture and art as a child. He learned to play piano, and at the age of eight he composed a song, *La Dame de Shalott,* to a poem by Tennyson. At 11 he entered the Paris Conservatory, where he specialized in organ, improvisation, and composition. He carried first prizes in all.

After graduation in 1930, Messiaen became the organist at Trinity Church in Paris. He taught at the École Normale de Musique and at the Schola Cantorum from 1936 to 1939. He also organized with other young composers the group La Jeune France (The Youth of France), with the aim of promoting modern French music.

Messiaen was in the French army at the outbreak of World War II in 1939. He was taken prisoner and spent two

PEOPLE IN MUSIC

Messiaen's mother wrote a book of poems about her yet-to-be-born son, giving his life special meaning to her.

Olivier Messiaen at a rehearsal, 1967. (Hulton-Deutsch Collection/Corbis) ▶

years in a German prison camp in Görlitz, Silesia. He composed there his *Quatuor pour la fin du temps*. He was repatriated in 1941 and resumed his post as organist at Trinity Church in Paris. Beginning in 1948, he was professor of harmony and analysis at the Paris Conservatory. He also taught at the Berkshire Music Center in Tanglewood, Massachusetts in the summer of 1948, and in Darmstadt from 1950 to 1953.

Young composers seeking instruction in new music became his eager pupils, among them PIERRE BOULEZ, KARLHEINZ STOCKHAUSEN, and IANNIS XENAKIS. He received numerous honors. He was made a Grand Officier of the Legion of Honor, was elected a member of the Institute de France, the Bavarian Academy of the Fine Arts, the Accademia di Santa Cecilia in Rome, the American Academy of Arts and Letters, and other organizations. He married the pianist Yvonne Loriod in 1961.

Messiaen was one of the most original of modern composers. In his music he made use of a wide range of styles, from GREGORIAN CHANT to Oriental rhythms (he called himself a "rhythmic mathematician"). A mystic by nature and Roman Catholic by religion, he sought a relationship between progressions of musical sounds and religious concepts. Ever in quest of new musical resources, he employed in his scores the early electronic musical instrument the ONDES MARTENOT and exotic percussion instruments. His large-scale and ambitious orchestral work *Turangalîla-Symphonie* used many of these unusual instruments.

In 1983 Messiaen's only opera, *St. François d'Assise,* premiered, to international acclaim, at the Paris Opéra. In addition to this masterpiece, Messiaen's oeuvre includes orchestral, chamber, and vocal works, and compositions for organ. Messiaen discussed his theories of rhythm and mode in *Technique de mon langage musical* (Technique of my musical language; two volumes, 1944). He also published individual articles on the music of bird calls and other subjects.

Messiah. Religious ORATORIO by GEORGE FRIDERIC HANDEL, 1742. He wrote this work in an astonishingly brief three and a half weeks, when he was living in Dublin, where it was first performed, with Handel himself conducting at the organ.

The municipal council of Parowan, Utah, resolved to name a local mountain Mt. Messiaen in 1978. This is where Messiaen wrote his work *Des canyons aux étoiles,* glorifying the natural beauties of the state of Utah.

A Dublin paper reported, "Words are wanting to express the exquisite Delight it afforded to the admiring crowded Audience. The Sublime, the Grand, and the Tender, adapted to the most elevated, majestick and moving words, conspired to transport and charm the ravished Heart and Ear."

Although *Messiah* was a Lenten ORATORIO, it eventually became a standard choral work performed at Christmastime as well. The score of *Messiah* lends itself to large-scale productions. Some London performances numbered more than 3,000 singers, and as many as 27 bassoons and other instruments in proportion.

Remember: the title is simply *Messiah*, not *The Messiah*, as persistently misapplied.

The English LIBRETTO is selected from the King James Bible, detailing the world's response to Jesus, before, during, and after his presence. Although Handel never learned to speak English grammatically and his German accent was thick, he revealed an extraordinary sensitivity to the rhythm of the English text.

Handel's working score of *Messiah* was published in facsimile in 1974, and it shows graphically the many changes Handel made in subsequent years, with some sections practically composed anew. Of the many famous numbers in the score, the *Hallelujah Chorus* is the most familiar.

Metamorphosen. THRENODY, a mournful piece by RICHARD STRAUSS, scored for 23 string instruments. He wrote it at the end of World War II and concluded his manuscript with the words "In Memoriam." The work contains quotations from the funeral march from LUDWIG VAN BEETHOVEN's *Eroica* Symphony. It was performed for the first time in Zurich the following year.

metamorphosis. Extensive VARIATIONS on a theme. In a metamorphosis, the key, rhythm, and intervallic structure of a theme may be changed, with only the basic line discernible. The IDÉE FIXE in HECTOR BERLIOZ's *Symphonie fantastique* undergoes a radical metamorphosis in the course of the work. PAUL HINDEMITH composed a *Symphonic metamorphosis on themes of Carl Maria von Weber.*

PEOPLE IN MUSIC

Metastasio, Pietro (born Antonio Domenico Bonaventura Trapassi), Italian poet and opera librettist; b. Rome, Jan. 3,

1698; d. Vienna, April 12, 1782. Metastasio was the son of a papal soldier named Trapassi. However, in his professional career he took the Greek translation of the name, both Trapassi (or Trapassamento) and Metastasio meaning "transition."

Metastasio was a learned classicist. He began to write plays as a young boy and studied music with Nicola Porpora. He achieved great fame in Italy as a playwright. In 1729 he was appointed court poet in Vienna by Emperor Charles VI. He wrote 27 opera texts, which were set to music by GEORGE FRIDERIC HANDEL, CHRISTOPH WILLIBALD GLUCK, WOLFGANG AMADEUS MOZART, Johann Adolf Hasse, Porpora, Niccolò Jommelli, and many other celebrated composers, some 60 or more times. His LIBRETTOS were remarkable for their melodious verse, which naturally suggested musical associations.

Metastasio's LIBRETTO to the opera by Niccolo Conforto, *La Nitteti* (1754; Madrid, 1756), was on the same subject as GIUSEPPE VERDI's *Aïda*, anticipating the latter by more than a century.

meter (U.K. metre; Ger. *Taktart*). 1. The placing of musical rhythms into beats, then beats into symmetrical or asymmetrical, regular or irregular groupings. 2. In verse, the division into symmetrical lines. The meter of English hymns is classified into three types, according to the kind of feet used (the figures show the number of syllables in each line):

Iambic: *Common meter* (C.M.), 8 6 8 6

Long meter (L.M.), 8 8 8 8

Short meter (S.M.), 6 6 8 6

These have regularly four lines to each stanza; when doubled to eight lines they are called *Common meter double* (C.M.D.), *Long meter double* (L.M.D.), and *Short meter double* (S.M.D.). They may also have six lines in each stanza and are then named *Common particular meter* (C.P.M.), 8 8 6 8 8 6; *Long particular meter* (L.P.M.) or *Long meter six lines*, 8 8 8 8 8 8; and *Short particular meter* (S.P.M.), 6 6 8 6 6 8.

Besides the above, there are *Sevens and sixes*, 7 6 7 6; *Tens*, 10 10 10 10; *Hallelujah meter*, 6 6 6 6 8 8 (or 6 6 6 6 4 4 4 4), etc. Trochaic: *Sixes*, 6 6 6 6; *Sixes and fives*, 6 5 6 5; *Sevens*, 7 7 7 7; *Eights and sevens*, 8 7 8 7, etc.

Dactylic: *Elevens*, 11 11 11 11; *Elevens and tens*, 11 10 11 10, etc.

These are most of the meters in general use. Hymnbooks use the system as a means of cross-reference and allow the possibility of putting a different text to a melody, or vice versa.

metric modulation. In the broadest sense, a change of time signature. In modern usage, applied by CHARLES IVES and systematically developed by ELLIOTT CARTER (who coined the term), a technique in which one rhythmic pattern is superimposed on another, then supersedes it and becomes the basic meter. Usually, such time signatures are mutually prime (e.g., $\frac{4}{4}$ and $\frac{3}{8}$), and so have no common divisors. Thus, the change of the basic meter decisively alters the numerical content of the beat, but the minimal denominator ($\frac{1}{8}$ when $\frac{4}{4}$ changes to $\frac{3}{8}$; $\frac{1}{16}$ when, e.g., $\frac{1}{8}$ changes to $\frac{7}{16}$, etc.) remains constant in duration.

MUSICAL
INSTRUMENT

Electric (left) *and mechanical* (right) *metronomes. (Benson Collection)* ▶

metronome (Gr., *metro* + *nomos,* law of measurement; Ger. *Taktmesser*). A mechanical device that beats time, indicating

the tempo of a composition. It consists of a graduated pendulum that is adjusted by sliding a small weight up or down its length.

The design most commonly used was invented by J. N. Maelzel about 1816. The first metronome was developed a few years earlier by an obscure Amsterdam mechanic named Winkel, whose invention lacked the gradations. Winkel subsequently accused Maelzel of stealing his idea. However that might be, the initials MM (Maelzel metronome, or metronome marking) have for a century and a half adorned most student editions of classical works.

The marking MM [quarter note] = 120 indicates that there are 120 quarter notes per minute. By setting the weight on the pendulum at 120, the proper beat is obtained whereby each tick of the pendulum counts for one quarter note (as it happens, a half-second).

LUDWIG VAN BEETHOVEN, who believed in the power of modern inventions, seized upon Maelzel's metronome as the perfect instrument to perpetuate the correct tempos of his works. It is the traditional view that (1) he trusted Maelzel too well, (2) the machine that he had at his disposal was defective (the usual interpretation), or (3) (perish the thought!) Beethoven's own sense of tempo had betrayed him, because he assigned metronome marks that would accelerate the logical tempos beyond rational limits, in one instance converting an *allegretto* into a *prestissimo*. As a consequence, performers of Beethoven's late works usually ignore his metronome marks. It should be noted that some conductors have begun to follow the markings that, with a smaller orchestra, seem at least possible.

Until recently, the metronome was a familiar pyramidal accoutrement perched on the piano in the drawing room of every teacher and student, but with the advance of technology it has been replaced by a variety of small contraptions that emit electronic beeps or light pulses.

Some modern composers discovered that the metronome clicks make legitimate percussive effects. GYÖRGY LIGETI, one of the most imaginative of the musical AVANT-GARDE, wrote a piece for 100 mechanical metronomes beating different tempos. Visually, the spectacle is extraordinary.

Mexican Hayride. Musical by COLE PORTER, 1944. The plot involves an American female bullfighter in Mexico and the chargé d'affaires of the U.S. embassy in Mexico City. He is enraptured by the matadora but is upset when she appears to throw the defeated bull's ear at an American fugitive from justice. Not only does she prove to the diplomat that this was a mistake, but she takes part in a successful hunt after the outlaw. Includes *I Love You* and *Count Your Blessings*.

Meyerbeer, Giacomo (born Jakob Liebmann Beer), German composer; b. Vogelsdorf, near Berlin, Sept. 5, 1791; d. Paris, May 2, 1864. Meyerbeer was a son of a prosperous Jewish family of merchants named Beer. He added the name

PEOPLE IN MUSIC

Meyer to his surname and later changed his first name for professional purposes.

Meyerbeer began piano studies with Franz Lauska; he also received some instruction from Muzio Clementi. He made his public debut in Berlin when he was 11. He then studied composition with Carl Friedrich Zelter from 1805 to 1807, and subsequently with B. A. Weber. It was as Weber's pupil that he composed his first stage work, the ballet-pantomime *Der Fischer und das Milchmädchen* (The Fisher and the Milkmaiden), which was produced at the Berlin Royal Theater in 1810. He then went to Darmstadt to continue his studies with Abbé Vogler until late 1811, numbering among his fellow pupils CARL MARIA VON WEBER.

While under Vogler's tutelage Meyerbeer composed the oratorio *Gott und die Natur* (God and Nature; 1811) and also the operas *Der Admiral* (1811; not performed) and *Jephthas Gelübde* (1812). Meyerbeer's next opera was also unsuccessful. In 1813 he traveled to Vienna, where he found success as a pianist in private musical settings. In November 1814 he proceeded to Paris, and in December 1815 to London.

Meyerbeer went to Italy early in 1816, and there turned his attention fully to dramatic composition. His Italian operas—*Romilda e Costanza* (1817), *Semiramide riconosciuta* (1819), *Emma di Resburgo* (1819), *Margherita d'Angiu* (1820), *L'Esule di Granata* (1821), and *Il Crociato in Egitto* (1824)—brought him fame there, placing him on a par with the celebrated GIOACCHINO ROSSINI in public esteem. The immense success of *Il Crociato in Egitto* in particular led to a successful staging at London's King's Theatre, followed by a triumphant Paris production, both in 1825, which made Meyerbeer famous throughout Europe.

To secure his Paris position, he revamped *Margherita d'Angiu* for the French stage as *Margherita d'Anjou* in 1826. He began a long and distinguished association with the dramatist and librettist Eugène Scribe in 1827 as work commenced on the opera ROBERT LE DIABLE. It was produced at the Paris Opéra in 1831, with extraordinary success.

Meyerbeer began work on what was to become the opera LES HUGUENOTS in 1832. Set to a LIBRETTO mainly by Scribe, it was accorded a spectacular premiere at the Opéra in 1836. Late in 1836 he and Scribe began work on a new opera, LE

PROPHÈTE. He also commenced work on the opera *L'AFRI-CAINE* in 1837, again utilizing a libretto by Scribe. Initially written for the famous soprano Marie-Cornelie Falcon, after the loss of her voice, Meyerbeer set the score aside. It was destined to occupy him on and off for the rest of his life.

In 1839 RICHARD WAGNER sought out Meyerbeer in Boulogne. Impressed with Wagner, Meyerbeer extended him financial assistance and gave him professional recommendations. However, Wagner soon became disenchanted with his prospects and berated Meyerbeer in private, so much so that Meyerbeer was compelled to end the friendship.

Meyerbeer began work on *Le Prophète* in earnest in 1838, completing it by 1840. However, its premiere was indefinitely delayed as the composer attempted to find capable singers. In 1842 *Les Huguenots* was performed in Berlin. On June 11, 1842, Meyerbeer was formally installed as Prussian Generalmusikdirektor. From the onset of his tenure, disagreement with the Intendant of the Royal Opera, Karl Theodor von Küstner, made his position difficult. Finally, in late 1848, Meyerbeer was dismissed from his post, although he retained his position as director of music for the royal court. In this capacity he composed a number of works for state occasions, including the opera *Ein Feldlager in Schlesien,* which reopened the opera house in 1844, following its destruction by fire. The leading role was sung by JENNY LIND, one of Meyerbeer's discoveries. It had some success after its first performance in Vienna under the title *Vielka* in 1847, although it never equaled the success of his Paris operas.

In 1849 Meyerbeer again took up the score of *Le Prophète.* As he could find no tenor to meet its demands, he completely revised the score for the celebrated soprano Pauline Viardot-García. With Viardot-García as Fidès and the tenor Gustave Roger as John of Leyden, it received a brilliant premiere at the Paris Opéra in 1849, a success that led to Meyerbeer's being made the first German Commander of the Legion of Honor.

Meyerbeer's next opera was *L'Étoile du nord* (The Star of the North), which used music from *Ein Feldlager in Schlesien.* Its first performance at the Opéra-Comique in 1854 proved an outstanding success. Equally successful was his opera *Le Pardon de Ploërmel* (Opéra-Comique, 1859). In 1862 he composed a special work for the London World Exhibition, the *Fest-Ouverture im Marschstyl,* and made a visit to England during the festivities.

In the meantime, work on *L'Africaine* had occupied Meyerbeer fitfully for years. Given Scribe's death in 1861 and Meyerbeer's own failing health, he was compelled to finally complete it. In April 1864 he put the finishing touches on the score, and rehearsals began under his supervision. However, he died on the night of May 2, 1864, before the work was premiered. His body was taken to Berlin, where it was laid to rest in official ceremonies attended by the Prussian court, prominent figures in the arts, and the public at large. François-Joseph Fétis was subsequently charged with making the final preparations for the premiere of *L'Africaine,* which was given at the Paris Opéra to notable acclaim in 1865.

Meyerbeer established himself as the leading composer of French grand opera in 1831 with *Robert le diable,* a position he retained with distinction throughout his career. Indeed, he became one of the most celebrated musicians of his era. Although the grand conceptions and stagings of his operas proved immediately appealing to audiences, his dramatic works were more than mere theatrical spectacles. His vocal writing was truly effective, because he often composed and tailored his operas with specific singers in mind. Likewise, he had a great gift for orchestration, using the instrumental forces in unique, new ways. Nevertheless, his stature as a composer was eclipsed after his death by Wagner. As a consequence, his operas disappeared from the active repertoire, although revivals and recordings saved them from total oblivion in the modern era.

med′zōh-sōh-prah′nōh

PEOPLE IN MUSIC

mezzosoprano (*mezzo;* It.). The female voice between SOPRANO and ALTO, partaking of the quality of both. It is usually a small-ranged voice ($a–f^2$, or $a–g^2$), but very full-toned in the medium register.

Miaskovsky, Nikolai (Yakovlevich), Russian composer and teacher; b. Novogeorgievsk, near Warsaw, April 20, 1881; d. Moscow, Aug. 8, 1950. Miaskovsky's father was an officer of the department of military fortification. Nikolai attended military schools in Nizhny-Novgorod in 1893 and St. Petersburg beginning in 1895, graduating in 1899.

Developing an interest in music, Miaskovsky took lessons with Nikolai Kazanly, his first influences being FRÉDÉRIC CHOPIN and PIOTR ILYICH TCHAIKOVSKY. In 1902–03 he was in Moscow, where he studied harmony with RHEINHOLD GLIÈRE. Returning to St. Petersburg in 1903, he took lessons with Ivan Kryzhanovsky, from whom he acquired a taste for modernistic composition in the IMPRESSIONIST style. In 1906, at the age of 25, he entered the St. Petersburg Conservatory as a pupil of Anatoli Liadov and NIKOLAI RIMSKY-KORSAKOV, graduating in 1911.

At the outbreak of World War I in 1914, Miaskovsky was called into active service in the Russian army. In 1916 he was removed to Reval to work on military fortifications. He remained in the army after the Bolshevik Revolution of 1917, and in 1918 he became an officer in the Maritime Headquarters in Moscow. He was finally demobilized in 1921. In that year he became professor of composition at the Moscow Conservatory, remaining at that post to the end of his life.

A composer of extraordinary ability, Miaskovsky wrote 27 symphonies, much chamber music, piano pieces, and songs. His music is tightly structured but at the same time expressive of deep emotions. Unlike other Russian national composers, he used folk rhythms or melodies in only a few of his works. While he stretched the bounds of traditional harmony and melody, he did not adopt the most extreme elements of modern music.

Michelangeli, Arturo Benedetti, Italian pianist and teacher; b. Brescia, Jan. 5, 1920; d. Lugano, June 12, 1995. Michelangeli received formal training at the Venturi Institute in Brescia on violin. At the age of 10, he entered the Milan Conservatory as a piano pupil of Giuseppe Anfossi, obtaining his diploma at the age of 13. In 1939 he won the Concours International de piano in Geneva, and later joined the piano faculty at the Martini Conservatory in Bologna.

During World War II, Michelangeli was a lieutenant in the Italian air force. After the formal surrender of Italy to the

PEOPLE IN MUSIC

Allies and the German occupation, he was active in the country's anti-Fascist underground. He was taken prisoner by the Germans but escaped after a few months. He somehow managed to practice, acquiring a formidable virtuoso technique.

Michelangeli toured the U.S. in 1950 and 1966, playing in the Soviet Union in 1964, and also giving concerts in South America. Eventually he returned to Italy and dedicated himself mainly to teaching. He organized an International Academy for pianists in a rented palazzo in Brescia with a multitude of pianos in soundproof studios. Among his pupils were Jörg Demus, Walter Klien, Mauizio Pollini, and Martha Argerich.

Michelangeli was as well known for his unusual character as for his playing. He often canceled scheduled performances and engaged in such distracting (and dangerous) activities as automobile racing, skiing, and mountain climbing. Both his virtuosity and his eccentricities contributed to his legend, and his rare concerts were invariably public successes.

microtime. Term invented by KARLHEINZ STOCKHAUSEN in 1955 to designate the number of vibrations corresponding to individual pitch. He contrasted this with MACROTIME, which he applied to the duration of each rhythmic pulse.

microtonality. Division of the octave into intervals smaller than the HALF TONE (or semitone), the smallest interval used within the 12-step, EQUAL-TEMPERED SCALE.

Intervals smaller than semitones were used in ancient Greece, but were abandoned in Western music with the establishment of the ecclesiastical modes. When greater sensitivity toward tonal elements developed in modern times, composers and theorists began investigating the acoustical, coloristic, and affective aspects of intervals smaller than a semitone, particularly QUARTER TONES.

The Mexican composer Julián Carrillo (1875–1965) experimented with microtonal intervals as early as 1895. That year, he published his *Sonido 13* (13th Sound), the title referring to the tonal possibilities that lay beyond the 12 notes of the CHROMATIC scale. Later he organized an international

society for the exploration of microtonality under the grandiose name Cruzada Intercontinental Sonido 13 (The International Crusade for the 13th Sound). He devised special instruments for performance of microtonal intervals and
proposed a numerical notation of 96 divisions of the octave,
which enabled him to designate precise intervallic values for
half tones, quarter tones, sixth tones, eighth tones, and sixteenth tones.

The English musician John Foulds (1880–1939) experimented with quarter tones in 1898. He writes in his book
From Music Today (1934):

As an exercise in microtonality, Carrillo arranged LUDWIG
VAN BEETHOVEN'S FIFTH SYM-
PHONY in quarter tones by dividing each interval into two.
In so doing, the entire range
of the work shrank to about
three octaves.

> In the year 1898 I had tentatively experimented in a
> string quartet with smaller divisions than usual of the in-
> tervals of our scale, quarter-tones. Having proved in per-
> formance their practicability and their capability of ex-
> pressing certain psychological states in a manner
> incommunicable by any other means known to musi-
> cians, I definitely adopted them as an item in my com-
> posing technique.

The most systematic investigation of the theory and
practice of quarter tones was undertaken by Alois Hába in
Czechoslovakia. "As a boy of 12," he writes,

> I played with my three older brothers in my father's vil-
> lage band. We were poor; there were ten children in the
> family, and I had to contribute to household expenses.
> When we played for village festivals it often happened
> that folk singers used intervals different from the tem-
> pered scale, and they were annoyed that we could not ac-
> company them properly. This gave me the idea to prac-
> tice at home playing nontempered scales on my violin in
> intervals smaller than a semitone. This was my first "con-
> servatory" for music in quarter-tones and in 6th-notes.

Probably the first entirely self-consistent work in quarter
tones was the string quartet written by Hába in 1919. He
also compiled the first manual containing detailed instructions on composing in quarter tones, third tones, and sixth

tones, which he published under the fitting title *Neue Harmonielehre* in 1928.

Under Hába's supervision the August Foerster piano manufacturing company of Czechoslovakia constructed the first model of a quarter-tone piano, which was patented on March 18, 1924. At the same time Hába established the first seminars of microtonal music, at the Prague Conservatory. He and his students published a number of works in quarter tones, in Hába's special notation containing symbols for half a sharp, a sharp and a half, half a flat, and a flat and a half.

The first quarter-tone piano manufactured in the U.S. was patented by Hans Barth on July 21, 1931. His instrument had two keyboards of 88 notes each. The upper keyboard was tuned at the regular international pitch and had the usual five black keys and seven white. The lower keyboard was tuned a quarter tone down, and its keys were blue and red. James Paul White, a Boston musician, constructed in 1883 a microtonal keyboard, which he called the *harmon,* and used a notation in which deviations from regular pitch were indicated by plus and minus signs. He theorized that 612 equal divisions of an octave would provide the most practical approximation to pure intonation. His instrument is preserved at the New England Conservatory of Music.

In 1917 the Russian composer Ivan Wyschnegradsky devised a system of quarter tones with a motto, inspired by Heraclitus, "Everything flows." In 1924, then living in Paris, he formulated the concept of "pansonority," which was his term for a specific scale made up of quarter tones. To produce fairly accurate quarter tones, he used two pianos or two pairs of pianos tuned a quarter tone apart. In November 1945 he conducted in Paris an entire program of his works, including a symphonic poem for four pianos entitled *Cosmos.*

In Russia itself quarter-tone music had a brief period of success in the early 1920s, cultivated by the Quarter-Tone Society of Leningrad, founded by NIKOLAI RIMSKY-KORSAKOV's grandson, Georg. The American composer CHARLES IVES contributed some pieces written in quarter tones. He claimed that he became aware of the new resources of microtonal music when his father, a bandleader in the Union Army during the Civil War, experimented in tuning band instruments a quarter tone apart.

Quarter tones have been used by composers to suggest the Greek enharmonic mode through the centuries. FRO-MENTAL HALÉVY incorporated a few quarter tones in his symphonic poem *Prométhée enchaîné*. HECTOR BERLIOZ wrote an interesting account of its first performance in *Revue et Gazette Musicale de Paris* (March 1849): "The employment of quarter tones in Halévy's work is episodic and very short, and produces a species of groaning sound in the strings, but its strangeness seems perfectly justified here and enhances considerably the wistful prosody of the music."

NICOLAS SLONIMSKY composed an overture for strings, trumpet, and percussion in the Phrygian mode. He took as his theme an ancient Greek tune from the accompaniment to the tragedy *Orestes* produced in Athens in 400 B.C. He conducted this arrangement at the Hollywood Bowl in 1933. In order to produce the needed two quarter tones, the open strings of the violins, violas, and cellos were tuned a quarter tone up, with the rest of the string instruments preserving the ordinary pitch. The Romanian composer Georges Enescu inserted a transitional passage in quarter tones in his opera *Oedipe,* produced in Paris in 1936. In this case, too, the composer's intention was to evoke the effect of the ancient Greek enharmonic scale.

Other EQUAL TEMPERAMENTS have been proposed. Perhaps the most complete research in this direction was done by Joseph Yasser in his book *A Theory of Evolving Tonality* (N.Y., 1932), in which he proposed a system of "supra-tonality," with accidentals designated by special symbols for supra-sharp, supra-flat, and supra-natural of the synthetic scale. He believed that 19-note equal temperament was the most logical step after the present system. Ernst Krenek experimented with 13-equal temperament. KARLHEINZ STOCK-HAUSEN used temperaments for which the basic interval was something other than the octave. (There is also the concept of *macrotonality,* in which there are fewer than 12 equally tempered notes per octave.)

The return to ancient Greek theory also inspired composers to revive the JUST INTONATION system, where intervallic relationships were determined rationally, not logarithmically. Perhaps the most ambitious project in justly tuned music was undertaken by the American composer HARRY

PARTCH, who devised an asymmetrical scale of 43 unequal intervals in an octave. To play these intervals, he adapted or constructed a number of special instruments, among them a microtonal viola, a reed organ, MARIMBAS (including one in diamond shape), plucked dulcimers, and modern versions of the Greek kithara. His work has influenced many subsequent composers, instrument makers, and theorists.

In actual performance, quarter tones and other microtonal divisions are only rough approximations of their true acoustical value. With the advent of electronic instruments and computer music, it became possible to reproduce microtonal intervals with absolute precision.

middle C. The C (actually, c¹) in the middle of the piano keyboard:

MIDI (Music Instrument Digital Interface). Computer language used to connect computers, synthesizers, sequencers, and other electronic musical instruments so that they may "communicate with" (send data to) each other; also, the device carrying this information. This simplifies live electroacoustic processing and output. *MIDI compatible,* able to read MIDI data; *MIDI jack, port,* the connecting device on electronic musical instruments intended for the MIDI.

Midi, Le. FRANZ JOSEPH HAYDN's Symphony No. 7 (1761), a sequel to his Symphony No. 6, *Le Matin.* Its bright key of C major suggests the warm, midday sun.

Midler, Bette, American singer, actress, and comedienne; b. Paterson, N.J., Dec. 1, 1945. Midler's family moved to Hawaii shortly after her birth. She studied drama in Honolulu, then settled in N.Y. She sang in a variety of gay venues, including bathhouses and clubs, and on Broadway (*Fiddler on the Roof* and *Tommy*). She subsequently engaged Barry Manilow as her music director and a backup trio known as The Harlettes and developed a raucous cabaret routine through which she generated a loyal following, becoming known as "The Divine Miss M." Her 1972 album of that name won a gold record. Subsequent albums of note

PEOPLE IN MUSIC

include *Bette Midler* (1973), *Songs for the New Depression* (1976), *Live at Last* (1977), and *Broken Blossom* (1977).

Midler starred in the film *The Rose* (1979), based on the life of Janis Joplin, for which she received an Academy Award nomination. Her soundtrack LP sold into the millions. Other successful films were *Down and Out in Beverly Hills* (1986), *Ruthless People* (1986), *Outrageous Fortune* (1987), and *Beaches* (1989), for which she sang the Grammy Award–winning

Two divas: Bette Midler and Elton John, 1975. (UPI/ Corbis-Bettmann)

title song, *Wind Beneath My Wings.* Her covers of songs by artists as varied as BRUCE SPRINGSTEEN, KURT WEILL, HOAGY CARMICHAEL, and Tom Waits show her stylistic diversity.

Her comedic gifts, an integral aspect of her live performances, are captured on the recording *Mud Will Be Flung Tonight* (1985), in which she revitalizes the spicy, sometimes lewd anecdotes of the late Sophie Tucker. She authored the comic memoirs *A View from a Broad* (1980) and a children's book, *The Saga of Baby Divine* (1983).

Midori (born Goto Mi Dori), prodigiously gifted Japanese wunderkind of the violin; b. Osaka, Oct. 25, 1971. Midori studied with her mother, Setsu Goto. In 1981 she went to the U.S., where she took lessons at the Aspen Music School and at N.Y.'s Juilliard School.

Midori attracted the attention of ZUBIN MEHTA when she was 10 years old. He subsequently engaged her as a soloist with the N.Y. Philharmonic, with which she traveled on an

PEOPLE IN MUSIC

extensive Asian tour. There followed concerts with the Berlin Philharmonic, the Boston Symphony Orchestra, the Chicago Symphony Orchestra, the Cleveland and Philadelphia Orchestras, the Los Angeles Philharmonic, the London Symphony Orchestra, and other European and American orchestras. Midori performed in programs that included not only classical concertos but also modern works, under the direction of such renowned conductors, besides Mehta, as LEONARD BERNSTEIN, ANDRÉ PREVIN, LORIN MAAZEL, RAYMOND LEPPARD, and DANIEL BARENBOIM.

Midori won the admiration of orchestra members for her remarkable artistic dependability. On one occasion, when a string broke on the concertmaster's violin during an orchestral introduction, she demonstrated remarkable calm: because she had a few minutes to spare before her entrance as a soloist, she handed her own violin to the player and coolly changed the broken string in time to continue the performance without pause.

In 1990 Midori made her N.Y. recital debut at CARNEGIE HALL. In 1992 she created the Midori Foundation to promote the cause of classical music.

Midsommarvaka (Midsummer Vigil). First of three Swedish Rhapsodies for orchestra by Hugo Alfvén, 1904, his most celebrated piece, first performed in Stockholm. It was produced as a ballet under the title *La Nuit de Saint-Jean* in Paris in 1920 and received over 25 performances in four years.

Midsummer Night's Dream, A. Incidental music by FELIX MENDELSSOHN to Shakespeare's play. The overture, op.21, was composed in 1826, when he was 17. He later composed songs and additional instrumental music in 1842, including the *Wedding March,* often used in marriage ceremonies ever since. The music was first performed in its entirety in Potsdam in 1843.

Midsummer Night's Dream, A. Opera by BENJAMIN BRITTEN, 1960, based on Shakespeare, first performed in Aldeburgh, England. The score is subdivided into set pieces. Britten purposely uses many different styles, with elements of IMPRESSIONISM applied to the magical creatures, and the realistic scenes depicted in a folklike manner.

Mignon. Opera by Ambroise Thomas, 1866, first performed in Paris. The opera is based on Goethe's novel *Wilhelm Meister's Years of Apprenticeship.*

The gypsy girl Mignon, maltreated by her people, is rescued by Meister, who makes her his maidservant. They are joined by a wandering minstrel who is searching for his daughter kidnapped by gypsies. Lo and behold, Mignon turns out to be his daughter and all is made right.

Mikado, The, or The Town of Titipu. Comic opera by Gilbert and Sullivan, 1885, first produced in London.

Yum-Yum is a delicious Japanese maiden whom her guardian hopes to marry. The heir to the Japanese throne, disguised as a minstrel, also loves her. Because in Japan flirting is punishable by death, periodical beheadings are scheduled. However, the Lord High Executioner has an innate aversion to killing. When the Mikado's son reveals his identity, the Emperor is elated, cancels all executions, and lets his son marry Yum-Yum.

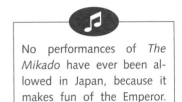

No performances of *The Mikado* have ever been allowed in Japan, because it makes fun of the Emperor.

Miki, Minoru, Japanese composer; b. Tokushima, March 16, 1930. Between 1951 and 1955 Miki studied at the National University of Fine Arts and Music in Tokyo. In 1964 he was a founder of the Nihon Ongaku Shudan (Pro Musica Nipponia), an ensemble dedicated to performing new music for traditional Japanese instruments. He later served as its artistic director. He lectured at the Tokyo College of Music, and also was founder-director of Utayomi-za in 1986, a musical-opera theater.

PEOPLE IN MUSIC

Miki's works include operas, symphonies, and Western and Japanese orchestral music. He has also composed concertos for KOTO, MARIMBA, Japanese classical trio, percussion, solo, and chamber works, most involving Japanese instruments, and vocal and choral works.

Mikrokosmos. Set of six books of progressive piano pieces by BÉLA BARTÓK, 1926–39. The remarkable innovation of this collection is its introduction of MODAL scales and ASYM-

METRIC rhythmic patterns. Many pieces bear picturesque titles, such as *From the Diary of a Fly*, while others reflect the underlying technique, as in *Imitation Reflected, Accents,* etc. The concluding *Six Dances in Bulgarian Rhythm* give an informative glance at the rhythmic and harmonic structures that the composer discovered during his many years of collecting and studying traditional folk melodies and rhythms.

Milanov, Zinka (Kunc), famous Croatian-American soprano; b. Zagreb, May 17, 1906; d. N.Y., May 30, 1989. Milanov studied at the Zagreb Academy of Music, then with Milka Ternina, Maria Kostrencic, and Fernando Carpi. After making her debut as Leonora in IL TROVATORE in Ljubljana in 1927, she was principal soprano of the Zagreb Opera from 1928 to 1935, where she sang in over 300 performances in Croatian.

After appearing at Prague's German Theater in 1936, Milanov was invited by ARTURO TOSCANINI to sing the Verdi Requiem at the Salzburg Festival a year later. That same year, she made her Metropolitan Opera debut in N.Y. as Leonora. She continued to perform at the Met intermittently until her farewell performance as Maddalena in ANDREA CHÉNIER in April 1966.

In addition to appearing in San Francisco and Chicago, Milanov sang at Buenos Aires's Teatro Colón (1940–42), Milan's La Scala (1950), and London's Covent Garden (1966–67). She married Predrag Milanov in 1937, but they were divorced in 1946. She then married Ljubomir Ilic in 1947.

Blessed with a voice of translucent beauty, Milanov became celebrated for her outstanding performances of roles in operas by GIUSEPPE VERDI and GIACOMO PUCCINI. Her brother was the pianist and composer Bozidar Kunc (1903–64).

Milhaud, Darius, French composer; b. Aix-en-Provence, Sept. 4, 1892; d. Geneva, June 22, 1974. Milhaud was a descendant of an old Jewish family, which had settled in Provence for many centuries. His father was an almond merchant. There was a piano in the house, and Milhaud improvised melodies as a child. He then began violin lessons.

Milhaud entered the Paris Conservatory in 1909. He played violin in the student orchestra under Paul Dukas. He received first "accessit" in violin and counterpoint, second "accessit" in fugue, and the Prix Lepaulle for composition. While still a student, he wrote music in a bold, modernistic manner. He became associated with the composer ERIK SATIE, the author Jean Cocteau, and the poet Paul Claudel. When Claudel was appointed French minister to Brazil, he engaged Milhaud as his secretary. They sailed for Rio de Janeiro early in 1917, returning to Paris (via the West Indies and N.Y.) shortly after the end of World War I in November 1918.

In 1920 Milhaud's name became known to a larger public as a result of a newspaper article by Henri Collet. Collet grouped him with five other modern French composers (GEORGES AURIC, LOUIS DUREY, ARTHUR HONEGGER, FRANCIS POULENC, and GERMAINE TAILLEFERRE) under the name LES SIX, even though the association was slight. In 1922 Milhaud visited the U.S., where he lectured at Harvard, Princeton, and Columbia Universities and also appeared as pianist in his own works. In 1925 he traveled in Italy, Germany, Austria, and Russia. Returning to France, he devoted himself mainly to composition and teaching.

At the outbreak of World War II, Milhaud was in Aix-en-Provence. In July 1940 he went to the U.S. and taught at Mills College in Oakland, California. In 1947 he returned to France. He was appointed professor at the Paris Conservatory, but continued to visit the U.S. as conductor and teacher almost annually, despite arthritis, which compelled him to conduct while seated. He retained his post at Mills College until 1971, when he settled in Geneva.

Exceptionally prolific from his student days, Milhaud wrote a great number of works in every genre. He introduced a modernistic type of music drama, "opera à la minute," and also the "miniature symphony." He experimented with new stage techniques, incorporating techniques borrowed from film. He also successfully revived the Greek type of tragedy with vocal accompaniment.

Milhaud also composed works for electronic instruments. He demonstrated his contrapuntal skill in such compositions as his two string quartets (No. 14 and No. 15),

Milhaud's ballet *La Création du monde* (The Creation of the World) of 1923 portrays the Creation in terms of African beliefs. It is the earliest example of the use of the blues and jazz in a symphonic score, predating GEORGE GERSHWIN.

which can be played together as a string octet. He was the first to exploit POLYTONALITY in a consistent and deliberate manner. He applied the exotic rhythms of Latin America and the West Indies in many of his lighter works, including his *Saudades do Brasil,* which are particularly popular. Brazilian movements are also found in his *Scaramouche* and *Le Boeuf sur le toit* (The Cow on the Roof).

Despite this mastery of many different styles and forms, Milhaud succeeded in establishing a style that was distinctly his own. His melodies are nostalgically lyrical or vivaciously rhythmical, according to mood. His instrumental writing is of great complexity and difficulty, and yet entirely within the capacities of modern virtuoso technique. For so prolific and gifted a composer, Milhaud's music is remarkably consistent in quality.

Among Milhaud's works are operas, incidental music, orchestral works, numerous sets of songs, many set to the poems of Claudel, several psalms and other religious works, and works for piano. His essays were first collected in *Études* (1926).

Military Symphony. FRANZ JOSEPH HAYDN's Symphony No. 100 in G Major, 1794, the eighth of 12 symphonies written for performance in London during his tours there. The work's nickname refers to the orchestration of the second movement, which includes not only the standard timpani, but a triangle, cymbals, and the bass drum. This and the *Surprise* Symphony are among the most popular of Haydn's symphonies.

Miller, (Alton) **Glenn,** famous American trombonist and bandleader, b. Clarinda, Iowa, March 1, 1904; d. Dec. 15, 1944. Miller spent his formative years in Fort Morgan, Colorado. He played with the local Boyd Senter Orchestra in 1921 and took courses at the University of Colorado.

After performing with Ben Pollack's band on the West Coast from 1924 to 1928, Miller followed Pollack to N.Y. and became active as a freelance musician. He helped to found an American-based orchestra for British bandleader Ray Noble in 1934, and subsequently studied orchestration

PEOPLE IN MUSIC

with the famous theorist and teacher Joseph Schillinger. He began experimenting with special effects, combining clarinets with saxophone in the same register.

Miller organized his first band in 1937, but it failed to find an audience and dissolved in 1938. That same year he organized another band, which caught on in 1939 through its radio broadcasts and recordings. It subsequently became one of the most successful groups of the day, producing such popular recordings as *Moonlight Serenade* and *In the*

Glenn Miller in his U.S. Army uniform, c. 1942. (Hulton-Deutsch Collection/Corbis)

Mood (both 1939), *Tuxedo Junction* (1940), and *Chattanooga Choo Choo* and *A String of Pearls* (both 1941). It also appeared in the films *Sun Valley Serenade* (1941) and *Orchestra Wives* (1942).

Miller joined the U.S. Army Air Force as a captain in 1942 and put together a band for entertaining the troops. It was based in England from 1944. Tragically, at the end of 1944, Miller died in an airplane accident while flying from London to Paris. A film, *The Glenn Miller Story,* was produced in 1953.

Millöcker, Carl, Austrian conductor and composer; b. Vienna, April 29, 1842; d. Baden, near Vienna, Dec. 31, 1899. Millöcker's father was a jeweler, and he was destined for that trade but showed irrepressible musical inclinations. He played the flute in a theater orchestra at the age of 16, and later took courses at the Conservatory of the Gesellschaft der Musikfreunde in Vienna.

PEOPLE IN MUSIC

Upon the recommendation of FRANZ VON SUPPÉ, Millöcker received a post as theater conductor in Graz in 1864. In 1866 he returned to Vienna, where, from 1869 to 1883, he was second conductor of the Theater an der Wien. He suffered a stroke in 1894, which left him partially paralyzed.

As a composer, Millöcker possessed a natural gift for melodious music. Although his popularity was never as great as that of JOHANN STRAUSS, JR. or FRANZ LEHÁR, his operettas effectively captured the spirit of Viennese life.

PEOPLE IN MUSIC

Milnes, Sherrill (Eustace), distinguished American baritone; b. Downers Grove, Ill., Jan. 10, 1935. Milnes learned to play piano and violin at home, then played tuba in a school band. After a period as a medical student at North Central College in Naperville, Illinois, he turned to music. He subsequently studied voice with Andrew White at Drake University in Des Moines and with Hermanus Baer at Northwestern University.

Milnes sang in choral performances under Margaret Hillis in Chicago, then was a member of the chorus at the Santa Fe Opera, where he first sang minor operatic roles. In 1960 he joined Boris Goldovsky's Boston-based opera company and toured widely with it. He met ROSA PONSELLE in Baltimore in 1961, and she coached him in several roles. He first appeared with the Baltimore Civic Opera as Gerard in *ANDREA CHÉNIER* in 1961.

Milnes made his European debut as Figaro in *IL BARBIERE DI SIVIGLIA* at the Teatro Nuovo in Milan in 1964. Later that year, he made his first appearance at the N.Y. City Opera, singing Valentin in *Faust*. His Metropolitan Opera debut in N.Y. followed in the same role in 1965. He rose to a stellar position at the Metropolitan, being acclaimed for both vocal and dramatic abilities. He also sang with other opera houses in the U.S. and Europe. His notable roles include Don Giovanni, Escamillo, the Count di Luna, Tonio, Iago, Barnaba, Rigoletto, and Scarpia.

Milnes left the Met shortly after his 30th year with the company. He has continued to perform in recital through the '90s, as well as making appearances with various opera companies throughout the world. He also has made a second career as a teacher and conductor.

Milstein, Nathan (Mironovich), celebrated Russian-born American violinist; b. Odessa, Dec. 31, 1903; d. London, Dec. 21, 1992. Milstein's father was a well-to-do woolen merchant, his mother an amateur violinist who gave him his first lessons. He began to study with the well-known violin teacher Piotr Stoliarsky in Odessa, remaining with him until 1914. He then went to St. Petersburg, where he entered the class of Leopold Auer at the St. Petersburg Conservatory from 1915 to 1917.

PEOPLE IN MUSIC

Milstein began his concert career in 1919, with his sister as piano accompanist. In Kiev he met VLADIMIR HOROWITZ, and they began giving duo recitals in 1921. Later they were joined by cellist Gregor Piatigorsky, and organized a trio. Russia was just emerging from a devastating civil war, and communications with western Europe were not established until much later.

In 1925 Milstein was able to leave Russia. He went to Berlin and then to Brussels, where he met the Belgian conductor/violinist Eugène Ysäye, who encouraged his career. He gave several recitals in Paris, then proceeded to South America. On Oct. 28, 1929, he made his American debut with the Philadelphia Orchestra conducted by LEOPOLD STOKOWSKI. In 1942 he became an American citizen.

After World War II, Milstein appeared regularly in all of the principal music centers of the world. He performed with most of the great orchestras, gave numerous recitals, and recorded in many different settings. Milstein also gave master classes at the Juilliard School and in Zurich.

Milstein celebrated the 50th anniversary of his American debut in 1979 by giving a number of solo recitals and appearing as soloist with numerous orchestras.

Milstein was renowned for his technical virtuosity and musical integrity. He also composed a number of violin pieces, including *Paganiniana* (1954), and prepared cadenzas for the violin concertos of LUDWIG VAN BEETHOVEN and JOHANNES BRAHMS.

mimodrama. A dramatic or musical spectacle in which performers convey dramatic action by gestures and choreography, without speaking. Mimodrama is the same as PANTOMIME (1).

PEOPLE IN MUSIC

Mingus, Charles, African-American jazz double-bass player, pianist, bandleader, and composer, b. Nogales, Ariz., April 22, 1922; d. Cuernavaca, Mexico, Jan. 5, 1979. Mingus was reared in Los Angeles where, during his high school years, he studied double bass with Red Callender and Herman Rheinschagen and composition with Lloyd Reese.

After working with Barney Bigard in 1942, LOUIS ARMSTRONG in 1943, and LIONEL HAMPTON in 1947–48, he led his own groups as "Baron Mingus" before attracting notice as a member of Red Norvo's trio in 1950–51. Mingus then settled in N.Y., where he worked with Billy Taylor, DUKE ELLINGTON, STAN GETZ, ART TATUM, and BUD POWELL. He was head of his own recording company, Debut Records, from 1952 to 1955, and also became active as a composer. He worked with various musicians in small combos and eventually developed a close association with saxophonist ERIC DOLPHY.

A highly explosive individual, Mingus became known as the "angry man of jazz" for his opposition to the white commercial taint of his art form. After his second recording company (Charles Mingus label, 1964–65) failed and his financial situation became desperate, he retired from the public scene from 1966 to 1969. After resuming his career, he was awarded a Guggenheim fellowship in 1971 and subsequently devoted much time to composing. He also led his own groups until being stricken with amyotrophic lateral sclerosis, which sidelined him in 1978. He died a year later.

Mingus was a master instrumentalist and a versatile composer, producing both conventionally notated works and dictated pieces. In his unique series of works *Fables and Meditations,* he achieved a style that effectively erased the lines between jazz improvisation and notated composition. Mingus's most important work, the two-hour *Epitaph* for 30 instruments, discovered by his wife several years after his death, received its premiere posthumously in N.Y. on June 3, 1989.

Mingus recorded prolifically, both as a sideman and as a leader.

Shortly before his death, Mingus collaborated with the singer/songwriter JONI MITCHELL.

miniature score. An orchestral score reproduced in a small size. Full scores of symphonic works, chamber music, and even complete operas were first published in miniature versions in Germany in the 19th century. In pocket size, they were convenient to carry around for study purposes, or for reading while listening to music as it was played. The most active music publisher of miniature scores was Eulenberg of Leipzig.

minimalism. A school of composition influenced by JOHN CAGE and the N.Y. school of painters of the 1950s. More recently, minimalism has been used to describe musical works based on the repetition and gradual alteration of short rhythmic and/or melodic figures. It is also referred to as *process music.*

Minimalism was influenced by traditional compositions from the Pacific Rim, India, Indonesia, and Africa. These traditional musics included hypnotic drone effects and repetitive interlocking musical and rhythmic patterns.

Among minimalist American pioneers were LA MONTE YOUNG, TERRY RILEY, STEVE REICH, and PHILIP GLASS. In Riley's 1964 piece *IN C* for any instruments, musicians play in the key of C major until the last few measures, where he allows the passing entry of an F♯. Reich reinforced his technique by a study of African drumming, utilizing shifting phase and other repetitive techniques in works for similar and mixed ensembles. Glass enriched the uniformity of repetitive music by writing music to accompany visually spectacular stage plays and films.

Minkus, Léon (Aloisius Ludwig), Austrian violinist and composer; b. Vienna, March 23, 1826; d. there, Dec. 7, 1917. Minkus went to Russia in his youth and was engaged by Prince Yusupov as concertmaster of his serf orchestra in St. Petersburg from 1853 to 1856.

PEOPLE IN MUSIC

From 1862 to 1872 Minkus was concertmaster of the Bolshoi Theater in Moscow. In 1869 the theater staged his ballet *Don Quixote* to the choreography of the famous Russian ballet master Marius Petipa. Its success was extraordinary: its appeal to the Russian audiences proved to be so durable that the work retained its place in the repertoire of Russian ballet companies for more than a century. Equally popular was his ballet *La Bayadère,* produced by Petipa in St. Petersburg in 1877. Another successful ballet was *La Fi-*

ametta or The Triumph of Love, originally produced in Paris in 1864.

From 1872 to 1885 Minkus held the post of court composer of ballet music for the Imperial theaters in St. Petersburg. He remained in Russia until 1891, when he returned to Vienna, where he lived in semiretirement.

PEOPLE IN MUSIC

Minnelli, Liza (May), successful American singer of popular music and actress, daughter of the legendary singer JUDY GARLAND by her second husband, the film director Vincente Minnelli; b. Los Angeles, March 12, 1946. Minnelli dropped out of high school to devote herself exclusively to singing, making her professional debut in the 1963 off-Broadway revival of *Best Foot Forward.* In 1965 she appeared in the Broadway musical *Flora, The Red Menace,* for which she won a Tony Award. She established herself as a film actress in *The Sterile Cuckoo* in 1969. She also starred in the highly acclaimed film *Cabaret* in 1972, perhaps her most famous role, for which she won an Academy Award. She further won Tony awards for her one-woman show *Liza* in 1974 and for her appearance in the Broadway musical *The Act,* three years later.

Minnelli appeared opposite Dudley Moore in the romantic film comedy *Arthur* in 1981 and its sequel, *Arthur on the Rocks,* made seven years later. After starring in the musical *The Rink* in 1983–84, she underwent treatment for drug and alcohol dependency in 1984. Following rehabilitation, she made extensive tours in the U.S. and abroad.

Minnelli's career has been uneven in the '90s, as she continues to battle drug and alcohol abuse. In 1997 she briefly took over the lead from JULIE ANDREWS in *Victor, Victoria.*

min´ne-zing´er **Minnesinger** (Ger.). The German aristocratic poet-musicians of the 12th through 14th centuries, predecessors to the MEISTERSINGERS.

Minnesingers traveled through central Europe singing lyric songs in royal German courts, ducal castles, and villages. Like their counterparts, the TROUVÈRES and TROUBADOURS, they were mostly of noble birth. They regarded their profession as an expression of knightly valor and idealistic dedication to the real or imaginary ladies of their hearts

(*Minne* is Old German for "love"). With the end of the Crusades, and with a certain stabilization of the German states, the role of the Minnesingers declined. The performance and creation of lyric or heroic songs gradually was transferred to the town guilds and local craftsmen represented by them (*Meistersinger*).

minor (from Lat., small; It. *minore;* Fr. *mineur;* Ger. *moll*). 1. Intervals within a NATURAL MINOR SCALE between the TONIC (first degree) and the second, third, sixth, and seventh scale DEGREES. 2. A type of scale (e.g., A minor), key (A minor), or triad (A minor chord, with a minor third and perfect fifth above the root). In each case, the third degree of the scale forms an INTERVAL of a minor third with the ROOT.

minstrel (Fr. *ménestrel*). 1. In the Middle Ages, professional musicians who sang or recited poems, often of their own composition, to simple instrumental accompaniment. They were employed by royalty and feudal lords in Europe during the Middle Ages. They served as entertainers, players upon the lute or the flute, jesters, and sometimes as participants in domestic and political intrigues.

The term *minstrel* first appeared in the 14th century, and was derived from the French title *ménéstrier* (minister). With the decay of feudal society, the profession of minstrels disappeared.

2. Nineteenth-century white American performers portraying African-American characters in elaborate stage shows.

In the 1820s and '30s, individual circus performers began to wear blackface, performing "authentic" African-American songs, often accompanied on a new musical instrument called the BANJO. These acts became so popular that small groups of minstrel performers came together. They developed a set routine with a group of characters: Jim Crow, the Southern slave character, and Zip Coon, the uptown, city dweller; Mr. Tambo and Mr. Bones, two musicians playing tambourine and animal bones; and the Interlocutor and Endman, who exchanged comic dialogue.

Originally, the actors would sit in a line or circle and perform individual numbers broken up by the dialogue and introductions of the Interlocutor and Endman. However, in order to offer a full evening of entertainment, short plays were then added to the acts, often on sentimental topics such as "life on the old plantation." Finally, a CAKEWALK or elaborate dance number would end the evening's festivities.

Modern re-creation of a minstrel show, 1969. (Hulton-Deutsch Collection/Corbis)

As part of the minstrel shows, performers introduced many songs. These songs were in imitation of African-American folk songs, and also reflected the style of the sentimental songs of the day. STEPHEN FOSTER was the greatest composer of such songs, even though he never lived in the South and was not personally familiar with the conditions of African-American life or slavery. Many of Foster's songs— OLD FOLKS AT HOME, OH SUSANNAH, CAMPTOWN RACES— have gained the status of American folk songs.

Minstrel show troupes were popular not only in the U.S. but also on tours of Europe. By the 1870s and '80s, "authentic" African-American performers—still wearing blackface—were introduced onto the minstrel stage, as an "added attraction." Blackface performers continued to be popular into the 1920s, both black and white: AL JOLSON and African-American comedian Bert Williams are only two better-known examples.

minuet (Fr. *menuet;* It. *Minuetto;* Ger. *Menuett*). The most popular court dance in triple time. It was danced by couples, distinguished by the stately grace of its choreography and its balanced musical structure. The standard minuet consisted of three sections, of which the first and third were identical. The middle section, set in the DOMINANT, SUBDOMINANT, or RELATIVE KEY, was called the "trio" because it was written usually for three instruments, whereas the minuet proper was usually arranged for a fuller ensemble.

It is generally believed that the minuet was derived from a provincial French dance tune, but as a mature form it was introduced at the court of Louis XIV. JEAN-BAPTISTE LULLY, his court musician, wrote a number of minuets for royal balls.

The vogue of minuet dancing spread to all the courts of Europe, becoming tremendously popular in Russia, Spain, and Italy, but less so in England and Germany. Eventually the minuet became an integral part of the BAROQUE instrumental SUITE, and in CLASSIC SONATAS and SYMPHONIES.

In the 19th century the minuet yielded its place in sonatas and symphonies to the more whirlwind mood of the SCHERZO. However, this new form usually conserved the $\frac{3}{4}$ time signature as well as the characteristic trio.

Minute Waltz. Nickname for FRÉDÉRIC CHOPIN's Waltz in D Flat Major, op.64, which is supposedly possible to negotiate in about one minute. Omitting the repeats, the time can be cut to 48 seconds.

miracle plays. Sacred dramas, often with music, popular in England in the Middle Ages. The stories were usually on biblical subjects or parables. Later examples of this genre were called *moralities.*

Miranda, Carmen (born Maria do Carmo Miranda da Cunha), charismatic Portuguese-American singer of popular music and actress; b. Marco de Canaveses, near Lisbon, Feb. 9, 1909; d. Beverly Hills, Calif., Aug. 5, 1955. Miranda spent her formative years in Rio de Janeiro. After performing throughout South America, she made her first appearance on Broadway in 1939 in the revue *The Streets of Paris,*

It is said that the king himself often danced to Lully's music—although his mature, commanding size was ill-suited for dancing or any energetic movement.

PEOPLE IN MUSIC

where she was dubbed the "Brazilian Bombshell." She went on to gain an extensive following via many film appearances, recordings, nightclub engagements, and television appearances. She is particularly remembered for her spiky high-heeled shoes and fantastic headdresses made of fruit. In the movie musical *The Gang's All Here* (1943), with lavish choreography by Busby Berkeley, she comically careened her way through the number *The Lady with the Tutti Frutti Hat*.

meer-lĕ′tŏhn

MUSICAL INSTRUMENT

mirliton (Fr.). Small tubular musical instrument, the sound of which is produced by a membrane set vibrating by the human voice; same as the KAZOO.

Miroirs (Mirrors). Piano SUITE by MAURICE RAVEL, 1906, in five movements:

Noctuelles (nocturnal moths)

Oiseaux tristes (wistful birds)

Un Barque sur l'océan (a lonesome boat on the ocean)

Alborada del gracioso (the morning serenade of a jester)

La Vallée des cloches (the valley of bells)

These movements are among the finest examples of IMPRESSIONIST piano writing. The suite was first performed in Paris.

Miserere. The opening Latin word of the 50th Psalm, in the Roman Catholic (Vulgate) numbering; thereby, musical settings of the Psalm. The imploration "Have mercy" is a part of the Holy Week Service known as TENEBRAE (darkness).

There is a credible story that WOLFGANG AMADEUS MOZART as a young boy attended the performance of a Miserere by Gregorio Allegri (1582–1652) in the Vatican, memorized the entire setting for nine voices, and wrote it down shortly afterward. Allegri's Miserere was an exclusive property of the papal choir, so Mozart's feat was undoubtedly disturbing to church officials, but the piece was eventually published and became famous.

Miss Julie. Opera by NED ROREM, 1965, after the drama by Strindberg, first produced in N.Y. Miss Julie is of noble birth. Strangely, she falls under the spell of the family servant, who dominates her so fully that at his behest she robs her own father. Distressed and repentant, she commits suicide. The music is appropriately melodramatic, set in a moderately modernistic manner.

Miss Liberty. Musical by IRVING BERLIN, 1949. In 1885 N.Y. City, two famous newspaper editors (James Gordon Bennett and Joseph Pulitzer) are waging a publicity war for the coverage of the recently arrived Statue of Liberty, presented by France to N.Y. Their representatives are trying to locate the Paris model for the statue. Pulitzer's reporter finds a girl he believes was the model for the statue and brings her to N.Y. She is accused of fraudulent misrepresentation, but Pulitzer proves her innocence. In the finale she sings a song to the text engraved at the base of the statue, "Give me your tired, your poor."

Missa Papae Marcelli. MASS by GIOVANNI PIERLUIGI DA PALESTRINA, published in 1567. It bears the name of Pope Marcellus II, whose reign lasted three weeks in 1555. It is set in a HOMOPHONIC (single-melody) style quite different from his earlier POLYPHONIC works.

Some church leaders—perhaps Marcellus among them—had been critical of the many ornate settings of psalms that featured many interlocking melodic parts. Some historians believe that this piece was written by Palestrina at Marcellus's request to simplify religious music. While this story may be legendary, it is not inconceivable that Palestrina chose to honor a deceased pope in this way.

Missouri Waltz. Popular piece, 1914, by Frederick Knight Logan (1871–1928). It was first published as a piano solo, with Logan credited only as its "arranger." Two years later, when the words were added, the sheet music sold a million copies, and Logan took full credit for the work. It was quickly adopted by the state of Missouri as its official song.

President Harry Truman loved to play the piano, and the *Missouri Waltz* was one of his favorite pieces.

Mr. Broucek's Excursion to the Moon and Mr. Broucek's Excursion into the 15th Century. Two fantasy operas by LEOŠ JANÁČEK (1908–17), premiered in Prague, 1920. The hero is a typical middle-class citizen who, when drunk, imagines himself first traveling to the moon and then back in time.

Sadly, Berlin's last Broadway musical was a gigantic flop. It soured him on composing, and for the next decades until his death he rarely appeared in public.

Mister President. Musical by IRVING BERLIN, his last, 1962. The president of the U.S. makes an informal trip to Moscow, where he engages in friendly talk, not with Soviet officials but with simple workers. But his unusual method of diplomacy arouses an uproar in the U.S., and he is defeated at the next election. A romance between the president's daughter and a secret service man provides love interest. Includes *Empty Pockets Full of Love* and *Meat and Potatoes.*

Mr. Tambourine Man. Folk rock ballad by BOB DYLAN that was the Byrds' first No. 1 hit in 1965.

Mrs. Robinson. Theme song from the 1968 film *The Graduate,* written by PAUL SIMON. It was a No. 1 hit for him and his then-partner, Art Garfunkel.

Misty. Song by ERROLL GARNER, 1955. This sentimental ballad became extremely popular in JOHNNY MATHIS's recording.

PEOPLE IN MUSIC

Mitchell, Joni (born Roberta Joan Anderson), Canadian singer and songwriter of popular music; b. McLeod, near Lethbridge, Alberta, Nov. 7, 1943. Mitchell was raised in Saskatoon and took piano lessons in childhood, later learning to play guitar. She attended the Alberta College of Art in Calgary for a year and sang in a local coffeehouse. She then performed in Toronto, where she met and married the folksinger Chuck Mitchell, whose last name she kept after their divorce.

Mitchell wrote the hit song *Both Sides Now* (1968), made famous in JUDY COLLINS's recording. Mitchell included it in her album *Clouds* (1969), which captured a Grammy Award for best folk recording in 1970. Her album *Ladies of the Canyon* (1970) attained gold status, and the subsequent album *Court and Spark* (1974) also proved highly popular. Other popular songs of the '70s included her minor hit *Big Yellow Taxi,* a comment on the ecological damage done to the earth by man.

In her interpretations, she closely followed the folk-song style, with an admixture of jazzy syncopation and unusual guitar tunings. For a while she collaborated with CHARLES MINGUS. After his death in 1979, she wrote a moving song in his memory, *God Must Be a Boogie Man.* Other albums of note include *Hejira* (1976), *Don Juan's Reckless Daughter* (1978), *Dog Eat Dog* (1986), *Chalk Mark in a Rain Storm* (1988), *Night Ride Home* (1991), and *Turbulent Indigo* (1994).

Mitridate, Re di Ponto. Opera by WOLFGANG AMADEUS MOZART, 1770, first performed in Milan. Mozart was only 14 when he wrote this work. The LIBRETTO is based on a play by French playwright Jean Racine.

Mithridates, king of Pontus, loves a young Greek girl who is loved also by his two sons. Many complications follow as the story unravels. Finally, Mithridates is fatally wounded in battle and urges his second son to marry the girl they all love.

Mitropoulos, Dimitri, Greek-born American conductor and composer; b. Athens, March 1, 1896; d. Nov. 2, 1960. Mitropoulos studied piano and harmony at the Odeon Conservatory in Athens. While still a student, his opera after Maeterlinck, *Soeur Beatrice,* was performed in 1919.

PEOPLE IN MUSIC

In 1920, after his graduation, Mitropoulos went to Brussels, where he studied composition. In 1921 he went to Berlin, where he took piano lessons with the Italian modern composer FERRUCCIO BUSONI at the Hochschule für Musik until 1924. Concurrently, he was rehearsal pianist at the Berlin State Opera.

Mitropoulos became a conductor of the Odeon Conservatory orchestra in 1924, serving as co-conductor from 1927 to 1929, then its principal conductor. Beginning in 1930, he was also professor of composition there.

In 1930 Mitropoulos was invited to conduct a concert of the Berlin Philharmonic. When the soloist Egon Petri became suddenly indisposed, Mitropoulos substituted for him as soloist in SERGEI PROKOFIEV's Piano Concerto No. 3, conducting from the keyboard. He played the same concerto in Paris in 1932 as pianist-conductor, and later in the U.S. His Paris debut as a conductor in 1932 met with spontaneous success. He conducted the most difficult works from memory, a novelty at the time, and also led rehearsals without a score.

Mitropoulos made his American debut with the Boston Symphony Orchestra in 1936, with immediate acclaim. That same year he was engaged as music director of the Minneapolis Symphony Orchestra, where he frequently performed modern music, including works by ARNOLD SCHOENBERG, ALBAN BERG, and other representatives of the ATONAL school. He was able to give these works emotional performances that won over a sometimes skeptical audience.

Mitropoulos resigned from the Minneapolis Symphony Orchestra in 1949 to accept the post of conductor of the N.Y. Philharmonic. He shared the podium with LEOPOLD STOKOWSKI for a few weeks, and in 1950 he became music director. In 1956 LEONARD BERNSTEIN was engaged as associate conductor with Mitropoulos, and in 1958 succeeded him as music director. With the N.Y. Philharmonic, Mitropoulos continued his policy of bringing out important works by European and American modernists. He also programmed modern operas (*Elektra, Wozzeck*) in concert form.

Sadly, after leaving the N.Y. Philharmonic, Mitropoulos's career was brief. He died after suffering a heart attack while rehearsing GUSTAV MAHLER's Third Symphony with the orchestra of the Teatro alla Scala, Milan.

A musician of astounding technical ability, Mitropoulos became very successful with the general public as well as with the modern composers whose works he often championed. While he spent most of his time in the U.S., Mitropoulos continued to appear as guest conductor in Europe. He also appeared on numerous occasions as conductor at the Metropolitan Opera in N.Y. (debut conducting *Salome*, 1954) and at various European opera theaters. He became an American citizen in 1946.

As a composer, Mitropoulos was one of the earliest among Greek composers to write in a distinctly modern idiom.

mixed media. Works in which musical, dramatic, verbal, literary, and other elements are joined in a single composition, usually in novel ways.

Musicians of the AVANT-GARDE are increasingly laboring toward the unification of modern musical productions with those of other arts: painting, sculpture, phonograph recording, theater, radio, television, and electronics. The practice represents in fact a return to the ancient ideal of unity of liberal arts, with music occupying the honorable position as *ancilla artis.*

Mixolydian mode. *See* AUTHENTIC MODES.

Mlada. Opera by NIKOLAI RIMSKY-KORSAKOV, 1892, premiered in St. Petersburg. Although the action takes place in the Slavic settlement on the Baltic shore in the 10th century, the cast of characters is mostly supernatural. Mlada is a dead princess who visits her fiancé in his dreams. Slavic apparitions tell him that Mlada was murdered by the girl he now plans to marry. He swears vengeance and kills the accused murderess. He dies too, and is reunited with Mlada in heaven.

M.M. 1. Trademark of Johannes Nepomuk Maelzel's METRONOME, invented 1816. 2. More commonly, an abbreviation for "metronome marking."

modal harmony. The harmonic possibilities derived from the traditional MODES. It is thus separate from TONAL HARMONY, which concerns the common MAJOR and MINOR KEYS. Modal harmony may or may not operate on the TONIC-DOMINANT principle. Some modes are free from tonal RESOLUTION altogether.

modality. A 20th-century term applied to a revival of diatonic MODES other than the MAJOR and MINOR SCALES. Often, composers use modes to evoke an exotic style or subject matter; MODEST MUSSORSKY, for instance, used modes in his music to describe the essence of the Russian soul. Some have borrowed modes from traditional folk melodies

mode. 1. A generic term applied to ancient Greek melodic progressions. More particularly, the modes were church scales established in the Middle Ages and codified in the system of GREGORIAN CHANT.

The intervals of the Greek modes were counted downward, while those of the medieval modes were counted upward, so the actual scale notes were different between the Greek and the church systems. However, the church modes retained the Greek names of the modes. The modes continued to underlie all Western music through the 17th century, then gradually gave way to the tonal major and minor keys.

Originally there were eight modes based on the "white keys" of the C major scale. They began on D, E, F, or G with a range of about an octave. Each of these four notes produced two modes: an AUTHENTIC MODE (beginning on the ROOT note itself) and a PLAGAL MODE (running from the fourth below to the fifth above). In the 16th century, four more scales were added (beginning on A and C and their respective SUBDOMINANTS), bringing the total to 12.

THE CHURCH MODES AND THEIR NAMES			
Name	**Root Note (Finalis)**	**Lowest note**	**Type**
1. Dorian	D	D	authentic
2. Hypodorian	D	A	plagal
3. Phryigian	E	E	authentic
4. Hypophrygian	E	B	plagal
5. Lydian	F	F	authentic
6. Hypolydian	F	C	plagal
7. Mixolydian	G	G	authentic
8. Hypomixolydian	G	D	plagal
9. Aeolian	A	A	authentic
10. Hypoaeolian	A	E	plagal
11. Ionian	C	C	authentic
12. Hypoionian	C	G	plagal

2. The distinction between a major key (mode) and minor key (mode). 3. Any scalar pattern of intervals, either indigenous to a culture (Indian, Japanese, Indonesian, etc.) or

newly invented. 4. A system of rhythmic notation used in the 13th century (MENSURAL NOTATION).

modern music. In present classical usage, modern music refers to works written since 1900. Variants may include *20th-century music, new music,* and *contemporary music.*

modernism. Musical composition as it developed early in the 20th century. Key elements included:

MODULATION from one key to another broke completely free from DIATONIC and CHROMATIC progressions.

DISSONANCES acquired equal rights with CONSONANCES.

Several KEYS could be combined in a technique called POLYTONALITY.

MELODY was allowed to veer away from its TONAL foundations.

The sensibility of progress and "the new" that emerged c.1910 was expressed in the paintings of Pablo Picasso and Wassily Kandinsky, the novels of James Joyce and Marcel Proust, and the music of ARNOLD SCHOENBERG and IGOR STRAVINSKY.

Modernism was later supplanted by POSTMODERNISM, a reaction to many of the excesses of the modern movement.

modinha. Brazilian and Portuguese art song of the 18th and 19th centuries. Sentimental in tone, the modinha was usually accompanied by GUITAR. Its originally simple qualities changed with the influence of operatic ARIA, leading to elaborate melodies and some ornamentation. In its latter Brazilian stage, the modinha became truly lyrical and folk song-like.

modulation. Transition from one key or mode to another within a single composition.

The idea of modulation dates back to the system of HEXACHORDS of GUIDO D'AREZZO. This theory was not based on modern rules of tonal harmony; rather, d'Arezzo came up with an elaborate system based on substituting scale notes from one hexachord to another. Some of the resulting modulations sound very odd to modern ears, because they rarely occur in modern tonality.

When the idea of the major and minor keys was established as dual counterparts of tonality, the rules of modulation were drawn according to the principle of kinship of keys having the same number of sharps or flats in the key signature, or of neighboring keys having one more or one less sharp or flat relative to the initial key. This relationship was incorporated in a scientific-looking CIRCLE OF FIFTHS in the image of the face of a clock in which the sharps move clockwise and flats move counterclockwise. Any composer desiring to modulate from one key to another that was not adjacent in the circle of fifths had to move through the intermediate stopovers, step by step.

Departing from C major (virginally clear of accidentals), with a goal of A major (which has three sharps), one has to traverse successively the stops that have one and two sharps in the key signature. This could be done by moving, for variety's sake, first to a minor key having one sharp (E minor), then to a major key having two sharps (D major), and from there landing in A major via a regular CADENCE.

But what if a modulating traveler had to go to a key four or five sharps away from the starting point? Surely movement by steps across the clock of the circle of fifths would be tedious. Luckily, each minor key has a major DOMINANT, which enables the modulating composer to jump four stops in the direction of sharps, clockwise. For instance, the dominant of A harmonic minor is E major, a key that has four sharps in its key signature. Starting from C major, we can detour to its relative minor key (A minor) and from there make a direct transition to E major. We append a nice cadence, and the job is done.

The circle of fifths is not the only itinerary for modulation. There is a powerful chromatic resource in *enharmonic modulation.* Let us take a common, ordinary DOMINANT SEVENTH CHORD in the key of C, G–B–D–F. Change F enharmonically to E♯, a note identical to F in sound but not in meaning. E♯ functions as the top note of an AUGMENTED SIXTH CHORD whose bottom note is the former dominant,

G. Thus the E♯ has an irresistible instinct to rise to F♯, while the bottom note G has a hardly more resistible instinct to sink to the lower F♯. When both notes, following their instincts, land on an F♯ octave, we find ourselves in the tonic $\frac{6}{4}$ chord of B minor.

In *chromatic modulation,* chords can be ever-changing. Consider the DIMINISHED SEVENTH CHORD. Depending on one of its 24 musically possible spellings, it can instantly modulate to any of the 24 major or minor keys. No wonder it was called by Italian opera composers ACCORDE DI STUPE-FAZIONE, because it stunned the listener into catatonic suspense, particularly when played TREMOLO in the strings. Because the diminished seventh chord consists of minor thirds that are free to move in parallel motion, dramatic chromatic rises and falls are most effective. ROMANTIC operas, even by respectable composers, are full of such crawling chords. But even nonoperatic composers are not averse to taking advantage of this facility. In the coda of his B flat minor Scherzo for piano (op.20), FRÉDÉRIC CHOPIN uses a series of ornamented diminished seventh chords with nerve-tingling embellishments in the middle voices that finally resolve into the long-anticipated key of D flat major. FELIX MENDELSSOHN portrays a storm with diminished sevenths in his *FINGAL'S CAVE* overture.

Other types of modulations are *diatonic modulation,* one effected by use of diatonic intervals; *final modulation,* one in which the new key is retained, or still another follows; *passing, transient, transitory modulation,* one in which the original key is speedily regained.

modus (Lat., mode). In MENSURAL NOTATION, the ratio of note values between the *maxima* and *longa,* and between the *longa* and *brevis.* The former ratio is called *modus major;* the latter, *modus minor.*

Like other mensural note values, these ratios can either be *perfect* (a PERFECTION), containing three units of the lesser note values, or *imperfect* (an IMPERFECTION), containing only two units of the lesser note values. Thus *modus major imperfectus* is a measure containing two longas; *modus minor imperfectus* contains two *breves.*

Moldau *(Vlatava).* The second and most famous movement of BEDŘICH SMETANA's symphonic cycle *MÁ VLAST,* 1874. It is a tribute to the river on which the city of Prague is situated.

The main theme, in E minor, is ingratiatingly ROMAN-TIC. Whether by actual borrowing or through extraordinary coincidence, this melody was adopted for the Zionist AN-THEM at the first International Zionist Conference in Basel in 1897. It eventually evolved into the Israeli national anthem *Hatikvah* (hope). Investigators also found that the melody of *Moldau* was remarkably similar to a Swedish song written in 1822, and the melody has also been traced to folk songs of Dutch and Polish origin.

moment musical (Fr.). ROMANTIC character piece, usually for piano. FRANZ SCHUBERT wrote six pieces so titled, published under the incorrect French title *Moments musicals.*

Momente. Work by KARLHEINZ STOCKHAUSEN, 1962, scored for SOPRANO, four choruses (who sing, speak, scream, and clap), 13 instruments, and PERCUSSION, first performed in Cologne. In the score, Stockhausen introduced the term *Moment-Groups* to designate the planned (or unplanned) simultaneous production of certain sounds by voices and instruments.

PEOPLE IN MUSIC

Mompou, Federico, significant Catalan composer; b. Barcelona, April 16, 1893; d. there, June 30, 1987. After preliminary studies at the Barcelona Conservatory, Mompou went to Paris, where he studied piano and composition. He returned to Barcelona during World War I, then was again in Paris from 1921 to 1941, when he once more returned to Spain.

Mompou's music is inspired by Spanish and Catalan melodies, but its harmonic and instrumental treatment is entirely modern. His works, mostly for piano, include *Scènes d'enfants* (1915), *Trois pessebres* (1918), *Cants magics* (1919), *Festes Llunyanes* (1920), *Charmes* (1921), *Dialogues* (1923), *Canción y Danza* (1918–62), 10 preludes (1927–51), *Paisajes* (1942, 1947, 1960), and *Música callada* (Silent music; four albums, 1959–67). He also composed *Suite com-*

◀

Federico Mompou at the piano, 1978. (Colita/Corbis)

postelana for guitar (1963), as well as choral works and songs.

Mond, Der (The Moon). Opera by CARL ORFF, 1939, to his own text after a fairytale by the Brothers Grimm, first produced in Munich. The story tells of four boys who steal the moon and use it as a bedside lamp. When they die, they arrange to take the moon with them to their graves. The sudden illumination arouses the dead. St. Peter comes down to restore order and puts the moon up in the sky where it belongs.

Like most of Orff's operas, *Der Mond* is a theatrical spectacle, containing spoken dialogue, a PANTOMIME, and several symphonic interludes in which a large group of percussion instruments make interesting noises.

Mondo della luna, Il (The World of the Moon). OPERA BUFFA by FRANZ JOSEPH HAYDN, 1777, first performed at the Prince Esterházy estate. An astronomer, fittingly named Dr. Ecclittico (ecliptic), drugs a rich Venetian man. He convinces the man that he is on the moon and that the lunar authorities have ordered him to let his daughter marry her impoverished suitor. The music is spirited and pleasing to the ears of inhabitants of any celestial body.

money and music. Musicians do not manufacture material goods and therefore, like poets, must subsist through patronage. In times of catastrophic social disturbances—wars, famine, and plagues—music stops. In times of prosperity, musicians attach themselves to the dominant powers, to the church, to the royal court, to educational institutions (which themselves must depend on the powers of the state), or to wealthy merchants.

In the church, and particularly in the most organized historical church of Rome, musicians performed the essential duties of writing for sacred services. When great royal courts emerged in the Middle Ages, kings, emperors, dukes, and other secular potentates employed musicians to lend decorum to their mundane preoccupations. With the emergence of industrial civilization, many kings took pleasure in sponsoring musical activities. Singers found easy employment in the church, instrumentalists were less in demand, and composers had the least opportunity unless they acted also as performers, conductors of military bands, or instructors in universities.

In public demand of their services, a similar order exists. Popular singers can make a fortune, but artists specializing in classical music often find it hard to earn a dime.

A curious inverse ratio exists in relation to a singer's musical education or professional excellence and commercial success. Some of the most successful jazz and rock 'n' roll performers could never learn to read music. Even the most celebrated opera TENOR, ENRICO CARUSO, sang by ear, even though he was already an international star.

Instrumentalists come second in popular acclaim. Among them pianists enjoy the greatest opportunity of monetary success, followed by violinists and cellists. Symphonic conductors may be described as instrumentalists of the baton. Sometimes they have rivaled performing artists in public admiration, but because symphonic music is the food for the sophisticates and the connoisseur, and because they cannot pursue their profession with a maximum of proficiency without an orchestra of great excellence, they may remain philosophers of music, even when they become idols of the audience.

Infinitely more successful financially are the leaders of dance bands, from the "Waltz King" JOHANN STRAUSS, JR. and the "March King" JOHN PHILIP SOUSA to the leaders of some big bands.

In terms of both popular success and financial reward, composers find themselves on the lowest rung of the ladder. Some composers of semiclassical music and popular songs have achieved a certain prosperity, but authors of large symphonic works or chamber music have little hope of attaining even a moderate income.

The history of musical biography is a study in impoverished beginnings and unhappy endings:

WOLFGANG AMADEUS MOZART wrote pathetic letters to a friendly banker asking for petty loans. (One of these letters sold some 200 years later to an autograph collector for a sum a thousand times as large as the loan requested by Mozart.)

LUDWIG VAN BEETHOVEN flaunted his poverty with proud assertion of his status as a "brain owner."

PIOTR ILYICH TCHAIKOVSKY had a rich admirer in the person of Mme. von Meck, who gave him an annual grant.

RICHARD WAGNER was put in a debtor's prison in Paris when he was already a well-known composer.

BÉLA BARTÓK complained bitterly during his last years of life in America that he could not even find piano pupils to provide pocket money. A friendly Hungarian emigré arranged for him to make a recording of his piano music, but sales were so poor that his friend decided to doctor his royalty account to make it appear more respectable. (A picture postcard with Bartók's handwriting sold after his death for $165.)

ARNOLD SCHOENBERG applied to the Guggenheim Foundation for a grant to enable him to complete his opera *Moses und Aron* but was turned down. (A few pages of Schoenberg's orchestration of a Viennese operetta that he composed as a young man was priced at several thousand dollars at an auction after his death.)

ALEXANDER SCRIABIN suffered desperate financial difficulties after the death of his patron, the publisher Belaieff. Sometimes, living in Switzerland, he even lacked enough money for a postage stamp.

The situation of composers has considerably improved in the 20th century: in Europe, by the creation of government grants, prizes, and other awards, and in the U.S., by the formation of ASCAP and BMI to protect royalty interests. Furthermore, "prestige" payments are often made by publishers to composers, the sale of whose works is not profitable commercially.

Moniuszko, Stanislaw, Polish composer; b. Ubiel, Minsk province, Russia, May 5, 1819; d. Warsaw, June 4, 1872. In 1827 Moniuszko's family went to Warsaw, where he first studied music. He continued his training in Minsk and finally in Berlin during 1837.

Moniuszko went to Vilnius in 1840, where he served as organist at St. John's chapel. He gained notice as a composer when he published volume 1 of his *Śpiewnik domowy* (Songbook for Home Use; 1843). He gained the support of various Polish figures in the arts and also won the admiration of fellow composers MIKHAIL GLINKA, ALEXANDER DARGOMIZHSKY, and CÉSAR CUI in Russia. In 1848 a concert performance of the two-act version of his opera *Halka* was given for the first time in Vilnius. After he expanded it to four acts, it was staged in Warsaw in 1858, scoring a great success.

In 1859 Moniuszko settled in Warsaw, becoming conductor of opera at the Grand Theater. He continued to compose for the stage and also taught at the Music Institute from 1864. He published *Pamiętnik do nauki harmonii* (Textbook on Harmony; 1871).

Moniuszko holds a revered place in Polish music history as the outstanding composer of opera in his era, but he also excelled as a composer of songs. His other works include incidental music to 14 plays, ballets, orchestral and chamber music, and both sacred and secular choral works.

Monk, Meredith (Jane), American composer, singer, and filmmaker; b. Lima, Peru (of American parents), Nov. 20, 1942. Monk studied EURYTHMICS from an early age. She was educated at Sarah Lawrence College (B.A., 1964), then was a pupil in voice of Vicki Starr, John Devers, and Jeanette Lovetri, in composition of Ruth Lloyd, Richard Averee, and Glenn Mack, and in piano of Gershon Konikow.

Monk has pursued an active career as a singer, film-maker, director, choreographer, recording artist, and composer. In 1968 she organized The House in N.Y., a company devoted to interdisciplinary approaches to the arts. In 1978 she founded her own vocal chamber ensemble, with which she toured widely in the U.S. and abroad. In 1972 and 1982 she held Guggenheim fellowships. She has also received various ASCAP awards and many commissions. In 1995 she was awarded a MacArthur fellowship.

Monk's powerful SOPRANO vocalizations employ a wide range of ethnic and AVANT-GARDE influences. As one of the first and most natural of PERFORMANCE ARTISTS, Monk developed a flexible, imaginative theatrical style. Many of the "plots" of her works are influenced by dream narrative and psychoanalysis. All of her works include physical movement.

Among Monk's best-known works are *Education of the Girlchild,* opera for six voices, electric organ, and piano (1972–73); *Dolmen Music* for six voices, cello, and PERCUSSION (1979); *Turtle Dreams (Waltz)* for four voices and two electric organs (1980–81); *Book of Days,* film score for 10 voices, cello, SHAWM, SYNTHESIZER, HAMMERED DULCIMER, BAGPIPE, and HURDY-GURDY (1988); *Atlas,* opera (1991); and *Denkai Krikiki Chants* for four voices (1995).

Monk, Thelonious (Sphere), noted African-American jazz pianist and composer; b. Rocky Mount, N.C., Oct. 10, 1917; d. Englewood, N.J., Feb. 17, 1982. Monk is one of the most famous eccentrics in all of jazz. A gifted pianist and composer, he was one of the creators of BEBOP.

Monk was born in Hell's Kitchen on the West Side of N.Y., where he spent most of his life. In the late '40s, he joined a group of jazz musicians playing in a small Harlem club called Minton's Playhouse, which included DIZZY GILLESPIE and CHARLIE PARKER. Monk composed at this time a number of classic pieces—including his signature tune, *'Round Midnight*—which helped define the bebop style. At about the same time, he made his first recordings as a soloist and leading a small group.

Through the '50s, Monk built his reputation as one of the most innovative of all jazz pianists. He worked with a number of important jazz players, including both older mu-

PEOPLE IN MUSIC

sicians like COLEMAN HAWKINS and young newcomers like JOHN COLTRANE. He also composed a long list of standards, including *Blue Monk, Well You Needn't,* and *In Walked Bud.*

Monk's behavior became increasingly eccentric in the '60s. He would go through periods of time without speaking to his family or friends. Meanwhile, he composed little new music, although he continued to perform many of his own pieces and standards. In the early '70s, he performed on several "Giants of Jazz" tours while continuing to lead his own group, including his son, T. S., on drums. However, his periods of illness increased, and by 1976 he abandoned playing. He spent the last six years of his life living in a small apartment in Weehawken, N.J., funded by a wealthy jazz fan. He did not play and rarely spoke. He died in 1982.

Monk's piano playing was unique. It is often described as "angular" because of the spiky melodies, long pauses, and jagged chords that he used. His pieces managed to have memorable melodies that were easy to hum while at the same time being very complicated to play correctly. Numerous jazz and rock musicians have said they were influenced by his music.

Monk's *'Round Midnight* is thought to be among the most-recorded of all jazz standards.

PEOPLE IN MUSIC

Monkees, The. (Guitar/vocal: Michael Nesmith, b. Houston, Tex., Dec. 30, 1942; Vocal/tambourine: Davy Jones, b. Manchester, England, Dec. 30, 1945; Bass/vocal: Peter Tork [Torkelson], b. Washington, D.C., Feb. 13, 1944; Drums/vocal: Michael "Micky" Dolenz, b. Tarzana, Calif., March 8, 1945.) Known as the "Pre-Fab Four," the Monkees were a group created to cash in on the popularity of the BEATLES and their films for the TV/teenage market. They achieved great popularity from 1966, when their TV show premiered, until 1969, when the group disintegrated.

Auditioned for looks as much as musical talents, they scored hits primarily with songs written by pop tunesmiths such as Goffin-King, Neil Diamond, and, particularly, Tommy Boyce and Bobby Hart. Hits included Boyce and Hart's *Last Train to Clarksville* and *Valleri,* Leiber and Stoller's *D. W. Washburn,* John Stewart's *Daydream Believer,* and Goffin-King's *Pleasant Valley Sunday.*

Aspiring to transcend their teenybopper roots, the group made the impressionistic film *Head* (1968), working with director Bob Rafaelson and Jack Nicholson. It perplexed their younger fans while failing to win over the sophisticated crowd, although today it is considered something of a cult classic. That same year, they toured the country to prove that they could indeed play their own instruments. As an opening act, they enlisted a then little-known guitarist named JIMI HENDRIX, but their teenage fans were dismayed by his pyrotechnics and he was quickly dropped from the tour.

After the group disbanded, Nesmith formed a country-rock group known as the First National Band and enjoyed some success as a songwriter (his *Different Drum* was a hit for Linda Ronstadt and the Stone Ponys in 1969). In the '70s, Nesmith became involved in the new field of music video, developing a prototype for what would become MTV, and producing various films.

In 1986, with the re-release of Monkee recordings again selling briskly, Jones, Tork, and Dolenz reunited for a comeback album and tour. Nesmith resisted the temptation to join the mass cash-in until the mid-'90s, when he too took to the road with his old ape-mates.

monochord. An ancient CHORDOPHONE. As the name indicates, it had a single string, stretched over a soundbox, and a shifting bridge that allowed the string to be adjusted to different pitches. It is used to test acoustic theories.

> MUSICAL
> INSTRUMENT

monodrama. A stage work in which only one actor, speaker, or singer acts, recites, or sings. ARNOLD SCHOENBERG introduced a type of singing recitation, SPRECHSTIMME, in which the actor speaks his lines in an inflected manner following the melody and rhythmic design of the music, a technique that came to its full fruition in his *PIERROT LUNAIRE.* The classic example of a staged monodrama is his *Erwartung.* In Schoenberg's *Die glückliche Hand,* the central character sings and mimes the story, and a chorus comments on the action in Sprechstimme.

The Russian composer Vladimir Rebikov evolved a novel type of monodrama that he described as psychodrama. In it an actor recites his state of mind with musical accompaniment.

monody (from Lat., single song). Usually, the recitative-like BASSO CONTINUO song style of early-17th-century Italy.

monophonic. 1. Texture of unaccompanied melody. 2. Instrument capable of producing but one tone at a time.

monothematism and polythematism. In the 19th and 20th centuries, composers turned to monothematism, in which a single subject might govern an entire composition.

Monothematism, an extension of organicism ("growing" a piece from one melody or even motif) and related to thematic transformation, is basic to the structure of a theme with variations. However, if variations depart too widely from the theme, the result may be polythematic. Rigid monothematism carries an intrinsic danger of monotony. On the other hand, extreme polythematism courts the opposite danger of discontinuity.

In monothematism the single theme must recur a sufficient number of times to produce an impression of uniformity. In polythematic constructions, overt similarities among successive themes must be avoided.

monotone 1. A single unaccompanied and unvaried tone. 2. Recitation (intoning, chanting) on such a tone.

PEOPLE IN MUSIC

Monroe, Bill (William Smith), American country music singer, mandolin player, and songwriter; b. near Rosine, Ky., Sept. 13, 1911; d. Springfield, Tenn., Sept. 9, 1996. Monroe studied with his uncle, Pendleton Vandiver, a fiddler, then played fiddle in a band formed by his brothers Birch and Charlie. Charlie and Bill performed as the Monroe Brothers for a few years. In 1938 Bill organized his own band, the Blue Grass Boys, which gained fame through appearances on the *Grand Ole Opry* radio program in Nashville.

Monroe's innovations in string-band music led to the development of the BLUEGRASS style. His most famous band included LESTER FLATT and EARL SCRUGGS, who introduced bluegrass style BANJO (fingerpicking melodies using three fingers equipped with metallic picks). This group lasted from about 1946 to 1949. Monroe composed many bluegrass standards, including the waltz *Blue Moon of Kentucky,*

Uncle Pen (in honor of his fiddling relative), and many other vocal works, as well as dozens of classic instrumentals, including *Rawhide, Wheelhoss,* and *Scotland.*

Many notable bluegrass and newgrass musicians played in Monroe's band, including Stringbean (Dave Akeman), Jimmie Martin, Sonny Osborne, Vassar Clements, Buddy Spicher, Kenny Baker, Ralph Rinzler, Richard Greene, Bill Keith, and Peter Rowan. In 1970 Monroe was elected into the Country Music Hall of Fame.

Monroe continued to perform over the decades, with little change in either the lineup of his band or the music that it performed. He was still performing and recording at the time of his death.

Montemezzi, Italo, Italian opera composer; b. Vigasio, near Verona, Aug. 4, 1875; d. there, May 15, 1952. Montemezzi was a pupil at the Milan Conservatory and graduated in 1900. His graduation piece, conducted by ARTURO TOSCANINI, was *Cantico dei Cantici,* for chorus and orchestra. He then devoted himself almost exclusively to opera. In 1939 he went to the U.S., living mostly in California. In 1949 he returned to Italy.

Montemezzi's chief accomplishment was the maintenance of the best traditions of Italian dramatic music. His masterpiece was *L'amore dei tre re* (Milan, April 10, 1913), which entered the standard repertoire of opera houses all over the world.

Monteux, Pierre, celebrated French-born American conductor; b. Paris, April 4, 1875; d. Hancock, Maine, July 1, 1964. Monteux studied violin, harmony, and composition at the Paris Conservatory, receiving first prize for violin in 1896. He then was a viola player in the Colonne Orchestra, and later chorus master there. He also played viola in the orchestra of the Opéra-Comique in Paris.

In 1911 Monteux organized his own concert series, the Concerts Berlioz, at the Casino de Paris. That same year, he also became conductor for Sergei Diaghilev's Ballets Russes, and his performances of modern ballet scores established him as one of the finest technicians of the baton. He led the world premieres of IGOR STRAVINSKY's *PETROUCHKA, LE SACRE*

In 1954 Elvis Presley took BILL MONROE's waltz, *Blue Moon of Kentucky,* and sped it up to make his first big hit as a rock and roller. Monroe frequently performed the piece both in waltz time and in the new version arranged by Elvis.

PEOPLE IN MUSIC

PEOPLE IN MUSIC

DU PRINTEMPS, and *LE ROSSIGNOL,* MAURICE RAVEL's *DAPHNIS ET CHLOÉ,* and CLAUDE DEBUSSY's *JEUX.* He also conducted at the Paris Opéra in 1913–14 and founded the Societé des Concerts Populaires in Paris in 1914. He appeared as guest conductor in London, Berlin, Vienna, Budapest, and other major European cities.

In 1916–17, Monteux toured the U.S. with the Ballets Russes, and in 1917 he conducted the Civic Orchestra Society in N.Y. From 1917 to 1919 he conducted at the Metropolitan Opera there. In 1919 he was engaged as conductor of the Boston Symphony Orchestra, holding this post until 1924. From 1924 to 1934 he was associate conductor of the Concertgebouw Orchestra in Amsterdam, and from 1929 to 1938 he was principal conductor of the newly founded Orchestre Symphonique de Paris.

From 1936 until 1952 Monteux was conductor of the reorganized San Francisco Symphony Orchestra. He became a naturalized U.S. citizen in 1942. He appeared as a guest conductor with the Boston Symphony Orchestra from 1951, and also accompanied it on its first European tour in 1952 and again in 1956. Likewise he was again on the roster of the Metropolitan Opera from 1953 to 1956. In 1961 (at the age of 86) Monteux became principal conductor of the London Symphony Orchestra, retaining this post until his death.

Monteux was married in 1927 to Doris Hodgkins (b. Salisbury, Maine, 1895; d. Hancock, Maine, March 13, 1984), an American singer who co-founded in 1941 the Domaine School for Conductors and Orchestral Players in Hancock, Maine, of which Monteux was director. After Monteux's death, she established the Pierre Monteux Memorial Foundation.

As an interpreter, Monteux tried to bring out the inherent essence of music, without imposing his own artistic personality. Unemotional and restrained in his podium manner, he nonetheless succeeded in producing brilliant performances in an extensive repertoire ranging from the classics to the 20th century.

PEOPLE IN MUSIC

Monteverdi (Monteverde), **Claudio** (Giovanni Antonio), outstanding Italian composer who established the foundations of modern opera; b. Cremona (baptized), May 15, 1567; d. Venice, Nov. 29, 1643. Monteverdi was the son of a chemist who practiced medicine as a barbersurgeon. Claudio studied singing and theory with Marc' Antonio Ingegneri, maestro di cappella at the Cathedral of Cremona, and also learned to play the organ. He acquired mastery of composition at a very early age. He was only 15 when a collection of his three-part motets

Title page of a collection of Monteverdi's works, 1594. (New York Public Library)

was published in Venice. There followed several sacred madrigals, published in 1583, and canzonettas, a year later.

In 1589 Monteverdi visited Milan and made an appearance at the court of the Duke of Mantua. By 1592 he had obtained a position at the court in the service of Vincenzo I as *suonatore* (performer) on the viol (VIOLA DA GAMBA) and violin (VIOLA DA BRACCIO). He came into contact with the Flemish composer Giaches de Wert, maestro di cappella at the Mantuan court, whose command of COUNTERPOINT greatly influenced Monteverdi.

In 1592 Monteverdi published his third book of madrigals, a collection marked by many innovative harmonic accompaniments. In 1595 he accompanied the retinue of the Duke of Mantua on forays against the Turks in Austria and Hungary, and also went with him to Flanders in 1599. He married Claudia de Cattaneis, one of the Mantuan court singers, in 1599, with whom he had two sons (a daughter died in infancy). In 1601 he was appointed maestro di cappella in Mantua following the death of Benedetto Pallavicino. The publication of two books of madrigals in 1603 and 1605 further confirmed his mastery of the genre.

Having already composed some music for the stage, Monteverdi now turned to the new form of the opera. *L'ORFEO,* his first, was given before the Accademia degli Invaghiti in Mantua in February 1607. In this pastoral, he effectively moved beyond the Florentine model of recitative-dominated drama by creating a more flexible means of expression. The score is a combination of MONODY, madrigal, and instrumental music of diverse kinds.

In 1607 Monteverdi was made a member of the Accademia degli Animori of Cremona. However, he suffered a grievous loss in the death of his wife in Cremona that September. Although greatly depressed, he accepted a commission to compose an opera to celebrate the marriage of the heir apparent to the court of Mantua, Francesco Gonzaga, to Margaret of Savoy. The result was *L'Arianna,* to a text by Ottavio Rinuccini, presented in Mantua in 1608. Although the complete manuscript has been lost, the surviving versions of the *Lamento d'Arianna* from the score testify to Monteverdi's genius in expressing emotion in moving melodies.

In 1614 Monteverdi prepared a five-part arrangement of his sixth book of madrigals, also published separately in Venice in 1623. He wrote two more works for wedding celebrations, the prologue to the pastoral play *L'Idropica* (which is lost) and the French-style ballet *Il ballo delle ingrate.*

Monteverdi's patron, Duke Vincenzo of Mantua, died in 1612, and his successor, Francesco, did not retain Monteverdi's services. However, Monteverdi had the good fortune of being called to Venice in 1613 to occupy the vacant post of maestro di cappella at San Marco, at a salary of 300 ducats, which was raised to 400 ducats in 1616. His post at San Marco proved to be the most auspicious of his career, and he retained it for the rest of his life. He composed mostly church music but did not neglect the secular madrigal forms. He accepted important commissions from Duke Ferdinando of Mantua. His ballet *Tirsi e Clori* was given in Mantua in 1616.

In 1619 Monteverdi published his seventh book of madrigals, significant in its bold harmonic innovations. In

1624 his dramatic cantata, *Il combattimento di Tancredi e Clorinda,* after Tasso's *Gerusalemme liberata,* was performed at the home of Girolamo Mocenigo, a Venetian nobleman. The score is noteworthy for the effective role played by the string orchestra. In 1630 Monteverdi composed the opera *Proserpina rapita* for Venice, of which only one trio has survived.

Following the plague of 1630–31, Monteverdi wrote a MASS of thanksgiving for performance at San Marco (the GLORIA survives). In 1632 he took holy orders. His *Scherzi musicali* for one and two voices was published in 1632. Then followed his *Madrigali guerrieri et amorosi,* an extensive retrospective collection covering some 30 years, which was published in 1638.

In 1637 the first public opera houses were opened in Venice, and Monteverdi found a new outlet for his productions. His operas *Il ritorno d'Ulisse* in patria (1640), *Le nozze d'Enea con Lavinia* (1641; not extant), and *L'incoronazione di Poppea* (1642) were all given in Venice. The surviving works may be considered the first truly modern operas in terms of presenting dramatically compelling stories.

Monteverdi died at the age of 76 and was accorded burial in the church of the Frari in Venice. A commemorative plaque was erected in his honor, and a copy remains in the church to this day.

Monteverdi's place in the history of music is of great importance. He established the foundations of modern opera conceived as a drama in music. For greater dynamic expression, he enlarged the orchestra, in which he selected and skillfully combined instruments accompanying the voices. He was one of the earliest, if not the first, to employ such coloristic effects as string TREMOLO and PIZZICATO. His RECITATIVE assumes dramatic power, at times approaching the dimensions of an ARIOSO.

Monteverdi expanded the harmonic palette available to composers. He also championed a new style of composition that emphasized a single melody line over the POLYPHONIC compositions of the past. Many older, more conservative theorists and composers criticized him greatly for these innovations.

Monteverdi's son, a medical student, was arrested in 1627 for reading books that were on the church's list of banned items. However, his name was soon cleared, much to his father's relief.

Mood Indigo. Instrumental work, later a hit song by DUKE ELLINGTON, 1930, popularized by his orchestra. It generated a whole series of imitations, depicting colorful moods from the deepest blue to the most cheerful red.

Moody Blues, The. (Best-known lineup: Guitar/vocal/keyboard/sitar: Justin Hayward, b. Swindon, Wiltshire, Oct. 29, 1944; Keyboards/guitar: Mike Pinder, b. Birmingham, Dec. 27, 1941; Bass/vocals: John Lodge, b. Birmingham, July 20, 1945; Bass: Ray Thomas, b. Stourport-on-Severn, Dec. 29, 1942; Drums: Graeme Edge, b. Rochester, Kent, March 30, 1944.) British art-rock group best remembered for its symphonic/rock fusions that greatly influenced future groups including Genesis; Emerson, Lake, and Palmer; Yes; and ELO.

Originally centering on singer/songwriter Denny Laine, the group first scored a pop hit with the song *Go Now* in 1965. However, Laine left a year later, and the group radically changed directions. With new hands Hayward and Lodge, the band released the concept album *Days of Future Passed,* in 1968, featuring the London Symphony Orchestra. It produced the hit *Tuesday Afternoon* and also included *Nights in White Satin,* which, four years later, became another chartbuster.

The group, which disbanded in 1973, produced richly textured thematic albums, featuring many orchestra and electronic instruments, including the mellotron. It has since reunited from time to time, achieving hits with *The Voice* (1981) and *Your Wildest Dreams* (1986).

Moog, Robert (Arthur), American designer of electronic musical instruments; b. Flushing, N.Y., May 23, 1934. Moog studied at Queens College (B.S. in physics, 1957), Columbia University (B.S. in electrical engineering, 1957), and Cornell University (Ph.D. in engineering physics, 1965). He founded the R. A. Moog Company in 1954 for the purpose of designing electronic musical instruments.

In 1964 Moog introduced the first SYNTHESIZER modules. His company was incorporated in 1968, with its headquarters at Trumansburg, N.Y. In 1970 he brought out the Minimoog, a portable MONOPHONIC (capable of playing only one voice at a time) instrument. In 1971 the company

Robert Moog playing a keyboard synthesizer, 1986. (UPI/Corbis-Bettmann)

became Moog Music and went to Buffalo, N.Y. In 1973 it became a division of Norlin Industries, with which Moog was associated until 1977.

In the '80s, Moog founded another firm, Big Briar, in Leicester, N.C., which manufactured devices for precision control of ANALOG and DIGITAL synthesizers. He was associated with Kurzweil Music Systems of Boston from 1984 to 1989.

Moog's synthesizers and other electronic devices were used by both classical and rock musicians. He has also built reproductions of the THEREMIN, one of the first electronic instruments.

Moon River. Song by HENRY MANCINI and JOHNNY MERCER, 1961, the theme for the film *Breakfast at Tiffany's*. It was a hit that year for both Mancini in his instrumental version and as a song for Jerry Butler.

Moonlight Sonata. Popular nickname for LUDWIG VAN BEETHOVEN's piano sonata *Quasi una fantasia,* op.27, No. 2, composed in 1801. Its name came from an imaginative and sentimental German writer who said that the slowly rolling arpeggios of the opening movement reminded him of moonlight on the quiet surface of Lake Lucerne in Switzerland. The work is in C sharp minor, in three movements. In the finale the wind whips up a storm on the lake, and the moonlight is reflected violently.

PEOPLE IN MUSIC

While a student at Yale, Moore wrote several school songs, among them the football song *Good Night, Harvard,* which became popular among students.

Moore, Douglas (Stuart), American composer and music educator; b. Cutchogue, N.Y., Aug. 10, 1893; d. Greenport, N.Y., July 25, 1969. Moore studied at Yale University with D. S. Smith and Horatio Parker. After obtaining his bachelor's and music degrees in 1915 and 1917, respectively, he joined the U.S. Navy.

Following the end of World War I in 1918, Moore attended classes led by the well-known educator Vincent d'Indy at the Schola Cantorum in Paris. He also took lessons in organ and in composition with NADIA BOULANGER. Returning to the U.S., he studied with ERNEST BLOCH in Cleveland, where he also served as organist at the Cleveland Museum of Art from 1921 to 1923 and at Adelbert College, Western Reserve University, from 1923 to 1925. In 1925 he received a Pulitzer traveling scholarship in music and spent a year in Europe. In 1926 he was appointed to the faculty of Columbia University, where, in 1940, he became head of the music department, numbering many American composers among his students. He retired in 1962.

A fine craftsman, Moore applied his technical mastery to American subjects in his operas and symphonic works. He achieved popular success with his "folk opera" *The Ballad of Baby Doe,* dealing with the true story of a historical figure who lived in a Colorado silver mining camp. The opera was staged in 1956, at Central City, Colorado, where its action took place. It had numerous revivals in the U.S. and Europe.

Moore is best known for his operas, which, in addition to *The Ballad of Baby Doe,* include *The Devil and Daniel Webster* (1939), *Giants in the Earth* (1949; 1951; awarded the Pulitzer Prize in music), *The Wings of the Dove* (1961), and *Carry Nation,* based on the story of the notorious temperance fighter (1966). He also scored a ballet, *Greek Games,* and wrote incidental music and film scores.

Moore's orchestral works include *The Pageant of P. T. Barnum,* suite (1924); *Moby Dick,* symphonic poem (1927); *A Symphony of Autumn* (1930); *Overture on an American Tune* (1932); *In Memoriam,* symphonic poem (1944); Symphony No. 2 in A major (1946); *Farm Journal,* suite for chamber orchestra (1948); and *Cotillion,* suite for strings (1952). He also wrote chamber works, piano pieces, organ music, choral works, and songs. In the field of music education, Moore wrote the books *Listening to Music* (1932) and *From Madrigal to Modern Music: A Guide to Musical Styles* (1942).

Moore, Gerald, renowned English piano accompanist; b. Watford, July 30, 1899; d. Penn, Buckinghamshire, March 13, 1987. Moore first studied piano at the local music school. After his family moved to Canada in 1913, he made appearances as a solo recitalist and accompanist.

Moore returned to England in 1919 and began recording two years later. He first gained distinction as accompanist to the well-known tenor John Coates in 1925. He subsequently achieved legendary fame as the preeminent accompanist of the day, appearing with such celebrated singers as Kathleen Ferrier, Dietrich Fischer-Dieskau, Elizabeth Schwarzkopf, and Janet Baker.

Moore retired from the concert circuit in 1967 but continued to make recordings. He was given numerous awards and honorary degrees during his career. He wrote a number of books, including *Singer and Accompanist: The Performance of 50 Songs* (1953), *The Schubert Song Cycles* (1975), and *"Poet's Lore" and Other Schumann Cycles and Songs* (1984).

Moorman, (Madeline) **Charlotte,** AVANT-GARDE American cellist; b. Little Rock, Ark., Nov. 18, 1933; d. N.Y., Nov. 8, 1991. Moorman received a B.A. in music at Centenary College in Shreveport, Louisiana, before studying cello with Horace Britt at the University of Texas in Austin and then completing her training in the late '50s at the Juilliard School in N.Y.

Moorman founded the N.Y. Avant-Garde Art Festival in 1963, with which she remained active until 1982. She was a prime influence in the FLUXUS movement, a group of artists who combined humor, audience participation, and self-made art. She first attracted attention in 1965 when she performed the *Cello Sonata No. 2 for Adults Only.*

In 1967 she became something of a sensation when she performed NAM JUNE PAIK's *Opéra Sextronique* in accordance with the composer's instructions (i.e., nude from the waist up). Her performance was halted by her arrest, and although she was tried and convicted for unseemly exposure, her sen-

PEOPLE IN MUSIC

PEOPLE IN MUSIC

tence was eventually suspended and she resumed her championship of the avant-garde.

Among other notable performances were *TV Bra for Living Sculpture* (1969), which called for a bra made of two small televisions, and Paik's *The TV Cello* (1971), in which she played a cello made out of three television sets. EDGARD VARÈSE was so taken with Moorman that he dubbed her the "Jeanne d'Arc of New Music."

She succumbed to breast cancer, a relatively forgotten figure, in 1991.

moralities. A later form of the MIRACLE PLAYS.

Moran, Robert (Leonard), important American composer of the AVANT-GARDE; b. Denver, Jan. 8, 1937. Moran studied piano, then went to Vienna in 1957 and took lessons in 12-TONE composition. Returning to the U.S., he enrolled at Mills College in Oakland, California, where he attended seminars of Luciano Berio and DARIUS MILHAUD, earning a master's degree in music in 1963. Later that year, he completed his training with Roman Haubenstock-Ramati in Vienna.

With Howard Hersh, Moran was founder and co-director of the San Francisco Conservatory's New Music Ensemble. He also was composer-in-residence at Portland (Oregon) State University from 1972 to 1974 and at Northwestern University in 1977–78 in Evanston, Illinois, where he led its New Music Ensemble. He appeared extensively as a pianist in the U.S. and Europe in programs of contemporary music.

In his compositions, Moran combines the "found art" style with ALEATORY (chance) techniques. Some of his works are in GRAPHIC NOTATION, while others are inspired by an earlier piece, place, or era. Moran has composed mixed media works of the environmental type. Among the most unusual are *Smell Piece for Mills College* for Frying Pans and Foods (Mills College, 1967; originally intended to produce a fire sufficiently hot that it would burn down the college); *39 Minutes for 39 Autos* for 30 skyscrapers, 39 auto horns, Moog synthesizer, and players, employing 100,000 persons, and making use of autos, airplanes, searchlights, and local

PEOPLE IN MUSIC

radio and television stations (San Francisco, Aug. 20, 1969, the night of the moon landing); *Hallelujah,* "a joyous phenomenon with fanfares" for marching bands, drum and bugle corps, church choirs, organs, carillons, rock 'n' roll bands, television stations, automobile horns, and any other sounding implements, commissioned by Lehigh University for the city of Bethlehem, Pennsylvania, with the participation of its entire population of 72,320 inhabitants (Bethlehem, April 23, 1971); and *From the Market to Asylum* for performers (1982). He also collaborated with PHILIP GLASS on *The Juniper Tree,* a children's opera, in 1985.

morceau (Fr.). A piece, composition. *Morceau de genre,* characteristic piece; *morceau de musique,* a piece of music; *morceaux choisis,* an anthology of popular piano pieces appropriate to the diligent student, provincial teacher, or sincere amateur.

mor-sōh′

moresca (It.; Sp. *morisca*). A Moorish dance. It achieved popularity in Spain during the final phase of the struggle against Moorish power in southern Spain. It often contained a representation of a sword fight.

mōh-rĕs′căh

Apparently the English MORRIS DANCE is a late derivation of the moresca. Interludes of Moorish dances in exotic costumes were often included in French ballets of the 18th and 19th centuries.

Moreschi, Alessandro. *See* CASTRATO.

Morganfield, McKinley. *See* WATERS, MUDDY.

Morley, Thomas, English composer; b. Norwich, 1557 or 1558; d. London, Oct. 1602. Morley studied with William Byrd. From 1583 to 1587 he was organist and master of the choristers at Norwich Cathedral. In 1588 he received his music degree from Oxford University. About this time he became organist at St. Paul's Cathedral.

In 1592 Morley was sworn in as a Gentleman of the Chapel Royal and was made Epistler and then Gospeller. He was also active as a printer, holding a monopoly on all music published under a patent granted to him by the government

PEOPLE IN MUSIC

Beginning around 1590, Morley worked as a spy for the British government.

in 1598. In addition to publishing his own works (CAN-ZONETS, MADRIGALS, BALLETS, and AIRES), he acted as editor, arranger, translator, and publisher of music by other composers. Notable among his editions was *The Triumphes of Oriana* (1601), a collection of madrigals by 23 composers, all dedicated to Queen Elizabeth I.

Morley also gained distinction as a music theorist. *A Plaine and Easie Introduction to Practicall Musicke* (1597) became famous as a description of British musical schooling of his time.

Morris dance. A characteristic and highly structured English dance for men only, adorned in exotic costumes or wearing animal masks, apparently borrowing several features of the Spanish MORESCA.

The dancers typically are clothed in white shirts and trousers, with a criss-crossed sash over the chest. Bells are tied to the ankles, and the dancers carry either handkerchiefs or large sticks. Movements are executed in patterns, with a verse consisting of one set of figures varying with a repeated chorus.

The tempo is moderate and can be played by one or more traditional instrumentalists. The use of swords in a noncombatant manner in some of the dances suggests the presence of symbolic character play. Also suggestive of an original dramatic origin is the inclusion on occasion of non-dancing characters, including a man dressed as a woman (a "Maid Marian") and/or a jester, who interact with the dancers.

The Morris dance went into hibernation until its conscious revival by British ethnomusicologists early in the 20th century.

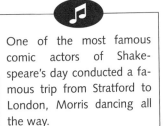

One of the most famous comic actors of Shakespeare's day conducted a famous trip from Stratford to London, Morris dancing all the way.

PEOPLE IN MUSIC

Morris, James (Peppler), American bass-baritone; b. Baltimore, Jan. 10, 1947. After studies with a local teacher, Morris won a scholarship to the University of Maryland, concurrently receiving invaluable instruction from ROSA PONSELLE. He then continued his studies at the Peabody Conservatory of Music in Baltimore from 1966 to 1968.

Morris made his debut as Crespel in *The Tales of Hoffmann* with the Baltimore Civic Opera in 1967. After further training with Nicola Moscona at the Philadelphia Academy of Vocal Arts from 1968 to 1970, he made his Metropolitan Opera debut in N.Y. as Amonasro in *AIDA* in 1971. He also appeared with the Opera Orchestra of N.Y. and sang widely in Europe. In 1975 he scored a notable success as Don Giovanni at the Metropolitan.

Although closely associated with the Italian and French repertoires, Morris appeared as Wotan in *Die Walküre* at the Baltimore Civic Opera in 1984. He subsequently sang that role in the San Francisco Opera's *Ring* cycle in 1985, eliciting extraordinary critical acclaim.

Morrison, Jim (James). *See* DOORS, THE.

Morrison, Van (real name, George Ivan), Irish-American rock singer, guitarist, saxophonist, and songwriter; b. Belfast, Aug. 13, 1945. Morrison taught himself to sing and play guitar, harmonica, and saxophone. After dropping out of high school when he was 16, he set off with his rhythm-and-blues outfit, the Monarchs, for Germany.

PEOPLE IN MUSIC

Returning to Belfast, he put together the group called Them in 1963, with which he began his recording career. The group's biggest U.S. hit was *Gloria,* released in 1966, just as the band was breaking up. Later that year, Morrison went to the U.S., where he produced the hit song *Brown-Eyed Girl* in 1967 and brought out his first solo album, *Blowin' Your Mind.*

Influenced by the music of BOB DYLAN and the hippie movement in general, Morrison issued his most influential albums, 1968's *Astral Weeks* and 1970's *Moondance,* featuring the hit single of the same name. He moved to California in 1971 and continued to produce minor hits in an R&B style, including *Wild Night.*

After a period (1973–76) in Ireland, in 1976 Morrison was living again in California. He made a guest appearance at the Band's famous *Last Waltz* that year. Morrison continued to record in the late '70s and '80s, combining a mystical outlook with funky, blues- and R&B-influenced music. Toward the end of the '80s, he turned toward Celtic-themed concerns and musical influences, recording an album with the Irish folk revival band, the Chieftains.

PEOPLE IN MUSIC

Morrison has continued to record, perform, and write new material in the '90s. He has produced a mix of R&B and blues-flavored material, and even has cut an album of jazz and blues covers.

Morton, "Jelly Roll" (Ferdinand Joseph Lemott, LaMothe, La Menthe), pioneer Creole American composer and pianist of ragtime, blues, and jazz; b. New Orleans, Oct. 20, 1890; d. Los Angeles, July 10, 1941. Born into a French-speaking family that proudly recalled its former days of wealth and position, Morton grew up surrounded by musical instruments and frequently attended performances at the New Orleans French Opera House.

Morton took up piano when he was 10 and began working in the bordellos of Storyville when he was 12. By the time he was 14 he was traveling throughout Louisiana, Mississippi, Alabama, and Florida, while making New Orleans his main haunt. He was a colorful and flamboyant figure, given to extravagant boasting and flashy living. In addition to his being a musician, he was a professional gambler (excelling at cards and billiards), nightclub owner, and producer. As a result of his travels, he learned various black, white, and Hispanic musical idioms to produce a form of music akin to jazz.

After performing in Los Angeles from 1917 to 1922, he went to Chicago. There he made his first solo recordings in 1923 of his own *New Orleans Blues* (1902), *Jelly Roll Blues* (1905), and *King Porter Stomp* (1906) and, with a sextet of his own, *Big Foot Ham* (1923). With his own New Orleans–style band, the Red Hot Peppers, he recorded *Grandpa's Spells* (1911), *The Pearls* (1919), and *Black Bottom Stomp* (1925).

Morton went to N.Y. in 1928 but found himself outside the mainstream of jazz developments. He later ran a jazz club in Washington, D.C., where he made infrequent appearances as a pianist.

In 1938 folklorist ALAN LOMAX recorded Morton for the Library of Congress, capturing him on disc playing piano, singing, relating anecdotes, and preserving his view of the history of jazz. This led to a few more commercial recordings just before his death.

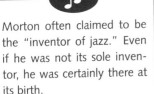

Morton often claimed to be the "inventor of jazz." Even if he was not its sole inventor, he was certainly there at its birth.

Mose in Egitto (Moses in Egypt). Opera by GIOACCHINO ROSSINI, 1818, first produced in Naples. The libretto follows the biblical narrative of the escape of the Israelites across the miraculously distended Red Sea and the destruction of the pursuing Egyptian army when the waters converge on them.

The opera was selected by Benito Mussolini to be performed at the gala reception for Adolf Hitler in Rome in 1935. Mussolini was apparently oblivious to the fact that his anti-Semitic partner could hardly have enjoyed watching Jews escape persecution.

Moses und Aron. Opera by ARNOLD SCHOENBERG, 1930–32, to his own text. Acts 1 and 2 were completed, while act 3 was probably never started. The libretto is extant, and the work was produced posthumously in Hamburg in 1954. The score is in the 12-TONE idiom, with many episodes written in SPRECHSTIMME. The religious conflict between spirituality and materialism, personified by Moses and his brother Aaron, underlies the text.

Schoenberg gives indications in the score that an orgy staged around the idol of the Golden Calf should include the burning of four naked virgins and other scenes of ancient depravity. A realistic production along these lines was attempted in London in 1965, but the alleged virgins wore loincloths. Subsequent productions have left the loincloths in the dressing room.

Many theories abound as to why Schoenberg left this worked uncompleted. Some feel he identified too closely with its central characters.

mosh pit. An area on a popular dance floor where patrons are permitted to practice such sports as slam dancing, pogoing, and lifting individuals above the floor involuntarily. Because of the damage that has been done, clubs now warn that patrons who enter the pit do so at their own risk.

Mosh pits have also been formed at the front of concert halls, in the space between the first row of seats and the lip of the stage.

Mosolov, Alexander (Vasilievich), Russian composer; b. Kiev, Aug. 11, 1900; d. Moscow, July 12, 1973. Moslov

The omission of the second *a* in the German title was due to Schoenberg's triskaidecaphobia (fear of the number 13). If "Aaron" were spelled with the double a, the sum of the letters in the complete title would have been 13.

PEOPLE IN MUSIC

1163

fought in the civil war in Russia from 1918 to 1920, where he was wounded and decorated twice with the Order of the Red Banner for heroism. After the war, he studied composition with the composer RHEINHOLD GLIÈRE in Kiev, then studied harmony and counterpoint with Glière, composition with NIKOLAI MIASKOVSKY, and piano with SERGEI PROKOFIEV at the Moscow Conservatory from 1922 to 1925.

Mosolov played his first Piano Concerto in Leningrad in 1928. In his earliest works he adopted modernistic devices and even wrote songs to texts of newspaper advertisements. His ballet *Zavod* (Iron Foundry; 1927) attracted attention because of its attempt to imitate the sound of a factory at work. One member of the orchestra shook a large sheet of metal in order to re-create the noise of the factory. However, Mosolov was sharply criticized by Soviet authorities for attempting to introduce these realistic elements into his work.

In 1936 Mosolov was expelled from the Union of Soviet Composers for staging drunken brawls and behaving rudely to waiters in restaurants. He was sent to Turkestan to collect folk songs as a move toward his rehabilitation. After returning to Moscow in 1939, he continued to make excursions to collect folk songs in various regions of Russia until just before his death in the early 1970s.

Mosolov wrote five symphonies, two piano concertos, one concerto each for harp and cello, four operas, oratorios, choral and solo vocal works, five piano sonatas, two string quartets, and other music.

Most Happy Fella, The. Musical by FRANK LOESSER, 1956. The story centers on a middle-aged Italian California grape grower in love with a young waitress in a San Francisco restaurant. He courts her by mail, but when she asks for his picture, she gets a photo of one of his workers. When she finally arrives at his ranch vineyard, she is shocked to learn that her fiancé is old but consoles herself by a lightning affair with the young man in the photograph. Meanwhile, the grape grower breaks his leg. Eventually the waitress returns to her aging suitor in search of emotional and financial security.

The score, composed as an almost continuous stream of music, has many fine songs, among them *Young People, How*

Beautiful the Day Is, Big "D", Somebody Somewhere, Standing on the Corner, and *Abbondanza.*

motet (from Mid. Fr. *mot,* word; Ger. *Motette;* It. *mottetto*). A sacred vocal composition in CONTRAPUNTAL style, without accompaniment until the BAROQUE period (when motets were often called ANTHEMS). This modest term embraces half a millennium of the most fruitful developments of POLYPHONIC music, stretching from the Middle Ages to the RENAISSANCE, and continuing through the period of the Baroque.

The motet was developed in the church, in both Roman Catholic and Protestant rites, as well as in secular practices. In Middle French, *mot* signified a VERSE, STROPHE, or STANZA. This is corroborated by the fact that the contrapuntal voice above the TENOR, originally called DUPLUM, acquired in the 13th century the term *motet* and carried a text. Franco of Cologne, writing in the 13th century, describes the motet as *discantus cum diversis litteris* (a contrapuntal part with different texts). In the course of two centuries, the motet was supplemented by more contrapuntal parts, some of them in the French vernacular.

During the Renaissance, the Latin motet was separated from the secular motet that absorbed numerous folk elements. Further developments are found in the great polyphonic works of the masters of the Flemish school: JOHANNES OCKEGHEM, JACOB OBRECHT, and JOSQUIN DES PRES. Later, GIOVANNI PIERLIUGI DA PALESTRINA in Italy, TOMÁS LUIS DE VICTORIA in Spain, THOMAS TALLIS in England, HANS LEO HASSLER in Germany, and CLAUDE GOUDIMEL in France contributed to the art. In England the motet assumed HOMOPHONIC (single-melody) forms, leading to the formation of a specific British type of anthem. In Germany, Heinrich Schütz and, nearly a century later, the great JOHANN SEBASTIAN BACH (whose greatest work in the motet style was written for double chorus and eight solo voices) created the specific form of the German motet.

The motet suffered an irreversible decline in the 19th century. The few composers who stubbornly cultivated it, particularly in Germany, did so more out of reverence to its Gothic past than out of inner imperative. In the 20th century, the motet suffered its final *rigor mortis.*

Mother of Us All, The. Opera by VIRGIL THOMSON, 1947, to a libretto by Gertrude Stein, first produced in N.Y. The universal matriarch is Susan B. Anthony, the American suffragette who fought for the right to vote for women. The cast of characters are two modestly abbreviated names, Virgil T. and Gertrude S., representing the composer and author, respectively.

Like Stein's writing, which is apparently simple but actually very complex, Thomson's music at first hearing seems relatively unsophisticated, with much of the harmony written in simple TRIADS.

Mothers of Invention, The. *See* ZAPPA, FRANK.

motion (Lat. *motus*). 1. The progression or conduct of a single part or MELODY, *conjunct* when progressing by steps, *disjunct* when progressing by skips. 2. The movement of one part in relation to that of another.

In *contrary* or *opposite* motion (*motus contrarius*), one part ascends while the other descends, and in *oblique* motion (*motus obliquus*), one part remains on a single note while the other moves. In *parallel* motion (*motus rectus*), both parts move up or down by the same interval, and in *similar* motion, both move up or down together by dissimilar intervals. In *mixed* motion, two or more of the above varieties occur at once between several parts.

motive (Ger. *Motiv;* Fr. *motif*). 1. A short phrase or figure used in development or imitation. 2. A leading motive. *Measure motive,* one whose accent coincides with that of the measure's downbeat.

Motown. *See* GORDY, BERRY, JR.

Mourning Becomes Electra. Opera, 1967, by Martin David Levy (b. 1932), first performed in N.Y., based on Eugene O'Neill's play.

The ancient Aeschylus drama is here adapted into a tragedy of conflicting emotions in the wake of the American Civil War. The wife of a returning soldier poisons him in order to continue her affair with another. Her son kills his mother's lover, then the mother kills herself. Horrified by his part in the tragedy, the son also commits suicide, and the daughter is doomed to live alone in mourning.

The score is written in a modern, ATONAL style, but occasional harmonious arias are given to the singers.

mouth organ. Colloquialism for HARMONICA.

movable Do[h]. A SOLFÈGE (*solfeggio*) method used primarily to teach sight-singing. The major DIATONIC scale is sung to the original syllables of the method developed by Guido d'Arrezo (Doh, Rey, Me, Fah, Soh, Lah), with the leading tone designated by the syllable *Te.* For minor scales and chromatic progressions, the vowels are changed to *e* for sharp and *a* (pronounced "aw") for flat.

The distinction of movable Doh is that the tonic note is also called Doh, whatever the key. This system, widely accepted in English-speaking countries, has the unfortunate consequence of divorcing the absolute sound from its adopted name. The British call this system *tonic Sol-fa.*

movement. 1. TEMPO. 2. A principal division or section of a composition.

Mozart, Franz Xaver Wolfgang, Austrian pianist and composer, grandson of (Johann Georg) LEOPOLD MOZART, nephew of Maria Anna "Nannerl" Mozart Berchthold zu Sonnenburg, son of WOLFGANG AMADEUS MOZART and often called by his father's name; b. Vienna, July 26, 1791; d. Carlsbad, July 29, 1844. Franz studied piano with Franz Xaver Niemetschek in Prague while living with the Dusek family. He then continued his training in Vienna, working with many major musicians and composers.

After a period as a teacher in Lemberg and environs from 1807 to 1819, Franz embarked upon a major tour of Europe as a pianist from 1819 to 1821. In 1822 he returned to Lemberg as a teacher, receiving additional instruction in counterpoint from Johann Mederitsch of Gallus in 1826. That same year he organized the Lemberg Cacilien-Chor. He settled in Vienna in 1838, where, in 1841, he was named honorary Kapellmeister of the Dom-Musik-Verein

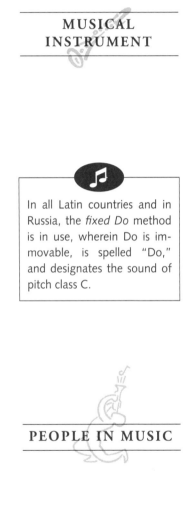

MUSICAL INSTRUMENT

In all Latin countries and in Russia, the *fixed Do* method is in use, wherein Do is immovable, is spelled "Do," and designates the sound of pitch class C.

PEOPLE IN MUSIC

and the Mozarteum in Salzburg. Franz was made maestro compositore onorario of Rome's Congregazione ed Accademica Santa Cecilia in 1842.

As a composer, Franz Mozart revealed a gift for writing for the piano. Among his works are two piano concertos, *Konzertvariationen* for piano and orchestra (1820) and Sinfonia in D Major. He also composed Piano Quintet, op.1, two violin sonatas, a *Grande Sonate* in E major for violin or cello and piano, op.19 (1820), and Rondo (Sonate) for flute and piano. He composed many works for solo piano, including Sonata, op.10 (1808), three sets of polonaises, and 11 sets of variations. Other works include four cantatas (one for FRANZ JOSEPH HAYDN's birthday in 1805, which has not survived), unaccompanied choral pieces, and songs.

PEOPLE IN MUSIC

Mozart, (Johann Georg) **Leopold,** German-born Austrian composer, violinist, and music theorist, father of WOLFGANG AMADEUS MOZART and Maria Anna "Nannerl" Mozart Berchthold zu Sonnenburg, and grandfather of FRANZ XAVER WOLFGANG MOZART; b. Augsburg, Nov. 14, 1719; d. Salzburg, May 28, 1787. A bookbinder's son, Leopold studied at the Augsburg Gymnasium from 1727 to 1735, then at the lyceum attached to the Jesuit school of St. Salvator until 1736. In 1737 he went to Salzburg, where he studied philosophy and law at the Benedictine University, earning a bachelor of philosophy degree in 1738.

After earning his degree, Leopold entered the service of Johann Baptist, Count of Thurn-Valsassina and Taxis, as both valet and musician. In 1743 he became fourth violinist in the Prince-Archbishop's Court Orchestra. He also taught violin and keyboard to the choirboys of the cathedral oratory. In 1757 he became composer to the court and chamber, and in 1758 he was promoted to second violinist in the court orchestra. In 1762 he was appointed vice-Kapellmeister.

Leopold married Anna Maria Pertl of Salzburg (1747), with whom he fathered seven children, only two of whom, Maria Anna ("Nannerl") and Wolfgang Amadeus, survived infancy. He dedicated himself to the musical education of his children, but his methods at times approached frank exploitation, and his advertisements of their appearances were in poor taste. However, there is no denying his great role in fostering his son's career.

Leopold was a thoroughly competent composer, and the mutual influence between father and son was such that works long attributed to his son proved to be his. He was also important as a theorist. He produced an influential violin method in 1756. His *Nannerl-Notenbuch,* published in 1759, is a model of a child's music album. His vocal works include sacred CANTATAS, MASSES, litanies, school dramas, and secular lieder. Orchestral works include several symphonies and concertos, among them *Die musikalische Schlittenfahrt* (1755). He also composed chamber music and keyboard works.

Mozart, Wolfgang Amadeus, prodigious Austrian composer whose works in every genre are unsurpassed in lyric beauty, rhythmic variety, and effortless melodic invention, son of (Johann Georg) LEOPOLD MOZART, father of FRANZ XAVER WOLFGANG MOZART, and brother of Maria Anna "Nannerl" Mozart Berchthold zu Sonnenburg; b. Salzburg, Jan. 27, 1756; d. Vienna, Dec. 5, 1791. Wolfgang and his sister were the only two among the seven children of Anna Maria and Leopold Mozart to survive infancy. Mozart's sister was four and a half years older. She took harpsichord lessons from her father, and Mozart as a

The famous *Kindersinfonie,* long attributed to FRANZ JOSEPH HAYDN, was in all probability a work by Leopold Mozart.

PEOPLE IN MUSIC

Mozart (at the keyboard) with his father, Leopold, and sister, Nannerl, c. 1763. (The National Gallery, London/Corbis)

very young child eagerly absorbed the sounds of music. He soon began playing the harpsichord himself and later studied the violin.

Leopold was an excellent musician, but he also appreciated that his children could draw a large (and well-paying) audience. In January 1762 he took them to Munich, where they performed before the Elector of Bavaria. That September, they played for Emperor Francis I at his palace in Vienna. The family returned to Salzburg in January 1763, and in June the children were taken to Frankfurt, where Wolfgang showed his skill in improvising at the keyboard.

In November they arrived in Paris, where they played before Louis XV. It was in Paris that Wolfgang's first compositions were printed (four sonatas for harpsichord, with violin ad libitum). In April 1764 they proceeded to London, where Wolfgang played for King George III.

In London Mozart was befriended by JOHANN SEBASTIAN BACH's son Johann Christian, who gave exhibitions improvising four-hands at the piano with the younger Mozart. By that time Mozart had tried his hand at composing serious works. He wrote two symphonies for a London performance, and the manuscript of another very early symphony, purportedly written by him in London, was discovered in 1980. Leopold wrote home with undisguised pride: "Our great and mighty Wolfgang seems to know everything at the age of seven that a man acquires at the age of 40." Knowing the power of publicity, he diminished Wolfgang's age, for at the time the child was nine years old. In July 1765 the family journeyed to the Netherlands, then set out for Salzburg, visiting Dijon, Lyons, Geneva, Bern, Zurich, Donaueschingen, and Munich on the way.

Arriving in Salzburg in November 1766, Wolfgang applied himself to serious study of counterpoint under the tutelage of his father. In September 1767 the family proceeded to Vienna, where Wolfgang began work on an opera, *La finta semplice*. His second theater work was a SINGSPIEL, *Bastien und Bastienne*, which was produced in Vienna at the home of Dr. Franz Mesmer. In December 1768 Mozart led a performance of his *Missa solemnis* in C minor before the royal family and court at the consecration of the Waisenhauskirche.

Dr. Franz Mesmer used hypnosis to treat his patients. The word "mesmerized" comes from his name, meaning to be in a state of stupor or temporary unconsciousness.

Upon Mozart's return to Salzburg in January 1769, Archbishop Sigismund von Schrattenbach named him his konzertmeister, without remuneration. Still determined to broaden Mozart's artistic contacts, his father took him on an Italian tour, beginning in late 1769 and running through 1770. Legends of Mozart's extraordinary musical ability grew. It was reported, for instance, that he wrote out the entire score of *Miserere* by Gregorio Allegri, which he had heard in the Sistine Chapel at the Vatican only twice. Young Mozart was subjected to numerous tests by famous Italian musicians, among them Giovanni Sammartini, Niccolò Piccini, and Padre Martini.

Mozart was given a diploma as an elected member of the Accademia Filarmonica in Bologna after he had passed examinations in harmony and counterpoint. In October 1770 the pope made him a Knight of the Golden Spur. He was commissioned to compose an opera. The result was *Mitridate, re di Ponto,* which was performed in Milan on December. Mozart himself conducted three performances of this opera from the harpsichord. After a short stay in Salzburg, the family returned to Milan in 1771, where Mozart composed the serenata *Ascanio in Alba* for the wedding festivities of Archduke Ferdinand held that October. He returned to Salzburg late in 1771. His patron, Archbishop Schrattenbach, died about that time, and the successor, Archbishop Hieronymus Colloredo, seemed to be indifferent to Mozart as a musician.

Once more Mozart went to Italy, where his newest opera, *Lucio Silla,* was performed in Milan in December 1772. He returned to Salzburg in March 1773, but in July of that year he went to Vienna, where he became acquainted with the music of FRANZ JOSEPH HAYDN, who greatly influenced his instrumental style. Returning to Salzburg once more, he supervised the production of his opera *Il Re pastore,* which was performed on April 23, 1775.

In March 1778 Mozart visited Paris again for a performance of his PARIS SYMPHONY (No. 31) at a Concert Spirituel. His mother died in Paris on July 3, 1778. Returning to Salzburg in January 1779, he resumed his duties as konzertmeister and also obtained the position of court organist at a salary of 450 gulden. In 1780 the Elector of Bavaria com-

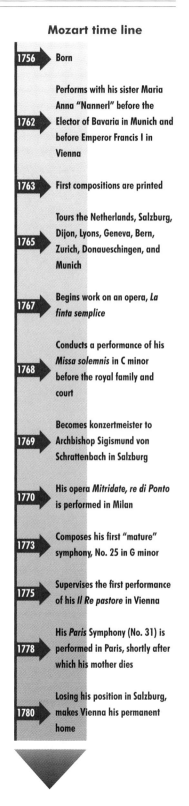

Mozart time line

1756 Born

Performs with his sister Maria Anna "Nannerl" before the **1762** Elector of Bavaria in Munich and before Emperor Francis I in Vienna

1763 First compositions are printed

Tours the Netherlands, Salzburg, Dijon, Lyons, Geneva, Bern, **1765** Zurich, Donaueschingen, and Munich

1767 Begins work on an opera, *La finta semplice*

Conducts a performance of his *Missa solemnis* in C minor **1768** before the royal family and court

1769 Becomes konzertmeister to Archbishop Sigismund von Schrattenbach in Salzburg

1770 His opera *Mitridate, re di Ponto* is performed in Milan

1773 Composes his first "mature" symphony, No. 25 in G minor

1775 Supervises the first performance of his *Il Re pastore* in Vienna

1778 His *Paris* Symphony (No. 31) is performed in Paris, shortly after which his mother dies

1780 Losing his position in Salzburg, makes Vienna his permanent home

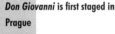

1782 Marries Constanze Weber and produces his operatic masterpiece *Die Entführung aus dem Serail* at the Burgtheater

1782–83 Composes two fine symphonies—No. 35 in D major, the *Haffner,* and No. 36 in C major, the *Linz,* respectively

1785 Completes his set of six string quartets dedicated to Franz Joseph Haydn

1786 *Le nozze di Figaro* is produced in Vienna

1787 *Don Giovanni* is first staged in Prague

1788 Composes his last three symphonies, No. 39 in E flat major, No. 40 in G minor, and No. 41 in C major (*Jupiter*)

1789 Appears as soloist in one of his piano concertos before the Elector of Saxony in Dresden and also plays the organ at the Thomaskirche in Leipzig

1790 *Così fan tutte* is performed for the first time in Vienna

1791 *Die Zauberflöte* is first produced in Vienna, just months before his youthful death

Mozart received only 800 gulden per year as against Gluck's salary of 2,000.

missioned from him an opera seria, *IDOMENEO,* which was successfully produced in Munich in January 1781. However, that May Mozart lost his position with the Archbishop in Salzburg and decided to move to Vienna, which became his permanent home. There he produced the operatic masterpiece *Die Entführung aus dem Serail* (THE ABDUCTION FROM THE SERAGLIO), staged at the Burgtheater (July 1782, with excellent success). In August 1782 he married Constanze Weber, the sister of Aloysia Weber, with whom he had previously been in love.

Two of Mozart's finest symphonies—No. 35 in D major, the *Haffner,* written for the Haffner family of Salzburg, and No. 36 in C major, the *Linz*—date from 1782 and 1783, respectively. From this point forward, Mozart's productivity reached extraordinary dimensions, but despite the abundance of commissions and concert appearances, he was unable to earn enough to sustain his growing family. Still, melodramatic stories of Mozart's abject poverty are gross exaggerations.

In 1785 Mozart completed a set of six string quartets which he dedicated to Haydn. Unquestionably, the structure of these quartets owed much to Haydn's CONTRAPUNTAL art. Haydn himself paid tribute to Mozart's genius. Mozart's father quoted him as saying, "Before God and as an honest man I tell you that your son is the greatest composer known to me either in person or by name."

In May 1786 Mozart's great OPERA BUFFA, *LE NOZZE DI FIGARO* (The Marriage of Figaro), was produced in Vienna, to a triumphant reception. It was performed in Prague early in 1787, with Mozart in attendance. It was during that visit that Mozart wrote his 38th Symphony in D Major, known as the *PRAGUE* SYMPHONY. It was in Prague, also, that his operatic masterpiece *DON GIOVANNI* was produced, in October 1787. That November, Mozart was appointed kammermusicus in Vienna as a successor to CHRISTOPH WILLIBALD GLUCK, albeit at a smaller salary.

The year 1788 was a glorious one for Mozart and for music history, being the year that he composed his last three symphonies: No. 39 in E flat major, No. 40 in G minor, and No. 41 in C major, known under the name *JUPITER.* In the spring of 1789 Mozart went to Berlin. On the way he appeared as soloist in one of his piano concertos before the Elector of Saxony in Dresden, and also played the organ at the Thomaskirche in Leipzig. His visits in Potsdam and Berlin were marked by private concerts at the court of Friedrich Wilhelm II. The king commissioned from him a set of six string quartets and a set of six piano sonatas, but Mozart died before completing them.

Returning to Vienna, he began work on his opera buffa *COSÌ FAN TUTTE,* first performed in Vienna in January 1790. That October, Mozart went to Frankfurt for the coronation of Emperor Leopold II. Returning to Vienna, he saw Haydn, who was about to depart for London. In 1791 Mozart completed the score of *DIE ZAUBERFLÖTE* (The Magic Flute), with a German libretto by Emanuel Schikaneder. It was performed for the first time on Sept. 30, 1791, in Vienna.

There followed a mysterious episode in Mozart's life. A stranger called on him with a request to compose a requiem. The caller was an employee of Count Franz von Walsegg, who intended to have the work performed as his own in memory of his wife. In many tellings of this story, Mozart took this as a portent of his own death and labored mightily to finish the funereal score. Sadly, he was unable to finish the score, which was completed by his pupil Franz Xaver Süssmayr and by Joseph Leopold Eybler.

The immediate cause of Mozart's death at the age of 35 has been the subject of much speculation. Almost immediately after this sad event, myths and fantasies appeared in the press. The most persistent was that Mozart had been poisoned by the court composer ANTONIO SALIERI out of professional jealousy. This particularly morbid piece of invention gained circulation in European journals. The story was further elaborated upon by a report that Salieri confessed his unspeakable crime on his deathbed in 1825. Aleksandr Pushkin used the tale in his drama *Mozart and Salieri,* which NIKOLAI RIMSKY-KORSAKOV set to music in his opera of the same title. A fanciful dramatization of the rivalry was made into a successful play, *Amadeus,* by Peter Shaffer, produced in London in 1979 and in N.Y. in 1980. The rivalry subsequently gained wider currency through the award-winning film version of *Amadeus* in 1984.

Another myth related to Mozart's death that found its way into the majority of Mozart biographies and even into respectable reference works was that a blizzard raged during his funeral and that none of his friends could follow his body to the cemetery. This story is easily refuted by the records of the Vienna weather bureau for the day. It is also untrue that Mozart was buried in a pauper's grave. His body was removed from its original individual location because the family neglected to pay the mandatory dues.

The universal recognition of Mozart's genius during the two centuries since his death has never wavered. In his music, smiling simplicity was combined with somber drama, lofty inspiration was contrasted with playful diversion, profound meditation alternated with fleeting moodiness, and religious concentration was filled with human tenderness.

The variety of technical development in Mozart's works is all the more remarkable considering the limitations of musical instruments in his time. The topmost note on his keyboard was F above the third ledger line, so that in the RECAPITULATION in the first movement of his famous C major piano sonata, the SUBJECT had to be dropped an octave lower to accommodate the MODULATION. The vocal technique displayed in his operas is amazing in its perfection. To be sure, the human voice has not changed since Mozart's time, but he knew how to exploit vocal resources to the utmost. This adaptability of his genius to all available means of sound production is the secret of the eternal validity of his music and the explanation of the present popularity of mini-festivals, such as the N.Y. concert series "Mostly Mozart."

The standard system of identification for Mozart's scores was established by L. von Köchel in his *Chronologisch-thematisches Verzeichnis sämtlicher Tonwerke Wolfgang Amadé Mozarts* (Leipzig, 1862; 6th edition, revised by F. Giegling, A. Weinmann, and G. Sievers, Wiesbaden, 1964). The catalog numbers of the original catalogue are known as K, and the revised numbers of the 6th edition, which follow, are often referred to as K^6. Mozart also kept a catalogue during the latter part of his life, known as *Mozarts Werkverzeichnis 1784–1791.*

Although the traditional count is 41 symphonies, present estimates list more than 50 such works; however, a few early works remain in dispute. The problem occurs because Mozart used the normal way of learning music in his day— by writing it down—so that works found in his handwriting have been mistaken for his own compositions. This occurs in early symphonies and piano concertos.

While it is impossible to describe the stylistic development in the symphonies here, it can be stated that No. 25 in G minor, K.183, 173dB (late 1773) is the first of the "mature" symphonies. It forecasts the haunting effect of the later G minor symphony (No. 40).

Included in the traditional count of 27 piano concertos are four pastiches of other composers' pieces, done as exercises. For Mozart, the piano concerto was the best way to show off his talents as keyboard player, composer, leader, and provider of the newest musical novelties. Fashion and fad were as much a part of the CLASSIC music scene as they are of today's popular music, a fact that Mozart struggled with for most of his career.

Mozart composed two rondos for piano and orchestra, and five authentic violin concertos, as well as concertos for bassoon, flute, oboe, horn, flute and harp, and clarinet.

Mozart also composed numerous functional and occasional works, including Serenata notturna in D Major, K.239 (1776); Serenade in D Major, K.250, 248b, *Haffner* (1776); Divertimento in D Major, K.251 (1776); Serenade in D Major, K.320, *Posthorn* (1779); *Maurerische Trauermusik* in C Minor, K.477, 479a (1785); *Ein musikalischer Spass* (A Musical Joke) in F Major, K.522 (1787); *Eine kleine Nachtmusik* in G major, K.525 (1787); divertimentos for wind ensemble; marches (two not extant); over 100 German dances; ländler; and contredanses.

Mozart's chamber music includes 23 string quartets, including the six quartets dedicated to Haydn; six string quintets (two violins, two violas, and cello), the finest examples of this genre ever written; four quartets for flute, violin, viola, and cello; as well as quintets featuring piano, horn, clarinet, and oboe. He also wrote various string chamber works. Mozart composed over 30 keyboard and violin sonatas, many unfinished (1762–88), 17 solo keyboard sonatas (1775–89), five sonatas for keyboard duet, Sonata in D Major for two keyboards, K.448, 375a (1781), 16 variations for keyboard solo and one for keyboard duet, and many miscellaneous pieces, including 17 sonatas for organ, most with two violins and bassoon.

In addition to his operas, Mozart wrote a great deal of vocal music, including many MASSES, ORATORIOS, and CANTATAS.

Mozart's sister, Maria Anna "Nannerl" Berchthold zu Sonnenburg, b. Salzburg, July 30, 1751; d. there, Oct. 29, 1829, was a pianist and teacher. She was taught music by her father from her earliest childhood and appeared in public as a pianist with her brother. After their travels together in Europe, she returned to Salzburg and eventually devoted herself mainly to teaching. In 1784 she married Baron von Berchthold zu Sonnenburg, who died in 1801. She went blind in 1825. Although nearly five years older than Wolfgang, she survived him by 38 years.

Mozart i Salieri. Opera by NIKOLAI RIMSKY-KORSAKOV, 1898, to a LIBRETTO after Aleksandr Pushkin's poem, first produced in Moscow. Pushkin's text is based on the legend that spread shortly after WOLFGANG AMADEUS MOZART's death, accusing the eminently respectable Italian composer Antonio Salieri (for a time a teacher of LUDWIG VAN BEETHOVEN) of poisoning Mozart. In Pushkin's poem and in the opera, Salieri declares that were Mozart allowed to live on, other composers—honest, industrious, but not blessed by genius—would be condemned to futility.

Rimsky-Korsakov used authentic excerpts from Mozart's compositions as well as musical allusions to Salieri's opera *Tarare,* which Mozart prized highly in this work.

Mozartiana. The fourth orchestral suite by PIOTR ILYICH TCHAIKOVSKY, 1887, arranged from various instrumental and choral works by WOLFGANG AMADEUS MOZART. It was first performed in Moscow.

MUSICAL
INSTRUMENT

mṛidaṅgam. Classical drum of southern India, in an elongated barrel shape with two heads of different diameters. It is made of wood, although its name refers to clay.

The heads, as in many other wooden MEMBRANOPHONES, are attached to hoops and tightened by leather thongs. The instrument is tuned by inserting tension wedges between the hoop and the heads and also by applying a paste to each head. The two heads are tuned an octave apart.

Muddy Waters. *See* WATERS, MUDDY.

Muette de Portici, Le (The Mute Girl of Portici; also called *Masaniello*). Opera by DANIEL-FRANÇOIS-ESPRIT AUBER, 1828, first performed in Paris.

The Neopolitan fisherman Masaniello, the brother of the mute girl of Portici (a small fishing village near Naples), leads a rebellion against the Spanish rule. He is mysteriously murdered just as he achieves his goal of overthrowing the Spanish viceroy in Naples. His deaf-mute sister throws herself into the crater of Mt. Vesuvius during an eruption.

The story has a historical foundation: an actual Masaniello led a successful uprising in 1647. He was murdered, but Mt. Vesuvius erupted 16 years before the event.

Mulligan, Gerry (Gerald Joseph), American jazz baritone saxophonist and arranger; b. N.Y., June 4, 1927; d. Darien, Conn., Jan. 19, 1996. Mulligan's childhood years were spent in Philadelphia, where he learned to play piano. He played reed instruments and worked professionally as an arranger while still in his teens, then went to N.Y. in 1946, where he played reed instruments and wrote arrangements for drummer Gene Krupa's big band. After performing with MILES DAVIS from 1948 to 1950, he acquired a reputation as one of the finest baritone saxophonists of his era.

In 1952 Mulligan formed the first of several "pianoless" quartets, with which he toured extensively and made recordings. Mulligan was one of the leaders of the COOL JAZZ school. His playing was highly melodic, and many of his compositions showed the influence of classical composition.

Mulligan led his own big band on a tour of Europe in 1960 and of Japan in 1964. He also made appearances with various jazz notables and began playing the soprano saxophone. He remained active through the '70s, '80s, and '90s, until his death. Although he occasionally showed the influence of current pop music, his style changed little over the years.

When the opera was performed in Brussels in 1830, the people in the audience became so excited by this operatic cry for freedom that they spilled out into the streets, demanding independence for Belgium. A year or so later they achieved it.

PEOPLE IN MUSIC

multiphonics. A modern method of wind sound production that through OVERBLOWING and special fingerings results in two or more sounds simultaneously by a single performer on a MONOPHONIC instrument.

PEOPLE IN MUSIC

Munch (born Münch), **Charles** (1891–1968), eminent Alsatian conductor; b. Strasbourg, Sept. 26, 1891; d. Richmond, Va., Nov. 6, 1968. His father, Ernst Münch (b. Niederbronn, Dec. 31, 1859; d. Strasbourg, April 1, 1928), was an organist and choral conductor. Charles studied violin at the Strasbourg Conservatory and with Lucien Capet in Paris.

In 1914, at the outbreak of World War I, Munch enlisted in the German army. He was made a sergeant of artillery and was gassed at Peronne and wounded at Verdun. A year after the end of the war in 1919, he returned to Alsace-Lorraine and became a French citizen. Having received further violin training from Carl Flesch in Berlin, Munch pursued a career as a soloist. He was also professor of violin at the Leipzig Conservatory and concertmaster of the Gewandhaus Orchestra there. In 1932 he made his professional conducting debut in Paris with the Straram Orchestra. He also studied conducting with Alfred Szendrei there from 1933 to 1940.

Munch quickly rose to prominence. He was conductor of Paris's Orchestre de la Société Philharmonique from 1935 to 1938 and became a professor at the École Normale de Musique in 1936. In 1938 he became music director of the Société des Concerts du Conservatoire de Paris, remaining in that post during the years of the German occupation during World War II. Refusing to collaborate with the Nazis, he gave his support to the Resistance, being awarded the Legion of Honor in 1945.

Munch made his U.S. debut as a guest conductor of the Boston Symphony Orchestra in 1946, followed by a transcontinental tour of the U.S. with the French National Radio Orchestra in 1948. In 1949 he was appointed music director of the Boston Symphony Orchestra, which he and PIERRE MONTEUX took on its first European tour in 1952. They took it again to Europe in 1956, also touring in the Soviet Union, the first U.S. orchestra to do so.

After retiring from his Boston post in 1962, Munch made appearances as a guest conductor and also helped to launch the Orchestre de Paris in 1967. He died a year later in Richmond, Virginia.

Munch acquired an outstanding reputation as an interpreter of the French repertoire, his performances being marked by spontaneity, color, and elegance. French music of the 20th century also occupied a prominent place on his programs. He introduced new works by ALBERT ROUSSEL, DARIUS MILHAUD, ARTHUR HONEGGER, and others. He wrote *Je suis chef d'orchestre* (I Am the Orchestra's Leader; 1954).

Munrow, David (John), gifted English recorder player; b. Birmingham, Aug. 12, 1942; d. (suicide) Chesham Bois, Buckinghamshire, May 15, 1976. Munrow studied English at Pembroke College, Cambridge during 1961–64. In addition to his studies, he founded an ensemble to promote early English music and organized a recorder consort. In 1967 he formed the Early Music Consort of London, with which he gave many successful concerts of medieval and RENAISSANCE music. He also was active with his own BBC radio program.

Munrow lectured on early music at the University of Leicester from 1967 and was professor of recorder at London's Royal Academy of Music from 1969. He published the volume *Instruments of the Middle Ages and Renaissance* in 1976.

Muradeli, Vano (Ilyich). *See* GREAT FRIENDSHIP, THE.

murky bass. A curious term of puzzling origin. It is applied to rudimentary accompaniment in broken OCTAVES in the bass, much in use in ROCOCO music. Some theorists suggest that *murky* is taken from the English word that means exactly what it says: unclear and confusing.

musette (Fr.). 1. A small OBOE. 2. A reed stop on the organ. 3. A small French BAGPIPE, very popular in the BAROQUE era. It was much more ornate in appearance than the Scottish bagpipe and was used in BALLETS given at the French court. Music was written for the instrument by Nicolas Hotteterre, Joseph Bodin de Boismortier, JEAN-PHILIPPE RAMEAU, and

PEOPLE IN MUSIC

MUSICAL INSTRUMENT

♪

Musettes are found in many BAROQUE instrumental suites by French composers, and also in the English Suite No. 3 of JOHANN SEBASTIAN BACH. As late as 1925, ARNOLD SCHOENBERG included one in his op.25 piano suite.

Michel Pignolet de Montéclair. 4. A pastoral dance of the French ballet, characterized by a DRONE accompaniment and $\frac{12}{8}$ meter.

The middle section of the GAVOTTE is often called *Musette,* when it has a sustained drone on the TONIC and DOMINANT.

An older name for the musette is *cornemuse.*

PEOPLE IN MUSIC

Musgrave, Thea, Scottish composer; b. Barnton, Midlothian, May 27, 1928. Musgrave pursued preliminary medical studies at the University of Edinburgh and concurrently studied composition and counterpoint, receiving a bachelor's of music degree in 1950 and winning the Donald Tovey Prize. From 1952 to 1954 she studied at the Paris Conservatory with NADIA BOULANGER, and later was a scholarship student of AARON COPLAND at the Berkshire Music Center in Tanglewood, Massachusetts, in 1959.

Musgrave taught at the University of London from 1958 to 1965, then was a visiting professor of composition at the University of California, Santa Barbara in 1970. She also lectured at various other U.S. and English universities and made appearances as a conductor on both sides of the Atlantic. She held two Guggenheim fellowships (1974–75; 1982). In 1971 she married the American violinist Peter Mark, who later served as conductor of the Virginia Opera Association in Norfolk, Virginia. She was named Distinguished Professor of Music at Queens College in N.Y. in 1987.

At the outset of her career, Musgrave followed the acceptable modern style of composition. Soon the lyricism of the initial period of her creative evolution gave way to increasingly CHROMATIC constructions. She eventually adapted SERIAL organization. She described her theatrical works as "dramatic abstracts" in form, because even in the absence of a programmatic design, they revealed some individual dramatic traits.

Appreciated by critics and audiences alike, Musgrave's compositions, in a variety of styles but invariably effective and technically accomplished, enjoyed numerous performances in Europe and America. She is best known for her vocal works, including the operas *Abbott of Drimock,* chamber opera (1955), *The Decision* (1964–65), *The Voice of Ariadne* (1972–73), *Mary, Queen of Scots* (1976), *A Christmas Carol* (1979), *An Occurrence at Owl Creek Bridge,* radio opera (1981), *Harriet, the Woman Called Moses* (1985), and *Simón Bolívar* (1994). Among her many orchestral works are Clarinet Concerto (1969), a deft, chic virtuoso piece requiring the soloist to promenade among members of the orchestra; *Moving into Aquarius* (1984; in collaboration with R. R. Bennett); *The Seasons* (1988); *Rainbow* (1990); *Autumn Sonata,* bass clarinet concerto (1993); *Journey Through a Japanese Landscape,* concerto for MARIMBA and wind orchestra (1994); and *Helios,* oboe concerto (1995). She also composed music for ballets and numerous chamber works.

music (It. *musica;* Ger. *Musik;* Fr. *musique*). The word *music* is derived from the Greek, *mousikē,* an art of the muses (sing. *Mousa*). Euterpe, the muse of tragedy and FLUTE playing, and Polyhymnia, the muse of singing, are regarded as the inspiring deities of music: Euterpe, because in ancient Greece music was closely connected with tragedy, and theatrical spectacles were invariably accompanied by the playing of the flute; and Polyhymnia, because the beginning of music was marked by a multiplicity of songs.

In present terms, *music* may be defined as a meaningful succession of perceptible sounds in temporal motion. These sounds may be single sonorous units (as in MELODY) or combinations of several such units (as in HARMONY and COUNTERPOINT). Temporal motion may consist of sounds of equal duration (simple chant) or of unequal duration (rhythmed melody, or MELORHYTHM). Melorhythms may be patterned symmetrically, in well-demarcated periods (corresponding to unchanged meter in versification), or in asymmetrical fragments.

The perfection of a melorhythmic figure is determined by the balance between MELODY and RHYTHM. When melodic elements (TONES) vary greatly in pitch, the rhythm may be allowed to remain steady. When the melody is confined to a few notes, and in extreme cases to a single note, then rhythm must show variety.

Music is written down by means of symbols or notes. A medieval monk, St. Isidore of Seville, stated in the 7th cen-

> *"If music be the food of love, play on."*
>
> —William Shakespeare,
> *A Midsummer Night's Dream*

tury that music is an art that can be preserved by oral tradition only because tones can never be notated (*scribi non possunt*). The history of musical notation has indeed been arduous, but for the last four centuries it has assumed a fairly uniform aspect. The height of a musical tone is measured by its relative position on a STAFF of five lines, with CLEFS indicating the selected pitch of a specific note, usually G, C, or F, placed on any of the five lines on the staff. The rest of the notes are calculated from the clef note, with each space and each line representing one DIATONIC degree.

The concept of music does not necessarily signify beauty or attractiveness. Indeed, music of primitive peoples, which is beautiful to them, may appear chaotic and ugly to an outsider. Within the memory of many musicians, compositions by modern masters were condemned by critics as pure noise.

The German philosopher Emmanuel Kant described music as "an artistic arrangement of sensations of hearing," which is logically acceptable, because it includes any subjectively artistic succession of musical elements. Georg Wilhelm Friedrich Hegel declared that the aim of music is "to render in sounds the innermost self which moves in itself according to the subjective feeling for one's ideal soul." This statement is so involved that it may signify any sound, or any combination of sounds, that expresses an emotion.

Theorists seeking to separate music from other arts emphasize its unique capacity to convey emotions and meaning, to express spiritual and sensory phenomena in terms that use no language and no pictorial representation. Hegel himself admitted that music is "sufficient unto itself and therefore self-explanatory."

Great poets extolled music as a catalyst of passion and a motive force for bravery. Shakespeare expressed this quality in the ringing lines "The man that hath no music in himself / nor is not moved with concord of sweet sounds / . . . let no such man be trusted." In his *Ode on a Grecian Urn,* Keats said that music should be perceived in silence: "Heard melodies are sweet, but those unheard are sweeter." Henry Wadsworth Longfellow followed the philosophers in saying that "music is the universal language of mankind."

In the Middle Ages music was part of mathematics, included in the curriculum of the universities. In poetic language, the word *numbers* means music. "Will no one tell me what she sings?" William Wordsworth questioned, and surmised: "Perhaps the plaintive numbers flow / For old, unhappy, far-off things." German philosopher Gottfried Wilhelm Leibniz said: "Music is a kind of counting performed by the mind without knowing that it is counting." This definition comes remarkably close to British philosopher Bertrand Russell's description of mathematics as "the subject in which we never know what we are talking about, nor whether what we are saying is true."

music(al) box (Fr. *boîte à musique*). Mechanical musical instrument perfected shortly after the invention of clockwork, about the year 1200.

The first such mechanical instrument was the BARREL ORGAN, manufactured for the Archbishop of Salzburg in 1502. It had 350 pipes; each pipe would be opened or stopped as a barrel with pins rotated. This was followed by the mechanical CARILLON, the best of which were made in Flanders and Holland in the 17th century. Chiming watches that played tunes appeared in France in the 18th century.

The Swiss music box has steel tongues of definite pitch that are plucked by pins on a rotating metal cylinder or barrel, turned by clockwork. The first models were made by Antoine Favre of Geneva in 1796. The music box industry reached its greatest development about 1870. It declined with the appearance of the phonograph, a ri-

MUSICAL
INSTRUMENT

◀

Music box that operates by playing removable discs, c. 1890. (UPI/Corbis-Bettmann)

val too mighty for tinkling pins and tongues. Apart from chiming watches, music boxes were manufactured in the form of snuff boxes and sewing boxes. Musical dolls are music boxes that survive into the present time.

In 1994 a collection of new music boxes commissioned for "The Music Box Project," supported by the Reuge Music Company in Sainte-Croix, Switzerland, and curated by Claudia Gold, was unveiled. These included new works by a variety of modern composers and visual artists, including JOHN CAGE (*Extended Lullaby*), Laurie Anderson (*Tilt #1*), and NAM JUNE PAIK (*I Wrote It in Tokyo in 1954*).

Music Box Revue, The. An annual series of revues, 1921–24, with songs composed by IRVING BERLIN, that took place at the Music Box Theater, which he co-owned. Among the songs that were written for these shows are *Say It With Music, Lady of the Evening, What'll I Do?,* and *All Alone.*

music drama. The original description of opera as it evolved in Florence early in the 17th century (*dramma per musica*). RICHARD WAGNER adopted this term in order to emphasize the dramatic element in his spectacles (*Musikdrama*).

Music for Strings, Percussion, and Celesta. A multimovement work by BÉLA BARTÓK, 1937, in which percussion instruments play a major part. The four-part structure can be viewed as the slow-fast VERBUNKOS form (played twice), or perhaps the late BAROQUE SINFONIA. The opening string FUGUE is as powerful as any since LUDWIG VAN BEETHOVEN's late quartets. The piece was first performed in Basel.

music hall. A place and type of light entertainment popular in British cities in the Victorian and Edwardian eras, modeled after the Paris CAFÉ CHANTANT.

Music halls usually featured songs and dances spiced by an infinitesimal display of sensuality, sufficient to make moral guardians shudder with horror at the depravity of the thing. A further degradation was afforded by the adjacent *cabinets particuliers,* where a peer or a lord might entertain a lady of a lower class. As the 20th century proceeded, music hall performers entered the traveling VAUDEVILLE circuits, which persisted in Britain until World War II.

Music in the Air. Musical by JEROME KERN and OSCAR HAMMERSTEIN, 1932. The story describes a love affair between a schoolteacher and the daughter of the leader of a local choral society in Bavaria. The two collaborate on a song and try to get it published in Munich, where the young schoolteacher is attracted to a prima donna and the girl flirts with an opera librettist. Not achieving professional success and tired of extracurricular romances, the couple return to their mountain town. Includes *I've Told Ev'ry Little Star* and *The Song Is You.*

music journals. Before the advent of mass publications or general newspapers that included a special department devoted to concert reviews, music criticism existed only in the form of theoretical discussions in specially printed pamphlets. Germany was a pioneer in musical journalism, where essays on technical subjects were published in connection with public performances. The first musical periodical that published critical evaluations of musical works was the *Allgemeine musikalische Zeitung,* founded in 1798 and published, with an occasional hiatus, until 1881.

In 1834 ROBERT SCHUMANN founded his own publication, *Neue Zeitschrift für Musik,* dedicated to the propaganda of "new music" of a ROMANTIC mold. After many interruptions it was reincarnated after World War I. The German music weekly *Signale für die musikalische Welt,* founded in 1841, lasted almost a century until World War II finally killed it off. The informative weekly *Allgemeine Musikzeitung* was also the victim of World War II after 70 years of relatively prosperous existence. With the exception of Schumann's journal, these publications adopted a conservative, not to say reactionary, attitude toward the novel musical tendencies of each successive period.

In France, *La Revue Musicale* continued its uncertain existence from 1827 to 1880, was reincarnated under the same title in 1920, only to falter and die. *Le Ménèstrel* lasted more than 100 years after its founding in 1833, with the inevitable collapse during the Paris Commune and World War I. World War II put a finish to it. Its critical attitudes

It was for *Allgemeine musikalische Zeitung* that ROBERT SCHUMANN wrote, at the age of 19, his unsigned article saluting FRÉDÉRIC CHOPIN as a genius.

during the first century of its existence were definitely reactionary: it damned RICHARD WAGNER and CLAUDE DEBUSSY with equal fervor.

In England, the most durable monthly is *The Musical Times,* founded in 1844 and still going strong after nearly 150 years. In the U.S., musical journals of opinion had a relatively brief life. In the 19th century, *Dwight's Journal of Music* enjoyed respect. It was dull, and it damned Wagner.

In the meantime, artists of varying degrees of excellence, music teachers, and minor musicians of all calibers, mostly of European birth, came to the U.S. in search of employment. In the U.S. these demands were met by commercial music periodicals, of which *The Musical Courier* and *Musical America* were particularly prominent. They published weekly issues that featured dispatches by specially assigned European correspondents and reproduced excellent photographs of the current celebrities who bought advertising space.

As interest in the artistic and amorous goings-on in the musical world waned, these journals began to languish and finally expired. *Musical America* survived as a shriveled appendix to *High Fidelity,* but it, too, has disappeared. *The Etude* purveyed mainly to music lovers and amateurs. It published sentimental biographies of contemporary musicians, as well as simplified selections of their easier-to-play compositions, but it, too, succumbed. In place of these publications there arose a crop of commercialized periodicals devoted to recordings, radio, and television, with only a sprinkling of informative material. Musicological journals carried on a subsidized existence.

In the U.S., *The Musical Quarterly* was the most important publication in the scholarly field. In England, *Music and Letters* and *Music Review* purveyed selective information. There were also music journals of some value in Italy. In Russia, the monthly *Sovietskaya Musica* furnished information on Soviet music. In Latin America, only the *Revista Musical Chilena* appeared with some regularity.

The international AVANT-GARDE has put out sporadic issues of great interest to their particular audiences. The most extreme was *Source,* published in California, without visible financial support, printing the most fantastic samples of ultra-modern productions lavishly illustrated in a variety of colors. It existed for several years before collapsing.

Music for Airports. Landmark work by BRIAN ENO, 1978, expressing the composer's interest in composed environmental sounds. Eno composed it entirely for SYNTHESIZER.

The work was later performed by the lively downtown N.Y. ensemble Bang on a Can, whose personnel includes Michael Gordon, David Lang, Julia Wolfe, and Evan Ziporyn, each of whom arranged one of its four movements (*1/1, 1/2, 2/1, 2/2*). For their 1998 recording, the instrumentation of the Bang on a Can All-Stars was enhanced by voices, brass, winds, and pipa, filling out the orchestra of sound in order to re-create the sounds of Eno's original synthesized work.

Music Man, The. Musical by MEREDITH WILSON, 1957. An affable flim-flam man cons officials in a small town in the Midwest to form a school band, collects money for instruments, then moves on to the next town to trick other victims. But his would-be victims are so inspired by his rhetoric, and he so influenced by a librarian named Marian, that he decides to see the thing through, resulting in a splendid marching band. Many songs have endured, including *76 Trombones; Trouble; Goodnight My Someone; My White Knight; Till There Was You;* and *Gary, Indiana.*

Music of Changes. Landmark work for solo piano by JOHN CAGE, 1951. In *Music of Changes,* charts containing 64 cells (arranged into eight rows of eight columns each) are employed, with each relating in a one-to-one correspondence with the 64 hexagrams (a figure in the shape of a six-pointed star) of the Chinese book used to predict the future, the *I Ching*. To select an element from a chart, Cage would toss coins. The random numbers produced would be matched to one of the 64 symbols of the *I Ching,* then the corresponding cell in the chart. In this work, chance, for the first time, is used as a means to compose a work, and not simply an end. As might be expected, silence is equally represented as sound in the finished work.

Music of Changes was first performed by Cage's close collaborator, David Tudor, at N.Y.'s Cherry Lane Theater on Jan. 1, 1952.

music of the spheres. *See* HARMONY OF THE SPHERES.

music stand (Ger. *Pult;* Fr. *pupitre*). A metal (occasionally wooden) rack placed in front of musicians to hold scores during rehearsal or performance.

music theater (U.K. *theatre*). Any small to moderate musical stage work involving a dramatic element in its performance, frequently distinguished from opera by its scale and scope.

music therapy. The study and use of musical stimuli and activity in the evaluation, remediation, or maintenance of health. It developed into a bona fide profession at about the time of World War II in the U.S., with university curricula following within the decade.

In earlier times, anecdote served the role that research does now. A Sicilian youth suspected that his beloved was faithless. His suspicions were further inflamed by the sounds of FLUTE music in the PHRYGIAN MODE. Seized by madness, he rushed into her house. Pythagoras, taking temporary leave of his mathematical calculations, took notice of the young man's condition and ordered the flute player to change from the Phrygian to the DORIAN MODE. This MODULATION had an immediate soothing effect on the youth, who became philosophically calm.

At a time when tempers were short and modes were untempered, Alexander the Great was so sensitive that when a musician played a Phrygian air on the lyre Alexander unsheathed his sword and slew one of his guests. The musician precluded further slaughter by switching to a less exciting mode. Aristotle tells of alleviating the pain of slaves by causing flute music to be played while they were being punished by flogging. Terpander pacified a menacing crowd of rebellious citizens by singing in pleasing modes, accompanying himself on a seven-string lyre of his invention. So impressed were his listeners that they burst into tears and rushed to kiss the feet of their tyrant.

The ancient Greek Phrygian mode (which corresponds to the IONIAN MODE in GREGORIAN CHANT, identical with C major), was regarded by the Greeks as most apt to cause hyperventilation in a human being.

Tyrtacus, the Athenian, was sent to Sparta on a mission to undermine the savage Spartan spirit by playing an elegy, *Eunomia* (good law), to them. However, when he inadvertently changed to the militaristic Dorian mode, the Spartans rose in wrath and marched belligerently on Athens.

Plato declared that civil obedience can be achieved by means of music. Indeed, public decrees were often recited in ancient Greece to the melodious accompaniment of the lyre. Damon of Athens succeeded in quieting drunken youths by playing tunes on the flute. Maecenas, the legendary patron of Roman poetry, cured his chronic insomnia by listening to distant sounds of music.

The Phrygian mode was recommended by Theophrastus, favorite disciple of Aristotle, for cure of sciatica, with the vertical flute to be held close to the affected nerve ganglion. Many victims of melancholy regained their self-confidence when Phrygian tunes were played for them, Theophrastus reports. Flute playing in the Phrygian mode was also proposed by Caelius Aurelianus for temporary relief from lumbago and arthritis. At the sound of the flute, the ailing person would begin to tremble, thus stimulating the nerves affected and curing the disease.

Belief in the beneficial and curative properties of music persisted even when the model dichotomy of the Phrygian and Dorian modes were replaced by "scientific" reasoning and experimentation. In *The Musical Doctor,* published in 1811, Peter Lichtenthal suggests musical remedies for a variety of human ills.

"Music has charm to soothe the savage breast," William Congreve wrote, but the statement is not always true. If the chroniclers can be trusted, Eric the Good, king of Denmark, ordered all weapons removed from his reach before the court lutenist began to play for fear that he might be moved to violence by the sounds of music. So strong was this impulse, it is said, that the moment the lutenist began to play, the king rushed out, seized a sword, and killed four men.

On the other side of the ledger, King Philip II of Spain engaged the famous CASTRATO Farinelli to sing for him every night to allay his chronic melancholy. Farinelli sang the same four songs for the king every night for 25 years, until the royal sufferer finally gave up the ghost.

One of the most bizarre chronicles of musical therapy concerns *tarantism,* an uncontrollable compulsion to dance, which erupted in Taranto, Italy in the 15th century. This morbid choreographic condition was caused by the bite of the tarantula spider, and according to contemporary reports, it could be cured by playing the Italian tarantella, a rapid dance in $\frac{6}{8}$ time.

A plausible claim can be made, however, for the psychiatric benefit of music for retarded or autistic children. Playing rhythmic dance music, particularly in binary meter (which corresponds to the natural alternation of steps, inspirations and expirations of breath, and the diastolic and systolic heartbeats), may well have a soothing effect on disturbed individuals. The most beneficial tempo is 80 beats per minute, which corresponds to the normal pulse rate.

What kind of music should be played for medicinal purposes? As long ago as 1852, a German physiologist wrote: "A careful study of melodies shows that we are completely ignorant of the circumstances under which the change from one type of nerve excitation to another corresponds to the physical substratum of the aesthetic sensations generated by the music."

Some music-loving physicians assert that music can directly affect the seat of emotion in the cerebral cortex. Numerous experiments have been conducted on mental patients to establish what particular type of music is best for them, with no conclusive results. Musical statistics have been compiled by psychologists to prove that the piano music of FRÉDÉRIC CHOPIN and SERGEI RACHMANINOFF was good for unbalanced persons, while IGOR STRAVINSKY and ARNOLD SCHOENBERG upset their mental equilibrium. This is probably based on a natural bias against modern music as opposed to styles that are more familiar.

For a most conspicuous resurgence of music therapy in the present age, see NEW AGE MUSIC.

The Institute of Musical Therapy, organized in Poland in 1974, suggested the following musical program be played prior to open-heart surgery for the beneficial effect on the patient as well as the surgeon:

Gavotte in A Major by Christoph Willibald Gluck

Clair de lune by CLAUDE DEBUSSY

Siciliana by Johann Sebastian Bach

Adagio attributed to Tomasso Albinoni

---

moo′zē′kăh

musica (Lat.). MUSIC. As a medieval term, it is incorporated in several expressions of the period: *musica artificialis,* composed music; *musica chordae,* string music; *musica da camera,* chamber music; *musica da chiesa,* church music; *musica divina,* sacred music; *musica harmonica,* vocal music; *musica* *humana,* harmony of body and soul; *musica instrumentalis,* music as performed and heard; *musica mundana,* music of the universe; *musica organica,* organ or wind music; *musica pulsus,* percussive music; *musica rhythmica,* music produced by finger-striking; *musica sacra,* sacred music; *musica ventus,* wind music; *musica vocalis,* vocal music; *musica vulgaris,* secular (not vulgar) music.

Musica enchiriadis. Important anonymous Latin treatise, dating from c.900, which includes discussion of the TETRA-CHORD, parallel ORGANUM, and NOTATION.

musica ficta (Lat.). In music from the 10th through 16th centuries, the introduction of ACCIDENTALS, mainly sharps, to accommodate MODULATION (or changing from one scale to another). The term, which means "manufactured music," originated in the 14th century to replace the misleading derogatory term *musica falsa.*

    Compilers of medieval Latin treatises fully realized how inadequate these terms were. In one, an anonymous author speaks of the new type of modulation as *non tamen falsa musica, sed inusitata* (not so much false music, but useless music). But another anonymous author terms this "useless" music as *causa necessitatis et causa pulchritudinis cantus per se* (for the reason of necessity and beauty, an independent melody). Still another writer claims that *falsa musica non est inutilis immo necessaria* (false music is not useless, but quite necessary), an opinion echoed by the positive pronouncement of Philippe de Vitry that *musica ficta sive falsa est musica vera et necessaria* (musica ficta or musica falsa is true and necessary music).

    The practical consequences of musica ficta, whatever the term itself might connote, were far-reaching. Medieval theorists had slavishly followed the GUIDONIAN HAND. Their cautious modulations had to be *in manu* (in the hand). However, musica ficta led music to the regions *extra manum* (outside the hand), venturing into the territory that required remote sharps and flats, at first only F♯ and B♭, but later C♯ and other accidentals.

    In the meantime, musica ficta generated related terms such as *vox ficta,* a CONTRAPUNTAL part containing extra

moo′zē′kăh fík′tah

sharps or flats, and *cantus fictus,* a theme written in an alien key. Not until the reluctant admission on the part of theorists that all keys are intervallically alike and that notation was the *anicilla musicae* (servant of music) were musica ficta and musica falsa freed from the suspicion of falsity.

moo'zē'kăh fi'gyoor-a'tah

musica figurata (Lat.). Music arranged in contrasting CONTRAPUNTAL figurations.

moo'zē'kăh rě-zer-văh'tah

musica reservata (Lat.). A 16th-century term applied to a particularly sophisticated type of CONTRAPUNTAL music, related to MUSICA FICTA and "reserved" for masters of the craft.

Musica transalpina. A collection of Italian MADRIGALS with English translations, 1588. This anthology greatly influenced the development of the English madrigal school.

musical. American or English MUSICAL COMEDY or REVUE.

MUSICAL
INSTRUMENT

musical bow. Generic name for the MONOCHORD, consisting of a flexible rod curved by a string and played with a stick. A resonator may be attached, or the mouth may be used as one.

The instrument is found almost universally at one time or another. Despite earlier theories, many cultures that play a musical bow do not hunt with bow and arrow.

musical comedy. A generic term applied to a play with music or opera with a comic or at least nontragic LIBRETTO. At its broadest, the term can be applied to works beginning in the 16th century. However, the word *comedy* derives from the Italian *commedia,* which simply means "story" or "play," and does not guarantee the presence of humor. Similarly, the French OPÉRA COMIQUE may not necessarily leave them laughing (i.e., the story of GEORGES BIZET's *CARMEN*).

Early American musicals were closer in essence to revues. THE BLACK CROOK, first presented in 1866 and revived for decades afterward, is a good example. It included chorus lines, songs, and a very loose plot.

In the last century, the term has been shortened to *musical* and refers generally to a work with dialogue and songs. Works that present songs only are descendants of VAUDEVILLE and are considered examples of the REVUE. Either type is known colloquially as a *show.* The American musical began developing in the post–Civil War era. The genre was influenced by French dancing chorus lines, Viennese operettas, and British musical comedy (GILBERT AND SULLIVAN) and music hall.

At the turn of the century, VICTOR HERBERT brought the OPERETTA to Broadway, followed closely by RUDOLF FRIML and SIGMUND ROMBERG. At the same time, GEORGE M. CO-HAN developed a more American genre, full of vibrancy, with songs, choruses, dance numbers, and the thinnest of plots.

After World War I, many musicals reflected political and social issues of the day, however flippantly. JEROME KERN's great *Show Boat,* staged in 1927, was a profound exception, with its close study of racism. GEORGE and IRA GERSHWIN, RICHARD RODGERS and LORENZ HART, COLE PORTER, and IRVING BERLIN were the best known of many who scored these musical plays. While the quality of the songs continued to improve, lyrically and musically, the librettos remained mostly flimsy, using familiar comic opera devices such as mistaken identity, disguise, and satire. Gershwin's most serious work, *Porgy and Bess,* was written as an opera.

With the 1943 *Oklahoma!,* Richard Rodgers and OSCAR HAMMERSTEIN reintroduced the "serious musical comedy" on a steadier basis. Whether the subject matter (WEST SIDE STORY) or the source (KISS ME KATE, MY FAIR LADY) was the strength behind the show, the postwar musical was a more total work of art than any of its predecessors.

In the last decades of the 20th century, this kind of musical survived and expanded in the hands of STEPHEN SOND-HEIM and ANDREW LLOYD WEBBER. The other major development, musicals based on independently popular music such as ROCK and SOUL, has produced mixed results.

musical saw. A novelty musical instrument. A player places the handle of the saw against the inside of the thigh, then bends up the blade. Against the nontoothed edge, a violin bow is run to produce a tone. By bending the blade up and down, different tones are created.

Any saw can be used, but flexible saws made specifically for this purpose work best.

musicale. A musical presentation or concert given as part of a social gathering of affluent music lovers. An abbreviation of *soirée musicale* (musical evening).

MUSICAL INSTRUMENT

musicology. The science of music, a concept that includes all branches of music (i.e., theory, history, aesthetics, lexicography, bibliography, etc.)

The term originated in France early in the 19th century (*musicologie*), was later adopted by German music theorists (*Musikwissenschaft*), and domesticated in England and the U.S. as musicology. Musicology at first emphasized abstruse historical and semantic subjects. But as the teaching of musicology expanded and embraced general historiography of music and even biography, Ph.D. degrees were awarded by leading universities for dissertations with such titles as "Plausible Deciphering of Beethoven's Notes to His Housekeeper Instructing Her to Buy Candles and Yellow Soap" (the specification *gelbe* for the color of the soap was credited by the author to an eminent Beethovenologist) and "New Data Establishing Schumann's Syphyllitic Infection."

Analysis of works, bibliographical studies of all kinds, and newfangled theories dealing with melody, harmony, or counterpoint, all gradually fell in the category of musicology until it truly became a science of music history, theory, and biography. The only requirement to qualify, so it seemed, was a profusion of learned footnotes, some of which actually contradicted the author's postulates. Several musicological journals give space for the publication of such esoteric subjects, which, it must be admitted, occasionally furnish useful information.

musicus (Lat.; Ger. *Musikant*). Medieval designation of a learned musician, profoundly versed in the mathematical theory (and theology) of materials of which music is made, This term was used in contrast with a mere CANTOR, who could sing or play music without understanding what it was.

moo-zēk′ **Musik** (Ger.). MUSIC. *Musikalien,* printed musical compositions; *Musikdruck,* music printing or publishing; *Musikfest,* music festival; *Musikforschung,* music research; *Musikgeschichte,* music history; *Musikgesellschaft,* music society; *Musikschule,* music school; *Musikverein,* music association; *Musikwissenschaft,* musical science, MUSICOLOGY; *Musikzeitung,* music periodical.

musique (Fr.). MUSIC. *Musique de chambre,* chamber music; *musique de scène,* INCIDENTAL MUSIC; *musique d'ameublement,* FURNITURE MUSIC, BACKGROUND MUSIC; *musique funèbre,* funeral music; *musique mesurée,* late-16th-century settings of *vers mesurés,* French poetry that utilizes classical Greek and Latin versifying principles; *musique populaire,* folk (not popular) music; *musique sacrée,* sacred music; *musique d'ecurie* (music of the stable), field music, that is, music played in unison by trumpets and signal horns.

mü-zēk′

musique concrète (Fr., concrete music). Composition on recording tape, using recorded natural sounds and editing and processing them to produce a piece.

mü-zēk′ con-crĕt′

Musique concrète was named in April 1948 by PIERRE SCHAEFFER, a French radio engineer. Experimenting with the newly invented magnetic tape recorder, he found that noises, conversations, and radio commercials recorded on tape could be made into a composition by splicing the tape in various ways, running it at different speeds, or backwards, and so on. Overtracking—recording repeatedly over the same length of tape—makes it possible to create a multi-voiced composition of great complexity.

In the U.S., OTTO LUENING, VLADIMIR USSACHEVSKY, and EDGARD VARÈSE were the most important early exponents of musique concrète. Later, pop musicians discovered the possibilities of making tape collages. John Lennon of the BEATLES introduced the use of backward-running tape in songs like *Rain, Strawberry Fields Forever,* and *Tomorrow Never Knows.* He also composed a series of tape collages with AVANT-GARDE artist YOKO ONO.

Today, digital SAMPLERS have replaced old-fashioned tape recorders as a means of recording and reconstituting sounds. The sound collages used to accompany rap music, made up of samples of other recordings added to other sounds and rhythms, are good examples of digitally produced musique concrète.

Mussorgsky, Modest (Petrovich), Russian composer, the greatest of the "Mighty Five"; b. Karevo, Pskov district, March 21, 1839; d. St. Petersburg, March 28, 1881. Mus-

PEOPLE IN MUSIC

Modest Mussorgsky. (New York Public Library) ▶

sorgsky received instruction on the piano from his mother. At the age of 10, he was taken to St. Petersburg, where he had piano lessons with Anton Herke, remaining his pupil until 1854.

In 1852 Mussorgsky entered the cadet school of the Imperial Guard. He composed a piano piece entitled *Porte-enseigne Polka,* which was published that year. After his graduation in 1856, he joined the regiment of the Guard. In 1857 he met Alexander Dargomyzhsky, who introduced him to the composers CÉSAR CUI and MILY BALAKIREV. He also became friendly with Vladimir Stasov, the critic and chief champion of Russian national music. These associations prompted his decision to become a professional composer. Balakirev helped him to acquire a knowledge of form. Mussorgsky tried to write music in classical style, but without success. As Mussorgsky himself expressed it, his inner drive was directed toward "new shores."

However, Mussorgsky's family estate had to be liquidated to pay off debts, making it necessary for him to find a full-time job. He became a clerk in the Ministry of Communications in 1863, being dismissed four years later. During this time, he continued to compose, but his lack of technique compelled him time and again to leave his pieces unfinished. He eagerly sought professional advice from his friends Stasov (for general aesthetics) and NIKOLAI RIMSKY-KORSAKOV (for problems of harmony).

To the very end of his life, Mussorgsky regarded himself as being only half-educated in music and constantly acknowledged his inferiority as a craftsman. But he yielded to no one in his firm faith in the future of national Russian music. When a group of composers from Bohemia visited St. Petersburg in 1867, Stasov published an article in which for the first time he referred to the "mighty handful of Russian musicians" (i.e., the "Mighty Five") pursuing the ideal of national art. The expression was picked up derisively by some journalists, but it was accepted as a challenge by Mussorgsky and his comrades-in-arms, Balakirev, ALEXANDER BORODIN, Cui, and Rimsky-Korsakov.

In 1869 Mussorgsky once more entered government service, this time in the forestry department. He became an alcoholic and had epileptic fits. He died a week after his 42nd birthday.

The significance of Mussorgsky's genius did not become apparent until some years after his death. Most of his works were prepared for publication by Rimsky-Korsakov, who corrected some of his harmonic crudities and reorchestrated the symphonic works. Original versions of his music were preserved in manuscript, and eventually published. Despite the availability of the authentic scores, his works continue to be performed in Rimsky-Korsakov's editions, made familiar to the whole musical world.

In his dramatic works and songs, Mussorgsky draws a boldly realistic vocal line, in which inflections of speech are translated into natural melody. His first attempt in this genre was an unfinished opera, *The Marriage,* based on Russian writer Nikolai Gogol's comedy, which demonstrated Mussorgsky's penetrating sense of musical humor. His ability to depict tragic moods is revealed in his cycle *Songs and Dances of Death,* while his understanding of intimate poetry is shown in the children's songs.

Mussorgsky's greatest work is the opera *BORIS GODUNOV,* which has no equal in its stirring portrayal of personal destiny against a background of social upheaval. In it, Mussorgsky created a true national music drama, without a trace of the Italian conventions that had theretofore dominated the operatic works by Russian composers.

The set of pieces *PICTURES AT AN EXHIBITION* (somewhat after the manner of ROBERT SCHUMANN's *Carnaval*) is Mussorgsky's best known work for the piano. It is remarkable for its vivid representation of varied scenes (it was written to commemorate his friend, the painter Victor Hartmann, whose pictures were the subjects of the music). The work became famous in MAURICE RAVEL's brilliant orchestration.

Mussorgsky's orchestral works include *Ivanova noch'na Lisoy gore* (St. John's Night on Bald Mountain; 1860–67; reorchestrated by Rimsky-Korsakov; 1886) and *Vyzatiye Karsa* (The Capture of Kars, March, 1880). He also composed choral works, songs, and piano works. Mussorgsky wrote no chamber music, perhaps because he lacked training in contrapuntal technique.

Although Mussorgsky was a Russian national composer, his music influenced many composers outside Russia. He came to be regarded as the strongest talent of the Russian national school.

Nearly 100 transcriptions of *Pictures at an Exhibition* have been made to date.

MUSICAL INSTRUMENT

mute. 1. A piece of metal fitted to the bridge of a violin or other stringed instrument, designed to deaden the sound when put into position. The direction for putting on the mutes is *con sordini;* for taking them off, *senza sordini.* 2. A leather-covered pad, pasteboard cone, or wooden cylinder inserted in the bell of brass instruments to modify the tone.

PEOPLE IN MUSIC

Muti, Riccardo, Italian conductor; b. Naples, July 28, 1941. His father was a physician who possessed a natural Neapolitan tenor voice. After receiving instruction in violin and piano from him, Riccardo studied composition at the Conservatorio di Musica San Pietro a Majella in Naples, earning a diploma in piano. He then studied conducting and composition at the Verdi Conservatory in Milan.

After winning the Guido Cantelli Competition in 1967, he made his formal debut with the RAI (Italian Radio Orchestra) in 1968. He then conducted in major Italian music centers. His success led to his appointment as principal conductor of the Teatro Comunale in Florence in 1970. He also conducted at the Maggio Musicale Fiorentino, becoming its artistic director in 1977. In the meantime, he began his advancement to international fame with guest conducting appearances at the Salzburg Festival in 1971 and with the Berlin Philharmonic in 1972.

In 1972 Muti made his U.S. debut with the Philadelphia Orchestra. A year later, he conducted at the Vienna State Opera and that same year became principal conductor of the New Philharmonia Orchestra in London (it resumed its original name of Philharmonia Orchestra in 1977). In 1974 he conducted the Vienna Philharmonic and in 1977 appeared at London's Covent Garden.

Muti's successful appearances with the Philadelphia Orchestra led to his appointment as its principal guest conductor in 1977. In 1979 he was also named music director of the Philharmonia Orchestra. In 1980 he succeeded EUGENE ORMANDY as music director of the Philadelphia Orchestra, and subsequently relinquished his posts in London and Florence in 1982. In 1986 he became music director of Milan's La Scala but retained his Philadelphia position. He announced his resignation as music director of the Philadelphia Orchestra in 1990 but agreed to serve as its laureate conductor from 1992. In 1993 he conducted his own edition of Spontini's *Vestale* at La Scala.

Muti's brilliance as a symphonic conductor enabled him to maintain, even enhance, the illustrious reputation of the Philadelphia Orchestra established by LEOPOLD STOKOWSKI and carried forward by Ormandy. Unlike his famous predecessors, he excels in both the concert hall and the opera pit.

Mutter, Anne-Sophie, German violinist; b. Rheinfeldin, June 29, 1963. At the age of six, Mutter won First Prize with Special Distinction at the Jungen Musiziert National Competition, the youngest winner in its annals.

In 1976 Mutter came to the notice of the conductor HERBERT VON KARAJAN during her appearance at the Lucerne Festival. In 1977 he invited her to be a soloist with him and the Berlin Philharmonic at the Salzburg Easter Festival,

PEOPLE IN MUSIC

which marked the beginning of an auspicious career. She subsequently appeared regularly with Karajan and the Berlin Philharmonic, and also recorded standard violin concertos with him. She likewise appeared as soloist with many other leading conductors and orchestras on both sides of the Atlantic.

Beginning in 1986 she held the first International Chair of Violin Studies at London's Royal Academy of Music. In 1988 she made her N.Y. recital debut. In 1998 she made a world tour playing the Beethoven violin sonatas, with Lambert Orkis as pianist.

Muzak. Trademark of the first U.S. company to produce, distribute, and transmit background music for public consumption. Known colloquially as "canned" or "elevator" music, Muzak is also supplied to restaurants, stores, malls, doctors' offices, transit terminals, and waiting rooms. The kinds of music purveyed by Muzak consist of saccharine instrumental arrangements of popular or semiclassical songs.

Muzak executives liked to describe themselves as "Specialists in the Physiological and Psychological Applications of Music," and their product as "a nonverbal symbolism for the common stuff of everyday living in the global village, promoting the sharing of meaning because it massifies symbolism in which not few but all can participate." However, not all shared joyfully. Driven to desperation, N.Y. commuters brought a class action suit to show cause why this "tonal pollution" at the Grand Central Terminal in N.Y. should be declared a public nuisance. Surprisingly, they won.

My Blue Heaven. Song by Walter Donaldson, 1924. It became a tremendous hit in 1927 on the radio, and its recordings sold into millions of copies. It was also incorporated in several movie musicals.

My Country 'Tis of Thee. The first line of the patriotic hymn *America*.

My Fair Lady. Musical by ALAN JAY LERNER and FREDERICK LOEWE, 1956, based on George Bernard Shaw's play *Pygmalion*.

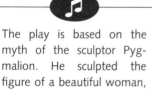

The play is based on the myth of the sculptor Pygmalion. He sculpted the figure of a beautiful woman, only to fall in love with his creation.

In the Shavian and musical version, Professor Henry Higgins is fascinated by the speech of a Cockney flower girl and takes her on as a challenge, aiming to improve her diction and demeanor. He succeeds, but romance rears its head, not without difficulties.

It is a tribute to Lerner and

Audrey Hepburn portraying the transformed Eliza Doolitle in the 1964 film of My Fair Lady. (UPI/Corbis-Bettmann)

Loewe that they succeeded in making a musical out of a play about linguistics, that they could turn such a British-seeming play into a Broadway hit, and that Shaw gave his blessing to this attempt shortly before his death. The great British music hall performer Stanley Holloway was a cast member, and the play also launched the career of singer Julie Andrews. The excellent score includes *The Rain in Spain, I Could Have Danced All Night, On the Street Where You Live, Get Me to the Church on Time,* and *I've Grown Accustomed to Her Face.*

My Girl. A 1965 No. 1 pop and R&B hit for Motown group the TEMPTATIONS, penned by the famous Holland-Dozier-Holland trio.

My Heart Belongs to Daddy. Song by COLE PORTER, 1938, written for the musical *Leave It to Me.* Broadway vocalist MARY MARTIN made the song famous. The "daddy" referred to is not a relative.

My Heart Stood Still. Song by RICHARD RODGERS and LORENZ HART, 1927, from the musical *A CONNECTICUT YANKEE.* A hit in London, its popularity was helped by the future

Duke of Windsor (then Prince of Wales), who liked to sing it himself.

My Melancholy Baby. Song by Ernie Burnett, 1912. The lyrics were by his wife, but he divorced her and had his publisher rearrange the words. She promptly sued him, and the courts awarded her damages.

This was not the end of Burnett's tribulations. In 1965 the son of a nightclub pianist named Ben Light claimed that the song was actually his father's and that Burnett had lifted it from him. By that time everyone concerned with the song's origin was deceased, so that the loyal son of the supposed composer had to drop his claim.

My Old Kentucky Home. Song by STEPHEN FOSTER, 1853, popularized in the MINSTREL shows. It is both the state song of Kentucky and the anthem of the Kentucky Derby.

My Sweet Lord. George Harrison's 1970 tribute to the Indian God Krishna. The song later got him into secular hot water when Ronald Mack, the songwriter of *He's So Fine,* realized that Harrison had unintentionally borrowed his tune for the hit. Harrison settled out of court with Mack.

My Way. Adapted in 1969 from the French song *Mon Habitude* by Paul Anka, with music by Claude François and Jacques Revaux. This became singer FRANK SINATRA's unofficial theme song in the '70s.

My Wild Irish Rose. Song by Chauncey Olcott, 1899, made popular by him in VAUDEVILLE. It became one of the most successful sentimental Irish ballads.

Mysterious Mountain. Symphony No. 2 by ALAN HOVHANESS, 1955. It was inspired by the mystic vision of a phantom peak somewhere in the Himalayas. The score is written in an IMPRESSIONISTIC manner emphasizing colorful instrumental contrasts. It was first performed in Houston, Texas, with LEOPOLD STOKOWSKI conducting.

Mysterium. An unfinished, in fact virtually unbegun, crowning work of ALEXANDER SCRIABIN.

This work had the grand plan to embody the synthesis of all arts and of all human senses, visual, auditory, tactile, gustatory, and olfactory. Scriabin envisioned the *Mysterium* as a final sacrament, with himself as the high priest of the production. The nearest approximation to *Mysterium* was Scriabin's *Poem of Ecstasy.* He planned an intermediate link between it and *Mysterium,* a work for all media that he called a Preliminary Act.

An attempt was made by a group of Russian musicians to orchestrate several of Scriabin's piano pieces of his last period and arrange them in a suite approximating the idea of *Mysterium.* The project was totally unsuccessful.

mystery plays. Medieval Bible plays, often with vocal and instrumental music. In the form called moralities, abstract ideas were portrayed on the stage. For example, a character named "Faith" might encounter another named "Charity," and so forth.

Modern versions of the mysteries have been successfully revived in Britain and elsewhere.

Mystic Chord. The name that Russian composer ALEXANDER SCRIABIN attached to a chord consisting of six notes, C–F♯–B♭–E–A–D, which lies at the foundation of his last symphonic work, *Promethée.* It is also known as the Prometheus chord.

The chord was stated in several of Scriabin's previous compositions in which it usually resolved into the DOMINANT NINTH CHORD by moving A to B♯ and F♯ to G, thus resolving the two suspensions.

No composer since Scriabin's day has made use of the Mystic Chord.

Nabucco. Opera by GIUSEPPE VERDI, 1842, first performed in Milan. It is based on the biblical story of the Hebrews and Nebuchadnezzar (Daniel 1-4), the Babylonian king who defeated them and held them in "Babylonian captivity." The king eventually goes mad but saves himself by converting to the religion of the Hebrews. One of Verdi's early works, *Nabucco* has had several revivals in the 20th century.

MUSICAL INSTRUMENT

nail fiddle. A primitive instrument in use for a time in the 18th century. It consisted of a wooden board with nails of different sizes affixed in a semicircle. It was played with an ordinary violin bow on the nails.

MUSICAL INSTRUMENT

naker (Mid. Eng.; Arab. *naqqāra;* Fr. *nacaire;* It. *nacchera*). A small KETTLEDRUM of the Middle East, played in pairs. It was subsequently introduced in India and Europe, where it was briefly in vogue.

PEOPLE IN MUSIC

Nancarrow, Conlon, remarkable American-born Mexican composer, innovator in the technique of recording notes on a PLAYER-PIANO roll; b. Texarkana, Ark., Oct. 27, 1912; d. Mexico City, Aug. 10, 1997. Nancarrow played the trumpet in jazz orchestras, then took courses at the Cincinnati College Conservatory of Music from 1929 to 1932. He subsequently traveled to Boston, where he became a private student of NICOLAS SLONIMSKY, WALTER PISTON, and ROGER SESSIONS.

In 1937 Nancarrow volunteered to fight the Fascist forces in Spain. When the freedom fighters lost, he was refused a U.S. passport and moved to Mexico City, where he remained for 40 years, eventually obtaining Mexican citizenship in 1956. In 1981, with political pressures defused in the U.S., Nancarrow was able to revisit his native land and to participate in the New Music America Festival in San Francisco. In 1982 he was a composer-in-residence at the Cabrillo Music Festival in Aptos, California. He also traveled to Europe, where he participated in festivals in Austria, Germany, and France. In 1982 he was awarded the "genius grant" of $300,000 by the MacArthur Foundation of Chicago, enabling him to continue his work without financial concerns.

The unique quality of most of Nancarrow's compositions is that he composed them by cutting PLAYER-PIANO rolls to mark the notes and rhythms. They can therefore be performed only by a player piano. This method of composition gave him total freedom in creating the most complex contrapuntal, harmonic, and rhythmic combinations that no human pianist or number of human pianists could possibly perform. The method itself is extremely laborious. A bar containing a few dozen notes might require an hour to stamp out on the piano roll.

In 1984 Nancarrow gave a concert of his works in Los Angeles, in a program including his *Prelude and Blues* for ACOUSTIC PIANO and several of his studies. In 1988 his Third String Quartet was given its premiere performance in Cologne, Germany, by the London-based Arditti Quartet, one of the very few ensembles in the world capable of realizing Nancarrow's exceedingly complex scores.

napolitana (It.). An old type of Italian MADRIGAL, revived in modern times in the form of a popular song.

napura (Sans., Beng. *nūpura*). Indian vessel rattle. It is in the form of a hollow copper ring filled with pebbles and worn on the ankles by dancers.

MUSICAL
INSTRUMENT

narrator. A speaking part in Baroque ORATORIOS, corresponding to the Italian *testo,* designed to promote the continuity of the plot.

In the 20th century, the narrator plays an important part in IGOR STRAVINSKY's *OEDIPUS REX* and *HISTOIRE DU SOLDAT,* and, in a lighter vein, SERGEI PROKOFIEV's *PETER AND THE WOLF.*

national anthems. Songs that by accident or intention assume the status of a patriotic HYMN. Most of them are anonymous, and few transcend their functional role and possess genuine musical beauty. Only one, the former Austro-Hungarian anthem (*Gott erhalte unsern Kaiser*), was written by a major composer (FRANZ JOSEPH HAYDN). The same melody has been used as Germany's anthem with different texts during the 20th century.

nationalism. A late 19th- and early 20th-century movement, prominent in Russia, Bohemia, and other parts of Eastern Europe. Nationalist composers consciously strived to embody and reveal aspects of their national identity in their music.

natural. 1. The sign (♮), canceling a sharp (♯)or flat (♭). 2. A white key on the keyboard.
   Natural harmonics, those produced on an open string; *natural horn,* one without valves; *natural interval,* one found between any two tones of a diatonic major scale; *natural key,* C major; *natural pitch,* that of any wind instrument when not overblown (*see* OVERBLOWING); *natural scale,* one having neither sharps nor flats, i.e., C major; *natural tone,* any tone obtained on a wind instrument with cupped mouthpiece, without using keys, valves, or the slide.

natural minor scale. The basic minor scale, without CHROMATIC alterations, and therefore lacking the LEADING TONE. The scale uses the sharps or flats indicated in the key signature shared by its RELATIVE MAJOR SCALE, whose TONIC is a MINOR THIRD above the minor tonic.

naturalism. In musical usage, naturalism appears as an extreme case of VERISMO (or realism). Naturalistic opera emphasizes the negative phenomena of life without the redeeming quality of romance.

Nature Boy. Song by Eden Ahbez, 1946. It skyrocketed in popularity in the post–World War II years, when the ideas of living according to nature, eating organic food, and doing yoga were in the air, particularly in California.

Naughty Marietta. OPERETTA by VICTOR HERBERT, 1910, first performed in N.Y.

The action takes place in 18th-century New Orleans. Marietta is an Italian girl from Naples who travels to Louisiana in search of a marriage of convenience. She has a peculiar dream in which she hears an enchanting melody, which remains unfinished as she wakes up. Anxious to complete it, she promises her hand to a man who can find a satisfactory ending to the tune. A dashing army captain offers a reasonable ending, and she marries him.

Navarraise, La (The woman of Navarra). Opera by JULES MASSENET, 1894, first produced in London. The heroine becomes involved with a royal officer during the internal political strife of 16th-century Spain. When he is killed, she goes insane. The score makes use of techniques associated with Italian VERISMO.

Navarro, "Fats" (Theodore), American jazz trumpeter; b. Key West, Fla., Sept. 24, 1923; d. N.Y., July 7, 1950. Navarro first took up the tenor saxophone, then mastered the trumpet. He subsequently played with several groups, including those of Andy Kirk (1943–44) and Billy Eckstine (1945–46). Navarro later worked in N.Y. as a leading exponent of the BOP style. Sadly, his life and career were cut short by ill health, which was further damaged by his use of heroin.

Nazareth (Nazare), Ernesto (Julio de), Brazilian pianist and composer; b. Rio de Janeiro, March 20, 1863; d. there, Feb. 4, 1934. Nazareth was a pioneer in fostering a national Brazilian type of composition.

Nazareth wrote pieces using European forms but incorporating Brazilian melodies and rhythms. Among the genres he invented were *fado brasileiro, tango brasileiro, valsa brasileira,* and *marcha brasileira.* He also composed original dances in the rhythms of the SAMBA and CHÔRO.

Neapolitan sixth. The FIRST INVERSION of a flatted SUPERTONIC chord (♭II⁶). In C major, this would be the notes F–A♭–D♭. The Neapolitan sixth chord is used as a functional substitute for the SUBDOMINANT in a CADENCE.

The dream tune is *Ah, Sweet Mystery of Life,* one of the greatest songs Herbert ever wrote. It was used in a comic way by Mel Brooks in his film *Young Frankenstein,* when the monster finally finds his mate.

PEOPLE IN MUSIC

PEOPLE IN MUSIC

In his declining years, Nazareth became totally deaf.

While the composers of the BAROQUE Neapolitan school did not invent the chord, they used it so often as to become associated with it.

PEOPLE IN MUSIC

Near, Holly, American popular vocalist, songwriter, and actress; b. Ukiah, Calif., June 6, 1949. Near sang in public from childhood. She also worked in film and television and had a leading role on Broadway in the rock musical *HAIR*.

She took a commercially and artistically independent stance with her music, forming the Redwood label to record a series of albums in the '70s and '80s, all of which became known largely by word of mouth. Near was unique in writing socially conscious lyrics set to Broadway-type popular melodies. In the late '70s, she "came out" as a lesbian and began to give concerts only for women audiences.

While preferring smaller venues for her performances, Near has appeared at Carnegie Hall in N.Y. and the Royal Albert Hall in London. She also made film and television appearances, participated in benefit concerts, and engaged in philanthropic work.

With Meg Christiansen and Cris Williamson, Near is one of the most important and influential musicians in the feminist and lesbian communities. Her excellent voice, flexible acting skills, and fiery personality have won her a large and general audience.

Nearer My God to Thee. Protestant HYMN by LOWELL MASON, c.1850. It became a standard song in Christian churches throughout the world. CHARLES IVES quotes the tune in his Fourth Symphony and other works to evoke the devotional atmosphere of old America.

nā-ben-shtim-meh

Nebenstimme (Ger., adjacent voice). A term invented by ARNOLD SCHOENBERG to denote the second POLYPHONIC voice. *See* HAUPTSTIMME.

MUSICAL INSTRUMENT

neck. On some CHORDOPHONES, the section of the body by which strings are held. Also called the *handle*.

Nelson Mass. A nickname for FRANZ JOSEPH HAYDN's Mass in D minor, 1798. A trumpet flourish in the Benedictus was supposed to suggest Nelson's victory at Abukir (Egypt). Also called *Imperial Mass.*

Nelson, Judith (Anne Manes), American soprano; b. Chicago, Sept. 10, 1939. Nelson studied at St. Olaf College in Northfield, Minnesota, then sang with music groups of the University of Chicago and the University of California, Berkeley. She made her operatic debut as Drusilla in CLAUDIO MONTEVERDI's *L'INCORONAZIONE DI POPPEA* in Brussels in 1979, then appeared widely as a soloist and recitalist. In 1987 she sang Stefano Landi's *Sant' Alessio* (1634) at Innsbruck.

Although particularly noted for her performances of BAROQUE music, she also introduced compositions by American and English composers.

Nelson, Prince Roger. *See* PRINCE.

PEOPLE IN MUSIC

Nelson, Willie (Hugh), American country-music singer, guitarist, and songwriter; b. Abbott, Tex., April 30, 1933. For a short time, Nelson attended Baylor University in Waco, Texas. He then made appearances in local honky-tonk bars and also began to write songs, which included *Hello Walls, Crazy,* and *Night Life,* which were covered by artists like RAY PRICE and PATSY CLINE.

In the early '60s, Nelson went to Nashville. He played bass in Ray Price's band. However, his own recordings were marred, he believed, by the producers' lack of sympathy for his unusual way of singing and playing the guitar. Discouraged by his lack of success in Nashville, he returned to Texas in the late '70s.

Nelson settled in Austin, where he organized a series of annual picnics and befriended other new country singers and songwriters. Because they were rebelling against the standard "Nashville sound," these country performers became known as "outlaws." Nelson also took control of his recording career. His first independent production was of the 1975 theme album *Red-Headed Stranger,* which was based on the story of a Western gunman.

Nelson continued to stretch the boundaries of country music in 1978, when he released an album of pop song stan-

PEOPLE IN MUSIC

dards, *Stardust.* It was an unexpected best-seller. Meanwhile, he had country hits with his songs O*n the Road Again* in 1980 and *Always on My Mind,* two years later.

Nelson continued to write and perform through the '80s and '90s. Although still a popular performer on stage, he has had fewer hits of late. He also became a competent actor, making appearances in the films *Electric Horseman* (1979), *Honeysuckle Rose* (1980), and *Wag the Dog* (1998).

neoclassicism. A revival, in 20th-century compositions, of 18th-century (or earlier) musical ideas.

Neoclassicism has been associated with many of the post–World War I works of both IGOR STRAVINSKY and ARNOLD SCHOENBERG, but it was anticipated by French composers at the turn of the century. When the harmonic richness of IMPRESSIONISM reached its saturation point, it became clear to many composers that further amplification of coloristic devices was no longer stimulating or novel. This artistic reaction coincided with the European economic collapse following World War I, so that it became financially impossible to engage large orchestras or grandiose operatic companies.

The cry went all over Europe, "Back to Bach!" To this was added the slogan of NEW SIMPLICITY. But the past could not be recaptured in its literal form, and the new movement was launched under the name of neoclassicism.

Neoclassicism is characterized by the following traits:

a return to the DIATONIC scale and associated harmonies

elimination of all programmatic and ROMANTIC associations either in the titles or the tonal content of individual works

a revival of the BAROQUE forms of SONATA, SERENADE, SCHERZO, PASSACAGLIA, TOCCATA, CANON, FUGUE, and the florid type of VARIATION

cultivation of compact forms, such as symphonies and sonatas in one movement and operas without a chorus and with a reduced orchestral contingent (usually containing 13 instruments) reconstruction of old Baroque instruments, particularly the HARPSICHORD, and their employment in modernized classical techniques

restrained use of ornamentation; very little thematic development or RECAPITULATION

Depending on your point of view, neoclassicism was either a dangerously conservative trend or a healthy turning away from the excesses of both ROMANTICISM and ultra-MODERNISM.

Other 20th-century revival movements include *neomedievalism,* which reclaims medieval techniques for modern composition; *neomodality,* a return to using the ancient system of MODES; *neoprimitivism,* a revival of "primitive" or folk/traditional musical forms; *neoromanticism,* works embodying 19th-century musical ideas, such as programmatic content and orchestral color.

Nesterenko, Evgeni (Evgenievich), distinguished Russian bass; b. Moscow, Jan. 8, 1938. Nesterenko first studied architectural engineering, graduating from the Leningrad Structural Institute in 1961. He then enrolled in the Leningrad Conservatory, where he studied voice.

Nesterenko began his opera career at the Maly Theater in Leningrad from 1963 to 1967, then was a member of the Kirov Opera and Ballet Theater there until 1971. In 1970 he won first prize at the Tchaikovsky Competition in Moscow and in 1971 joined the Bolshoi Theater. Nesterenko then engaged on a European concert tour and also sang in the U.S. In 1975 he was appointed chairman of the voice department at the Moscow Conservatory. He excelled in such roles as Boris Godunov and Méphistophélès. In 1982 he was awarded the Lenin Prize. He sang GIUSEPPE VERDI's Zaccaria (*NABUCCO*) in Barcelona in 1984, BÉLA BARTÓK's Bluebeard in Budapest in 1988, GIOACCHINO ROSSINI's Don Basilio in Munich in 1990, and Verdi's Attila in Antwerp in 1993 and his King Philip in Helsinki in 1995.

Neue Sachlichkeit (Ger.). A movement launched in Germany after World War I to describe the "new objectivity"

PEOPLE IN MUSIC

in drama, art, and music as a reaction against the hyper-romantic tendencies of 19th-century culture. The economic necessity of cutting down the production cost of musical presentations resulted in the creation of new types of chamber opera, without a chorus, and a partial return to the classical type of orchestral composition. In many respects, the movement coincided with the aims of GEBRAUCHSMUSIK. *See also* NEOCLASSICISM.

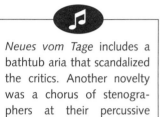

Neues vom Tage includes a bathtub aria that scandalized the critics. Another novelty was a chorus of stenographers at their percussive typewriters.

Neues vom Tage (*Daily news*). Opera by PAUL HINDEMITH, 1929, first produced in Berlin. It tells the story of two unhappily married couples living in a modern urban center.

neumes. MENSURAL NOTATION signs used in the later Middle Ages to represent PITCH and RHYTHM. *See also* NOTATION.

Never on Sunday. Song by Manos Hadjidakis, 1960, for the film of the same name. It featured Melina Mercouri as a pious Greek prostitute who refuses to ply her trade on the Sabbath.

New Age music. "Music that employs time, space, and silence as a sonic vehicle to get the listener into closer contact with his/her spiritual nature," as defined by Steven Halpern in his introduction to *The International Guide to New Age Music,* published in 1988.

New Age music tends toward simple means and effects. It ignores the traditional verse and chorus structures of pop music. Instead, it often uses newly developed or adapted ELECTRONIC textures and incorporates exotic sounds in the form of musical materials from other cultures, including traditional music. New Age works are also overwhelmingly instrumental and often make use of AMBIENT sounds, particularly of nature.

The terms commonly used to describe New Age music say much about its ideology and agenda, which shares much with MUSIC THERAPY: this music is described as relaxing, tranquil, healing, meditative, celestial, mystical, and nourishing. Since its rise to commercial popularity in the mid-1970s, New Age music has spawned some 50 closely related subgenres, including ambient music, space music, and, especially, contemporary instrumental music.

Other, more established genres of music have taken on a New Age tinge, such as New Age JAZZ, New Age POP music, New Age FOLK music, New Age PROGRESSIVE music, etc. Countless radio stations, programs, and conferences devoted to its promulgation have sprung up in the last decade. New Age music is also often a featured component at such popular conventions as the Whole Life Expo and the Festival of Mind-Body-Spirit.

New England Triptych. Orchestral work by WILLIAM SCHUMAN, 1956. It uses themes from hymns and other tunes by the 18th-century composer WILLIAM BILLINGS. It was first performed in Miami.

New Moon, The. Musical by Sigmund Romberg, 1928.

The story deals with an 18th-century Frenchman who is a slave indentured to a rich man in New Orleans, then under French rule. He is sought by the French royalist police on the suspicion of political intrigue, and a ship called *The New Moon* is sent to New Orleans to bring him back to France for trial. But there is a mutiny on board, and *The New Moon* alights on a small Caribbean island. In the meantime, the news arrives of the French Revolution, and the fugitive slave becomes a hero. He takes possession of the island in the name of the French Revolutionary government, summons the girl he loves from New Orleans, and marries her.

The popular score includes *Softly as in a Morning Sunrise, One Kiss,* and the chorus *Stout-Hearted Men.*

new music. The term became current about 1920. It denoted a type of modern music marked by a DISSONANT COUNTERPOINT, ATONALITY, and brevity of expression. Later, new music became synonymous with ULTRA-MODERN MUSIC.

new romanticism. A U.S. movement, begun in the 1970s, wherein composers returned to the gestures, forms, genres, and harmonies of the 19th century.

new simplicity. 1. During the NEOCLASSICAL flowering of the 1920s, the slogan "New Simplicity" was raised among composers eager to divest themselves of an enforced sophistication of the period. In practice, New Simplicity meant a return to elementary melodic and harmonic practices. 2. A 1970s movement, especially among central European, Scandinavian, and Dutch composers, toward a simplified style of composition highly influenced by the American MINIMALISTS.

New Wave. *See* ROCK.

New World Symphony. *See* FROM THE NEW WORLD.

New York Skyline, The. A graphic score by HEITOR VILLA-LOBOS, 1940, based on an outline of the actual skyline. The musical result was broadcast from Rio de Janeiro to N.Y. for the opening of the Brazilian Pavillion at the N.Y. World's Fair.

PEOPLE IN MUSIC

Newman, Alfred, American film composer and conductor, uncle of RANDY NEWMAN; b. New Haven, Conn., March 17, 1900; d. Los Angeles, Feb. 17, 1970. Newman studied piano with the Polish-born pianist Sigismund Stojowski and composition with the Austrian-born composer RUBIN GOLDMARK. He also had private lessons with ARNOLD SCHOENBERG in Los Angeles.

Newman began his career in vaudeville shows and was billed as "the Marvelous Boy Pianist." Later, when he led theater orchestras on Broadway, he was hailed as "the Boy Conductor" and "the Youngest Conductor in the U.S." In 1930 he went to Hollywood and devoted himself entirely to writing film music. Of his 230-odd film scores, 45 were nominated for Academy Awards, and nine were winners. Among his most successful scores were *The Prisoner of Zenda* (1937), *The Hunchback of Notre Dame* (1939), *Wuthering Heights* (1939), *Captain from Castille* (1947), *The Robe* (1953), and *The Egyptian* (1954; partly written by the original assignee, Bernard Herrmann).

Stylistically, Newman borrowed from the great ROMANTIC composers such as PIOTR ILYICH TCHAIKOVSKY, SERGEI

RACHMANINOFF, RICHARD WAGNER, and FRANZ LISZT. In doing so, he created a category of composition that was to become known, with some disdain, as "movie music."

Newman, Randy, American societal singer, pianist, and
songwriter, nephew of ALFRED NEWMAN; b. Los Angeles,
Nov. 28, 1943. Newman's father, Lionel, and his uncle, Alfred, were both prominent film composers. He studied music with his father and privately with others through high
school.

PEOPLE IN MUSIC

Newman absorbed the lush romanticism of his family's
melodies but added to them lyrics that were often ironic.
The "narrators" of his songs also were often bigoted or in
some other way out of the mainstream. Unlike most singer/
songwriters, Newman's songs do not necessarily reflect his
personal opinions.

Newman is a fine pianist, who can mimic many popular
styles. His vocal capabilities are more limited, but he is able
to capture the irony of his lyrics in his often gravelly voice.

At the beginning of his career, many of Newman's early
songs were covered by other artists, like his wistful love ballad
I Think It's Gonna Rain Today, a minor hit for singer JUDY
COLLINS in the late '60s. He then began his own recording
career. Newman himself had a minor hit with the title song
from his 1972 album *Sail Away,* a song that ironically entices
Africans to come to America in order to be slaves.

In 1977 Newman had the greatest hit of his career with
Short People, a song told by a person who supposedly hates
all people under a certain height. The song was widely criticized by those who failed to recognize that Newman was in
fact satirizing bigotry in it by selecting such an obviously absurd reason for the narrator's hatred. (Newman himself is
short.) The jaunty melody also is absurdly unsuited to the
anger in the lyrics. Similarly, *I Love L.A.* (1983), a parody of
those who live the sun-and-surf life-style, was successfully
adopted as a song in praise of Los Angeles by most listeners!

While continuing to issue albums on his own, Newman
has become a prominent film scorer, like his famous uncle
and his father. Among his many successful scores is *Ragtime*
(1981). He has also turned his hand to writing for the stage.
In 1995 he released an album version of his stage work, an

adaptation of Goethe's *Faust*. A year later, it was staged in Los Angeles and N.Y.

In 1998 a boxed set of Newman's own recordings and film work was issued to celebrate his 30-year career.

Nichols, "Red" (Ernest Loring), American jazz cornetist and bandleader; b. Ogden, Utah, May 8, 1905; d. Las Vegas, June 28, 1965. Nichols's father taught him cornet, and he played in his father's brass band from the age of 12.

Nichols then formed his own band, advertised as *Red Nichols and His Five Pennies*. He enticed some of the best jazz players into working with him, including such future celebrities as JIMMY DORSEY, BENNY GOODMAN, and GLENN MILLER. Unlike some other early jazz men, Nichols led a conservative life and was a good businessman, enabling him to continue performing through the '50s, and to retire with a good income.

Nicolai, (Carl) **Otto** (Ehrenfried), famous German composer and conductor; b. Königsberg, June 9, 1810; d. Berlin, May 11, 1849. Nicolai studied piano at home and at the age of seventeen went to Berlin, where he took lessons in theory with the well-known teacher CARL FRIEDRICH ZELTER. He also took courses at the Royal Institute for Church Music.

In 1833 Nicolai made his concert debut in Berlin as a pianist, singer, and composer. He then was engaged as organist to the embassy chapel in Rome by the Prussian ambassador. While in Italy, he also studied COUNTERPOINT with the music critic Giuseppe Baini.

In 1837 Nicolai proceeded to Vienna, where he became a singing teacher and kapellmeister at the Kärntnertortheater. In 1838 he returned to Italy, and in 1839 he presented in Trieste his first opera, *Rosmonda d'Inghilterra,* given under its new title as *Enrico II.* His second opera, *Il Templario,* was staged in Turin a year later.

In 1841 he moved to Vienna, where he was appointed court kapellmeister. Nicolai was instrumental in establishing symphony concerts utilizing the musicians of the orchestra of the Imperial Court Opera Theater. In 1842, he conducted this ensemble, featuring LUDWIG VAN BEETHOVEN's Seventh Symphony. This became the inaugural concert of

PEOPLE IN MUSIC

Despite their name, there were usually eight, and more often ten, "pennies" accompanying Nichols.

PEOPLE IN MUSIC

the celebrated Vienna Philharmonic. In 1848 Nicolai was appointed kapellmeister of the Royal Opera in Berlin.

In 1849 Nicolai's famous opera *DIE LUSTIGEN WEIBER VON WINDSOR* (The merry wives of Windsor), after Shakespeare, was given at the Berlin Royal Opera. This work was to become his only enduring creation, because Nicolai died only two months after its production.

Nicolai also composed sacred choral music, secular vocal music for vocal ensemble and piano, two symphonies (1831; 1835), overtures, chamber music, and solo songs.

In 1887 Hans Richter, then conductor of the Vienna Philharmonic, inaugurated an annual "Nicolai-Konzert" in his memory, and it became a standard event. It was subsequently conducted by GUSTAV MAHLER (1899–1901), FELIX WEINGARTNER (1909–27), WILHELM FURTWÄNGLER (1928–31, 1933–44, and 1948–54), KARL BÖHM (1955–57 and 1964–80); and CLAUDIO ABBADO (1980 and 1983).

Nielsen, Carl (August), greatly significant Danish composer; b. Sortelung, near Nørre-Lyndelse, June 9, 1865; d. Copenhagen, Oct. 3, 1931. Nielsen received violin lessons in childhood from his father and from the local schoolteacher. He played second violin in the village band and later in its amateur orchestra. After studying cornet with his father, he played in the Odense military orchestra from 1879 to 1883, serving as its signal horn and alto trombone player. He also taught himself to play piano.

While in Odense, Nielsen began to compose, producing several chamber pieces. He then received financial assistance to continue his training at the Royal Conservatory in Copenhagen, where he studied violin, theory, and music history between 1884 and 1886.

Nielsen was a violinist in Copenhagen's Royal Chapel Orchestra from 1889 to 1905. In the interim, he achieved his first success as a composer with his *Little Suite* for strings in 1888. In 1901 he was granted an annual pension by the Danish government. He was conductor of the Royal Theater from 1908 to 1914 and the Musikforeningen from 1915 to 1927 in Copenhagen, and also appeared as a guest conductor in Germany, the Netherlands, Sweden, and Finland. From 1916 to 1919 he taught theory and composition at

PEOPLE IN MUSIC

There are instances of bold experimentation in some of Nielsen's works: for example, the insertion of a snare drum solo in his Fifth Symphony, playing independently of the rest of the orchestra.

the Royal Conservatory and was appointed its director a few months before his death.

Nielsen's early music, ROMANTIC in essence, was influenced by EDVARD GRIEG, JOHANNES BRAHMS, and FRANZ LISZT. However, he later experienced the powerful impact of modern music, particularly in HARMONY, which in his works grew more and more CHROMATIC and DISSONANT. Yet he reserved simple DIATONIC progressions, often in a folk-song manner, for his major climaxes. In his orchestration he applied rich sonorities and colorful instrumental COUNTERPOINT.

Nielsen is sometimes described as the JEAN SIBELIUS of Denmark, despite obvious differences in their styles and sources of inspiration. While the music of Sibelius is deeply rooted in national folklore, both in subject matter and melody, Nielsen seldom drew on Danish popular music. And Sibelius remained true to the traditional style of composition, while Nielsen sought new ways of expression.

It was only after his death that Nielsen's major works entered the world repertoire. Festivals of his music were organized on his centennial in 1965. His symphonies in particular were played and recorded in England and America, bringing him belated recognition as one of the most important composers of his time. In 1988 Queen Margrethe II dedicated the Carl Nielsen Museum in Odense.

Nielsen's best-known works are the six symphonies: No. 1, op.7 (1890–92; 1894), No. 2, op.16, *Die fire temperamenter* (The four temperaments; 1902), No. 3, op.27, *Sinfonia espansiva,* with two solo singers (1912), No. 4, op.29, *Det uudslukkelige* (The inextinguishable, 1916), No. 5, op.50 (1922), and No. 6, *Sinfonia semplice* (an oddly sarcastic work, 1925). He composed two great operas in Danish: the tragedy *Saul og David* (1902) and the comedy *MASKARADE* (1906), as well as a melodrama, *Snefrid* (1894). He also composed incidental music for many plays. He wrote many other orchestral, chamber, solo, and vocal works. His writings include *Levende musik* (Living music, Copenhagen, 1925) and *Minfynske barndom* (My childhood in Funen, Copenhagen, 1927).

Nielsen's son-in-law was the Hungarian Emil Telmanyi, a violinist, conductor, and teacher (b. Arad, June 22, 1892;

d. June 12, 1988). Telmanyi studied with Hubay at the Royal Academy of Music in Budapest. In 1911 he began an active career as a violinist, and in 1918 married Ann Marie, Nielsen's daughter. In 1954 Telmanyi supervised the creation of a curved bow to play JOHANN SEBASTIAN BACH's violin works; it became known as the *Vega* bow.

Night and Day. Song by COLE PORTER, 1932. Its effect lies in the constant shifts of HARMONY, while the tune itself remains mesmerisingly monotonous.

Night Flight (*"Volo di notte"*). Opera by LUIGI DALLAPIC-COLA, 1940. It is based on the novel *Vol de nuit* (1931) by Antoine de St.-Exupéry, first produced in Florence. The story deals with a dramatic night flight over the Andes in a single-engine monoplane. The score includes spoken dialogue and a wordless passage of a disembodied voice warning the pilot of dangers.

Night on Bald Mountain, A. Symphonic poem by MODEST MUSSORGSKY, 1867. The original Russian name translates as "St. John's Night on the Bare Mountain."

Russian composers have been partial to the subject of devilry. Mussorgsky's contribution pictures broom-riding witches who celebrate a Black Mass, but the church bells at midnight scare them away.

Mussorgsky left the score half finished. NIKOLAI RIMSKY-KORSAKOV completed it in his usual well-meaning fashion and conducted its first performance, five years after Mussorgsky's death, in St. Petersburg, 1886.

Night Piece, A. Work for flute and strings by ARTHUR FOOTE, 1919, one of his finest instrumental pieces.

Nightingale, The (*Le Rossignol*). Opera by IGOR STRAVINSKY, 1914, first produced in Paris. The Chinese Emperor is dying, and his life is sustained by the singing of a nightingale. But when the Japanese Ambassador thoughtlessly presents the Emperor with a mechanical nightingale, the real bird flies away, and the Emperor's health declines dangerously. As a discordant funeral march is played, the real nightingale is brought in, and the Emperor regains his strength. The moral seems to be that human ills ought to be left to natural cures.

The first two acts were composed before the ground-breaking ballets *Petrouchka* and *The Rite of Spring*; the last act was composed afterward. For this reason, the work straddles the change in Stravinsky's music from more traditional to modern style. The score mixes Russian melodies, tone color reminiscent of CLAUDE DEBUSSY, and the occasional harsh DISSONANCE.

Nights in the Gardens of Spain (*Noches en los jardines de España*). Symphonic impression for piano and orchestra by MANUEL DE FALLA, 1916, first performed in Madrid. The three-movement work describes music and dancers in Andalusia.

PEOPLE IN MUSIC

Nilsson, (Märta) **Birgit,** greatly renowned Swedish soprano; b. Västra Karups, May 17, 1918. Nilsson studied with Joseph Hislop at the Royal Academy of Music in Stockholm, making her debut as Agathe in CARL MARIA VON WEBER's *Der Freischütz* at the Royal Theater there in 1946.

Nilsson gained her first success as GIUSEPPE VERDI's Lady Macbeth in 1947, then sang major roles in operas by RICHARD WAGNER, GIACOMO PUCCINI, and RICHARD STRAUSS with increasing success. She first appeared as Brünnhilde in RICHARD WAGNER's *Götterdammerung* in Stockholm during the 1954–55 season and sang this role in the *Ring* cycle for the first time in Munich during the same season. She likewise appeared at the Vienna State Opera and at the Bayreuth Festival, both in 1954, and returned there regularly from 1959 to 1970.

In 1956 Nilsson made her U.S. debut at the Hollywood Bowl. That same year, she sang Brünnhilde in Wagner's *Die Walküre* at the San Francisco Opera, after which she made her first appearance at London's Covent Garden in 1957. She made her long-awaited Metropolitan Opera debut as Isolde in 1959, remaining with the company until 1974.

After an absence of five years, she returned to the Metropolitan Opera for a gala concert in 1979. She then rejoined the company, appearing as Elektra in 1980. She retired from the operatic stage in 1982.

Nilsson was universally acclaimed as one of the greatest Wagnerian dramatic sopranos.

ninth. *See* INTERVAL.

ninth chord. Although ninth chords are defined as chords consisting of a series of four superimposed THIRDS on any degree of the SCALE, their use is confined in practice to DOMINANT ninth chords. These chords were cultivated systematically by RICHARD WAGNER, FRANZ LISZT, and ANTON BRUCKNER, always within a given tonality.

The ninth chord requires five-part harmony for its totality, because in four-part harmony, the fifth above the root is left out. The necessity of the resolution into the DOMINANT SEVENTH CHORD is felt very strongly in CADENCES, as, for instance, toward the end of the overture of Wagner's *Die Meistersinger.* The dramatic attraction of the ninth chord led ALEXANDER SCRIABIN to the formation of his so-called MYSTIC CHORD, a harmonic extension of it.

CLAUDE DEBUSSY emancipated the dominant ninth chord by moving it in parallel formation, either chromatically or by minor thirds, without resolution. Numerous composers of the 20th century used this device to create a feeling of harmonic uncertainty. Fascination with the ninth chord ceased abruptly with the decline of musical IMPRESSIONISM in the second quarter of the 20th century. Parallel ninth chords, once the darlings of modernism, were relegated to a type of "mood music."

Nine. Musical, 1982, by Maury Yeston. Until *Nine* opened, Yeston was known as a classical music theorist.

Based on Fellini's movie *8 ½,* it includes echoes of BAROQUE and ROMANTIC STYLES, continuing the operatic trend in musical theater established by FRANK LOESSER, STEPHEN SONDHEIM, and ANDREW LLOYD WEBBER.

Ninth Symphonies. Many composers have reached number nine in their symphonic production, among them GUSTAV MAHLER and ANTON BRUCKNER. However, when musicians speak simply of "The 9th," it is generally understood to mean LUDWIG VAN BEETHOVEN's great *Choral Symphony.*

Ninth Symphony. Symphony by GUSTAV MAHLER, 1908 – 09. The work is in four movements, and it is one of his longest symphonies. Mahler constantly breaks the rules of traditional harmony in this work. For example, although the work begins in D major, it ends in D-flat major!

Psychologically motivated analysts perceive Mahler's premonition of his own death in the music.

PEOPLE IN MUSIC

Nirvana. (Guitar/vocal: KURT COBAIN, b. Hoquiam, Wash., Feb. 20, 1967; d. Seattle, Wash., April 5, 1994; Bass: Krist Novoselic, b. Los Angeles, May 16, 1965; Drums: David Grohl, b. Warren, Ohio, Jan. 14, 1969.) The most successful and famous GRUNGE-ROCK group.

Cobain and Novoselic were childhood friends in Aberdeen, Washington. They formed Nirvana together in 1987. Playing locally with various supporting members, they were signed to the small Sub Pop label, recording their first album, which featured the single *Love Buzz* backed with *Negative Creep,* both hits among the growing grunge community. Grohl joined the lineup in time for their major label debut, *Nevermind,* released on DGC Records in 1990. The song *Smells Like Teen Spirit* made the album an immediate chart-busting hit and established the group as the voice of their (plaid-clad) generation.

The band produced a second album, *In Utero,* banned by Wal-Mart and other chain stores but still happily consumed by teens everywhere. An appearance on *MTV Unplugged* helped listeners actually understand the group's lyrics—previously nearly obliterated by their ear-crunching sound—and some were surprised by Cobain's sensitivity and others by his disturbing sentiments.

In 1992 Cobain wed COURTNEY LOVE, the big-lunged vocalist and songwriter with the group Hole, and the couple's escapades were soon making tabloid headlines. Cobain himself had trouble adjusting to adulation and fame, attempting suicide in March 1994 and, one month later, shooting himself in the head at his home. An outpouring of grief-stricken grungers held a vigil outside his residence.

Following Cobain's death, Grohl formed the Foo Fighters. Love continued to record and perform, and also co-starred in the film *The People vs. Larry Flynt,* in 1996.

Nixon in China. Opera by JOHN ADAMS, 1987. It depicts, in fancifully realistic scenes, President Nixon's historical trip to China in 1972, with Nixon's role assigned to a baritone, Mao Zedung as a Wagnerian HELDENTENOR, and his wife as a mindless ingenue. The world premiere was given, of all places, in Houston, Texas, with quite a few people making the trip from N.Y. and other large cities to see it. The production was directed by Peter Sellers, and the LIBRETTO written by Alice Goodman.

Two orchestral excerpts from *Nixon in China, Short Ride in a Fast Machine* and *The Chairman Dances,* are frequently programmed separately.

Nixon, Marni (born Margaret Nixon McEathron), American soprano; b. Altadena, Calif., Feb. 22, 1930. Nixon studied with Carl Ebert at the University of Southern California in Los Angeles, Jan Popper at Stanford University, and BORIS GOLDOVSKY and SARAH CALDWELL at the Berkshire Music Center at Tanglewood, Massachusetts.

PEOPLE IN MUSIC

Nixon pursued a multifaceted career. She sang on the soundtrack of the films *The King and I, West Side Story,* and *My Fair Lady,* and also starred in her own children's program on television. She also appeared in musical comedy and opera and was a soloist with major orchestras in the U.S. and abroad. She taught at the California Institute of the Arts in Valencia from 1969 to 1971 and, beginning in 1980, at the Music Academy of the West in Santa Barbara.

No, No, Nanette. Musical by VINCENT YOUMANS, 1924. The plot centers on a publisher of Bibles who has affairs with a series of young women, to the chagrin of his proper wife. In the end he straightens out his difficulties. While the best-known song is the beloved *Tea for Two,* others include the title song and *I Want to Be Happy.*

The play became one of the most popular of the 1920s. It was subsequently revived in the 1970s and was again a smash hit.

No Strings. Musical by RICHARD RODGERS, 1962. An American writer in Paris falls in love with a black model. He wants to take her back to the U.S., but she recoils at the thought of the reaction to their interracial romance. Still, he feels that only in America can he write his projected novel, and they part wistfully. Highlights include the title song and *The Sweetest Sounds.*

Nobody Knows the Trouble I've Seen. African-American spiritual. It was first collected in Charleston, South Carolina, before the American Civil War and published in the collection *Slave Songs of the United States,* in 1867. The melody possesses a type of syncopation similar to that of RAGTIME and JAZZ.

Nobody Knows You When You're Down and Out. A 1923 song by James Cox. It became a blues hit for BESSIE SMITH, among others, and a favorite in the Depression era. It was covered quite effectively by ERIC CLAPTON on his *UNPLUGGED* CD.

Noces, Les (The wedding). Choreographic scenes by IGOR STRAVINSKY, 1923, first produced by Sergei Diaghilev's Ballets Russes in Paris. It is scored for chorus, soloists, 4 pianos, and 17 percussion instruments, and may generically be called a staged CANTATA. The music is rooted in Russian folk song, but it is harmonized in a modern, DISSONANT style.

The libretto consists of four scenes, tracing the rituals of a peasant betrothal and wedding. The Russian title is *Svadebka* (Little wedding).

Nocturnal. Work by EDGARD VARÈSE, based on Anaïs Nin's novel *The House of Incest.* The work was never completed by Varèse, but edited in 1973 by Varèse's student CHOU WEN-CHUNG. A portion of the work was premiered in N.Y., 1961. *Nocturnal* is scored for soprano, bass chorus, small orchestra, piano, and percussion.

Varèse planned another work, *Nocturnal II,* even as *Nocturnal* lay unfinished, but this second work never got beyond sketches.

nŏhk-tŭrn′

ROBERT SCHUMANN also wrote nocturnes, but, in conformity with the prevalent nationalistic sentiment of the time, he assigned to them a German name, *Nachtstück.*

nocturne (Fr., night piece; Ger. *Nachtstück;* It. *notturno*). A piece of dreamily ROMANTIC or sentimental character, set in pleasing MELODY and HARMONY, and without fixed form.

The nocturne emerged as a distinct genre of Romantic piano pieces early in the 19th century, primarily through the poetic creations of FRÉDÉRIC CHOPIN. The pioneer of piano nocturnes was the Irish composer JOHN FIELD, but his pieces fall far below those of Chopin in quality. Even though nocturnes are creatures of the night, Chopin often includes dramatic turbulence in the middle sections.

Nocturnes. Orchestral SUITE by CLAUDE DEBUSSY, 1901, in three movements: *Nuages* (Clouds), *Fêtes* (Festivals), and *Sirènes* (Sirens). It was first performed in its entirety in Paris.

The first movement is a musical monochrome, the clouds simply white and grey. The second movement is full of rhythmic sounds and light. The third movement, which includes a female chorus, depicts the laughing sirens singing their mysterious songs.

Nocturns. A portion of the MATIN service of the Roman Catholic daily hours, held during the night.

node (nodal point). A point in a vibrating body (such as a string, soundboard, trumpet, bell) that remains at rest during the vibration of the other parts of the body.

noël (Fr.; from Lat. *natalis,* birthday). A Christmas carol or HYMN with sacred or secular texts, including drinking songs.

noise. Scientifically speaking, sound with indefinite pitch, but used as a compositional element in many 20th-century compositions. A collection of tonally unrelated simultaneous sounds of different frequencies and intensities, meaningless to musical or even unmusical ears.

WHITE NOISE is an integral assembly of sounds of numerous frequencies, but more or less equal intensities. In radio transmission, noise is called *static,* and a similar electromagnetic disturbance in television is called *snow.* Metaphorically, conservative music critics often describe unfamiliar music as noise.

Non nobis Domine. A famous vocal CANON of the latter 16th century, usually attributed to WILLIAM BYRD. It is set in three parts. The treble enters first, the middle voice then comes in a perfect fourth below, and the bass enters a fifth below that. One of the voices may even be inverted without disastrous consequences to the harmony.

MUSICAL
INSTRUMENT

Because the canon is not written out, it must be classified as a RIDDLE CANON. Indeed, it can be sung in several different formations, all of them quite harmonious. In England, this canon was often sung as a grace before meals.

non vibrato (It.). A marking in a score for stringed instruments and singers warning them against their natural tendency to play VIBRATO. Modern editions of early music scores, where vibrato was unknown, might be marked in this way. Many modern scores are also marked non vibrato, because vibrato is considered an undesirable technique remaining from the ROMANTIC era.

nōhn vē-brăh′tōh

None. A daily service, part of the Roman Catholic Divine Office, celebrated at 3 P.M., the time when Jesus died on the cross (counted as the ninth hour from sunrise, hence the name). This service is one of the four so-called Little Hours.

nonet. A composition for nine voices or instruments. Usually, the instrumentation involves more than one instrumental family, but AARON COPLAND wrote a nonet for three violins, three violas, and three cellos, in 1961.

Nono, Luigi, remarkable Italian composer who earned a unique place in the history of modern music through his devotion to addressing social problems; b. Venice, Jan. 29, 1924; d. there, May 8, 1990. Nono became a student at the Venice Conservatory in 1941, where he received instruction in composition. He also studied law at the University of Padua, graduating in 1946, and later had advanced harmony and counterpoint lessons.

A man of extraordinary courage, Nono joined the Italian Communist Party while the country was still under the dictatorship of Mussolini. He was an active participant in the Italian Resistance movement against the Nazis. In 1975 he was elected to the Central Committee of the Communist Party, and remained a member until his death.

Although Nono's works are extremely difficult to perform and practically all of them are devoted to Communist propaganda, he found support among a number of liberal composers and performers. At the end of his life, he ac-

PEOPLE IN MUSIC

quired an enormous reputation as a highly original composer in a novel technical idiom as well as a fearless political agitator.

As a composer he followed the ideas of ARNOLD SCHOENBERG without adhering to the literal scheme of 12-TONE composition. Unlike other Communist composers who followed the strict rules of Soviet realism, writing music that would appeal to the average listener, Nono did not water down his style to suit popular tastes. He made use of a variety of techniques: SERIALISM, ALEATORY, CONCRETE music, and ELECTRONICS.

Nono's most militant composition, both politically and musically, is his opera *INTOLLERANZA 1960,* utilizing texts by progressive authors Bertolt Brecht, Paul Eluard, Jean-Paul Sartre, and Victor Mayakovsky. The work is a powerful protest against imperialist policies and social inequities. At its production in Venice in 1961, a group of neo-Fascists showered the audience with leaflets denouncing Nono for his alleged contamination of Italian music.

Nono married Schoenberg's daughter, Nuria, in 1955, with whom he had two daughters. They separated on friendly terms after several years. After their divorce, Nuria settled in her father's last residence in Los Angeles, and Nono traveled widely in Europe. After his death of a liver ailment at the age of 66, Nuria established the Nono Archives in Venice.

Nordic Symphony. First Symphony by HOWARD HANSON, 1923, containing elements of Scandinavian folk rhythms. First performed in Rome.

Norfolk Rhapsody No. 1. Symphonic picture by RALPH VAUGHAN WILLIAMS, 1906, first performed in London. The melodic materials are taken from authentic English songs. The composer wrote two more rhapsodies but decided not to include them in his catalogue.

Norma. Opera by VINCENZO BELLINI, 1831, first produced in Milan. Norma is the high priestess of the Druid temple in ancient Gaul (France) during its occupation by the Romans. As behooves many operas, natural enemies fall in love. Here, not only Norma herself becomes involved with Pollione, a Roman proconsul, and bears him a couple of children, but a virgin of the temple also loves him, in violation of her vow of chastity. The proconsul is caught desecrating the temple of the Druids, but Norma cannot bring herself to put him to death as she ought to do in her capacity as high priestess. She confesses her own unchastity and ascends the sacrificial funeral pyre with Pollione for ritual burning.

Norma is Bellini's most melodious and most harmonious opera, a perennial favorite of the public. The aria *Casta diva,* in which Norma appeals to the goddess of the moon, is a paragon of melodic beauty.

The aria *Casta diva* was used to great effect in the 1996 film *Philadelphia,* starring Tom Hanks as an ostracized homosexual lawyer stricken with AIDS.

PEOPLE IN MUSIC

Norman, Jessye, exceptionally gifted African-American soprano; b. Augusta, Ga., Sept. 15, 1945. Norman studied on scholarship at Howard University in Washington, D.C., in 1961, where she had vocal lessons from Carolyn Grant. She

Jessye Norman, c. 1973. (Hulton-Deutsch Collection/ Corbis) ▶

then continued her training at the Peabody Conservatory of Music in Baltimore and at the University of Michigan, where her principal teacher was Pierre Bernac.

In 1968 Norman won the Munich Competition, making her operatic debut a year later as Elisabeth in *Tannhäuser* at the Berlin Deutsche Opera. She appeared in the title role of GIACOMO MEYERBEER's *L'AFRICAINE* at Florence's Maggio Musicale in 1971 and the following year sang Aida at Milan's La Scala and Cassandra in HECTOR BERLIOZ's *LES TROYENS* at London's Covent Garden. In 1973 she made major recital debuts in London and N.Y.

After an extensive concert tour of North America in 1976–77, Norman made her U.S. stage debut as Jocasta in IGOR STRAVINSKY's *OEDIPUS REX* and as HENRY PURCELL's Dido on a double bill with the Opera Company of Philadelphia in 1982. A year later, she made her Metropolitan Opera debut as Cassandra.

In 1986 Norman appeared as soloist in RICHARD STRAUSS's *Vier letzte Lieder* with the Berlin Philharmonic during its tour of the U.S. In 1989 she was the featured soloist with ZUBIN MEHTA and the N.Y. Philharmonic in its opening concert of its 148th season, which was telecast live to the nation by PBS. In 1992 she sang Jocasta in the first operatic production at the new Saito Kinen Festival in Matsumoto, Japan. In 1996 she sang Emilia Marty in LEOŠ JANÁČEK's *THE MAKROPULOS AFFAIR* at the Metropolitan Opera.

Norman's extraordinary repertory ranges from Purcell to RICHARD RODGERS. She also commended herself in MODEST MUSSORGSKY's songs, which she performed in Moscow in Russian. In her recitals she gave performances of the classical German repertory as well as contemporary masterpieces, such as ARNOLD SCHOENBERG's *GURRELIEDER* and *Erwartung*, and the French moderns, which she invariably performed in the original tongue. This combination of scholarship and artistry contributed to her consistently successful career as one of the most versatile concert and operatic singers of her time.

Norrington, (Sir) **Roger** (Arthur Carver), scholarly English conductor; b. Oxford, March 16, 1934. Norrington was educated at Clare College, Cambridge, and the Royal College of Music in London. He began his career performing as a tenor.

In 1962 Norrington founded the Schütz Choir in London, with which he first gained notice as a conductor. From 1966 to 1984 he was principal conductor of the Kent Opera,

PEOPLE IN MUSIC

where he produced scores by CLAUDIO MONTEVERDI, utilizing his own performing editions. He served as music director of the London Baroque Players from 1975 and the London Classical Players from 1978. He also was principal conductor of the Bournemouth Sinfonietta during 1985–89.

In 1989 Norrington made an auspicious N.Y. debut at Carnegie Hall conducting LUDWIG VAN BEETHOVEN's Eighth and Ninth Symphonies. In 1990 he became music director of the Orchestra of St. Luke's in N.Y., which post he held until 1994. In 1980 he was made an Officer of the Order of the British Empire, in 1990, a Commander of the Order of the British Empire, and in 1997 he was knighted.

In 1990 Norrington conducted WOLFGANG AMADEUS MOZART's *DIE ZAUBERFLÖTE* at the Promenade concerts in London. In 1997 he conducted Mozart's *MITRIDATE* in Salzburg, where he also became chief conductor of its Camerata Academica.

Norrington became a controversial figure in the classical world by insisting that the classical tempo is basic for all interpretation. He also insisted that Beethoven's metronome markings, not usually accepted by performers, are in fact accurate reflections of Beethoven's inner thoughts. He obtained numerous defenders of his ideas (called "inspired literalism") for the interpretation of classical music, which aroused sharp interest as well as caustic rejection. However that might be, his performances, especially in the U.S., received a great deal of attention, and he was particularly praised for his accuracy and precision.

In 1985 Norrington began an annual series of musical "experiences": weekends devoted to in-depth exploration of some major classical work, comprising lectures, open rehearsals, research exhibits, and performances of other works by the same composer (which have included FRANZ JOSEPH HAYDN and HECTOR BERLIOZ as well as the inevitable Beethoven) and his contemporaries.

North, Alex, gloriously gifted American composer and conductor with a predilection for uniquely colored film music; b. Chester, Pa., Dec. 4, 1910; d. Pacific Palisades, Calif., Sept. 8, 1991. North's father, a blacksmith, emigrated from Russia. North studied piano and theory at the Curtis Insti-

PEOPLE IN MUSIC

tute of Music in Philadelphia and later received a scholarship to study at the Juilliard School of Music in N.Y., where he took courses in composition from 1929 to 1932.

A decisive change in North's life came with his decision to go to Russia as a technology specialist at a time when Russia was eager to engage American technicians. He became fascinated with new Russian music and received a scholarship to attend the Moscow Conservatory, where he studied composition from 1933 to 1935. He also was music director of the propaganda group of German Socialists called "Kolonne links" (Column to the left).

North mastered the Russian language and acquired a fine reputation in Russia as a true friend of Soviet music. Returning to the U.S., he took additional courses in composition with AARON COPLAND (1936–38) and ERNST TOCH (1938–39). In 1939 he conducted 26 concerts in Mexico as music director of the Anna Sokolow Dance Troupe, during which stay (in Mexico City), he had some instruction from Silvestre Revueltas.

In 1942 North entered the U.S. Army, where, promoted to captain, he became responsible for entertainment programs in mental hospitals. He worked closely with the psychiatrist Karl Menninger in developing a theatrical genre called psychodrama, which later became an accepted mode of therapy. During his Army years, North also worked with the Office of War Information, composing scores for over 25 documentary films.

Through all of his experiences, North developed a distinct flair for theater music, while continuing to produce estimable works in absolute forms. His concerto, *Revue* for clarinet and orchestra, was performed by BENNY GOODMAN in N.Y. under the baton of LEONARD BERNSTEIN in 1946. North's concentrated efforts, however, became directed mainly toward the art of film music, a field in which he triumphed. Among North's outstanding film scores are *A Streetcar Named Desire* (1951), *Death of a Salesman* (1951), *The Bad Seed* (1956), *The Rainmaker* (1956), *Spartacus* (1960), *The Misfits* (1961), *Cleopatra* (1963), *The Agony and the Ecstasy* (1965), *Who's Afraid of Virginia Woolf?* (1966), *Under the Volcano* (1984), *Prizzi's Honor* (1985), *The Dead* (1987), and *Good Morning, Vietnam* (1988).

But success is rarely without disheartening frustration. North was commissioned to write the score for *2001: A Space Odyssey,* on which he worked enthusiastically. Much to his dismay, however, its director, Stanley Kubrick, replaced it. North refused to be downhearted by this rejection and used the discarded material for his Third Symphony.

North was nominated 15 times for an Academy Award, but it was not until 1986 that the Academy of Motion Picture Arts and Sciences finally awarded him an Oscar for lifetime achievement. His song *Unchained Melody* (1955) became a popular hit. He also composed ballets, children's theater pieces, orchestral music, choral works, and chamber pieces.

PEOPLE IN MUSIC

Norvo, Red (born Kenneth Norville), American jazz xylophonist, vibraphonist, and bandleader; b. Beardstown, Ill., March 31, 1908. He played piano and XYLOPHONE while attending classes in mining engineering at the University of Missouri in 1926–27. He then was hired by famous dance band leader PAUL WHITEMAN. Like many other early jazz bands, the xylophone was used primarily as a novelty instrument in Whiteman's group.

Norvo met the singer Mildred Bailey in Whiteman's group, and the pair relocated to N.Y. in 1933. They were known as "Mr. and Mrs. Swing" during their brief marriage. In 1935 he organized his own band in N.Y., where he also worked with BENNY GOODMAN in 1944–45 and WOODY HERMAN in 1945–46.

After World War II, Norvo began playing with the young BEBOP musicians. He relocated to California, where he worked in a trio with bassist CHARLES MINGUS and guitarist Tal Farlow. He became one of the leading performers of bebop on the xylophone and was known for his energetic and crisp melody lines.

Norvo continued to work through the mid-'70s, when he briefly retired. He then returned to performing in the '80s, working on his own and with saxophonist BENNY CARTER and Farlow.

Nose, The. Opera by DMITRI SHOSTAKOVICH, 1930. It is based on the fantastic story by Gogol, and was first produced in Leningrad.

The story deals with the nose of a government functionary that mysteriously disappears from his face during shaving and goes off as an independent individual. All sorts of absurdities occur, interspersed with satirical darts at Czarist bureaucracy. In the end, the nose resumes its rightful place, much to the owner's relief.

The score is a brilliant exercise in grotesquerie. It includes an OCTET of janitors in DISSONANT counterpoint, gigantic orchestral sneezes, and other effects. The production was greeted with great exhilaration by Soviet musicians but received a chilly reception by the Kremlin bureaucracy, and Shostakovich was charged with imitating decadent Western models. Many years elapsed before *The Nose* was revived on the Soviet stage.

nose flutes. Family of wind instruments blown with nasal rather than oral breath, although some can be blown in both ways. The materials used and form (e.g., TRANSVERSE, END-BLOWN) vary widely.

Examples may be found on all continents, most notably in Melanesia and Polynesia.

nóta (Hung.). An urban song, such as *Rákóczi-nóta,* a song about Rákóczi.

notation (Ger. *Notierung*). The art of representing musical tones, and their modifications, by means of written characters. Also the craft of writing symbols that represent sounds.

It took a millennium to develop a musical notation capable of even an approximate rendition of pitch and duration. The Spanish theologian Isidore of Seville, who flourished in the 7th century, asserted that musical sounds could be transmitted from one generation to another only by oral tradition because they could not be properly notated.

Music of ancient Greece was notated by letters, some of them turned backwards, or put upside down, apparently to indicate a certain type of INTERVAL. Toward the end of the first millennium A.D., an early system of notation appeared in the form of *NEUMES*, a Greek word for a nod, a sign, or a signal, indicating single notes or groups of notes (LIGATURES).

MUSICAL INSTRUMENT

Neumes were placed directly in the text, above the lines. They indicated the rise or fall of the vocal inflection, graphically derived from the acute, grave, and circumflex accents. An acute accent represented by a slant to the right denoted the rise of a second, a third, or another small interval. With the establishment of square notation, the intervallic norms became more definite. Rhythmic values were determined according to an elaborate set of rules that varied from century to century and from country to country, so that the transcription of medieval CHANTS becomes a matter of editorial discretion.

In time the neumes developed into groups of notational cells that were embodied in graphic shapes and assumed expressive Latin names, such as *punctum* (point), *virga* (comma), *pes* (foot), *clivis* (declivity), *scandicus* (ascent), *climacus* (climaxing), *torculus* (torque), and *porrectus* (erect). These gave rise to symbols for ornaments in BAROQUE music.

MENSURAL NOTATION, or notation that can be measured, emerged in the middle of the 13th century. Its invention, or at least its standardization, is usually ascribed to FRANCO OF COLOGNE. In the early centuries of mensural notation, white notes of different shapes were used. Black notes appeared in the course of time when it became necessary to write rapid passages. The standard notation of note lengths was the following: *maxima, longa, brevis* (or *breve*), *semibrevis* (or *semibreve*), *minima, semiminima, fusa,* and *semifusa.* Each of these equaled two or three notes of the next smaller durations. Thus *maxima* had two or three *longas,* a *longa* had two or three *breves,* a *breve* had two *semibreves,* etc. As if *maxima* were not long enough, a *larga* was introduced, which had the value of two or three *maximas.*

It is ironic that the *semibreve* (half-brief) note of mensural notation became in time the longest note of modern notation, designated as a WHOLE NOTE, which occupied an entire bar in $\frac{4}{4}$ time. It appears that in the Middle Ages time was running at a slower tempo. The shapes of these notes were either oblongs or rhomboids, with or without stems attached. *Semiminima* was notated either as a black rhomboid with a stem stuck into it from above like a toothpick in an olive, or else as a white rhomboid with a flag. As time passed, and as musicians became more and more agitated in their rhythmical mores, additional flags were attached to the stems of small notes, and theorists ran out of qualifying prefixes, such as demi-, semi-, hemi-, etc., in order to designate these very fast notes.

Arithmetically, in modern notation a whole note equals two half notes, a half note equals two quarter notes, a quarter note equals two eighth notes, etc. But in mensural notation a note could equal either two or three of the next smaller note. In modern notation a dotted half-note equals three quarter notes, etc., but in mensural notation the operation had to be indicated verbally or by a system of ligatures that are most misleading in view of the absence of BARLINES and other symbols. The verbal clues were contained in the adjectives *perfectum* or *imperfectum*. These words did not mean perfection or imperfection in the moral or physical sense, but in the Latin sense of completion and incompletion. *Perfectio* (perfection) was the subdivision of a note into three smaller note values, subdivisions into two being *imperfectio* (imperfection).

Furthermore, there were special terms for the mutual relationships between each pair of adjacent note values. The relationship between *brevis* and *semibrevis* was called *tempus*. The relationship between a *semibrevis* and *minima* was *prolatio* (prolation). If both *tempus* and *prolatio* were perfect, the result was a bar of nine whole-notes subdivided into three groups. If the *tempus* were perfect and the *prolatio* imperfect, this denoted three groups, each of which had two beats. If the *tempus* were imperfect but the *prolatio* perfect, then there were two divisions of three beats each.

The perfection was symbolized by a perfect circle in the time signature, while the imperfection was indicated by a semicircle. We inherited the sign of imperfection in the $\frac{4}{4}$ time signature that looks like the capital letter C.

Complications ensue as we plunge more deeply into ligatures, groups of notes glued together, or hanging to one another precariously by the corner of an oblong or to the side of a rhombus. Musicologists who are willing to devote their lives to the mysteries of mensural notation come figuratively to blows in their attempts to reach common understanding of these scores. As a result, transcriptions of medieval manuscripts in mensural notation are rarely in agreement.

Theologically minded music theorists of the Middle Ages suggested that triple time is perfect because it stands for the Trinity.

In modern usage, fractional names designate musical notes: whole note, half note, quarter note, eighth note, 16th note, 32nd note, 64th note, etc. Individual eighth notes have flags attached to them, while groups of eighth notes are united by black beams. Sixteenth notes have two flags, and their groups are united by double beams. Thirty-second notes have three flags and are united by triple beams, and so forth.

Identical graphic symbols are used in all Western music, but the names may differ. Thus, in British usage quarter notes are called *crotchets,* eighth notes are *quavers,* 16th notes are *semi-quavers,* 32nd notes are *demisemiquavers,* 64th notes are *hemidemisemiquavers,* and 128th notes are called *semi-hemidemisemiquavers.*

A dot next to the note head adds 50 percent to the value of the note. Thus a half note has two quarter notes and a dotted half note has three. In British usage, a *minima* has two *crochets* and a dotted *minima* has three. A *crochet* has two *quavers,* and a dotted *crochet* has three. A *quaver* has two *semiquavers,* a dotted *quaver* has three, and so on. The same augmentations by 50 percent are effected by dots placed after rests.

With the virtual disappearance of special signs indicating ornamentation in the 19th century, the present system of notation became an entirely workable method of writing down notes corresponding precisely to intended pitch and duration. The invention of the METRONOME made it possible to measure metrical units in fractions of a second. The addition of the BARLINE in the notational system is a great metric support, but the persistent habit of stressing the first beat has been an unfortunate byproduct of this innovation. Interpretation remained a personal matter, but liberties could be taken only in dynamics, variations in tempo, and ornamentation.

True, the written notes did not always reflect the composer's ideal, and some great masters wrote passages that could not be performed adequately or even approximately. LUDWIG VAN BEETHOVEN wrote sustained chords in some of his piano sonatas that could not be held by pedal without muddying up the harmony, or by the fingers that were occupied elsewhere. ROBERT SCHUMANN has a melody in his

ÉTUDES SYMPHONIQUES (1834) for piano that is to be played LEGATO in the bass but cannot be carried on without interruption.

There are numerous examples in great masterpieces in which the composer seems to be following a different beat in the rhythmic design from the one that appears in the metric arrangement. A most extraordinary incongruence between the visual notation and auditory perception occurs in the first movement of the First Symphony of JOHANNES BRAHMS, where a rhythmic period of three eighth notes enters on the second beat of $\frac{6}{8}$, with the accented notes overlapping the barlines. A modern composer would probably write a bar of $\frac{1}{8}$ and then resume $\frac{6}{8}$ time until the notated rhythm and meter coincide. Quite often, the ear groups several bars into one unit in a fast tempo. When Beethoven indicates that the scherzo of his Ninth Symphony is to be perceived in *ritmo di tre battute* (rhythm of three bars), he reveals the inadequacy of notation and its incompatibility with auditory perception.

A system that pursued a totally different track from the universally accepted notation was TABLATURE, which indicated graphically the position of each note on the LUTE, GUITAR, UKULELE, and keyboard instruments. Tablatures were widely used by lute players beginning in the 15th century and went out of use in the 18th, together with the lute itself. After three centuries of almost total disuse, tablature was revived in published editions for the guitar to enable popular performers who could not read music to pick out the necessary chords. The notation for the ukulele was always in the form of a tablature, resembling that of the lute but having no historic connection with it. A modern keyboard tablature, *Klavarskribo* (clavier notation in Esperanto), which indicates the positions of notes on a diagram of the piano keyboard, was launched in Holland.

Ultramodern composers of the second half of the 20th century tried to remedy the ills of musical notation with the aid of science, at least as far as meter and rhythm were concerned. Instead of the uncertainties of tempo marks, time signatures, and rhythmical units in metrical frames, some ultramodern notation specifies the duration of each note in time units, usually in seconds or fractions of seconds. Visually, too, a whole note occupies all the room of a bar of $\frac{4}{4}$ time, a half-note takes up exactly one half of such a bar, and passages in smaller notes are notated proportionately to the time they consume. In dynamics, the newest notation blithely specifies differences between pianissimo (*pp*) and pianississimo (*ppp*), fortissimo (*ff*) and fortississimo (*fff*), and so forth, up and down the dynamics range. The trouble, of course, is that human performers cannot execute such scientific niceties with any degree of precision or with a requisite aplomb. Electronic instruments have come to the rescue, therefore.

Such is the perversity of human nature that just as musical notation seemed to achieve a scientific precision, composers of the avant-garde developed a yen for indeterminacy. Of course, indeterminacy is itself a respectable scientific doctrine, and the theory of probabilities, which is closely related to it, possesses a mathematical aura that is quite idiosyncratic in its application. But a human being is also a tangle of probabilities. It is logical, therefore, that ultramodern notation should have absorbed the human element.

IANNIS XENAKIS, KARLHEINZ STOCKHAUSEN, EARLE BROWN, SYLVANO BUSSOTTI, JOHN CAGE, and many others in Europe, America, Japan, and Greece have adopted a graphic notation that not only deals in probabilistic elements but also resorts to pictorial representations of human faces experiencing prescribed emotions, from saintly tranquility to raging madness. When an occasional music staff is inserted in such scores, it may be covered with blobs of black ink or surrealistic geometrical curves. Verbalization of the basic elements of notation expands enormously here, and the performer is often urged to play or sing anything at all. Some modern musicians are possessed by a desire to represent new music by visual images, while others have returned to older notational and stylistic modes.

note (Lat. *figura*). One of the signs used to express the relative pitch and time value of TONES. *Note against note,* COUNTERPOINT in equal notes.

Notre Dame school. A religious compositional school that flourished in Paris in the 12th and 13th centuries. Its greatest masters were LEONINUS and PEROTINUS. But whether they were actually attached to the present cathedral of Notre Dame itself is a matter of conjecture, because the cornerstone of the famous church was not laid until the middle of the 12th century, and the construction was not completed for two more centuries.

notturno (It., night piece). 1. NOCTURNE. 2. Instrumental genre of the 18th century, akin to the DIVERTIMENTO, SERENADE, and CASSATION.

nōht-toor′nōh

FRANZ JOSEPH HAYDN and WOLFGANG AMADEUS MOZART were among the many composers of notturnos.

nŏh-vel-let′tĕ

novachord. *See* HAMMOND, LAURENS.

novellette (Ger.). Character piece, usually for piano solo, introduced by ROBERT SCHUMANN. These pieces were usually free in form, bold in HARMONY, ROMANTIC in character, and of considerable length. They are distinguished by a number of melodically unrelated THEMES that are united by a common rhythm.

"Novelette" does not mean "a little novel," as may be imagined. Schumann invented it (op.21, 1838) to express his admiration for the English singer Clara (Anastasia) Novello (1818–1908). But this was not the first time that Schumann engaged in such verbal trickery. He also wrote pieces that he described as "Wiecketten," after the maiden name of his beloved wife, Clara.

However, novelette was such an attractive name that many composers have knowingly adopted Schumann's playful title, using the term precisely in the sense of little novels or stories.

novelty. Popular instrumental piece or song not easily classified, such as nonsense songs, rhymes for children, pieces with unusual orchestration (e.g., typewriter, clock, toy balloons, tinkling bells), and so on.

LEROY ANDERSON specialized in orchestral novelties, such as *The Syncopated Clock* (1950).

Noye's Fludde. Opera by BENJAMIN BRITTEN, 1958, based on the medieval Chester MIRACLE PLAY, first performed in Oxford. Except for Noye (Noah), the roles are to be filled by children.

Nozze di Figaro, Le. *See* MARRIAGE OF FIGARO, THE.

number. 1. A subdivision of an opera or ORATORIO. 2. A smaller, and more or less complete, portion of a large work, such as a SONG, ARIA, INTERLUDE, etc. 3. Any single piece on a program. 4. An OPUS NUMBER.

number opera (Ger. *Nummernoper*). An opera in which the principal ingredients—ARIAS, vocal ensembles, instrumental INTERLUDES, etc.—are clearly separated from each other, or are connected by RECITATIVE or spoken dialogue.

Virtually all operas before RICHARD WAGNER were number operas, but an argument can be advanced that transitions between separate numbers create a continuity characteristic of "music drama" of the Wagnerian type. Wagner's theories virtually determined the operatic practice of the second half of the 19th century, but a return to the more formal type of number opera occurred in the 20th century. Twentieth-century composers, especially IGOR STRAVINSKY, successfully revived the seemingly extinct genre and even took delight in emphasizing its outdated traits.

number pieces. A designation for the late works by JOHN CAGE bearing numbers as titles (*Seventy-Four, Thirteen, One⁵*, etc.). The numbers refer to the number of players called for in the score or occasionally the number of parts. Superscript numbers are added to differentiate multiple compositions with the same number of players, and thus the same number title (e.g., *Two⁴*, the fourth work composed for two players). Cage's number pieces all utilize his TIME-BRACKET NOTATION.

numbers. The Latin word *numeri* had a second meaning, music, which was governed by the law of proportions between two different sounds.

In the fourth century, St. Augustine drew a distinction between *numeri sonantes,* the actual musical tone perceived by the senses, and *numeri recordabiles,* music that is remembered. In St. Augustine's concept, a melody was formed by a single sound instantaneously perceived and memorably associated with several preceding sounds. Long before St. Augustine, Aristoxenus (b. 354 B.C.) likened the musical tones of a melody to letters in a language.

So intimate was the connection felt between numbers and music that in medieval universities music was taught as part of the quadrivium (curriculum) of exact sciences, along with arithmetic, geometry, and astronomy. This association with numbers was lost in CLASSICAL and ROMANTIC music. Not until the 20th century did the numerical element in music regain its status.

Mathematical parameters lie at the foundation of SERIAL music. The calculus of sets is an important tool in rhythmic serialization. Some composers have used the FIBONACCI SERIES (a group of numbers) to determine meter, rhythm, or intervals. Simple arithmetical progressions also yield material for rhythmic arrangements. The application of numbers to composition is limitless, with the difficulty being to select numerical sets that would provide material for purely musical structures.

numerology. Several composers, superstitiously believing the importance of certain numbers in their lives, reflected these beliefs in their musical compositions.

There are indications that JOHANN SEBASTIAN BACH favored mystic numbers derived from the position of the letters of his last name in the alphabet. B–A–C–H would then equal $2 + 1 + 3 + 8 = 14$. According to the same ordering, the numerical value of J–S–B–A–C–H equals 41. One of Bach's late portraits has 14 buttons on the breast. In his last completed composition, *Vor deinen Thron,* the initial staff has 14 notes, the entire melody 41.

The curious, and quite serious, case of triskaidekaphobia (fear of the number 13) that preoccupied GIOACCHINO ROSSINI and ARNOLD SCHOENBERG had an apparent bearing on the date of their deaths. Rossini died on Friday the 13th (like many Italians, he was superstitiously fearful of such a combination). Schoenberg, who regarded the number 13 as ominous because he was born on the 13th of the month, went so far as to remove the second *A* in the title of his unfinished work *Moses und Aron* (i.e., Aaron, composed 1930–32) because the sum of the letters in the title added up to 13. He died on the 13th of the month, at the age of 76, the digits of which add up to 13.

Nun's fiddle. *See* TROMBA MARINA.

nuove musiche, Le (It., the new music). Originally the title of a selection of monodies by GIULIO CACCINI (1602), which became a slogan of the Florentine CAMERATA.

So potent was the desire on the part of music lovers to return to the original sources of vocal music uncomplicated by artful devices that soon the entire period of the early 17th century was designated as the period of *nuove musiche.* Its MONODIC style gave birth to OPERA, ORATORIO, and CANTATA, and inaugurated the era of the BAROQUE.

The creators of nuove musiche also established the historically important principle that the text should be the determining factor of musical expression rather than be subordinated to the prearranged melodic structure. The extreme development of BAROQUE POLYPHONY reversed the stream once more toward greater complexity, but the predominance of the text over polyphony was once more proclaimed a century and a half later by CHRISTOPH WILLIBALD GLUCK and basically subscribed to by RICHARD WAGNER and CLAUDE DEBUSSY.

PEOPLE IN MUSIC

Nurock, Kirk, innovative American composer and originator of "natural sound"; b. Camden, N.J., Feb. 28, 1948. Nurock held scholarships for study at the Juilliard School in N.Y. and at the Eastman School of Music in Rochester, N.Y. His teachers in composition were the noted composers VINCENT PERSICHETTI, ROGER SESSIONS, and LUCIANO BERIO. He was awarded the Elizabeth Sprague Coolidge Prize in chamber music in 1970.

From his earliest essays in composition, Nurock used extraordinary and unusual sound production. He became active as a conductor of idiosyncratic theater productions, among them the popular musical *Hair* (1968). He further developed a natural ability to perform advanced keyboard JAZZ music.

In 1971 Nurock developed an experimental vocal technique, "natural sound," founded on the assumption that every person's vocal cords, as well as other parts of their bodies, are capable of producing different sounds.

In several works Nurock annexed animal noises, the most challenging among the works being his Sonata for Piano and Dog, composed in 1983. Audience participation is welcomed, as several of Nurock's works are specifically scored for untrained participants who are called on to improvise their parts.

nut (Fr. *talon;* Ger. *Frosch;* It. *tallone*). 1. The ridge over which the strings pass at the end of the FINGERBOARD next to the head of a VIOLIN, etc. 2. The sliding projection at the lower end of the violin bow, by means of which the hair is tightened or slackened; also called FROG. 3. The "lower nut" on the violin is the ridge between the TAILPIECE and TAILPIN (or button).

MUSICAL INSTRUMENT

Nutcracker, The. BALLET by PIOTR ILYICH TCHAIKOVSKY, 1892, first performed in St. Petersburg. The subject of the ballet is taken from the fairy tale *Casse-Noisette* by Alexander Dumas *père,* itself borrowed from a tale by E.T.A. Hoffmann.

A girl dreams of a fight between a nutcracker and mice. She helps the nutcracker, who then is trans-

Antoinette Sibley and Anthony Dowell in a 1968 production of The Nutcracker. (Hulton-Deutsch Collection/Corbis)

formed into a beautiful prince and takes her into the magic land of sweets.

The Nutcracker is a full-length ballet. An instrumental suite drawn from it contains an overture, a march, and six dances: *Dance of the Sugar Plum-Fairies,* in which Tchai-

Tchaikovsky's masterpiece was given new life in 1992 by modern dancer Mark Morris, whose tongue-in-cheek adaptation of the classic ballet under the title *The Hard Nut* has become a holiday favorite to rival *The Nutcracker.*

PEOPLE IN MUSIC

MUSICAL
INSTRUMENT

kovsky includes the CELESTA for the first time in any orchestral work, *Ukrainian Dance, Trepak, Arabian Dance* (coffee), *Chinese Dance* (tea), *Pastorale,* and *Waltz of the Flowers.*

The fact that Tchaikovsky could write this sunlit music in the same year as his mournful *Pathétique Symphony* proves that musical inspiration and accomplishment often have nothing to do with the psychological states of a composer.

N.W.A. (Vocals: Ice Cube [O'Shea Jackson], b. Los Angeles, June 15, 1969; Dr. Dre [Andre Young], b. Los Angeles, Feb. 18, 1965; Eazy-E [Eric Wright], b. Los Angeles, Sept. 7, 1963; d. there, Mar. 26, 1995; MC Ren [Lorenzo Patterson], b. Los Angeles, June 16, year unknown; DJ Yella [Antoine Carraby], b. Los Angeles, Dec. 11, year unknown.) Popular RAP group of the early '90s. The group formed around the performer/record company owner Wright (aka Eazy-E) and composers Jackson (Ice Cube) and Young (Dr. Dre). Eazy-E had a hit with Cube and Dre's *Boyz-n-the-Hood,* inspiring them to join forces in the group N.W.A. (Niggaz Wit Attitude).

N.W.A.'s debut album, *Straight Outta Compton* (1989), featured early gangster rap attitudes, including *F–k the Police* and *Dopeman.* Despite its success, Cube felt he was shortchanged by the group and left it soon after. He has since enjoyed a successful solo recording and acting career.

The group's second album, *Efil4zaggin* ("Niggaz 4 life" spelled backwards), was another smash hit. On it, they spouted antifemale lyrics, while attacking ex-member Ice Cube (establishing the dissing wars so favored by rap acts). However, the group soon splintered into individual activities. Eazy-E gained notoriety on his own as a producer/performer, as did Dr. Dre.

Eazy-E died of AIDS in March 1995.

nyckelharpa (Swed.). Keyed folk FIDDLE, dating from the RENAISSANCE and still played.

Like the HURDY-GURDY, the strings are stopped by keys, but, unlike it, the nyckelharpa strings rest on a flat bridge and are bowed. The number of strings has remained flexible: between one and two melody strings, and between two and three DRONES. In instruments constructed after the 18th century, up to 11 sympathetic strings were added.

O

o. 1. When placed over G, D, A, or E in a VIOLIN part (or the equivalent for other string instruments), the lowercase *o* stands for the word *open* and indicates that the notes so marked must be played on an OPEN STRING. 2. In a BASSO CONTINUO part, as a sign that only the bass NOTE or its OCTAVE should be used in the accompaniment to a given passage without filling in the HARMONY. 3. Placed above a note, usually in string parts, it signifies the use of HARMONICS. 4. In chord TABLATURE, a DIMINISHED FIFTH or CHORD.

O Sole Mio! One of the most famous Neapolitan ballads, composed in 1899 by Eduardo Di Capua (1864–1917).

obbligato (It., obligatory; Ger. *obligato*). Originally, an instrumental part that was essential in the performance, such as the many SONATAS for piano and another instrument *obbligato.* The meaning expanded to any instrumental or vocal part that is a concerted (and therefore an essential) part.

ōh-blē-gah′tōh

However, through some unexplained twist of fate, *obbligato* began to be used, particularly in popular arrangements, to indicate an optional part. For example, a song with *cello obbligato* would mean that such a part would be a desirable addition to the accompaniment, but not essential.

Oberon. Opera by CARL MARIA VON WEBER, 1826, first produced in London, the composer conducting. The plot shares characters with Shakespeare's *A Midsummer Night's Dream.*

Oberon is King of the Elves, and Titania his Queen. There are numerous exotic characters springing up here and there. Oberon's appointed task in life is to find a pair of lovers undeterred by any misadventure. He succeeds with the help of his magic horn. There is a grand reunion at the end, at the court of Charlemagne.

This opera's original text is in English, because the work was commissioned by the famous Covent Garden opera company in London.

The LIBRETTO is magnificent in its absurdity. The glorious overture survives on the concert podium, but the opera is rarely performed in its entirety.

Oberto, Conte di San Bonifacio. Opera by GIUSEPPE VERDI, 1839, produced in Milan, the first of his operas to be performed.

Oberto is killed by his daughter's lover in a duel. The murderous seducer leaves Italy never to return, and the abandoned girl is left to her futile lamentations. The opera was successful and still maintains a spark of life at its infrequent revivals on the Italian stages.

objets trouvés (Fr.). A term rather defiantly introduced by avant-garde painters and sculptors, meaning quite literally "found objects." Marcel Duchamp was probably the first to exhibit an *objet trouvé,* a urinal from a men's lavatory. Man Ray exhibited a sewing machine wrapped in a piece of canvas, and Andy Warhol managed to create a sensation by selling a realistic representation of a Campbell's soup can for a reputed sum of $70,000. A plate with remnants of an unfinished dinner was exhibited as an *objet trouvé,* as was "bagel jewelry," an actual bagel set in a jewelry box. Found or ready-made objects are also incorporated by modern artists as part of sculpture or montage.

Ultramodern composers sometimes insert passages from works by other composers as a token of homage and partly as an experiment in construction. Such *objets trouvés* need not harmonize with their environment, which may be completely alien to the nature of the implant. An early example is the sudden appearance of the tune *Ach, du lieber Augustin* in ARNOLD SCHOENBERG's Second String Quartet (1908).

Others make use of musical *objets trouvés* by the simple device of playing another composer's music. An example of an embroidered *objet trouvé* is LUCIANO BERIO's *Sinfonia* (1968), which incorporates whole chunks of music from GUSTAV MAHLER, MAURICE RAVEL, and others.

MUSICAL INSTRUMENT

oboe (Fr. *hautbois,* high wood; Ger. *Hoboe/Oboe;* It. *oboe*). 1. An orchestral instrument with a conical wooden tube, 9

◀ *Oboe players in an orchestra. (Jim Seere)*

to 14 keys, and a DOUBLE REED. Its present RANGE is two oc-TAVES and a seventh, from b^0 to a^3.

The oboe first made its appearance toward the middle of the 17th century in France.

Its tone is very reedy and penetrating, although not harsh. Only two kinds are in ordinary use, the treble oboe (just described), and the ENGLISH HORN (alto oboe) of lower pitch. The oboe is rather limited in its agility, in contrast to the melodious FLUTE or the wide-ranging CLARINET. But the oboe compensates for these real or imaginary deficiencies by the precision of its intonation and by the strength of its sound; indeed, it can pierce through the entire orchestral fabric as easily as the trumpet.

In orchestral writing, oboes are commonly used in pairs, like flutes, clarinets, and BASSOONS. As a solo instrument, the oboe is not as popular as the flute, clarinet, or even bassoon, but GEORGE FRIDERIC HANDEL wrote several concertos for it. Subsequently, solo recitals, even by great oboe virtuosos, are rare.

2. In the organ, an 8′ reed stop, with conical pipes surmounted by a bell and cap.

oboe da caccia (It., hunting oboe). An instrument tuned a FIFTH below the OBOE. It was in use during the RENAISSANCE period but was eventually replaced by the ENGLISH HORN.

Because of its piercing tone, the oboe stands unchallenged as it gives the introductory A to tune up the orchestra.

oh′boh-eh dăh că′tchăh

MUSICAL INSTRUMENT

oboe d'amore (It., love oboe; Fr. *hautbois d'amour;* Ger. *Liebeshoboe/Liebesoboe*). An oboe pitched in A, a MINOR THIRD below the standard instrument, with either a standard oboe or bulbous bell. It was the most popular of the woodwind d'amore instruments but like the others is essentially obsolete.

Obrecht (Obreht, Hobrecht, Obertus, Hobertus), **Jacob,** famous Netherlandish composer; b. probably in Bergen-op-Zoom, Nov. 22, 1450 or 1451; d. Ferrara, 1505. Obrecht is first mentioned as *zangmeester* (director of singing) in Utrecht c.1476–78, after which he became choirmaster for the Corporation of Notre Dame at St. Gertrude in Bergen-op-Zoom in 1479. In 1840 he took holy orders and said his first MASS as an ordained priest.

Obrecht was made *maître des enfants* (choir master) at Cambrai in 1484 but was dismissed a year later for his neglect of the choirboys as well as using the choir's money for his own purposes. He then was made succentor at St. Donatian in Bruges in 1486. At the invitation of the Duke of Ferrara, he obtained a leave of absence to travel to Italy. He arrived in Ferrara in late 1487, returning to Bruges in 1488. He was made *maître de chapelle* (master of the chapel choir) there in 1490 but was excused from that position a year later.

By 1494 Obrecht was at Notre Dame in Antwerp, serving as CAPELLANIE MAGISTER (chapel master; i.e., director of the choir) in 1495. He returned to St. Gertrude in Bergen-op-Zoom in 1496–97 and then received a benefice connected to the altar of St. Josse in Notre Dame at Antwerp in 1498. He was again at St. Donatian in Bruges from 1499 until his retirement in 1500. He then lived in Bergen-op-Zoom and made visits to Antwerp, and in 1504 he returned to the ducal court in Ferrara, where he died of the plague.

Obrecht was one of the leading composers of his era, his MASSES and MOTETS being of particular importance. He also wrote CHANSONS, many to Dutch texts.

ocarina (It., little goose). A bulbous flute in the shape of a bird. Ocarinas are usually manufactured from terra-cotta, with finger holes and a whistle mouthpiece. They are often used as whistles.

NIKOLAI RIMSKY-KORSAKOV includes an ocarina tuned in an alternating scale of WHOLE TONES and SEMITONES in the score of his OPERA-BALLET *Mlada* (1892).

Ocean. The final collaborative work of choreographer MERCE CUNNINGHAM and composer JOHN CAGE, 1994, a 90-minute landmark in modern dance in its circular conception and execution. Cunningham was aided in his work, much of which was determined by CHANCE, by LifeForms, a computer program developed specifically for choreographers at Simon Fraser University in Canada.

The music is comprised of two discrete, overlaid works, one ELECTRONIC (DAVID TUDOR's *Soundings: Ocean Diary*) and one ACOUSTIC (Andrew Culver's *Ocean 1-95* for 112 musicians located above and around the audience, based upon Cage's ideas and instructions pieced together after his death in 1992).

Ocean Symphony. ANTON RUBINSTEIN's Second Symphony, 1854, in C major, first performed in Leipzig. He wrote it when he was only 24 years old, and it became his most popular symphonic work. It was criticized as having "too much water and too little ocean," but it endured for half a century as long as its kind of expansive Germanic ROMANTICISM held sway.

It was a sort of ritual for the N.Y. Philharmonic to open its seasons with the *Ocean Symphony.* Then, suddenly, something snapped. The work became unacceptable to aesthetically minded music lovers, and it simply vanished from the repertory. *Sic transit Oceanus!*

Ochs, Phil, American social-protest singer/songwriter, b. El Paso, Tex., Dec. 19, 1940; d. Far Rockaway, N.Y., April 19, 1976. A contemporary of BOB DYLAN's in the early '60s, to whose work his was often compared, Ochs was a more polished performer and wrote a variety of satirical songs on issues of the day.

Although born in Texas, Ochs first performed while a college student in Cleveland, as half of a duo who became known as the *Sundowners.* In 1961 he relocated to N.Y.'s Greenwich Village, where he became a solo act. His work

PEOPLE IN MUSIC

was quickly championed by *Broadside* magazine, a folk publication specializing in topical songs. He was signed to the folk label Elektra, where he recorded his first album, *All the News That's Fit to Sing*. Early hits included *I Ain't a Marchin' Anymore* and *There but for Fortune* (covered in 1965 by Joan Baez).

In 1967 Ochs relocated to California and began writing in a more personal, confessional style. He had some minor hits, including *Pleasures of the Harbor* (1967) and *Small Circle of Friends* (1968), an ironic contemporary song on people's apathy when it came to the violence occurring around them.

Taking yet another odd turn in his career, he returned to N.Y. to perform at Carnegie Hall in 1971, oddly dressed in a gold lamé suit. He had worn a similar costume on the cover of his ironically titled *Greatest Hits* album, which, in fact, did not contain any hits at all but was entirely made up of new material. The audience, stunned by his personality shift, was not pleased.

Ochs traveled in the early '70s to Africa and England and then returned to the N.Y. area by 1974, taking up new causes, including organizing a concert against the dictatorial government of Chile. Depressed by his lack of success, he took his own life by hanging himself while on a visit to his sister in 1976.

Ochs's music enjoyed a revival in the '90s, with several compilations of his earlier recordings reissued and two different biographies published.

PEOPLE IN MUSIC

Ockeghem (Okeghem, Okengheim, Ockenheim, etc.), **Johannes** (Jean, Jehan de), great Flemish composer; b. c. 1410; d. probably in Tours, Feb. 6, 1497. He may have been a pupil of GILLES BINCHOIS, the Flemish MADRIGAL composer. Ockeghem is first listed among the *vicaires-chanteurs* (vicar-singers) at Notre Dame in Antwerp in 1443 and served there until 1444. By 1446 he was in the service of Charles I, Duke of Bourbon, in Moulins, remaining there until at least 1448.

By 1452 Ockeghem was in the service of Charles VII of France as first among the singer-chaplains who were non-priests, and by 1454 he was *premier chapelain*. He subsequently served Louis XI and Charles VIII, who, in 1459, made him treasurer of the Church of St. Martin-de-Tours. Under Louis XI, he also was a canon at Notre Dame in Paris from 1463 to 1470. He likewise was a chaplain at St. Benoit. In January 1470 he traveled to Spain at the King's expense. In 1484 he journeyed to Bruges and Dammes.

With his contemporaries GUILLAUME DUFAY and JOSQUIN DES PREZ, Ockeghem ranks among the foremost masters of the Franco-Flemish style of composition in the second half of the 15th century. Among his settings of the MASS is the earliest surviving POLYPHONIC REQUIEM. The inventiveness displayed in his Masses is only excelled in his superb MOTETS. His achievements in the art of imitative COUNTER-POINT unquestionably make his music a milestone on the way to the A CAPPELLA style of future generations.

octave (Eng., Fr.; from Lat. *octava,* eighth; It. *ottava;* Ger. *Oktave*). 1. A series of eight consecutive DIATONIC tones. 2. The INTERVAL. Different octaves bear special names, more or less acceptable in international nomenclature (see SCALE(s)). The earliest type of POLYPHONIC singing was at the interval of an octave, with boys singing an octave higher than men.

Concealed, covered, or *hidden octaves* (or *fifths*), PARALLEL octaves (or fifths) suggested by the progression of two parts in similar motion to the interval of an octave (or fifth); *parallel octave,* CONSECUTIVE OCTAVES; *rule of the octave,* a series of HARMONIES written over the DIATONIC scale as a bass; *short octave,* the lowest octave of some old ORGAN MANUALS, in which some keys (and pipes) are omitted.

3. In the organ, a stop whose pipes sound tones an octave higher than the keys touched, e.g., the PRINCIPAL. Also *octave coupler,* one uniting the 8′ tones of one keyboard with those an octave higher on another; *octave flute,* 1. The piccolo. 2. An organ stop of 4′ pitch; *octave sign, see* OTTAVA; *octave stop, see* OCTAVE (3).

octet (Fr. *octour;* It. *ottetto;* Ger. *Oktett*). A composition for eight solo voices or instruments.

ode. 1. A chorus in ancient Greek plays. 2. A musical work of praise.

Upon Ockeghem's death, Guillaume Crétin wrote a poetic *Déploration* in his honor. JOSQUIN DES PREZ and JOHANNES LUPI, both important contemporary composers, composed musical epitaphs for him also.

A curious explanation as to why the octave is the most perfect interval is given in an anonymous medieval music treatise. According to this writer, it was because *octavo die Abraham circumcisus erat* (because it was "on the 8th day that Abraham was circumcised").

Ode to Billy Joe. BOBBIE GENTRY's self-penned country and pop smash hit of 1967.

The song was considered scandalous for its time, particularly for a country number, because of the implication that the protagonist threw her baby off of the Tallahatchie Bridge. It also inspired a B-grade feature film.

Ode to Joy. The standard English title of the choral finale of LUDWIG VAN BEETHOVEN's Ninth Symphony. It is set to the words of Friedrich von Schiller's poem *An die Freude,* expressing faith in the ultimate brotherhood of men.

Odhecaton. The first printed collection of POLYPHONIC music, published by Ottaviano dei Petrucci, in 1501. The title means "100 Songs" (*ode* + *hecaton*).

Actually, there are only 96 songs in the collection, but its historical value would have been great no matter what the number. Only nine are furnished with texts, but at the time the *Odhecaton* was published, instrumental tunes were commonly sung, and songs were often played on instruments.

Oedipus Rex. Opera-oratorio by IGOR STRAVINSKY, 1927, first performed in concert form in Paris. The stage premiere took place in Vienna one year later.

In order to make the legend of Oedipus more timeless, Stravinsky arranged to have French playwright Jean Cocteau's LIBRETTO translated into Latin. The music follows this impulse; it is majestically static like a row of Greek marble columns. Significant musical phrases are relentlessly reiterated to drive their meaning into the mind of the listener; but Italian opera also provides models for Stravinsky (e.g., Jocasta's aria).

A somewhat ironic narrator recites the events in between the musical numbers.

oeuvre (Fr.). A work. *Oeuvres choisies,* selected works; *oeuvres complètes,* complete works; *oeuvres inédites,* unpublished works; *oeuvres posthumes,* posthumous works.

Of Mice and Men. Opera by CARLISLE FLOYD, 1970, based on John Steinbeck's novel. Two migrant workers, George and Lennie, work on a farm and dream of buying a ranch of their own. After the simple-minded Lennie commits murder, George shoots him dead to save him from execution.

Of Thee I Sing. Musical by GEORGE GERSHWIN, 1931. The work is a satire on American Presidential campaigns.

The candidate, Wintergreen, runs on a "platform of love," vowing to marry the winner of the Miss White House contest if he is elected. He wins, but instead of marrying the contest's winner he selects a plainer girl since she can really make corn muffins for the White House functions. An impeachment process is avoided when Vice President Throttlebottom marries the beauty contest winner instead.

The lyrics, by Gershwin's brother Ira, are incisive. The leading songs are the title song, *Love Is Sweeping the Country,* and *Who Cares?* The critic Brooks Atkinson found the work "funnier than the government, and not nearly so dangerous." It was the first MUSICAL to win the Pulitzer Prize.

off-beat. A peculiar feature of RAGTIME and JAZZ, or of SYNCOPATION in general, in which the metrically unaccented parts of the MELODY are played with a strong rhythmic stress.

Offenbach, Jacques (Jacob), famous French composer of German descent; b. Cologne, June 20, 1819; d. Paris, Oct. 5, 1880. Offenbach was the son of a Jewish cantor, whose original surname was Eberst. Offenbach was the town in which his father lived.

Offenbach studied violin before taking up the cello when he was nine. After training with Joseph Alexander and Bernhard Breuer in Cologne, he settled in Paris in 1833. Following cello studies at the Paris Conservatory in 1833–34, he played in the orchestra of the Opéra-Comique. He pursued a career as a soloist and chamber music artist beginning in 1838. From 1850 to 1855 he was a conductor at the Théâtre-Français. His *Chanson de Fortunio* for Alfred de Musset's comedy *Chandelier,* composed in 1850, proved tremendously popular.

In 1855 Offenbach opened his own theater, the *Bouffes-Parisiens,* at the Salle Marigny. Late that year it moved to the Salle Choiseul, where he scored his first great success with

The book's and opera's title is taken from Robert Burns's famous line "The best laid schemes o' mice and men."

PEOPLE IN MUSIC

Jacques Offenbach. (Library of Congress/Corbis)

the OPERETTA *Orphée aux enfers* (Orpheus in hell; 1858). His *La Belle Hélène* (The beautiful Helen, 1864) proved to be one of his most celebrated works, soon taken up by theatrical enterprises all over the world.

Having abandoned the management of the Bouffes-Parisiens in 1866, Offenbach nevertheless continued to write for the stage. His *La Vie parisienne* (Parisian life; 1866), *La Grande-Duchesse de Gérolstein* (The Grand Duchess of Gerolstein; 1867), and *La Périchole* (1868) were notably successful. In 1873 he took over the management of the Théâtre de la Gaité, where he brought out his revised version of *Orphée aux enfers* as an *opéra-féerique* (fantastic opera; 1874).

In 1876 Offenbach undertook a tour of the U.S., describing his impressions in *Notes d'un musicien en voyage* (Notes of a traveling musician; 1877) and *Offenbach en Amerique* (Offenbach in America; 1877).

Offenbach's only grand opera, the masterpiece *Les Contes d'Hoffmann* (THE TALES OF HOFFMANN) remained unfinished at his death. Recitatives were added by Ernest Guiraud with the famous barcarolle from Offenbach's *Die Rheinnixen* from 1864, in which the tune was used for a ghost song. The completed score was premiered at the Opéra-Comique in Paris in 1881 with instantaneous success, and subsequently was performed on both sides of the Atlantic.

Offenbach is a master of the operetta. His music is characterized by an abundance of flowing, rollicking melodies, seasoned with ironic humor, suitable to the extravagant burlesque of the situations. His irreverent treatment of mythological characters reflected the atmosphere of precarious gaiety in the Paris of his day.

In addition to his more than 60 operettas and opéras-comiques, Offenbach wrote several pieces for the cello, including six works with orchestra, several pieces for cello and piano, solo works, and teaching pieces.

Offertory (Fr. *Offertoire;* It. *Offertorio;* Lat. *Offertorium*). In the Roman Catholic MASS, the verses or ANTHEM following the CREDO, and sung by the choir while the priest is placing the consecrated elements on the altar, during which the offerings of the congregation are collected. This is the fourth division of the PROPRIUM of the Mass. Its original name was *Antiphona ad offerendum.*

The earliest musical procedure of the Offertory contained the reading of psalms, followed by a responsorial chant or some other ANTIPHONAL singing. Many organ pieces bear the title *Offertory,* but most works of the Offertory type are religious MOTETS in a POLYPHONIC setting.

Officium Divinum (Lat.). Divine Office. *See* CANONICAL HOURS.

Oh, Bury Me Not on the Lone Prairie. A famous American song, the origin of which is unknown.

It was first published as an "authentic folksong" in 1907 by John Lomax and was included in his 1910 collection *Cowboy Songs* under the title *The Dying Cowboy.* However, Lomax did not realize that the song was in fact based on a sentimental poem, written by E. H. Chapin in 1839 and called *The Ocean Burial,* where the injunction was not against a prairie burial but rather a watery one. It was set to music by George N. Allen a decade later, and subsequently the lyrics were transmuted into a classic of cowboy expression.

Oh! Dear, What Can the Matter Be? An English song published in London as long ago as 1792 and possibly earlier. It has retained its popularity as a nursery song.

Oh, How I Hate to Get Up in the Morning. Song by IRV-ING BERLIN, 1918, ruefully lamenting the sound of the army REVEILLE. Berlin wrote it during his stint as an American soldier in World War I; he subsequently performed it again during World War II.

Oh, Kay! Musical by GEORGE GERSHWIN, 1926. Kay is a sister of an English duke. They use their family yacht for liquor smuggling during Prohibition. The plot detours into a love story when an American playboy falls in love with Kay.

There are several fine songs in the score, including *Do, Do, Do, Clap Yo' Hands,* and *Someone to Watch Over Me.*

This song provided the title for the popular Julia Roberts–Richard Gere film about a prostitute with a heart of gold.

Oh, Pretty Woman. ROY ORBISON's No. 1 1964 hit, with his famous growled interjection, a pop favorite. Covered by HEAVY-METALISTS Van Halen in 1982.

Oh, Promise Me! This lyric promissory note was a last-minute insertion in the operetta *Robin Hood* (1890) by REGINALD DE KOVEN, produced in Chicago in 1890. The song became popular at weddings, second only to *Here Comes the Bride,* the bridal chorus from RICHARD WAGNER's *LOHENGRIN* (1850).

Oh! Susanna. Song by STEPHEN FOSTER, 1848, which became a favorite during the California Gold Rush of 1849. The rapid POLKA time fits the words perfectly, and the BANJO accompaniment is equally pleasing.

Oh, What a Beautiful Mornin'. An outburst of melodious morning pleasure by RICHARD RODGERS and OSCAR HAMMERSTEIN II, 1943, from the musical *OKLAHOMA!*

Oh Where, Oh Where Has My Little Dog Gone? A German song, 1847. In the original, the narrator laments a lost sock, not a lost dog. In 1864 the popular songwriter Septimus Winner (1827–1902) set English lyrics to the melody. He called it *Der Deitcher's dog* (The German's Dog) and set it in a pseudo-German dialect. Later it was transformed into its popular final version.

Ohana, Maurice, French composer and pianist; b. Casablanca (of Spanish parents), June 12, 1914; d. Paris, Nov. 13, 1992. Ohana studied piano in Barcelona and at the Paris Conservatory. He also had lessons in COUNTERPOINT at the Schola Cantorum from 1937 to 1940.

Following service in the British Army during World War II, Ohana completed his training at Rome's Accademia di Santa Cecilia from 1944 to 1946, then settled in Paris. In 1981 he was made a Commandeur des Arts et Lettres. He won the Prix National de Musique (1975) and the Honegger (1982) and Ravel (1985) prizes.

Ohana's music combines elements of his Spanish background and the world of IGOR STRAVINSKY'S *THE RITE OF SPRING* (1913) and *LES NOCES* (1923) with a keen ear for percussion and timbre. However, he was resolutely against the avant-garde world of PIERRE BOULEZ. He composed operas, orchestral and chamber works, piano music, including 24 Preludes (1972–73), and group and solo vocal works.

Oiseaux exotiques (exotic birds). Work by OLIVIER MESSIAEN, 1956, for piano, wind instruments, and percussion. In it, instrumental approximations of bird songs from exotic lands are incorporated. It was first performed in Paris.

Oistrakh, David (Fyodorovich), great Russian violinist; b. Odessa, Sept. 30, 1908; d. Amsterdam, Oct. 24, 1974. Oistrakh studied violin as a child in Odessa, where he made his debut at the age of six. He then continued his studies at the Odessa Conservatory from 1923 to 1926.

Oistrakh appeared as soloist in ALEXANDER GLAZUNOV'S Violin Concerto under the composer's direction in Kiev in 1927. In 1928 he went to Moscow, and in 1934 he was appointed to the faculty of the Moscow Conservatory. His name attracted universal attention in 1937 when he won first prize at the Ysaÿe Competition in Brussels, in which 68 violinists from 21 countries took part.

Oistrakh played in Paris and London in 1953 with extraordinary success. He made his first American appearances in 1955, as soloist with major American orchestras and in recitals, winning enthusiastic acclaim. He also made appearances as a conductor from 1962. He died while on a visit to

PEOPLE IN MUSIC

PEOPLE IN MUSIC

Violinists David (right) *and Igor Oistrakh, 1961. (Hulton-Deutsch Collection/Corbis)* ▶

Amsterdam as a guest conductor with the Concertgebouw Orchestra.

Oistrakh's playing was marked, apart from a phenomenal technique, by stylistic fidelity to works by different composers of different historical periods. Soviet composers profited from his advice as to technical problems of violin playing. He collaborated with SERGEI PROKOFIEV in making an arrangement for violin and piano of Prokofiev's Flute Sonata. (He also played a chess match with Prokofiev.)

A whole generation of Soviet violinists were numbered among Oistrakh's pupils, first and foremost his son Igor (b. Odessa, April 27, 1931), who has had a spectacular career in his own right. He won first prize at the International Festival of Democratic Youth in Budapest in 1949 and the Wieniawski Competition in Poznan in 1952. Some critics regarded him as equal to his father in virtuosity.

Okeghem, Johannes. *See* OCKEGHEM, JOHANNES.

Oklahoma! Musical by RICHARD RODGERS and OSCAR HAMMERSTEIN II, 1943, the first collaboration between one of the great Broadway teams.

The action takes place in the old Indian Territory. A love triangle results in a fight between two suitors in which one of them, Jud (the real aggressor) is accidentally killed by Curly. After being freed of all blame by a judge on the spot,

Curly and his fiancée, Laurey, pack off to join the land rush in the future state of Oklahoma.

The musical was tremendously successful and became a classic of the modern American musical theater. Among its many imperishable tunes are the title song, *OH WHAT A BEAUTIFUL MORNIN'*, *People Will Say We're in Love,* and *The Surrey with the Fringe on Top.*

oktoechos. A system of eight ECHOI as practiced in Byzantine chant. The doctrine and practice of oktoechos probably originated in Syria early in the 6th century, possibly by analogy with the ancient Greek MODES.

Ol' Man River. Song by JEROME KERN and OSCAR HAMMERSTEIN II, from the musical *SHOW BOAT,* 1927 Next to STEPHEN FOSTER's *OLD FOLKS AT HOME ("Way Down upon the Swanee River"),* it is the greatest American river song, glorifying the mighty Mississippi that "just keeps rollin' along." Winston Churchill quoted it as a song symbolizing the greatness of America. Implicit in the song, however, is the difficult life of the black population of the Delta.

Old Black Joe. Song by STEPHEN FOSTER, 1860. According to an accepted legend, Joe was a black servant in the house of Foster's fiancée.

Old Folks at Home. Song by STEPHEN FOSTER, 1851, one of his most famous. He sold it for a tiny sum of money to the famous MINSTREL performer and manager E. P. Christy, who published it as his own. Only after Christy's copyright expired was the injustice righted and Foster's name given as composer in the new edition, but by that time he was dead.

The song is commonly known under the title *Swanee River.*

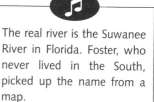

The real river is the Suwanee River in Florida. Foster, who never lived in the South, picked up the name from a map.

Old Gray Mare, The. An anonymous American song, 1858. The original melody was also called *Down in Alabam'.* The text has gone through several changes.

Old Hundred. A tune originally set to the words of the 100th Psalm (*Make a Joyful Noise unto the Lord, All Ye*

Lands), also known as a hymn of praise, *All People That on Earth Do Dwell*. The hymn *Old Hundred* was first printed in the English Psalter in 1563. It also appears in the First Bay Psalm Book in 1640. CHARLES IVES quotes the tune in his music.

Old MacDonald Had a Farm. An old nursery rhyme with imitations of animal sounds. The lyrics have been traced back to an English song by THOMAS D'URFEY that appeared in print as early as 1706, while the first known American publication of the melody was printed under the title *Litoria! Litoria!* in 1859.

In 1917 the first appearance of words and music as we know them today came under the title "Ohio," although the farmer was called "MacDougal." Surprisingly, today's version was not published until 1920, when it was included in a Boy Scout book, which helped regularize the name of the farmer and the cast of animal characters.

Old Maid and the Thief, The. Opera by GIAN CARLO MENOTTI, 1939, written for radio and the first such work broadcast over the NBC network. It was not performed on stage until 1949 in Philadelphia.

An old maid takes a stranger into her home. She grows dependent on him, and, yielding to his increasing demands, she engages in theft. When the thefts are discovered, everyone suspects the stranger. Irritated by this injustice, he robs her of all her possessions and disappears.

¡Olé! Spanish exclamation used as a refrain in various song genres. *See also* APPLAUSE.

MUSICAL INSTRUMENT

PEOPLE IN MUSIC

oliphant (Old Fr. *olifant*, elephant). Abbreviation for *cor d'olifant*, a Byzantine signal TRUMPET, sometimes made of elephant's tusk. It was imported from the Orient and employed for ceremonial occasions. The instrument came to Europe during the Middle Ages.

Oliver, "King" (Joseph), outstanding African-American JAZZ cornetist and bandleader, uncle of ULYSSES (Simpson) KAY; b. on a plantation near Abend, La., May 11, 1885; d.

Savannah, Ga., April 8, 1938. In 1907 Oliver was working in Storyville (the red-light district of New Orleans) with the Melrose Brass Band. After working with several other bands, he formed his own group in 1915, which was eventually known as the Creole Jazz Band. By 1917 he had acquired the nickname "King," traditionally reserved for leading jazz musicians. However, it was also in 1917 that the city government closed the bordellos in Storyville, putting most of the musicians out of work.

The following year Oliver moved his band to Chicago, leading a migration of jazz musicians to the city that was largely responsible for the spreading of the black New Orleans jazz style throughout the country. In 1922 LOUIS ARMSTRONG, whom Oliver had known in New Orleans, joined the band, helping to make it the most polished exponent of New Orleans's collectively improvised jazz. The group's 1923 recordings were the most influential early jazz recordings ever made. They have been reissued by the Smithsonian Institution.

Subsequent bands formed by Oliver remained a potent force in jazz until around 1928. For the next few years, Oliver struggled to keep up with the times, but BIG-BAND jazz had replaced New Orleans-style groups in popularity. He died penniless and forgotten in 1938.

Oliveros, Pauline, American composer; b. Houston, May 30, 1932. Oliveros's mother and grandmother, both piano teachers, taught her the rudiments of music. She studied violin, accordion, and horn as a teenager. She then studied composition and accordion at the University of Houston from 1949 to 1952 and then continued her studies at San Francisco State College, earning her bachelor's degree in 1957, and privately with Robert Erickson from 1954 to 1960.

Oliveros became involved early on with avant-garde music. From 1961 to 1965, she was codirector of the San Francisco Tape Music Center, and, after it became the Mills Tape Music Center, was its director until 1967. She then taught at the University of California, San Diego, from 1967 to 1981.

Oliveros has won numerous awards, including a Guggenheim Fellowship in 1973, and ASCAP awards from 1982

PEOPLE IN MUSIC

Pauline Oliveros, playing the accordion, 1981. (Becky Cohen)

to 1994. In 1984, 1998, and 1990 she won an NEA composer's fellowship, and in 1994 she was awarded the Foundation for Contemporary Performance Arts grant.

Introduced by Erickson to modern harmony, asymmetrical rhythms, group improvisation, and acoustical sounds, she began to explore the range of subliminal sounds derived from the OVERTONE SERIES, DIFFERENTIAL TONES, and other sources. In 1960 she composed a Piano Sextet that explored a variety of such elusive tonal elements. It received the Pacifica Foundation National Prize. Advancing further into the domain of new sounds, she wrote the choral work *Sound Patterns* to wordless voices in 1962; it received a prize in the Netherlands.

While in San Diego, Oliveros was able to develop her ideas still further. Taking advantage of her skill as a gardener, she arranged garden hoses and lawn sprinklers as part of a musical ensemble accompanied by the sounds of alarm clocks and various domestic utensils. Occasionally, a musician was instructed to bark. To this enriched artistic vocabulary was soon added a physical element. Performers acted the parts of a magician, a juggler, and a fortune-teller. Page turners, piano movers, and floor sweepers were listed as performing artists.

In her later works, Oliveros reduced these movement activities. She gradually began to compose ceremonial works of sonic meditation. She used various vocal effects, including soft murmuring, chanting, and joyful yodeling, with the purpose of inducing an altered state of consciousness. She often presided over such sessions, singing and playing her faithful accordion.

ombra scene (It.). Shadow scene; a dramatic operatic episode taking place in the nether regions, in a cemetery, or in a place where ghosts congregate. It is usually cast as an accompanied RECITATIVE; for some reason, it was usually in the key of E-flat major.

Ombra scenes feature many general pauses, tremolos, exclamations, and other emotional outbursts. The clarinet, French horn, and trombone are favorite instruments for shadow scenes in BAROQUE operas.

omnitonality. Modern musicologists have used the term *omnitonality* to indicate a totality or tonalities with frequent collisions of different KEYS. Omnitonality enjoyed a certain vogue as a compromise definition for modern techniques that retained the basic sense of tonality but expanded it to the entire cycle of MAJOR and MINOR SCALES. It is almost synonymous with PANTONALITY.

Omnitonic, having or producing all tones; CHROMATIC (as in an instrument).

On a Clear Day You Can See Forever. Musical by ALAN JAY LERNER (text) and BURTON LANE (music), 1965.

The whimsical plot deals with a girl who is not only clairvoyant, but who can also see back in time. Her skeptical psychiatrist is astounded by her ability to locate misplaced objects, to anticipate the exact moment when the phone will ring, and to make flowers grow unnaturally fast. When in a trance she identifies herself with an 18th-century English lady, and research proves that there was such a person, the psychiatrist falls in love with both her former and present selves.

Among Oliveros's works are:

Double Basses at 20 Paces, theater piece for two basses, their seconds, and a referee with slide and tape (1966)

Spiral Mandala for clarinets, tuned crystal glasses, and bass drum with four players and chant (1978)

Lion's Eye for Javanese GAMELAN and SAMPLER (1985)

All Fours for the Drum Bum for solo drum set (1990)

WOLFGANG AMADEUS MOZART introduces the ghostly statue of the Commendatore in *DON GIOVANNI* with an ominous TROMBONE passage.

Includes the title song, *Come Back to Me,* and *What Did I Have That I Don't Have Now?*

On Hearing the First Cuckoo in Spring. Symphonic poem by FREDERICK DELIUS, 1913, one of his most popular orchestral works, first performed in Leipzig, 1913. Its style is ROMANTIC, with impressionistic touches.

On the Banks of the Wabash, Far Away. Ballad by Paul Dresser (1868–1906), 1897, describing the place where he grew up. The ballad swept the country and was an enormous hit. In 1913 it was adopted as the state song of Indiana.

On the Good Ship Lollipop. Song by Richard Whiting, 1934. It was made famous by six-year-old Shirley Temple in the movie *Bright Eyes.*

On the Road to Mandalay. Song, 1907, by Oley Speaks (1874–1948). Based on Rudyard Kipling's poem, the song became a great favorite of overweight baritones. Mandalay is in the former Burma.

On the Sunny Side of the Street. Song by Jimmy McHugh, with lyrics by Dorothy Fields, 1930, featured in the *International Revue.* It was subsequently used in several movies as a sentimental declaration of an optimistic philosophy of life.

On the Town. Musical by LEONARD BERNSTEIN, 1944, his first, premiered in Boston. The score is an adaptation of his BALLET *Fancy Free* (1944). It deals with the amorous frolics of three sailors on leave in N.Y. The famous opening episode pictures the city in the number *New York, New York.*

On Top of Old Smokey. A mountain folk song popularized in 1951 by PETE SEEGER, originally known as *Little Mohee.* Satirized by Tom Glazer as *On Top of Spaghetti* ("all covered with cheese/I lost my poor meatball/When somebody sneezed") to become a No. 14 hit in 1963.

On Your Toes. Musical by RICHARD RODGERS and LORENZ HART, 1936. A lowly vaudeville hoofer decides to get class through classical ballet but fails utterly at it. On the advice of a Russian ballerina, he stages a modern dance show under the topical title *Slaughter on Tenth Avenue,* which scores an immediate hit. The music that accompanied this ballet sequence, a symphonic JAZZ poem, remains popular. The song *There's a Small Hotel* has also remained a favorite.

Once upon a Mattress. Musical by Mary Rodgers (b. N.Y., Jan. 11, 1931), daughter of RICHARD RODGERS, 1959. The story is taken from the classical fairy tale by the Brothers Grimm, *The Princess and the Pea.*

A queen wishes to make sure that her son marries a real princess. When a bedraggled girl arrives at the palace after a journey from her own land, the prince is charmed by her. The wily queen subjects her to an unfailing test of lineage by placing a pea under 20 mattresses in the bed the girl is to sleep on, since only a real princess would be sensitive to this encumbrance and be unable to sleep. Surprisingly, the girl passes. Only after her engagement to the prince is announced is the horrible truth discovered: the sympathetic court jester filled the mattresses with all kinds of sharp metal objects. But by now the prince loves her too much to give her up.

Ondes Martenot. An ELECTRONIC KEYBOARD instrument named after its French inventor, MAURICE MARTENOT. He originally named it the *Ondes musicales.* It was first exhibited in Paris in 1928. Several works have been written for it, including ANDRÉ JOLIVET's full-fledged concerto (1947).

One Touch of Venus. Musical by KURT WEILL, 1943. A romantic New Yorker puts the engagement ring he has bought for his best girl on the little finger of a statue of Venus in an art museum. The love goddess becomes imbued with a vital spark and makes a tour of N.Y. with her bemused companion. In the end he returns to his fiancée-to-be, and Venus is restored to her rightful place in the art gallery.

Includes the songs *Speak Low* and *I'm a Stranger Here Myself.*

Ono, Yoko, Japanese-born American vocalist, songwriter, and performance artist; b. Tokyo, Feb. 18, 1933. Ono was

MUSICAL INSTRUMENT

PEOPLE IN MUSIC

born to a wealthy banking family. In 1947 she moved to N.Y., where she entered Sarah Lawrence College in 1953. She became active in Manhattan conceptual-art circles, notably the FLUXUS group. She made films, performance pieces, and artwork that invited audience participation.

In 1966 Ono met JOHN LENNON of the BEATLES. They became companions and collaborators, eventually marrying in 1969. Under her influence, Lennon became interested in avant-garde ideas that drew him away from rock, contributing to the breakup of the Beatles in 1970. Ono also became interested in rock music, and the two often performed together. After Lennon's death in 1980, Ono produced several posthumous albums.

Ono's work is often bizarre, her shrill TREMOLO voice moving over a fluid, arrhythmic background reflecting Asian influences. Some of her recordings, notably those between 1980 and 1984, are more popular in style. A musical retrospective of her career was issued in the early 1990s as the CD set called *Onobox*.

onomatopoeia. Imitations of natural or industrial sounds in music. These abound in CLASSIC, ROMANTIC, and MODERN MUSIC.

Familiar examples are the thunderstorms of LUDWIG VAN BEETHOVEN's *Pastoral Symphony* and in the overture to GIOACCHINO ROSSINI's opera *WILLIAM TELL* (1829). Bird calls are natural resources for musical imagination, such as in the famous "Spring" concerto of ANTONIO VIVALDI's *Four Seasons*.

Sounds of industry were reproduced with varying degrees of verisimilitude in numerous modern works. In his *PACIFIC 231* (1924), ARTHUR HONEGGER created a stimulating impression of an American locomotive gathering speed by the simple device of increasing the number of accented beats in each successive bar. The whirring of an early airplane propeller is realistically imitated in a piece entitled *The Aeroplane* (1920) by the American composer Emerson Whithorne. The Italian Futurists attempted to emulate the noises of 20th-century city life by the use of megaphones.

The stroke of midnight is sounded by the chimes in the score of MODEST MUSSORGSKY's *Night on Bald Mountain* (1867). The clatter of steel-making is realistically illustrated by the shaking of a sheet of metal in the ballet *Iron Foundry* (1927) by the Soviet composer Alexander Mosolov.

A realistic piece of grim onomatopoeia occurs in *Robespierre's Overture* (1856) by Henry Charles Litolff, in which the fall of Robespierre's head after his execution on the guillotine is rendered by a thud of the bass drum.

Amusing attempts to illustrate a sneeze are found in *THE NOSE* (1930) by DMITRI SHOSTAKOVICH and *HÁRY JÁNOS* (1926) by ZOLTÁN KODÁLY.

Only You. The Platters' DOO-WOP classic, originally recorded in 1955, and quickly covered by a white group, the Hilltoppers. The Platters sang it in the Bill Haley teen flick *Rock Around the Clock.*

oompah(-pah). An onomatopoeic vocable to describe an alternating TONIC and the DOMINANT bass line as played by the TUBA, OPHICLEIDE, SERPENT, and other deep bass instruments. This is particularly found in marches and galops, as played by military bands.

open form. *See* MOBILE FORM.

open form composition. Open form composition often delegates the ordering of component parts of a piece to the performer. Among the first to develop such techniques was the American composer EARLE BROWN, whose *Folio* (1952) allows the performers great latitude in arranging given materials.

KARLHEINZ STOCKHAUSEN further developed this technique in his *Klavierstücke,* consisting of separate sections that can be performed in any order. TERRY RILEY's now-classic *IN C* (1965) inspired an entire generation of MINIMALISTS. In it, notated fragments are played any number of times at will by the members of the ensemble.

open harmony. In FOUR-PART HARMONY, an arrangement of voices such that the three upper voices have a total range of more than an OCTAVE (as in C, G, E, C). Open harmony is most suitable for choral writing, as opposed to CLOSE HARMONY, which is easier for keyboard harmony.

open string. On any CHORDOPHONE with a FINGERBOARD, a string in its natural, unstopped state; similarly, it is played

MUSICAL
INSTRUMENT

without being stopped by the finger. When an open string is to be played, a small circle is placed above the note. Because the sound of open strings are so distinctive from STOPPED notes, they are avoided in melodic passages. They become increasingly essential in double-, triple-, and quadruple-stops.

Some works exploit open strings for reasons of sound or symbolism. CAMILLE SAINT-SAËNS builds his *Danse macabre* (1875) on the open strings of the solo violin, suggesting a witch tuning her fiddle. ALBAN BERG insists on open strings in passages of his Violin Concerto (1936). A string quartet falsely attributed to Benjamin Franklin, the manuscript of which was discovered in 1945, is written entirely for open strings so that even beginners could play it. But the strings are tuned in an unusual way to allow unexpected and even DISSONANT harmonics to be formed.

opera. A form of drama, of Italian origin, in which vocal and instrumental music are essential and predominant. The several acts, often preceded by instrumental introductions,

Paris Bastille Opera House, 1994. (Owen Franken/Corbis)

consist of vocal scenes, RECITATIVES, songs, ARIAS, duets, trios, choruses, etc., accompanied by the orchestra. This is the *grand* or *heroic* opera.

A *comic* opera is a versified comedy set to music; an OPERETTA or SINGSPIEL has spoken interludes.

opera buffa (It.; Fr. *opéra bouffe*). Comic opera, as opposed to OPERA SERIA. In a typical cast there are standard comic characters, some of which are borrowed from the COMMEDIA DELL'ARTE.

    Opera buffa thrives on schemes and strategems found in comedies of Shakespeare, Molière, and other classics of dramatic literature. Such plays are filled with mistaken identities, disguises, deceptions, and intrigues, but virtue triumphs in the end. The dupes forgive their tormentors, young couples are united, and the spirit of entertainment overcomes all the stumbling blocks of blatant absurdities.

ôh′pā-răh boof′fah

opéra comique (Fr.). French opera with spoken dialogue instead of RECITATIVE, not necessarily humorous in nature. The music of these operas was of a light dramatic texture, often introducing concepts of morality and proper social behavior.

    In 19th-century France, opéra-comique denoted opera with spoken dialogue. The Paris Opéra-Comique was originally the theater intended for the production of French dramatic works that contained musical numbers and spoken dialogues in about equal measure. But this opera house also saw productions, such as GEORGES BIZET's *Carmen* (1875), which could hardly be called comical.

ŏh-pā-răh kŏh-mēk′

opera in musica (It., musical work; usually abbrev. to *opera*). A dramatic presentation for singers and instruments performing in costume on the stage. Spoken dialogue may alternate with musical sections.

opera seria (It.). Serious (grand, heroic, tragic) opera. It is virtually identical with the concept of grand opera. It denotes an eloquent music drama replete with emotional upheavals, tragic conflicts, scenes of triumph and disaster, with insanity, murders, and suicides filling the action. By tradition, an opera seria ought to have at least three acts but may well extend into five. It can also include BALLET. Its opposite is OPERA BUFFA.

ŏh-pā-răh sā′rē-ăh

operetta (It.; Fr. *opérette*). A "little opera" in which the libretto is in a comic, mock-pathetic, parodistic, or anything-

ŏh-pĕh-rĕt′tăh

but-serious vein. The music is light and lively, often inter-rupted by dialogue.

ŏf′ĭ′klīd

ophicleide (from Grk. *ophis* + *kleidos,* serpent with keys; Fr. *ophicléide;* Ger. *Ophikleide;* It. *oficleide*). A large, deep-toned keyed BUGLE with U-shaped conical tube with slightly flared bell and cup mouthpiece, invented c.1817.

George Bernard Shaw volunteers that his uncle played it and then "perished by his own hand." The ophicleide itself became extinct shortly after Shaw's uncle's suicide and was replaced by the tuba.

MUSICAL
INSTRUMENT

opus (Lat., abbrev. *Op.* or *op.*). Work. *Opus number,* the number assigned for chronological identification of a work, or group of works, by a particular composer.

Unfortunately, composers and their publishers seldom were entirely accurate in coordinating the chronology with the opus numbers. For instance, FRÉDÉRIC CHOPIN's Piano Concerto in F minor (composed 1829–30), bearing the opus number 21, was actually composed a year earlier than his Piano Concerto in E minor, which bears the opus number 11. Sometimes, competing publishers would have their own sets of opus numbers for a particular composer, thus creating more than one op.1, op.2, etc. The use of opus numbers became an established practice in the 19th century, but it fell off among many modern composers.

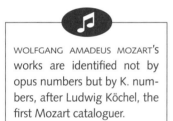

WOLFGANG AMADEUS MOZART's works are identified not by opus numbers but by K. numbers, after Ludwig Köchel, the first Mozart cataloguer.

ōh-răh-tô′rē-ōh

oratorio (It.). An extended, more or less dramatic composi-tion for vocal solos and chorus, with accompaniment by orchestra and/or organ, sung without stage play or scenery. The genre, known also as *historia,* developed in 17th-century Italy as a way for operatic composers to keep busy during Lent, when theaters were closed.

PEOPLE IN MUSIC

Orbison, Roy (Kelton), American rock singer, guitarist, and songwriter; b. Wink, Tex., April 23, 1936; d. Henderson-ville, Tenn., Dec. 6, 1988. He studied geology at North Texas State College. After performing with local rockabilly bands, he began a recording career in 1956. He also was ac-tive as a songwriter in Nashville. Roy possessed an excellent lyric tenor voice, unusual among the common breed of rockers. His song OH, PRETTY WOMAN became his signature tune. He also had hits with *Crying* and *Blue Bayou.*

Shortly before his death in 1988, he joined George Harrison, BOB DYLAN, Tom Petty and Jeff Lynne to produce the album *The Traveling Wilburys,* on which he added prominent vocals to the songs *Not Alone Anymore, End of the Line,* and *Handle with Care.* He also recorded a final solo album produced by Jeff Lynne, which provided a minor hit with *You Got It,* revived in 1995 by Bonnie Raitt.

orchestra (Ger. *Orchester;* Fr. *orchestre*). A company of musicians performing on the instruments usually employed in opera, oratorio, or symphony. Hence, also the instruments taken together. *Orchestral,* pertaining to, or resembling, the orchestra.

orchestration. The art of writing music for performance by an orchestra. The science of combining, in an effective manner, the instruments constituting the orchestra.

orchestrion. A large stationary BARREL ORGAN, generally played by clockwork.

Ordinary (Lat. *Ordinarium*). In the Roman Catholic High MASS, the sung sections with fixed texts: KYRIE, GLORIA, CREDO, SANCTUS, AGNUS DEI (and the closing *Ite, missa est* or *Benedicamus Domino*). These sections are interwoven with the PROPRIUM, with changing texts according to the church calendar.

ordre. A term used by FRANÇOIS COUPERIN and other French musicians for a group of KEYBOARD pieces in the manner of the instrumental SUITE.

The ordre usually contains, in addition to the traditional movements of the suite, pieces with whimsical descriptive titles, designed to appeal to the amateurs who played them, such as *Les petits moulins à vent* (The small windmills), *Les Barricades mystérieuses* (The mysterious barricades), etc.

Orfeo ed Euridice. "Azione teatrale per musica" by CHRISTOPH WILLIBALD GLUCK, 1762, first produced in Vienna in

MUSICAL INSTRUMENT

Italian, with the part of Orfeo sung by the famous CASTRATO Gaetano Guadagni.

The work acquired its greatest historical significance after its performance with a French LIBRETTO in Paris in 1774. It demonstrated Gluck's doctrine of subordinating music to the text so as to achieve the maximum degree of dramatic verity.

The story follows the Greek myth of the singer Orpheus trying to recover his beloved Euridice from the land of death and losing her when he fails to obey the injunction not to look back at Hell's entrance.

The customary BALLET required of all works at the Paris Opéra is fulfilled by the famous *Dance of the Blessed Spirits.*

Orfeo, L'. A "fable in music" by CLAUDIO MONTEVERDI, 1607, first performed privately in Mantua. The LIBRETTO follows the familiar legend of Orpheus trying to recover his beloved Euridice from Hades.

For aesthetic reasons, Monteverdi omitted the original ending, the dismembering of Orpheus by a crazed mob. Instead, Orpheus is taken to Elysium by Apollo. The historical significance of *L'Orfeo* lies in its skillful alternation of MONODY and more old-fashioned textures, providing the first balanced approach to early opera.

Also of interest is its orchestration, which includes CLAVICEMBALOS, HARPS, TROMBONES, CORNETS, a CLARINO, RECORDERS, ORGANS, and a large contingent of string instruments.

PEOPLE IN MUSIC

Orff, Carl, outstanding German composer; b. Munich, July 10, 1895; d. there, March 29, 1982. Orff attended the Munich Academy of Music, graduating in 1914. He later had additional instruction in Munich from the leading German composer Heinrich Kaminski.

From 1915 to 1917 Orff was a conductor at the Munich Kammerspiele. After military service during World War I, he conducted at the Mannheim National Theater and the Darmstadt Landestheater in 1918–19. He was conductor of Munich's Bach Society from 1930 to 1933.

Orff developed a highly important method of musical education, which was adopted not only in Germany but in England, America, and Russia. It stemmed from the Günther School for gymnastics, dance, and music that Orff cofounded in 1924 with dancer Dorothee Günther in Munich, with the aim of promoting instrumental playing and understanding of rhythm among children.

Orff commissioned the piano manufacturer Karl Maendler to construct special percussion instruments that would be easier for children to play. These "Orff instruments" became widely adopted in American schools. Orff's ideas of rhythmic training owe much to the EURHYTHMICS of ÉMILE JAQUES-DALCROZE, but he simplified them to reach the elementary level. As a manual, he compiled a set of musical exercises, *Schulwerk* (Schoolwork; 1930–35; revised 1950–54). He also taught composition at the Munich Staatliche Hochschule für Musik from 1950 to 1955.

As a composer, Orff sought to revive and adapt the early music forms to modern tastes by means of DISSONANT COUNTERPOINT, with lively rhythm in asymmetrical patterns. His most famous score is the scenic oratorio *CARMINA BURANA,* from 1937. Its words (in Latin and middle German) are taken from 13th-century student poems found in the Benediktbeuren monastery in Bavaria.

Orff's other works were primarily for the stage, including operas, musical plays, and vocal works. He also wrote three stage works in 1925 after works by CLAUDIO MONTEVERDI: *Klage der Ariadne, Orpheus,* and *Tanz der Spröden,* all three of which were revised in 1940.

organ (Ger. *Orgel;* Fr. *orgue;* It. *organa*). The pipe organ is the largest keyboard instrument. Its very appearance is most imposing with its several rows of vertical pipes, usually arranged in a tasteful symmetrical position.

The pipes, of which there are two main divisions—FLUTE and REED—are made to speak by wind admitted from the bellows upon pressing the keys. The organ has two or more MANUALS or keyboards and a complex system of STOPS or registers that govern the tone color. It also has a pedal keyboard. A master organist must therefore be a virtuoso with the feet as well as the hands.

Modern organs usually have five keyboards or manuals:

The most prominent manual bears the proud name of the Great Organ, which is supplied with the loudest stops.

MUSICAL
INSTRUMENT

Manufacturing an organ, 1937. (Hulton-Deutsch Collection/ Corbis) ▶

The second manual is the Swell Organ, which enables the organist to produce a tremendous CRESCENDO.

The third manual is called Choir Organ. It is used for the purpose of accompaniment.

The fourth manual, the Solo Organ, is designed to bring out a special instrumental tone color.

The fifth manual, the Echo Organ, produces the effect of a distant sound.

The manuals are arranged in staircaselike steps, so that the Great Organ is the nearest to the player, and the Echo Organ the highest up. The order of the lower manuals may differ depending on the manufacturer.

The PEDAL ORGAN sounds an octave below the manuals. The stops of the pedal are so fixed that the sound may be lowered two and even three octaves. The stops are named according to the sizes of the sets of pipes that they activate. The normal pitch of the manual commands an eight-foot stop, called the *open diapason* stop, which opens a pipe approximately eight feet long. Other pipes, four feet and two feet long, sound, respectively, an octave or two octaves higher. In the low range, there is a 16-foot pipe and a 32-

foot pipe, and even a 64-foot pipe, which will produce sounds two, three, and four octaves lower than the given note. Both the manuals and the pedals possess special stops that can bring into play upper or lower octaves, or indeed all of them together, producing a gigantic unison that lends the particular magnificence to a cathedral organ.

And that is not all. There are COUPLERS by which two manuals can be connected, so that the organist can amplify the sound by playing on only one of these coupled manuals. And it is also possible to double the sound an octave above or below by using these couplers. Furthermore, the organist can prepare the REGISTRATION, the system of stops, in advance in order to start playing in octaves or double octaves, both in the manuals and in the pedals, and in desired tone colors. Special registers or stops can be interconnected selectively or for the entire organ.

The names of the organ stops provide a whole inventory of acoustical terms. The king of the stops is the DIAPASON STOP, which implies a totality of tones (*diapason* means "through all" in Greek). Metaphorically, the word can be used in the same sense as GAMUT, meaning the entire compass of audible sounds from the lowest to the highest. Other stops are named after the instruments they attempt to duplicate (flute, oboe, clarinet, bassoon, strings, etc.). Two registrations have poetic names—*vox angelica* and *vox humana*. Obviously, the first is supposed to convey the impressions of an angel singing solo, and the second a human.

Large organs traditionally were placed in great cathedrals, to fill the halls with their massive sound, "to the glory of God." In the U.S., electronic organs have found a place in such varied venues as the large-scale motion picture palaces of the '20s and '30s to the roller rinks of the '50s. Today's modern cathedrals—baseball stadiums—make use of massive electronic organs, often playing repeated patterns, to inspire the fans and players to new levels of excitement.

The expression "pulling out all the stops" comes from the organ literature, to mean to play an organ with all of its many forces working at the same time. (The metaphor obviously has sarcastic connotations when applied to a salesman or politician.)

organetto (It.). 1. A PORTATIVE ORGAN, used in the MEDIEVAL and RENAISSANCE periods. It is placed on the left knee and played as a melody instrument with the right hand, while the left hand operates the bellows. 2. Street or BARREL ORGAN.

MUSICAL INSTRUMENT

organista (Lat.). 1. Organ player. 2. Composer of ORGANUM; Leoninus was praised as *optimus organista.*

MUSICAL
INSTRUMENT

organistrum. Medieval HURDY-GURDY in a fiddle shape with three strings.

organized sound. Sound is an acoustical phenomenon, which by itself does not make music. COMPOSITION begins at the point when two sounds are connected horizontally (as a series of NOTES forming a MELODY) or vertically (as two or more notes played at the same time; i.e., HARMONY or COUNTERPOINT).

The rules of composition have changed over the centuries. What was once considered musical sin—such as the Medieval fear of the TRITONE (the diminished fifth)—is now considered ordinary practice.

In the 20th century, all rules were overthrown. To avoid the associations with the word *music,* experimental composer EDGARD VARÈSE advanced the concept of organized sound. In his view, this term described any progression of acoustic phenomena—even noise—that is formed into a coherent work by a composer.

ôr′găn-ŭm

MUSICAL
INSTRUMENT

organum (Lat.). 1. An ORGAN. 2. The earliest attempts at harmonic or POLYPHONIC music. This practice first developed between 900 and 1200 A.D. Its earliest forms consisted of a TENOR part, with the addition of one, two, or at most three contrapuntal parts. The only INTERVALS used were OCTAVES and FIFTHS, but perfect FOURTHS resulted when the fifth note was inserted between two octave points. This was known as *parallel organum.*

To the modern ear, this type of counterpoint may at first sound extremely mechanical and unsatisfying. However, the masters of organum were much freer in their harmonizations than the naked definitions implied. Indeed, CONTRARY (one voice moves up while the other moves down) and OBLIQUE (one voice moves while the other remains stationary) motion between the tenor and the contrapuntal voices were introduced as soon as the practice spread in general church usage. It became possible, then, to move from an octave to a fifth in contrary motion, and vice versa, and even use DISSONANT passing tones when moving from one "legitimate" interval to another.

The 13th century saw the development of *melismatic organum,* in which contrapuntal parts were assigned florid passages while the principal voice continued to hold the original tone—hence the term TENOR for that voice, i.e., a "tenant," or "one who holds." With the advent of MENSURAL counterpoint and notation, the art of organum became a complex discipline of polyphonic writing. The most notable achievements in this highly developed organum were reached by the two great masters of the NOTRE DAME SCHOOL in Paris, LEONINUS and PEROTIN. The peak of the organum era of composition was achieved with the impressive *organum quadruplum,* in which the principal voice was accompanied by three intricate contrapuntal voices.

Ormandy, Eugene (born Jenö Blau), outstanding Hungarian-born American conductor; b. Budapest, Nov. 18, 1899; d. Philadelphia, March 12, 1985. Ormandy studied violin with his father. He entered the Royal Academy of Music in Budapest at the age of 5 and received an artist's diploma at 13. He received a teacher's certificate in 1917, then was concertmaster of the Blüthner Orchestra in Germany. He also gave recitals and played with orchestras as a soloist.

PEOPLE IN MUSIC

◀

Eugene Ormandy, c. 1955. (Library of Congress/Corbis)

In 1921 he went to the U.S. In 1924 he made his conducting debut with the Capitol Theater Orchestra, N.Y., where he became concertmaster, remaining for two and a half years. In 1929 he conducted the N.Y. Philharmonic at

Lewisohn Stadium and in 1930 became guest conductor with the Robin Hood Dell Orchestra, Philadelphia. In 1931 he conducted the Philadelphia Orchestra for the first time. That same year, he was appointed music director of the Minneapolis Symphony Orchestra.

In 1936 Ormandy was engaged as associate conductor of the Philadelphia Orchestra (with LEOPOLD STOKOWSKI), becoming its music director in 1938. He remained with the orchestra until his retirement, becoming its most famous conductor. He traveled with it on numerous transcontinental tours from 1937 to 1977, making an extended tour in England in 1949. In the spring of 1955 he presented concerts with it in 10 European countries. In the summer of 1958 he led it on another European tour (including Russia). In 1973 he took the Philadelphia Orchestra to China and led it in several cities there. This marked the first appearance of an American symphony orchestra in the People's Republic of China.

Ormandy was given numerous international awards and honorary degrees. In 1970 he received the Presidential Medal of Freedom. In 1976 he was named an honorary Knight Commander of the Order of the British Empire by Queen Elizabeth II in honor of the American Bicentennial.

In his interpretations, Ormandy revealed himself as a ROMANTICIST. He excelled in the works of LUDWIG VAN BEETHOVEN, ROBERT SCHUMANN, and RICHARD STRAUSS, conducting all scores from memory.

After 42 seasons as music director of the Philadelphia Orchestra, Ormandy retired at the close of the 1979–80 season and was named conductor laureate.

Ormindo. Opera by PIER FRANCESCO CAVALLI, 1644, premiered in Venice at Carnival time. Two young army men are in love with the queen of the land. The king discovers the intrigue but forgives the youthful adventurers. *Ormindo* is one of the earliest extant MONODIC operas.

ornament (Ger. *Verzierungen*). A GRACE NOTE, an embellishment.

ornamentation (Ger. *Verzierung;* Fr. *agréments;* It. *fioretti*). The art of ornamenting a composition.

While composers have added many indications to scores as to how they wish a piece of music to be played, it is not always clear what was originally intended. Moreover, in EARLY MUSIC scores there is little guidance for the player. For this reason, scholars have attempted to come up with general rules for ornamentation. However, this remains very much an individual choice among players.

Ornamente. Piano piece by BORIS BLACHER, 1950, in which he introduced VARIABLE METERS. Blacher used this technique in the 1953 *Orchester Ornament,* a SUITE in three movements, first performed in Venice.

Orontea. Opera by ANTONIO CESTI, 1659, premiered in Innsbruck in Italian. The story deals with a seriocomic confusion between princely characters and their lowly servants. One of the servants, Orontea, turns out to be a princess in her own right who was registered in the wrong column in the church birth records. The style is MONODIC, the dialogue mostly in RECITATIVE, and there is no CHORUS.

Orphée aux enfers (Orpheus in hell). OPERETTA by JACQUES OFFENBACH, 1858, first produced in Paris, his first major success.

The gods of Olympus are here exposed as bumbling creatures intent on having their pleasure on earth rather than in heaven. The score includes a can-can, which shocked the sensibilities of some proper Parisians.

CAMILLE SAINT-SAËNS borrows the can-can from *Orphée aux enfers,* in his CARNIVAL OF THE ANIMALS (composed 1886), in the section called *Tortoise.* The connection here is that Orpheus made his lute out of a tortoise shell.

Orphéon. A 19th-century French choral society with a membership recruited mainly among AMATEURS. It was named, of course, after the mythical singer Orpheus, whose art could enchant humans and animals alike and move inanimate objects. The Orphéon became an important branch of musical education in France. Several periodicals were published devoted to its activities, among them *La France Orphéonique* and *L'Echo des Orphéons.* CHARLES GOUNOD, HECTOR BERLIOZ, and other notable composers wrote pieces for the group.

In Barcelona, the Orfeo Catalan was organized with the purpose of performing choral and other music. In Brazil, Heitor Villa-Lobos founded an "Orpheonic concentration," in which thousands of schoolchildren participated. In England, an Orpheonic Choral Festival was staged in 1860, with the participation of thousands.

Toward the end of the 19th century, the extent of activities of the original French Orphéon abated. In the 20th century, the movement itself went into decline.

Orpheus. BALLET by IGOR STRAVINSKY, 1948, first performed in N.Y. It is written in the NEOCLASSICAL style.

Ory, "Kid" (Edward), African-American jazz trombonist and bandleader; b. La Place, La., Dec. 25, 1886; d. Honolulu, Jan. 23, 1973. Ory played the BANJO as a child, then took up TROMBONE. He first played in the famous band led by "KING" OLIVER and then joined LOUIS ARMSTRONG's Hot Five and Seven. After a hiatus in performing from 1933 to 1942, he organized his own band and toured Europe from 1956 to 1959.

Ory was known for his "tailgate" style of trombone playing. In this style, the player slides up to the melody note in a dramatic style. He also composed the well-known *Muskrat Ramble.*

oscillator. An ELECTRONIC device used to produce a WAVE FORM.

ōh-stē-nah′tōh

The vendor's cry "fresh strawberries, wild blackberries" is repeated in a French medieval MOTET.

ostinato (It. *obstinate*). A repeated or constant theme that is accompanied by a changing CONTRAPUNTAL part.

Long before the term became part of musical terminology, the practice of repeating the thematic phrase became common in MOTETS and CANONS. Secular motives in MEDIEVAL POLYPHONIC compositions are particularly notable when regarded as early occurrences of ostinato figures.

The true ostinato is the creation of the BAROQUE, and the forms in which it is applied properly and consistently are the PASSACAGLIA, CHACONNE, GROUND BASS, and related forms. In these forms, the ostinato appears invariably in the bass and therefore becomes a true BASSO OSTINATO. The majestic creations of JOHANN SEBASTIAN BACH in these forms are justly compared with the greatest achievements of Gothic architecture or epic poems in literature.

With the decline of the Baroque in the middle of the 18th century, the use of the basso ostinato gradually declines also. In CLASSIC music, melody was queen and the bass her faithful servant. Obviously, such a servant could not be obstinate. Indeed, WOLFGANG AMADEUS MOZART and FRANZ JOSEPH HAYDN found the use of the governing basso ostinato artificial and "unnatural." Samples of *ritmo ostinato* (persistent rhythm) in the bass part are found in Mozart's sacred music, but even in such works a certain variation of rhythmic figures is easily heard.

Interest in the artificial devices of the ostinato technique revived toward the end of the 19th century. The finale of the Fourth Symphony of JOHANNES BRAHMS is a passacaglia. MAX REGER, a Baroque enthusiast, wrote passacaglias to resemble a Bach incarnate. The first opus number by ANTON WEBERN bears the title *Passacaglia*. In his opera *Lulu* (1937), written in the 12-TONE idiom, ALBAN BERG includes a passacaglia movement. Implicit formations peculiar to the ostinato technique may be found in piano works of BÉLA BARTÓK and PAUL HINDEMITH. And, naturally, composers of NEOCLASSICAL music find the ostinato formula very attractive.

Finally, in the 20th century, the ostinato technique has shifted in some cases from the bass to the middle and even melodic voices, as a structurally unifying device. In CARL NIELSEN's Fifth Symphony (1922), the violas play a tremolo of a minor third for the first several minutes of the work. IGOR STRAVINSKY's *PETROUCHKA* and LEOŠ JANÁČEK's Sinfonietta (1926) feature OSTINATO-like melodies. Stravinsky's *THE RITE OF SPRING* (1913) is filled with ostinato figures.

Otello. Opera by GIUSEPPE VERDI, 1887, first produced in Milan. The masterly libretto by Arrigo Boito is generally faithful to Shakespeare's play, from which it is derived, and the Italian text is exemplary. (The spelling Otello, without an *h,* is proper in Italian.)

Otello is a Moor who leads the Venetian army to victories over the Turks. Provoked by Iago, his malicious aide-de-camp, he suspects his wife Desdemona of infidelity and strangles her. When he finds out his monstrous error he stabs himself to death.

Vladimir Bogachov (Otello) and Kallen Esperian (Desdemona) in a 1994 production of Otello. *(Robbie Jack/Corbis)* ▶

The opera, which Verdi completed at the age of 73, is remarkable for its departure from the style and idiom of his previous operas. Instead, it points the way toward the modern concept of MUSIC DRAMA.

Otello, ossia Il Moro di Venezia. Opera by GIOACCHINO ROSSINI, 1816, after Shakespeare, first produced in Naples. While revivals have occurred on occasion, it cannot match the musical and popular success of GIUSEPPE VERDI's opera on the same source.

ottava (It.). OCTAVE. *All' ottava* (written *8ᵛᵃ*------ or *8*------), "at the octave," an octave higher; *coll' ottava,* "with the octave," that is, in octaves; *ottava alta,* the higher octave; *ottava bassa* (*8ᵛᵃ bassa*), the lower octave, an octave below.

PEOPLE IN MUSIC

Otter, Anne-Sofie von, Swedish mezzosoprano; b. Stockholm, May 9, 1955. Otter began her training at the Stockholm Musikhogskölan, then studied with Erik Werba in Vienna and Geoffrey Parsons in London, and later with Vera Rozsa.

In 1982 Otter joined the Basel Opera, and in 1984 she sang at the Aix-en-Provence Festival. She made her first appearance at London's Covent Garden in 1985 as Cherubino. That same year she made her U.S. debut as soloist in WOLFGANG AMADEUS MOZART's C-minor Mass with the Chicago Symphony Orchestra. In 1987 she sang at La Scala in Milan and at the Bavarian State Opera in Munich. In 1988 she appeared as Cherubino at the Metropolitan Opera in N.Y. In 1989 she made her first appearance at the Salzburg Festival as Marguerite in LA DAMNATION DE FAUST with GEORGE SOLTI and the Chicago Symphony Orchestra. In 1992 she returned to Salzburg to sing Ramiro. On May 6, 1998, she made her Carnegie Hall recital debut in N.Y.

Otter sang widely as a soloist with major orchestras and as a recitalist. Her other roles include Gluck's Orfeo, Mozart's Idamantes and Dorabella, Tchaikovsky's Olga, and Strauss's Octavian.

oud. *See* 'Ūd.

Over the Rainbow. Song by HAROLD ARLEN and E. Y. HARBURG, 1939. It was made extraordinarily popular by JUDY GARLAND in the film *The Wizard of Oz.*

Over There. Celebrated patriotic song by GEORGE M. COHAN, 1917, written shortly after the U.S. entered the war against Germany. It sold over two million copies of sheet music and over a million phonograph records. ENRICO CARUSO sang it for the American troops. It was featured in Cohan's movie biography, *Yankee Doodle Dandy* (1942).

overblowing. With wind instruments, forcing the wind through the tube in such a way as to cause any HARMONIC to sound, in order to play the upper REGISTERS.

overstring. To arrange the strings of a piano in two sets, one lying over and diagonally crossing the other. A piano so strung is called an *overstrung* piano, in comparison to a *vertical* one. This technique is used primarily in spinet or upright pianos, in order to fit the long bass strings into a smaller box.

overtone (overtone series; Ger. *Oberton*). *See* HARMONICS.

overture (from Fr. *ouverture,* opening). 1. (Ger. *Ouvertüre*) Alternate name for the BAROQUE instrumental SUITE. 2. Originally, a musical introduction to a play, opera, or bal-

MUSICAL INSTRUMENT

Cohan received the Congressional Medal of Honor for writing *Over There.*

let. In the 19th century, the overture also became an independent concert piece, the CONCERT OVERTURE.

An overture to an OPERA served often as a thematic table of contents, with the tunes of the most important ARIAS, CHORUSES, and instrumental INTERLUDES passing in review and preparing the listener for the melodic joys to come during the course of the work itself.

As a musical form, the overture made its first appearance in France in the 17th century. The practice of JEAN-BAPTISTE LULLY gave rise to a special form of the FRENCH OVERTURE, which consisted of two contrasting sections, the first being in a slow tempo marked by dotted rhythms and concluding on the DOMINANT of the principal key, and the second in a faster tempo, often culminating in a fugal development. This BINARY form later expanded into a TERNARY (three-part) structure by the simple expedient of returning to the initial slow part, varied at will. The French overture was also much in use in instrumental suites.

In the 18th century, the French overture went into decline and was replaced by the more vivacious ITALIAN OVERTURE. The slow movement was placed in the middle between two fast sections. Such a formation was obviously more exhilarating to the listener than the French genre in which the overture began and ended with a slow section.

In early Italian operas, the overture was called a SINFONIA, that is, an instrumental section without singing, and, in more recent times, a PRELUDIO. The type of "summary overture" that incorporates materials from the opera itself is exemplified by WOLFGANG AMADEUS MOZART's overtures to *DON GIOVANNI* and *THE MAGIC FLUTE,* LUDWIG VAN BEETHOVEN's three *LEONORE Overtures,* CARL MARIA VON WEBER's *DER FREISCHÜTZ* overture, any overture by GIACOMO MEYERBEER, and virtually all overtures by Russian composers of the 19th century.

RICHARD WAGNER's overtures to his early operas and *DIE MEISTERSINGER* belonged to the category of "summary overtures." However, in his MUSIC DRAMAS of the later period, and particularly in *DER RING DES NIBELUNGEN,* he abandoned the idea of using material from the opera itself and returned to a type of prelude, usually of short duration, to introduce the opera. RICHARD STRAUSS followed the Wagnerian type of introduction in his own operas, and so did a great majority of later opera composers, including GIACOMO PUCCINI and composers of the VERISMO school. Only the Russians of the Soviet period remained faithful to the Italian type of summary overture.

Overtures form an integral part of scores of incidental music for dramatic performances. In numerous cases, operas, even by famous composers, drop out of the repertory, while their overtures continue to have independent lives on the concert stage. Performances of Beethoven's *FIDELIO* are relatively rare, but his *Leonore Overtures* are played constantly. GIOACCHINO ROSSINI's opera *WILLIAM TELL* has virtually disappeared from the repertory, but its overture is one of the most popular pieces of the concert repertory.

Finally, there is the concert overture, neither connected to nor intended for any opera. Among the most famous are *FINGAL'S CAVE* by FELIX MENDELSSOHN, the *Faust Overture* by Wagner, and two by JOHANNES BRAHMS, the *ACADEMIC FESTIVAL Overture* and the *Tragic Overture*. Among overtures in a lighter vein, the concert overture *POET AND PEASANT* by FRANZ VON SUPPÉ achieved a tremendous popularity that showed no signs of abating for well over a century.

The *William Tell* overture is famous as the theme music to the popular radio/television series *The Lone Ranger*.

Owens, "Buck" (Alvis Edgar, Jr.), American country-music singer, guitarist, and songwriter; b. Sherman, Tex., Aug. 12, 1929. Buck got his nickname at age three, after a favorite family horse. The family moved to Mesa, Arizona, when Owens was ten years old. Soon thereafter, Owens took up the MANDOLIN, and then electric GUITAR. He began playing in honky-tonks when he was 16 and married singer Bonnie Campbell a year later (she later became popular as Bonnie Owens).

In 1951 the Owens relocated to Bakersfield, California, where there was a thriving country music scene. Owens partnered with singer Tommy Collins, making a few recordings with him. He made his first solo records in 1955–56 for a small local label.

In 1957 Owens signed with Capitol Records, where he would have most of his hits. His first major country hit was *Under Your Spell Again*. Owens then scored a series of No. 1 country hits from 1963 to 1969, all backed by his group, the

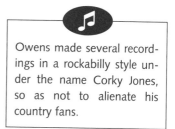

PEOPLE IN MUSIC

Owens made several recordings in a rockabilly style under the name Corky Jones, so as not to alienate his country fans.

Buckaroos. These included *Act Naturally* (1963; covered by the Beatles in 1966), *I've Got A Tiger by the Tail* (1965), and *Waitin' in Your Welfare Line* (1966). Most of Owens's material was upbeat, in a HONKY-TONK vein, marked by his slightly tongue-in-cheek delivery.

From 1969 to 1986 Owens was cohost (with Roy Clark) of the highly popular *Hee Haw* television program. Its combination of cornpone humor and songs made it hugely successful.

In 1988 newcomer star Dwight Yoakam helped revive Owens's career by cutting a duet with him on his *Streets of Bakersfield*.

Ox Minuet (*Ochsenmenuette*). A piece misattributed to FRANZ JOSEPH HAYDN, but actually composed by Ignaz Seyfried as part of his light opera of the same name in 1823.

In an unsubstantiated anecdote, Haydn composed a minuet for his favorite butcher. The butcher asked its name, and Haydn humorously replied, "Ox Minuet." The butcher sent him an ox as a token of gratitude.

While the tune of the minuet was by Seyfried, the rest of the opera was arranged from various authentic tunes by Haydn. Fortunately for Haydn, he was long dead when *The Ox Minuet* was produced.

Oxford Symphony. Symphony No. 92 by FRANZ JOSEPH HAYDN (1789), in the key of G major. The title is misleading, because Haydn did not compose it especially for the university town of Oxford, England, but rather had it performed there during his trip to England. He was rewarded for it by an honorary Doctor of Music degree.

Ozawa, Seiji, brilliant Japanese conductor; b. Fenytien, China (of Japanese parents), Sept. 1, 1935. Ozawa's father was a Buddhist, his mother a Christian. The family returned to Japan in 1944 at the end of the Japanese occupation of Manchuria. Ozawa then began to study piano.

At age 16, Ozawa enrolled at the Toho School of Music in Tokyo, where one of his teachers, Hideo Saito, profoundly influenced his development as a musician. He graduated in 1959 with first prizes in composition and conduct-

PEOPLE IN MUSIC

◄

*Seiji Ozawa, 1968. (UPI/
Corbis-Bettmann)*

ing. By that time he had already conducted concerts with
the NHK (Japan Broadcasting Corporation) Symphony Orchestra and the Japan Philharmonic. Upon Saito's advice, he
went to Europe. To defray his expenses, he became a motor-
scooter salesman for a Japanese firm and promoted the product in Italy and France.

In 1959 Ozawa won first prize at the international competition for conductors in Besançon and was befriended by
CHARLES MUNCH and Eugène Bigot. He then studied conducting with Bigot in Paris. Munch arranged for Ozawa to
go to the U.S. and to study conducting at the Berkshire Music Center in Tanglewood, Massachusetts. In 1960 he won
its Koussevitzky Prize, and was awarded a scholarship to
work with HERBERT VON KARAJAN and the Berlin Philharmonic. LEONARD BERNSTEIN heard him in Berlin and engaged him as an assistant conductor of the N.Y. Philharmonic.

In 1961 Ozawa made his first appearance with the orchestra at Carnegie Hall. Later that year he accompanied
Bernstein and the orchestra on its tour of Japan. In 1962 he
was invited to return as a guest conductor of the NHK Symphony Orchestra, but difficulties arose between him and the
players, who objected to being commanded in an imperious
manner by one of their own countrymen. Still, he succeeded
in obtaining engagements with other Japanese orchestras,
which he conducted on periodic visits to his homeland.

After he served as sole assistant conductor of the N.Y.
Philharmonic in 1964–65, Ozawa's career advanced signifi-

cantly. From 1964 to 1968 he was music director of the Ravinia Festival, the summer home of the Chicago Symphony Orchestra. In 1969 he served as its principal guest conductor. From 1965 to 1969 he also was music director of the Toronto Symphony Orchestra, which he took to England in 1965. From 1970 to 1976 he was music director of the San Francisco Symphony Orchestra and then its music adviser in 1976–77. He took it on an extensive tour of Europe, garnering exceptional critical acclaim.

Even before completing his tenure in San Francisco, Ozawa began a close association with the Boston Symphony Orchestra. With GUNTHER SCHULLER he became co-artistic director of its Berkshire Music Center in 1970, and in 1972 he assumed the post of music adviser of the Boston Symphony Orchestra. In 1973 he became its music director and sole artistic director of the Berkshire Music Center. This was an astonishing event in American music annals, marking the first time an Asian musician was chosen solely by his merit to head the Boston Symphony Orchestra, which since its foundation had been the exclusive preserve of German, and later French and Russian, conductors.

In 1976 Ozawa took the Boston Symphony Orchestra on a tour of Europe. In 1978 he escorted it to Japan, where those among Japanese musicians who had previously been skeptical about his abilities greeted his spectacular ascendance with national pride. Another unprecedented event took place in the spring of 1979, when Ozawa traveled with the Boston Symphony Orchestra to the People's Republic of China. Later that year Ozawa and the orchestra went on a tour of European music festivals.

The centennial of the Boston Symphony Orchestra in 1981 was marked by a series of concerts under Ozawa's direction that included appearances in 14 American cities and a tour of Japan, France, Germany, Austria, and England. On Sept. 24, 1991, he conducted the Saito Kinen Orchestra of Japan at its first appearance in the U.S. at N.Y.'s Carnegie Hall. On Sept. 5, 1992, he inaugurated the Saito Kinen Festival in Matsumoto. He made his Metropolitan Opera debut in N.Y. on Dec. 4, 1992, conducting *Eugene Onegin*. In 1994 the Boston Symphony Orchestra's new concert hall at Tanglewood was named the Seiji Ozawa Hall in his honor.

Ozawa's reputation received universal recognition. He proved himself a consummate master, equally penetrating in the classical and modern repertoire. His performances of such demanding scores as Gustav Mahler's Eighth Symphony and Arnold Schoenberg's *Gurrelieder* constituted proof of his commanding technical skill, which was affirmed by his assured presentation of the rhythmically and contrapuntally intricate Fourth Symphony of CHARLES IVES. All these challenging scores Ozawa conducted from memory, an astonishing feat in itself. He also prepared the Boston Symphony Orchestra for its first performance of John Cage's *101.*

Ozawa was married twice: first to the Japanese pianist Kyoko Edo, and then to a Eurasian, Vera Ilyan. He received honorary doctorates from the University of San Francisco (1971) and the New England Conservatory of Music (1982). His remarkable career was the subject of the documentary film *Ozawa,* telecast by PBS in 1987.

P. Abbreviation for pedal (P.; *Ped.*); pianoforte (*Pf*). Dynamics: start softly, then suddenly loud (*pf*); soft (*p*); softer (*pp*); even softer (*ppp*); loud, then suddenly soft (*fp*); somewhat soft (*mp*); somewhat loud (*mf*).

pachanga, la. A Cuban dance step and song, originally performed by Havana bands playing drums, flutes, piano, and strings. The music resembles a MERENGUE with a refrain. It emerged in the 1960s and superseded the MAMBO and CHACHA in popularity. The name means a wild party in Caribbean slang.

Pachelbel, Johann, celebrated German organist, teacher, and composer; b. Nuremberg (baptized), Sept. 1, 1653; d. there (buried), March 9, 1706. Pachelbel studied music in Nuremberg with Heinrich Schwemmer. He received instruction in composition and instrumental performance from the German organist/composer Georg Caspar Wecker and pursued academic studies at the local St. Lorenz School. He also attended lectures at the Auditorium Aegidianum.

In 1669–70, Pachelbel took courses at the University of Altdorf and served as organist at the Lorenzkirche there. He subsequently was accepted as a scholarship student at the Gymnasium Poeticum in Regensburg and took private music lessons with Kaspar Prentz. In 1673, Pachelbel went to Vienna as deputy organist at St. Stephen's Cathedral. In 1677 he assumed the position of court organist in Eisenach. In 1678 he became organist at the Protestant Predigerkirche in Erfurt.

It was in Erfurt that Pachelbel established his reputation. He was a friend of the Bach family and teacher of Johann Christoph Bach, who in turn taught JOHANN SEBASTIAN

BACH. In 1681, Pachelbel married Barbara Gabler. She and their infant son died during the plague of 1683. He then married Judith Drommer in 1684, with whom he had five sons and two daughters.

In 1690 Pachelbel accepted an appointment as Württemberg court musician and organist in Stuttgart. However, with the French invasion in the fall of 1692, he fled to Nuremberg. In November of that year he became town organist in Gotha. In 1695, he succeeded Wecker as organist at St. Sebald in Nuremberg, a position he held until his death.

Pachelbel was one of the most significant predecessors of Bach. His liturgical organ music was of the highest order, particularly his splendid organ CHORALES. His nonliturgical keyboard music was likewise noteworthy, especially his FUGUES and VARIATIONS (of the latter, his *Hexachordum Apollinis* of 1699 is extraordinary).

Pachelbel was equally gifted as a composer of vocal music. His MOTETS, sacred CONCERTOS, and concertato settings of the MAGNIFICAT are fine examples of German church music. He was a pioneer in using pitch levels to correspond to the meaning of the words. Thus, his setting of the motet *Durch Adams Fall* is accomplished by a falling figure in the bass, exaltation is expressed by a rising series of arpeggios in a major key, steadfast faith is conveyed by a repeated note, and satanic evil is translated into an ominous figuration of a broken diminished-seventh chord. Generally speaking, joyful moods are portrayed by major keys, mournful states of soul by minor keys, a practice that became a standard mode of expression through the centuries.

His organ works include numerous chorales, 95 Magnificat fugues, 26 nonliturgical fugues, 16 toccatas, 7 preludes, 6 fantasias, 6 ciacconas, 3 ricercari, the set of arias with variations called *Hexachordum Apollinis: sex arias exhibens … quam singulis suae sunt subjectae variationes* (1699), 17 suites, and chorale variations. He also composed seven string and basso continuo PARTITAS.

Pachelbel's vocal works include several German motets for two four-part choruses, two Latin motets, sacred German concertos, ARIAS with basso continuo, music for Vespers, Magnificat settings, and two MASSES.

Pachelbel is responsible for the famous Canon and Gigue in D major, for three violins and basso continuo. It has been published and republished in numerous arrangements for various instruments. It is often performed at wedding services.

Honegger explained that he was as passionately infatuated with locomotives as other men are with horses or women.

PEOPLE IN MUSIC

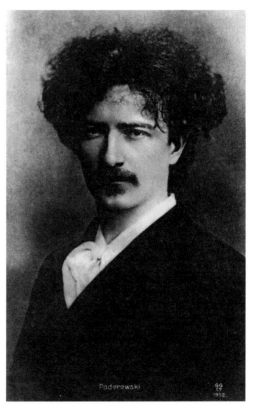

Ignacy Paderewski, c. 1895. (Michael Nicholson/Corbis) ▶

Pacific 231. Symphonic movement by ARTHUR HONEGGER, 1924, first performed in Paris. The designation 231 indicates the number of wheels (2–3–1) on this type of American locomotive.

The score is a highly effective if rudimentary representation of accelerated motion, beginning with one note to a bar, and progressing through two, three, four, five, and six, picking up the tempo as a locomotive gains speed. There is a lyric middle section before *Pacific 231* slows to a stop.

Paderewski, Ignacy (Jan), celebrated Polish pianist and composer; b. Kurylowka, Podolia (Russian Poland), Nov. 18, 1860; d. N.Y., June 29, 1941. Paderewski's father was an administrator of country estates, and his mother died soon after his birth. From early childhood, Paderewski was attracted to piano music. He received some instruction from pianist Peter Sowinski, who taught him four-hand arrangements of operas.

Paderewski's first public appearance was in a charity concert at the age of 11, when he played piano with his sister. His playing aroused interest among wealthy patrons, who took him to Kiev. He was then sent to Warsaw, where he entered the Conservatory, learned to play trombone, and joined the school band. He also continued serious piano study.

In 1875 and 1877 Paderewski toured in provincial Russian towns with a Polish violinist. In the interim periods he took courses in composition at the Warsaw Conservatory, and upon graduation in 1878 he was engaged as a member of its piano faculty. In 1880 he married a young music student named Antonina Korsak, but she died nine days after giving birth to their child later that year.

In 1882 Paderewski went to Berlin to study composition with Friedrich Kiel. There he met ANTON RUBINSTEIN, who gave him encouraging advice and urged him to compose piano music. He resigned from his teaching job at the Warsaw Conservatory and began to study orchestration in Berlin with Heinrich Urban.

While on vacation in the Tatra Mountains (which inspired his *Tatra Album* for piano), Paderewski met the celebrated Polish actress Modjeska, who offered to finance his further piano studies with Theodor Leschetizky in Vienna. After several years as Leschetizky's student, he continued his career as a concert pianist. In 1888 he gave his first Paris recital. Later that year, he played a concert in Vienna. He also began receiving recognition as a composer. Anna Essipoff (Leschetizky's wife) played his piano concerto in Vienna under the direction of HANS RICHTER. Paderewski made his London debut in 1890.

In 1891 Paderewski played for the first time in N.Y. and was greeted with an adulation rare for pianists. By some accounts he gave 107 concerts in 117 days in N.Y. and other American cities and attended 86 dinner parties. His wit, already fully developed, made him a social lion in wealthy American salons.

American ladies beseeched him for a lock of his luxurious mane of hair. He invariably obliged, and when his valet observed that at this rate he would soon be bald, he said, "Not I, my dog." There is even a story related by a gullible biographer that Paderewski could charm beasts by his art and that a spider used to come down from the ceiling in Paderewski's lodgings in Vienna and sit at the piano every time Paderewski played a certain étude by FRÉDÉRIC CHOPIN. Paderewski eclipsed even opera star ENRICO CARUSO as an idol of the masses.

At one party, it was reported, the hostess confused him with a famous polo player who was also expected to be a guest and greeted him effusively. "No," Paderewski is supposed to have replied, "he is a rich soul who plays polo, and I am a poor Pole who plays solo."

In 1890 Paderewski made a concert tour in Germany. He also toured South America, South Africa, and Australia. In 1898 he purchased a beautiful home, the Villa Riond-Bosson, on Lake Geneva, Switzerland. In 1899 he married Helena Gorska, the Baroness von Rosen. In 1900, by a deed of trust, Paderewski established a fund of $10,000, the interest from which was to be used for triennial prizes given "to composers of American birth without distinction as to age or religion" for works in the following categories: symphonies, concertos, and chamber music.

In 1910, on the occasion of the centennial of Chopin's birth, Paderewski donated $60,000 for the construction of the Chopin Memorial Hall in Warsaw. In the same year he contributed $100,000 for the erection of the statue of King Jagiello in Warsaw, on the quinquecentennial of his victory over the Teutonic Knights in 1410. In 1913 he purchased a ranch in Paso Robles, California.

Although cosmopolitan in his culture, Paderewski remained a great Polish patriot. During World War I he donated the entire proceeds from his concerts to a fund for the Polish people caught in the war between Russia and Germany. After the establishment of the independent Polish state, Paderewski served as its representative in Washington, D.C. In 1919 he was named prime minister of the Polish Republic, the first musician to occupy such a post in any country at any period. He took part in the Versailles Treaty conference.

Paderewski resigned his post in late 1919 but reentered politics in 1920 in the wake of the Russian invasion of Poland that year, when he became a delegate to the League of Nations. He resigned in 1921 and resumed his musical career. In 1922 he gave his first concert after a hiatus of many years at CARNEGIE HALL in N.Y.

In 1939 Paderewski made his last American tour. Once more during his lifetime Poland was invaded, this time by both Germany and Russia, and once more Paderewski was driven to political action. He joined the Polish government-in-exile in France and was named president of its parliament in early 1940. He returned to the U.S. later that year, a few months before his death. At the order of President Roosevelt, his body was given state burial in Arlington National

At the Versailles conference, Prime Minister Clemenceau of France welcomed Paderewski with the famous, if possibly apocryphal, remark: "You, a famous pianist, [are now] a prime minister! What a comedown!"

Cemetery, pending the return of his remains to a free Poland.

As an artist Paderewski was a faithful follower of the RO-MANTIC school, which allowed free, almost improvisatory changes from the written notes, tempos, and dynamics. Judged by 20th-century standards of precise rendering of the text, Paderewski's interpretations appear surprisingly unrestrained, but this very personal freedom of performance moved contemporary audiences to ecstasies of admiration. Although his virtuoso technique, which astonished his listeners, has been easily matched by any number of pianists of succeeding generations, his position in the world of the performing arts remains undiminished.

As a composer Paderewski also belongs to the ROMANTIC school. At least one of his piano pieces, the *Menuet in G* (a movement of his set of *Six Humoresques* for piano), achieved enormous popularity. His other compositions, however, never sustained interest and were eventually relegated to the archives of unperformed music. His opera MANRU (1897–1900), dealing with folk life in the Tatra Mountains, was produced in Dresden in 1901 and, a year later, by the Metropolitan Opera in N.Y. Another major work, the B-minor Symphony, was first performed by the Boston Symphony Orchestra in 1909.

Paderewski's other works included the Piano Concerto in A minor (1888), *Fantaisie polonaise* for piano and orchestra (1893), Violin Sonata (1880), songs, and solo piano works.

padovana (It.). A fast dance whose name was used interchangeably with PAVANE, although the latter was more stately.

pǎh-dōh-vah′nǎh

paean. Song of praise or thanksgiving, often used to invoke the spirit of ancient Greece. The term is derived from the Greek *paian,* a reverential epithet found in the Hymn to Apollo.

Paër, Ferdinando. *See* LEONORA.

Paganini, Niccolò (Nicolò), legendary Italian violinist; b. Genoa, Oct. 27, 1782; d. Nice, May 27, 1840. Paganini's father, a poor dockworker, gave him his first lessons on MAN-

PEOPLE IN MUSIC

DOLIN and VIOLIN. He then studied with Giovanni Servetto, a violinist in the theater orchestra. By this time the young Paganini was already composing. He also began to study harmony with Francesco Gnecco and subsequently studied violin with Giacomo Costa, who arranged for him to play in local churches.

Paganini's first documented public appearance took place at the church of S. Filippo Neri in 1794. It was about this time that he first heard the Franco-Polish violin virtuoso Auguste Frederic Durand (later billed as Duranowski), who was a brilliant showman. Paganini later incorporated many of Durand's tricks into his own performance style.

Having made phenomenal progress in his studies, Paganini was sent to Parma in 1795 to study with Alessandro Rolla. Upon Paganini's arrival there, Rolla is reported to have told him that there was nothing left to teach him and suggested that he study composition with Ferdinando Paër instead. Paër, in turn, sent him to his own teacher, Gasparo Ghiretti. After study with both Ghiretti and Paër, Paganini returned to Genoa in 1796, appearing as a violinist in private performances.

A caricature of Niccolò Paganini. (Library of Congress/Corbis)

SIGNOR PAGANINI,
The Celebrated Violin Performer on One String.

With Napoleon's invasion of Italy, the Paganini family moved to Ramairone. By 1800 Paganini was with his father in Livorno, where he gave concerts. He also appeared in Modena. They returned to Genoa in 1801. That same year, in the company of his older brother Carlo, also a violinist, he made a brilliant and successful appearance in Lucca at the

Festival of Santa Croce. He settled there, becoming concert-master of the national orchestra.

As a soloist, Paganini captivated his audience by his pyrotechnics. During an engagement in Livorno, he so impressed a wealthy French merchant that he was rewarded with a valuable violin. With the arrival of Princess Elisa Baciocchi, the sister of Napoleon, as ruler of Lucca in 1805, musical life there was reorganized. The two major orchestras were dissolved and replaced by a chamber orchestra. Paganini was retained as second violinist and then was made solo court violinist in 1807. After the chamber orchestra itself was dissolved a year later, he played in the court string quartet and also served as violin teacher to Prince Felix Baciocchi. Dissatisfied with his position, he broke with the court in December 1809 and pursued a career as a virtuoso.

Paganini came to national prominence in 1813 with a series of sensationally successful concerts in Milan. He subsequently toured throughout Italy, his renown growing from year to year. In 1824 he met the singer Antonia Bianchi, who became his mistress. She bore him a son, Achilles, in 1825, whom Paganini legitimized in 1837. In 1827 he was made a Knight of the Golden Spur by Pope Leo XII.

When Paganini left Italy for his first tour abroad in 1828, he immediately gained a triumph with his opening concert in Vienna. He gave 14 concerts during his stay in Vienna and was accorded the honorary title of chamber virtuoso by the Emperor and presented with the city's medal of St. Salvator. Paganini made his first appearance in Berlin in 1829, then played in Frankfurt, Darmstadt, Mannheim, and Leipzig. In 1831 he made his Paris and London debuts, then gave concerts throughout Great Britain from 1831 to 1833. Paganini's artistic fortunes began to decline in 1834. His long-precarious health was ruined, but he had managed to retain his fame and considerable wealth. He continued to give sporadic concerts, but he spent most of his time at his villa in Parma, making occasional visits to Paris. A critical illness in October 1838 led to the loss of his voice. In November 1839 he went to Nice for his health but died there the following spring. Paganini's stupendous technique, power, and control, as well as his ROMANTIC passion and intense en-

One of Paganini's most famous tricks was to play the *Witches' Dance* on one string of the violin, after cutting the other three strings with a pair of scissors in front of the audience!

PEOPLE IN MUSIC

ergy, made him the marvel of his time. He also was not above employing certain tricks of virtuosity, such as tuning up the A string of his violin by a semitone. He was a highly effective composer for the violin and gave regular performances of his works at his concerts, with great success. Outstanding among his violin works are the 24 solo caprices (1805), 6 concertos, *Moto perpetuo,* and other works with orchestra, three string quartets (1800–05), 21 quartets for various combinations of instruments (1806–20), and sonatas.

Page, Patti (born Clara Ann Fowler), American popular singer; b. Claremore, Okla., Nov. 8, 1927. Page was one of the most popular singers of the '50s, selling over 60 million albums and singles. She began singing in her local church choir and then on Tulsa radio. She entered a local contest for a singer to appear as a spokesperson for the Page Milk Company. After winning, she adopted the name Patti Page, which stuck with her.

In the late '40s Page was discovered by bandleader/promoter Jack Rael, who later became her manager. He landed her a job on the popular Breakfast Club radio program, originating from Chicago, in 1948. She made her first recordings then, scoring immediately with the hit *Confess,* which Page performed as an entire vocal quartet, thanks to overdubbing. This became Page's trademark on a number of following hits, including *With My Eyes Wide Open I'm Dreaming* (1949), her first million-selling disc. In 1950 Page recorded what would become her theme song, *Tennessee Waltz,* which also became the state song of Tennessee. Several dozen hits followed, including the sugary sweet *(How Much Is that) Doggie in the Window,* which was recorded for a children's album but became a major adult pop hit. Page also became a popular figure on television, hosting her own variety shows, as well as appearing on many others. She was in a few movies in the early '60s, but never became a movie star like Doris Day. Page's last major hit was the theme from the 1965 thriller *Hush, Hush, Sweet Charlotte.* Page continued to record through the '70s, '80s, and '90s, primarily in a country vein. She made a return to nightclub singing in 1988, performing in N.Y.

page turner. A necessary adjunct to the pianist in a chamber music ensemble, and to a piano accompanist in song recitals. He or she sits on the left side of the player and turns the music page holding the right tip of the page delicately between the fingers.

Under no circumstances should the page turner put his or her arm across the pianist's field of vision, and any facial expression of aesthetic delight or, still worse, a grimace of disgust are impermissible. Any attempt at humming, rhythmic breathing, or similar musical or unmusical sounds are *verboten.* An ideal page turner, therefore, must be unobtrusive, respectful, and helpful.

PAULINE OLIVEROS raised the concert status of a page turner in a piece she wrote explicitly titled *Trio for Violin, Piano, and Page Turner* (1961). In his *Love and Conception* (1968–69), DANIEL LENTZ orchestrates an amorous moment for the page turner and pianist under the lid of the piano.

Pagliacci. Opera by RUGGERO LEONCAVALLO, 1892, first performed in Milan. Here, Leoncavallo made a deliberate effort to emulate the success of PIETRO MASCAGNI's *CAVALLERIA RUSTICANA,* produced about two years before, succeeding beyond all expectations. Because the two operas are short and similar in tone, they are invariably paired like symmetric twins on operatic playbills, affectionately referred to as *Cav* and *Pag.* With these two works, Leoncavallo and Mascagni inaugurated a realistic movement in opera which came to be known as VERISMO.

The story of *Pagliacci* is derived from an actual event where an actor killed his unfaithful wife after a theatrical performance in which they both took part. (Leoncavallo's father was the judge at the murder trial.) The opera is set as a play within a play, with a group of traveling actors performing in a booth in the center of the stage. The cast of characters is that of the COMMEDIA DELL'ARTE.

Just before the curtain rises in the booth, Canio the *pagliaccio* (clown) learns that his wife Nedda, who plays Columbina in the play within the play, has a lover. Canio sings his famous aria *Vesti la giubba* (with which ENRICO CARUSO moved a generation of operagoers to tears), lamenting the necessity of putting on a clown's garb when his heart is breaking. As the play progresses, he begins to identify with the character of the drama. He demands to know the name of his wife's lover. Horrified at the reality of his actions, she refuses, and he stabs her to death. Her lover, Silvio, rushes in from the stage audience and is killed in turn. The clown

The correct title of Leoncavallo's opera is *Pagliacci,* not *I pagliacci,* as it is often listed.

then announces to the shocked spectators, "La commedia è finita" (the comedy is over).

Paik, Nam June, Korean-American avant-garde composer and experimenter in the visual arts; b. Seoul, July 20, 1932. Paik studied at the University of Tokyo, then took courses in music theory in Munich and in Freiburg im Breisgau. Turning toward electronics, he conducted experimental work at the Electronic Music Studio in Cologne from 1958 to 1960. He also attended the summer seminars for new music at Darmstadt from 1957 to 1961.

Paik initially attracted attention at his duo recitals with the cellist CHARLOTTE MOORMAN, who performed topless. He acted as a surrogate cello, with his spinal column serving as the fingerboard for Moorman's cello bow, while his bare skin provided an area for intermittent PIZZICATI. Both were associated with the FLUXUS group, a group of N.Y. artists who encouraged audience participation in their works and who tried to introduce humor into serious artwork.

About 1963 Paik began experimenting with videotape as a medium for sounds and images. His initial work in this field was *Global Groove,* a high-velocity collage of intermingled television bits, which included instantaneous commercials, fragments from news telecasts, and subliminal extracts from regular programs. Paik's list of works includes:

Ommaggio a Cage for piano demolition, breakage of raw eggs, spray painting of hands in jet black, etc. (1959)

Symphony for 20 Rooms (1961)

Variations on a Theme of Saint-Saëns for cello and piano, with the pianist playing *The Swan* while the cellist dives into an oil drum filled with water (1965)

Performable Music, wherein the performer is ordered to make an incision with a razor of no less than ten centimeters on his left forearm (1965)

Opera sextronique (1967) and *Opera electronique* (1968) several video works, including *Video Buddha* (1974),

PEOPLE IN MUSIC

VIDEA (1980), *The More the Better* (1988), *My Faust/The Stations* (1988–91), and *Video Opera* (1993)

Of uncertain attribution is Symphony No. 3, which Paik delegated to Ken Friedman. Friedman worked on it in Saugus, California, the epicenter of the earthquake of Feb. 9, 1971. The earthquake itself constituted the finale of the piece.

Paine, John Knowles, prominent American composer and teacher; b. Portland, Maine, Jan. 9, 1839; d. Cambridge, Mass., April 25, 1906. Paine's father ran a music store and conducted the band in Portland. John Knowles studied organ, piano, harmony, and counterpoint in his hometown. From 1858 to 1961, he went to Berlin to further his music education, while also appearing as an organist and pianist in Germany and England.

PEOPLE IN MUSIC

In 1861 Paine settled in Boston, becoming organist of the West Church. He joined the faculty of Harvard University in 1862, where he also was organist at its Appleton Chapel. He was professor of music at Harvard University from 1875 to 1906, the first to hold such a position at a U.S. university. He was made a member of the National Institute of Arts and Letters in 1898.

Paine greatly distinguished himself as an educator, serving as mentor to many American composers and music teachers. He published *The History of Music to the Death of Schubert* in 1907. His compositions include two symphonies (1876, 1880), *As You Like It,* overture (c.1876), two symphonic poems: *The Tempest* (c.1876) and *An Island Fantasy* (c.1888), Duo Concertante for violin, cello, and orchestra (c.1877), chamber and choral works, songs, and keyboard works.

Paint Your Wagon. Musical by ALAN JAY LERNER and FREDERICK LOEWE, 1951. The action takes place during the gold rush in Northern California, in a mid-19th-century mining camp. A prospector discovers gold but suffers from loneliness and purchases one of the wives of a traveling Mormon at an auction. But the gold is soon depleted, the town falls into decay, and she falls in love with another. The sentimental ballad *I Talk to the Trees* is among the show's better-known songs.

Paisiello, Giovanni. *See* BARBER OF SEVILLE, THE.

The Pajama Game. Musical by RICHARD ADLER and Jerry Ross, 1954. The story rhapsodizes the efforts of workers at the Sleep-Tite Pajama Factory for a pay raise of 7 ½ cents an hour. The score includes a memorable tango, *Hernando's Hideaway.*

Pal Joey. Musical by RICHARD RODGERS and LORENZ HART, 1940. Pal Joey is a sleazy character employed as a dancer in a Chicago nightclub, but he is liked by the ladies. One of them, an affluent matron, sets him up in an apartment, and he willingly abandons his loving girlfriend for a life of luxury. Eventually, both women give him up and he is left alone and penniless. Includes *Bewitched, Bothered, and Bewildered.*

Palestrina, Giovanni Pierluigi da, great Italian composer; b. probably in Palestrina, near Rome, 1525 or 1526; d. Rome, Feb. 2, 1594. Palestrina is first listed as a choirboy at S. Maria Maggiore in 1537. In 1544 he was appointed organist of the cathedral of S. Agapit in Palestrina, where his duties also included teaching music to the canons and choirboys.

On June 12, 1547, Palestrina married Lucrezia Gori, with whom he had three sons. In 1550 the bishop of Palestrina, Cardinal Giovanni Maria

PEOPLE IN MUSIC

In his letters he customarily signed his name Giovanni Petraloysio.

Giovanni Pierluigi da Palestrina. (New York Public Library) ▶

Ciocchi del Monte, was elected pope, taking the name Julius III. On Sept. 1, 1551, he appointed Palestrina maestro of the Cappella Giulia to succeed Robin Mallapert. Palestrina dedicated his first book of masses to the Pope in 1554. In 1555 the Pope rewarded him by making him a member of the Cappella Sistina, even though he was a married man. He was admitted without taking the entrance examination and without receiving the approval of the other singers.

In September 1555 Pope Paul IV dismissed Palestrina and two other singers after invoking the celibacy rule of the chapel, granting each a small pension. A month later Palestrina became maestro di cappella of the great church of St. John Lateran, where his son Rodolfo joined him as a chorister. Palestrina's tenure was made difficult by inadequate funds for the musical establishment, and he resigned his post in July 1560. From 1561 to 1566 he was maestro di cappella of S. Maria Maggiore.

In 1562–63 the Council of Trent took up the matter of sacred music. Out of its discussions arose a movement to advance the cause of intelligibility of sacred texts when set to music. Palestrina's role with this Council remains a matter of dispute among historians, but his *Missa Pape Marcelli* is an outstanding example of a number of its reforms.

From 1564 Palestrina was also in charge of the music at the summer estate of Cardinal Ippolito II d'Este in Tivoli, near Rome. He apparently took up a full-time position in the cardinal's service from 1567 to 1571. During this period, he also taught at the Seminario Romano, where his sons Rodolfo and Angelo were students. In 1568 the court of Emperor Maximilian II offered him the position of imperial choirmaster in Vienna, but Palestrina demanded so high a salary that the offer was withdrawn.

In April 1571, upon the death of Giovanni Animuccia, Palestrina resumed his post as maestro of the Cappella Giulia. In 1575 his salary was increased to forestall his move to S. Maria Maggiore. In 1577, at the request of Pope Gregory XIII, Palestrina and Annibale Zoilo began the revision of the PLAINSONG of the Roman Gradual and Antiphoner. Palestrina never completed his work on this project; the revision was eventually completed by others and published in 1614.

In 1580, having lost his eldest sons and his wife to the plague, Palestrina decided to enter the priesthood. He soon changed his mind and married Virginia Dormoli, the widow of a wealthy furrier, in 1581. In succeeding years he devoted much time to managing her fortune while continuing his work as a musician. In 1583 he was tendered an offer to become maestro at the court of the Duke of Mantua, but again his terms were rejected as too high. In 1584 he published his settings of the Song of Solomon. In 1593 he began plans to return to Palestrina as choirmaster of the cathedral, but he was overtaken by death early the next year. He was buried in the Cappella Nuova of old St. Peter's Church.

With his great contemporaries WILLIAM BYRD and OR-LANDO DI LASSO, Palestrina stands as a foremost composer of the POLYPHONIC style of the Franco-Flemish school, creating works of unsurpassing beauty and technical difficulty. His sacred music remains his most glorious achievement. Highly prolific, he composed 104 MASSES, over 375 MOTETS, 68 offertories, over 65 HYMNS, 35 MAGNIFICATS, over 140 MADRIGALS (both sacred and secular), LAMENTATIONS, LITA-NIES, and PSALMS.

MAX REGER, whose last name is a palindrome, replied wit-tily to an admirer who com-plained that he could see only his back while he con-ducted a concert: "I am no different front or back."

palindrome. Words and sentences that do not change when they are read backwards.

Musical palindromes are synonymous with retrograde movements. In a palindromic section in ALBAN BERG's opera *LULU*, the music revolves backward to depict the story of Lulu's incarceration and escape. Samplers of palindromic canons are found in NICOLAS SLONIMSKY's *Thesaurus of Scales and Melodic Patterns*.

Panama Hattie. Musical by COLE PORTER, 1940. The hero-ine is a top canary at a low-grade cabaret in the Panama Canal Zone, who is in love with a Philadelphia blue-blood official. She makes the grade when she thwarts a plot to blow up the canal locks. She also acquires manners and eventually marries her Philadelphia friend.

Among the best tunes are *I've Still Got My Health; Let's Be Buddies; Make It Another Old Fashioned, Please;* and *I'm Throwing a Ball Tonight.*

pandora. A plucked CHORDOPHONE, akin to a bass CITTERN, with fixed frets and six double courses. It is reported in the period between 1560 and 1670 and commonly used in BASSO CONTINUO. The name was also applied to the THEORBO-LUTE.

MUSICAL
INSTRUMENT

panpipes. The most ancient of wind instruments, consisting of several reeds of different sizes bound together. Its name is explained by the legend that it was invented by the god Pan.

Panpipes exist in all cultures. In South American countries they are known under various names: *antara* (Peru), *rondador* (Ecuador), *capador* (Colombia), and *sico* (Bolivia). In China, panpipes are arranged in two mutually exclusive WHOLE-TONE SCALES, one symbolically masculine and the other feminine.

MUSICAL
INSTRUMENT

pantaleon. Large CIMBALOM invented by the great performer Pantaleon Hebenstreit (1667–1750), given its name by Louis XIV in 1705. The instrument was appreciated for its breadth of dynamic variation. While it was eventually superseded by the FORTEPIANO, it lent its name to the new instrument for a brief time.

MUSICAL
INSTRUMENT

pantomime (Grk., all imitating). 1. A BALLET-like performance without speech or singing in which action is suggested by gestures and choreography. 2. In the U.K., a pageant holiday play with songs, slapstick, and cross-dressing; an outgrowth of MUSIC HALL.

pantonality. ARNOLD SCHOENBERG's preferred synonym for ATONALITY, denoting the possibility of all tonalities, or the conscious absence of a single, preeminent TONALITY. Pantonality is almost synonymous with OMNITONALITY, the only difference being that pantonality includes atonal melodic progressions and uninhibited DISSONANT textures, while omnitonality tends to enhance the basic sense of tonality.

Panufnik, Andrzej, eminent Polish-born English conductor and composer; b. Warsaw, Sept. 24, 1914; d. London, Oct. 27, 1991. Panufnik's father was a Polish manufacturer

PEOPLE IN MUSIC

of string instruments, his mother an Englishwoman who studied violin in Warsaw. He began training with his mother.

After studying composition at the Warsaw Conservatory, earning his diploma in 1936, Panufnik took conducting lessons with FELIX WEINGARTNER at the Vienna Academy of Music in 1937–38. He subsequently completed his training with Philippe Gaubert in Paris and also studied in London in 1938–39. He returned to Warsaw in 1939, remaining there during the Nazi occupation, playing piano in the underground.

After the liberation of Poland in 1945, he conducted the Krakow and Warsaw Philharmonics. However, in 1954 Panufnik left his homeland in protest of the Communist regime, settling in England, where he became a naturalized British citizen in 1961. After serving as music director of the City of Birmingham Symphony Orchestra from 1957 to 1959, he devoted himself to composition. His wife, Scarlett Panufnik, published *Out of the City of Fear* (London, 1956), recounting his flight from Poland. His autobiography was published as *Composing Myself* (London, 1986).

In 1988 Panufnik appeared as a guest conductor of his own works with the N.Y. Chamber Symphony and in 1990 with the Chicago Symphony Orchestra. He was knighted in 1991.

In his early years Panufnik belonged to the vanguard group of Polish composers. He used advanced techniques, including QUARTER TONES, and made certain innovations in notation. In several of his orchestral works, he left blank spaces in the place of rests to indicate inactive instrumental parts. In his later music he adopted a more circumspect idiom—expressive, direct, and communicative. His compositions to 1944 were destroyed during the Warsaw uprising.

Panufnik composed ten symphonies and other orchestral works, four string quartets, other chamber and piano works, and choral works.

Papillons. Piano SUITE of 12 pieces by ROBERT SCHUMANN, 1831, published as op.2, descriptive of fleeting butterflies in feminine disguises. Schumann was inspired by the Romantic novel *Flegeljahre* (Years of Indiscretion) by Jean-Paul Richter.

The sad melody might well reflect Schumann's own youthful indiscretion. It is based on the notes A, E♭, C, and B, spelling, in German nomenclature (where E♭ is *Es,* i.e., S), the town of Asch where he experienced his first infatuation. He used the same theme in his later *Carnaval* (1833 – 35).

parable aria. A type of ARIA, much in vogue in the 18th century, in which the singer expresses emotion by way of parable or metaphor. A famous example is the protestation of one of the ladies in WOLFGANG AMADEUS MOZART'S *COSÌ FAN TUTTE* (1790) that she would remain as firm as a rock in resisting temptation. The rock is the crux of the metaphor in the parable.

Parade. "Realistic ballet" by ERIK SATIE, 1917, premiered in Paris. It was in the form of a vaudeville show, a series of disconnected scenes, with imitations of early JAZZ. With the collaboration of playwright Jean Cocteau and artist Pablo Picasso (whose designs are decidedly cubist), Satie created a model for dadaist art while inspiring almost as much of an uproar as IGOR STRAVINSKY'S *THE RITE OF SPRING* did in 1913.

parameter. A term denoting any one of the four principal aspects of musical sound, i.e., PITCH, DURATION, DYNAMICS, and TIMBRE.

paraphrases and transcriptions. An adaptation of a vocal or instrumental piece to a different medium, sometimes with variations.

When music became a more democratic art in the 19th century, not only the aristocracy but the middle class had PIANOS or HARMONIUMS in their drawing rooms, and professional musicians found a new outlet for their wares. OPERA and SYMPHONY had to be reduced to manageable proportions to make them accessible to the masses. Popular ARIAS, MARCHES, and BALLET numbers from favorite operas were arranged for the piano by highly capable musicians. Amateur adults and young children were offered arrangements of classical masterpieces that were not only musically adequate but also provided a social means of musical communication

Today, we can hear a symphonic performance in recorded form. However, in the 19th century, the only way for an individual to hear a symphony at home was to play a piano version (or reduction) of the piece.

and entertainment. German publishers put out reams of musical literature for piano, four-hands or solo.

Some great pianists, themselves composers of stature, participated in this democratization of music. FRANZ LISZT made piano transcriptions of opera and symphonic compositions (including the complete symphonies of LUDWIG VAN BEETHOVEN), as well as songs of FRANZ SCHUBERT and ROBERT SCHUMANN. He also wrote fantasies on the motives of current opera favorites. CARL CZERNY took time off from writing his myriad piano exercises to publish arrangements of operatic airs. Such arrangements pursued an eminently practical aim, namely, to acquaint music lovers with the operatic and symphonic music of the day.

Paris Symphonies. The traditional classification for FRANZ JOSEPH HAYDN's symphonies Nos. 82 – 87, written especially for performances in Paris in 1786.

PEOPLE IN MUSIC

Parker, Charlie (Charles Christopher, Jr.), noted African-American jazz alto saxophonist, also called *Bird* or *Yardbird;* b. Kansas City, Kans., Aug. 29, 1920; d. N.Y., March 12, 1955. Parker was self-taught on an alto saxophone given to him at age 13 by his mother. At 15 he left school and became a professional musician. He was a member of Jay McShann's band from 1937 to 1944, with which he toured and made his first recordings in 1941.

Charlie Parker, c. 1950. (New York Public Library) ▶

Parker moved to N.Y. in 1942, performing in Earl Hines's band for the next two

years. The group included DIZZY GILLESPIE and other young jazz artists. Gillespie and Parker then joined Billy Eckstine's band in 1944–45. After work they would meet in a club called Minton's, and there gradually evolved the new style of BEBOP. Parker became the acknowledged leader of this style, as he developed an improvising technique characterized by virtuosic speed, intense tone, complex harmonies, and highly embellished melodies having irregular rhythmic patterns and asymmetric phrase lengths.

After the mid-1940s, Parker usually worked in small combos led either by himself or by one of the other members of the small, close-knit circle of boppers. Occasionally, he also worked with larger ensembles (including a string orchestra for which he wrote arrangements). As a composer he usually worked with the 12-bar blues patterns (but always in an unique manner), or with chord progressions of well-known standards. His *Ornithology,* for instance, is based on the progressions of *How High the Moon.*

Although he achieved a prominence that made him a living legend (a leading N.Y. club, Birdland, was named after him), his life, in addition to being tragically short, was plagued by the consequences of heroin addiction (acquired when he was in his mid-teens) and alcoholism. He had a nervous breakdown in 1946 and was confined at Camarillo State Hospital in California for six months. Because of his suspected narcotics possession, the N.Y. City police took away his cabaret license in 1951, thereby denying him the right to work in N.Y. clubs. He attempted suicide twice in 1954 and subsequently entered Bellevue Hospital in N.Y. He died a year later.

Parker's music has become part of the essential jazz canon. His saxophone style has been emulated by countless younger players. His many compositions have become standards in the jazz repertoire. His recordings have been available continuously over the last four decades and will remain in print undoubtedly as long as recorded music is available in one form or another.

Parker, Horatio (William), eminent American composer and teacher; b. Auburndale, Mass., Sept. 15, 1863; d. Cedarhurst, N.Y., Dec. 18, 1919. Parker studied piano, theory,

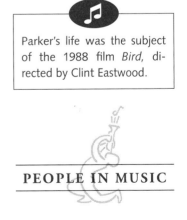

Parker's life was the subject of the 1988 film *Bird*, directed by Clint Eastwood.

PEOPLE IN MUSIC

and composition in Boston. He subsequently took courses in organ and composition with Joseph Rheinberger in Munich from 1882 to 1885, under whose tutelage he wrote the CANTATA *King Trojan* in 1885.

Horatio Parker, c. 1910. (Library of Congress/Corbis) ▶

Returning to the U.S., Parker settled in N.Y. and taught at the cathedral schools of St. Paul and St. Mary from 1886 to 1890, the General Theological Seminary in 1892, and the National Conservatory of Music in 1892–93. He was organist and choirmaster at St. Luke's from 1885 to 1887, St. Andrew's in 1887–88, and the Church of the Holy Trinity from 1888 to 1893.

In 1893 he went to Boston as organist and choirmaster at Trinity Church, remaining there until 1902. In 1893 Parker attracted attention with the first performance of his oratorio *Hora novissima* in N.Y. In this work, he demonstrated his mastery of choral writing, while his HARMONIC and CONTRAPUNTAL style remained securely tied to German practices. In 1894 he was engaged as a professor of theory at Yale University.

In 1895 Parker founded the New Haven Symphony Orchestra, which he conducted until 1918. Parker conducted performances of his works in England in 1900 and 1902. He received an honorary degree of Mus.D. at Cambridge University in 1902.

In 1904 Parker became dean of its School of Music, remaining there until his death. Many American composers received the benefit of his excellent instruction, including CHARLES IVES, who spoke highly of his teacher even though he pursued a different musical path. Parker also served as organist and choirmaster at the collegiate church of St. Nicholas in Boston from 1902 to 1910. He continued to compose industriously, without conceding to the emerging modern schools of composition. His choral works are particularly notable.

In 1911 his opera MONA won the $10,000 prize offered by the Metropolitan Opera in N.Y. and was produced there in 1912. He also won a prize offered by the National Federation of Women's Clubs for his second opera, *Fairyland,* which was produced in Los Angeles in 1915. Neither opera possessed enough power to survive in the repertoire. Other important compositions are orchestral works, including *Regulus,* overture héroïque (1884), Symphony in C major (Munich, 1885), *A Northern Ballad,* symphonic poem (Boston, 1899), and the Organ Concerto (Boston, 1902).

Among Parker's other compositions are chamber music pieces, including a string quartet (1885), suite (trio) for piano, violin, and cello (1893), string quintet (1894), and suite for piano and violin (1894), secular and religious choral music, songs, and many organ works, including the E-flat sonata (op.65).

parody. 1. A literary or musical genre that emerged in the 18th century and flourished in the 19th, particularly in OPERA. It usually followed on the heels of a successful or at least notorious theatrical production.

CARL MARIA VON WEBER's opera *DER FREISCHÜTZ* (1821) was lampooned in England in 1824 as "a new muse-sick-all and see-nick performance from the new German uproar, by the celebrated Funny-bear." RICHARD WAGNER's *TANNHÄUSER* (1845), which suffered a notorious failure at its first Paris production in 1861, engendered a number of French parodies, among them *Ya-Meine Herr, Cacophonie de l'Avenir.* Occasionally, a parody anticipates the main event. One, *Tristanderl und Süssholde,* was produced in Munich several days before Wagner's *TRISTAN UND ISOLDE* (1865) itself.

2. (from Grk. *para* + *aidein,* side-song) A type of MASS or MOTET, common in the RENAISSANCE, in which com-

posers borrowed whole pieces or parts of pieces (usually motets) and built new pieces around them. This method is distinct from the CANTUS FIRMUS and PARAPHRASE types, which borrow one melodic line.

Parsifal. "Sacred festival drama" by RICHARD WAGNER, 1882, produced in Bayreuth less than a year before his death. Wagner's libretto is drawn from the legend of the Holy Grail, the chalice from which Jesus drank at the Last Supper.

The religious symbolism of *Parsifal* requires some explanation. Before the opera begins, Amfortas, the King of the Grail, allows himself to be seduced by the sorceress Kundry in the service of Klingsor, the magician, who inflicts a grievous wound on the King. The wound can be healed only by the touch of the sacred spear. Only one pure of heart who has acquired wisdom through pity can take the spear away from Klingsor, who has it in his possession.

Young Parsifal satisfies these requirements. He is sent by the Knights of the Holy Grail to Klingsor's domain. Realizing the danger, Klingsor mobilizes a gardenful of flower maidens to lure and confuse Parsifal, and as a further inducement, Kundry kisses him on the lips. This elicits from Parsifal one of the most unexpected responses in all operatic literature, "Amfortas! The spear wound!" Whatever connection may exist between Kundry's lips and the King's wound, she instantly grasps its significance and suddenly changes from a sorceress into a humble supplicant for salvation, having been cursed for laughing at Jesus on his way to Golgotha. Parsifal seizes the spear that Klingsor has hurled at him and makes the sign of the cross with it. The power of the Christian symbol utterly destroys Klingsor's kingdom.

Parsifal makes his way to the Temple of the Holy Grail, where Kundry precedes him. He is named King of the Grail. Amfortas bares his wound and Parsifal heals it with the touch of the sacred spear. Parsifal then raises the Holy Grail in the air; at the sight of it Kundry collapses and dies, free of her curse at last.

In *Parsifal,* Wagner preserves his system of leading motives, but because of the religious content of the work, he also makes use of CHORALES and other sacred melodies. The harmonic and contrapuntal structure is purer and simpler than in Wagner's *Ring* tetralogy and his other MUSIC DRAMAS.

part (Fr. *partie*). 1. The series of tones written for and executed by a voice or instrument, either as a solo or together with other voices or instruments. 2. A division of a HOMOPHONIC movement devoted to the exposition of one melody, or musical idea, e.g., the two- and three-part song forms.

Part music, concerted or harmonized vocal music; *part singing,* the singing of part music, usually without instrumental accompaniment; *part song,* homophonic composition for at least three equal or mixed voices in harmony, without accompaniment; melody with choral harmony, with any reasonable number of voices to each part.

Pärt, Arvo, remarkable Estonian composer; b. Paide, Sept. 11, 1935. Pärt studied composition at the Tallinn Conservatory, graduating in 1963. From 1958 to 1967 he was attached to the music division of Estonian Radio.

In 1982, Pärt settled in West Berlin. He began to compose in a traditional manner, writing instrumental pieces in a neo-BAROQUE style, following classical forms but introducing DISSONANT, modern harmonies. Gradually, he began to explore several different modern composition styles, being particularly interested in examining different sound textures.

Pärt was the first Estonian composer to use ARNOLD SCHOENBERG's 12-TONE method of composition to form melodic and harmonic structures. He applied it in his arresting *Nekrolog,* composed in 1960, dedicated to the victims of the Holocaust. He has also expanded Schoenberg's theories to combine SERIAL structures with CHANCE techniques of composition.

Pärt's other orchestral works include three symphonies (*Polyphonic,* 1963; 1966; 1971), *Tabula rasa,* double concerto for two violins or violin and viola, strings, and prepared piano (1977), *Fratres* for strings and percussion (1977; 1991; also for violin, string orchestra, and percussion, 1992), chamber works, including *Arbos* for seven flutes and three triangles ad libitum (1977; also for eight brass and percussion, 1977–86), *Psalom* for string quartet (1986–91), and *Darf ich* . . . for violin, tubular bells ad libitum, and

PEOPLE IN MUSIC

One of Pärt's specialities is a technique he calls "tintinnabula," in which he uses shifting phases of a given chord.

strings (1995). Among his extensive vocal works are *Te Deum* for three choruses, piano, strings, and tape (1984–85; revised 1986), *Miserere* for soloists, chorus, ensemble, and organ (1989; revised 1990), and *Litany: Prayers of St. John Chrysostom for Each Hour of the Day and Night* for soloists, chorus, and orchestra (1994). Pärt also composed various keyboard pieces.

partbooks. Separate parts for singers or instrumentalists, in common use in the 16th century. Singers were seated around a table, each with an individual partbook, without using a general score. The practice of singing from partbooks has been recently revived by various English singing groups.

Partch, Harry, innovative American composer, performer, and instrument maker; b. Oakland, Calif., June 24, 1901; d. San Diego, Sept. 3, 1974. Largely self-taught, Partch began experimenting with instruments capable of producing fractional INTERVALS, which led him to the formulation of a 43-tone SCALE. He expounded his findings in his book *Genesis of a Music* (1949; 2nd edition, revised and augmented, 1974).

Partch built or adapted instruments to fit his theories and to compose with. Among these are:

PEOPLE IN MUSIC

a viola with elongated neck

a chromelodeon (reed organ)

kitharas with 72 strings

harmonic canons with 44 strings

boos (made of giant Philippine bamboo reeds)

cloud-chamber bowls

blow-boys (a pair of bellows with an attached automobile horn)

As more instruments were added to his ensemble, Partch revised earlier works to avail himself of new possibilities while adjusting to the changes or elimination of an instrument.

During the '30s and '40s, Partch wandered across the country, collecting traditional songs and stories, inscriptions on public walls, and recording speech-song for texts in his works. Partch's later theatrical pieces were often based on Greek tragedy and other mythological sources. Partch wrote a wide variety of compositions, mostly for ensembles of instruments of his own design, based on his own microtonal scale. Notable among them are:

17 Lyrics by Li Po for voice and adapted viola (1930–33)

The Wayward Barstow: 8 Hitchhiker Inscriptions from a Highway Railing at Barstow, California for voice and adapted guitar (1941; revised 1954)

U.S. Highball: A Musical Account of a Transcontinental Hobo Trip for voices, guitar I, kithara, and chromelodeon (1943; revised 1955)

The Bewitched, dance satire for soprano and ensemble of traditional and original instruments (1955)

Revelation in the Courthouse Park for 16 solo voices, four speakers, dancers, and large instrumental ensemble (1960)

Delusion of the Fury: A Ritual of Dream and Delusion, dramatic piece for large ensemble (1965–66)

Partch also wrote the score for the prize-winning biographical film *The Dreamer That Remains* (1972), produced by Betty Freeman, his longtime friend and patron.

partials (partial tones). *See* HARMONICS.

particella (It., particle). A reduced SCORE.
Some composers prefer writing down symphonic scores or even OPERAS in arrangements for two or three staves, one for woodwinds, one for brass, one or two for strings, with the vocal part, if any, in small printing on top. A vocal score of a choral work such as an ORATORIO is usually published in the form of particella, with the orchestral part arranged for piano.
FRANZ SCHUBERT and RICHARD WAGNER wrote some of their works first in particella form. SERGEI PROKOFIEV sys-

Many publishers now issue abridged scores for conductors, often with optional instrumental parts written in.

tematically adopted this abridged form of orchestral writing and engaged a knowledgeable assistant to convert such a particella into a full orchestral score according to indications of instrumentation given by him. A major part of the musical legacy of CHARLES IVES consists of piano arrangements with instrumental cues written in. IGOR STRAVINSKY composed *THE RITE OF SPRING* first for piano four-hands, which is essentially a particella.

partimento (It., division). The 17th- and 18th-century practice of improvising melodies over a given bass, which necessarily determined harmonic progressions. The practice had educational uses, but it waned at the end of the BAROQUE, when the BASSO CONTINUO gave way to fully written-out scores.

par-tē′täh

partita (*parthia;* It.). Originally, a VARIATION; by the BAROQUE era, a SUITE.

Examples of partitino include the "Turkish" percussion in WOLFGANG AMADEUS MOZART'S *THE ABDUCTION FROM THE SERAGLIO,* the trombone and the chorus in his *DON GIOVANNI,* and the children's chorus in GIACOMO PUCCINI'S *LA BOHÈME.*

partitino (It., little score). Supplementary parts, printed separately, for a work with instruments or vocal part that do not appear often in the complete SCORE. This helps keep the complete score from being overly cluttered.

Parton, Dolly (Rebecca), successful American singer and songwriter of country and popular music; b. Locust Ridge, near Sevierville, Tenn., Jan. 19, 1946. Born into a poverty-stricken family, Parton began to sing as a child. After graduating from high school, she went to Nashville to seek her fortune in the early '60s.

Parton recorded a few singles on her own, scoring a minor hit in 1966 with *Dumb Blonde,* a song that in many ways fit her original image. In 1967, she joined the cast of Porter Wagoner's television show, working as his duet partner and comic foil. She continued to record on her own, scoring hits with her autobiographical song *Coat of Many Colors* (telling how her mother made her childhood clothing out of any scraps of fabric she could find) and *Joshua.* She also had hits with Wagoner, including a remake of folksinger TOM PAXTON'S *Last Thing on My Mind.*

In 1974 Parton made a painful split from Wagoner, who felt he should continue to control the singer/songwriter's career. She had a hit immediately with *Jolene.* In 1977, she "crossed over" onto the pop charts with the sprightly song *Here You Come Again.* Parton's image—featuring lavish costumes, outrageous blond wigs, and her often-commented upon figure—made her the object of some satire, but also helped draw attention to her. She became a pop phenomenom, scoring on country and pop charts.

To top it all, Parton made herself famous by appearing as one of the three secretaries (with Jane Fonda and Lily Tomlin) in the comedy film *9 to 5* (1981), for which she wrote and recorded the theme song. In the film Parton showed a talent for light comic acting.

Parton's career in the balance of the '80s and '90s has been more spotted. Her acting career has been uneven, and she has appeared usually only in supporting roles. Meanwhile, she has had trouble regaining her position on the country charts, having been replaced by younger singers who appeal to a new generation of listeners.

Nonetheless, Parton has had a number of successes. Her Dollywood theme park, placed in the impoverished Tennessee county where she was raised, has been a financial success. And her songs continue to be recorded. In 1991 Whitney Houston scored a massive hit with Parton's *I Will Always Love You,* which was used as the theme for the movie *The Bodyguard.*

Parton's sister, Stella (b. Locust Ridge, near Sevierville, Tenn., May 4, 1949) had a short period of success also as a country-pop singer in the mid-'70s.

Pasatieri, Thomas, talented American opera composer; b. N.Y., Oct. 20, 1945. Pasatieri was self-taught on the piano. Between the ages of 14 and 18 he wrote some 400 songs, again without any guidance.

When Pasatieri was 15, he corresponded with the famous French teacher NADIA BOULANGER, persuading her to take him as a student. They worked together through the mail! At 16 he entered the Juilliard School of Music, where he studied with VITTORIO GIANNINI and VINCENT PERSICHETTI. He also took a course with DARIUS MILHAUD in Aspen, Colorado, where his first opera, *The Women,* to his own LIBRETTO, was performed when he was only 19.

PEOPLE IN MUSIC

It became clear to Pasatieri that opera was his natural medium. Unlike other modern composers, he was most comfortable following the traditional rules of Italian opera. While his productions were applauded by audiences, they shocked music critics and other composers, an attitude akin to that taken by some toward Giannini and GIAN CARLO MENOTTI.

From 1967 to 1969 Pasatieri taught at the Juilliard School. He then was engaged at the Manhattan School of Music until 1971. From 1980 to 1983 Pasatieri was Distinguished Visiting Professor at the University of Cincinnati College-Conservatory of Music.

Among his other operas are *The Seagull,* after Anton Chekhov (Houston, March 5, 1974), *Washington Square,* after Henry James (Detroit, Oct. 1, 1976), *Three Sisters,* after Chekhov (1979; Columbus, Ohio, March 13, 1986), *The Goose Girl,* children's opera (Fort Worth, Texas, Feb. 15, 1981), and *Maria Elena* (Tucson, April 8, 1983). He also composed works for vocal groups and instrumental accompaniment, as well as two piano sonatas (1976).

păhs-săh-cahl′yăh

passacaglia (It.; from Sp. *pasar una calle,* pass along a street; Fr. *passacaille*). Originally, a procession of a chorus playing and singing in MARCH time, probably derived from the Spanish *pasacalle.*

In the 17th century it acquired the characteristics of a VARIATION form in TRIPLE METER. Its most common feature is an OSTINATO BASS progression with melodic and harmonic variations in the upper voices.

In the BAROQUE period, the passacaglia became one of the most important instrumental forms for keyboard. JOHANN SEBASTIAN BACH, GEORGE FRIDERIC HANDEL, FRANÇOIS COUPERIN, and JEAN-PHILIPPE RAMEAU all wrote in this form. Many 18th-century composers used the terms *passacaglia* and *chaconne* to describe the same instrumental form. While the distinction between the two forms is not always clear, some musicologists have pointed out that the true passacaglia is written in rigorous COUNTERPOINT, while the chaconne is often chordal and HOMOPHONIC.

passage. 1. A portion or section of a piece, usually short, not necessarily developmental in nature. 2. A rapid repeated figure, ascending or descending, especially in piano writing. *See* RUN.

passing notes or tones. NOTES or TONES foreign to the CHORDS that they accompany, and passing by a step from one chord to another. They differ from SUSPENSIONS in not being prepared, and in entering (usually) on an unaccented BEAT.

Passion, Passion music. A musical setting of a text descriptive of Christ's sufferings and death on the cross. It retains its original Latin meaning of suffering. The text is usually drawn from the Latin text of the Bible.

There is a great deal of conventional symbolism in these compositions: the passion, that is, the actual pain experienced by Jesus, is rendered in CHROMATIC SCALES, the resurrection is set in clear MAJOR ARPEGGIOS, while the powers of the dark are expressed in falling BASSES in BROKEN DIMINISHED-SEVENTH CHORDS.

In the great Passions of JOHANN SEBASTIAN BACH, the characters, including Jesus and the apostles, speak and sing in German, while the chorus supplies the narrative.

pastiche (also Fr.; It. *pasticcio,* pie). A musical MEDLEY of extracts from different works, pieced together and provided with new words so as to form a "new" composition. Today, the word is often used disdainfully to designate a motley medley of unrelated tunes by unrelated composers, arranged in a sequence with artificial connective tissue between numbers.

Historically, the pastiche performed a useful function in acquainting music lovers with popular opera ARIAS, dance movements, and concert pieces, presented as an appetizing sampler plate of musical dishes. Unfortunately, the term began to be applied indiscriminately to sets of variations by several composers, musical gifts offered to friends, and other lesser compositions. Among some of the more famous pastiches are:

pᾰhs-tēsh′

Diabelli Variations—Anton Diabelli commissioned 51 composers (including FRANZ LISZT who, as a child of 11, contributed one) to write variations on a waltz tune of his own. LUDWIG VAN BEETHOVEN obliged with 33 variations which made Diabelli's name immortal.

Several Russian composers (ALEXANDER BORODIN, NIKO-LAI RIMSKY-KORSAKOV, CÉSAR CUI, and ANATOLI LIADOV) got together to create variations on *Chopsticks,* to which Liszt later added one of his own.

The *Hexameron* for piano on the march theme from VINCENZO BELLINI's opera *I PURITANI* (1835), written in 1837 by six composers, including FRÉDÉRIC CHOPIN and Liszt.

Luciano Berio concocted a musical stew with chunks of JOHANN SEBASTIAN BACH, CLAUDE DEBUSSY, MAURICE RAVEL, and GUSTAV MAHLER. He called the result *Sinfonia.*

See also POTPOURRI.

pastoral (Fr.; It. *pastorale*). 1. A scenic CANTATA representing pastoral life; a pastoral OPERA. 2. An instrumental piece imitating in style and instrumentation rural and idyllic scenes.

Pastoral Symphony (*Sinfonia Pastorale*). The Sixth Symphony of LUDWIG VAN BEETHOVEN, 1808 (op.68), first performed in Vienna.

It is set in the key of F major and is the only work of Beethoven having a PROGRAM.

It is in five movements, and Beethoven's descriptions are very specific:

1. *Revival of Pleasant Feelings upon Arriving in the Country Scene*

2. *By the Brook*

3. *Merry Gathering of Country Folk*

4. *Thunderstorm*

5. *Shepherd's Song of Joyful Gratitude after the Storm.*

Like many composers who first sketch out a descriptive program for their compositions and then soberly retract it, Beethoven added here a word of caution: "It is rather an expression of feeling than pictorial representation." However, the literalness of birdsongs in the score cannot be denied: the trill of the nightingale, the syncopated rhythm of the quail, and the familiar falling third of the cuckoo. And what could be more pictorial than the lightning bolts and heavy rainfall graphically depicted in the score? Finally, the serene conclusion gives the listener the feeling of the Austrian landscape after an invigorating rainfall.

Pastoral Symphony, A. The Third Symphony of RALPH VAUGHAN WILLIAMS, 1922, first performed in London. As was the case with LUDWIG VAN BEETHOVEN, when speaking of his *Pastoral Symphony,* so Vaughan Williams insisted that his *Pastoral Symphony* should be judged as pure music.

The work, in four traditional movements, is typical of the contemplative nature of Vaughan Williams as a composer, for the music seems to bear an unspoken message. The finale contains a wordless vocal part.

pastourelle (Fr.). PASTORAL song in the repertoire of the TROUBADOURS and TROUVÈRES.

Pathétique Sonata. LUDWIG VAN BEETHOVEN's Piano Sonata in C Minor, 1797–98 (op.13). The "pathetic"—that is, emotional—quality is dramatically expressed in the extreme contrast between its slow introduction and subsequent ALLEGRO. The complete title is *Grande Sonate pathétique,* written down in French by Beethoven himself, as was the fashion of the day. The second movement in A-flat major is a set of variations on one of Beethoven's most engaging ROCOCO themes.

Pathétique Symphony. PIOTR ILYICH TCHAIKOVSKY's Sixth Symphony, 1893, first conducted by the composer in St. Petersburg nine days before he died. Its four movements are set in the somber key of B minor. The title was suggested to Tchaikovsky by his brother Modest after the work was already completed.

The music epitomizes Tchaikovsky's obsession with Fate and possesses some extraordinary moments, such as a quotation in the trombones from the Russian Mass for the Dead. An exceptional feature is a "waltz in $\frac{5}{4}$ time," as it came to be known, in the second movement.

Tchaikovsky dedicated the *Pathétique* to his favorite nephew, Bob. He confessed that he loved the *Pathétique*

Another feature of the Sixth Symphony is the lack of pauses (ATTACCA) between the last three movements. This expands on a structural concept Beethoven first introduced in his Fifth Symphony.

more than any of his works, and that he actually wept while composing the music. He suffered when Bob failed to acknowledge receipt of the score that Tchaikovsky sent to him.

Patience, or Bunthorne's Bride. Comic opera by WILLIAM S. GILBERT and ARTHUR S. SULLIVAN, 1881, first performed in London. The poet Bunthorne (a combination of the names John Bunyan and Nathaniel Hawthorne?) is admired by aesthetically inclined young women, but he spurns them in favor of Patience, a milkmaid. He loses her to a dragoon, however, who puts on aesthetic airs.

The opera is a transparent satire on Oscar Wilde, whose postures were then both an amusement and irritation to much of Victorian society.

patter song. A rapid, syllabic humorous song, particularly effective in comic dialogues. The TESSITURA (range of the voice) is in the middle register, and the singing approximates the PARLANDO (semispoken) style.

WOLFGANG AMADEUS MOZART and GIOACCHINO ROSSINI excelled in Italian patter song. The greatest master in English was ARTHUR S. SULLIVAN in setting WILLIAM S. GILBERT's witty lines in their comic operas.

One of the most famous patter songs is Gilbert and Sullivan's *(I Am the Very Model of a) Modern Major General.*

Paukenmesse. *See* MASS IN TIME OF WAR.

Paul Bunyan. OPERETTA by BENJAMIN BRITTEN, 1941, to a LIBRETTO by British poet W. H. Auden, first performed at Columbia University, N.Y., when both men were in America. The story recounts the exploits of the legendary American frontiersman Paul Bunyan in a series of tuneful episodes.

After being laid aside for 35 years, the opera was revived at the 29th Musical Festival at Aldeburgh, England, 1976, as a bicentennial tribute to America.

pah′oo-zăh   **pause** (It. *pausa*). 1. A full stop. 2. A REST. 3. A FERMATA.

păh-vah′năh   **pavane** (It. *pavana*). A stately court dance in deliberate $\frac{4}{4}$ time. The supposed derivation of the word is from the Latin word *pavo* (peacock), because of the imagined similarity of the dance with the strutting step of the bird. Actually, the pavane originated in the 16th century in Padua, Italy, *Pava* being Padua's dialect name.

Because of its dignified choreography, the pavane became a favorite court dance in Europe and particularly in England during Elizabethan times. The tempo indication *Alla pavana* is also found. Many modern composers stylized the pavane in various novel ways, e.g., RALPH VAUGHAN WILLIAMS, in his orchestral *Pavane* with choral AD LIBITUM composed in 1887. A common misspelling *pavanne* has taken root in some American samples of the pavane style.

Pavane pour une infante défunte (Pavane for a dead princess). Piano piece by MAURICE RAVEL, 1899, first performed in Paris, 1902. It is a fine stylization of the slow courtly dance.

Pavarotti, Luciano, greatly renowned Italian tenor; b. Modena, Oct. 12, 1935. Pavarotti's father, a baker by trade, sang in the local church choir. Luciano learned to read music and began singing with the boy altos. He later joined his father in the choir and also sang in the chorus of the local Teatro Comunale and the amateur Chorale Gioacchino Rossini.

PEOPLE IN MUSIC

To prepare himself for a career as a schoolteacher, Pavarotti attended the local Scuola Magistrale. He then taught in an elementary school, augmenting his income by selling insurance. In the meantime, he began vocal studies with Arrigo Polo in Modena in 1955, then went to Mantua, where he continued his training with Ettore Campogalliani in 1960. He made his operatic debut as Rodolfo in *LA BOHÈME* at the Teatro Municipale in Reggio Emilia in 1961.

In 1962 Pavarotti obtained his first major engagement when he appeared as the Duke of Mantua at the Teatro Massimo in Palermo. His first important appearance outside his homeland was as Edgardo with the Netherlands Opera in Amsterdam a year later. That same year he made his Vienna State Opera debut as Rodolfo, a role he also sang for his first appearance at London's Covent Garden.

In 1965 Pavarotti made his U.S. debut as Edgardo opposite JOAN SUTHERLAND's Lucia with the Greater Miami Opera. After his first appearance at Milan's La Scala as Alfredo that year, he made a summer tour of Australia with the Joan Sutherland Williamson International Grand Opera Company, a venture featuring the celebrated DIVA. He subsequently scored his first triumph on the operatic stage when he took the role of Tonio in *LA FILLE DU RÉGIMENT* at Covent Garden in 1966. In this performance, he tossed off the aria *Pour mon âme,* replete with nine successive high Cs, winning an ovation. He was dubbed the "King of the High Cs," and a brilliant international career beckoned.

In 1967 Pavarotti made his debut at the San Francisco Opera as Rodolfo, a role he chose for his first appearance at the Metropolitan Opera in N.Y. in the following year. In subsequent seasons he became a mainstay at both houses and also appeared regularly with other opera houses on both sides of the Atlantic. Pavarotti also made frequent appearances in solo recitals and concerts with orchestras. In 1977 he starred as Rodolfo in the first *Live from the Met* telecast by PBS. In 1978 he made an acclaimed solo recital debut at the Metropolitan Opera, which was also telecast by PBS.

In 1980 he founded the Opera Company of Philadelphia/Luciano Pavarotti International Voice Competition. In 1983 he was a featured artist at the Metropolitan Opera Centennial Gala. In 1984 he gave a concert before 20,000 admirers at N.Y.'s Madison Square Garden, also seen by millions on PBS. He celebrated the 25th anniversary of his operatic debut by singing his beloved Rodolfo at the Teatro Comunale in Modena in 1986. In 1988 he sang Nemorino at the Berlin Deutsche Oper, eliciting no less than 15 curtain calls. In 1989 he appeared in concert with the N.Y. City Opera Orchestra in a special program at Avery Fischer Hall at N.Y.'s Lincoln Center, televised live by PBS. In 1990 he appeared at the Bolshoi Theater in Moscow.

Pavarotti has won widespread fame performing with JOSÉ CARRERAS and PLACIDO DOMINGO as the "3 Tenors." What started as a one-time fund-raising concert has become a semi-regular series. Their recordings and videos have set records for classical music sales.

Pavarotti spent much of the '90s coasting on his reputation. He has become the object of international gossip, leaving his long-time wife in 1995 to cohabitate with his far younger assistant. In 1998 he celebrated his 30th anniversary with the Metropolitan Opera, after having a knee and hip replacement. A much trimmer figure, he held his own in the performance, silencing many critics who had written him off as a has-been.

Nonetheless, Pavarotti remains one of the most popular opera performers of the day. The most idolized tenor since ENRICO CARUSO, he has made such roles as Nemorino in *L'ELISIR D'AMORE,* Riccardo in *UN BALLO IN MASCHERA,* Fernando in *LA FAVORITE,* Manrico in *IL TROVATORE,* Cavaradossi in *TOSCA,* and Radames in *AIDA,* as well as the ubiquitous Rodolfo, virtually his own. Through recordings and television appearances, he won an adoring global following.

pavillon d'amour (Fr., love bell; Ger. *Liebesfuss,* love foot). A bulbous opening at the end of the ENGLISH HORN, which has the effect of dampening the sound. The same type of extension was characteristic of the manufacture of a clarinetto d'amore, fagotto d'amore, oboe d'amore, and other "amorous" instruments, now largely obsolete.

payola. American slang for bribes to disc jockeys for "plugging" (promoting) particular records of popular music on radio.

Peacock Variations. Name sometimes used for ZOLTÁN KODÁLY's orchestral *Variations on a Hungarian Folksong,* 1939, first performed in Amsterdam. The work is based on an authentic Hungarian folk tune, *Fly, Peacock, Fly.*

Peanut Vendor, The. An arrangement of the Latin American tune *El Mansiero.* It was popularized by several orchestras and added into the 1953 remake of the film *A Star is Born.*

Pearl Jam. (Lead vocal: Eddie Vedder, b. Chicago, Dec. 23, 1964; Guitar: Mike McCready, b. Seattle, April 5, 1965; Rhythm Guitar: Steve "Stone" Gossard, b. Seattle, July 20, 1966; Bass: Jeff Ament, b. Big Sandy, Montana, March 10, 1963; Drums: Dave Krusen, replaced by Dave Abbruzzese in 1992 and Jack Irons in 1995.) Seattle

The so-called "payola" scandal in the late '50s destroyed the careers of several disc jockeys. Most notably, Alan Freed, who was the first DJ to use the term "rock 'n' roll" and promoted tours and films of early rock acts, lost his job because of the accusation that he took money in return for playing certain records.

PEOPLE IN MUSIC

grunge-rock band who, with Nirvana, launched thousands of plaid-shirted rockers. They are famous also for waging battle with Ticketmaster, refusing to play in venues that use the popular ticketing agency, who, they claim, over-charges for its services.

The group formed in 1990 and signed quickly to Epic Records. They scored an immediate success with their 1991 LP, *Ten*, which produced the hits *Even Flow, Jeremy, Alive*, and *Release*. They joined the alternative-rock tour Lolla-palooza in 1992 on its second outing, cementing their reputation with the grunge crowd. The year 1993 brought a second album, *Vs.*, and an appearance on the popular *MTV Unplugged* program. They also toured Europe with Neil Young, leading to a long association with the grandfather of all things grungy (the group backed Young on his album *Mirror Ball* in 1995).

Vitalogy came in 1994, which they released first on vinyl, and then, two weeks later, on CD and cassette. Band fans ended up buying both, lining the denim pockets of the group's members. Their 1995 summer tour was plagued by their ongoing fight with Ticketmaster.

In 1998 Pearl Jam released the album *Yield*, featuring a slightly softer image of the group. The hit song *Wishlist* from the album saw lead singer Vedder wishing for a better world!

PEOPLE IN MUSIC

Pears, (Sir) **Peter** (Neville Luard), renowned English tenor; b. Farnham, June 22, 1910; d. Aldeburgh, April 3, 1986. Pears began his career as temporary organist at Hertford College, Oxford in 1928–29, then was director of music at the Grange School, Crowborough, from 1930 to 1934. He was a scholarship student at the Royal College of Music in London during 1933–34, concurrently singing in the BBC chorus, and then with the BBC Singers from 1934 to 1938 and New English Singers from 1936 to 1938. During this period he received vocal instruction from Elena Gerhardt and Dawson Freer.

In 1936 Pears met the famed British composer BEN-JAMIN BRITTEN. They gave their first joint recital in 1937 and thereafter remained lifelong personal and professional companions. After singing in the Glyndebourne chorus in 1938, he accompanied Britten to the U.S. in 1939, where he continued his vocal training with Therese Behr and Clytie Hine-Mundy.

In 1942 Britten and Pears returned to England. Pears made his stage debut that same year in the title role of *LES CONTES D'HOFFMAN* at London's Strand Theatre. In 1943 he joined the Sadler's Wells Opera Company, gaining fame when he created the title role in Britten's *PETER GRIMES* in 1945. In 1946 he became a member of the English Opera Group and thereafter greatly distinguished himself in operas by Britten. Among roles he created were Albert Herring, the Male Chorus in *THE RAPE OF LUCRETIA*, Captain Vere in *BILLY BUDD*, Essex in *GLORIANA*, Quint in *THE TURN OF THE SCREW*, Flute in *A MIDSUMMER NIGHT'S DREAM* (and also was the colibrettist with the composer), the Madwoman in *CURLEW RIVER*, Sir Philip Wingrave in *OWEN WINGRAVE*, and Aschenbach in *DEATH IN VENICE*, a role he repeated for his Metropolitan Opera debut in N.Y. in 1974. He helped to found the Aldeburgh Festival in 1948, serving as a director and teacher of master classes until his death.

Pears also sang in several first performances of Britten's nonoperatic works, including the *Serenade* for tenor, horn, and strings, the *Michelangelo Sonnets,* and the *WAR REQUIEM.* He also excelled in works of other English composers, among them EDWARD ELGAR, GUSTAV HOLST, RALPH VAUGHAN WILLIAMS, and WILLIAM WALTON. He was made a Commander of the Order of the British Empire in 1957 and was knighted in 1978.

Pêcheurs de Perles, Les (The pearl fishers). Opera by GEORGES BIZET, 1863, premiered in Paris. Two fishermen in Ceylon are rivals in love, but their object of adoration is Leila, a priestess bound to chastity. One of the suitors, Zurga, is elected a tribal chief and promises her a priceless pearl if she remains chaste. She spurns the pearl and flees the island with Nadiv, the other fisherman.

pedal. 1. A foot KEY on the ORGAN or pedal piano. 2. A foot lever, as the piano pedals, or the organ swell-pedal. 3. A treadle, like those used for blowing the REED ORGAN. 4. A stop knob or lever worked by the foot (organ). 5. A contraction for PEDAL POINT.

MUSICAL
INSTRUMENT

Pedal note or *tone,* a sustained or continuously repeated note (tone); *pedal organ,* the set of stops controlled by the organ pedals; *pedal piano,* a piano provided with a PEDALIER.

pedal point (organ point; Fr. *point d'orgue;* Ger. *Orgelpunkt;* Sp. *bajo de organo,* organ bass). A sustained NOTE, usually in the BASS (Fr. *pedale inférieure*), and usually on the DOMINANT or TONIC, or both simultaneously. It is called pedal point because on the ORGAN, on which it is particularly effective, it is played on a pedal by the foot.

A protracted organ point on the DOMINANT usually heralds the AUTHENTIC CADENCE on the TONIC. So great is the bond, so strong the harmonic hold of the pedal point on the dominant, that it can support chords on all degrees of the DIATONIC scale as well as modulations into the lowered SUPERTONIC or the lowered SUBMEDIANT in a MAJOR KEY. Among examples of this holding power are the conclusion of the church scene in CHARLES GOUNOD's *FAUST,* the relevant passages in the OVERTURE to RICHARD WAGNER's *DIE MEISTERSINGER,* and in the wedding procession in NIKOLAI RIMSKY-KORSAKOV's *LE COQ D'OR,* which contains modulations into several unrelated keys before finally resolving into the tonic.

CADENZAS in piano concertos are based on a prolonged pedal point on the dominant in the bass. Cadences in fugal compositions are often reinforced by the pedal point in the bass, as for instance in the second FUGUE of the first book of JOHANN SEBASTIAN BACH's *WELL-TEMPERED CLAVIER* (1722). Pedal points in the bass can be sustained on the modern piano by the use of the middle (sustaining) pedal.

Pedal point in the middle voices (Fr. *pedale intérieure*) are relatively rare, but there are examples to be found, as are examples of pedal points in the high treble, as in the conclusion of Rimsky-Korsakov's *SCHEHERAZADE* (1888).

Remarkably, some composers writing in an ATONAL idiom or employing 12-TONE techniques occasionally use pedal points to establish the binding element missing in a system of composition that theoretically eliminates both the tonic and the dominant.

pedalier. A set of pedals, either (1) so adjusted as to play the low octaves of the PIANO, after the manner of organ pedals;

ALEXANDER SCRIABIN maintains a pedal point on the tonic in the finale of his *Poème de l'extase* (Poem of ecstasy) for about five minutes!

MUSICAL
INSTRUMENT

or (2) provided with separate strings and action, to be placed underneath the piano.

Pedrell, Felipe, eminent Spanish musicologist and composer; b. Tortosa, Feb. 19, 1841; d. Barcelona, Aug. 19, 1922. Pedrell became a chorister at Tortosa Cathedral when he was about seven, receiving instruction from Juan Antonio Nin y Serra. In 1873 he went to Barcelona as deputy director of the Light Opera Company, where he produced his first opera, *L'ultimo Abenzeraggio* a year later.

PEOPLE IN MUSIC

After a visit to Italy in 1876–77, and a sojourn in Paris, Pedrell settled in Barcelona in 1881, where he devoted himself mainly to the study of music. In 1882 he founded the journals *Salterio Sacro-Hispano* and *Notas Musicales y Literarias,* both of which ceased publication in 1883. He then was founder-editor of the important journal *La Ilustración Musical Hispano-Americana* from 1888 to 1896. During this period he worked on his operatic masterpiece, the trilogy *Los Pirineos/Els Pirineus* (1890–91). He also published the book *Por nuestra música* (For our music; 1891), which served as its introduction and as a plea for the creation of a national lyric drama based on Spanish folk song.

In 1894 Pedrell went to Madrid, where he was named professor of choral singing at the Conservatory and professor of advanced studies at the Ateneo. He was also elected a member of the Royal Academy of Fine Arts. Upon his return to Barcelona in 1904, he devoted himself to writing, teaching, and composing. Among his outstanding pupils were ISAAC ALBÉNIZ, MANUEL DE FALLA, ENRIQUE GRANADOS, and ROBERTO GERHARD.

Although Pedrell was admired as a composer by his contemporaries, his music has not obtained recognition outside his homeland. His lasting achievement rests upon his distinguished musicological work, which did much to restore interest in both historical and contemporary Spanish sacred music. Pedrell contributed studies of Spanish, Catalan, Latin American, and Portuguese music, bibliographies, early and new music studies, dictionaries, studies of Spanish liturgy and religious festivals, composer monographs, and examinations of opera and Spanish song. He also edited several collections of religious and secular works.

Peer Gynt. Incidental music by EDVARD GRIEG, 1876, for Norwegian playwright Henrik Ibsen's drama, premiered in Christiania (now Oslo).

Two orchestral suites were drawn from Grieg's music for the play, the first being particularly celebrated. It contains the poetic pastorale *In the Morning,* followed by the mournful dirge *Ase's Death,* a mazurka-like *Anitra's Dance,* and the sinister rollicking piece *In the Hall of the Mountain King.*

The second suite, performed separately in Christiania in 1891, includes *Ingrid's Lament, Arabian Dance, Stormy Evening on the Seashore,* and *Solveig's Song.*

PEOPLE IN MUSIC

Peerce, Jan (born Jacob Pincus Perelmuth), noted American tenor; b. N.Y., June 3, 1904; d. there, Dec. 15, 1984. Peerce played violin in dance bands and sang at various entertainment places in N.Y. In 1932, he was engaged as a singer at N.Y.'s Radio City Music Hall.

Peerce made his operatic debut in Philadelphia as the Duke of Mantua in 1938 and gave his first solo recital in N.Y. a year later. His lyrical voice attracted attention, and he was engaged by the Metropolitan Opera in N.Y., where he made his debut as Alfredo in 1941. He also sang Cavaradossi, Rodolfo, and Gounod's Faust there, remaining on its roster until 1966, appearing again in 1967–68.

Peerce retired in 1982. He was the brother-in-law of noted opera tenor RICHARD TUCKER.

Peggy-Ann. Musical by RICHARD RODGERS and LORENZ HART, 1926. A girl in a small town in N.Y. tries to escape her uninteresting environment and an impending marriage to an unglamorous local man by retreating to a world of fantasy. In her dreams she is an adventuress in N.Y., where she is a guest on a yacht and the bride of a rich playboy. Eventually, she returns to the bittersweet reality of the only existence granted her by fate. Includes *A Tree in the Park* and *Maybe It's Me.*

Peggy Sue. BUDDY HOLLY's 1957 No. 3 hit, his biggest in the U.S. during his lifetime. It inspired the follow-up song and later a film entitled *Peggy Sue Got Married.*

Pelléas et Mélisande. Lyric drama by CLAUDE DEBUSSY (1893–1902), to a libretto drawn from Belgian dramatist Maurice Maeterlinck's tragedy of the same name. It was first performed in Paris in 1902.

Golaud finds Mélisande wandering in a forest. He marries her, but soon an affectionate though innocent alliance develops between Mélisande and Golaud's half-brother, Pelléas. When she lets her long hair fall from her window, Pelléas caresses it. Golaud's jealousy is aroused, and he becomes violent. In a famous scene he drags Mélisande on the floor by her hair, and in a triumph of understatement she whispers, "I am not happy today."

When Golaud finds her with Pelléas at the fountain in the park, he kills Pelléas. Mélisande is about to bear Golaud's child; dying in childbirth, she forgives her husband for his crime.

So unusual is the music, so dramatic its departure from traditional French opera, that Paris music critics were bewildered. When RICHARD STRAUSS attended a performance of *Pelléas et Mélisande* in Paris, he turned to a friend during the first act and asked: "Is it going to go on and on like this?" To an uninitiated listener Debussy's music may appear static and monotonous.

Debussy's free use of unresolved DISSONANCES, frequent progressions of DOMINANT-NINTH CHORDS, and unstable tonality, all contributed to critical incomprehension. It took many years for *Pelléas et Mélisande* to take its rightful place among operatic masterpieces.

A Paris critic admitted by way of a compliment, "True, this music makes little noise, but it is a nasty little noise."

Pelléas et Mélisande. Symphonic poem by ARNOLD SCHOENBERG, 1905, based on the same play as CLAUDE DEBUSSY's masterpiece, first performed in Vienna, the composer conducting. The work is in the late-ROMANTIC style.

pelog. One of two principal SCALE categories in GAMELAN music. It is a PENTATONIC (five-note) group, in various tunings. A common example resembles the tempered scale E–F–G–B–C, i.e., with two SEMITONES and a large gap between C and E.

Penderecki, Krzysztof, celebrated Polish composer; b. Debica, Nov. 23, 1933. Penderecki was educated in Krakow,

PEOPLE IN MUSIC

1331

where he took courses at the Jagellonian University. After private composition studies, he received instruction in theory at the State Higher School of Music from 1955 to 1958. He was a lecturer in composition there from 1958 to 1966, remaining with it when it became the Academy of Music as rector (from 1972 to 1987) and as professor (from 1972). He also was professor of composition at the Essen Folkwang Hochschule für Musik from 1966 to 1968 and at Yale University from 1973.

Penderecki rapidly acquired a reputation as one of the most original composers of his time, receiving numerous international honors and honorary degrees. After a few academic works, he developed a hypermodern technique of composition in a highly individual style in which no line is drawn between CONSONANCE and DISSONANCE, TONAL or ATONAL MELODY, or traditional or innovative instrumentation. An egalitarian attitude toward all available resources of sound prevails. While his idiom is naturally complex, he does not disdain tonality, even in its most traditional forms.

Penderecki's music follows an athematic course, in constantly varying metrical and rhythmic patterns. He utilizes an entire spectrum of modern sonorities, expanding the domain of TONE to unpitched elements, making use of many novel effects (shouting, hissing, verbal interjections, tapping, rubbing, or snapping the fingers against the body of an instrument, etc.). For this he designed a complex NOTATION system using special symbols. He applies these modern devices to religious music, including MASSES in the orthodox Roman Catholic ritual.

Penderecki's most impressive (and most frequently performed) work is *Tren pamieci ofiarom Hiroszimy* (Threnody in memory of victims of Hiroshima) for 52 string instruments, composed in 1959–60. It is rich in dynamic contrasts and ends on a two-octave TONE CLUSTER.

Pennies from Heaven. Sentimental song by Arthur Johnston, 1936, introduced by BING CROSBY in a movie musical of the same name.

PEOPLE IN MUSIC

Penniman, Richard Wayne, called **Little Richard,** pioneering African-American rock 'n' roll singer and songwriter, extolled by his followers as the "King of Rock 'n' Roll"; b. Macon, Ga., Dec. 5, 1932. One of the most powerful performers in all of rock 'n' roll, Little Richard has had a long and varied career.

He was reared in a religious family. Both his grandfather and two uncles were ministers. Richard began singing and playing the piano in church, although his parents disapproved of even this music-making. He left home at age 13 (in several interviews decades later, he claimed his parents were upset by his developing homosexuality) and moved in with a white couple who owned a local bar, where he began performing.

Richard won a talent contest in 1951 in Atlanta, leading to a brief recording contract with RCA. He then relocated to Houston, Texas, where he recorded and toured, without much success, through 1955. That year, he made a demo tape for the Los Angeles-based Specialty label, where he teamed up with the producer Bumps Blackwell. In the initial sessions, Richard was cutting up and performing an off-color song that he played at his club gigs. After the lyrics were reworked, the result was *Tutti Frutti*—and a massive hit with both white and black audiences.

Richard's high-powered vocal performance, replete with whoops and hollers, and passionate piano pounding made *Tutti Frutti* an irresistible record. Naturally, the follow-ups repeated the formula, including: *Long Tall Sally; Rip It Up; Lucille; Jenny Jenny;* and *Good Golly, Miss Molly* through 1958. Richard also appeared on television variety shows and in a couple of teen-oriented films. However, in 1957 Richard had a vision of the world coming to an end, a sign that he had created sinful music. Flooded with remorse, he enrolled in a Bible college, emerging as a minister in the Seventh Day Adventist church, the home church of his family. He began recording gospel material and working as a minister, leaving behind his secular recordings.

The conversion stuck for seven years. In 1964 Richard made the first of many comebacks. Despite the fact that the Beatles were covering his songs, and even imitating his trademark "Whooos," Richard's time had passed. He continued to alternate between God and rock 'n' roll through the '70s, making another highly publicized return to the church at the decade's end.

Richard made a comeback again in 1985, when he had a cameo role in the hit social commentary film *Down and Out in Beverly Hills.* This led to renewed work on television series and commercials, as well as appearances in documentaries on the early days of rock. Richard never failed to claim to have invented rock 'n' roll.

Little Richard was in the first class of ten performers inducted into the Rock and Roll Hall of Fame in 1986. In 1993, he won a lifetime achievement Grammy award.

In a memorable sequence in the film *Hail, Hail, Rock and Roll* on the life and times of CHUCK BERRY, he shares stories with Berry and BO DIDDLEY about racism in the rock world.

pentachord. The first five notes of a SCALE.

pentatonic scale. A five-TONE SCALE, usually avoiding SEMITONIC steps by skipping the FOURTH and SEVENTH degrees in MAJOR, and the SECOND and SIXTH in natural MINOR.

Pentatonic scales are tonal progressions that can be played on the black keys of the piano keyboard. Such Westernized scales can be classified as major and minor, major pentatonic being simulated by a scale starting on F-sharp of the "black key scale," and the minor pentatonic by one starting on E♭. Consecutive FIFTHS and FOURTHS are the formative intervals, with harmonization usually based on pedal points on the presumed TONIC and DOMINANT. This type of music sounds alluringly exotic.

Many traditional and classical musics of the non-Western world use pentatonic scales as the basis of their melodies. These actually employ tones that fall outside the tempered Western scale, so that using the black notes of the piano to approximate these scales is, at best, a compromise.

The best examples of pentatonic music in Western classical music are found in the works of CLAUDE DEBUSSY and MAURICE RAVEL. Debussy uses the pentatonic scale in the middle section of his piano piece *Voiles,* and Ravel, in the third piece of his suite *MA MÈRE L'OYE* (1910), entitled *The Empress of the Pagodas.* Among modern operas containing materials from the pentatonic structures of the East are GIACOMO PUCCINI's *MADAMA BUTTERFLY* (1904), which employs Japanese melodic patterns, and *TURANDOT* (1926), presenting examples of pseudo-Chinese melodies.

Actually, the most common Japanese mode, although pentatonic, contains a semitone and so cannot be reduced to a "black key" scale. On the other side of the world, Irish and Scottish melodies contain pentatonic scales that in their structural aspects are quite different from Eastern examples.

Pepper, Art(hur Edward, Jr.), American jazz alto saxophonist; b. Gardena, Calif., Sept. 1, 1925; d. Los Angeles, June 15, 1982. Pepper's father was of German origin, and his mother was Italian. He played jazz clarinet and alto saxophone in school bands. He got married at 17 and then was drafted into the U.S. Army.

After his discharge, Pepper joined saxophonist STAN KENTON's band from 1946 to 1952. Pepper played in rich, emotional, and melodic style, influenced by his mentor, CHARLIE PARKER. He began making records, sometimes under the punning pseudonym Art Salt. However, his highly promising career was ruined by his addiction to heroin and other narcotic drugs. He squandered his earnings and, driven by the need for expensive drugs, descended into thievery and brawls. He was busted in 1952 on narcotics charges and served time in the Los Angeles County jail.

In 1953 Pepper was paroled to the U.S. Public Health Service Hospital at Fort Worth. He got in trouble again and was sentenced to jail in Los Angeles, where he served from 1954 to 1956 and again in 1960–61. Unable to control his habits, he was arrested and sent to San Quentin, where he served from 1961 to 1964 and, after another transgression, in 1965–66. In 1968–69, he played with drummer Buddy Rich's Big Band.

Pepper finally overcame his drug habit in the mid-'70s. He played mostly in small-band settings, although he recorded in a number of different accompaniments, including strings. Pepper's final style showed the same power and drive that he had in the '50s, with some more modern influences. He frankly told of his struggles with drug addiction in his autobiography, *Straight Time,* released in 1979, and in a documentary film on his life made in 1982.

Perahia, Murray, outstanding American pianist of Spanish-Jewish descent; b. N.Y., April 19, 1947. Perahia studied pi-

PEOPLE IN MUSIC

PEOPLE IN MUSIC

ano privately from 1953 to 1964. He then entered the Mannes College of Music, where he studied conducting and composition, earning his bachelor's degree in 1969. He also continued his piano studies with Artur Balsam and Mieczyslaw Horszowski.

In 1968 Perahia made his CARNEGIE HALL debut in N.Y. In 1972 he became the first American to win (by unanimous vote) the Leeds International Pianoforte Competition. In 1975 he was awarded the first Avery Fisher Prize, sharing it with the cellist Lynn Harrell. He appeared as soloist with leading orchestras of the U.S. and Europe and also gave many recitals in the U.S. and abroad. In 1982 he was appointed coartistic director of the Aldeburgh Festival, a post he held until 1989.

In 1992 Perahia suffered from a crippling hand injury that led him to retire briefly from public performances. He returned to the concert stage in 1994 as a soloist in LUDWIG VAN BEETHOVEN's Fourth Piano Concerto, in London. It took a further two years before the real problem was discovered—a bone spur in his right thumb—and Perahia could return to a full schedule of recording and performing.

Perahia excels in CLASSICAL music, having mastered all of WOLFGANG AMADEUS MOZART's concertos, often conducting from the keyboard. Despite focusing on the Classical repertoire, he is known for his emotional playing, which has intensified since his recovery from his hand problems in the early '90s.

MUSICAL INSTRUMENT

percussion (from Lat. *percutere,* strike, beat). The striking or beating of one body against another. Instruments of percussion are the DRUMS, TAMBOURINE, CYMBALS, BELLS, TRIANGLE, etc., as well as the DULCIMER and PIANO.

Not all instruments now classified in the percussion group really "percuss" (*percussus* is the past participle of *percutere,* meaning to strike or beat). There are instruments of concussion (from Lat. *concutere,* shake violently), shaken instruments such as the popular Latin American MARACAS, and instruments of friction, such as the GUIRO; CASTANETS that are clapped together, rather than struck, also do not fit easily into the category of percussion.

◀ *Percussionists in the orchestra.*
(Jim Seere)

Because most percussion instruments perform a rhythmic function, perhaps the term *rhythm instruments,* which has been gaining increasing acceptance not only in JAZZ but also in serious music, should be considered as an alternative.

There is a tendency to include KEYBOARD instruments among percussion instruments, but this would be historically and functionally wrong. Although the piano and its predecessor, the HARPSICHORD, are indeed percussed, their function, at least traditionally speaking, is not rhythmical par excellence. Perhaps the concept should be limited to some orchestral and ensemble pieces of the 20th century. On the other hand, the CELESTA, MARIMBA, VIBRAPHONE, and XYLOPHONE, which possess keyboards, are customarily included in the percussion section.

In the orchestral scores of the BAROQUE and CLASSICAL periods, percussion was relegated to a subordinate position and often notated on a supplementary line. Instruments of indefinite pitch—BASS DRUM, cymbals, triangles—were exotic imports described as JANIZARY MUSIC. The use of ethnic percussion continued into the following centuries. Other special sounds, such as the whip, were added as needed.

The first percussion instruments of definite pitch in the 18th-century orchestra, the TIMPANI, were usually found in pairs, tuned to the TONIC and the DOMINANT, and performed the function of reinforcing the bass. Their parts were often placed below the bass line in the score.

> 🎵
>
> The German terms for percussion, *Schlaginstrumente* (striking instruments) and *Schlagzeug* (literally, striking things), also fail to include the rhythmic effects produced by concussion and friction instruments.

Among percussion instruments of definite pitch, the largest group are the KEYBOARDS, all of them playing in the treble. The GLOCKENSPIEL has a penetrating bell-like sound and is often used whenever exotic color is invoked, i.e., the magic "instrument of steel" in WOLFGANG AMADEUS MOZART'S *DIE ZAUBERFLÖTE*. PIOTR ILYICH TCHAIKOVSKY makes effective use of the glockenspiel in the *Chinese Dance* of his *Nutcracker Suite*. Its keyboard equivalent, the CELESTA, patented in 1866, is used in his *Dance of the Sugar-Plum Fairies*. Another type of celesta manufactured in the 20th century is called *dulcitone*. Its "dulcet" tone is obtained through the substitution of steel bars by clear and OVERTONE-free tuning forks.

The XYLOPHONE (from Grk., wood sound) is a relative newcomer in Western orchestral literature, although it was known under the name of *Holzharmonika* (Ger., wood harmonica) in the 16th century. CAMILLE SAINT-SAËNS used it most effectively in his *Danse macabre* to imitate the clatter of skeleton bones. It is quite frequently used in modern scores because of its clear and articulate timbre.

The MARIMBA, a Latin-American import, is a keyboard instrument with resonators attached underneath. The VIBRAPHONE is made with steel bars and is electrically amplified. Both the vibraphone and the marimba are recent entries in popular and serious modern music. DARIUS MILHAUD wrote a concerto for the marimba, and many composers have included the vibraphone in their scores.

Russian OPERA composers often use church bells in their scores: Pyotr Ilyich Tchaikovsky in his *1812 OVERTURE* (1882), NIKOLAI RIMSKY-KORSAKOV in his *THE LEGEND OF THE INVISIBLE CITY OF KITEZH* (1907), and MODEST MUSSORGSKY in the conclusion of his witch-riddled *NIGHT ON BALD MOUNTAIN* (1886, actually added by Rimsky-Korsakov in his revision of the work). ARAM KHACHATURIAN used bells in his Second Symphony (1943) to glorify the Russian resistance to the Nazi invasion in World War II. In fact, this symphony has been called *SYMPHONY WITH A BELL*.

Tubular bells, also called *orchestral chimes*, are often used to represent church bells, such as the *Witches' Sabbath* in HECTOR BERLIOZ'S *SYMPHONIE FANTASTIQUE* (1830). Bell-like sounds are produced by other instruments made of metal: the cymbals, a pair of which is struck together; large GONGS (pitched) and TAM-TAMS (unpitched); the TRIANGLE; and a variety of shaken jingles such as sleigh bells. The TAMBOURINE has a drum head with little cymbals attached.

Drums, big and small, have furnished realistic effects in a number of scores in which military references are made, or to portray an execution, as in *TILL EULENSPIEGEL* (1895) by RICHARD STRAUSS or the *Robespierre Overture* (1856) by Henry Charles Litolff. In his Fifth Symphony, CARL NIELSEN has a long passage for a SNARE (side) DRUM in which the player is instructed to keep drumming, as if determined to interrupt the progress of the music itself. The BASS DRUM looks and sounds impressive enough to suggest ominous events.

CHINESE BLOCKS have a percussive sound almost as clear and penetrating as the xylophone, except that their pitch is indefinite. Among other percussion instruments, CLAVES are an integral part of Latin-American popular bands, but the instrument has also been adopted in modern scores, e.g., STEVE REICH's *Music for Pieces of Wood* for five pairs of tuned claves from 1973. Its sound is produced by striking together two pieces of resonant hardwood.

A tremendous expansion of the role of the percussion section in modern orchestral scores has put drummers in a privileged position in the orchestra. Some percussion parts demand real virtuosity, as for instance in IGOR STRAVINSKY's *L'HISTOIRE DU SOLDAT* (1918), in which a single performer must be able to handle several instruments in a truly acrobatic fashion. MORTON FELDMAN's virtuosic *The King of Denmark* from 1964 is another good example.

Percussion ensembles specializing in music expressly written for percussion have proliferated in Europe and America. For much of his early career, JOHN CAGE was known as a percussion composer, and his *Second Construction* for four percussionists (Portland, Ore., Feb. 14, 1940) remains quite popular. And there is at least one masterpiece of percussion literature for large ensemble, *IONISATION*, by EDGARD VARÈSE (1931), scored for 42 percussion instruments and two sirens.

CARL ORFF elevated the rhythm instruments to a commanding position in elementary music education. His specially designed instruments, including many xylophones and bells, are used to teach children the basics of music.

Perfect Day, A. Song, 1910, by Carrie Jacobs Bond (1862–1946), the tune of which was filched none too discreetly from ANTON RUBINSTEIN's *Melody in F.*

The song fits into any kind of social function, from a private club's entertainment to nondenominational funerals, even for singing in pubs. Five million copies of sheet music were sold, and the pursuit of happiness of millions of American single women was encouraged.

perfect pitch. Ability to name instantly and correctly any note sounded; also called *absolute pitch.*

This is an innate faculty, which appears in a musical child at a very early age. It is distinct from relative pitch, common among all musicians, in which a note can be named through an identification of its distance from one previously played. Perfect pitch is rare, even among professional musicians, and its presence is not a sure indication of great musical talent. For example, RICHARD WAGNER, HECTOR BERLIOZ, PIOTR ILYICH TCHAIKOVSKY, MAURICE RAVEL, and IGOR STRAVINSKY lacked it, while many obscure musicians have possessed it. Despite repeated claims by music educators, perfect pitch cannot be attained by ear training.

perfection (Lat., *perfectio*). *See* MENSURAL NOTATION; NOTATION.

Pergolesi, Giovanni Battista, remarkable Italian composer; b. Jesi, near Ancona, Jan. 4, 1710; d. Pozzuoli, near Naples, March 16, 1736. The original family name was Draghi. The name Pergolesi was derived from the town of Pergola, where Pergolesi's ancestors lived. Pergolesi was the only surviving child of his parents, three others having died in infancy. His childhood seems to have been plagued by ill health.

Pergolesi first studied with Francesco Santi, the maestro di cappella of the Jesi Cathedral. He also studied violin with Francesco Mondini. He then was given a stipend by the Marchese Cardolo Maria Pianetti, which enabled him to enter the Conservatorio dei Poveri di Gesù Cristo in Naples, where he studied violin with Domenico de Matteis and composition with Gaetano Greco, its maestro di cappella, Leonardo Vinci, and Francesco Durante. He became highly

PEOPLE IN MUSIC

A later caricature depicts Pergolesi as having a deformed leg.

proficient, playing at the Conservatory and throughout Naples.

Pergolesi's first performed work was the dramma sacro *Li prodigi della divina grazia nella conversione di S. Guglielmo Duca d'Aquitania,* given by the Conservatorio at the monastery of S. Agnello Maggiore in 1731. He graduated shortly thereafter and received a commission for his first opera, *La Salustia,* presented in Naples in January 1732. He then became maestro di cappella to Prince Ferdinando Colonna Stigliano. That September, his OPERA *Lo Frate 'nnamorato* proved highly successful. In December he composed several sacred works for performance at the church of S. Maria della Stella as an offering following a series of severe earthquakes in Naples.

He was next commissioned to write an OPERA SERIA to celebrate the birthday of the empress in 1733, *Il Prigionier superbo.* It contained the two-act intermezzo LA SERVA PADRONA, which became his most celebrated stage work. He was named deputy to the maestro di cappella of Naples in 1734. During a brief sojourn in Rome, his Mass in F major was performed at the church of S. Lorenzo in Lucina.

After returning to Naples, Pergolesi became maestro di cappella to Marzio Domenico IV Carafa, the Duke of Maddaloni. For the birthday of the king's mother, he was commissioned to write the opera *Adriano in Siria.* It was premiered, without success, in Naples in 1734, with the intermezzo *La Contadina astuta* (subsequently staged under various titles). He then was commissioned to write an opera for Rome's Teatro Tordinona, resulting in his unsuccessful opera seria *L'Olimpiade.* His last popular success for the stage was the commedia musicale *Il Flaminio.* Both works were premiered in 1735.

By 1735 Pergolesi's health had seriously declined, most likely from tuberculosis. Early in 1736 he went to the Franciscan monastery in Pozzuoli, where he soon died, at the age of 26. He was buried in the common grave adjacent to the Cathedral.

Following his death, Pergolesi's fame spread rapidly through performances of *La Serva padrona* and several other stage works. The Paris revival of the work in 1752 precipitated the "querelle des bouffons" between the partisans of the Italian and French opera. His fame was further increased by performances of the *Salve regina* in C minor and the *Stabat Mater* in F minor.

Peri was nicknamed "Il Zazzerino" (the long-haired one) because of his abundant head of hair.

Peri, Jacopo, significant Italian composer, b. Rome, Aug. 20, 1561; d. Florence, Aug. 12, 1633. Peri was descended from a noble Florentine family. At an early age he went to Florence, where he entered the convent of Ss. Annunziata in 1573 and became a singer. He also studied with Cristofano Malvezzi. He was organist at the Badia from 1579 to 1605 and a singer at the church S. Giovanni Battista by 1586.

In 1588 Peri entered the service of the Medici court of Grand Duke Ferdinando I. He was also in the service of the Mantuan court from the early 1600s. The Florentine CAMERATA met at the home of Count Giovanni de' Bardi in the 1580s, and it is likely that Peri participated in its activities.

As early as 1583, Peri collaborated with other composers on music to be played between the acts of Giovanni Fedini's dramatic comedy *Le due Persilie.* In the 1590s the home of Jacopo Corsi became the meeting place for many Florentine musicians, poets, and philosophers. Peri undoubtedly attended these meetings, because Corsi collaborated with him in setting Ottavio Rinuccini's pastoral *Dafne* to music. The first known performance of this work was a private one in Florence in 1598. *Dafne* is generally recognized as the first opera in monodic style, or STILE RAPPRESENTATIVO.

Peri's next opera was *Euridice,* again to a text by Rinuccini. Some of the music was rewritten by GIULIO CACCINI for the first performance, which was given for the wedding of Maria de' Medici and Henri IV of France at the Palazzo Pitti in Florence in 1600. Peri composed the opera *Tetide* (libretto by Cini) for Mantua in 1608, but it was not performed. Peri's next opera, *Adone* (libretto by Cicognini), was finished by 1611, but a performance scheduled for Mantua in 1620 never took place. Another work of the period, *La liberazione di Tirreno e d'Arnea,* from 1617, may be by Peri. It is also possible that he collaborated with Marco da Gagliano on the score, or it may be totally the work of Gagliano.

In 1619 Peri definitely collaborated with Gagliano on the opera *Lo sposalizio di Medoro e Angelica.* It was given at the Palazzo Pitti, Florence in honor of the election of Emperor Ferdinand III. He also composed the role of Clori for the opera *La Flora*, the remainder of the music being by Gagliano. It was first performed in honor of the wedding of Margherita de' Medici and Duke Odoardo Farnese of Parma, again at the Palazzo Pitti in Florence in 1628. Peri also collaborated with Gagliano on three ORATORIOS, none of which have survived.

In addition to individual songs published in various collections of the time, Peri also brought out *La varie musiche* (for one to three voices) *con alcune spirituali in ultimo, per cantare, harpsichord, chitarrone, ancora la maggior parte di esse per sonare semplicemente, organ,* which was published in Florence in 1609.

Péri, La. Choreographic poem by PAUL DUKAS, 1912, first performed in Paris. The exotic story centers on a sleeping beauty who vanishes into thin air when approached by an eager youth in search of immortality. This ingratiatingly, impressionistic piece is often performed as a concert work.

Périchole, La. OPERETTA by JACQUES OFFENBACH, 1868, first performed in Paris. The heroine is a Peruvian street singer in the 18th century, when the country was under Spanish rule. She loves her singing partner, but the Spanish viceroy hires her as a staff member at his court. She undergoes all kinds of temptations, but in the end returns to her lover.

This is one of Offenbach's most famous works, and several of its tunes remain exceedingly popular.

period. A complete musical thought of 8, 12, or 16 MEASURES ending with an AUTHENTIC CADENCE. A typical structure is that of the question-answer (ANTECEDENT-CONSEQUENT) type, where the first half of the period ends in the DOMINANT and the second half in an authentic cadence in the TONIC.

périodique (Fr. adj., periodic). A publisher's catalogue, as produced in London and Paris in the 18th century, sometimes focusing on a single work. These publications facilitated the purchase of published music by concert societies and individual musicians. Gradually, literary annotations and short analyses of the work(s) offered for sale were added, eventually giving rise to the publication of music magazines.

Perkins, Carl, noted rockabilly guitarist and songwriter; b. near Tiptonville, Tenn., April 9, 1932; d. Nashville, Tenn., Jan. 19, 1998. Perkins grew up in rural Tennessee, where he learned guitar from an early age. He formed a family band with his brothers Jay and Clayton and local drummer W. S. Holland by his teen years, playing for local dances and events.

By Carl's early 20s, the band earned a recording contract with the tiny Flip label. In 1955 it signed with Memphis-based Sun Records, hot off its success with another Southern crooner, ELVIS PRESLEY. Perkins's second release, *Blue Suede Shoes,* topped the country, pop, and R&B charts, selling over two million copies. Booked to appear on national television, the band was involved in a serious automobile accident on route to the performance in which brother Jay died and Carl was seriously injured. Although Perkins had other hits, his career never regained its momentum.

Perkins signed with Columbia records in 1958, but by the early '60s he was more popular in England than at home. One of his British fans, guitarist GEORGE HARRISON, did much to popularize Perkins's songs, recording with the mop-topped Beatles' versions of *Honey Don't, Everybody's Trying to Be My Baby,* and *Matchbox* (itself a remake of "BLIND LEMON" JEFFERSON's classic '20s blues song).

Perkins became part of JOHNNY CASH's roadshow in the '60s, touring with the deep-voiced country singer through the mid-'70s. Perkins continued to perform through the '70s, '80s, and '90s, recording on occasion, but never really achieving much success. He was inducted into the Rock and Roll Hall of Fame in 1987. In 1995 he published his autobiography. He died of cancer and heart failure in 1998.

Perlman, Itzhak, brilliant Israeli-American violinist; b. Tel Aviv, Aug. 31, 1945. Perlman was stricken with polio when he was four, which left his legs paralyzed. Despite this handicap, he began to play the violin and gave regular recitals in Tel Aviv.

In 1958 Perlman was discovered in Israel by Ed Sullivan, the TV producer, and appeared on his show in N.Y. a year later. Perlman's courage and good humor endeared him to the public at once. He remained in N.Y., where his parents soon joined him, and was accepted as a scholarship student in the classes of Ivan Galamian and Dorothy DeLay at the Juilliard School of Music.

Perlman made his professional American debut in 1963, playing with the National Orchestra Association in N.Y. In 1964 he won first prize in the Leventritt Competition, which carried, besides the modest purse ($1,000), a significant bonus: an appearance with the N.Y. Philharmonic. It also brought about a lasting friendship with the well-known violinist ISAAC STERN, who promoted him with all the enthusiasm of a sincere admirer. Perlman toured the U.S. from coast to coast in 1965–66 and toured Europe in 1966–67. In 1975 he joined the faculty of Brooklyn College.

Perlman seemed to be overflowing with a genuine love of life. He played not only classical music but also TIN PAN ALLEY song arrangements, RAGTIME, and JAZZ. He became quite a habitué of the White House, being particularly popular with President Reagan, who savored Perlman's show-biz savvy. In 1986 he was awarded the U.S. Medal of Freedom.

Perlman has continued to tour widely through the '70s, '80s, and '90s. He is a favorite figure on public television. In 1995, he made a television documentary on traditional Jewish KLEZMER music, called *In My Father's House;* the record accompanying the program was an unexpected hit.

permutation. In SERIAL music, a theoretical term for the changing of the order of individual notes in the basic series, either through the three basic operations (RETROGRADE, INVERSION, RETROGRADE INVERSION), cell operations (exchanging three- or four-note ROW fragments with the same intervallic content), arithmetic processes (taking every other pitch, etc.), or rotation (transposing the row according to its own constituents).

Perotin (called Perotinus Magnus and Magister Perotinus), celebrated composer who flourished in the 12th century.

PEOPLE IN MUSIC

Perotin's very identity, as well as a general outline of his life, remains speculative. Some researchers believe that he was born between 1155 and 1160, may have studied with LEON-INUS, carried out his major work on the revision of the *Magnus liber* (a collection of two-part music covering the entire religious calendar, originally compiled by Leoninus) between 1180 and 1190, was involved in the early development of the MOTET between 1190 and 1200, wrote his works for four voices at the close of the century, and died between 1200 and 1205. Another chronology maintains that he wrote the works for four voices in the 1190s, worked on the *Magnus liber* during the first years of the new century, wrote elaborate CLAUSULAS about 1210, was instrumental in creating Latin motets between 1210 and 1220, and died about 1225.

perpetuum mobile (Lat., *perpetual motion,* It., Moto perpetuo). A type of short and rapid composition, usually for a solo instrument.

Perséphone. Ballet by IGOR STRAVINSKY, 1934, with song and narration, premiered in Paris. The plot involves the mythical tale of Persephone's descent into Hades and subsequent ascent to earth.

Persichetti, Vincent (Ludwig), remarkable American composer and teacher; b. Philadelphia, June 6, 1915; d. there, Aug. 13, 1987. Persichetti's father was a native of Abruzzi, Italy, who emigrated to the U.S. in 1894. His mother was of German extraction, hailing from Bonn.

Vincent studied piano, organ, double bass, tuba, theory, and composition as a youth. He began his career as a professional musician when he was only 11, becoming a church organist at 15. He took courses in composition with Russell King Miller at the Combs Conservatory, gaining his music degree in 1936, then served as head of the theory and composition department there. He concurrently studied conducting with FRITZ REINER at the Curtis Institute of Music, earning a diploma in 1938, and piano with Olga Samaroff and composition with Paul Nordoff at the Philadelphia Conservatory, earning his master's degree and doctorate in

PEOPLE IN MUSIC

Persichetti's middle name was given not to honor LUD-WIG VAN BEETHOVEN but to commemorate his maternal grandfather, who owned a saloon in Camden, New Jersey.

1941 and 1945, respectively. He also studied composition with ROY HARRIS at Colorado College.

From 1941 to 1947 Persichetti was head of the theory and composition department of the Philadelphia Conservatory. In 1947 he joined the faculty of the Juilliard School of Music in N.Y., and, in 1963 he was named chairman of its composition department. In 1952 he became director of music publishing of Elkan-Vogel, Inc. With F. Schreiber, he wrote a biography of William Schuman that was published in 1954. He also published a valuable manual, *Twentieth Century Harmony: Creative Aspects and Practice,* in 1961.

Persichetti's music is remarkable for its fusing of the ostensibly incompatible idioms of CLASSICISM, ROMANTICISM, and stark modernism. He has created great lyrical melodies despite his use of modern harmonies. His significance for American music is comprised in his nine symphonies (1942–70), and, most particularly, in his 12 piano sonatas (1939–80) and six piano sonatinas (1950–54).

Although Persichetti stood far from the turmoil of musical politics, he unexpectedly found himself in the center of a controversy when he was commissioned by the 1973 Presidential Inauguration Committee to write a work for narrator and orchestra for a performance at President Richard Nixon's inauguration. Persichetti selected the text of Abraham Lincoln's second inaugural address, but, surprisingly, objections were raised by certain groups to the passionate denunciation of war in the narrative, at a time when the Vietnam War was very much in the news. The scheduled performance by the Philadelphia Orchestra was hurriedly canceled, and the work's premiere was deferred to a performance by the St. Louis Symphony Orchestra in Jan. 1973.

In 1987 Persichetti was diagnosed with lung cancer, but even when racked by disease he continued to work on his last opus, *Hymns and Responses for the Church Year,* Vol. 2. He requested that his body be donated to medical science. His devoted wife suffered a stroke and died on Thanksgiving Day in the same year.

In addition to those works cited above, Persichetti's compositions include the opera *Parable XX: The Sibyl* (1976; Philadelphia, 1985), other orchestral works, chamber compositions, including four string quartets (1939; 1944; 1959;

1972), numerous other keyboard compositions, including eight harpsichord sonatas (1951–84), choral works and a number of songs, including the major cycle for soprano and piano entitled *Harmonium,* after the work of the American poet Wallace Stevens (1952).

pes (Lat.). Harmonic support or accompaniment to a ROUND.

Peter and the Wolf. Symphonic fairytale by SERGEI PROKOFIEV, 1936, for narrator and orchestra. He wrote it for the Moscow Children's Theater in a couple of weeks, to his own text.

Peter is a Russian lad who takes care of his pets, including a bird, duck, and cat. When a wolf invades his outdoor menagerie, Peter organizes a hunt, rounds up the predator, and saves his beloved creatures, except for the duck, who is caught by the wolf.

The score pursues a didactic purpose, each animal being represented by a different instrument and theme. It was first performed in Moscow and became enormously popular all over the world.

Peter Grimes. Opera by BENJAMIN BRITTEN, 1945, his most popular, first produced in London. The libretto is taken from George Crabbe's 19th-century poem *The Borough.* The music is alternately lyric and tragic. The symphonic interludes, descriptive of the sea, and particularly one imitating the cries of the gulls, are very fine.

Peter Grimes is a fisherman whose young apprentice is lost at sea. Everyone suspects Grimes of murder. A hearing is held, and although Grimes is not found guilty, he is enjoined not to hire other apprentices. He disobeys the order and hires a new helper, who accidentally falls off a cliff to his death. A sympathetic sea captain, Balstrode, advises the by-now demented Grimes to sail off and "sink the boat" so that he perishes at sea, rather than at the hands of the enraged populace.

PEOPLE IN MUSIC

Peter, Paul, and Mary. (Guitar/vocal: Peter Yarrow, b. N.Y., May 31, 1938; Guitar/vocal: Noel Paul Stookey, b. Baltimore, Md., Nov. 30, 1937; Vocal: Mary Travers, b. Louisville, Ky., Nov. 7, 1937.) Famed folk trio of the '60s who introduced the songs of BOB DYLAN to a mass audience.

Formed by canny promoter Albert Grossman, the group first hit it big with its interpretations of traditional folksongs like *900 Miles* and modern folk-styled compositions like PETE SEEGER's *Where Have All the Flowers Gone*. They had a major hit with Dylan's *Blowin' in the Wind* in 1963, followed by his *Don't Think Twice, It's All Right,* and subsequently recorded songs by other young singer/songwriters, including Tom Paxton, JOHN DENVER, and Gordon Lightfoot. The group had their greatest success in 1967 with Denver's *Leaving on a Jet Plane,* along with Yarrow's composition *The Song Is Love.* A children's album, playfully titled *Peter, Paul and Mommy,* produced a major hit with *Day Is Done* and helped revive their 1962 hit *Puff, the Magic Dragon.*

They broke up in 1970 to pursue solo careers with varying degrees of success. They reunited in 1978, continuing to record and perform. Since then, they have had several reunion concerts, many broadcast on public television.

Peterson, Oscar (Emmanuel), noted Canadian jazz pianist; b. Montreal, Aug. 15, 1925. Peterson first played the trumpet, but a childhood illness led him to change to the piano. After winning a talent contest in 1940, he began playing on Canadian radio. Between 1944 and 1947 he played with the popular Canadian orchestra led by Johnny Holmes.

Peterson made his N.Y. debut in 1949 as part of the Jazz at the Philharmonic series held at CARNEGIE HALL. This all-star concert was put together by entrepreneur/record producer Norman Granz, who began recording Peterson in a variety of settings. Over the next four decades, Peterson continued to tour and record, often with Granz as his producer.

Peterson's style combines the rich harmonies of ART TATUM with the melodic lyricism of popular jazz-pianists like ERROLL GARNER and George Shearing. This combined with a pleasant stage personality has made him attractive to not only jazz but more mainstream audiences as well.

Petri, Egon, eminent German pianist and teacher, of Dutch descent; b. Hannover, March 23, 1881; d. Berkeley, Calif.,

PEOPLE IN MUSIC

PEOPLE IN MUSIC

May 27, 1962. Petri's father, Henri Wilhelm Petri (1856–1914), was a Dutch violinist who served as concertmaster in Hannover and of the Leipzig Gewandhaus orchestra. His mother was a singer. Petri studied violin, organ, and piano from an early age. His most famous teacher was FERRUCCIO BUSONI, the Italian-German piano virtuoso and composer, and Petri would do much to keep Busoni's style alive in his playing.

Having pursued a career as an orchestral violinist and as a member of his father's string quartet, Petri launched his career as a piano virtuoso in 1902, subsequently touring extensively in Europe. He was also active as a teacher, serving on the faculties of the Royal Manchester College of Music from 1905 to 1911 and the Berlin Hochschule für Musik from 1921 to 1926.

In 1932 Petri made his U.S. debut in N.Y., then performed on both sides of the Atlantic until the outbreak of World War II. He also taught at Boston's Malkin Conservatory in 1934–35. After World War II, he resumed his extensive tours. Having taught at Cornell University from 1940 to 1946, he then settled in California to teach at Mills College from 1947 to 1957 and the San Francisco Conservatory from 1952 to 1962. He made his farewell concert appearance in a recital in 1960.

As Busoni's foremost student, Petri followed his mentor's grand manner of piano virtuosity. His performances of JOHANN SEBASTIAN BACH and FRANZ LISZT were formidable, but he also championed the works of Busoni, Charles-Valentin Alkan, and Nicolai Medtner.

Petri, Michala, gifted Danish recorder player; b. Copenhagen, July 7, 1958. Petri began to play at the incredibly young age of three and appeared on Danish radio when she was five. She made her concert debut as a soloist in Copenhagen in 1969. She studied with Ferdinand Conrad at the Hannover Staatliche Hochschule für Musik from 1970 to 1976.

Petri formed a trio with her mother, a harpsichordist, and her cellist brother, and toured widely with it. In addition to chamber music performances, she toured extensively as a soloist.

PEOPLE IN MUSIC

Petri made her U.S. debut with N.Y.'s 92nd St. Y Chamber Orchestra in 1982 and first played in Japan in 1984. Since then she has made tours all over the world as a soloist with orchestras and as a recitalist. Her repertoire ranges from the early BAROQUE era to contemporary music, including works commissioned by her from such notables as Malcolm Arnold, Vagn Holmboe, Thomas Kippel, and Per Nørgård. She was made a Knight of Dannebrog in 1995.

Petrouchka (*Pétrouchka, Petrushka*). IGOR STRAVINSKY wrote this most strikingly Russian work while in Switzerland in 1911, when he was only 28 years old. The famous BITONAL combination in the score, which became known as the "Petrouchka chord," is a superposition of C-major and F-sharp major TRIADS, white keys against black keys on the piano keyboard, falling easily under the fingers of both hands.

Stravinsky played sketches of a piano and orchestral work for the famous Russian impresario Serge Diaghilev, who thought the music would make an excellent ballet. The piano work was reconceived as a dance work (although a large piano part remains).

The scenario represented the Russian spring carnival, featuring a puppet show that evolves into the ballet. One puppet is named Petrouchka, an affectionate peasant form of the name Peter. He woos a beautiful ballerina puppet but is thwarted by a rich Moor puppet, who throws poor Petrouchka out of her quarters. There is a pathetic interlude, with Petrouchka's MOTIVE derived from the BROKEN bitonal chord. Eventually, the Moor murders Petrouchka, whose ghost appears at the ballet's end to haunt the puppeteer.

For his basic materials, Stravinsky made ample use of popular street songs of old Russia, but he also borrowed some Austrian WALTZES and even French CHANSONETTES. There is an imitation of the BARREL ORGAN, with its seductive disharmonies.

Petrouchka was performed in the Diaghilev series of Russian ballets in Paris, where it was an immediate success.

Strangely enough, *Petrouchka* was criticized by some Russian critics, who said that Stravinsky betrayed his national heritage by offering a vulgar and distorted treatment of native songs to please decadent Parisian tastes. Some

CLAUDE DEBUSSY was greatly impressed by it. In a private letter he described Stravinsky as a young savage who swept away all the musical rules and conquered the listeners.

American critics found the score unfit for concert performance because it recalled circus and vaudeville music. But all such fault-finding was soon forgotten. The score of *Petrouchka* still stands, after 75 years, as a remarkable specimen of true musical modernism.

PEOPLE IN MUSIC

Pettersson, Gustaf Allan, remarkable Swedish composer; b. Västra Ryd, Sept. 19, 1911; d. Stockholm, June 20, 1980. Pettersson's father was a blacksmith, his mother a devout woman who could sing. The family moved to Stockholm and lived in dire poverty. Pettersson sold Christmas cards and bought a violin from his meager returns. He also practiced on a church organ.

In 1930 Pettersson entered the Stockholm Conservatory, studying violin, viola, and theory. From 1940 to 1951 he played viola in the Stockholm Concert Society Orchestra and also studied composition privately. In his leisure hours he wrote poems, 24 of which he set to music. In 1951 he went to Paris to study with the noted composers ARTHUR HONEGGER and RENÉ LEIBOWITZ. Returning to Sweden, he devoted himself to composition in large forms.

Pettersson's music is filled with dark moods, and he supplied deeply pessimistic descriptions for his symphonies and other works. In 1963 he began suffering from painful rheumatoid arthritis, but he stubbornly continued to compose while also proclaiming his misfortunes. He described himself as "a voice crying out, drowned in the noise of the times." The Stockholm Philharmonic played several of his symphonies, but when his Seventh Symphony, originally scheduled for its American tour in 1968, was taken off the program, Pettersson forbade performance of any of his music in Sweden.

Stylistically, Pettersson's music is related to GUSTAV MAHLER's symphonic manner, in its grand designs and its passionate, exclamatory power. Most of his symphonies are cast in single movements, with diversity achieved by frequent changes of mood, TEMPO, METER, and RHYTHM. Characteristically, 15 of the 16 are set in minor keys (No. 10 is in major).

Pettersson also composed other orchestral works, including three concertos for string orchestra (1949–50; 1956;

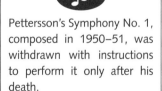

Pettersson's Symphony No. 1, composed in 1950–51, was withdrawn with instructions to perform it only after his death.

1956–57), and chamber and vocal works, notably *24 Barfo-tasånger* (24 barefoot songs) for voice and piano (1943–45), and *Vox humana,* 18 songs for soprano, alto, tenor, baritone, mixed chorus, and string orchestra, to texts by Native Americans (1974; Stockholm, 1976).

Petty, Tom, noted American rock 'n' roll singer and songwriter, leader of the group the Heartbreakers, b. Gainesville, Fla., Oct. 20, 1953. The nasal-voiced Petty has enjoyed a long career, both as the leader of the Heartbreakers and as a solo artist. He is greatly influenced by his '60s predecessors, including the Byrds, BOB DYLAN (with whom he has performed), and Neil Young, creating music that sounds eerily reminiscent of their earlier hits.

PEOPLE IN MUSIC

Petty began performing during high school in Gainesville, joining the band Mudcrutch on his graduation, along with guitarist Mike Campbell and pianist Benmont Tench. By the early 1970s they were in Los Angeles, where they gained a recording contract with Shelter Records. Known as Tom Petty and the Heartbreakers, they recorded two albums for the label, producing some minor hits. But when the label was sold to MCA, they entered a long legal battle, which led to a break in recording.

Returning on their own Backstreets label, Petty and the group produced their first major hit in 1979 with *Refugee.* Two years later, a duet with popular California rock singer Stevie Nicks on *Stop Draggin' My Heart Around* elevated Petty's stature greatly among pop fans. The band took a break to pursue individual projects from 1983 to 1985, returning to the charts with *Don't Come Around Here No More.*

In 1986 Petty and the band toured and recorded with Dylan, giving audiences a chance to hear two nasal-toned singers on the same bill! Two years later, joining with Dylan, GEORGE HARRISON, ROY ORBISON, and producer Jeff Lynne, Petty became a member of the mock-band, the Traveling Wilburys, who scored a series of surprise hits. A year later, he produced a successful solo album with several hits, including *I Won't Back Down* and *Free Fallin'.*

The Heartbreakers returned to recording and touring with Petty in 1991. Petty has since continued to record with the band, even for "solo" projects like *Wildflowers* (1994).

He scored the film *She's the One* in 1995, which produced the hit *Heart So Big.* In 1999, Petty and the band issued a new album, *Echo.*

PEOPLE IN MUSIC

Pfitzner, Hans (Erich), eminent German composer and conductor; b. Moscow (of German parents), May 5, 1869; d. Salzburg, May 22, 1949. Pfitzner studied piano with James Kwast at the Hoch Conservatory in Frankfurt. In 1899 he eloped with Kwast's daughter and took her to England, where they married.

From the early 1890s Pfitzner taught piano and theory at several leading German conservatories, while also conducting opera and theatrical orchestras. From 1908 to 1918 Pfitzner served as dean at the Strasbourg Conservatory and also conducted at the Strasbourg Opera. From 1920 to 1929 he led a master class at the Berlin Academy of Arts, and then was in Munich where he taught composition at the Akademie der Tonkunst until 1934.

Being of "pure" German parentage, Pfitzner was favored by the Nazi authorities and became an ardent supporter of the Third Reich. He even dedicated an overture, *Krakauer Begrüssung,* to Hans Frank, the murderous leader of occupied Poland, in 1944. After the collapse of Hitler's regime, Pfitzner had to face a war crimes court in Munich in 1948. Because of his advanced age, he was freed. He was taken to a home for the aged in Munich and later was transferred to Salzburg, where he died in misery. Eventually, his body was honorably laid to rest in a Vienna cemetery.

Pfitzner was hailed in Germany as a great national composer. He presented a concert of his works in Berlin in 1893, which was widely praised. After the premiere of his opera *Der arme Heinrich* in Mainz in 1895, the critics, among them the prestigious composer ENGELBERT HUMPERDINCK, praised the work in extravagant terms. Even more successful was his opera *Palestrina,* composed during 1911–15. The Pfitzner Society was formed in Munich as early as 1904, and a Hans Pfitzner Association was established in Berlin in 1938, with Wilhelm Furtwängler as president.

Although Pfitzner's music is traditional in style and conservative in HARMONY, he was regarded as a follower of the modern school, a comrade-in-arms of his close contemporary RICHARD STRAUSS. Very soon, however, his fame dwindled, and there were fewer performances of his operas and still fewer of his instrumental works. It was a miserable end for a once important and capable musician.

phase shifting. A technique of electronic music or recording in which a single melody line is doubled, with the second part played slightly "out of phase" (either slightly slower or faster) with the first.

Philharmonic Concerto. Variations for orchestra by PAUL HINDEMITH, 1932, for the 50th anniversary of the Berlin Philharmonic, which gave its first performance. There are six variations played with changing emphasis on one or another orchestral group.

Philidor, André Danican (L'Aîné), father of FRANÇOIS-ANDRÉ DANICAN PHILIDOR; b. Versailles, c.1647; d. Dreux, Aug. 11, 1730. Philidor was the son of Jean Danican (c.1620–1679), a composer and royal musician. In 1659 André entered the *grande écurie,* succeeding Michel Danican (c.1600–59), a family member. In it he played the cromorne, trompette marine, and drums. He subsequently played the oboe, bassoon, and bass cromorne in the royal chapel and *chambre du roi* (king's chamber or household).

In 1684 King Louis XIV appointed Philidor royal music librarian, a position he held until his death. During his long tenure, he acquired operas, ballets, sacred music, and partbooks from various periods of French history for the collection. A large portion of this collection eventually passed to St. Michael's College, Tenbury. It is now part of the collections at the Bibliothèque Nationale in Paris and the Bibliothèque Municipale in Versailles.

Philidor continued to serve as a musician in the royal chapel until 1722 and in the royal service until 1729. By his first wife he had 16 children, and by his second, 5. André's best-known works are his *opéras-ballets.* He also composed instrumental works, including dances and marches.

Philidor, François-André Danican, the greatest in a long line of eminent musicians, son of ANDRÉ DANICAN PHILIDOR;

Players of electric guitars and other amplified instruments can use a phase shifter, an electronic device, to achieve this result.

PEOPLE IN MUSIC

PEOPLE IN MUSIC

b. Dreux, Sept. 7, 1726; d. London, Aug. 31, 1795. Philidor was a page boy in the royal chapel in Versailles, where he studied music with the maître de chapelle, ANDRÉ CAMPRA. It was also at that time that he learned to play chess, a game at which he would later excel. A motet by him was performed in the royal chapel when he was 12.

In 1740 Philidor went to Paris, where he supported himself by copying music and teaching. His interest in chess continued, and he gained distinction as an outstanding player by defeating a number of celebrated masters of the day. He published a fundamental treatise on chess, *L'Analyze du jeu des échecs* in 1749. As a member of the St. James Chess Club in London, he gave lectures and demonstrations as a master.

At the same time, Philidor began a successful career as a composer for the theater. His first success was *Le Maréchal ferrant* (The blacksmith; 1761), which was given numerous performances. His *Le Sorcier* (The sorcerer; 1764) was also a triumph. Although *Tom Jones* (1765) was an initial failure, it enjoyed great popularity after its LIBRETTO was revised and it was performed in 1766. The same fate attended his *Ernelinde, princesse de Vorvège* when it was first given at the Paris Opéra in 1767. It was subsequently revised and performed most successfully as *Ernelinde* in Versailles in 1773.

Philidor continued to compose for the stage until his death, but he allowed his love for chess to take more and more of his time. He made frequent trips to London after 1775 to play at the St. James Chess Club.

Philidor was one of the finest early composers of OPÉRA-COMIQUE. Although his scores are often hampered by poor librettos, his orchestral writing is effective. He was an inventive composer and introduced the novelty of a vocal quartet a cappella (in *Tom Jones*). His choral work, *Carmen saeculare,* after Horace, proved most successful at its premiere in London in 1779. Other vocal works include *12 ariettes périodiques.*

Philippe de Vitry. *See* VITRY, PHILIPPE DE.

phonograph (U.K., gramophone). A mechanical device for reproducing sound or music.

A famous chess opening was named after Philidor.

The idea of preserving the sound of speech or music occupied the minds of poets and scientists for centuries. When the nature of sound was proved to be waves that could be recorded by attaching a stylus to a tuning fork and traced on a rotating blackened cylinder, the problem seemed near solution. All that had to be done was to play back the grooves on the cylinder with a sharp point, and the original sound produced by the tuning fork would be returned.

In 1877 Thomas Alva Edison attached a sensitive membrane to a stylus that impressed grooves on a wax cylinder. By retracing the grooves with the same stylus, the membrane was set in reciprocal motion and Edison heard the sound of his own voice reciting *Mary Had a Little Lamb*. Edison named this new invention *phonograph* (Grk., sound writing).

Many epoch-making inventions appear simultaneously, and indeed Edison had a close rival in the Paris inventor Charles Cros, who developed a talking machine that he named *parlephone* (speaking sound). Edison exhibited his phonograph at fairs and scientific expositions, but for many years it was regarded merely as an amusing toy. The rendition of the voice was squeaky and scratchy, but progress was rapid. A horn was attached to the recording membrane above the cylinder that amplified the sound so that it could be heard at a distance.

A decisive step in transforming an entertaining toy into an important musical instrument was the invention by Emile Berliner of a phonograph disc in 1888. Despite the obvious advantages of the disc, Edison continued to manufacture cylinders, introducing some improvements, finally yielding the field to the disc in 1929. In the meantime, the phonograph became a major industry, particularly in America. In 1900 the Victor Talking Machine Company adopted as its advertising symbol a picture of a dog listening to "His Master's voice" on a disc phonograph. So famous did the dog (named Nipper) and the slogan become that the phonograph itself became generally known after the name of this company, Victrola. The standard speed was established as 78 revolutions per minute (rpm).

The great drawback of the early phonograph disc was its limited length and its bulk. Each side of the disc could play

Edison visited Russia in 1890 and showed his instrument to eminent musicians, who were tremendously impressed. NIKOLAI RIMSKY-KORSAKOV signed an endorsement: "I heard the phonograph and I marveled at this invention of genius. Being a musician I can foresee the possibility of wide application of this device in the domain of musical art. A precise reproduction of talented interpretations of musical compositions, of outstanding singing voices, recording of folk songs, and improvisations by the means of the phonograph can be of incalculable importance to music. The phonograph also possesses the amazing capacity of accelerating and slowing down the tempo and to transpose [*sic*]. Glory be to great Edison!"

only four minutes and 30 seconds, and when recordings were made of SYMPHONIES and OPERAS, individual movements had to be split into several sections. The amount of music that could be held on a single disc was substantially enlarged by a seemingly obvious improvement in the late 1940s. By increasing the number of grooves on the disc and simultaneously slowing down the number of rpms from 78 to 33⅓ (or 45 rpms), it became possible to produce the 12-inch (diameter) long-playing record ("LP"), with each 33⅓ disc accommodating nearly half an hour of music. (The "45" disc is a seven-inch disc that accommodates up to about seven or eight minutes.) Furthermore, manufacturers began making records out of an unbreakable plastic material that was lighter than the shellac of the fragile 78s. An opera recorded on a "78" required many discs that weighed several pounds, whereas on the new 33⅓ LPs, the same opera could be recorded on two or three discs.

At the same time, progress was made in improving the sound quality of recordings. The first step toward a more realistic sound was the introduction of binaural recording, in which two separate monophonic channels were combined. By 1958 the technique was expanded to stereophonic recording ("stereo"), from the Greek word *stereos* (solid), in which sound could be distributed freely between the two channels by "mixing" the recorded sound. Recording through four channels, giving a vivid impression of being "surrounded" by sound, was introduced in 1970 under the name QUADRAPHONIC. It was, at the time, a commercial failure.

Finally, in the 1980s a remarkable improvement was made with the invention of the COMPACT DISC ("CD"). The stylus and analog recording are dispensed with, and, instead, sound is registered as a series of numbers (i.e., digitally) and transferred onto the metal-coated disc by laser.

phrase. Half of an eight-MEASURE PERIOD. Also, any short figure or PASSAGE complete in itself and unbroken in continuity.

phrase mark. A curved line connecting the notes of a PHRASE.

PHRASING: 1. The bringing into proper relief the phrases (whether MOTIVES, FIGURES, SUBJECTS, or PASSAGES). 2. The signs of notation devised to further this end.

Phrygian mode. *See* AUTHENTIC MODES.

Piaf, Edith (born Giovanna Gassion), noted French chanteuse; b. Paris, Dec. 19, 1915; d. there, Oct. 11, 1963. Piaf's childhood was tragic. After being abandoned by her mother, an Italian café singer and prostitute, she traveled with her father, a circus contortionist, acting as a shill for his street-corner acrobatics. She then became a street singer in Paris, earning the nickname "la môme Piaf" (the waif sparrow, in Parisian argot) because of her ragged and emaciated appearance.

PEOPLE IN MUSIC

Piaf was befriended by a cabaret owner, but when he was murdered, she was held by the French police as a material witness. During World War II and the German occupation, she entertained French prisoners in Germany. As a result, she was accused of collaboration but was eventually cleared. She made her first tour of the U.S. in 1947, then sang widely in subsequent years, making appearances in films and on television.

Although musically uneducated, Piaf developed a type of BALLAD singing that was filled with deep sentiment and expressive artistry. Her performances drew enthusiastic responses from nightclub audiences and sophisticated music critics. Not a songwriter, she made many CHANSONETTES internationally famous, including *La Vie en rose, What Can I Do?, I'll Remember Today, Hymne à l'amour,* and *Les Trois cloches.*

piano (It.). 1. Soft, softly (sign *p*). *Piano pedal,* the soft (or left) pedal of the pianoforte. 2. Standard abbreviation for *pianoforte* used in this dictionary. The piano is a KEYBOARD stringed instrument whose tones are produced by hammers striking the strings. The principal parts are the frame, the SOUNDBOARD, the strings, the ACTION, and the PEDALS.

pē-ah′nōh

MUSICAL
INSTRUMENT

The most popular musical instrument in the home and on the concert stage, the piano was invented in the first decade of the 18th century by Bartolommeo Cristofori, who

The internal mechanism of a piano. (Smithsonian Institution) ▶

called it a *Gravicembalo col piano e forte* (large keyboard with soft and loud). This rather clumsy description was soon abbreviated to pianoforte or (particularly in Russia) fortepiano. Subsequently, it became known under its present name.

The most important innovation of the piano, as distinguished from its keyboard predecessors, the HARPSICHORD and CLAVICHORD, was in its sound production mechanism. In the piano, the sound is produced by hammers striking the strings from below. Although the mechanism activating the hammers seems simple, the construction of the piano required a great deal of ingenuity. The hammers had to fall back to their original position after striking the strings without accidentally rebounding. Then, a soft damper that was lifted when the key was struck had to quickly fall back on the string to avoid its continued sounding. But if rapid repetition of the same note was needed, a special device had to be provided to make the hammer drop to an intermediate height between the original position and the strings, so that it could strike the string again in an instant. All of these requirements were met by the mechanism called the ESCAPEMENT.

In order to produce a sound an octave deeper, a string had to be doubled in length. If all piano strings were of the same thickness, then the string for the lowest C in the bass, seven octaves below the highest C on the keyboard, would have to be 128 times as long as the string for the high C, an obvious impossibility. An examination of the soundboard under the lid of the grand piano will show that the bass strings are much thicker than the treble strings, and it is through a combination of greater thickness and increased length that the bass strings can be accommodated within the wing-like shape of the piano.

The piano strings in the bass range are single for each tone. In the middle range, they are paired in order to give more sound, and in the extreme treble there are three strings to each tone to enhance the resonance still more. Dampers are absent in the extreme upper register of the piano because the thin strings do not sustain enough resonance to require dampening. Modern pianos have three pedals:

The German word for the grand piano is *Flügel*, wing. Curiously enough, LUDWIG VAN BEETHOVEN adopted the German name *Hammerklavier* for the sonatas of his last period. The word simply means "hammer keyboard."

The RIGHT-HAND (damper, loud) PEDAL releases all the dampers. All the keys played while the pedal is held down will continue to sound until the pedal is released.

The LEFT-HAND (soft) PEDAL shifts the entire keyboard slightly to the right. The result is that the hammers strike the bass strings obliquely, thus diminishing their volume, and strike only two out of three strings for each tone in the middle and upper registers. That is why the application of this pedal is often marked in classical scores as *una corda* (one string), or, more rarely, *due corde* (two strings), depending on the extent of the shift. When the left pedal is taken off, the action is indicated by the words *tre corde*.

Grand pianos and most modern pianos contain a MIDDLE PEDAL, the *sostenuto* (sustaining), which releases the dampers off any notes that are being held down by the fingers when this pedal is applied. Like the damper pedal, these notes are kept sounding until the sostenuto pedal is released.

The range of the early pianoforte was about the same as that of the contemporary HARPSICHORD, about four-and-a-half octaves, the upper limit being F above the staff of the treble clef (f^3). Because of the lack of higher notes, 18th-century composers for piano often had to transpose the RECAPITULATION section in SONATA form an octave lower in the middle of a sequence, as in WOLFGANG AMADEUS MOZART's famous C-major Piano Sonata, K. 545 (1788). Similar sudden transpositions occur in Beethoven's early sonatas.

Editors of classic piano music have been preoccupied with the problem of adapting these works written for a limited range so as to make use of the normal keyboard of modern pianos. Such a revision raises the speculative question whether Mozart would have taken advantage of the newly available higher notes in the recapitulation of his C-major Sonata K. 545 to avoid the awkward shift of register. As for Beethoven, he actually had a chance to revise his earlier sonatas for publication when the range of the keyboard was considerably extended within his own lifetime, but he failed to do so, possibly because he felt disinclined to spend time on such a revision, more likely because he felt there was no need to do so. But it certainly would be worthwhile to change the low A_2 to $G\sharp_2$ in the octave cascade in MAURICE RAVEL's *JEUX D'EAU* (1902), whenever this piece is performed on a piano with the extra notes in the bass.

The range of the piano keyboard was extended rapidly in the 19th century and soon stabilized in its present standard keyboard of seven octaves and a minor third, from A_2 to c^5. The Austrian firm of Bösendorfer manufactured early in the 20th century a piano that extended to C_2 (an added sixth below the standard low A), but it remains a curiosity and is seldom used in concert.

In the 19th century, the French manufacturer PLEYEL invented the PÉDALIER, a pedalboard akin to that of an organ, designed to be attached to the piano and played with the feet.

piano quartet. Composition for piano, violin, viola, and cello. *Piano quintet,* composition for piano and string quartet; *piano trio,* composition for piano, violin, and cello.

piano score. An ARRANGEMENT or REDUCTION of an orchestral work for PIANO.

pē-ăh-nōh-fôr′tĕh   **pianoforte** (It., loud-soft). Full name of PIANO; also dynamic mark.

pianola. *See* PLAYER PIANO.

Piatigorsky, Gregor, great Russian-born American cellist and teacher; b. Ekaterinoslav, April 17, 1903; d. Los Angeles, Aug. 6, 1976. Piatigorsky received his first lessons from his father, a violinist, then took cello lessons at the Moscow Conservatory. He played in various orchestras in Moscow.

In 1921 Piatigorsky left Russia. He took cello lessons with Julius Klengel in Leipzig. After serving as first cellist of the Berlin Philharmonic from 1924 to 1928, he devoted himself to a solo career. He played the solo part in DON QUIXOTE by RICHARD STRAUSS under the composer's direction many times in Europe and was probably unexcelled in this part. Strauss himself called him "mein Don Quixote."

Piatigorsky went to America in 1929 and made his American debut in Oberlin, Ohio. Later that year, he played ANTONÍN DVOŘÁK's Concerto with the N.Y. Philharmonic, eliciting great praise.

Piatigorsky was regarded as the world's finest cellist after PABLO CASALS. He continued giving solo recitals and appearing with major European and American orchestras for many years. He gave first performances of several cello works commissioned by him from PAUL HINDEMITH, Vladimir Dukelsky, MARIO CASTELNUOVO-TEDESCO, and others.

Piatigorsky became a naturalized U.S. citizen in 1942. He taught at the Curtis Institute of Music in Philadelphia from 1942 to 1951 and at the Berkshire Music Center in Tanglewood, Massachusetts. He was a professor at the University of Southern California in Los Angeles from 1962 to 1976.

Piatigorsky also presented a series of trio concerts with JASCHA HEIFETZ and Leonard Pennario. He was the recipient of honorary doctor of music degrees from many universities. He published an autobiographical volume, *Cellist,* in 1965.

PEOPLE IN MUSIC

Piazzolla, Astor, fiery Argentine bandoneón player, bandleader, composer, and arranger; b. Mar del Plata, March 11, 1921; d. Buenos Aires, July 5, 1992. Piazzolla was taken to N.Y. in 1924, where he took up the BANDONEÓN at age 12. Upon settling in Buenos Aires in 1937, he began a career as a bandoneón player and arranger. He also pursued training with ALBERTO GINASTERA and later was a scholarship student

PEOPLE IN MUSIC

in Paris of NADIA BOULANGER in 1954–55. He organized his own band and in 1960 founded the innovative Quinteto Nuevo Tango. From 1974 to 1985 he made his home in Paris, then returned to his homeland.

Piazzolla was a master of the modern TANGO, embracing the avant-garde style incorporating classical and JAZZ elements with a touch of modern DISSONANCES. His other works include OPERAS, theater music, film scores, CONCERTOS (including one for bandoneón, 1979), and chamber music.

MUSICAL INSTRUMENT

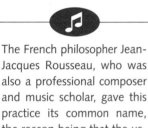

pibcorn (Welsh). A HORNPIPE dating from the Middle Ages to the 18th century, recently revived. It consists of a single or double cylindrical tube with a single beating REED, protected by a cowhorn mouth bell, terminating in a cowhorn bell. The tube, made of bone, wood, or cane, generally had six fingerholes and one rear fingerhole.

pē′brŏh

The French philosopher Jean-Jacques Rousseau, who was also a professional composer and music scholar, gave this practice its common name, the reason being that the usage was particularly strong in the French region of Picardy, where there were numerous cathedrals and organs.

pibroch (Gael.). Genre in VARIATION form for the Scottish Highland BAGPIPE.

Picardy third. The frequent practice in BAROQUE music of ending a minor-key piece with a MAJOR TONIC CHORD. The Picardy third in this case is the major third from the tonic.

Acoustic reasons suggest the preference of ending with a major third, an INTERVAL that is within the OVERTONE series, whereas the tonic minor third is not. Examples can be found literally by the millions, in the CADENCES of CHORALES, in the CODA of each of JOHANN SEBASTIAN BACH'S FUGUES in minor keys, and so on.

The principle of the Picardy third is also extended into whole SONATAS and SYMPHONIES in minor keys, the most resplendent illustration of which is found in LUDWIG VAN BEETHOVEN's Fifth Symphony in C minor, which ends in resounding C major.

PEOPLE IN MUSIC

Piccinni, (Vito) **Niccolò** (Nicola) (Marcello Antonio Giacomo), significant Italian composer; b. Bari, Jan. 16, 1728; d. Passy, near Paris, May 7, 1800. Piccinni's father was a violinist at Bari's Basilica di San Nicola, and his maternal uncle was the composer Gaetano Latilla. His precocity manifested itself at an early age.

Thanks to the archbishop of Bari, Piccinni was able at age 14 to enter Naples's Conservatory di S. Onofrio, where he studied with Leonardo Leo and Francesco Durante. Upon his graduation in 1754, he commenced his career as a composer for the stage with his comic opera *Le Donne dispettose,* which was produced in Naples.

Piccinni's theatrical instinct led him to select LIBRETTOS rich in dramatic content. He had a keen ear for melody and wrote ARIAS that fell naturally in the vocal range of each singer. He elaborated the conventional climactic scenes so that dramatic interest was sustained to the end, and he varied the TEMPOS and the HARMONIES in the ensembles, which further contributed to the quality of his works.

Piccinni's *Zenobia,* staged in Naples in 1756, was his first attempt at a serious opera. After several other operas for Naples, he received a commission to write an opera for Rome, *Alessandro nelle Indie,* in 1758. It was followed in 1760 by his comic opera *La Cecchina, ossia La buona figliuola,* which proved a great success at home and abroad. In subsequent years he wrote prolifically for the stage, producing well over 100 operas for the major Italian theaters.

Making his home in Naples, Piccinni served as second maestro di cappella at the Cathedral, was active as an organist in convents, and taught singing. Piccinni's fortunes in Rome declined with the rise of Pasquale Anfossi, his former pupil and protegé, in 1773. However, he still found success in Naples with a second *Alessandro nelle Indie* in 1774 and *I Viaggiatori,* a year later.

In 1776 Piccinni was called to Paris by the French court, where his presence precipitated the famous quarrel between the "Gluckists" and "Piccinnists."

Piccinni's first French opera, *Roland,* staged in 1778, won considerable success. He then served as director of an Italian troupe in Paris through 1779. Although he was promised by the Paris Opéra that his *Iphigénie en Tauride* would be produced before Gluck's masterpiece with the same title, it was not given until 1781, some two years after

The "Gluckists" supported the operas of Christoph Willibald Gluck, who pioneered a new French style of operatic composing. The "Piccinnists" supported the more traditional Italian style of Piccinni. Each side heatedly supported its position through pamphlets and letters to the popular press.

the Gluck premiere. While it was fairly successful, Piccinni gained his only major success with the opera *Didon* in 1783, the same year in which he finally was granted a pension by the French court. In 1784 he was appointed maître de chant at the École Royale de Chant et de Déclamation Lyrique in Paris.

In spite of their rivalry, Piccinni held the highest regard for Gluck. Indeed, he suggested that an annual memorial concert be given in Gluck's memory, but financial support was not forthcoming. Upon the death of another rival, AN-TONIO SACCHINI, Piccinni spoke in homage at his funeral.

With the coming of the French Revolution, Piccinni lost his post and pension. In 1791 he returned to Naples. Upon his daughter's marriage to a French Jacobite, he was placed under house arrest in 1794. He finally gained freedom in 1798 and returned to Paris, where he obtained partial restoration of his pension. His appointment as sixth inspector at the Conservatory came when he was too ill to pursue an active life.

Piccinni demonstrated a remarkable facility in writing both comic and serious operas. His historical importance rests upon his establishment of the Italian operatic style as the model for his French and German successors.

Piccinni's son Luigi (Lodovico) Piccinni (b. 1764; d. Passy, July 31, 1827) was also a composer. After studies with his father he wrote operas for Paris and several Italian cities. He was kapellmeister to the Swedish court in Stockholm from 1796 to 1801, then taught singing.

Piccinni had another son, Giuseppe, who in turn sired an illegitimate son, Louis Alexandre (Luigi Alessandro; Lodovico Alessandro) Piccinni (b. Paris, Sept. 10, 1779; d. there, April 24, 1850), who also became a composer. He was active as an accompanist and rehearsal pianist in several Parisian theaters, and as a conductor. He taught in various French cities, serving as director of the Toulouse music school from 1840 to 1844. He wrote numerous works for the theater.

pik′kōh-lō

MUSICAL
INSTRUMENT

piccolo (*flauto piccolo, ottavino,* It., little; Fr. *petite flûte;* Ger. *kleine Flöte*). The small octave FLUTE, pitched an OCTAVE higher than the orchestral flute.

pick. An instruction to pluck or twang the strings of a GUITAR, MANDOLIN, etc. Also the PLECTRUM with which to do this.

Pictures at an Exhibition. When his friend, an otherwise mediocre Russian painter named Victor Hartmann, died, MODEST MUSSORGSKY was disconsolate. After going to a posthumous exhibition of Hartmann's pictures, he wrote in 1874 a SUITE of short piano pieces, each descriptive of one of the paintings. That Hartmann's name is remembered at all is owed to Mussorgsky's genius of musical pictorialism.

Among the more striking musical portraits are *An Old Castle, Ballet of Unhatched Chickens in Their Eggshells, The Hut of Baba Yaga,* and the triumphant closing *Great Gate of Kiev.* Music lovers know *Pictures at an Exhibition* mainly in the brilliant orchestration made by MAURICE RAVEL in 1922, although nearly 100 other versions have been made of this public domain work to date.

piece. 1. (It. *pezzo;* Fr. *pièce;* Ger. *Stück*). A musical COMPOSITION, i.e., *Klavierstücke,* PIANO pieces. 2. An INSTRUMENT, taken as a member of an ORCHESTRA or BAND.

Pierrot Lunaire. Song cycle for speaking voice, piano, flute/piccolo, clarinet/bass clarinet, violin/viola, and cello by ARNOLD SCHOENBERG, 1912, first performed in Berlin.

As in his *Gurre-Lieder,* which set poems by a non-German translated into German, so the text of *Pierrot Lunaire* (Moonstruck Pierrot) is taken from 21 poems by a Belgian poet, Albert Giraud, rendered into German. The music is a tour de force of fascinating COUNTERPOINT, a genuine ATONAL masterpiece, with instrumental TIMBRES and the speaking voice (SPRECHTSTIMME) forming an absorbing network of aural impressions.

Pijper, Willem, renowned Dutch composer and teacher; b. Zeist, Sept. 8, 1894; d. Leidschendam, March 18, 1947. Pijper received a rudimentary education from his father, an amateur violinist, then went to the Toonkunst School of Music in Utrecht, where he studied composition and piano from 1911 to 1916.

PEOPLE IN MUSIC

From 1918 to 1923 Pijper was music critic of *Utrecht Dagblad,* and from 1926 to 1929, coeditor of the monthly *De Muziek.* He taught theory at the Amsterdam Conservatory from 1918 and then was a professor of composition there from 1925 to 1930. He served as director of the Rotterdam Conservatory from 1930 until his death.

In his music, Pijper continued the ROMANTIC tradition of GUSTAV MAHLER, but also adopted IMPRESSIONISTIC harmonies. He developed a "germ-cell theory," in which an opening CHORD or MOTIF is the source of all succeeding harmonic and melodic development (similar to ARNOLD SCHOENBERG's gestalt theory). He also used the octatonic scale of alternating WHOLE TONES and SEMITONES, regarding it as his own, not realizing that it was used abundantly by NIKOLAI RIMSKY-KORSAKOV (in Russian reference works it is termed the "Rimsky-Korsakov scale"). The "Pijper scale," as it became known in the Netherlands, was also used by Anton von der Horst and others.

During the German bombardment of Rotterdam in May 1940, nearly all of Pijper's manuscripts were destroyed by fire, including the unpublished reduced scoring of his large Second Symphony (restored in 1961 by Pijper's student Karel Mengelberg). Also destroyed was the unpublished Divertimento for piano and string orchestra.

Pilgrim's Progress, The. Morality play by RALPH VAUGHAN WILLIAMS, 1951, first performed in London. Based on John Bunyan's classic allegory, the score contains several scenes passed by the Pilgrim on his journey: the City of Destruction, Valley of Humiliation, Vanity Fair, and the Delectable Mountains.

Pines of Rome, The (*I pini de roma*). Symphonic poem by OTTORINO RESPIGHI, 1924, first performed in Rome. The music describes four pine groves in and around Rome. The score introduces an innovation, the playing of a recording of a nightingale. The piece has become a perennial favorite at symphony concerts.

Pink Floyd, British art-rock group. (Guitar/vocal: Roger "Syd" Barrett, b. Cambridge, Jan. 6, 1946; Keyboard/vocal: Rick Wright, b. London, July 28, 1945; Bass/piano/vocal: Roger Waters, b. Great Bookham, Sept. 6, 1944; Drums: Nick Mason, b. Birmingham, Jan. 27, 1945; Barrett was replaced by David Gilmour, b. Cambridge, March 6, 1944, in

PEOPLE IN MUSIC

1968; band dissolved in 1983; regrouped in 1987, without Waters.) Originally a leader in psychedelic ROCK, and then one of the originators of progressive rock, the band is best remembered for the concept opus *The Dark Side of the Moon* (1973), still a best-seller more than 25 years later.

The band members came together in London in the mid-'60s while attending art and architecture schools. Taking their name from two American blues singers (Pink Anderson and Floyd Council), they became a favorite at trendy clubs like London's Marquee and UFO. Originally led by guitarist/songwriter Roger "Syd" Barrett, the group produced a major hit with their second release, *See Emily Play,* a single so complex that it could not be reproduced on stage. Their first album, *The Piper at the Gate of Dawn,* continued the psychedelic trend, with moody arrangements complementing Barrett's often dense lyrics. However, Barrett soon began displaying disturbing behavior, and by early 1968 he was ousted from the group, to be replaced by David Gilmour. Although he made a few more recordings, Barrett disappeared from public view, becoming a cult figure in his absence.

With Barrett gone, Roger Waters came to the foreground as the main creative force in the band. A series of albums and elaborate tours followed, culminating in Waters's masterpiece, *Dark Side of the Moon,* which featured the group's first chart-busting, U.S. hit, *Money.* The album remained on the U.S. charts for over 14 years, a major achievement.

Further recordings and mammoth tours followed, with the group's massive sound equipment complemented by equally massive set pieces (the famed flying pig being one of their better efforts). Another megahit concept album came in 1979 with *The Wall,* which produced a hit theme song, a spectacular tour unparalleled in the annals of rock, and a 1982 film. However, this proved to be something of a swansong, as by 1983 the group had disbanded.

In 1987 the group reunited without Waters, who complained bitterly that they were treading on his creative toes. Gilmour took control of the group, writing the material for their *A Momentary Lapse of Reason* album, which was another steady seller. Waters retaliated with several solo efforts, as well as a mammoth production of *The Wall* in 1990 staged at (where else?) the Berlin Wall.

Although continuing to record without Waters into the '90s, the band has failed to achieve recent success. However, they gained a place in the Rock and Roll Hall of Fame in 1996.

Pinocchio. Concert OVERTURE by ERNST TOCH, 1936, premiered in Los Angeles. This "merry overture" depicts the classic tale of the puppet come to life whose nose grows longer with each lie he tells.

Pins and Needles. Political revue by HAROLD ROME, 1937. This was produced by the International Ladies' Garment Workers' Union and featured union members in its original cast. Its subject dealt with the labor problems of the 1930s. The opening song *Sing Me a Song of Social Significance* sets the character of the production. Others include *One Big Union for Two* and *It's Better With a Union Man.*

PEOPLE IN MUSIC

Pinza, Ezio (baptized Fortunio), celebrated Italian bass; b. Rome, May 18, 1892; d. Stamford, Conn., May 9, 1957. The family moved to Ravenna when Ezio was an infant. He studied engineering and also was active in sports. He began to study voice at the age of 18 at the Bologna Conservatory.

In 1914 Pinza made his opera debut as Oroveso in *Norma* in Soncino. After military service in World War I, he resumed his career, making his first important appearance as the Chevalier Des Grieux in Rome in 1920. He then sang at La Scala in Milan from 1922 to 1924. In May 1924 he was selected by ARTURO TOSCANINI for the leading part in the world premiere of ARRIGO BOITO's *Nerone.*

In 1926 Pinza made his American debut at the Metropolitan Opera in N.Y. as Pontifex Maximus in GASPARE SPONTINI's *La Vestale* and remained a company member until 1947. He appeared also in San Francisco, Chicago, and other major U.S. cities, and also sang in Europe and South America. His most celebrated roles were Mephistopheles in CHARLES GOUNOD's *FAUST,* Don Giovanni, and Boris Godunov.

In 1949 Pinza appeared in the musical *South Pacific* by RICHARD ROGERS and OSCAR HAMMERSTEIN II and immediately became successful in this new career. He also appeared in films.

pipa (Chin.). Short-necked, Chinese wooden LUTE used since antiquity. The body is pear-shaped, with a wooden soundboard, crescent soundholes, a fingerboard with four frets (the other 6 to 13 are on the belly), and four silk strings. The instrument does not have great RESONANCE, so each note sounds sharply and briefly. It is the predecessor of the Japanese BIWA.

Many compositions for pipa depict military engagements or battles. VARIATIONS for the instrument have been written and published.

Pirates of Penzance, The, or The Slaves of Duty. Comic opera by WILLIAM S. GILBERT and ARTHUR S. SULLIVAN, 1879, first produced in London.

The hero of the work, Frederic, is to be apprenticed a pirate on the hero's 21st birthday. However, as Frederic was born in a leap year, he would not reach majority until 1940, at the time a very remote date indeed. The pirates' strict code prevents them from doing any real damage to him and, after many verbal confusions, they abandon their dismal calling and proclaim their undivided loyalty to Queen Victoria.

A popular version was staged on Broadway in the mid-'80s with pop singer Linda Ronstadt and was later made into a film.

Pistol Packin' Mama. Song by Al Dexter, 1943, made famous by BING CROSBY and the ANDREWS SISTERS.

piston. *See* VALVE.

Piston, Walter (Hamor, Jr.), outstanding American composer and teacher; b. Rockland, Maine, Jan. 20, 1894; d. Belmont, Mass., Nov. 12, 1976. The family name was originally Pistone; Piston's paternal grandfather was Italian.

MUSICAL
INSTRUMENT

The Pirates of Penzance includes the chorus that eventually became known as *Hail, Hail, the Gang's All Here.*

PEOPLE IN MUSIC

Piston received his primary education in Boston, then took courses in architectural drawing at the Massachusetts Normal Art School, graduating in 1916. He then took piano lessons with Harris Shaw and also studied violin, playing in restaurants and places of public entertainment as a youth. During World War I, he was in the U.S. Navy.

After the armistice, Piston entered Harvard University, graduating in 1924. While at Harvard, he conducted concerts of the university orchestra, the Pierian Sodality. In 1924 he went to Paris on a John Knowles Paine Traveling Fellowship and became a student of the renowned teacher of music theory NADIA BOULANGER. He also took courses with PAUL DUKAS at the École Normale de Musique in 1925.

Returning to the U.S. in 1926, Piston was appointed to the faculty of Harvard University, and in 1944, he became a professor of music there. He was named professor emeritus in 1960.

As a teacher, Piston was greatly esteemed, not only because of his thorough knowledge of music and teaching ability, but also because of his kindness to his students. Among his grateful disciples was LEONARD BERNSTEIN. As a composer, Piston followed CLASSICAL forms while extending his harmonic structures in a modern style. He was particularly expert in contrapuntal writing.

Beginning about 1965, Piston adopted a modified system of 12-TONE COMPOSITION, particularly in initial thematic statements. His Symphony No. 8 (1965) and Variations for Cello and Orchestra (1966) are in this late style. Piston rejected the narrow notion of ethnic Americanism in his music and stated once that an artist could be as American working in the Library of the Boston Atheneum as roaming the Western prairie. Yet he employed upon occasion the syncopated rhythms of JAZZ.

Piston received Pulitzer Prizes for his Symphony No. 3 (1947) and Symphony No. 7 (1961), and N.Y. Music Critics' Circle Awards for his Symphony No. 2 (1943), Viola Concerto, and String Quartet No. 5 (1962). He held the degree of D.Mus. *honoris causa* from Harvard University and was elected a member of the National Institute of Arts and Letters in 1938, the American Academy of Arts and Sciences in 1940, and the American Academy of Arts and Letters in 1955.

Among Piston's works is the well-known ballet *The Incredible Flutist* (Boston, 1938; suite, Pittsburgh, 1940). He wrote many orchestral works, including eight symphonies (1938–65), and chamber pieces, including five string quartets (1933–62). He also composed vocal and keyboard works. With two exceptions, he never wrote for voices.

Piston also wrote several textbooks that have become classics in the study of music: *Principles of Harmonic Analysis* (1933), *Harmony* (1944; 5th edition, revised and enlarged by M. DeVoto, 1987), *Counterpoint* (1947), and *Orchestration* (1955).

pitch. The position of a TONE in the musical SCALE.

Pitch is relative or absolute. The *relative* pitch of a tone is its position (higher or lower) as compared with some other tone. (*See* INTERVAL.) Its *absolute* pitch is its fixed position in the entire range of musical tones.

To indicate absolute pitch, the musical scale is divided into a fixed series of octaves, named and lettered as in "The Table of Clefs" (see p. x). The number of vibrations made by a tone establishes its absolute pitch.

Acoustically, pitch is determined by the frequency of vibrations of a given tone. The smaller the sound-producing instrument, the higher the pitch. A whistle is small, thus its pitch is high; the bass tuba is large, so its pitch is very low. On string instruments and the piano, the shorter and thinner the string, the higher the pitch.

A relatively small minority of musicians possess the faculty of PERFECT PITCH, which enables them to name any note within the audible range. Relative pitch, however, which can be acquired, enables a person to name the interval between two pitches.

The present standard pitch for A in the middle octave is 440 vibrations per second. In the orchestra, the oboe gives out the standard A, to which all the other instruments tune because it is an instrument little affected by changes of temperature and humidity. However, this standard pitch has been fluctuating widely through the centuries. In the 19th

If WOLFGANG AMADEUS MO-
ZART listened to a 20th-cen-
tury rendition of his JUPITER
SYMPHONY (1788), he would
think that it had been transposed to C-sharp major instead of the written key of C
major.

**MUSICAL
INSTRUMENT**

century, the middle A was considerably lower than that of today's standard pitch.

pitch class. A term denoting a set of all pitches with the same name, e.g., pitch class A, inclusive of all possible As, regardless of register.

pitch pipe. A small wooden or metal reed pipe that sounds one or more tones of fixed pitch, to give the tone for tuning an instrument, or for a choir.

pivot chord. In MODULATION, a chord pivotal to both the old KEY and the new key, that is, belonging to both keys. Particularly in CHROMATIC modulation, the DIMINISHED SEVENTH CHORD functions as such a device.

plainchant, plainsong. The unison vocal music of the Christian church, probably dating from the first centuries of the Christian era. The style is still used in the Roman Catholic ritual, although now the lyrics are sung in the vernacular rather than in church Latin.

Planets, The. Orchestral SUITE by GUSTAV HOLST, composed in 1914–16. It was first performed publicly in its entirety in London in 1920.

There are seven movements, corresponding to the seven planets known before the discovery of Pluto, and the designations of these movements are mythological:

> *Mars, the Bringer of War;*
>
> *Venus, the Bringer of Peace;*
>
> *Mercury, the Winged Messenger;*
>
> *Jupiter, the Bringer of Jollity;*
>
> *Saturn, the Bringer of Old Age;*
>
> *Uranus, the Magician;*
>
> *Neptune, the Mystic* (with a wordless female chorus).

The work is by far the most celebrated of Holst's productions and is often quoted. The Jovian joviality of the

Jupiter movement is particularly striking. Yet, *The Planets* is atypical of Holst's music, and he himself never understood its popularity.

Planquette, (Jean-) **Robert.** *See* CLOCHES DE CORNEVILLE, LES.

platter. Slang for PHONOGRAPH record, especially in the 1950s.

player piano. A mechanical PIANO that "plays itself," allowing nonperformers to enjoy music in the home in the days before the PHONOGRAPH.

A roll of heavy paper is perforated with holes that correspond in pitch and duration to the notes originally played on the piano. The pitches are represented by the horizontal parameter, and the duration, including rests, by the vertical. The roll is placed on a cylinder, which revolves slowly. To reproduce the original performance, a stream of air is passed through the perforations and activates the corresponding hammers, which then strike the piano strings and simultaneously depress the keys of the piano keyboard. The visual impression of such automatic piano playing is that of a magical performance by the invisible fingers of a phantom pianist.

The player piano, under various trademarks such as the *Pianola* and the *Welte-Mignon* became highly popular after its introduction late in the 19th century, and its popularity did not diminish until the advent of the modern phonograph. Several composers, among them IGOR STRAVINSKY and PAUL HINDEMITH, composed and recorded pieces for the player piano. Many famous early pianists, including IGNACY PADEREWSKI, GEORGE GERSHWIN, and SCOTT JOPLIN, made piano rolls, and therefore we are able to get a sense of their playing style.

The player piano possesses the unique capacity of enabling a composer to make perforations directly on the roll guided by desired measurements. Most remarkable results were achieved in this technique by CONLON NANCARROW, who constructed a number of ETUDES and other pieces by punching holes directly into the roll, resulting in melodic, harmonic, and rhythmic patterns of extreme complexity and utmost precision.

MUSICAL INSTRUMENT

In the digital world, a new type of automatic piano has come on the scene, manufactured by the Yamaha corporation. The trade name for this instrument is the *Disklavier.* Here, a digital CD (like that used in a CD player for recordings) activates the piano's mechanism.

Please Mr. Postman. Early Motown No. 1 pop hit for the Marvelettes in 1962. It was covered in 1964 by the BEATLES and in 1975 by the CARPENTERS.

JOHN LENNON said the punning title was inspired by a Bing Crosby song in which the crooner asks his loved one to "please listen to my pleas."

Please Please Me. The BEATLES's first British No. 1 hit (although it only made No. 3 in the U.S.).

plectrum. A PICK; a small piece of ivory, tortoise shell, metal, or plastic, held between the forefinger and thumb, or fitted to the thumb by a ring, and used to pluck or twang the strings of the MANDOLIN, ZITHER, GUITAR, Asian zithers and lutes, etc.

plena (Sp.). Puerto Rican ballad similar to the CALYPSO songs of Trinidad.

PEOPLE IN MUSIC

Pleyel, Ignace Joseph (Ignaz Josef), eminent Austrian-French pianist, piano manufacturer, music publisher, and composer; b. Ruppertsthal, near Vienna, June 18, 1757; d. on his estate near Paris, Nov. 14, 1831. Pleyel was the 24th of 38 children in the impoverished family of a schoolteacher. Nonetheless, he received sufficient education, including music lessons. Thanks to the generosity of Count Ladislaus Erdödy, he became FRANZ JOSEPH HAYDN's pupil and lodger in Eisenstadt (c.1772–77) and then was enabled to go to Rome.

In 1783 Pleyel became second kapellmeister at the Strasbourg Cathedral, advancing to the rank of first kapellmeister in 1789. However, he lost his position during the turbulent times of the French Revolution. He conducted the Professional Concerts in London during the 1791–92 season and honored his teacher Haydn by playing a work of Haydn's at the opening concert. After several years he returned to Strasbourg to liquidate his estate there.

In 1795 Pleyel went to Paris, where he opened a music store that was in business until 1834, and in 1807 he founded a piano factory, which manufactured famous French pianos. The firm eventually became known as Pleyel et Cie., and it continued to prosper for over a century and a half.

The name Pleyel is mainly known through his piano manufacture, but he was a prolific and an extremely competent composer. His productions are so close in style to those of Haydn that specialists are still inclined to attribute certain works in Haydn's catalogues to Pleyel. He composed about 45 symphonies, six symphonie concertantes, two violin concertos, five cello concertos, other concertos, 16 string quintets, a septet, a sextet, more than 70 string quartets, many trios and duos. He also wrote some vocal music, including two operas, and some songs.

Pleyel's son (Joseph Stephen) Camille (b. Strasbourg, Dec. 18, 1788; d. Paris, May 4, 1855) was a pianist, piano manufacturer, and composer. Camille's wife, Marie-Félicité-Denise Moke Pleyel (b. Paris, Sept. 4, 1811; d. St.-Josse-ten-Noode, near Brussels, March 30, 1875), was a fine pianist, teacher, and composer. HECTOR BERLIOZ fell in love with her in 1830, but she married the younger Pleyel that same year, while Berlioz was in Rome. However, she separated from Pleyel in 1835.

Plow that Broke the Plains, The. Orchestral suite by VIRGIL THOMSON, 1936, arranged from the score of a documentary film depicting the joys and miseries of American farming.

plugging. American slang for the promotion, by means fair or foul, of books, films, records, videos, etc. *See also* PAYOLA.

Plunderphonic. A CD anthology compiled in 1989 by the Canadian composer and sound engineer John Oswald (b. Kitchener-Waterloo, May 30, 1953), comprised of "plunderphones" ("electroquotes or macrosamples of familiar sound") derived from revised recorded performances by well-known artists across genres, including JAMES BROWN, LORIN MAAZEL and the Cleveland Orchestra, GEORGE HARRI-

SON, DOLLY PARTON, GLENN GOULD, BING CROSBY, MICHAEL JACKSON, and COUNT BASIE, among others.

Oswald's plunderphonic snippets are the substance of each of 24 tracks, themselves sequenced into typical genre groupings. This technique, under the name of electronic SAMPLING, is common in rap recordings as a means of creating a background track.

Remarkably innovative at its release, *Plunderphonics*'s essence was soon usurped by a variety of commercial practitioners, not least apparently in hodge-podge radio spots that percussively superimpose fragments of songs, ads, and station identifications. Not surprisingly, Oswald has been actively involved in issues of copyright morality. *Plunderphonics* itself carries no copyright warning, having in its place a "shareright" insignia, with a prominent "not for sale" stamped on both disc and case. The disc itself is also stamped "All copying lending public performance and broadcast of this disc permitted," while the reverse of its case holds the following statement: "Any resemblance to existing recordings is unlikely to be coincidental." Both sampling and Oswald's work raises the question of copyright protection of a performance. To avoid lawsuits, most producers today acknowledge the sources of their samples and pay a permission fee for their use.

pluralism. As in COLLAGE, the use of different styles within a single composition, sometimes simultaneously.

pŭ-shĕt′

MUSICAL INSTRUMENT

pochette (Fr., little pocket; Ger. *Taschengeige*). A very small VIOLIN that could be carried in the pocket of a dancing master, used to accompany his pupils in rehearsal. *See also* KIT.

Poème de l'extase, Le (Poem of ecstasy). Symphonic poem by ALEXANDER SCRIABIN, 1905–08, first performed in N.Y. by the Russian Symphony Society conducted by Modest Altschuler in 1908.

The work justified its title. Scriabin provided a multitude of sectional subtitles, in French, detailing the intermediate states leading to ecstasy. The final triumphant moment is represented by 53 consecutive bars in resonant C major.

Poème divin, Le (Divine poem). Symphony No. 3 by ALEXANDER SCRIABIN, 1902–04, first performed in Paris, 1905. It is Scriabin's first work of mystic inspiration, and the titles of its four movements (all in the original French) are indicative: *Grandiose* (Great/Large), *Luttes* (Strife), *Voluptes* (Sensuality), and *Jeu divin* (Divine game).

The work is in C minor, with an ending in resonant C major, "avec une joie éclatante" (to be played "with an explosion of joy").

Poème électronique. Environmental musical work by EDGARD VARÈSE, 1958, for sounds entirely electronically produced and recorded on tape. It was commissioned for the Philips Pavilion at the Brussels World Exposition in 1958, with the sound projected stereophonically from 400 loudspeakers distributed throughout the building.

Poème satanique. Piano piece by ALEXANDER SCRIABIN, 1903. Curiously, this devilish piece is written in the celestial key of C major. The satanism of the music is symbolic and is defeated, musically, by heavenly forces.

Pohjola's Daughter. Symphonic poem by JEAN SIBELIUS, 1906, first performed in St. Petersburg.

Pohjola is the northern land, protected by Louhi; her daughter makes her home sitting on a rainbow. Her enticing beauty lures Väinämöinen, the hero of the *Kalevala,* but he cannot create the talisman she demands of him. He engages a smith, who succeeds, but the daughter prefers the smith to the hero and ends up marrying him.

point d'orgue (Fr., organ point). 1. PEDAL POINT. 2. PAUSE. 3. CADENZA.

pwŏhn dôrg

pointillism. In the nomenclature of modern art, pointillism is a method of applying colored dots to the canvas, forming a cumulative design.

In modern music the term is descriptive of ATONAL and athematic styles. Separate notes are distributed individually rather than as parts of an integral melorhythmic curve. This

Stewart Copeland, drummer and founder of the Police, 1979. (Neal Preston/Corbis) ▶

emphasis upon single notes in a serially organized process was developed by ANTON WEBERN.

Police, The. (Lead vocal/bass: Gordon Sumner, aka "STING," b. Wallsend, Northumberland, Oct. 2, 1951; Guitar: Andrew Summers, b. Poulton-le-Fylde, Dec. 31, 1942;

Drums/vocals: Stewart Copeland, b. Alexandria, Va., July 16, 1952.) Hit-making British new-wave band, formed originally in the mid-'70s out of the remains of various minor progressive-ROCK bands.

Schoolteacher and semiprofessional musician Gordon Sumner (known in his youth as "Sting" because he wore a black-and-yellow striped soccer shirt), originally from the Newcastle area, and London-based drummer Stewart Copeland were joined by guitarist Henri Padovani for the group's first single in 1976. However, Padovani was soon replaced by Andrew Summers, who had previously worked with Soft Machine and the Animals.

Signed to the American A&M label, the group toured the U.S. at their own expense in 1978, achieving their first chart recognition with Sting's song *Roxanne* in early 1979. Their second album sold steadily for two years on the American charts, although it produced only a minor hit, *Message in a Bottle.*

However, in 1980 the Police broke through big time with *Don't Stand So Close to Me,* followed a year later by

Every Little Thing She Does Is Magic, both Sting-penned, rollicking pop songs. The group produced the classic album *Synchronicity* in 1983, showing a diversity of influences from world rhythms to JAZZ and rock. Critically acclaimed, it proved to be their last effort. Sting pursued a successful acting and solo career, scoring many major hits through the '80s and '90s, while Copeland became a successful soundtrack composer and Summers sessioned and recorded on his own.

polka (Bohem. *pulka;* It. *polca*). A lively round dance in $\frac{2}{4}$ time, originating about 1830 as a peasant dance in Bohemia, despite a name suggesting Polish origin (*polka* means a Polish girl). It generated suddenly in Prague in 1847 and almost immediately spread all over Europe. In this process it lost its specific Bohemian characteristics and became a popular salon dance. JOHANN STRAUSS, JR. wrote a famous *Pizzicato Polka,* and many other composers followed suit. IGOR STRAVINSKY wrote the *Circus Polka* (1942) for a dance of elephants in the Ringling Brothers circus.

Polka mazurka, a form of mazurka accommodated to the steps of the polka; *polka schnell,* a fast polka; a designation used by Johann Strauss (e.g., *Vergnügungszug,* pleasure train) and others.

pōl′kăh

Polka dots were named for the decorated shirts that many polka dancers wore in the 19th century.

Pollini, Maurizio, famous Italian pianist and conductor; b. Milan, Jan. 5, 1942. A precocious child, Pollini began piano studies at an early age with Carlo Ambrogio Lonati. He made his debut at age nine, then studied at the Milan Conservatory. After sharing second prize in the Geneva Competition in 1958, he took his diploma in piano at the Milan Conservatory in 1959. He also studied with ARTURO BENE-DETTI MICHELANGELI.

After capturing first prize in the Chopin Competition in Warsaw in 1960, Pollini launched an acclaimed career as a virtuoso, appearing throughout Europe as a soloist with leading orchestras and as a recitalist. In 1968, he made his U.S. debut at N.Y.'s CARNEGIE HALL. In later years, he made appearances as a conductor, leading concerts from the keyboard and also mounting the podium and taking charge in the opera pit.

PEOPLE IN MUSIC

Pollini is a foremost master of the keyboard. He has won deserved renown for making his phenomenal technical resources a means of exploring a vast repertoire, ranging from JOHANN SEBASTIAN BACH to the modern avant-garde. In 1987 he was awarded the Ehrenring of the Vienna Philharmonic, and in 1997 he gave a LUDWIG VAN BEETHOVEN sonata cycle at the Royal Festival Hall in London.

pŏh-lŏh-näz′ **polonaise** (Fr.; It. *polonese, polacca*). A dance of Polish origin, in $\frac{3}{4}$ time and moderate tempo. It was formerly in animated processional style but now is merely a slow promenade opening a ball.

Examples of polonaises are found in instrumental works of JOHANN SEBASTIAN BACH, LUDWIG VAN BEETHOVEN, and FRANZ SCHUBERT. However, it was FRÉDÉRIC CHOPIN who elevated the polonaise to the heights of artistry in his piano music.

polymeter. The simultaneous use of several different meters.

Polymeter dates back to the RENAISSANCE. For example, Spanish dance music used double TIME SIGNATURES, $\frac{3}{4}$ against $\frac{6}{8}$. In operatic usage, polymeter is encountered in scenes descriptive of simultaneous uncoordinated action, known under the name IMBROGLIO. IGOR STRAVINSKY used this technique in *PETROUCHKA*. However, it is primarily in 20th-century music that polymeter has come to the fore. ELLIOTT CARTER employs METRIC MODULATION by changing meter and TEMPO in polyphonic writing. At the points of modulation, some players would be thinking in the present meter and tempo, while others would be viewing their music in terms of the next meter and tempo. Ben Johnston's *Knocking Piece* (1962) for two percussionists and piano lid is a *tour de force* of reinterpreting time and MEASURE, virtually measure by measure.

Perhaps the most remarkable instance of contrapuntal polymeter is found in the second movement of *THREE PLACES IN NEW ENGLAND* (composed 1903–14) by CHARLES IVES. This famous section illustrates the meeting of two marching bands, each playing similar marching tunes at the same time, although they are playing at different tempi, in the ratio $\frac{4}{3}$, so that four bars of the faster march equal three bars of the slower. In his original manuscript Ives coordinated these different tempos within the uniform measures in $\frac{4}{4}$ time, marking cross-accents wherever they occurred. Ives incorporated in the published score an alternative arrangement with non-coincidental barlines, in clear polymetric notation.

Among examples of implicit polymetry not marked as such by time signatures is the coda of ROBERT SCHUMANN's Piano Concerto (1845), where the systematic SYNCOPATION in the piano part in $\frac{3}{4}$ time results in a polymetric combination of $\frac{3}{2}$ in the piano part versus two bars of $\frac{3}{4}$ in the orchestra.

In GEORGE GERSHWIN's *I GOT RHYTHM*, the implicit polymetry consists of one bar in $\frac{2}{16}$ time, four bars of $\frac{3}{16}$ time, and one bar of $\frac{2}{16}$ time, adding up to $\frac{16}{16}$, that is, $\frac{4}{4}$, which is the notated time signature. Sometimes the term *polymetry* is applied, inaccurately, to a succession of different time signatures. The proper term for such usages is *changing meters*.

polymodality. Polymodality is a special case of POLYTONALITY in which the principal melodic lines are modal rather than tonal.

polyphonic. 1. *See* POLYPHONY. 2. Describing an instrument capable of producing two or more tones simultaneously, like the PIANO, HARP, or ORGAN. 3. In SYNTHESIZERS, the ability to sound more than one voice at the same time. Originally, synthesizers were MONOPHONIC; i.e., they could play only one part at a time.

polyphony (from Grk., *poly* + *phone,* many sounds). The combination in harmonious progression of two or more independent MELODIES. The independent treatment of the parts, or COUNTERPOINT, in its widest sense.

In ancient Greek, the word bore a derogatory meaning of multivoiced chatter. However, in a medieval treatise, polyphony is described as *modus canendi a pluribus diversam observantibus melodiam* (a method of singing a diverse melody from many components). In the musical lexicon published by J. G. Walther in 1732, polyphony is defined simply as "a many-voiced composition."

In the 19th century, polyphony was identified with COUNTERPOINT in which each voice has its own individual-

In his performances of the work, NICOLAS SLONIMSKY conducted three bars in $\frac{4}{4}$ time with his right hand and four bars in alla breve time with his left. Those in the orchestra who had parts with the faster march were to follow the conductor's left hand and the rest his right hand.

ity, as contrasted with HOMOPHONY, in which the melody is a dominating part, with the rest of the musical fabric subordinated to it harmonically.

To describe this better, a comparison has been made to a mathematical grid. Melody lines, which make up a polyphonic composition, have been described as moving horizontally, from left to right, or on the X-axis of a grid. Harmonies, which are made up of several notes played simultaneously, are described as being horizontal, or stacked up and down along the Y-axis. The term LINEAR COUNTERPOINT has been used to emphasize the horizontality of polyphonic compositions.

In a polyphonic composition, individual parts are interdependent and mutually accommodating in forming a pleasing ensemble. Contrapuntal IMITATION is a polyphonic system *par excellence,* the FUGUE being the summit of polyphonic technique.

Polyphony attained its culmination with the great works of JOHANN SEBASTIAN BACH and went on a decline almost immediately after his death. Indeed, the rush toward homophony was led by Bach's sons. In place of "diversity in unity," the essence of polyphonic composition, the masters of CLASSIC music of the second half of the 18th century and the succeeding four generations of ROMANTIC composers made melody paramount and harmony its servant.

In 20th-century music, polyphony has made a comeback. The technique of composition with 12 TONES related only to one another, as promoted by ARNOLD SCHOENBERG, is a model of strict polyphony. In this system, polyphonic voices are all derived from a single basic theme. Both the horizontal and vertical lines—melody and harmony—are formed in the governing series of 12 tones.

polyrhythm. The simultaneous occurrence of several fundamentally different RHYTHMS, each clearly recognizable through individual accents. All POLYPHONIC music entails the use of different rhythms at the same time, but to qualify as polyrhythm such rhythms must be maintained for a considerable number of BARS in each individual PART. In this sense polyrhythm is the product of new music developed mainly in the 20th century.

Polyrhythm differs from POLYMETER in that the former indicates a combination of two unrelated rhythmic groups, while the latter indicates the superposition of two different meters usually having the same note values as their common denominator.

polystylistic music. ECLECTICISM in composition, a term invented by ALFRED SCHNITTKE in 1971. Either term may apply to composers who use different historical or current styles in different works, or to a single piece that exhibits a variety of styles.

polytonality. The simultaneous use of several KEYS. In actual practice, it is difficult to sustain the acoustical separation of more than two different keys, thus reducing polytonality to BITONALITY.

An amusing example of polytonality is found in WOLF-GANG AMADEUS MOZART's *Ein musikalischer Spass,* where he makes the horns play in different keys from the rest of the orchestra. But Mozart's professed intention in this "musical joke" was to ridicule the ignorance of amateur musicians. He could not have anticipated the time when such a musical joke would become a new technique.

Pomo d'oro, Il (The golden apple). "Festa teatrale" by ANTONIO CESTI, 1667, performed in Vienna during Carnival. The work comprised a prologue and five acts, broken down into 66 "scenes." The production involved 24 set changes and lasted eight or more hours. As one can imagine, the expense of producing it was immense.

The plot is based on the mythological choice of Paris between three goddesses for their beauty. Selecting Aphrodite, he gets Helen, whom he kidnaps to Troy. This, of course, begins the famous Trojan War described in Homer's *Iliad.*

The music that has survived reveals a skillful use of MONODY. The work was never revived, unsurprisingly. As it is, *Il pomo d'oro* could have literally been the opera to end all operas.

Pomp and Circumstance. Five orchestral marches by EDWARD ELGAR, completed in 1930. The most famous of these

The expression "pomp and circumstance" comes from Shakespeare's *Othello*.

PEOPLE IN MUSIC

marches is the first. Its middle section has been set to the words *Land of Hope and Glory,* and it is used by almost every American school as a processional at graduation ceremonies. The first two marches were introduced in Liverpool, England, in 1901.

Ponce, Manuel (Maria), distinguished Mexican composer; b. Fresnillo, Dec. 8, 1882; d. Mexico City, April 24, 1948. Ponce studied piano with his older sister. In 1904 he went to Europe, where he took lessons in composition with the well-known composer Enrico Bossi in Bologna and in piano with music critic Theodor Krause in Berlin.

Upon his return to Mexico, Ponce taught piano at the Mexico City Conservatory from 1909 to 1915. He gave a concert of his compositions in Mexico City in 1912, which included a piano concerto. During World War I, he lived in N.Y. and in Havana. He then went to Paris for additional study with the French composer/teacher PAUL DUKAS. His contact with French music brought a radical change in his style of composition. His later works are more POLYPHONIC in structure and more economical in form.

Ponce possessed a great gift of melody. One of his songs, *Estrellita* (1914), became a universal favorite and was often mistaken for a folk song. In 1941 he made a tour in South America, conducting his own works.

Ponce was the first Mexican composer of the 20th century to employ an identifiably modern musical language, and his contributions to the guitar and orchestral repertoire are substantial. His place in the history of Mexican music is a very important one. A concert hall was named after him in the Instituto de Bellas Artes in Mexico City.

Ponchielli, Amilcare, celebrated Italian composer; b. Paderno Fasolaro, near Cremona, Aug. 31, 1834; d. Milan, Jan. 15, 1886. Ponchielli studied with his father, a shopkeeper and organist at the village church, and entered the Milan Conservatory as a nonpaying student when he was nine. While a student there he collaborated on the operetta *Il sindaco babbeo,* staged in 1851. He also wrote the symphonic *Scena campestre* a year later.

PEOPLE IN MUSIC

After his graduation in 1854, Ponchielli went to Cremona as a church organist. He was named assistant to Ruggero Manna, director of Cremona's Teatro Concordia a year later, where he brought out his opera *I promessi sposi* in 1856. He was conductor of the municipal bands in Piacenza and Cremona, where he also conducted opera while continuing to compose for the theater.

Ponchielli finally achieved notable success with the revised version of his *I promessi sposi,* which premiered in Milan in late 1872, and was subsequently performed throughout Italy. His subsequent LA GIOCONDA, also first staged in Milan four years later, secured his reputation.

Ponchielli was professor of composition at the Milan Conservatory in 1880 and again from 1881. He also served as maestro di cappella at Bergamo's S. Maria Maggiore cathedral from 1881 to 1886. He married the soprano Teresina Brambilla in 1874. His birthplace was renamed Paderno Ponchielli in his honor.

La Gioconda remains Ponchielli's only work to have acquired repertoire status. It includes the famous ballet number *Dance of the Hours.* In addition to his numerous stage works, he composed many band pieces, vocal chamber music, chamber works, and piano pieces.

Pop! Goes the Weasel. A famous Anglo-American nursery rhyme written in JIG time.

In the British version the word *weasel* had nothing to do with the rodent, but was the name of a household utensil, like a flatiron. Pop was the colloquial word for the pawnshop, so that the lines "that's the way the money went, pop goes the weasel" described a predicament of a poor Englishman who had to hock his flatiron. In the American version, the weasel is definitely an animal.

pop(ular) music. A general term to denote a wide variety of musical styles, generally characterized by their easy accessibility to wide audiences. Popular compositions are usually of modest length, with prominent and memorable melodies, and a simple, unassuming harmonic language.

Definitions and sources for popular music are broad and plentiful, from Tin Pan Alley to musicals, Anglo-Irish traditional to country, blues to soul, classical to environmental urban sound. In the last quarter of the 20th century, influences from around the world have become primary.

The term *popular music* can only be interpreted as music with a commercial aspect, unlike authentic folk music. In this sense it holds a social position similar to most CLASSICAL music, which has also had a monetary goal in most cases, as opposed to folk music. To a classical audience, popular may seem vulgar, downgraded, repellant, and socially divisive. But that attitude may suggest an inability or unwillingness to hear the multitude of differences in the many kinds of popular music.

Porgy and Bess. Opera by GEORGE GERSHWIN, 1935, to a libretto by his brother Ira. It was based on an American play by Dubose and Dorothy Heyward, first performed in Boston.

The startling innovation of the opera was its selection of a subject from African-American life, with its cast of characters consisting almost exclusively of African Americans. Porgy is a cripple, and Bess is his girl. He kills her former convict lover, Crown, and is arrested, but is released for lack of evidence. In the meantime, Bess is spirited away to N.Y. by a worldly gent with an engaging nickname, Sportin' Life. At the end of the opera, Porgy sets out to look for Bess.

Several songs from the opera have become American classics, including *Summertime, A Woman Is a Sometime Thing, My Man's Gone Now, I Got Plenty o' Nuthin', Bess You Is My Woman Now,* and *It Ain't Necessarily So.* The musical idiom of *Porgy and Bess* is an artistic re-creation of SPIRITUALS, JAZZ, and BLUES.

MUSICAL INSTRUMENT

PEOPLE IN MUSIC

portative organ. A small portable ORGAN used in religious processions.

Porter, Cole (Albert), remarkable American composer of popular music; b. Peru, Ind., June 9, 1891; d. Santa Monica, Calif., Oct. 15, 1964. Porter was educated at Yale University (B.A., 1913), then took academic courses at Harvard Law School, and later at the Harvard School of Music in 1915–16. He also received instruction in counterpoint, composition, or-chestration, and harmony from VINCENT D'INDY at the Paris Schola Cantorum in 1919.

While at Yale, Porter wrote foot-ball songs (*Yale Bull Dog Song, Bingo Eli Yale,* etc.) and also composed music for college func-tions. He first gained success as a composer for

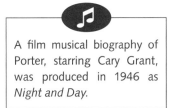

Cole Porter and his dachsund, 1926. (UPI/Corbis-Bettmann)

A film musical biography of Porter, starring Cary Grant, was produced in 1946 as *Night and Day.*

the stage with his *Wake Up and Dream,* produced in London, in 1929. There followed a cascade of musical comedies for which he wrote both lyrics and music, which placed him in the front rank of the American musical theater. His *Gay Divorcée* from 1932 was a hit for the great dancer Fred Astaire both on stage and screen. Another classic work from the '30s, ANYTHING GOES, has seen many revivals.

Porter's life and career were greatly changed in 1937, when he was injured while horseback riding. A series of painful operations followed, and eventually his right leg was amputated. Nonetheless, he continued to compose prolifically.

Porter's greatest success came with his musical comedy KISS ME, KATE, after Shakespeare's *The Taming of the Shrew,* which opened in N.Y. in 1948. The musical captured perfectly the spirit of the original play, cleverly interweaving the Shakespearean text with a modern subplot. Porter continued to write musicals into the '50s, including the hits *Can-can* (1953) and *Silk Stockings* (1955). His last work was a television musical, *Aladdin,* composed in 1958. He died six years later.

Porter was a master of subtle expression without senti-mentality, irony, and a natural blend of word poetry with the finest of harmonious melodies. Of his many songs, at least half a dozen became great favorites: *BEGIN THE BEGUINE, It's De-Lovely, Night and Day, MY HEART BELONGS TO DADDY, Don't Fence Me In,* and *Wunderbar.* He also composed numerous film scores, including *Rosalie* (1937), *You'll Never Get Rich* (1941), and *Les Girls* (1957).

Portuguese Hymn. Obsolete nickname of ADESTE FIDELIS (O, come, all ye faithful). It was regularly performed in the Portuguese chapel in London during the early 1800s.

position. 1. The place of the left hand on the FINGERBOARD of the VIOLIN, etc. In the first position, the forefinger stops the TONE (or SEMITONE) above the open string; by shifting up, so that the first finger takes the place previously occupied by the second, the second position is reached, and so on. In the half position the second, third, and fourth fingers occupy the places taken, in the first position, by the first, second, and third fingers.

    2. The arrangement of notes in a CHORD, with reference to the lowest part. In the first, or fundamental, position, the lowest part takes the ROOT; in the second, it takes the third, etc. 3. Close (open) position, *see* HARMONY.

MUSICAL INSTRUMENT

positive organ (Ger. *Positiv;* Fr. *positif*). Medieval portable ORGAN with a single MANUAL and no PEDAL. To operate the bellows that pumped air into the pipes, an assistant was required. It was often used at the homes of pious church musicians and parishioners.

MUSICAL INSTRUMENT

post horn. A HORN without VALVES or KEYS, used on post coaches. The sound of the post horn was associated with departure, sorrowful or joyful. LUDWIG VAN BEETHOVEN used such an association in his *LES ADIEUX* (1809), where the opening post horn call is sounded in the descending CADENCE known as HORN FIFTHS.

posthumous works. Commonly used to describe works first discovered, performed, or published after the composer's death.

postlude (Ger. *Nachspiel*). 1. A closing piece on the ORGAN. 2. A REFRAIN.

postmodernism. *See* MODERNISM.

potpourri (*mélange, méslange;* Fr., rotten pot; It. *mescolanza*). A musical medley, exhibiting a variety of unrelated refrains and fragments, connected in an arbitrary manner. In an enlarged sense *potpourri* was used by music publishers, particularly in Germany, for any collection of favorite ARIAS or instrumental pieces, and the word itself did not acquire its somewhat derogatory meaning until much later. Modern NEOCLASSICAL composers revived the potpourri in a nostalgically attractive manner, as a series of disconnected musical sketches.

pōh-poo-rē'

Poule, La. *See* THE HEN.

Poulenc, Francis (Jean Marcel), brilliant French composer; b. Paris, Jan. 7, 1899; d. there, Jan. 30, 1963. Poulenc was born into a wealthy family of pharmaceutical manufacturers. His mother taught him music in his childhood, and at 16 he began taking formal piano lessons.

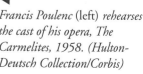

PEOPLE IN MUSIC

◄

Francis Poulenc (left) *rehearses the cast of his opera,* The Carmelites, *1958. (Hulton-Deutsch Collection/Corbis)*

A decisive turn in Poulenc's development as a composer occurred when he attracted the attention of ERIK SATIE. Deeply impressed by Satie's compositions in the then-shocking style of DADAISM, Poulenc joined an ostentatiously self-descriptive musical group called the *Nouveaux Jeunes* (New Youth). In a gratuitous parallel with the Russian Five, the French critic Henri Collet renamed the "New Youths" *Le Groupe de Six,* and the label stuck under the designation *LES SIX.* The six musicians included, besides Poulenc, Georges Auric, Louis Durey, ARTHUR HONEGGER, DARIUS MILHAUD, and GERMAINE TAILLEFERRE. Although quite different in their styles of composition and artistic inclinations, they continued collective participation in various musical events.

From 1918 to 1921 Poulenc served in the French army and then began taking lessons in composition with Charles Koechlin from 1921 to 1924. An excellent pianist, Poulenc became in 1935 an accompanist to the French baritone Pierre Bernac, for whom he wrote numerous songs.

Compared with his comrades-in-six, Poulenc appears a CLASSICIST. He never experimented with the popular devices of "MACHINE MUSIC," ASYMMETRICAL RHYTHMS, and POLY-HARMONIES as did Honegger and Milhaud. He was content to follow the gentle NEOCLASSICAL style of MAURICE RAVEL. Among his other important artistic contacts was the ballet impresario Sergei Diaghilev, who commissioned him to write music for his Ballets Russes.

Apart from his fine songs and piano pieces, Poulenc revealed himself as an inspired composer of religious music, of which his choral works *Stabat Mater* and *Gloria* are notable. He also wrote remarkable music for the organ, including a concerto that became a minor masterpiece. A master of artificial simplicity, he satisfies even sophisticated listeners by his pleasing harmonies, spiced with quickly passing discords.

Pound, Ezra (Loomis), greatly significant American man of letters and amateur composer; b. Hailey, Idaho, Oct. 30, 1885; d. Venice, Nov. 1, 1972. Pound was educated at Hamilton College (Ph.B., 1905) and the University of Pennsylvania (M.A., 1906). He went to England, where he established himself as a leading experimental poet and influential critic. He also pursued a great interest in EARLY

PEOPLE IN MUSIC

MUSIC, especially that of the TROUBADOURS, which led him to try his hand at composing.

With the assistance of American composer GEORGE AN- THEIL, he composed the opera *Le Testament,* after poems by François Villon in 1923, which was first performed three years later in Paris. It was followed by a second opera, *Calva- canti* in 1932, and a third, left unfinished, based on the po- etry of Catullus.

In 1924 Pound settled in Rapallo, Italy. Although mar- ried to Dorothy Shakespear, daughter of one of Yeats's friends, he became intimate with the American violinist Olga Rudge. Rudge bore him a daughter in 1925, and his wife bore him a son in 1926. Through the influence of Rudge, Pound's interest in music continued, and he became a fervent champion of ANTONIO VIVALDI. He also worked as a music reviewer and ran a concert series with Rudge.

A growing interest in economic history and an ill- considered admiration for the Fascist dictator Benito Mus- solini led Pound to promote increasingly controversial ideas. During World War II he made many broadcasts over Rome Radio on topics ranging from literature to politics. His con- demnation of Jewish banking circles in America and the American effort to defeat Fascism led to his arrest by the Al- lies after the collapse of Mussolini's regime. In 1945 he was sent to a prison camp in Pisa. In 1946 he was sent to the U.S. to stand trial for treason but was declared insane and confined to St. Elizabeth's Hospital in Washington, D.C. Fi- nally, in 1958 he was released and allowed to return to Italy, where he died in 1972.

Pound was an early champion of Antheil's modern musi- cal experiments, writing a pamphlet in 1924 promoting the American's music. He also composed several works for solo violin for Rudge, including *Fiddle Music* (1924) and *Al poco giorno,* which went unpublished until 1983. He also arranged Gaucelm Faidit's *Plainte pour la mort du roi Richart Coeur de Lion.* Pound's musical manuscripts at Yale Univer- sity include various musical experiments, such as rhythmic and melodic realizations of his poem *Sestina: Altaforte.*

Pousseur, Henri (Leon Marie Therese), Belgian composer of the ultramodern school; b. Malmedy, June 23, 1929.

Among composers who have set Pound's poems to music are AARON COPLAND, ELISABETH LUYTENS, and LUCIANO BERIO.

PEOPLE IN MUSIC

Pousseur studied at the Liège Conservatory from 1947 to 1952 and the Brussels Conservatory in 1952–53, and also had private lessons in composition from PIERRE BOULEZ. He taught music in various Belgian schools from 1950 to 1959.

Until 1959, Pousseur worked in the Cologne and Milan electronic music studios, where he came in contact with the experimental composers KARLHEINZ STOCKHAUSEN and LUCIANO BERIO. He was a member of the avant-garde group of composers called "Variation" in Liège. In 1958 Pousseur founded the Studio de Musique Electronique APELAC in Brussels, which in 1970 became a part of the Centre de Recherches Musicales in Liège. He served as its director until 1975, when he was named the director of the Liège Conservatory.

In his music, Pousseur uses the capabilities of magnetic tape, electronics/SYNTHESIZERS, CHANCE operations and INDETERMINACY, and a full range of human-produced vocal sounds for his multimedia representations. Among his recent compositions are *Traverser la forêt,* cantata for speaker, two vocal soloists, chorus, and 12 instruments (1987), *Ode No. 2, Mnemosyne (doublement) obstinée* for string quartet and soprano ad libitum (London, June 1989), *Leçons d'enfer,* musical theater (Metz, Nov. 14, 1991), and *Dichterliebesreigentraum,* grand paraphrase after Robert Schumann's cycle for two pianos, soprano, baritone, chamber chorus, and chamber orchestra (1992–93; Amsterdam, June 1993).

Powell, "Bud" (Earl), African-American jazz pianist; b. N.Y., Sept. 27, 1924; d. there, Aug. 1, 1966. Powell began playing piano in the classical style as a child. At age 15 he dropped out of high school and began hanging out at Minton's Playhouse, an after-hours club in Harlem that was home to the bebop pianist THELONIOUS MONK. Greatly influenced by Monk, Powell began playing in the then-new BEBOP style.

In 1943 he joined Cootie Williams's big band and toured with them. When the band played in Philadelphia, Powell was badly beaten by local police. This was the beginning of a lifelong struggle with mental problems, which may have been brought on by the severe beating. In 1945 he began to act erratically and had the first of several electroshock

PEOPLE IN MUSIC

treatments for mental illness. Through the '50s, Powell's mental state continued to deteriorate. Nonetheless, he recorded on his own and as a sideman for many of the leading jazz players of the day. In 1956, his brother, Richie, also a musician, died, which further aggravated Powell's mental health. He also began to drink heavily and use drugs, adding to his instability. From 1960 to 1964, Powell lived in Paris, France, where he recorded and performed. He returned to N.Y. in 1964 but performed only infrequently until his death two years later.

Praetorius, Michael, great German composer, organist, and music theorist; b. Creuzburg an der Werra, Thuringia, Feb. 15, 1571; d. Wolfenbüttel, Feb. 15, 1621. The surname of the family was Schultheiss (sometimes rendered as Schultze), which he Latinized as Praetorius.

PEOPLE IN MUSIC

Praetorius was the son of a Lutheran pastor. He studied with Michael Voigt, cantor of the Torgau Lateinschule. In 1582 he entered the University of Frankfurt an der Oder, and in 1584 he continued his studies at the Lateinschule in Zerbst, Anhalt. From 1587 to 1590 he was organist of St. Marien in Frankfurt. In 1595 he entered the service of Duke Heinrich Julius of Braunschweig-Wolfenbüttel as an organist. In 1604 he also assumed the duties of court kapellmeister.

Upon the death of his patron in 1613, the Elector Johann Georg of Saxony obtained Praetorius's services as deputy kapellmeister at the Dresden court. Praetorius retained his Dresden post until 1616 and then resumed his duties in Wolfenbüttel.

Praetorius devoted only a part of his time to Wolfenbüttel, because he had been named kapellmeister to the administrator of the Magdeburg bishopric and prior of the monastery at Ringelheim in 1614. He also traveled a great deal, visiting various German cities. These factors, coupled with a general decline in his health, led to the decision not to reappoint him to his Wolfenbüttel post in 1620. He died the following year a wealthy man. Deeply religious, he directed that the greater portion of his fortune go to organizing a foundation for the poor.

Praetorius was one of the most important and prolific German composers of his era. His *Musae Sioniae,* a significant collection of over 1,200 settings of Lutheran CHO-RALES, is a particularly valuable source for hymnology. He also published collections of MOTETS, PSALMS, sacred songs, MADRIGALS, LITANIES, works with BASS CONTINUO, and a collection of French instrumental dances under the title *Terpsichore, musarum aoniarum quinta a 4–6* in 1612. Praetorius is even better known for his *Syntagma musicum,* published in three volumes:

> *Syntagmatis musici tomus primus* (1614–15), a historical and descriptive treatise in Latin on ancient and ecclesiastical music, and ancient secular instruments.

> *Syntagmatis musici tomus secundus* (1618; with an appendix, *Theatrum instrumentorum,* 1620), in German, a most important source of information on musical instruments of the period, describing their form, compass, tone quality, etc. The organ is treated at great length, and the appendix contains 42 woodcuts of the principal instruments enumerated.

> *Syntagmatis musici tomus tertius* (1618), a valuable and interesting account of secular composition of the period, with a treatise on SOLMISATION, NOTATION, etc.

Prague Symphony. WOLFGANG AMADEUS MOZART's Symphony No. 38 in D major, performed for the first time in Prague in 1787. Mozart's work was highly regarded in that city, and was always better received even than in Vienna.

Prairie, The. Cantata by LUKAS FOSS, 1944, to texts by Carl Sandburg, premiered in N.Y. Although American in essence, the score does not quote actual folk songs.

Praise the Lord and Pass the Ammunition. Song by FRANK LOESSER, written shortly after the Japanese attack on Pearl Harbor, 1941. It was based on a quote attributed to, of all people, an army chaplain!

Pratella, Francesco Balilla. *See* FUTURISM.

precentor. A director and manager of a choir, and of musical services in general. In the Anglican church, the precentor is second in rank to the deacon.

prelude (from Lat. *praeludium,* preplay; Fr. *prélude;* It. *pre-ludio;* Ger. *Vorspiel*). A musical introduction to a large work or FUGUE. Also, an independent composition.

The earliest instrumental preludes consisted usually of introductory CHORDS and ARPEGGIOS and a brief MELODY with a HOMOPHONIC accompaniment. During the BAROQUE period preludes served as introductions to an instrumental SUITE, usually for PIANO or ORGAN.

In the 19th century, however, the prelude emancipated itself and became an independent form. FRÉDÉRIC CHOPIN's *Preludes* for piano are not preambles to anything but rather, self-sufficient compositions.

CLAUDE DEBUSSY, SERGEI RACHMANINOFF, and ALEXAN-DER SCRIABIN followed Chopin in fashioning their own piano preludes. The opening *Promenade* in MODEST MUSSORGSKY's piano suite PICTURES AT AN EXHIBITION (1874) is of the nature of a prelude, although when interposed between numbers in the rest of this suite they assume the role of interludes.

The opposite of the prelude is the POSTLUDE. In PAUL HINDEMITH's piano suite *Ludus Tonalis* (1944), the postlude is the physical inversion of the prelude, obtained by playing the pages of the prelude upside down and adjusting the accidentals.

The most famous introductory preludes are those paired with fugues in JOHANN SEBASTIAN BACH'S *WELL-TEMPERED CLAVIER* (1722), each in the key of the fugue that followed.

Prélude à l'après-midi d'un faune (Prelude to the afternoon of a faun). Symphonic poem by CLAUDE DEBUSSY, 1894, first performed in Paris. This is probably the most poetic creation of Debussy's IMPRESSIONISTIC genius, scored for a small orchestra in which the woodwinds, horns, harps, and a pair of antique cymbals form an exquisite image.

The *Prélude* is inspired by a poem by the French symbolist Stéphane Mallarmé. It depicts the silent contemplation by a sensuous faun of nymphs and other creatures of the woods on a sunny afternoon. For a performance subsequent to the premiere, a note was inserted explaining that the complete text of the poem could not be printed because young girls attended the concerts. An American music publishing house issued an arrangement of the work with a picture of a fawn on the cover. The publisher did not know the difference between the Greek demigod faun and a young animal of the deer family.

Préludes. Piano cycles by CLAUDE DEBUSSY, in two books (1909–10; 1910–13), although earlier pieces may have been included.

Préludes, Les. Symphonic poem by FRANZ LISZT, 1854, first performed in Weimar, with Liszt conducting.

The title is taken from a poem by French poet Alphonse Lamartine, in which he asks the rhetorical question, "What is life but a series of preludes?" The music is successively dramatic, lyrical, and solemn. It is a good example of how a composer takes a single theme and transforms it to depict many moods.

premiere (from Fr. *première audition,* first hearing; Ger. *Uraufführung*). The first performance of a musical (or other) work.

preparation. The preparation of a DISSONANCE consists in the presence, in the preceding CHORD and same part, of the TONE forming the dissonance.

MUSICAL
INSTRUMENT

prepared piano. An instrument whose timbre is altered by placing such objects as screws, bolts, nuts, metal paper clips, coins, safety pins, clothespins, cardboard, rubber wedges,

John Cage preparing a piano, c. 1960. (The John Cage Trust)

wires, pencil erasers, metal strips, and virtually anything that can be attached or placed between, on top of, or below the strings of a grand piano.

JOHN CAGE invented the term in the early 1940s, his masterpiece for the instrument being his *Sonatas and Interludes* (1946–48), performed in 1949 in Carnegie Hall. The work earned him awards from both the Guggenheim Foundation and the National Institute of Arts and Letters, for "having thus extended the boundaries of musical art."

Present Arms. Musical by RICHARD RODGERS and LORENZ HART, 1928. The action takes place in Hawaii, with an English lord's daughter being pursued by both a sailor from Brooklyn and a German baron. The sailor wins the lady after performing feats of heroism in a shipwreck. Pseudo-Hawaiian melodies enliven the score.

Presley, Elvis (Aron), fantastically popular American rock 'n' roll singer and balladeer; b. Tupelo, Miss., Jan. 8, 1935; d. Memphis, Aug. 16, 1977. Born in rural Mississippi, Elvis was raised in the city of Memphis, where there was a rich culture of black BLUES, GOSPEL, and white country music to be heard. He was employed as a mechanic and truck driver in his early youth. At about the age of 12, he taught himself guitar and began singing a wide variety of songs.

In 1953 Presley showed up one day at the small recording studios run by Sam Phillips, called the Memphis Recording Service, to make a record to give to his mother for her birthday. Phillips's studio manager noticed the boy and recommended him to her boss. About a year later, Phillips invited Presley to make a demo recording, pairing him with local musicians guitarist Scotty Moore and bassist Bill Black. In July 1954 they recorded their first single, a cover of the R&B classic *That's Alright, Mama* and the country/bluegrass song *Blue Moon of Kentucky.* It was issued on Phillips's Sun Records label.

The immediate success of this recording led to further recordings and tours. At first, Elvis was viewed as a "country" artist, appearing on the famous Louisiana Hayride radio show and playing country fairs and festivals in the South. However, his recordings began to attract a larger audience

PEOPLE IN MUSIC

Parker had been named an honorary "Kentucky Colonel" by the governor of Kentucky. Although this honor did not carry any real authority or rank, he insisted on being addressed as "the Colonel" from that point forward.

and also the attention of a well-known country-music promoter "Colonel" Tom Parker.

In late 1955 Phillips sold Presley's recording contract to RCA for a then-incredible amount of $35,000. Presley immediately scored with *Heartbreak Hotel,* followed by the two-sided hit, *Hound Dog/Don't Be Cruel.* Also in 1956, Presley made his first appearance on the Ed Sullivan television show (filmed only from the waist up, to avoid showing his "offensive" hip movements) and his first feature film, *Love Me Tender.*

1957 was another banner year for Presley. He made perhaps his best feature films, JAILHOUSE ROCK, featuring an imaginative dance sequence and a strong score by Mike Leiber and Jerry Stoller, and KING CREOLE. He also had a major hit with Otis Blackwell's R&B hit *All Shook Up.*

From 1958 to 1960 Elvis's sky-rocketing career was interrupted for two years when he was inducted into the Army. He served his time in Germany. Meanwhile, RCA had stockpiled enough material to keep Elvis on the charts, so that he continued to have hits during his absence, including *Wear My Ring around Your Neck* and *A Big Hunk o' Love.*

Upon his return, Elvis made a triumphant appearance on a FRANK SINATRA special and immediately returned to recording and making films. His first film on his return was *GI Blues,* taking advantage of the publicity that his service in the army had generated. Rather than the hard-rocking sounds of the '50s, Elvis now seemed to prefer heart-pumping ballads, scoring No. 1 singles with *It's Now or Never* and *Are You Lonesome Tonight?*

Presley's early to mid-'60s career was a major letdown from the quality of his earlier work. He appeared in a series of decidedly B- and C-grade movies. Most of his issued records were drawn from the film soundtracks, which were often filled with bottom-of-the-barrel material. The arrival of the BEATLES on the U.S. scene in 1964 also seriously hurt the popularity of older acts.

Presley made a stunning "comeback" in 1968. He returned to the charts with his first strong material in years, particularly Jerry Reed's song *Guitar Man.* He made a famous television special featuring an "informal" concert segment with his old bandmates from the '50s. The momentum carried over into 1969, when he returned to his home-town of Memphis to record two landmark albums. He scored his first top ten hit in years with the social-conscious ballad *In the Ghetto,* written by Mac Davis. He also returned to live performing, making a triumphant two-week engagement in Las Vegas.

However, Presley's comeback quickly turned into a prolonged burn-out. Addicted for years to amphetamines (to stay awake) and sleeping pills (to bring him down), Presley also ballooned in weight. By the mid-'70s, he was a walking parody of his earlier self, going through the motions of performing. On August 16, 1977, Presley finally succumbed to a heart attack, brought on by his excessive weight and long-time use of barbituates.

Since his death, Presley has become, if anything, more famous than he was when he was alive. Fans have made pilgrimages to his mansion/home in Memphis, Graceland, to visit his grave and see the place where he lived. His records—from budget CDs to lavish boxed sets—have been issued and reissued. His estate, which was bankrupt at the time of his death, is now one of the wealthiest in the nation, generating hundreds of thousands of dollars of income a year.

Pretty Girl Is Like a Melody, A. Song by IRVING BERLIN, 1919, written for the Ziegfeld Follies of that year. It became a permanent fixture of the Follies and was added to several movie musicals.

Previn, André (George) (born Andreas Ludwig Priwin), brilliant German-born American pianist, conductor, and composer; b. Berlin, April 6, 1929. Previn was of Russian-Jewish descent. He showed an unmistakable musical gift as a child. His father, a lawyer, was an amateur musician who gave him early training. At the age of six, he was accepted as a pupil at the Berlin Hochschule für Musik, where he studied piano. As a Jew, however, he was compelled to leave school in 1938. The family then went to Paris, where he continued his studies with Marcel Dupré at the Paris Conservatory.

In 1939 the family emigrated to America, settling in Los Angeles, where his father's cousin, Charles Previn, was music

PEOPLE IN MUSIC

director at Universal Studios in Hollywood. André took lessons in composition with Joseph Achron, ERNST TOCH, and MARIO CASTELNUOVO-TEDESCO. He became an American citizen in 1943. Even before graduating from high school, he obtained employment at MGM, becoming an orchestrator there and later one of its music directors. He also became a fine jazz pianist.

While serving in the U.S. Army from 1950 to 1952, Previn was stationed in San Francisco, where he took lessons in conducting with PIERRE MONTEUX, then music director of the San Francisco Symphony Orchestra. During these years he wrote much music for films, receiving Academy Awards for *Gigi* (1958), *Porgy and Bess* (1959), *Irma la Douce* (1963), and *My Fair Lady* (1964). Throughout this period he continued to appear as a concert pianist. In 1962 he made his formal conducting debut with the St. Louis Symphony Orchestra, and conducting soon became his principal vocation.

From 1967 to 1969 Previn was conductor-in-chief of the Houston Symphony Orchestra. In 1968 he assumed the post of principal conductor of the London Symphony Orchestra, retaining it with distinction until 1979, when he was made its conductor emeritus. In 1976 he became music director of the Pittsburgh Symphony Orchestra, a position he held with similar distinction until a dispute with the management led to his resignation in 1984.

Previn had already been engaged as music director of the Royal Philharmonic Orchestra of London in 1982, a position he held from 1985 to 1987. He then served as its principal conductor. Previn also accepted appointment as music director of the Los Angeles Philharmonic Orchestra. He formally assumed his duties there in 1985 but gave up this position in 1990 after disagreements with the management. From 1990 he appeared widely as a guest conductor with the world's foremost orchestras.

During his years as a conductor of the London Symphony Orchestra, Previn took it on a number of tours to the U.S., Russia, Japan, South Korea, and Hong Kong. He continued to compose popular music, including the scores for the musicals *Coco* (1969) and *The Good Companions* (1974). With words by Tom Stoppard, he composed *Every Good Boy*

Deserves Favour in 1977, a work for actors and orchestra. His other compositions include Symphony for Strings (1962), *Overture to a Comedy* (1963), *Elegy* for oboe and strings (1967), Cello Concerto (1967), Horn Concerto (1968), Guitar Concerto (1972), *Principals* for orchestra (1980), *Reflections* for orchestra (1981), *Divertimento* for orchestra (1982), and Piano Concerto (1985). His opera *A Streetcar Named Desire* was premiered in San Francisco on Sept. 19, 1998, Previn conducting. He edited the book *Orchestra* (Garden City, N.Y., 1979) and also published *André Previn's Guide to Music* (London, 1983).

Previn was married four times (and divorced thrice): to the jazz singer Betty Bennett, to the jazz poet Dory Langdon (who made a career of her own as composer and singer of pop songs), to the actress Mia Farrow, and in 1982 to Heather Hales. His nephew is the versatile critic and writer on contemporary music and art RICHARD KOSTELANETZ (b. N.Y., May 14, 1940).

Prey, Hermann, outstanding German baritone; b. Berlin, July 11, 1929; d. Munich, July 22, 1998. Prey studied at the Berlin Hochschule für Musik. In 1952 he won first prize in a vocal competition organized by the U.S. Army and that same year made his operatic debut as the second prisoner in *Fidelio* in Wiesbaden.

PEOPLE IN MUSIC

After appearing in the U.S., Prey joined the Hamburg State Opera in 1953. He also sang in Vienna and Berlin (beginning in 1956), and Salzburg (from 1959). In 1959 he became a principal member of the Bavarian State Opera in Munich. He made his Metropolitan Opera debut in N.Y. as Wolfram in 1960. In 1965, Prey appeared for the first time in England at the Edinburgh Festival and later sang regularly at London's Covent Garden, beginning in 1973. He also appeared as a soloist with major orchestras and as a recitalist, and starred in his own Munich television show. In 1982 Prey became a professor at the Hamburg Hochschule für Musik.

Among his finest operatic roles were Count Almaviva, Papageno, Guglielmo, and GIOACCHINO ROSSINI's Figaro, but he also sang a number of contemporary roles. As a lieder artist, he distinguished himself in songs by FRANZ SCHUBERT, ROBERT SCHUMANN, and JOHANNES BRAHMS. His autobiography appeared as *Premierenfieber* (1981; English translation as *First Night Fever: The Memoirs of Hermann Prey,* 1986).

Prez, Josquin des. *See* DESPREZ (DES PREZ), JOSQUIN.

PEOPLE IN MUSIC

Price, (Mary Violet) **Leontyne,** remarkably gifted African-American soprano; b. Laurel, Miss., Feb. 10, 1927. Price was taught piano by a local woman and also learned to sing. She went to Oak Park High School, graduating in music in 1944. She then enrolled in the College of Education and Industrial Arts in Wilberforce, Ohio, where she studied voice with Catherine Van Buren, earning her bachelors of arts degree in 1948.

Price was awarded a scholarship at the Juilliard School of Music in N.Y., where she received vocal training from Florence Page Kimball and also joined the Opera Workshop under the direction of Frederic Cohen. VIRGIL THOMSON heard her perform the role of Mistress Ford in GIUSEPPE VERDI's *FALSTAFF* and invited her to sing in the revival of his opera *FOUR SAINTS IN 3 ACTS* in 1952. She subsequently performed the role of Bess in GEORGE GERSHWIN's *PORGY AND BESS* on a tour of the U.S. during 1952–54 and in Europe in 1955.

In 1954 Price made a highly acclaimed debut as a concert singer in N.Y. Later that year, she sang at the first performance of SAMUEL BARBER's *PRAYERS OF KIERKEGAARD* with

Leontyne Price, 1978. (Ira Nowinski/©Corbis) ▶

the Boston Symphony Orchestra. In 1955 she performed Tosca on television, creating a sensation both as an artist and as an African American taking up the role of an Italian diva. Her career was soon assured.

In 1957 Price appeared with the San Francisco Opera, later that year singing Aida, a role suited to her passionate artistry. In 1958 she sang Aida again with the Vienna State Opera under the direction of HERBERT VON KARAJAN. On July 2, 1958, she sang this role at Covent Garden in London and again at La Scala in Milan in 1959, the first African-American woman to sing with that most prestigious company.

In 1961 Price made her first appearance with the Metropolitan Opera in N.Y. in the role of Leonora in *IL TROVATORE*. A series of highly successful performances at the Metropolitan followed: Aida, Madama Butterfly, Donna Anna (all 1961), Tosca (1962), and Pamina (1964). She created the role of Cleopatra in the premiere of Barber's *ANTONY AND CLEOPATRA* at the opening of the new Metropolitan Opera House at Lincoln Center in N.Y. in 1966.

In 1973 Price sang Madama Butterfly at the Metropolitan once more. In 1975, she appeared there in the title role of *Manon Lescaut*. She also sang Aida there, a role she repeated for her farewell operatic performance in a televised production broadcast live from the Metropolitan Opera by PBS on Jan. 3, 1985. She then continued her concert career, appearing with notable success in major music centers.

Price was married in 1952 to the baritone William Warfield (b. West Helena, Ark., Jan. 22, 1920), who sang Porgy opposite her Bess. They were separated in 1959 and finally divorced in 1972. She received many honors during her remarkable career. In 1964 President Johnson bestowed upon her the Medal of Freedom, and in 1985 President Reagan presented her with the National Medal of Arts. In 1992 she was made a Dame Commander of the Order of the British Empire.

Pride, Charley, African-American country-music singer and guitarist; b. on a cotton farm near Sledge, Miss., March 18, 1938. Pride learned to play guitar but, bent on a career in baseball, he played in the minor leagues from 1954 to 1964.

PEOPLE IN MUSIC

Meanwhile, he played guitar and followed country radio as a hobby.

In 1965 country producer Jack Clement recommended Pride to RCA records in Nashville. He scored an immediate hit with *Just Between You and Me,* despite the fact that country radio was not inclined to play a recording by an African-American singer. In 1967 he was made a member of the GRAND OLE OPRY, the important Nashville-based country music radio program.

Pride enjoyed his greatest success in the late '60s and early '70s, producing 29 No. 1 country records. His biggest hits were *Is Anybody Goin' to San Antone?* and *Kiss an Angel Good Morning.*

The new country movement of the '80s and '90s more or less left Pride behind. Nonetheless, he continues to record and perform. He regularly appears in Branson, Missouri, the popular country-music town that features many of the older country performers.

Prière d'une vièrge (The maiden's prayer). A salon masterpiece for piano by Thekla Badarzewska, 1851. At one time, it was undoubtedly the most celebrated piano piece ever written.

Serious musicians criticized it as a deplorable piece of sentimental salon music, but young pianists all over the world continued to play it at home. More than 100 separate editions of the piece have been published.

The composer, a 17-year-old Polish girl, died a few years after its publication. She never knew the impact it had on young pianists everywhere!

Příhody Lišky Bystroušky. *See* CUNNING LITTLE VIXEN, THE.

prima donna (It., first lady) The leading SOPRANO in OPERA, be it in a particular role or as a public figure to be admired. *Prima donna assoluta* is an absolute prima donna superior to the *seconda donna* or *prima donna altra.*

The cult of the prima donna reached its height in the 19th century. A typical prima donna was an amply bosomed Italian or German soprano, possessing great lung power. The chronicles of opera are replete with tales about temperamental prima donnas engaging in fistfights and verbal warfare with other prima donnas over the size of lettering in their names on theatrical posters, the space allocated in their dressing rooms, the extent of publicity, the efficiency of the hired CLAQUE, etc. More than one prima donna has lost an engagement over such seemingly minor matters.

prima prattica (It., first practice). A term used in early 17th-century Italian theoretical treatises to denote the dense POLYPHONIC style of the previous century, synonymous with *STILE ANTICO*. This was distinct from the SECONDA PRATTICA, also called the *STILE MODERNO*.

prē-mäh präh′tē-käh

primary accent. The DOWNBEAT or THESIS. The accent beginning the MEASURE, directly following the BAR.

primary triad. One of the three fundamental TRIADS of a KEY (those on the first, fifth, and fourth degrees).

prime. The first note of a SCALE. *Prime tone,* FUNDAMENTAL.

primitivism. As *primitive music,* a term generally applied to songs created spontaneously by untrained musicians of a culture other than one's own. The term also carries a suggestion of a certain condescension on the part of educated musicians.

Conversely, musicians who wished to expand the boundaries of art music have found fresh inspiration in folk songs and dances as a source of new techniques. Thus Pablo Picasso was inspired by the artless productions of primitive cultures in creating his own superprimitive art. Similarly, IGOR STRAVINSKY sought inspiration in the melodies and rhythms of ancient Russian songs.

primo,-a (It.). First; a first or leading part, as in a duet. *Prima buffa,* leading lady in comic opera; *PRIMA DONNA,* leading lady in opera; *primo uomo,* the male equivalent of the prima donna; *prima vista,* at first sight; *prima volta,* the first time (written *Ima volta,* or simply *I,* or *1*), indicates that the measure(s) under its brackets are to be played the first time, before the repeat, whereas, on repeating, those marked *seconda volta* (or *IIda volta,* or *II,* or *2*) are to be performed instead.

prē-mŏh, -mäh

Primrose, William, eminent Scottish-born American violist and teacher; b. Glasgow, Aug. 23, 1903; d. Provo, Utah, May 1, 1982. Primrose studied violin in Glasgow with Camillo Ritter, at London's Guildhall School of Music, and, from 1925 to 1927, in Belgium with Eugène Ysaÿe, who advised him to take up viola because there were already many talented violinists on the music scene.

Primrose became violist in the London String Quartet from 1930 to 1935, with which he made several tours. In 1937 he settled in the U.S. and was engaged as the principal violist player in the NBC Symphony Orchestra in N.Y. under ARTURO TOSCANINI, holding this post until 1942. In 1939 he established his own string quartet. In 1953 he was named a Commander of the Order of the British Empire, and in 1955 he became a naturalized U.S. citizen. From 1954 to 1962 he was the violist in the Festival Quartet.

Primrose also became active as a teacher, serving on the faculty of the University of Southern California in Los Angeles in 1962 and at the School of Music of Indiana University in Bloomington from 1965 to 1972. In 1972 he inaugurated a master class at the Tokyo University of Fine Arts and Music. Returning to the U.S., he taught at Brigham Young University in Provo, Utah from 1979 until his death in 1982.

Primrose was greatly esteemed as a viola virtuoso. He gave first performances of viola concertos by several modern composers. He commissioned a viola concerto from BÉLA BARTÓK, but the work was left unfinished at the time of Bartók's death. The task of reconstructing the score from Bartók's sketches remained to be accomplished by Bartók's friend and associate Tibor Serly. Primrose gave its first performance with the Minneapolis Symphony Orchestra on Dec. 2, 1949.

Primrose published *A Method for Violin and Viola Players* in 1960 and *Technique in Memory* in 1963. He also edited various works for viola and made transcriptions for the instrument.

Prince (born Prince Roger Nelson), provocative African-American rock singer, instrumentalist, and songwriter; b. Minneapolis, June 7, 1958. His father led a jazz group

called the Prince Roger Trio, and his mother sang with it. He took up piano, guitar, and drums in his youth.

Before graduating from high school, Prince formed a soul-rock band and soon learned to play a whole regiment of instruments and to write songs. When his group, renamed Champagne, proved less than a bubbling success, he traveled to Los Angeles to conquer the recording industry. After producing the albums *For You* (1978) and *Prince* (1979), he had his first success with his sexually explicit *Dirty Mind* (1980) and *Controversy* (1981) albums.

Prince continued to produce hit albums, notably the futuristic concept album *1999* (1982). It was followed by the sensationally acclaimed film and sound-track album *Purple Rain* (1984), which won an Academy Award in 1985. One of its songs, *Darling Niki,* inspired some conservative critics to call for the labeling of rock albums, to protect young listeners from "suggestive lyrics." After producing the album *Parade* (1986), he starred in the films *Sign o' the Times* (1987) and *Graffiti Bridge* (1990).

In 1995 Prince embarked on a protracted battle with his record company, Warner Brothers, claiming they were refusing to issue his music the way he wished it produced. He finally freed himself of his contract, entering into a new distribution deal in 1996 with EMI. Since then, Prince has continued to record prolifically, although his music has achieved less attention than previously.

In 1990 Prince changed his stage name into an unpronounceable symbol, forcing the media to refer to him as "the Artist Formerly Known As Prince."

Prince Igor. Opera by ALEXANDER BORODIN, 1890, produced posthumously in St. Petersburg. Borodin, a professor of chemistry, neglected his musical compositions and failed to complete many scores, among them *Prince Igor.* This task fell to NIKOLAI RIMSKY-KORSAKOV and ALEXANDER GLAZUNOV.

The libretto is based on a Russian 12th-century chronicle recounting the story of the heroic Russian warrior Prince Igor. He is about to lead his army against the Mongol invaders, the Polovtzi, when an unpredicted eclipse of the sun throws his superstitious soldiers into disarray. (*Prince Igor* is the only opera that has a solar eclipse.)

Igor suffers defeat and is captured. The Polovtzian Khan treats him royally in captivity, however, and is willing to let him go free provided he promises not to go to war against him again. The Khan also offers him a choice of beautiful slave girls who stage the famous Polovtzian dances. Igor rejects all these allurements, eventually escapes, and rejoins his loving wife.

The music of this opera is filled with pseudo-Oriental touches. It is one of the richest of all Russian scores.

principal chords. The basic CHORDS of a KEY, i.e., the TRIADS built on the TONIC, DOMINANT, and SUBDOMINANT, with the DOMINANT-SEVENTH chord.

printing and publishing of music. Almost immediately after the appearance of Gutenberg's Bible set from moveable type, experiments began to set musical NOTES in type. The first book with printed musical examples was *Psalterium,* set in type in 1457 in Gutenberg's workshop.

Early printing press, c. 1870. (Christel Gerstenberg/Corbis) ▶

An important development in music printing was the use of woodblocks in which complete musical examples, notes, and lines were carved out and inked. This method was particularly handy for books on music theory in which text alternated with musical examples. These early specimens were usually printed in very large notes and widely separated lines.

A significant advance toward modern printing was made by the Venetian printer Ottaviano dei Petrucci, who began printing vocal music books in the first year of the 16th century and who may well be considered the Gutenberg of music printing. He also printed the first TABLATURES for the LUTE.

In early printed music a double process was involved. The lines of the staff were printed first, usually colored in red, and black notes were superimposed on the staff. Toward the end of the 16th century metal plates began to be used, with both lines and notes engraved by hand.

In the 18th century music engraving reached the point of a graphic art, particularly when punches and hammers were applied. Professional craftsmen sometimes accepted work in music engraving. Paul Revere, a silversmith by trade, became the first American to engrave music. The 18th-century French violinist and composer Jean-Marie Leclair (L'Aîné) entrusted the engraving of his music to his wife, a trained toolmaker.

Decisive progress in music printing was made in applying lithography, that is, printing from a stone surface with a viscous ink, a process developed by the German printer Aloys Senefelder in 1796. CARL MARIA VON WEBER apprenticed himself to Senefelder and introduced some improvements of his own. Type printing, in which musical symbols had to be placed on the staff separately by hand, a method that was too laborious for music printing but that yielded artistic results, was perfected in the second half of the 18th century. This method was used concurrently with copperplating and lithography for special purposes, such as the reproduction of musical examples in theory books.

The greatest era of music printing from copper plates was reached in the middle of the 19th century. Beautiful editions of instrumental music, orchestral scores, and complete operas were published by the German publishers Schott, Peters, and particularly Breitkopf & Härtel. Excellent editions of works by Russian composers, financed by the wealthy Russian merchant Belaieff, were printed on German presses in Leipzig.

Leclair was stabbed to death in his home. The evidence strongly pointed to his wife as the killer, because the wounds were inflicted by metal punches such as are used in music engraving!

The 18th century was dominated in England by the publishing house of Walsh, which began publishing GEORGE FRIDERIC HANDEL's operas and also reprinted many works by continental composers. Several important publishing enterprises emerged in Great Britain in the 19th century and prospered unflaggingly into the last part of the 20th: Chappell, founded in 1810, and Boosey, founded in 1816. Boosey's competitor was Queen Victoria's trumpet player, Hawkes, who formed an independent printing shop specializing, like Boosey, in orchestral and chamber music. In 1930 the inheritors of both joined in a highly successful publishing house, Boosey and Hawkes. Another important British publishing house was Novello, established in 1829 and concentrating on choral music.

The U.S., even after its independence, continued to rely on England for its music, which was mostly imported from the former mother country. Among the earliest American publishers, or rather importers, of music was BENJAMIN CARR, who emigrated to America after the Revolution and set up the first American music store, Carr's Musical Depository, in Philadelphia in 1794. The first important American-born publisher of music was Oliver Ditson, who established a business as a music seller in Boston in 1835 and continued in business for about a decade.

The American dependence on Great Britain for music publishing continued until the middle of the 19th century, when the predominant influence on all branches of music in the U.S. was asserted by German immigrants. The year 1861 marked the foundation of the most important music publishing firm in America, established by Gustav Schirmer. Another German-born music publisher, Carl Fischer, settled in N.Y. and established an important publishing organization in 1872. Among American-born music publishers, Theodore Presser established his own firm in 1883. An important source of income for American music publishers was the representation of European publishers who held the rights for lucrative operas, popular orchestral pieces, and pedagogical literature.

Italy occupies an important position in music publishing, thanks to the almost exclusive rights on famous Italian operas. The firm of Ricordi, formed in 1808, holds the richest grants of Italian operatic literature. The entire stock of plates and publications was destroyed in a devastating air attack on Milan, the site of the Ricordi publishing house, in 1943, but like a musical phoenix it emerged from the ashes and resumed its important position.

In Austria, Hungary, and the Scandinavian countries, local publishers maintained a close cooperation with the large German or English publishing houses. Among French publishers the firm of Durand, founded in 1870, became the most important as well as the most prosperous. Editions Salabert, organized in 1896, went into the lucrative field of popular arrangements of theater music.

Before the Revolution, Russia had several important publishers that supplied the Russians with European music literature but also published works by Russian composers. Among them, Jurgenson, PIOTR ILYICH TCHAIKOVSKY's publisher, played a significant role in championing Russian music. Belaieff generously sponsored the publication of music by composers of the Russian national school. SERGE KOUSSEVITZKY and his wealthy wife founded his own firm with the specific purpose of publishing works by modern Russian composers, among them ALEXANDER SCRIABIN, IGOR STRAVINSKY, and SERGEI PROKOFIEV.

After the Revolution, the Soviet government nationalized all Russian publishing houses and established a Central State Publishing House. Because the Soviet government was the sole publisher, the costs of publishing were absorbed within the general budget of the state. It therefore became possible for Russia to publish music extensively, almost extravagantly. For instance, all 27 symphonies of NIKOLAI MIASKOVSKY were published from engraved plates, including the orchestral parts.

Collected works of Russian classical composers were systematically issued. But even composers less known in Russia and quite unknown abroad had their works published as a matter of routine. Similar policies in publishing music existed in Communist Poland, Yugoslavia, Czechoslovakia, Rumania, and Bulgaria. With the end of Communism in Eastern Europe, these countries now have to follow the examples of their Western capitalist counterparts.

It has become very expensive to publish contemporary orchestral scores. For this reason, many publishers no longer typeset the full scores, relying instead on reproducing handwritten copies, sometimes penned by the composers themselves! Often, the scores are printed in small quantities, just enough for performance use.

process music. *See* MINIMALISM.

processional. A hymn sung in church during the entrance of choir and clergy.

Prodigal Son, The. Church parable by BENJAMIN BRITTEN, 1968, first performed at the Aldeburgh Festival. The text is based on the biblical parable of a wandering son who is welcomed home by his lenient father, to the dismay of the prodigal's brothers.

Professor Longhair. *See* BYRD, HENRY ROELAND.

program music (programmatic music; Ger. *Programmusik;* Fr. *musique à programme*). A class of instrumental compositions intended to represent distinct moods or emotions, or to depict actual scenes or events, as opposed to ABSOLUTE MUSIC. Perhaps *descriptive music* would be a more adequate definition, but the terms above have become well established in English-speaking countries. In the 19th century, the preferable description of program music was *tone painting.*

A pioneer in program music was FRANZ LISZT. His ideas were eagerly accepted and developed by many German composers of the second half of the 19th century, culminating in the symphonic poems of RICHARD STRAUSS.

Imitation of sounds in nature, particularly the singing of birds, are obvious sources of literal program music and are found in a number of compositions centuries before the movement of ROMANTIC program music became pronounced. Among famous examples are *La Poule* by JEAN-PHILIPPE RAMEAU, imitating the cackling of hens, *Les abeilles,* with its murmurations of innumerable bees by FRANÇOIS COUPERIN, and *Le Coucou* (*The cuckoo*) by Louis-Claude Daquin. In the domain of literary musical narratives, the earliest examples are a set of biblical stories written for harpsichord by Johann Kuhnau, the *Four Seasons* concertos by ANTONIO VIVALDI, and KARL DITTERS VON DITTERSDORF's 12 symphonies illustrating Ovid's *Metamorphoses.*

Probably the most explicit piece of symphonic program music is the *SYMPHONIE FANTASTIQUE* (1830) of HECTOR BERLIOZ, written by him to express his love for the Shakespearean actress Miss Smithson. Among Liszt's symphonic poems, the ones that bear direct literary connections are *LES PRÉLUDES* (1854) and the *Faust Symphony* (1857). HENRY CHARLES LITOLFF composed the overture *Robespierre* (1856), in which the falling of the severed head of Robespierre into the basket is rendered as a thud on the bass drum.

The 19th century saw the greatest flowering of program music. This led to the regrettable practice of giving imaginative but more often trite nicknames to musical compositions whose composers never intended to write programmatic music. It is ironic that most of the familiar titles attached to FELIX MENDELSSOHN's *Songs without Words* are the products of the publisher's eagerness to attract romantically inclined players. FRANZ JOSEPH HAYDN's symphonies and string quartets received popular nicknames that represent the general desire to seek familiar images in the sounds of music. But even so, it is as difficult to trace the rationale of some of these titles as it is to find the animal figures in the constellations of the zodiac seen by ancient stargazers.

Among Haydn's symphonies we have *The Philosopher* (No. 22), *The Schoolmaster* (No. 55), and *The Absent-Minded Man* (No. 94). Only the *Surprise Symphony,* which in German has a more concrete description, *Paukenschlag* (Drumstroke), has a musical meaning behind the title, because in the second movement there is a sudden loud chord at the end of the theme, inserted there by Haydn supposedly to wake dozing members of the audience.

There is no explanation why WOLFGANG AMADEUS MOZART's great C-major Symphony, K.551, should be called the *JUPITER SYMPHONY* (1788). Nor is there any reason to call Beethoven's E-flat Piano Concerto the *EMPEROR CONCERTO* (1795). Both nicknames were apparently invented in England. The *MOONLIGHT SONATA* (1801) of Beethoven received its programmatic name thanks to a critic who said that its opening movement suggested to him moonlight on Lake

Lucerne. Although the *SONATA APPASSIONATA* seems appropriate to describe Beethoven's impassioned music, the title was invented by a publisher.

Even when the composer specifically denies any programmatic significance, descriptive nicknames are removed with difficulty. The so-called *Raindrop Prelude* of FRÉDÉRIC CHOPIN is supposed to have been inspired by his listening to raindrops fall on the roof of his house on the Island of Mallorca, but he expressly denied this. More to the point is the title *Revolutionary Étude,* because it is marked by rebellious upward passages in the left hand. It was composed by Chopin at the time Warsaw was captured by the Russians, leading to the partition of his beloved fatherland. The nickname for Chopin's *MINUTE WALTZ* seems obvious, but no human pianist can play it in 60 seconds flat, with all the repeats.

Personal references and all kinds of musical asides are found throughout music literature. Certainly ROBERT SCHUMANN's *Carnaval,* built on the four notes spelling the name of the Bohemian town of Asch in the German musical alphabet, is a piece of program music, with autobiographical allusions. It was in Asch that Schumann met a lady he had once loved (not Clara). Another famous autobiographical piece of program music is *Symphonia domestica* by RICHARD STRAUSS, in which the composer portrayed in music the nightly bath of his infant son. The exact time, 7 o'clock, is represented by the chimes striking seven.

PIOTR ILYICH TCHAIKOVSKY's *PATHÉTIQUE SYMPHONY* is a piece of program music after the fact, because the descriptive title was attached to it after the score was completed. What is interesting is that it contains a passage in the trombones from the Russian Mass for the Dead, as if Tchaikovsky had a premonition of his death, which occurred a few days after the first performance of the work.

Any composition, no matter how abstract or classically sober, can be interpreted as an image. Modern ballet composers often use movements from symphonic works for choreographic spectacles of a romantic nature with suitable titles attached to them. Some pieces of program music would lose their attraction if they were deprived of their titles. The witty interlude *Pianists* in *The Carnival of the Ani-*

mals of CAMILLE SAINT-SAËNS would be pointless were it not for the inclusion of pianists among the animals of the title.

In some pieces of program music the title becomes more important than the music itself. This is particularly true of the humorous creations of ERIK SATIE, whose music would hardly be the same without those fantastically imaginative and humorous titles, such as *Heures séculaires et instantanées* (Century-long instantaneous hours).

Sometimes composers yield to the temptation of attaching programmatic titles to their works only to rescind them later. GUSTAV MAHLER bestowed programmatic titles to several of his symphonies— *Titan* for the first, *Summer Morning's Dream* for the third, *The Giant* for the fifth—but subsequently insisted that he never authorized anyone to use them for identification. IGOR STRAVINSKY's *Scherzo fantastique* was originally published with a long quotation from Maeterlinck's *Life of the Bees.* He even added specific subtitles, such as *Queen Bee's Nuptial Flight,* to parts of his score, but later denied that the music was inspired by any insects whatsoever.

Communist countries tend to support program music, while they condemn "art for art's sake." The musical philosophy of the People's Republic of China is typical. In January of 1974, the official organ of the Communist Party of the Chinese Republic published a leading article entitled *Works of Music without Titles Do Not Reflect the Class Spirit,* and specifically condemned Piano Sonata No. 17 by "the German capitalist musician, Beethoven" and the Symphony in B minor by the "Romantic Austrian capitalist musician, Schubert."

CHARLES IVES was certainly a composer of program music, with America as his program. In his symphonic *Fourth of July,* he assembled a heterogenous orchestra with a wildly DISSONANT climax representing the explosion of multicolored fireworks. In his note on the work he wrote: "It is pure program music—it is also pure abstract music." He added a quotation from Mark Twain's *Huckleberry Finn,* "You pays yer money, and you takes yer choice."

progression. The advance from one TONE to another, or from one CHORD to another. The former is *melodic,* the latter *harmonic.*

progressive composition. In songwriting, the setting of each STROPHE (verse) to different music, following the changing mood of the piece. Compare with STROPHIC composition, where melody and harmony are generally the same for each verse. Also called THROUGH-COMPOSED.

progressive jazz. In the late '40s and early '50s, a group of jazz musicians hoped to combine techniques from modern classical music with the improvisation and energy of traditional jazz. This movement was also called THIRD STREAM, because it represented an alternative to pure classical or pure jazz performance. A handful of arrangers—most notably GIL EVANS—were instrumental in introducing modern harmonies, POLYRHYTHM, and POLYPHONY into jazz orchestration as part of this movement.

progressive rock. *See* ROCK.

Prokofiev (Prokofieff), **Sergei** (Sergeievich), great 20th-century Russian composer, creator of new and original formulas of rhythmic, melodic, and harmonic combinations that became the recognized style of his music; b. Sontsovka, near Ekaterinoslav, April 27, 1891; d. Moscow, March 5, 1953. Prokofiev's mother was born a serf in 1859, two years before the emancipation of the Russian serfs. She assumed (as was the custom) the name of the estate where she was born, Sontsov.

Prokofiev received his first piano lessons from his mother, who was an amateur pianist. He improvised several pieces and then composed a children's opera, *The Giant,* in 1900, which was performed at home. Following his bent for the theater, he put together two other operas, *On Desert Islands* (1902) and *Ondine* (1904–7). Fantastic subjects obviously possessed his childish imagination.

Prokofiev was 11 years old when he met the great Russian master Sergei Taneyev, who arranged for him to take private lessons with Reinhold Glière, who became his tutor at Sontsovka during the summers of 1903 and 1904 and by correspondence during the intervening winter. Under Glière's knowledgeable guidance in theory and harmony,

Prokofiev time line

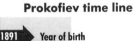

1891   Year of birth

1903–4   Studies with REINHOLD GLIÈRE

1910   His first published work, a piano sonata, is premiered in Moscow

1913   Travels to Paris, London, and Switzerland

1914   Graduates from the St. Petersburg Conservatory, receiving the Anton Rubinstein Prize with his Piano Concerto No. 1

1915   Composes his orchestral *Scythian Suite*

1916–17   Composes the first of seven symphonies, the famous *CLASSICAL SYMPHONY*

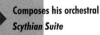

Prokofiev composed a symphony in piano version and still another opera, *Plague*, based upon a poem by Pushkin.

Finally, in 1904, at the age of 13, he enrolled in the St. Petersburg Conservatory, where he studied composition and piano. Later he was accepted by no less a master than NIKOLAI RIMSKY-KORSAKOV, who instructed him in orchestration. He also studied conducting with Nikolai Tcherepnin and form with Joseph Wihtol.

During the summers, Prokofiev returned to Sontsovka or traveled in the Caucasus and continued to compose, already in quite an advanced style. The Moscow publisher Jurgenson (PIOTR ILYICH TCHAIKOVSKY's publisher) accepted his first work, a piano sonata, for publication. It was premiered in Moscow on March 6, 1910. Prokofiev made his first visit to Paris, London, and Switzerland during 1913. In 1914 he graduated from the St. Petersburg Conservatory, receiving the Anton Rubinstein Prize (a grand piano) as a pianist-composer with his Piano Concerto No. 1, which he performed publicly at the graduation concert.

Prokofiev's early works showed an advanced appreciation of DISSONANT harmonies, and assymmetric rhythms and melodies. This was explicitly demonstrated in his *Sarcasms* and *Visions fugitives* for piano, which was percussive and sharp, yet not lacking in lyric charm. Grotesquerie and irony animated his early works. He also developed a strong attraction toward primitive subjects. His important orchestral work, the *SCYTHIAN SUITE* (arranged from music written for a ballet, *Ala and Lolly,* 1915), draws upon a legend of ancient Russian sun-worship rituals. While a parallel with IGOR STRAVINSKY's *THE RITE OF SPRING* (1913) may exist, there is no similarity between the styles of the two works.

During the same period, Prokofiev wrote his famous *CLASSICAL SYMPHONY* (1916–17), in which he adopted with remarkable acuity the formal style of FRANZ JOSEPH HAYDN. While the structure of the work was indeed classical, the sudden modulatory shifts and subtle elements of grotesquerie revealed decisively a new type of art.

After conducting the premiere of his *Classical Symphony* in Petrograd in 1918, Prokofiev left Russia by way of Siberia and Japan for the U.S. (the continuing war in Europe pre-

1918–19 Leaves Russia via Siberia, traveling to Japan and, later, to the U.S.

1920 Settles in Paris, where his ballets *Chout, Le Pas d'acier,* and *L'Enfant prodigue* are produced by Sergei Diaghilev and the Ballets Russes

1921 Visits America again for the production of THE LOVE FOR THREE ORANGES, commissioned by the Chicago Opera Company

1927 Returns to Russia as a pianist in a series of programs comprised of his own works

1929 After a second visit to Russia as a pianist, he decides to stay

1936–36 Composes the ballet *Romeo and Juliet*

1936 Composes the symphonic fairy tale PETER AND THE WOLF

1938 Composes his Cello Concerto, which evolves into the *Sinfonia Concertante* and is premiered by MSTISLAV ROSTROPOVICH in 1954, one year after Prokofiev's death

1939 Composes the historical cantata ALEXANDER NEVSKY

1940s Prokofiev is denounced as decadent and corrupted by Western influences by reactionary Soviet politicians, a situation which continues to his death

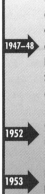

1947–48 In an (unsuccessful) attempt to appease the Soviet establishment, he composes the opera *A Tale about a Real Man,* based on a heroic exploit of a Soviet pilot during the war against the Nazis

1952 Completes work on his opera WAR AND PEACE, begun in 1941

1953 Dies of heart failure, a few hours before the death of Stalin

vented him from traveling westward). He gave concerts of his music in Japan and later in the U.S., playing his first solo concert in N.Y. Some American critics greeted his appearance as the reflection of the chaotic events of Russia in revolution, and Prokofiev himself was described as a "ribald and Bolshevist innovator and musical agitator." "Every rule in the realm of traditional music writing was broken by Prokofiev," one N.Y. writer complained. "Dissonance followed dissonance in a fashion inconceivable to ears accustomed to melody and harmonic laws."

Prokofiev's *Classical Symphony,* in particular, struck some critics as "an orgy of dissonant sound, an exposition of the unhappy state of chaos from which Russia suffers." Another N.Y. critic indulged in the following: "Crashing Siberians, volcano hell, Krakatoa, sea-bottom crawlers. Incomprehensible? So is Prokofiev." But yet another critic issued a word of caution, suggesting that "Prokofiev might be the legitimate successor of Borodin, Mussorgsky, and Rimsky-Korsakov." The critic was unintentionally right, as Prokofiev is firmly enthroned in the pantheon of Russian music.

In 1920 Prokofiev settled in Paris, where he composed for Sergei Diaghilev's Ballets Russes. Diaghilev produced Prokofiev's ballets *Chout* (a French transliteration of the Russian word for buffoon), *Le Pas d'acier* (The steps of steel; descriptive of the industrial development in Soviet Russia), and *L'Enfant prodigue* (The prodigal son). In 1921 Prokofiev again visited the U.S. for the production of the opera commissioned by the Chicago Opera Company, *The Love for Three Oranges.*

In 1927 Prokofiev was invited to be the pianist for a series of his own works in Russia. He gave a number of concerts in Russia again in 1929 and eventually decided to remain there. In Russia he wrote some of his most popular works, including the symphonic fairy tale *Peter and the Wolf* from 1936, staged by a children's theater in Moscow, the historical cantata *Alexander Nevsky* (1939; based on the soundtrack to the film by Sergei Eisenstein), the ballet ROMEO AND JULIET (1935–36), and the opera *War and Peace* (1941–52), which went through numerous revisions.

Unexpectedly, in the 1940s, Prokofiev was included in a list of modern Soviet composers who were denounced by reactionary Soviet politicians. He meekly confessed that he had been occasionally interested in ATONAL and POLYTONAL devices during his stay in Paris but insisted that he had never abandoned the ideals of classical Russian music. Indeed, when he composed his Seventh Symphony, he described it specifically as a youth symphony, reflecting the energy and ideals of the "new Russia."

There were also significant changes in Prokofiev's personal life. He separated from his Spanish-born wife, the singer Lina Llubera, the mother of his two sons, and established a liaison with Myra Mendelson, a member of the Young Communist League. She was a writer and assisted him on the libretto of *War and Peace*. He made one final attempt to gain favor with the Soviet establishment by writing the opera *A Tale about a Real Man* (1947–48), based on a heroic exploit of a Soviet pilot during the war against the Nazis. But this, too, was damned by the servile Communist press as lacking in true patriotic spirit, and the opera was quickly removed from the repertoire.

After a decade of illness, Prokofiev died suddenly of heart failure on March 5, 1953, a few hours before the death of his nemesis, Stalin. Curiously enough, the anniversary of Prokofiev's death was recognized by the Communist regime after Stalin's own passing.

Prokofiev composed numerous other operas and ballets, as well as incidental music, film music, and choral music. Among his orchestral works are seven symphonies, of which the *Classical* (No. 1) and No. 5 are the most popular, five piano concertos, with No. 4 written for the left hand alone, two violin concertos (1923, 1935), Cello Concerto (1938; evolved into the *Sinfonia Concertante,* premiered by MSTISLAV ROSTROPOVICH, 1954), and SUITES from the operas, ballets, and film scores. Among his many chamber pieces are two string quartets, two sonatas for violin, and sonatas for violin solo, violin duo, cello, flute. Prokofiev also composed various pieces for piano, including nine sonatas (1909–47; No. 10, 1953, unfinished), Toccata (1912), *Tales of an Old Grandmother* (1918), two sonatinas (1931–32), and *Pensées* (1933–34). His songs include *The Ugly Duckling,* after Andersen (1914).

proletarian music. A movement among Communist countries in the 20th century to create a musical art form that would appeal to the "masses." This music was meant to be uplifting and to contain a positive message about Communist ideology. Simplicity of form, utilization of popular dance rhythms and, in theatrical music, a selection of subjects from Revolutionary history or class warfare, were the main characteristics of music for the proletariat.

See SOCIAL REALISM.

RICHARD WAGNER described his music drama *Das Rheingold* as the *Vorabend* (literally, the evening before) to the main trilogy of the *Der Ring des Nibelungen* (first complete performance in 1876).

prologue. An introductory part of an opera.

A typical short prologue is that sung before the beginning of RUGGERO LEONCAVALLO's *PAGLIACCI* (1892). Here it is used in a Shakespearean sense, signifying a person who addresses the audience to explain the meaning of the play.

The prologue is usually short, usually sung or narrated, and prepares the audience for the action of the play. The overture is an instrumental table of contents of the opera to follow.

Prométhée. Symphonic work by ALEXANDER SCRIABIN, 1911, subtitled *Le Poème du feu* (The poem of fire). The title refers to the Greek god Prometheus, who stole fire from the gods.

The score calls for an important piano part, organ, choruses, full orchestra, and a "color organ" that Scriabin called, in French, *clavier à lumières,* and, in Italian, *luce.* The original idea was that the color organ would bathe the concert hall with different colors to follow the piece's moods. However, no such instrument was used at the piece's premiere. The score is musically built on the MYSTIC CHORD.

Prometheus. Symphonic poem by FRANZ LISZT, 1850, after British poet Percy Shelley's *Prometheus Unbound.* The work portrays Prometheus's release from his enchainment to a rock. His freedom is symbolized by a FUGATO.

Prometheus. Opera by CARL ORFF, 1968, first performed in Stuttgart. The libretto is the original Greek text of Aeschylus's *Prometheus Bound.* The work is scored for a large orchestra, including some 75 percussion instruments.

Promises, Promises. Musical by Burt Bacharach and Hal David, 1968, based on Neil Simon's screenplay *The Apartment.* A mild-mannered insurance clerk lends his apartment to executives in his company for after-hours affairs. He suffers a heartache when he discovers that his favorite restaurant waitress has been to his pad with the personnel director. Includes the title song, *I'll Never Fall in Love Again,* and *Whoever You Are.*

prompter. A rather important person in OPERA, seated in the proscenium with the score in front of him or her, who gives cues to singers. The "invisible" place that houses the prompter is called the *box.* In France, Germany, and Russia, the prompter is called *souffleur* (one who breathes), while in Italy, he or she is known as *maestro suggeritore* (a master suggester).

Depending on the acoustics of the hall, the prompter's voice may unexpectedly carry to some parts of the orchestra seats. Incautious prompters have been known to hum the tunes of the work in progress.

Proms, The. Affectionate abbreviation for the Promenade Concerts of London, which began in 1837 in imitation of popular concerts in Paris launched by Philippe Musard in 1833.

The programs consisted usually of ballroom dances, OVERTURES, and occasionally short pieces of choral music. In London, Promenade Concerts were given in the summer in Drury Lane Theatre, which was turned into an "agreeable promenade in hot weather." The name *Promenade* was firmly established by 1840.

The eccentric French conductor Julien was the first leader of these concerts. He was followed by the German August Manns in 1859. In 1875 the Italian Luigi Arditi conducted Promenade Concerts at Covent Garden. In 1893 Henry Wood took over the series, and his name became forever associated with the most brilliant period of the Promenade Concerts, which by then had become known as The Proms.

In 1944 The Proms were officially named The Henry Wood Promenade Concerts, as homage to the conductor,

On the night of May 10 to 11, 1941, the Queen's Hall was hit by Nazi aerial bombardment, but The Proms did not expire. The concerts were moved to the Royal Albert Hall.

who died that year. Among his successors were ADRIAN BOULT, MALCOLM SARGENT, SIR JOHN BARBIROLLI, and COLIN DAVIS. A great deal of avant-garde music was eventually included in The Proms programs, such as *The Whale* by JOHN TAVENER (1969), Tim Souster's *Triple Music II* and *The Soft Machine,* a rock piece offering including such tunes as *Esther's Nose Job* and *Out-Bloody-Rageous* (1970), and KARL-HEINZ STOCKHAUSEN's *Carré* for four orchestras.

Proper. *See* PROPRIUM.

Prophète, Le. Opera by GIACOMO MEYERBEER, 1849, first performed in Paris. The prophet is based on the historical John of Leyden, leader of the Anabaptist sect in the 16th century. In order to maintain his self-proclaimed divine status, he denies his identity and repudiates his mother. When his beloved Bertha realizes what he has become, she stabs herself to death.

The army of the Holy Roman Emperor advances on Leyden. They set John's palace afire, and he perishes in the cataclysm, along with his forgiving mother.

The coronation march accompanying the prophet's entry in the cathedral is well-known.

proportion. A term of MEDIEVAL music theory relating to the duration of the NOTES of the melody and also the ratio of vibrations of these notes.

proportional notation. A system of notation developed by Earle Brown in which durations of notes are shown proportionally, relative only to one another and independent of any strict metric system. Also called *time-space notation.*

Proprium (Lat.) The Roman Catholic MASS Proper. The portions of the liturgy that regularly occur, but with changing text, depending on the feast day and readings for that service. The Proper pertinent to one or more saints is called *proprium sanctorum.*

The musical sections of the Proper are interwoven with the sections of the ORDINARY as follows (Ordinary in italics): Introit, *Kyrie, Gloria,* Gradual, Alleluia (or Tract), Sequence,

Credo, Offertory, *Sanctus, Agnus Dei,* Communion, *Ite missa est* (or *Benedicamus Domino*).

Proud Mary (Rollin' on the River). John Forgerty-penned song that was a big hit for his group, Creedence Clearwater Revival, in 1967. It is also closely associated with the energetic version by Ike and Tina Turner released in 1969.

psalm (from Grk. *psallein,* pluck; Fr. *psaume;* It. *salmo;* Ger. *Psalm*). A HYMN; a sacred song.

The psalm is one of the most important categories of prayerful biblical poems to be sung with instrumental accompaniment. Innumerable works, beginning with the simplest type of PLAINCHANT, have been set to the texts from the Book of Psalms. Biblical tradition holds that King David wrote most of the psalms and sang them, and he is therefore known as the psalmist.

Psalmody, music sung in Protestant churches in England and the U.S. from the 17th century to the early 19th.

psalm tones. In Gregorian CHANT, the recitation formulas to be used by a soloist for intoning complete PSALMS. Each of the original eight church MODES has its own psalm tone. Each psalm tone begins with an ascent to a reciting tone (*tenor,* holding tone, sustaining tone) a FIFTH above the mode's TONIC degree. When the end of the verse is reached, the melody descends to the tonic.

There is an additional psalm tone called the *tonus peregrinus* (wandering tone), which can be used with any of the eight modes by changing the *tenor.*

psalmodicon. Swedish bowed ZITHER, invented in 1829 by Johann Dillner. In its original form, it resembled the one-stringed TROMBA MARINA but with the addition of metal drone strings. It was used as a substitute for the ORGAN in churches and schools and evolved a cello-like body and additional strings. The invention of the HARMONIUM ended its usefulness in accompanying singing.

MUSICAL
INSTRUMENT

Psalmus Hungaricus. Oratorio by ZOLTÁN KODÁLY, 1923, premiered in Budapest, scored for tenor, chorus, children's chorus *ad libitum,* organ, and orchestra.

psalter. Collection of PSALMS written in the vernacular (i.e., the language of the country where the collection was published, rather than Latin).

Numerous national psalters have been translated by various hands. Some psalters are known by their place of publication, such as the Calvinist *Geneva Psalter,* published with polyphonic settings from 1546, and the *Bay Psalm Book,* the first book published in America. Thirteen musical settings were added to the latter in 1698.

sôl′ter-ĭ **psaltery.** An ancient instrument in use to the 17th century, known to the ancient Hebrews as the *Kinnor* and to the Germans as the *Rotta.* A kind of harp-zither, with a varying number of strings plucked by the fingers or with a PLECTRUM.

pseudonyms. Common in literature, since historically, women novelists often assumed masculine names to facilitate publication of their works. In music pseudonyms are relatively rare, except in cases in which a dignified composer writes popular music. EDWARD MACDOWELL, in the beginning of his career, published a number of short pieces under various pseudonyms. Professional composers of popular songs often wrote under pseudonyms. Vladimir Dukelsky, a serious symphonic composer, adopted the *nom de plume* of Vernon Duke in writing popular songs.

More widespread is pseudonymity among singers, both in opera and on the popular stage. Because Italians have become proverbially associated with excellence in opera, many non-Italians anxious to make an opera career have assumed Italian names. Thus the American soprano Lillian Norton became Nordica.

At the turn of the century, the belief was that a musician bearing an Anglo-Saxon name could not write successful songs, and that a surname ending in "ski" (to imitate a Polish suffix) or "ska" (for women) was essential. Thus, the British pianist Ethel Liggins became Ethel Leginska, but it did not help her much in her American career.

A flight from obviously Jewish names was pronounced among musical performers until recently. In the beginning of his spectacular career, LEONARD BERNSTEIN was strongly encouraged to change his name, but he indignantly refused, and did rather well under his real name.

Public Enemy. (Members: Chuck D [born Carlton Ridenhauer], b. N.Y., Aug. 1, 1960; MC Flavor Flav (born William Drayton], b. N.Y., March 16, 1959; Professor Griff [born Richard Griffin]; Terminator X [born Norman Lee Rogers], b. N.Y., Aug. 25, 1966.) Landmark, socially conscious RAP group. Formed originally at N.Y.'s Adelphi University in 1982, the group scored massive hits in the mid-'80s with their commentaries on contemporary black life. Songs like *Prophets of Rage, Bring the Noise,* and *Party for Your Right to Fight* made them immediately successful. However, the group was shrouded in controversy; when group "Minister of Information" Professor Griff made some anti-Semitic statements, he was ousted from its membership in 1989.

The group quickly bounced back with *Fear of a Black Planet* (1990), featuring the hit *Fight the Power* (which became the theme for Spike Lee's film *Do the Right Thing,* in which they also performed). Not shying away from controversy, they released *By the Time I Get to Arizona* in 1991, denouncing that state's refusal to honor Martin Luther King, Jr. However, by the early '90s, their activities slowed. In 1994 they were producing more mainstream pop material, scoring a hit with *Give It Up.*

Puccini, Giacomo (Antonio Domenico Michele Secondo Maria), celebrated opera composer; b. Lucca, Dec. 22, 1858; d. Brussels, Nov. 29, 1924. Puccini was the fifth of seven children of Michele Puccini, who died when Giacomo was only five. His musical training was thus entrusted to his uncle, Fortunato Magi, a pupil of his father. However, Giacomo showed neither inclination nor talent for music. His mother, determined to continue the family tradition, sent him to the local Istituto Musicale Pacini, where the director, Carlo Angeloni—who had also studied with Michele Puccini—became his teacher. After Angeloni's untiring patience had aroused interest and then enthusiasm in his pupil, progress was rapid, and he soon became a proficient pianist and organist.

PEOPLE IN MUSIC

PEOPLE IN MUSIC

L'ASSIETTE AU BEURRE

PUCCINI Ce transalpin truculent, sonó réservé que sa musique est talaguse, a risqué une Manon Lescaut, qui ne recule pas, elle, devant la scène du Désert. (Qu'en pense Massenet?) On peut lui reconnaître une certaine vivacité accusee, mais quelle vanité intérieurement quelles harmonies creuses que celles de La Vie Bohème.
1905

A caricature of Puccini made in 1902. (Leonard de Selva/Corbis) ▶

Puccini began serving as a church organist in Lucca and environs when he was 14 and began composing when he was 17. After hearing GIUSEPPE VERDI's *AIDA* in Pisa in 1876, he resolved to win laurels as a dramatic composer. Having written mainly sacred music, it was self-evident that he needed further training after graduating from the Istituto in 1880. With financial support from his granduncle, Dr. Nicolao Ceru, and a stipend from Queen Margherita, he pursued his studies with Antonio Bazzini and AMILCARE PONCHIELLI at the Milan Conservatory from 1880 to 1883. For his graduation, he wrote a *Capriccio sinfonico,* which was conducted by Franco Faccio at a Conservatory concert, eliciting great praise from the critics.

In the same year, Ponchielli introduced Puccini to the librettist Fontana, who gave him the text for a one-act opera. In a few weeks the score was finished and sent to the Sonzongo competition. It did not win the prize, but in 1884, *LE VILLI* was produced at the Teatro dal Verme in Milan, with gratifying success. The famous Italian music publisher Giulio Ricordi, who was present, commissioned the young composer to write a new opera for him. But five years elapsed before this work, *EDGAR* (in three acts; text by Fontana), was produced at La Scala in Milan, scoring only a moderate success.

By this time, Puccini had become convinced that, in order to write a really effective opera, he needed a better LI-

BRETTO than Fontana had provided. Accordingly, he commissioned Domenico Oliva to write the text of MANON LESCAUT. During its composition, however, Puccini and Ricordi practically rewrote the entire book, and in the published score Oliva's name is not mentioned. With *Manon Lescaut* (in four acts), first produced at the Teatro Regio in Turin in 1893, Puccini won a veritable triumph. This was even surpassed by his next work, LA BOHÈME (in four acts; text by Illica and Giacosa), produced at the same theater in 1896. These two works not only made their composer's name known throughout the world, but also have found and maintained their place in the repertoire of every opera house.

With fame came wealth, and in 1900 Puccini built a magnificent villa at Torre del Lago, where he had been living since 1891. His next opera, TOSCA (in three acts; text by Illica and Giacosa), produced at the Teatro Costanzi in Rome in 1900, is Puccini's most dramatic work. It has become a fixture of the standard repertoire and contains some of his best-known arias.

At its premiere at La Scala in 1904, MADAMA BUTTERFLY (in two acts; text by Illica and Giacosa) was hissed. Puccini thereupon withdrew the score and made some slight changes (division into three acts, and addition of the tenor aria in the last scene). This revised version was greeted with frenzied applause in Brescia later that same year. Puccini was now the acknowledged ruler of the Italian operatic stage, his works rivaling those of Verdi in the number of performances.

In 1907 the first performance of *Madama Butterfly* at the Metropolitan Opera in N.Y. took place in the presence of the composer, whom the management had invited especially for the occasion. It was then suggested that he write an opera on an American subject, the premiere to take place at the Metropolitan. He found his subject when he witnessed a performance of the melodrama *The Girl of the Golden West*. He commissioned C. Zangarini and G. Civinini to write the libretto, and the world premiere of LA FANCIULLA DEL WEST was given in the presence of the composer, amid much enthusiasm, at the Metropolitan Opera in 1910. While it never equaled the success of his *Tosca* or *Madama Butterfly*, it returned to favor in the 1970s as a period piece.

Puccini then brought out the operetta-like *LA RONDINE* (in three acts; Monte Carlo, 1917) and the three one-act operas *IL TABARRO* (after Didier Gold's *La Houppelande*), *SUOR ANGELICA,* and *GIANNI SCHICCHI* (performed as *IL TRITTICO* at the Metropolitan Opera, 1918). His last opera, *TURANDOT* (after Gozzi), was left unfinished. The final scene was completed by FRANCO ALFANO and performed at La Scala, with ARTURO TOSCANINI conducting in 1926, in its complete version.

puk (Korean). DRUM.

Pulcinella. Ballet by IGOR STRAVINSKY, 1920, consisting of a number of Italian songs and dances based on works once attributed to GIOVANNI BATTISTA PERGOLESI. (It is clear that none of the source works are Pergolesi's; most remain anonymous.)

The score was first performed by the Ballets Russes in Paris. Stravinsky arranged a concert suite from it, first performed by the Boston Symphony Orchestra in 1922. He also transcribed some of the movements of the suite for cello and piano, and for violin and piano, under the title *Suite italienne.* Despite the feminine ending, Pulcinella is a male character who appeared in the Italian COMMEDIA DELL'ARTE in the 17th century, depicted as a deceitful rogue.

pulse. A BEAT or ACCENT.

punctus (Lat.). 1. A dot that serves as a bar of separation between rhythmic groups in MENSURAL NOTATION; *punctus divisionis.* 2. A dot that adds half of the duration of the note so dotted; *punctus additionis.*

punto (Sp.). A Cuban song combining $\frac{3}{4}$ and $\frac{6}{8}$ meters, with occasional injections of $\frac{2}{4}$. Although clearly of Spanish origin, the Caribbean punto developed its own style, marked by percussive syncopation.

Purcell, Henry, great English composer; b. London, 1659; d. Dean's Yard, Westminster, Nov. 21, 1695. Purcell's parentage remains a matter of dispute, because documentary

MUSICAL
INSTRUMENT

PEOPLE IN MUSIC

evidence is lacking. His father may have been Henry Purcell (d. Westminster, Aug. 11, 1664), a singer, Master of the Choristers at Westminster Abbey, and a Gentleman of the Chapel Royal. It is also possible that his father was Thomas Purcell (d. Westminster, July 31, 1682), a singer and composer, most likely the brother of the elder Henry Purcell, a Gentleman of the Chapel Royal, composer for the violins (with Pelham Humfrey), marshal of the Corporation of Music, and a musician-in-ordinary in the King's Private Musick.

Whatever the case, the young Henry Purcell became a chorister of the Chapel Royal under Humfrey in 1669 and also received instruction from John Blow. When his voice broke in 1673, he was appointed Assistant Keeper of the Instruments. In 1677 he was named composer-in-ordinary for the violins. He became Blow's successor as organist of Westminster Abbey in 1679 and one of the three organists of the Chapel Royal in 1682. In 1683 he was named organ maker and keeper of the king's instruments.

Purcell's first printed work was a song in Playford's *Choice Ayres* (volume 1, 1675; volume 2, 1679), which contains other songs and an elegy on the death of MATTHEW LOCKE. In 1680 Purcell published some of his finest instrumental works, the *Fantasias* for strings. In that same year he began writing odes and welcome songs. Although their texts are almost invariably insipid or bombastic, he succeeded in clothing them in some of his finest music. His incidental music for the stage also dates from that year.

In 1685 Purcell wrote the anthem *My Heart Is Inditing* for the coronation of King James II. With *DIDO AND AENEAS* he produced the first great English opera. In the remaining years of his life he devoted much time to composition for the theater. He also wrote some outstanding sacred music, the Te Deum and Jubilate in D. For the funeral of Queen Mary, he wrote the anthem *Thou Knowest, Lord, the Secrets of Our Hearts* in 1695. It was performed, along with his four canzonas for brass and two elegies, at his own funeral later that year.

Purcell's church music shows him to be an original melodist and a master of form, harmony, and all contrapuntal devices. His music for the stage is equally rich in invention, dramatic instinct, and power of characterization. His

Purcell was buried in the north aisle of Westminster Abbey. His burial tablet well expresses contemporary estimation of his talents: "Here lyes Henry Purcell, Esq.; who left this life, and is gone to that blessed place where only his harmony can be exceeded."

chamber works surpass those of his predecessors and contemporaries. Among his many works is the opera *Dido and Aeneas* (libretto by Tate; London, 1689; although evidence shows that the work may date from the mid-1680s). Among his semi-operas (plays with varying degrees of music) are *The Prophetess, or The History of Dioclesian* (1690), *King Arthur, or The British Worthy* (1691), *The Fairy Queen* (1692), *The Indian Queen* (1695; final masque by D. Purcell), and *The Tempest, or The Enchanted Island* (c.1695). He also composed incidental music to numerous plays, including several by D'Urfey, Tate, Dryden, Crowne, Southerne, Shadwell, Lee, Congreve, and D'Avenant.

Purcell also composed numerous anthems and services (c.1677–c.1693), a MAGNIFICAT and Nunc dimitiis (n.d.), Morning and Evening Service (1682), and Te Deum and Jubilate (1694), as well as other sacred works. Other vocal works include 24 odes and welcome songs, numerous songs for solo voice and BASSO CONTINUO, songs for two or more voices and basso continuo, and CATCHES. Among Purcell's instrumental works are various pieces for winds and strings, including 14 fantasias, 3 overtures, 5 pavans, and 24 sonatas. He also composed many harpsichord pieces.

Purcell's brother Daniel (b. London, c.1660; d. there [buried], Nov. 26, 1717) was an organist and composer. He completed one or more of his brother's pieces after the latter's demise.

Puritani di Scozia, I (The Puritans of Scotland). Opera by VINCENZO BELLINI, 1835, first performed in Paris, a few months before Bellini's untimely death. The LIBRETTO is derived, after several translations and retranslations from French and Italian, from Walter Scott's novel *Old Mortality* (1816).

The Puritans are the Roundheads, fanatical followers of Oliver Cromwell. The action takes place in 1649 after the execution of the Stuart King Charles I of England. A noble cavalier, faithful to the King's cause, is engaged to the daughter of a Puritan but fails to appear at the altar in order to rescue Charles's widowed queen from Cromwell's murderous clutches. His bride is bewildered by his unexplained defection and goes insane. Her mad scene rivals in effectiveness that of GAETANO DONIZETTI's *LUCIA DI LAMMERMOOR* (1835), which is also derived from Walter Scott.

Having saved the Queen, the faithful bridegroom returns to his beloved, causing her to regain her mental faculties. But, to their horror, they are surprised by Cromwell's soldiers, who carry the hapless youth to the execution block. Once more his bride-to-be lapses into madness. But lo! A trumpet fanfare announces a new victory for Cromwell and his subsequent magnanimous decision to grant amnesty to his foes. Once more the situation is saved. As if on cue, the bride regains her senses, and a happy chorus congratulates them.

The popularity of *I Puritani* in the 19th century was enormous. The famous male duet of two Roundheads was performed at the premiere by two of the loudest singers in Europe. As GIOACCHINO ROSSINI quipped, they must have been heard as far as Mt. Vesuvius. The same duet was the subject of the *Grandes variations de bravoure sur la marche des Puritans* for piano by FRANZ LISZT.

Purlie. Musical by Gary Geld, 1970. Purlie is a black preacher in the cotton region of Georgia. He is dedicated to the goal of building a black church but is opposed in this by a villainous old white overseer on the plantation. The old man dies when he discovers that his own son, an easygoing guitar picker, works with Purlie.

The score contains elements of African-American gospel songs, folk ballads, and rhythm and blues. The final number, *Walk Him Up the Stairs,* has an authentic flavor of old hymnody.

Chinese musician playing the q'in. (Benson collection) ▶

q'in (Ch'in). An early Chinese ZITHER, the most honored of all Chinese musical instruments. The qin is associated with

the Confucian ruling class, which played meditatively upon its strings while pondering life.

kwŏ-drĭl′

quadrille. A French ballroom square dance, the name of which is derived from the Spanish *quadrilla,* that is, four dancing pairs. It has five main figures: *le Pantalon, l'Été, la Poule, la Pastourelle (la Trenise),* and *la Finale.* The time alternates between $\frac{3}{8}$ $(\frac{6}{8})$ and $\frac{2}{4}$.

The quadrille attained its greatest popularity in the early 19th century, in Europe (including Russia) and America.

quadrivium. A faculty of four sciences in medieval universities, of which music was one, regarded as the doctrine dealing with the physical part of sound perception. The other three sciences were arithmetic, geometry, and astronomy.

quadruple meter or **time.** That characterized by four beats to the measure. *Quadruplet,* a group of four equal notes, to be executed in the time of three or six of the same kind in the established rhythm, written: ♪♪♪♪

Quantz, Johann Joachim, famous German flutist, writer on music, and composer; b. Oberscheden, Hannover, Jan. 30, 1697; d. Potsdam, July 12, 1773. Quantz's father was a village blacksmith. Young Johann revealed a natural gift for music and played the double bass at village festivals at age eight. His father died when he was ten, and he was apprenticed to his uncle, Justus Quantz, a "Stadtmusikus" in Merseburg, in 1708, and later to J. A. Fleischhack. He received instruction on string and wind instruments, becoming particularly adept on the violin, oboe, and trumpet. He also studied harpsichord with J. F. Kiesewetter.

◄

Johann Joachim Quantz holding an open-hole flute. (New York Public Library)

Quantz completed his apprenticeship in 1713 but remained a journeyman under Fleischhack until 1716. He then became a member of the Dresden municipal band. During a three-month leave of absence in 1717, he studied counterpoint with J. D. Zelenka in Vienna and then subsequently became oboist at the Polish chapel of Augustus II in 1718. He was active in Dresden and Warsaw but soon turned to the transverse flute, receiving some lessons from P. G. Buffardin.

In 1724 Quantz went to Italy in the entourage of the Polish ambassador and sought out FRANCESCO GASPARINI in Rome for further COUNTERPOINT training. After a sojourn in Paris in 1726–27, he visited England before returning to Dresden as a flutist in the court Kapelle. In 1728 he made his first visit to Berlin in the entourage of Augustus II, where he was engaged as teacher to Crown Prince Friedrich. He continued to visit Berlin regularly to instruct the Crown Prince while carrying out his duties in Dresden, which included the making of flutes from 1739.

Friedrich, better known as Frederick the Great, ascended the throne as King of Prussia in 1740 and the next year called Quantz to Berlin, where it was his special province to oversee the King's private evening concerts. He was granted an annual salary of 2,000 thalers, plus an honorarium for each new composition and flute he produced. Quantz was held in such high esteem by his patron that he was the only individual granted the right to criticize Friedrich's performances as a musician.

Quantz's extensive output included some 300 concertos for flute, strings, and basso continuo, seven concertos for two flutes, strings, and basso continuo, two concertos for horn, strings, and basso continuo (one dubious), two concertos for oboe, strings, and basso continuo, Concerto for oboe d'amore, strings, and basso continuo (not extant), about 200 sonatas for flute and basso continuo, some 60 trio sonatas, 12 duets for two flutes or other instruments, 12 capriccios for flute, 8 fantasias for flute, 22 hymns, 6 songs, etc. On the whole, these works reveal Quantz as a transitional figure in the movement from the BAROQUE to the CLASSIC style.

Quantz's famous guide to the transverse flute, *Versuch einer Anweisung die Flöte traversiere zu spielen,* was published in Berlin in 1752. It remains in print in English today as *On Flute Playing* and is one of the most valuable guides to the early style of performance on the instrument.

quartal harmony. A system of harmonic structure based on the superposition of the intervals of the FOURTHS, rather than the traditional THIRDS. Such harmonic structures became increasingly attractive to 20th-century composers seeking to break the chains of triadic tonality.

quarter tone (Ger. *Viertelton*). Half a SEMITONE. An INTERVAL used by some modern composers, and also used in some non-Western music.

Quarter tones are not modern inventions. They are found in the ancient Greek enharmonic scale. Many RO-MANTIC composers of the 19th century thought of reviving quarter tones. George Ives, father of CHARLES IVES and an Army bandleader during the Civil War, experimented with tuning his instruments a quarter tone apart.

The attraction of quarter tones for modern composers is explained by the desire to develop a finer and more subtle means of musical expression. A pioneer of the modern revival of quarter tones was Julián Carrillo of Mexico, who published a treatise on *Sonido 13* in 1895. Alois Hába of Czechoslovakia codified the usages of quarter tones in his *Neue Harmonielehre,* published in 1928.

The first quarter-tone piano (with two keyboards tuned a quarter tone apart) was built in 1924. NIKOLAI RIMSKY-KORSAKOV's grandson Georg founded a quarter-tone society in Leningrad in the 1920s. The Russian Ivan Wyschnegradsky wrote much music for two pianos tuned a quarter tone apart. Ives wrote a chorale for strings in quarter tones as early as 1914.

Several systems of notation for quarter tones have been proposed, the most logical of which is the one by Hába using slashed signs for flats and sharps. ERNST BLOCH used quarter tones in his Piano Quintet, notated simply as flatted or sharped notes. *See also* MICROTONALITY.

quartet (*quartette;* Fr. *quatour;* It. *quartetto;* Ger. *Quartett*). 1. A concerted instrumental composition for four performers, such as the string quartet, for two violins, viola, and cello. 2. A composition, movement, or number, either vocal or instrumental, in four parts. A vocal quartet might involve one each of the four standard voices, labeled SATB. 3. A particular ensemble designed to perform these genres.

Quartet for the End of Time (*Quatuor pour la fin du temps*). A work for violin, clarinet, cello, and piano by OLIVIER MESSIAEN, 1941, in eight movements, it is a devotional meditation on the end of time.

quatricinium (Lat.). A four-voice composition, or a wind quartet for German *Stadtpfeifer.* The term first appeared in the 17th century.

Messiaen wrote it while a prisoner of war in Germany. It was first performed in the prisoner's camp Stalag 8A, Görlitz, Silesia.

Quattro pezzi sacri (Four sacred pieces). Choral works by GIUSEPPE VERDI, 1896, written in very old age, when he turned toward religious music after the composition of his last opera, *FALSTAFF* (1893). They are *Ave Maria, Laudi alla Vergine Maria, Stabat Mater,* and *Te Deum.* In the *Ave Maria,* Verdi uses the curious SCALA ENIGMATICA.

Que Sera, Sera. Song by Jay Livingston and Ray Evans, 1955, flaunting the fatalism of love and death. It was sung by Doris Day in Alfred Hitchcock's film *The Man Who Knew Too Much.*

Queen. (Vocal/keyboards: Freddie Mercury (born Frederick Bulsana), b. Zanzibar, Sept. 5, 1946; d. Kensington, Nov. 24, 1991; Lead guitar: Brian May, b. Twickenham, July 19 1947; Bass: John Deacon, b. Leicester, Aug. 19, 1951; Drums: Roger Taylor, b. Kings Lynn, July 26, 1949.) British exponents of glitter ROCK. Led by flamboyant vocalist Freddie Mercury, Queen was one of the most critically reviled but commercially successful outfits in rock from the mid-'70s to the early '80s, whose career enjoyed another bump in popularity in the early '90s.

The group was formed out of the remnants of other bands in early 1971. It produced a series of albums through the mid-'70s, finally breaking through to pop stardom in 1975 with *Bohemian Rhapsody,* promoted through one of the first rock videos. It was followed by more chart-toppers expressing characteristic bombastic sentiments, including *We Will Rock You* (1976) and *Another One Bites the Dust* (1980).

The group's popularity waned in the early '80s, however, and it broke up by 1986. Mercury, long rumored to be homosexual, announced just a day before his death in November 1991 that he had contracted AIDS. This led to an overblown tribute concert and renewed Queenmania.

Queen, The. Symphony No. 85 in B-flat major (1785) by FRANZ JOSEPH HAYDN, the fourth in a series of six symphonies that Haydn wrote for Paris performances. The title, usually listed in French (*La Reine*), is explained by the fact that Marie Antoinette heard it seven years before she died on the guillotine.

PEOPLE IN MUSIC

Bohemian Rhapsody was affectionately revived in the film *Wayne's World* (1992), and the video and song enjoyed another run of success.

Queen of Spades. Opera in three acts by PIOTR ILYICH TCHAIKOVSKY, based on a short story by Aleksandr Pushkin. It was first produced in St. Petersburg, Dec. 19, 1890.

A Russian army officer, Hermann, tries to elicit the secret of three winning cards from an old woman who had received them from the magician Cagliostro. His strange demand frightens the old woman and she dies, but her ghost appears to him in a lifelike hallucination and gives him the three winning cards: three, seven, and ace. He gambles on these cards and wins on the first two. But instead of picking up the winning ace, he draws the Queen of Spades for the last card and loses all. The card face of the Queen grimaces at him and he recognizes the old woman in it. He goes out and kills himself.

The score is highly dramatic and remains in the repertoire in Russia; it is occasionally staged in the West.

quena (*quechua*). Generic term for a vertical flute made of bamboo or baked clay, popular among the Guaraní Indians in Argentina, Bolivia, Peru, and the Amazon basin.

MUSICAL INSTRUMENT

Querelle des Bouffons. *See* GUERRE DES BOUFFONS.

quijada (*qui jada del burro;* Sp., jawbone of an ass). An Afro-Cuban instrument made from a donkey's jawbone, with its teeth left in. The quijada can be used as a scraper, a rattle, or a percussive instrument (hit with the fist). It dates as far back as the 18th century.

MUSICAL INSTRUMENT

quickstep. 1. A march, usually in $\frac{6}{8}$ time. 2. A rapid American foxtrot that evolved c.1920.

Quintenquartett. String quartet op.76, no. 2 (1797), by FRANZ JOSEPH HAYDN, in the key of D minor. Its nickname refers to the interplay of FIFTHS in the first movement. The quartet is also known as *The Bell* or *The Donkey.* Furthermore, the MINUET in it became known as the *Witch Minuet* because of its supposedly bewitching quality.

quintet (Fr. *quintette, quintour;* It. *quintetto;* Ger. *Quintett*). 1. A concerted instrumental composition for five performers. 2. A composition, movement, or number, vocal or instrumental, in five parts. 3. Also the performers as a group.

quintuplets (It. *quintina;* Ger. *Quintole;* Fr. *quintolet*). A group of five NOTES of equal duration played against a normal grouping of four or three. An interesting example of a whole section of quintuplets in eighth notes against a waltz rhythm of $\frac{3}{4}$ is found in the *Dance of the Mermaids* in NIKOLAI RIMSKY-KORSAKOV's opera *SADKO* (1898).

Quintuple rhythm or *time,* grouping of five beats to the measure.

quodlibet (from Lat., as you like it). As cultivated by MEDIEVAL students in Central Europe, a free MEDLEY of popular melodies, religious HYMNS, and cosmopolitan MADRIGALS, rendered in French as *fricassée* (stewed meat). The secret of attraction of such fricassees was the joy of recognition of familiar tunes in an otherwise solemn context. Even JOHANN SEBASTIAN BACH himself succumbed to the lure of the quodlibet by combining two popular melodies in the last movement of his *GOLDBERG VARIATIONS.*

In modern times, a quodlibet formed by the superposition of the Russian song *Dark Eyes* and FRÉDÉRIC CHOPIN's F-minor étude was popular among Russian conservatory students. Another popular modern quodlibet is a combination of the tunes *La Matchiche* and *Petite Tonkinoise. See also* POTPOURRI.

quotation. In music, the inclusion of musical materials in a composition that allude to other compositions or musics. Folk songs, contrapuntal elaborations on a given CANTUS FIRMUS, and the doom-laden chant DIES IRAE have been a favorite resource for centuries.

Some famous examples of musical quotation include:

RICHARD STRAUSS inserted the theme of the funeral march from LUDWIG VAN BEETHOVEN's *Eroica Symphony* in the score of his *METAMORPHOSEN,* a dirge on the death of Germany, written during the last weeks of World War II.

ALBAN BERG quoted JOHANN SEBASTIAN BACH's chorale *Es ist genug* at the conclusion of his Violin Concerto as a memorial for Manon Gropius, the young daughter of GUSTAV MAHLER's widow by another marriage.

An extraordinary assembly of assorted thematic memos, memories, and mementos is found in *Sinfonia* by LUCIANO BERIO, in which he quotes metamorphosed fragments from works of Mahler, CLAUDE DEBUSSY, MAURICE RAVEL, and others.

JOHN CAGE's *EUROPERAS,* comprised of nothing but collaged fragments from extant operas across several centuries, epitomizes the practice.

The situation is different, of course, when a quotation of a famous song is deliberately made for purposes of characterization or historical reference, as for instance the *MARSEILLAISE* in PIOTR ILYICH TCHAIKOVSKY's *1812 OVERTURE* and in UMBERTO GIORDANO's *ANDREA CHENIER,* or *THE STARSPANGLED BANNER* in GIACOMO PUCCINI's *MADAMA BUTTERFLY.* Cage's works may also be construed in this light.

Index